TAKING SIDES

Clashing Views on

Economic Issues

THIRTEENTH EDITION

Selected, Edited, and with Introductions by

Frank J. Bonello
University of Notre Dame

Isobel Lobo
Benedictine University

D0070718

**Contemporary
Learning Series**

A Division of The McGraw-Hill Companies

This book is dedicated to Thomas R. Swartz, a co-editor through the first eleven editions of this volume. His contributions are still evident in this edition, especially in the Introduction. Perhaps he will find time to read the new portions of this edition as a part of his well-deserved retirement. It is also dedicated to Frank Bonello's children and grandchildren (John, David, Michael, Amanda, and Jack) and to Isobel Lobo's parents.

Cover image: farmers: Joeseph Sohm–Visions of America / Getty Images

Cover Acknowledgment
Maggie Lytle

Compositor: ICC Macmillan Inc.

Thirteenth Edition

123456789DOCDOC987

Library of Congress Cataloging-in-Publication Data
Main entry under title:
Taking sides: clashing views on controversial economic issues/selected, edited, and with introductions by Frank J. Bonello.—13th ed.
Includes bibliographical references and index.
1. United States—Economic policy—1971–1981. 2. United States—Economic policy—1981–1993.
3. United States—Economic policy—1993–.
I. Bonello, Frank J., *comp.*
338.9'22

MHID: 0-07-352725-4
ISBN: 978-0-07-352725-3
ISSN: 1094-7612

Preface

> Where there is much desire to learn, there of necessity will be much arguing.
>
> — John Milton (1608–1674), English poet and essayist

Presented here are 19 debates on important economic issues, which are designed to stimulate critical-thinking skills and initiate lively and informed discussion. These debates take economic theory and show how it is applied to current real-world public policy decisions, the outcomes of which will have an immediate and personal impact. How these debates are resolved will affect our taxes, jobs, wages, educational systems, and so on; in short, they will shape the society in which we live.

The goal throughout each of the 13 editions of *Taking Sides: Clashing Views on Economic Issues* has been to select issues that reveal something about the nature of economics itself and something about how economics relates to current everyday newspaper headlines and television news stories on public policy concerns. To assist the reader, we begin each issue with an issue introduction, which sets the stage for the debate as it is argued in the "yes" and "no" selections. Each issue concludes with a postscript that briefly reviews the arguments and makes some final observations. The introduction and postscript do not preempt what is the reader's own task: to achieve a critical and informed view of the economic issue at stake. Certainly, the reader should not feel confined to adopt one or the other of the positions presented. The views presented should be used as starting points, and the suggestions for further reading in each postscript offer additional resources on the topic. Internet site addresses (URLs) have been provided at the beginning of each unit, which should also prove useful as resources for further research. At the back of the book is a listing of all the contributors to this volume, which provides information about the economists, policymakers, political leaders, and commentators whose views are presented here.

Changes to this edition This new edition of *Taking Sides* represents a considerable revision. Of the 19 issues, seven are completely new, and eight are updated. Thus, as the journey into the new millennium continues, this substantially revised book will help us understand the implications of a changing set of economic issues that were not part of our world just a few years ago. The new issues are "Are CEOs Paid What They Are Worth?" (Issue 2), "Is the New Medicare Part D Drug Benefit Good Health Care Policy?" (Issue 4), "Are Health Savings Accounts the Right Medicine for the Ills of the Health Care Industry?" (Issue 5), "Should Minimum Wage and Living Wage Laws Be Eliminated?" (Issue 11), "Do Unskilled Immigrants Hurt the American Economy?" (Issue 12), "Are Spending Cuts the Right Way to Balance the Federal

Government's Budget?" (Issue 16), and "Will the Creation of an Ownership Society Make the American Economy More Efficient and More Equitable?" (Issue 19). The updated issue involves international trade: "Has the North American Free Trade Agreement Benefited the Economies of Canada, Mexico, and the U.S.?" (Issue 17).

As with all of the previous editions the issues in the thirteenth edition can be used in any sequence. Although the organization of the book loosely parallels the sequence of topics found in a standard introductory economics textbook, you can pick and choose which issues to read first, since they are designed to stand alone. Unit 3, "The World Around Us," is structured to allow coverage of a broader set of problems society faces in an ever-changing world.

A word to the instructor   An *Instructor's Manual with Test Questions* (multiple choice and essay) is available from the publisher. A general guidebook, *Using Taking Sides in the Classroom*, which discusses methods and techniques for integrating the pro/con approach into any classroom setting, is also available. An online version of *Using Taking Sides in the Classroom* and a correspondence service for *Taking Sides* adopters can be found at http://www.mhcls.com/usingts/.

Taking Sides: Clashing Views on Economic Issues is only one title in the Taking Sides series. If you are interested in seeing the table of contents for any of the other titles, please visit the Taking Sides Web site at http://www.mhcls.com/takingsides.

Acknowledgments   Friends and readers across the United States and Canada have offered helpful comments and suggestions. As always, their suggestions were welcomed and have markedly enhanced the quality of this edition of *Taking Sides*. If as you read this book, you are reminded of an essay that could be included in a future edition, we hope that you will drop either of us a note at either Bonello.1@nd.edu or ILobo@ben.edu. We very much appreciate your interest and help, and we are always pleased to hear from you.

We are most appreciative of the encouragement and effort from the staff of McGraw-Hill Contemporary Learning Series while expediting this edition of *Taking Sides*—especially Susan Brusch, Senior Developmental Editor. To all those we owe a huge debt, many thanks, and none of the blame for any short-comings that remain in this edition of *Taking Sides*.

Frank J. Bonello
University of Notre Dame
Isobel Lobo
Benedictine University

Contents In Brief

Contents

Health care administrator Mark McClellan believes that the Part D drug benefit is the most important new addition to Medicare in its history, providing million of Americans with better benefits "at a significantly lower cost than originally estimated." Cato Institute senior fellow Jagadeesh Gokhale believes that Medicare's Part D drug benefit is "bad and shortsighted economic policy." He believes this program will, among other things, increase private drug prices, impose higher fiscal burdens on future generations, and reduce national saving and investment.

Edward L. Langston, a medical doctor and a trustee of the American Medical Association, believes that Health Savings Accounts (HSAs) will create better conditions in the health care industry, including enhancement of the patient-physician relationship and provision of "incentives to utilize heath care in a cost conscious manner." Robert Greenstein, founder and executive director of the Center for Budget and Policy Priorities, argues that HSAs have several negative consequences. In particular, he asserts these accounts will weaken "the existing comprehensive employer-based health insurance market," without, at the same time, providing any "significant cost containment."

The U.S. Department of Health and Human Services (HHS) argues that although the United States has a health care system that "is the envy of the world," it is a system that is to be brought to its knees by aggressive attorneys who force the medical community to practice costly "defensive medicine." Jackson Williams, legal council for the watchdog group Public Citizen, charges that the position taken by HHS is factually "incorrect, incomplete, or misleading" and even contradicted by other governmental agencies.

The Los Angeles County Economic Development Corporation believes that the introduction of Wal-Mart supercenter stores into the Southern California market will generate significant savings for consumers on their grocery, apparel, and general merchandise spending, and the redirected spending from the savings will create over 35,000 new jobs. The Democratic Staff of the House Committee on Education and the Workforce believes that Wal-Mart, in its efforts to achieve and maintain low prices, has "come to represent the lowest common denominator in the treatment of working people."

The Bush White House identifies a number of problems with the present structure of the Social Security system and proposes personal retirement accounts as a way of resolving these problems, and "dramatically reduce the costs of permanently fixing the system." Dean Baker, co-director of the Center for Economic and Policy Research, argues that President Bush's plan for personal retirement accounts would not fix Social Security; instead, it would "undermine a system that has provided security for tens of million of workers and their families, for seven decades, and which can continue to do so for long into the future if it is just left alone."

Free-market economists Norbert J. Michel, Alfredo Goyburu, and Ralph A. Rector applaud the George W. Bush administration's initiative to eliminate the double taxation of corporate dividends. They assert that this action will improve economic efficiency and that, in the long run, this tax cut will pay for itself because it will stimulate economic growth. Economic policy analysts Joel Friedman and Robert Greenstein argue that there are no valid economic justifications to propose the elimination of the tax on dividends. All that cutting dividend taxes will really do, they say, is reduce the tax burden on high-income individuals.

Professor Robert D. Manning lists a number of the problems with credit cards, including high interest rates, misrepresentation of the cost of debt consolidation loans, use of double billing cycles, use of "bait and switch" techniques, improper use of personal consumer credit information, and the proliferation of a number of practices that are of little or no benefit to consumers. Lawyer Micheal F. McEneney stresses the benefits that consumers experience because of the "ever-expanding choices available to consumers," and he supports these claims by reporting that a Federal Reserve study found that "91% of credit card holders are satisfied with their credit card issuers."

Economics instructor MacKenzie believes that eliminating minimum wage laws would "reduce unemployment and improve the efficiency of markets for low productivity labor." He also believes that the "economic case for a living wage is unfounded." Economist Wicks-Lim stresses the ripple effects of minimum and living wage laws; these effects increase the "effectiveness" of minimum and living wage laws as "antipoverty strategies."

Columnist Steven Malanga believes the influx of unskilled immigrants into the U.S. economy has imposed large costs on the larger society, including job loss by native workers and lower investment in labor-saving technology. More importantly, he argues that this immigration has increased utilization of the "vast U.S. welfare and social-services apparatus." Diana Furchtgott-Roth, senior fellow at the Hudson Institute and director of Hudson's Center for Employment Policy, and a former chief economist at the U.S. Department of Labor, observes that annual immigration is "a tiny fraction of our labor force," and immigrant laborers are "complements, rather than substitutes for native born Americans." She also cites a National Academy of Sciences study that concluded that foreign-born households are no more likely to use "welfare" than native-born households.

Lester R. Brown, founder and president of the Earth Policy Institute, describes his vision of an environmentally sustainable economy, which includes food supplies, population growth issues, water availability, climatic changes, and renewable energy. Lenny Bernstein, head of L.S. Bernstein & Associates, which advises companies and trade associations on political and scientific developments on global environmental issues, acknowledges that ecosystems are sensitive to climate change, but he argues that the change that we have seen repeated again and again over the course of history can lead to benefits for our children and our children's children.

Chris Edwards, director of tax policy studies at the Cato Institute, believes that the federal government overspending is the cause of its current fiscal problems. Higher taxes are not the solution because they "would result in greater tax avoidance, slower growth, less reported income, and thus less than expected tax revenue, perhaps prompting policymakers to jack up tax rates even higher." Former Congressman Charlie Stenholm argues that in addressing the deficit and debt problems, everything should be on the table. He stresses that addressing long-term fiscal challenges will require "some combination of stronger economic growth, restraining health care costs, scaling back benefit promises of entitlement programs, increasing the eligibility age for Social Security and Medicare, increasing revenues, and other tough choices."

Deputy Assistant U.S. Trade Representative Melle outlines the benefits of NAFTA and concludes that the three NAFTA countries "have not only become better customers for each other but better neighbors, more committed partners, and effective colleagues in a wide range of trade-related international organizations." Sandra Polaski, director of the Trade, Equity and Development Project, argues that NAFTA has produced negative effects in all three countries, including contributing to wage inequality in the United States. But the largest negative effects have been felt by the rural poor in Mexico: they "have borne the brunt of the adjustment to NAFTA and been forced to adapt without adequate government support."

The House Education and the Workforce Committee lists a number of
positive results for the No Child Left Behind Act, including higher reading
and math test scores in several states as well as improved data and
information for teachers and parents. Professor Gerald W. Bracey
believes that the No Child Left Behind Act is, from the perspective of the
Republican party, a perfect law because it will ultimately transfer billions
from the public sector to the private sector, because it will reduce the size
of government, and because it will "wound or kill" a large Democratic
party power base.

The George W. Bush White House is promoting a plan to increase
"ownership" in American society. The plan consists of a series of initiatives
in health care, in home ownership, in small business, and in Social
Security. These initiatives, if adopted, will create more ownership and
more vitality and give more people "a vital stake in the future of this
country." Paul Glastris argues that persons have rejected the president's
initiatives to give them more choice because they "feel quickly
overwhelmed when they lack the information or expertise to decide
confidently, and turn downright negative when the choices themselves
seem to put what they already have at risk."

Introduction

Economics and Economists: The Basis for Controversy

I think that Capitalism, wisely managed, can probably be more efficient for attaining economic ends than any alternative system yet in sight, but that in itself it is in many ways extremely objectionable.

—Lord John Maynard Keynes, *The End of Laissez-Faire* (1926)

Although more than 80 years have passed since Lord Keynes penned these lines, many economists still struggle with the basic dilemma he outlined. The paradox rests in the fact that a free market system is extremely efficient. It is purported to produce more at a lower cost than any other economic system. But in producing this wide array of low-cost goods and services, problems arise. These problems—most notably a lack of economic equity and economic stability—concern some economists.

If the problems raised and analyzed in this book were merely the product of intellectual gymnastics undertaken by "egg-headed" economists, then we could sit back and enjoy these confrontations as theoretical exercises. Unfortunately, we are not afforded that luxury. The essays contained in this book touch each and every one of us in tangible ways. They are real-world issues. One set of issues deals with "microeconomic" topics. (We refer to these issues as "micro" problems not because they are small problems, but because they deal with small economic units, such as households, firms, or individual industries). An example here is government assistance for seniors in their purchases of prescription drugs. Another set focuses on "macroeconomic" topics, such as the minimum and living wages, topics that impact the whole economy, on many industries. A third set of issues deals with matters that do not fall neatly into the macroeconomic or microeconomic classifications, including three issues relating to the international aspects of economic activity and single issues dealing with government debt, pollution, education, and ownership.

The range of issues and disagreements raises a fundamental question: Why do economists disagree? One explanation is suggested by Lord Keynes' 1926 remark. How various economists will react to the strengths and weaknesses found in an economic system will depend on how they view the relative importance of efficiency, equity, and stability. These are central terms, and we will define them in detail in the following pages. For now, the important point is that some economists may view efficiency as overriding. In other cases, the same economists may be willing to sacrifice the efficiency generated by the market in order to ensure increased economic equity and/or increased economic stability.

Given this discussion of conflict, controversy, and diversity, it might appear that economists rarely, if ever, agree on any economic issue. We would be most misleading if we left the reader with this impression. Economists rarely challenge the internal logic of the theoretical models that have been developed and articulated by their colleagues. Rather, they will challenge either the validity of the assumptions used in these models or the value of the ends these models seek to achieve. For example, it is most difficult to discredit the internal logic of the microeconomic models employed by the "free market economist." These models are elegant, and their logical development is most persuasive. However, these models are challenged by such issues as the assumption of functioning, competitive markets, and the desirability of perpetuating the existing distribution of income. In this case, those who support and those who challenge the operation of the market agree on a large number of issues. But they disagree most assuredly on a few issues that have dramatic implications.

This same phenomenon of agreeing more often than disagreeing is also true in the area of economic policy. In this area, where the public is most acutely aware of differences among economists, these differences are not generally over the kinds of changes that will be brought about by a particular policy. Again, the differences more typically concern the timing of the change, the specific characteristics of the policy, and the size of the resulting effect(s). For example, a recent survey found that 85 percent of economists agree that the United States should eliminate tariffs and other trade restrictions (see "Do Economists Agree on Anything? Yes!" by Robert Whaples, *Economists Voice*, www.bwepress.com/ev, November 2006).

Economists: What Do They Represent?

Newspapers, magazines, and TV commentators all use handy labels to describe certain members of the economics profession. What do the headlines mean when they refer to the "Chicago school," the "Keynesians," the "institutional economists," or the "radical economists"? Since these labels are used throughout this book, we feel obliged to identify the principal groups or camps in our profession. Let us warn you that this can be a misleading venture. Some economists—perhaps most economists—defy classification. They drift from one camp to another, selecting a gem of wisdom here and another there. These are practical men and women who believe that no one camp has all the answers to all the economic problems confronting society.

Recognizing this limitation, four major groups of economists can be identified. These groups are differentiated on the basis of two criteria: how they view efficiency relative to equity and stability, and what significance they attach to imperfectly competitive market structures. Before describing the views of the four groups on these criteria, it is essential to understand the meaning of certain terms to be used in this description.

Efficiency, equity, and stability represent goals for an economic system. An economy is efficient when it produces those goods and services that people want and does so without wasting scarce resources. Equity in an economic sense has several dimensions. It means that income and wealth are distributed according to accepted principles of fairness, that those who are unable to care for themselves receive adequate care, and that mainstream economic activity is open to all persons. Stability is viewed as the absence of sharp ups and downs in business activity, in prices, and in employment. In other words, stability is marked by steady increases in output, little inflation, and low unemployment.

The term "market structure" refers to the number of buyers and sellers in the market and the amount of control they exercise over price. At one extreme is a perfectly competitive market where there are so many buyers and sellers that no one has any ability to influence market price. One seller or buyer obviously could have great control over price. This extreme market structure, which we call pure monopoly, and other market structures that result in some control over price are grouped under the broad label of imperfectly competitive markets. That is, imperfect competition is a situation where the number of market participants is limited and, as a consequence, the participants have the ability to influence price. With these terms in mind, we can begin to examine the various schools of economic thought.

Free-Market Economists

One of the most visible groups of economists and perhaps the easiest group to identify and classify is the "free-market economists." In general, this is also the group of economists that persons have in mind when they speak of conservative economists. These economists believe that the market, operating freely without interferences from government or labor unions, will generate the greatest amount of well-being for the greatest number of people.

Economic efficiency is one of the priorities for free-market economists. In their well-developed models, consumer sovereignty—consumer demand for goods and services—guides the system by directly influencing market prices. The distribution of economic resources caused by these market prices not only results in the production of an array of goods and services that are demanded by consumers, but this production is undertaken in the most cost-effective fashion. The free-market economists claim that at any point, some individuals must earn incomes that are substantially greater than other individuals. They contend that these higher incomes are a reward for greater efficiency or productivity and that this reward-induced efficiency will result in rapid economic growth that will benefit all persons in the society. They might also admit that a system driven by these freely operating markets will be subject to occasional bouts of instability (slow growth, inflation, and unemployment). However, they maintain that government action to eliminate or reduce this periodic instability will only make matters worse. Consequently, government, according to the free-market or conservative economist, should play a minor role in the economic affairs of society.

Although the models of free-market economists are dependent on functioning competitive markets, the lack of these competitive markets in the real world does not seriously jeopardize their position. First, they assert that large firms are necessary to achieve low per-unit costs; that is, a single large firm may be able to produce a given level of output with fewer scarce resources than a large number of small firms. Second, they suggest that the benefits associated with the free operation of markets are so great compared to government intervention that even a "second-best solution" of imperfectly competitive markets still yields benefits far in excess of government intervention.

These advocates of the free market have been given various labels over time. The oldest and most persistent label is "classical economists." This is because the classical economists of the eighteenth century, particularly Adam Smith, were the first to point out the virtues of the market. Smith captured the essence of the system with the following words:

> Every individual endeavors to employ his capital so that its produce may be of greatest value. He generally neither intends to promote the public interest nor knows how much he is promoting it. He intends only his own security, only his own gain. And he is in this led by an invisible hand to promote an end that was no part of his intention. By pursuing his own interest he frequently promotes that of society more effectively than when he really intends to promote it.

—Adam Smith, *The Wealth of Nations* (1776)

Liberal Economists

Another significant group of economists in the United States can be classified as liberal economists. "Liberal" in this instance refers to the willingness to intervene in the free operation of the market. These economists share with the free-market economists a great respect for the market. However, the liberal economist does not believe that the explicit and implicit costs of a freely operating market should or can be ignored. Rather, the liberal maintains that the costs of an uncontrolled marketplace are often borne by those in society who are least capable of bearing them: the poor, the elderly, and the infirm. Additionally, liberal economists maintain that the freely operating market sometimes results in economic instability (that is, bouts of inflation, unemployment, and slow or negative growth).

Consider for a moment the differences between free-market economists and liberal economists at the microeconomic level. Liberal economists take exception to the free market on two grounds. First, these economists find a basic problem with fairness in the marketplace. Since the forces of consumer spending drive the market, there are those people who through no fault of their own (they may be aged, young, infirm, physically, or mentally handicapped) may not have the wherewithal to participate in the economic system. Second, the unfettered marketplace does not and cannot handle spill-over effects (known as "externalities"). These are the third-party effects that may occur as a result of some action. Will a firm willingly compensate its neighbors for the pollutants it pours into the nearby lake? Will a truck driver willingly drive at the speed limit and in the process reduce the highway accident rate? Liberal economists think not. These economists are therefore willing to have the government intervene in these and other similar cases.

The liberal economists' role in macroeconomics is more readily apparent. Ever since the failure of free-market economics during the Great Depression of the 1930s, Keynesianism (still another label for liberal economics) has become widely known. In his 1935 book, *The General Theory of Employment, Interest, and Money,* Lord John Maynard Keynes laid the basic groundwork for this school of thought. Keynes argued that the history of freely operating market economies was marked by periods of recurring recessions, sometimes very deep recessions, which we call depressions. He maintained that government intervention through its fiscal policy—government tax and spending power—could eliminate, or at least soften, these sharp reductions in economic activity and as a result move the economy along a more stable growth path. Thus for the Keynesians, or liberal economists, one of the "extremely objectionable" aspects of a free-market economy is its inherent instability.

Liberal economists are also far more concerned about the existence of imperfections in the marketplace than are their free-market counterparts. They reject the notion that imperfect competition is an acceptable substitute for competitive markets. These economists may agree that the imperfectly competitive firms can achieve some savings because of their large size and efficiency, but they assert that since there is little or no competition, the firms are not forced to pass these cost savings on to consumers. Thus liberal economists, who in some circles are labeled "antitrusters," are willing to intervene in the market in two ways. In some cases, they are prepared to allow some monopolies, such as public utilities, to exist, but they contend that government must regulate these monopolies. In other cases, they maintain that there is no justification for monopolies and they are prepared to invoke the powers of antitrust legislation to break up existing monopolies, and/or prevent the formation of new monopolies.

The Mainstream Critics and Radical Reform Economists

There are two other groups of economists that we must identify. One group can be called mainstream critics. Included in this group are individuals like Thorstein Veblen (1857–1929), and his critique of conspicuous consumption, to John Kenneth Galbraith (1908–2006), and his views on industrial structure. One reasonably cohesive group of mainstream critics are the post-Keynesians, who believe that as the principal economic institutions have changed over time, they have remained closer to the spirit of Keynes than the liberal economists. As some have suggested, the key aspect of Keynes as far as the post-Keynesians are concerned is his assertion that "expectations of the future are not necessarily certain." On a more practical level, post-Keynesians assert, among other things, that the productivity of the economic system is not significantly affected by changes in income distribution, that the system can still be efficient without competitive markets, that conventional fiscal policies cannot control inflation, and that "income policies" are the means to an effective and equitable answer to the inflationary dilemma. (This characterization of post-Keynesianism is drawn from Alfred S. Eichner's "Introduction" in *A Guide to Post-Keynesian Economics,* M.E. Sharpe, Inc., 1978.)

The fourth and last group can be called radical reformist economists, who trace their ideas to the nineteenth-century philosopher-economist Karl Marx and his most impressive work, the three volumes of *Das Kapital.* As with the other three groups of economists, there are subgroups of radical reform economists. One subgroup, which may be labeled contemporary Marxists, is best represented by those who have published their research over the years in the *Review of Radical Political Economy*. These economists examine issues that have been largely ignored by mainstream economists, such as war, sexism, racism, imperialism, and civil rights. In their analyses of these issues, they borrow from and refine the work of Marx. In the process, they emphasize the role of class in shaping society and the role of the economy in determining class structures. Moreover, they see a need to encourage explicitly the development of some form of democratic socialism, for only then will the greatest good for the greatest number be ensured.

In concluding this section, we must warn you to use these labels with extreme care. Our categories are not hard and fast. There is much grayness around the edges and little that is black and white in these classifications. This does not mean, however, that they have no value. It is important to understand the philosophical background of the individual authors. This background does indeed color and shade their work.

Summary

It is clear that there is no shortage of economic problems. These problems demand solutions. At the same time, there is no shortage of proposed solutions. In fact, the problem is often one of oversupply. The nineteen issues included in this volume will acquaint you or, more accurately, reacquaint you with some of these problems. And, of course, there are at least two proposed solutions for each of the problems. Here we hope to provide new insights regarding the alternatives available and the differences and similarities of these alternative remedies.

If this introduction has served its purpose, you will be able to identify common elements in the proposed solutions to the different problems. For example, you will be able to identify the reliance on the forces of the market advocated by free-market economists as the remedy for several economic ills. This introduction should also help you understand why there are at least two proposed solutions for every economic problem; each group of economists tends to interpret a problem from its own philosophical position and to advance a solution that is grounded in that same philosophical framework.

Our intention, of course, is not to connect persons to one philosophic position or another. We hope instead to generate discussion and promote understanding. To do this, each of us must see not only a proposed solution, we must also be aware of the foundation that supports that solution. With greater understanding, meaningful progress in addressing economic problems can be achieved.

Internet References . . .

The Dismal Scientist

The Dismal Scientist provides, on a subscription basis, economic data, analysis, and forecasts on a variety of topics.

http://www.dismal.com

Economist.com

The Web edition of *The Economist* is available free to subscribers to the print edition or for an annual fee to those who wish to subscribe online. A selection of articles is available free to those who want to explore the journal.

http://www.economist.com

The Policy Action Network

The site offers timely information and analysis of national policy in the form of a virtual magazine. It also provides links to the home pages of a number of liberal organizations and publications.

http://www.movingideas.org

Resources for Economists on the Internet

This guide to economic resources on the Internet is sponsored by the American Economic Association. It is an excellent starting point for anyone who wants to do research on economic topics. It has many Web links.

http://rfe.org

Statistical Resources on the Web: Comprehensive Economics

This site provides links to a wide variety of economic data at the city, state, country, and global level.

http://www.lib.umich.edu/govdocs/stecon.html

WebEc: WWW Resources in Economics

This site is a virtual library that categorizes free information in economics available on the World Wide Web.

http://www.helsinki.fi/WebEc

Internet Resources for Economists

This site offers a number of links to economic blogs, classic works, textbooks, data sources, journals, etc.

http://www.oswego.edu/~economic/econweb.htm

UNIT 1

Microeconomic Issues

*E*conomic decisions made at the microeconomic level affect our lives in a variety of important ways. Public and private actions determine what goods and services are produced, as well as the prices we pay for them. The actions also affect our incomes and even our health. In this unit, we examine the profit decisions of business, the pay of business leaders, labor market discrimination, the prices the elderly have to pay for drugs, health savings accounts, and reform of medical malpractice litigation.

- Are Profits the Only Business of Business?

- Are CEOs Paid What They Are Worth?

- Is There Discrimination in U.S. Labor Markets?

- Is the New Medicare Part D Drug Benefit Good Health Care Policy?

- Are Health Savings Accounts the Right Medicine for the Ills of the Health Care Industry?

- Is It Time to Reform Medical Malpractice Litigation?

ISSUE 1

Are Profits the Only Business of Business?

YES: **Milton Friedman**, from "The Social Responsibility of Business Is to Increase Its Profits," *The New York Times Magazine* (September 13, 1970)

NO: **Robert Almeder**, from "Morality in the Marketplace: Reflections on the Friedman Doctrine," in Milton Snoeyenbos, Robert Almeder, and James Humber, eds., *Business Ethics,* rev. ed. (Prometheus Press, 1998)

ISSUE SUMMARY

YES: Free-market economist Milton Friedman contends that the sole responsibility of business is to increase its profits.

NO: Philosopher Robert Almeder maintains that if capitalism is to survive, it must act in socially responsible ways that go beyond profit making.

Every economic society—whether it is a traditional society in Central Africa, a fossilized planned economy such as Cuba's, or a wealthy capitalist society such as those found in North America, Western Europe, and the Pacific Rim—must address the basic economic problem of resource allocation. These societies must determine *what* goods and services they can and will produce, *how* these goods and services will be produced, and *for whom* these goods and services will be produced.

The *what, how,* and *for whom* questions must be answered because of the problem of scarcity. Even if a given society were indescribably rich, it would still confront the problem of scarcity—in the case of a rich society, "relative scarcity." It might have all the resources it needs to produce all the goods and services it would ever want, but it could not produce all these things simultaneously. Thus, even a very rich society must set priorities and produce first those goods and services with the highest priority and postpone the production of those goods and services with lower priorities. If time is of the essence, this society would determine *how* these goods and services should be produced. And since this wealthy society cannot produce all it wants instantly, it must also determine *for whom* the first bundle of goods and services will be produced.

Few, if any, economic societies are indescribably rich. On the other hand, there are many examples of economic societies that face grinding deprivation daily. In these societies and in all the societies that fall between poverty and great affluence, the *what, how,* and *for whom* questions are immediately apparent. Somehow these questions must be answered.

In some societies, such as the Amish communities of North America, the answers to these questions are found in tradition: Sons and daughters follow in their parents' footsteps. Younger generations produce *what* older generations produced before them. The methods of production—the horsedrawn plow, the hand-held scythe, the use of natural fertilizers—remain unchanged; thus, the *how* question is answered in the same way that the *for whom* question is answered—by following historic patterns. In other societies, such as self-sustaining religious communities, there is a different pattern of responses to these questions. In these communities, the "elder" of the community determines *what* will be produced, *how* it will be produced, and *for whom* it will be produced. If there is a well-defined hierarchical system, it is similar to one of the former stereotypical command economies of Eastern Europe.

Although elements of tradition and command are found in the industrialized societies of Western Europe, North America, and Japan, the basic answers to the three questions of resource allocation in these countries are determined by profit. In these economic societies, *what* will be produced is determined by what will yield the greatest profit. Consumers, in their search for maximum satisfaction, will bid for those goods and services that they want most. This consumer action drives the prices of these goods and services up, which, in turn, increases producers' profits. The higher profits attract new firms into the industry and encourage existing firms to increase their output. Thus, profits are the mechanism that ensures that consumers get what they want. Similarly, the profit-seeking behavior of business firms determines *how* the goods and services that consumers want will be produced. Since firms attempt to maximize their profits, they select those means of production that are economically most efficient. Lastly, the *for whom* question is also linked to profits. Wherever there is a shortage of goods and services, profits will be high. In the producers' attempts to increase their output, they must attract factors of production (land, labor, and capital) away from other economic activities. This bidding increases factor prices or factor incomes and ensures that these factors will be able to buy goods and services in the open marketplace.

Both Milton Friedman and Robert Almeder recognize the merits of a profit-driven economic system. They do not quarrel over the importance of profits. But they do quarrel over whether or not business firms have obligations beyond making profits. In the following selection, Friedman holds that the *only* responsibility of business is to make profits and that anyone who maintains otherwise is "preaching pure and unadulterated socialism." In the second selection, Almeder, who is clearly not a "socialist," contends that business must act in socially responsible ways "if capitalism is to survive."

The Social Responsibility of Business Is to Increase Its Profits

When I hear businessmen speak eloquently about the "social responsibilities of business in a free-enterprise system," I am reminded of the wonderful line about the Frenchman who discovered at the age of 70 that he had been speaking prose all his life. The businessmen believe that they are defending free enterprise when they declaim that business is not concerned "merely" with profit but also with promoting desirable "social ends; that business has a social conscience" and takes seriously its responsibilities for providing employment, eliminating discrimination, avoiding pollution and whatever else may be the catchwords of the contemporary crop of reformers. In fact they are—or would be if they or anyone else took them seriously—preaching pure and unadulterated socialism. Businessmen who talk this way are unwitting puppets of the intellectual forces that have been undermining the basis of a free society these past decades.

The discussions of the "social responsibilities of business" are notable for their analytical looseness and lack of rigor. What does it mean to say that "business" has responsibilities? Only people can have responsibilities. A corporation is an artificial person and in this sense may have artificial responsibilities, but "business" as a whole cannot be said to have responsibilities, even in this vague sense. The first step toward clarity in examining the doctrine of the social responsibility of business is to ask precisely what it implies for whom.

Presumably, the individuals who are to be responsible are businessmen, which means individual proprietors or corporate executives. Most of the discussion of social responsibility is directed at corporations, so in what follows I shall mostly neglect the individual proprietor and speak of corporate executives.

In a free-enterprise, private-property system, a corporate executive is an employee of the owners of the business. He has direct responsibility to his employers. That responsibility is to conduct the business in accordance with their desires, which generally will be to make as much money as possible while conforming to the basic rules of the society, both those embodied in law and those embodied in ethical custom. Of course, in some cases his employers may have a different objective. A group of persons might establish a corporation for an eleemosynary purpose—for example, a hospital or a school. The manager of such a corporation will not have money profit as his objective but the rendering of certain services.

In either case, the key point is that, in his capacity as a corporate executive, the manager is the agent of the individuals who own the corporation or establish the eleemosynary institution, and his primary responsibility is to them.

Needless to say, this does not mean that it is easy to judge how well he is performing his task. But at least the criterion of performance is straightforward, and the persons among whom a voluntary contractual arrangement exists are clearly defined.

Of course, the corporate executive is also a person in his own right. As a person, he may have many other responsibilities that he recognizes or assumes voluntarily—to his family, his conscience, his feelings of charity, his church, his clubs, his city, his country. He may feel impelled by these responsibilities to devote part of his income to causes he regards as worthy, to refuse to work for particular corporations, even to leave his job, for example, to join his country's armed forces. If we wish, we may refer to some of these responsibilities as "social responsibilities." But in these respects he is acting as a principal, not an agent; he is spending his own money or time or energy, not the money of his employers or the time or energy he has contracted to devote to their purposes. If these are "social responsibilities," they are the social responsibilities of individuals, not of business.

What does it mean to say that the corporate executive has a "social responsibility" in his capacity as businessman? If this statement is not pure rhetoric, it must mean that he is to act in some way that is not in the interest of his employers. For example, that he is to refrain from increasing the price of the product in order to contribute to the social objective of preventing inflation, even though a price increase would be in the best interests of the corporation. Or that he is to make expenditures on reducing pollution beyond the amount that is in the best interests of the corporation or that is required by law in order to contribute to the social objective of improving the environment. Or that, at the expense of corporate profits, he is to hire "hard-core" unemployed instead of better-qualified available workmen to contribute to the social objective of reducing poverty.

In each of these cases, the corporate executive would be spending someone else's money for a general social interest. Insofar as his actions in accord with his "social responsibility" reduce returns to stockholders, he is spending their money. Insofar as his actions raise the price to customers, he is spending the customers' money. Insofar as his actions lower the wages of some employees, he is spending their money.

The stockholders or the customers or the employees could separately spend their own money on the particular action if they wished to do so. The executive is exercising a distinct "social responsibility," rather than serving as an agent of the stockholders or the customers or the employees, only if he spends the money in a different way than they would have spent it.

But if he does this, he is in effect imposing taxes, on the one hand, and deciding how the tax proceeds shall be spent, on the other.

This process raises political questions on two levels: principle and consequences. On the level of political principle, the imposition of taxes and the expenditure of tax proceeds are governmental functions. We have established elaborate constitutional, parliamentary and judicial provisions to control these functions, to assure that taxes are imposed so far as possible in accordance with the preferences and desires of the public—after all, "taxation without representation" was one of the battle cries of the American Revolution. We have a system of checks and balances to separate the legislative function of imposing taxes and enacting expenditures from the executive function of collecting taxes and administering expenditure programs and from the judicial function of mediating disputes and interpreting the law.

Here the businessman—self-selected or appointed directly or indirectly by stockholders—is to be simultaneously legislator, executive and jurist. He is to decide whom to tax by how much and for what purpose, and he is to spend the proceeds—all this guided only by general exhortations from on high to restrain inflation, improve the environment, fight poverty and so on and on.

The whole justification for permitting the corporate executive to be selected by the stockholders is that the executive is an agent serving the interests of his principal. This justification disappears when the corporate executive imposes taxes and spends the proceeds for "social" purposes. He becomes in effect a public employee, a civil servant, even though he remains in name an employee of a private enterprise. On grounds of political principle, it is intolerable that such civil servants—insofar as their actions in the name of social responsibility are real and not just window-dressing—should be selected as they are now. If they are to be civil servants, then they must be selected through a political process. If they are to impose taxes and make expenditures to foster "social" objectives, then political machinery must be set up to guide the assessment of taxes and to determine through a political process the objectives to be served.

This is the basic reason why the doctrine of "social responsibility" involves the acceptance of the socialist view that political mechanisms, not market mechanisms, are the appropriate way to determine the allocation of scarce resources to alternative uses.

On the grounds of consequences, can the corporate executive in fact discharge his alleged "social responsibilities"? On the one hand, suppose he could get away with spending the stockholders' or customers' or employees' money. How is he to know how to spend it? He is told that he must contribute to fighting inflation. How is he to know what action of his will contribute to that end? He is presumably an expert in running his company—in producing a product or selling it or financing it. But nothing about his selection makes him an expert on inflation. Will his holding down the price of his product reduce inflationary pressure? Or, by leaving more spending power in the hands of his customers, simply divert it elsewhere? Or, by forcing him to produce less because of the lower price, will it simply contribute to shortages? Even if he could answer these questions, how much cost is he justified in imposing on his stockholders, customers and employees for this social purpose? What is the appropriate share and what is the appropriate share of others?

And, whether he wants to or not, can he get away with spending his stockholders', customers' or employees' money? Will not the stockholders fire him? (Either the present ones or those who take over when his actions in the name of social responsibility have reduced the corporation's profits and the price of its stock.) His customers and his employees can desert him for other producers and employers less scrupulous in exercising their social responsibilities.

This facet of "social responsibility" doctrine is brought into sharp relief when the doctrine is used to justify wage restraint by trade unions. The conflict of interest is naked and clear when union officials are asked to subordinate the interest of their members to some more general social purpose. If the union officials try to enforce wage restraint, the consequence is likely to be wildcat strikes, rank-and-file revolts and the emergence of strong competitors for their jobs. We thus have the ironic phenomenon that union leaders—at least in the U.S.—have objected to Government interference with the market far more consistently and courageously than have business leaders.

The difficulty of exercising "social responsibility" illustrates, of course, the great virtue of private competitive enterprise—it forces people to be responsible for their own actions and makes it difficult for them to "exploit" other people for either selfish or unselfish purposes. They can do good—but only at their own expense.

Many a reader who has followed the argument this far may be tempted to remonstrate that it is all well and good to speak of government's having the responsibility to impose taxes and determine expenditures for such "social" purposes as controlling pollution or training the hard-core unemployed, but that the problems are too urgent to wait on the slow course of political processes, that the exercise of social responsibility by businessmen is a quicker and surer way to solve pressing current problems.

Aside from the question of fact—I share Adam Smith's skepticism about the benefits that can be expected from "those who affected to trade for the public good"—this argument must be rejected on grounds of principle. What it amounts to is an assertion that those who favor the taxes and expenditures in question have failed to persuade a majority of their fellow citizens to be of like mind and that they are seeking to attain by undemocratic procedures what they cannot attain by democratic procedures. In a free society, it is hard for "good" people to do "good," but that is a small price to pay for making it hard for "evil" people to do "evil," especially since one man's good is another's evil.

I have, for simplicity, concentrated on the special case of the corporate executive, except only for the brief digression on trade unions. But precisely the same argument applies to the newer phenomenon of calling upon stockholders to require corporations to exercise social responsibility (the recent G.M. crusade, for example). In most of these cases, what is in effect involved is some stockholders trying to get other stockholders (or customers or employees) to contribute against their will to "social" causes favored by the activists. Insofar as they succeed, they are again imposing taxes and spending the proceeds.

The situation of the individual proprietor is somewhat different. If he acts to reduce the returns of his enterprise in order to exercise his "social responsibility," he is spending his own money, not someone else's. If he wishes to spend his money on such purposes, that is his right, and I cannot see that there is any objection to his doing so. In the process, he, too, may impose costs on employees and customers. However, because he is far less likely than a large corporation or union to have monopolistic power, any such side effects will tend to be minor.

Of course, in practice the doctrine of social responsibility is frequently a cloak for actions that are justified on other grounds rather than a reason for those actions.

To illustrate, it may well be in the long-run interest of a corporation that is a major employer in a small community to devote resources to providing amenities to that community or to improving its government. That may make it easier to attract desirable employees, it may reduce the wage bill or lessen losses from pilferage and sabotage or have other worthwhile effects. Or it may be that, given the laws about the deductibility of corporate charitable contributions, the stockholders can contribute more to charities they favor by having the corporation make the gift than by doing it themselves, since they can in that way contribute an amount that would otherwise have been paid as corporate taxes.

In each of these—and many similar—cases, there is a strong temptation to rationalize these actions as an exercise of "social responsibility." In the present climate of opinion, with its widespread aversion to "capitalism," "profits," the "soulless corporation" and so on, this is one way for a corporation to generate goodwill as a by-product of expenditures that are entirely justified in its own self-interest.

It would be inconsistent of me to call on corporate executives to refrain from this hypocritical window-dressing because it harms the foundations of a free society. That would be to call on them to exercise a "social responsibility"! If our institutions, and the attitudes of the public make it in their self-interest to cloak their actions in this way, I cannot summon much indignation to denounce them. At the same time, I can express admiration for those individual proprietors or owners of closely held corporations or stockholders of more broadly held corporations who disdain such tactics as approaching fraud.

Whether blameworthy or not, the use of the cloak of social responsibility, and the nonsense spoken in its name by influential and prestigious businessmen, does clearly harm the foundations of a free society. I have been impressed time and again by the schizophrenic character of many businessmen. They are capable of being extremely far-sighted and clear-headed in matters that are internal to their businesses. They are incredibly short-sighted and muddleheaded in matters that are outside their businesses but affect the possible survival of business in general. This short-sightedness is strikingly exemplified in the calls from many businessmen for wage and price guidelines or controls or income policies. There is nothing that could do more in a brief period to destroy a market system and replace it by a centrally controlled system than effective governmental control of prices and wages.

The short-sightedness is also exemplified in speeches by businessmen on social responsibility. This may gain them kudos in the short run. But it helps to strengthen the already too prevalent view that the pursuit of profits is wicked and immoral and must be curbed and controlled by external forces. Once this view is adopted, the external forces that curb the market will not be the social consciences, however highly developed, of the pontificating executives; it will be the iron fist of Government bureaucrats. Here, as with price and wage controls, businessmen seem to me to reveal a suicidal impulse.

The political principle that underlies the market mechanism is unanimity. In an ideal free market resting on private property, no individual can coerce any other, all cooperation is voluntary, all parties to such cooperation benefit or they need not participate. There are no "social" values, no "social" responsibilities in any sense other than the shared values and responsibilities of individuals. Society is a collection of individuals and of the various groups they voluntarily form.

The political principle that underlies the political mechanism is conformity. The individual must serve a more general social interest—whether that be determined by a church or a dictator or a majority. The individual may have a vote and a say in what is to be done, but if he is overruled, he must conform. It is appropriate for some to require others to contribute to a general social purpose whether they wish to or not.

Unfortunately, unanimity is not always feasible. There are some respects in which conformity appears unavoidable, so I do not see how one can avoid the use of the political mechanism altogether.

But the doctrine of "social responsibility" taken seriously would extend the scope of the political mechanism to every human activity. It does not differ in philosophy from the most explicitly collectivist doctrine. It differs only by professing to believe that collectivist ends can be attained without collectivist means. That is why, in my book "Capitalism and Freedom," I have called it a "fundamentally subversive doctrine" in a free society, and have said that in such a society, "there is one and only one social responsibility of business—to use its resources and engage in activities designed to increase its profits so long as it stays within the rules of the game, which is to say, engages in open and free competition without deception or fraud."

Robert Almeder

Morality in the Marketplace: Reflections on the Friedman Doctrine

Introduction

In seeking to create a climate more favorable for corporate activity, International Telephone and Telegraph allegedly contributed large sums of money to "destabilize" the duly elected government of Chile. Even though advised by the scientific community that the practice is lethal, major chemical companies reportedly continue to dump large amounts of carcinogens and mutagens into the water supply of various areas and, at the same time, lobby strongly to prevent legislation against such practices. General Motors Corporation, other automobile manufacturers, and Firestone Tire and Rubber Corporation have frequently defended themselves against the charge that they knowingly and willingly marketed a product that, owing to defective design, had been reliably predicted to kill a certain percentage of its users and, moreover, refused to recall promptly the product even when government agencies documented the large incidence of death as a result of the defective product. Finally, people often say that numerous advertising companies happily accept, and earnestly solicit, accounts to advertise cigarettes knowing full well that as a direct result of their advertising activities a certain number of people will die considerably prematurely and painfully. Most recently, of course, American Tobacco Companies have been charged with knowingly marketing a very addictive product known to kill untold numbers in slow, painful and costly deaths while the price of the stock of these companies has made fortunes for the shareholders. We need not concern ourselves with whether these and other similar charges are true because our primary concern here is with what might count as a justification for such corporate conduct were it to occur. There can be no question that such corporate behavior sometimes occurs and is frequently legal, or at least not illegal. The question is whether corporate behavior should be constrained by nonlegal or moral considerations. If so, to what extent and how could it be done? As things presently stand, it seems to be a dogma of contemporary capitalism rapidly emerging throughout the world that the sole responsibility of business is to make as much money as is *legally* possible. But the interesting question is whether this view is rationally defensible.

Sometimes, although not very frequently, corporate executives will admit to the sort of behavior depicted above and then proceed proximately to justify such behavior in the name of their responsibility to the shareholders or owners (if the shareholders are not the owners) to make as much profit as is legally possible. Thereafter, less proximately and more generally, they will proceed to urge the more general utilitarian point that the increase in profit engendered by such corporate behavior begets such an unquestionable overall good for society that the behavior in question is morally acceptable if not quite praiseworthy. More specifically, the justification in question can, and usually does, take two forms.

The first and most common form of justification consists in urging that, as long as one's corporate behavior is not illegal, the behavior will be morally acceptable because the sole purpose of being in business is to make a profit; and the rules of the marketplace are somewhat different from those in other places and must be followed if one is to make a profit. Moreover, proponents of this view hasten to add that, as Adam Smith has claimed, the greatest good for society in the long run is achieved not by corporations seeking to act morally, or with a sense of social responsibility in their pursuit of profit, but rather by each corporation seeking to maximize its own profit, unregulated in that endeavor except by the laws of supply and demand along with whatever other laws are inherent to the competition process. This, they say, is what has made capitalist societies the envy of the world while ideological socialisms sooner or later fail miserably to meet deep human needs. Smith's view, that there is an invisible hand, as it were, directing an economy governed solely by the profit motive to the greatest good for society in the long run,[1] is still the dominant motivation and justification for those who would want an economy unregulated by any moral concern that would, or could, tend to decrease profits for some *alleged* social or moral good.

Milton Friedman, for example, has frequently asserted that the sole moral responsibility of business is to make as much profit as is legally possible; and by that he means to assert that attempts to regulate or restrain the pursuit of profit in accordance with what some people believe to be socially desirable ends are in fact *subversive* of the common good because the greatest good for the greatest number is achieved by an economy maximally competitive and unregulated by moral rules in its pursuit of profit.[2] So, on Friedman's view, the greatest good for society is achieved by corporations acting legally, but with no further regard for what may be morally desirable; and this view begets the paradox that, *in business*, the greatest good for society can be achieved only by acting without regard for morality, at least in so far as moral rules are not reflected in the legal code. Moreover, adoption of this position constitutes a fairly conscious commitment to the view that while one's personal life may well need moral governance beyond the law, when pursuing profit, it is necessary that one's corporate behavior be unregulated by any moral concern other than that of making as much money as is legally possible; curiously enough, it is only in this way that society achieves the greatest good. So viewed, it is not difficult to see how a corporate executive could sincerely and consistently adopt rigorous standards of morality in his or her personal life and yet feel quite comfortable in abandoning those standards in the pursuit of profit. Albert Carr, for example, likens the conduct of business to that of playing poker.[3] As Carr would have it, moral busybodies who insist on corporations acting morally might do just as well to censure a good bluffer in poker for being deceitful. Society, of course, lacking a perspective such as Friedman's and Carr's is only too willing to view such behavior as strongly hypocritical and fostered by an unwholesome avarice.

The second way of justifying, or defending, corporate practices that may appear morally questionable consists in urging that even if corporations were to take seriously the idea of limiting profits because of a desire to be moral or more responsible to social needs, then corporations would be involved in the unwholesome business of selecting and implementing moral values that may not be shared by a large number of people. Besides, there is the overwhelming question of whether there can be any non-questionable moral values or non-controversial list of social priorities for corporations to adopt. After all, if ethical relativism is true, or if ethical nihilism is true (and philosophers can be counted upon to argue agressively for both positions), then it would be fairly silly of corporations to limit profits for what may be a quite dubious reason, namely, for being moral, when there are no clear grounds for doing it, and when it is not too clear what would count for doing it. In short, business corporations could argue (as Friedman has done)[4] that corporate actions in behalf of society's interests would require of corporations an ability to clearly determine and rank in noncontroversial ways the major needs of society; and it would not appear that this could be done successfully.

Perhaps another, and somewhat easier, way of formulating this second argument consists in urging that because moralists and philosophers generally fail to agree on what are the proper moral rules (if any), as well as on whether we should be moral, it would be imprudent to sacrifice a clear profit for a dubious or controversial moral gain. To authorize such a sacrifice would be to abandon a clear responsibility for one that is unclear or questionable.

If there are any other basic ways of justifying the sort of corporate behavior noted at the outset, I cannot imagine what they might be. So, let us examine these two modes of justification. In doing this, I hope to show that neither argument is sound and, moreover, that corporate behavior of the sort in question is clearly immoral if anything is immoral—and if nothing is immoral, then such corporate behavior is clearly contrary to the long-term interest of a corporation. In the end, we will reflect on ways to prevent such behavior, and on what is philosophically implied by corporate willingness to act in clearly immoral ways.

The "Invisible Hand"

Essentially, the first argument is that the greatest good for the greatest number will be, and can only be, achieved by corporations acting legally but unregulated by any moral concern in the pursuit of profit. As we saw earlier, the evidence for this argument rests on a fairly classical and unquestioning acceptance of Adam Smith's view that society achieves a greater good when each person is allowed to pursue her or his own self-interested ends than when each person's pursuit of self-interested ends is regulated in some way or another by moral rules or concern. But I know of no evidence Smith ever offered for this latter claim, although it seems clear that those who adopt it generally do so out of respect for the perceived good that has emerged for various modern societies as a direct result of the free enterprise system and its ability to raise the overall standard of living of all those under it.

However, there is nothing inevitable about the greatest good occurring in an unregulated economy. Indeed, we have good inductive evidence from the age of the Robber Barons that unless the profit motive is regulated in various ways (by statute or otherwise) untold social evil can, and *will,* occur because of the natural tendency of the system to place ever-increasing sums of money in ever-decreasing numbers of hands as a result of the nature of competition unregulated. If all this is so, then so much the worse for all philosophical attempts to justify what would appear to be morally questionable corporate behavior on the grounds that corporate behavior, unregulated by moral concern, is necessarily or even probably productive of the greatest good for the greatest number. Moreover, a rule utilitarian would not be very hard pressed to show the many unsavory implications to society as a whole if society were to take seriously a rule to the effect that, if one acts legally, it is morally permissible to do whatever one wants to do to achieve a profit. We shall discuss some of those implications of this rule below before drawing a conclusion.

The second argument cited above asserts that even if we were to grant, for the sake of argument, that corporations have social responsibilities beyond that of making as much money as is legally possible for the shareholders, there would be no noncontroversial way for corporations to discover just what these responsibilities are in the order of their importance. Owing to the fact that even distinguished moral philosophers predictably disagree on what one's moral responsibilities are, if any, it would seem irresponsible to limit profits to satisfy dubious moral responsibilities.

For one thing, this argument unduly exaggerates our potential for moral disagreement. Admittedly, there might well be important disagreements among corporations (just as there could be among philosophers) as to a priority ranking of major social needs; but that does not mean that most of us could not, or would not, agree that certain things ought not be done in the name of profit even when there is no law prohibiting such acts. Doubtless, there will always be a few who would do most anything for a profit; but that is hardly a good argument in favor of their having the moral right to do so rather than a good argument showing that they refuse to be moral. In sum, it is difficult to see how this second argument favoring corporate moral nihilism is any better than the general argument for ethical nihilism based on the variability of ethical judgments or practices; and apart from the fact that it tacitly presupposes that morality is a matter of what we all in fact would, or should, accept, the argument is maximally counterintuitive (as I shall show) by way of suggesting that we cannot generally agree that corporations have certain clear social responsibilities to avoid certain practices. Accordingly, I would now like to argue that if anything is immoral, a certain kind of corporate behavior is quite immoral although it may not be illegal.

Murder for Profit

Without caring to enter into the reasons for the belief, I assume we all believe that it is wrong to kill an innocent human being for no other reason than that doing so would be more financially rewarding for the killer than if he were to earn his livelihood in some other way. Nor, I assume, should our moral feeling on this matter change depending on the amount of money involved. Killing an innocent baby for fifteen million dollars would not seem to be any less objectionable than killing it for twenty cents. It is possible, however, that a self-professing utilitarian might be tempted to argue that the killing of an innocent baby for fifteen million dollars would not be objectionable if the money were to be given to the poor; under these circumstances, greater good would be achieved by the killing of the innocent baby. But, I submit, if anybody were to argue in this fashion, his argument would be quite deficient because he has not established what he needs to establish to make his argument sound. What he needs is a clear, convincing argument that raising the standard of living of an indefinite number of poor persons by the killing of an innocent person is a greater good for all those affected by the act than if the standard of living were not raised by the killing of an innocent person. This is needed because part of what we mean by having a basic right to life is that a person's life cannot be taken from him or her without a good reason. If our utilitarian cannot provide a convincing justification for his claim that a greater good is served by killing an innocent person in order to raise the standard of living for a large number of poor people, then it is hard to see how he can have the good reason that he needs to deprive an innocent person of his or her life. Now, it seems clear that there will be anything but unanimity in the moral community on the question of whether there is a greater good achieved in raising the standard of living by killing an innocent baby than in leaving the standard of living alone and not killing an innocent baby. Moreover, even if everybody were to agree that the greater good is achieved by the killing of the innocent baby, how could that be shown to be true? How does one compare the moral value of a human life with the moral value of raising the standard of living by the taking of that life? Indeed, the more one thinks about it, the more difficult it is to see just what would count as objective evidence for the claim that the greater good is achieved by the killing of the innocent baby. Accordingly, I can see nothing that would justify the utilitarian who might be tempted to argue that if the sum is large enough, and if the sum were to be used for raising the standard of living for an indefinite number of poor people, then it would be morally acceptable to kill an innocent person for money.

These reflections should not be taken to imply, however, that no utilitarian argument could justify the killing of an innocent person for money. After all, if the sum were large enough to save the lives of a large number of people who would surely die if the innocent baby were not killed, then one would as a rule be justified in killing the innocent baby for the sum in question. But this situation is obviously quite different from the situation in which one would attempt to justify the killing of an innocent person in order to raise the standard of living for an indefinite number of poor people. It makes sense to kill one innocent person in order to save, say, twenty innocent persons; but it makes no sense at all to kill one innocent person to raise the standard of living of an indefinite number of people. In the latter case, but not in the former, a comparison is made between things that are incomparable.

Given these considerations, it is remarkable and somewhat perplexing that certain corporations should seek to defend practices that are in fact instances of killing innocent persons for profit. Take, for example, the corporate practice of dumping known carcinogens into rivers. On Milton Friedman's view, we should not regulate or prevent such companies from dumping their effluents into the environment. Rather we should, if we like, tax the company after the effluents are in the water and then have the tax money used to clean up the environment.[5] For Friedman, and others, the fact that so many people will die as a result of this practice seems to be just part of the cost of doing business and making a profit. If there is any moral difference between such corporate practices and murdering innocent human beings for money, it is hard to see what it is. It is even more difficult to see how anyone could justify the practice and see it as no more than a business practice not to be regulated by moral concern. And there are a host of other corporate activities that are morally equivalent to deliberate killing of innocent persons for money. Such practices number among them contributing funds to "destabilize" a foreign government, selling cigarettes while knowing that they are highly addictive killers of innocent people, advertising cigarettes, knowingly marketing children's clothing having a known cancer-causing agent, and refusing to recall (for fear of financial loss) goods known to be sufficiently defective to directly maim or kill a certain percentage of their unsuspecting users because of the defect. On this latter item, we are all familiar, for example, with convincingly documented charges that certain prominent automobile and tire manufacturers will knowingly market equipment sufficiently defective to increase the likelihood of death as a direct result of the defect, and yet refuse to recall the product because the cost of recalling and repairing would have a greater adverse impact on profit than if the product were not recalled and the company paid the projected number of predictably successful suits. Of course, if the projected cost of the predictably successful suits were to outweigh the cost of recall and repair, then the product would be recalled and repaired, but not otherwise.

In cases of this sort, the companies involved may admit to having certain marketing problems or a design problem, and they may even admit to having made a mistake; but, interestingly enough, they do not view themselves as immoral or as murderers for keeping their product in the market place when they know people are dying from it, people who would not die if the defect were corrected.

The important point is not whether in fact these practices have occurred in the past, or occur even now; there can be no doubt that such practices have occurred and continue to occur. Rather the point is that when companies act in such ways as a matter of policy, they must either not know what they do is murder (i.e., unjustifiable killing of an innocent person), or knowing that it is murder, seek to justify it in terms of profit. And I have been arguing that it is difficult to see how any corporate manager could fail to see that these policies amount to murder for money, although there may be no civil statute against such corporate behavior. If so, then where such policies exist, we can only assume that they are designed and implemented by corporate managers who either see nothing wrong with murder for money (which is implausible) or recognize that what they do is wrong but simply refuse to act morally because it is more financially rewarding to act immorally.

Of course, it is possible that corporate executives would not recognize such acts as murder. They may, after all, view murder as a legal concept involving one non-corporate person or persons deliberately killing another noncorporate person or persons and prosecutable only under existing criminal statute. If so, it is somewhat understandable how corporate executives might fail, at least psychologically, to see such corporate policies as murder rather than as, say, calculated risks, tradeoffs, or design errors. Still, for all that, the logic of the situation seems clear enough.

Conclusion

In addition to the fact that the only two plausible arguments favoring the Friedman doctrine are unsatisfactory, a strong case can be made for the claim that corporations *do* have a clear and noncontroversial moral responsibility not to design or implement, for reasons of profit, policies that they know, or have good reason to believe, will kill or otherwise seriously injure innocent persons affected by those policies. Moreover, we have said nothing about wage discrimination, sexism, discrimination in hiring, price fixing, price gouging, questionable but not unlawful competition, or other similar practices that some will think businesses should avoid by virtue of responsibility to society. My main concern has been to show that because we all agree that murder for money is generally wrong, and since there is no discernible difference between that and certain corporate policies that are not in fact illegal, then these corporate practices are clearly immoral (that is, they ought not to be done) and incapable of being morally justified by appeal to the Friedman doctrine since that doctrine does not admit of adequate evidential support. In itself, it seems sad that this argument needs to be made and, if it were not for what appears to be a fairly strong commitment within the business community to the Friedman doctrine in the name of the unquestionable success of the free enterprise system, the argument would not need to be stated.

The fact that such practices do exist—designed and implemented by corporate managers who, for all intents and purposes appear to be upright members of the moral community—only heightens the need for effective social prevention. Presumably, of course, any company willing to put human lives into the profit and loss column is not likely to respond to moral censure. Accordingly, I submit that perhaps the most effective way to deal with the problem of preventing such corporate behavior would consist in structuring legislation such that senior corporate managers who knowingly concur in practices of the sort listed above can effectively be tried, at their own expense, for murder, rather than censured and fined a sum to be paid out of corporate profits. This may seem a somewhat extreme or unrealistic proposal. However, it seems more unrealistic to think that aggressively competitive corporations will respond to what is morally necessary if failure to do so could be very or even minimally profitable. In short, unless we take strong and appropriate steps to prevent such practices, society will be reinforcing a destructive mode of behavior that is maximally disrespectful of human life, just as society will be reinforcing a value system that so emphasizes monetary gain as a standard of human success that murder for profit could be a corporate policy if the penalty for being caught at it were not too dear.

Fortunately, a number of states in America have enacted legislation that makes corporations subject to the criminal code of that state. This practice began to emerge quite strongly after the famous Pinto case in which an Indiana superior court judge refused to dismiss a homicide indictment against the Ford Motor Company. The company was indicted on charges of reckless homicide stemming from a 1978 accident involving a 1973 Pinto in which three girls died when the car burst into flames after being slammed in the rear. This was the first case in which Ford, or any other automobile manufacturer, had been charged with a criminal offense. The indictment went forward because the state of Indiana adopted in 1977 a criminal code provision permitting corporations to be charged with criminal acts. At the time, incidentally, twenty-two other states had similar codes. At any rate, the judge, in refusing to set aside the indictment, agreed with the prosecutor's argument that the charge was based not on the Pinto design fault, but rather on the fact that Ford had permitted the car "to remain on Indiana highways knowing full well its defects." The fact that the Ford Motor company was ultimately found innocent of the charges by the jury is incidental to the point that the increasing number of states that allow corporations to fall under the criminal code is an example of social regulation that could have been avoided had corporations and corporate managers not followed so ardently the Friedman doctrine.

In the long run, of course, corporate and individual willingness to do what is clearly immoral for the sake of monetary gain is a patent commitment of a certain view about the nature of human happiness and success, a view that needs to be placed in the balance with Aristotle's reasoned argument and reflections to the effect that money and all that it brings is a means to an end, and not the sort of end in itself that will justify acting immorally to attain it. What that beautiful end is and why being moral allows us to achieve it, may well be the most rewarding and profitable subject a human being can think about. Properly understood and placed in perspective, Aristotle's view on the nature and attainment of human happiness could go a long way toward alleviating the temptation to kill for money.

In the meantime, any ardent supporter of the capitalistic system will want to see the system thrive and flourish; and this it cannot do if it invites and demands government regulation in the name of the public interest. A *strong* ideological commitment to what I have described above as the Friedman doctrine is counterproductive and not in anyone's long-range interest because it is most likely to beget an ever-increasing regulatory climate. The only way to avoid such encroaching regulation is to find ways to move the business community into the long-term view of what is in its interest, and effect ways of both determining and responding to social needs before society moves to regulate business to that end. To so move the business community is to ask business to regulate its own modes of competition in ways that may seem very difficult to achieve. Indeed, if what I have been suggesting is correct, the only kind of enduring capitalism is humane capitalism, one that is at least as socially responsible as society needs. By the same token, contrary to what is sometimes felt in the business community, the Friedman doctrine, ardently adopted for the dubious reasons generally given, will most likely undermine capitalism and motivate an economic socialism by assuring an erosive regulatory climate in a society that expects the business community to be socially responsible in ways that go beyond just making legal profits.

In sum, being socially responsible in ways that go beyond legal profit making is by no means a dubious luxury for the capitalist in today's world. It is a necessity if capitalism is to survive at all; and, presumably, we shall all profit with the survival of a vibrant capitalism. If anything, then, rigid adherence to the Friedman doctrine is not only philosophically unjustified, and unjustifiable, it is also unprofitable in the long run, and therefore, downright subversive of the long-term common good. Unfortunately, taking the long-run view is difficult for everyone. After all, for each of us, tomorrow may not come. But living for today only does not seem to make much sense either, if that deprives us of any reasonable and happy tomorrow. Living for the future may not be the healthiest thing to do; but do it we must, if we have good reason to think that we will have a future. The trick is to provide for the future without living in it, and that just requires being moral.[6]

This paper is a revised and expanded version of "Morality in the Marketplace," which appears in Business Ethics *(revised edition) eds. Milton Snoeyenbos, Robert Almeder and James Humber (Buffalo, N.Y.: Prometheus Press, 1992) 82–90, and, as such, it is a revised and expanded version of an earlier piece "The Ethics of Profit: Reflections on Corporate Responsibility," which originally appeared in* Business and Society *(Winter 1980, 7–15).*

Notes

1. Adam Smith, *The Wealth of Nations,* ed. Edwin Canaan (New York: Modern Library, 1937), p. 423.

2. See Milton Friedman, "The Social Responsibility of Business Is to Increase Its Profits," in *The New York Times Magazine* (September 13, 1970), pp. 33, 122–126 and "Milton Friedman Responds," in *Business and Society Review* no. 1 (Spring 1972), p. 5ff.

3. Albert Z. Carr, "Is Business Bluffing Ethical?" *Harvard Business Review* (January–February 1968).

4. Milton Friedman in "Milton Friedman Responds," in *Business and Society Review* no. 1 (Spring 1972), p. 10.

5. Ibid.

6. I would like to thank J. Humber and M. Snoeyenbos for their comments and criticisms of an earlier draft.

POSTSCRIPT

Are Profits the Only Business of Business?

Friedman dismisses the pleas of those who argue for socially responsible business action on the grounds that these individuals do not understand the role of the corporate executive in modern society. Friedman points out that the executives are responsible to the corporate owners, and if the corporate executives take a "socially responsible" action that reduces the return on the owners' investment, they have spent the owners' money. This, Friedman maintains, violates the very foundation of the American political-economic system: individual freedom. If the corporate executives wish to take socially responsible actions, they should use their own money; they should not prevent the owners from spending their money on whatever social actions they might wish to support.

Almeder argues that some corporate behavior is immoral and that defense of this immoral behavior imposes great costs on society. He likens corporate acts such as advertising cigarettes, marketing automobiles that cannot sustain moderate rear-end collisions, and contributing funds to destabilize foreign governments to murdering innocent children for profit. He argues that society must not condone this behavior but, instead, through federal and state legislation, must continue to impose regulations upon businesses until businesses begin to regulate themselves.

Perhaps no single topic is more fundamental to microeconomics than the issue of profits. Many pages have been written in defense of profits; see, for example, Milton and Rose Friedman's *Free to Choose: A Personal Statement* (Harcourt Brace Jovanovich, 1980). A classic reference is Frank H. Knight's *Risk, Uncertainty, and Profits* (Kelly Press, 1921). Friedrich A. Hayek, the author of many journal articles and books, is a guru for many current free marketers. There are a number of other books and articles, however, that are highly critical of the Friedman-Knight-Hayek position, including Christopher D. Stone's *Where the Law Ends: Social Control of Corporate Behavior* (Harper & Row, 1975). Others who challenge the legitimacy of the notion that markets are morally free zones include Thomas Mulligan, "A Critique of Milton Friedman's Essay 'The Social Responsibility of Business Is to Increase Its Profits,'" *Journal of Business Ethics* (1986); Daniel M. Hausman, "Are Markets Morally Free Zones?" *Philosophy and Public Affairs* (Fall 1989); and Andrew Henley, "Economic Orthodoxy and the Free Market System: A Christian Critique," *International Journal of Social Economics* (vol. 14, no. 10, 1987).

ISSUE 2

Are CEOs Paid What They Are Worth?

YES: Ira T. Kay, from "Don't Mess With CEO Pay," *Across the Board* (January/February 2006)

NO: Edgar Woolard, Jr., from "CEOs Are Being Paid Too Much," *Across the Board* (January/February 2006)

ISSUE SUMMARY

YES: Ira T. Kay, businessman and author, defends current CEO pay practices. He argues that "Empirical studies show that executive compensation has closely tracked corporate performance," and that rejecting pay-for-performance will hurt both workers and stockholders.

NO: Edgar Woolard, Jr., former CEO and chairman of Dupont, describes four myths regarding the compensation received by corporate business leaders. Dismissing the myths, he believes no one but CEOs get "paid excessively when they fail."

Perhaps the strongest argument for market economies rests on their ability to produce an efficient allocation of resources. There may be cases in which markets fail to produce these efficient outcomes, but these instances of market failure, as in the case of public goods or goods that involve positive or negative externalities, should be infrequent. In the process of producing these efficient outcomes, markets will also produce inequalities. Indeed, most people are willing to accept unequal outcomes because of the resulting efficiencies. In taking this position, these individuals distinguish between equality of outcomes from equality of opportunities; the former is accepted so long as the latter exists.

These abstract notions of inequality of outcomes become more real when we consider some of the actual differences in incomes and earnings. Take first the differences in the distribution of household income. In 2005 the poorest 20 percent of households in the United States received 3.4 percent of total household income while the richest 20 percent of households received more than 15 times as much, about 50 percent of total household income (there were 114 million households in 2005). The figures are perhaps even more striking if we consider the difference in the earnings of those working at the minimum wage and those who serve as the heads of the country's largest companies. The current federal minimum wage is $5.15 an hour, a level set by Congress in 1996. This translates into a yearly income of $10,300 (assuming the individual works 40 hours a week for 50 weeks per year). This compares with an estimated 2005 total compensation package of $13.5 million for the average chief executive of a Standard and Poor's 500 company (The Corporate Library's 2006 CEO Pay Survey, The Corporate Library, September 29, 2006). And while the federal minimum wage has not changed since 1996, the just-cited study estimated the change in average total executive compensation between 2004 and 2005 at 16.4 percent.

Some people do more than simply complain that executive compensation is excessive; they have taken legal action to take away a part of that compensation. Perhaps the most famous of these cases involves Eliot Spitzer, who before being elected governor of the state of New York served as its attorney general, and Richard Grasso, former president of the New York Stock Exchange (NYSE). The charge is that Mr. Grasso's $187.5 million pay package was excessive and that he must return a portion of his pay to the NYSE. At the time of this writing the outcome of this case has not been determined.

Although almost everyone would agree that a chief executive of a business should be paid more than the average employee of that business, the issue is one of how much more. Are the executives, in fact, worth the pay represented by the $13.5 million figure cited above? Ira T. Kay admits that there are abuses in executive compensation, but argues that in most cases CEOs really earn all that they get. Edward Woolard, Jr., takes the opposite position. He believes that CEO pay is excessive, and it is time to get the system of executive compensation back under control.

Don't Mess With CEO Pay

For years, headlines have seized on dramatic accounts of outrageous amounts earned by executives—often of failing companies—and the financial tragedy that can befall both shareholders and employees when CEOs line their own pockets at the organization's expense. Images of lavish executive life-styles are now engraved in the popular consciousness. The result: public support for political responses that include new regulatory measures and a long list of demands for greater shareholder or government control over executive compensation.

These images now overshadow the reality of thousands of successful companies with appropriately paid executives and conscientious boards. Instead, fresh accusations of CEOs collecting huge amounts of undeserved pay appear daily, fueling a full-blown mythology of a corporate America ruled by executive greed, fraud, and corruption.

This mythology consists of two related components: the myth of the failed pay-for-performance model and the myth of managerial power. The first myth hinges on the idea that the link between executive pay and corporate performance—if it ever existed—is irretrievably broken. The second myth accepts the idea of a failed pay-for-performance model and puts in its service the image of unchecked CEOs dominating subservient boards as the explanation for decisions resulting in excessive executive pay. The powerful combination of these two myths has captured newspaper headlines and shareholder agendas, regulatory attention and the public imagination. . . .

Fueling the Fiction

. . . In recent years, dozens of reporters from business magazines and the major newspapers have called me and specifically asked for examples of companies in which CEOs received exorbitant compensation, approved by the board, while the company performed poorly. Not once have I been asked to comment on the vast majority of companies—those in which executives are appropriately rewarded for performance or in which boards have reduced compensation or even fired the CEO for poor performance.

I have spent hundreds of hours answering reporters' questions, providing extensive data and explaining the pay-for-performance model of executive compensation, but my efforts have had little impact: The resulting stories feature the same anecdotal reporting on those corporations for which the process has gone awry. The press accounts ignore solid research that shows that annual pay for most executives moves up and down significantly with the company's performance, both financial and stock-related. Corporate wrongdoings and outlandish executive pay packages make for lively headlines, but the reliance on purely anecdotal reporting and the highly prejudicial language adopted are a huge disservice to the companies, their executives and employees, investors, and the public. The likelihood of real economic damage to the U.S. economy grows daily.

For example, the mythology drives institutional investors and trade unions with the power to exert enormous pressure on regulators and executive and board practices. The California Public Employees' Retirement System—the nation's largest public pension fund—offers a typical example in its Nov. 15, 2004, announcement of a new campaign to rein in "abusive compensation practices in corporate America and hold directors and compensation committees more accountable for their actions."

The AFL-CIO's website offers another example of the claim that managerial power has destroyed the efficacy of the pay-for-performance model: "Each year, shocking new examples of CEO pay greed are made public. Investors are concerned not just about the growing size of executive compensation packages, but the fact that CEO pay levels show little apparent relationship to corporate profits, stock prices or executive performance. How do CEOs do it? For years, executives have relied on their shareholders to be passive absentee owners. CEOs have rigged their own compensation packages by packing their boards with conflicted or negligent directors."

The ROI of the CEO

As with all modern myths, there's a grain of truth in all the assumptions and newspaper stories. The myths of managerial power and of the failed pay-for-performance model find touchstones in real examples of companies where CEOs have collected huge sums in cash compensation and stock options while shareholder returns declined. . . .

These exceptions in executive pay practices, however, are now commonly mistaken for the rule. . . . Never mind that these same CEOs stand at the center of a corporate model that has generated millions of jobs and trillions of dollars in shareholder earnings. Worse, using CEOs as scapegoats distracts from the real causes of and possible solutions for inequality.

The primary determinant of CEO pay is the same force that sets pay for all Americans: relatively free—if somewhat imperfect—labor markets, in which companies offer the levels of compensation necessary to attract and retain the employees who generate value for shareholders. Part of that pay for most executives consists of stock-based incentives. A 2003 study by Brian J. Hall and Kevin J. Murphy shows that the ratio of total CEO compensation to production workers' average earnings closely follows the Dow Jones Industrial Average. When the Dow soars, the gap between executive and non-executive compensation widens. The problem, it seems, is not that CEOs receive too much performance-driven, stock-based compensation, but that non-executives receive too little.

The key question is not the actual dollar amount paid to a CEO in total compensation or whether that amount represents a high multiple of pay of the average worker's salary but, rather, whether that CEO creates an adequate return on the company's investment in executive compensation. In virtually every area of business, directors routinely evaluate and adjust the amounts that companies invest in all inputs, and shareholders directly or indirectly endorse or challenge those decisions. Executive pay is no different.

Hard Realities

The corporate scandals of recent years laid bare the inner workings of a handful of public companies where, inarguably, the process for setting executive pay violated not only the principle of pay-for-performance but the extensive set of laws and regulations governing executive pay practices and the role of the board. But while I condemn illegal actions and criticize boards that reward executives who fail to produce positive financial results, I know that the vast majority of U.S. corporations do much better by their shareholders and the public. I have worked directly with more than a thousand publicly traded companies in the United States and attended thousands of compensation-committee meetings, and I have *never* witnessed board members straining to find a way to pay an executive more than he is worth.

In addition, at Watson Wyatt I work with a team of experts that has conducted extensive research at fifteen hundred of America's largest corporations and tracked the relationship between these pay practices and corporate performance over almost twenty years. In evaluating thousands of companies annually, yielding nearly twenty thousand "company years" of data, and pooling cross-sectional company data over multiple years, we have discovered that for both most companies and the "typical" company, there is substantial pay-for-performance sensitivity. That is, high performance generates high pay for executives and low performance generates low pay. Numerous empirical academic studies support our conclusions.

Our empirical evidence and evidence from other studies have produced the following key findings:

1. Executive pay is unquestionably high relative to low-level corporate positions, and it has risen dramatically over the past ten to fifteen years, faster than inflation and faster than average employee pay. But executive compensation generally tracks total returns to shareholders—even including the recent rise in pay.
2. Executive stock ownership has risen dramatically over the past ten to fifteen years. High levels of CEO stock ownership are correlated with and most likely the cause of companies' high financial and stock-market performance.

3. Executives are paid commensurate with the skills and talents that they bring to the organization. Underperforming executives routinely receive pay reductions or are terminated—far more often than press accounts imply.
4. CEOs who are recruited from outside a company and have little influence over its board receive compensation that is competitive with and often higher than the pay levels of CEOs who are promoted from within the company.
5. At the vast majority of companies, even extraordinarily high levels of CEO compensation represent a tiny fraction of the total value created by the corporation under that CEO's leadership. (Watson Wyatt has found that U.S. executives receive approximately 1 percent of the net income generated by the corporations they manage.) Well-run companies, it bears pointing out, produce significant shareholder returns and job security for millions of workers. . . .

Why CEOs Are Worth the Money

The huge gap between the realities of executive pay and the now-dominant mythology surrounding it has become even more evident in recent years. Empirical studies show that executive compensation has closely tracked corporate performance: Pay rose during the boom years of the 1990s, when U.S. corporations generated huge returns, declined during the 2001–03 profit slowdown, and increased in 2004 as profits improved. The myth of excessive executive pay continued to gain power, however, even as concrete, well-documented financial realities defied it.

The blind outrage over executive pay climbed even during the slow-down, as compensation dropped drastically. During this same period, in the aftermath of the corporate scandals, Congress and the U.S. regulatory agencies instituted far-reaching reforms in corporate governance and board composition, and companies spent millions to improve their governance and transparency. But the critics of executive pay and managerial power were only encouraged to raise their voices.

It might surprise those critics to learn that CEOs are not interchangeable and not chosen by lot; they are an extremely important asset to their companies and generally represent an excellent investment. The relative scarcity of CEO talent is manifested in many ways, including the frenetic behavior of boards charged with filling the top position when a CEO retires or departs. CEOs have significant, legitimate, market-driven bargaining power, and in pay negotiations, they use that power to obtain pay commensurate with their skills. Boards, as they should, use their own bargaining power to retain talent and maximize returns to company shareholders.

Boards understand the imperative of finding an excellent CEO and are willing to risk millions of dollars to secure the right talent. Their behavior is not only understandable but necessary to secure the company's future success. Any influence that CEOs might have over their directors is modest in comparison to the financial risk that CEOs assume when they leave other prospects and take on the extraordinarily difficult task of managing a major corporation, with a substantial portion of their short- and long-term compensation contingent on the organization's financial success. . . .

Properly designed pay opportunities drive superior corporate performance and secure it for the future. And most importantly, many economists argue, the U.S. model of executive compensation is a significant source of competitive advantage for the nation's economy, driving higher productivity, profits, and stock prices.

Resetting the Debate

Companies design executive pay programs to accomplish the classic goals of any human-capital program. First, they must attract, retain, and motivate their human capital to perform at the highest levels. The motivational factor is the most important, because it addresses the question of how a company achieves the greatest return on its human-capital investment and rewards executives for making the right decisions to drive shareholder value. Incentive-pay and pay-at-risk programs are particularly effective, especially at the top of the house, in achieving this motivation goal. . . .

A long list of pressures, including institutional-investor pushback, accounting changes, SEC investigations, and scrutiny from labor unions and the media, are forcing companies to rethink their executive-compensation programs, especially their stock-based incentives. The key now is to address the real problems in executive compensation without sacrificing the performance-based model and the huge returns that it has generated. Boards are struggling to achieve greater transparency and more rigorous execution of their pay practices—a positive move for all parties involved.

The real threat to U.S. economic growth, job creation, and higher living standards now comes from regulatory overreach as proponents of the mythology reject market forces and continue to push for government and institutional control over executive pay. To the extent that the mythology now surrounding executive pay leads to a rejection of the pay-for-performance model and restrictions on the risk-and-reward structure for setting executive compensation, American corporate performance will suffer.

There will be more pressure on boards to effectively reduce executive pay. This may meet the social desires of some constituents, but it will almost surely cause economic decline, for companies and the U.S. economy. We will see higher executive turnover and less talent in the executive suite as the most qualified job candidates move into other professions, as we saw in the 1970s, when top candidates moved into investment banking, venture-capital firms, and consulting, and corporate performance suffered as a result.

Our research demonstrates that aligning pay plans, incentive opportunities, and performance measures throughout an organization is key to financial success. Alignment means that executives and non-executives alike have the opportunity to increase their pay through performance-based incentives. As new regulations make it more difficult to execute the stock-based elements of the pay-for-performance model, for example, by reducing broad-based stock options, we will see even less alignment between executives' compensation and the pay packages of the rank-and-file. We are already witnessing the unintended consequences of the new requirement for stock-option expensing as companies cut the broad-based stock-option plans that have benefited millions of workers and given them a direct stake in the financial success of the companies for which they work.

Instead of changing executive pay plans to make them more like pay plans for employees, we should be reshaping employee pay to infuse it with the same incentives that drive performance in the company's upper ranks. A top-down regulatory approach to alignment will only damage the entire market-based, performance-management process that has worked so well for most companies and the economy as a whole. Instead of placing artificial limits on executive pay, we should focus squarely on increasing performance incentives and stock ownership for both executive and non-executive employees and rewarding high performers throughout the organization, from top to bottom. Within the context of a free-market economy, equal opportunity—not income equality by fiat—is the goal. . . .

In some ways, the decidedly negative attention focused on executive pay has increased the pressure that executives, board members, HR staffs, and compensation consultants all feel when they enter into discussions about the most effective methods for tying pay to performance and ensuring the company's success. The managerial-power argument has contributed to meaningful discussions about corporate governance and raised the level of dialogue in boardrooms. These are positive developments.

When the argument is blown into mythological proportions, however, it skews thinking about the realities of corporate behavior and leads to fundamental misunderstandings about executives, their pay levels, and their role in building successful companies and a flourishing economy. Consequently, the mythology now surrounding executive compensation leads many to reject a pay model that works well and is critical to ongoing growth at both the corporate and the national economic level. We need to address excesses in executive pay without abandoning the core model, and to return the debate to a rational, informed discussion. And we can safely leave Marie Antoinette out of it.

Edgar Woolard, Jr.

 **NO**

CEOs Are Being Paid Too Much

There's a major concern out there for all of us. I personally am extremely saddened by the loss of the respect that this country's corporate leaders have experienced. We've had a double blow in the last ten years or so. The first one we know way too much about—the fraud at Enron, Tyco, Adelphia, WorldCom, and many others.

The CEOs say there were a few rotten apples in that barrel, and maybe that's the answer—but there are a hell of lot more rotten apples than I would have ever guessed. But that's just the base of one of the issues that has eroded the trust and confidence in American business leaders.

The second one is the perception of excess compensation received by CEOs getting worse year by year. And if directors agree, they can be the leaders in making a very important change. I'd like to deal with it by describing several myths about compensation and trying to undermine them.

Myth #1: CEO Pay by Competition

The first is the myth that CEO pay is driven by competition—and to that I say "bull." CEO pay is driven today primarily by outside consultant surveys, and by the fact that many board members have bought into the concept that your CEO has to be at least in the top half, and maybe in the top quartile. So we have the "ratchet, ratchet, ratchet" concept. We all understand it well enough to know that if everybody is trying to be in the top half, everybody is going to get a hefty increase every year. If Bill and Sally get an increase in their total compensation, I have to get an increase so that I will stay in the top half.

How can we change that?

In 1990, we addressed this issue at DuPont. I became CEO in 1989, and I was concerned about what was evident even then. A 1989 *Business Week* article talked about executive pay—who makes the most and are they worth it: Michael Eisner, $40 million in 1988; Ross Johnson, $20 million; and others. I don't know Eisner, but I know that even fifteen years later he's one of the most criticized CEOs in the country.

What we did at DuPont was go to a simple concept: internal pay equity. I went to the board and the compensation committee and said, "We're going to look at the people who run the businesses, who make decisions on prices and new products with guidance from the CEO—the executive vice presidents—and we're going to set the limit of what a CEO in this company can be paid at 1.5 times the pay rate for the executive vice president—50 percent."

That to me seemed equitable. It had been anywhere from 30 to 50 percent in the past. I said, "Let's set it at 50 percent, and we're not going to chase the surveys." And this is the way DuPont has done it ever since. I think we have tweaked it up a little bit since then, but using a multiple still is the right way to go.

Board members can do this by suggesting that the HR and compensation people look at what's happened to internal pay equity, and seriously consider going in that direction. That will solve this problem in a great way.

Myth #2: Compensation Committees Are Independent

I give a "double bull" to this one. It could be that committees are becoming more independent, but over the last fifteen years they certainly haven't been.

Let me describe how it works: The compensation committee talks to an outside consultant who has surveys that you could drive a truck through and that support paying anything you want to pay. The consultant talks to the HR vice president, who talks to the CEO. The CEO says what he'd like to receive—enough so he will be "respected by his peers." It gets to the HR person, who tells the consultant, and the CEO gets what he's implied he deserves. The members of the compensation committee are happy that they're independent, the HR person is happy, the CEO is happy, and the consultant gets invited back next year.

There are two ways to change that as well. Here's the first one. When John Reed came back to the New York Stock Exchange to try to clean up the mess after Dick Grasso, he made the decision—which I admire him for—that the board was going to have its own outside consultant, one who was not going to be allowed to talk to internal people—not to the HR vice president, not to the CEO.

I'm the head of the comp committee at the NYSE, and when I talk with our outside consultant, he gives us his ideas of what he thinks the pay package ought to be. Then, with the consultant there, I talk to the compensation committee, and we make a decision. I talk to the HR vice president to see if he has any other thoughts, but the committee is totally independent.

The other way to change things is to truly insist on pay-for-performance, which everyone likes to talk about but no one does. Boards pay everybody in the top quartile whether they have good performance or bad performance—or even if they're about to be fired.

Well, I was on a board fifteen years ago, and four CEOs were on the compensation committee, and for two consecutive years, we gave the CEO and the executives there no bonus, no salary increase, and modest stock options, because their performance was lousy those years. After that, they did extremely well, and we paid them extremely well. That's how pay-for-performance should work.

Myth #3: Look How Much Wealth I Created

This one is really a joke. It was born in the 1980s and '90s during the stock-market bubble, when all CEOs were beating their chest about how much wealth they were creating for shareholders. And I'd look to the king, Jack Welch. Jack's the best CEO of the last fifty years, and I've told him this. But he likes to say, "I created $400 billion worth of wealth." No, Jack—no, you didn't. He said that when GE's stock was at 60, but when the bubble burst it went to 30, and it's in the low 30s now. So he created $150 to $200 billion.

But besides the actual figure, there are two things wrong with his claim. Now, I don't care how much money Jack Welch made. God bless him; I think he's terrific. But what did it do? It set a new level for CEO pay based on the stock-market bubble; all the other CEOs were saying, "Look how much wealth I created."

So you've got this more recent high level of executive pay, and then you've got the ratcheting effect in the system. Those things have to change.

Myth #4: Severance for Failing

The last one is the worst of all. Any directors who agree to give these huge severance pay packages to CEOs who fail—Philip Purcell of Morgan Stanley got $114 million, Carly Fiorina of Hewlett-Packard got $20 million—why are you doing that? No one else gets paid excessively when they fail. They get fired; they get fair severance.

All of this is killing the image of CEOs and corporate executives. When it comes to our image, we're in the league with lawyers and politicians. I don't want to be there, and I don't think you do either. We need the respect of our employees and the general public. And there's a lot of skepticism about leaders in politics and in churches and in the military—but we can't have it in the business community, because we're the backbone of the market system that has made this country great and created so many opportunities for people. We can't be seen as either dishonest or greedy.

What can you do about it?

Some of you CEOs need to show leadership and say, "We're going to do internal pay equity." It's easy to get the data, and then you can decide what you think is fair and how much you think the CEO contributes versus the other business leaders who make their companies so strong.

Compensation committees need to seriously consider implementing internal pay equity. Pay only for outstanding performance. Quit giving people money just because Bill and Sally are getting it. Consider going to an independent consultant that deals only with the board while you deal with HR and the CEO.

Last, take a look at stock-option packages. Not just for one year but the mega-grants that built up in the 1980s and '90s. If you've given huge stock-option packages for the last five years, look at their value. There's nothing in the Bible that says that you have to give increased stock options every year. Give a smaller grant; give a different kind of grant; put some kind of limits on.

There are many ways to do it, but it's important to get the system back under control. It's important for our image, for our reputation, for integrity, for trust, and for our leadership in this country.

POSTSCRIPT

Are CEOs Paid What
They Are Worth?

Ira T. Kay begins his defense of executive compensation by noting the common misperception that the high level of pay is undeserved. He believes this misperception rests on two myths. The first is that the pay-for-performance model no longer works as an explanation of executive compensation. The second myth is that executives control their own boards of directors and in this way determine their own compensation. He feels that these myths, which are fueled by the media's reporting of exceptional cases, may be damaging to the economy because various groups including institutional investors and trade unions exert pressure to change the pay-for-performance model. But the fact is, Kay maintains, the cases of abuse are the exception and not the rule. He then offers five key findings from various studies of executive compensation. One of these findings is that "Executives are paid commensurate with the skills and talents that they bring to the organization." He concludes by asserting that the real issue is how to spread the pay-for-performance model from the executive suite to all levels of the corporation.

Edgar Woolard, Jr., also considers some myths. He lists four. First, there is the myth that executive pay is determined by competition. He believes that in reality consultants pay a major role is setting the pay of business leaders. The second myth is that compensation committees, in the first instance, setting executive pay are independent. Woolard argues that over the last 15 years these committees have, in fact, not gotten more independent. The third myth holds that executive pay is tied to the wealth created by the executive. Woolard points to the fact that the rise in stock prices through the 1990s was a general phenomenon, not determined by the actions of business leaders but in large part the result of a stock market bubble. The last myth is that severance packages given to executives who have failed are fair. Instead, the opposite is true: The one group who gets excess severance pay is executives. Based on reality rather than myth, it is important to get the executive compensation system back under control.

There is a growing literature on executive compensation. The popular press certainly reports on the pay of corporate heads, sometimes as part of the business news and other times from the perspective that the pay is excessive or undeserved. For an example of the former, see "An Early Christmas at Lehman," by Randall Smith (*Wall Street Journal,* December 6, 2006). For an example of the latter, see "While Shares Fell, Viacom Paid Three $160 Million" (*New York Times*, April 16, 2005). Other articles include "Special Report: CEO Pay 'Business as Usual'" (*USA Today*, March 30, 2005) and "The

True Measure of a CEO" by James O'Toole (*Across the Board*, September/ October 2005). The issue has attracted the attention of various public officials, including Congressman Barney Frank who serves on the House Committee on Financial Services: His views are expressed in "The Problem of Executive Compensation" at http://www.house.gov/banking_democrats/ExecCompProblems.html. The views of labor as represented by the AFL-CIO can be found at http:// www.aflcio/corporatewatch/paywatch/pay/. For a more complete and critical analysis of executive compensation see *Pay Without Performance* by Lucian Benchuk and Jesse Fried (Harvard University Press, 2005).

ISSUE 3

Is There Discrimination in U.S. Labor Markets?

YES: William A. Darity, Jr., and Patrick L. Mason, from "Evidence on Discrimination in Employment: Codes of Color, Codes of Gender," *Journal of Economic Perspectives* (Spring 1998)

NO: James J. Heckman, from "Detecting Discrimination," *Journal of Economic Perspectives* (Spring 1998)

ISSUE SUMMARY

YES: Professor of economics William A. Darity, Jr., and associate professor of economics Patrick L. Mason assert that the lack of progress made since the mid-1970s toward establishing equality in wages between the races is evidence of persistent discrimination in U.S. labor markets.

NO: Professor of economics and Nobel Laureate James J. Heckman argues that markets—driven by the profit motive of employers—will compete away any wage differentials that are not justified by differences in human capital.

O ver 45 years have passed since Rosa Parks refused to give up her seat on a segregated Montgomery, Alabama, bus. America has had these years to finally overcome discrimination, but has it? Have the domestic programs of Presidents John F. Kennedy and Lyndon Johnson that were enacted after those turbulent years following Parks's act of defiance made it possible for African Americans to succeed within the powerful economic engine that drives American society? Or does racism still stain the Declaration of Independence, with its promise of equality for all?

Before we examine the economics of discrimination, perhaps we should look backward to see where America has been, what progress has been made, and what is left—if anything—to accomplish. American history, some say, reveals a world of legalized apartheid where African Americans were denied access to the social, political, and economic institutions that are the mainstays of America. Without this access, millions of American citizens were doomed to live lives on the fringes of the mainstream. Thus, the Kennedy/

Johnson programs left one legacy, which few now dispute: These programs effectively dismantled the system of legalized discrimination and, for the first time since the end of slavery, allowed blacks to dream of a better life.

The dream became a reality for many. Consider the success stories that are buried in the poverty statistics that were collected and reported in the 1960s. Poverty scarred the lives of one out of every five Americans in 1959. But poverty was part of the lives of fully one-half of all African American families. Over time fewer and fewer Americans, black and white, suffered the effects of poverty; however, even though the incidence of poverty has been cut in half for black Americans, more than 25 percent of African American families still live in poverty. Even more distressing is the reality that African American children bear the brunt of this economic deprivation. In 1997, 37.2 percent of the "next generation" of African Americans lived in families whose total family income was insufficient to lift them out of poverty. (Note that although black Americans suffer the effects of poverty disproportionately, white-not-Hispanic families are the single largest identifiable group who live in poverty: white-not-Hispanic people make up 46.4 percent of the entire poor population; white-Hispanic, 22.2 percent; and black, 25.6 percent.)

The issue for economists is why so many African Americans failed to prosper and share in the great prosperity of the 1990s. Few would deny that in part the lack of success for black Americans is directly associated with a lack of "human capital": schooling, work experiences, and occupational choices. The real question, however, is whether differences between blacks and whites in terms of human capital can explain most of the current wage differentials or whether a significant portion of these wage differentials can be traced to labor market discrimination.

In the following selections, William A. Darity, Jr., and Patrick L. Mason argue that a significant part of the reason for black Americans' lack of economic success is discrimination, while James J. Heckman maintains that the issue is all human capital differences.

YES

William A. Darity, Jr., and
Patrick L. Mason

Evidence on Discrimination in Employment

There is substantial racial and gender disparity in the American economy. As we will demonstrate, discriminatory treatment within the labor market is a major cause of this inequality. The evidence is ubiquitous: careful research studies which estimate wage and employment regressions, help-wanted advertisements, audit and correspondence studies, and discrimination suits which are often reported by the news media. Yet, there appear to have been periods of substantial reductions in economic disparity and discrimination. For example, Donohue and Heckman (1991) provide evidence that racial discrimination declined during the interval 1965–1975. Gottschalk (1997) has produced statistical estimates that indicate that discrimination against black males dropped most sharply between 1965 and 1975, and that discrimination against women declined during the interval 1973–1994. But some unanswered questions remain. Why did the movement toward racial equality stagnate after the mid-1970s? What factors are most responsible for the remaining gender inequality? What is the role of the competitive process in elimination or reproduction of discrimination in employment?

The Civil Rights Act of 1964 is the signal event associated with abrupt changes in the black-white earnings differential (Bound and Freeman, 1989; Card and Krueger, 1992; Donohue and Heckman, 1991; Freeman, 1973). Along with other important pieces of federal legislation, the Civil Rights Act also played a major role in reducing discrimination against women (Leonard, 1989). Prior to passage of the federal civil rights legislation of the 1960s, racial exclusion and gender-typing of employment was blatant. The adverse effects of discriminatory practices on the life chances of African Americans, in particular, during that period have been well-documented (Wilson, 1980; Myers and Spriggs, 1997, pp. 32–42; Lieberson, 1980). Cordero-Guzman (1990, p. 1) observes that "up until the early 1960s, and particularly in the south, most blacks were systematically denied equal access to opportunities [and] in many instances, individuals with adequate credentials or skills were not, legally, allowed to apply to certain positions in firms." Competitive market forces certainly did not eliminate these discriminatory practices in the decades leading up to the 1960s. They remained until the federal adoption of antidiscrimination laws.

From William A. Darity, Jr., and Patrick L. Mason, "Evidence on Discrimination in Employment: Codes of Color, Codes of Gender," *Journal of Economic Perspectives*, vol. 12, no. 2 (Spring 1998). Copyright © 1998 by The American Economic Association. Reprinted by permission. References and some notes omitted.

Newspaper help-wanted advertisements provide vivid illustrations of the openness and visibility of such practices. We did an informal survey of the employment section of major daily newspapers from three northern cities, the *Chicago Tribune,* the *Los Angeles Times* and the *New York Times,* and from the nation's capital, *The Washington Post,* at five-year intervals from 1945 to 1965. (Examples from southern newspapers are even more dramatic.) . . .

With respect to gender-typing of occupations, help-wanted advertisements were structured so that whole sections of the classifieds offered job opportunities separately and explicitly for men and women. Men were requested for positions that included restaurant cooks, managers, assistant managers, auto salesmen, sales in general, accountants and junior accountants, design engineers, detailers, diemakers, drivers, and welders. Women were requested for positions that included household and domestic workers, stenographers, secretaries, typists, bookkeepers, occasionally accountants (for "girls good at figures"), and waitresses.[1] The *Washington Post* of January 3, 1960, had the most examples of racial preference, again largely for whites, in help-wanted ads of any newspaper edition we examined. Nancy Lee's employment service even ran an advertisement for a switchboard operator—presumably never actually seen by callers—requesting that all *women* applying be white! Advertisements also frequently included details about the age range desired from applicants, like men 21–30 or women 18–25. Moreover, employers also showed little compunction about specifying precise physical attributes desired in applicants.[2]

Following the passage of the Civil Rights Act of 1964, none of the newspapers carried help-wanted ads that included any explicit preference for "white" or "colored" applicants in January 1965. However, it became very common to see advertisements for "European" housekeepers (a trend that was already visible as early as 1960). While race no longer entered the help-wanted pages explicitly, national origin or ancestry seemed to function as a substitute. Especially revealing is an advertisement run by the Amity Agency in the *New York Times* on January 3, 1965, informing potential employers that "Amity Has Domestics": "Scottish Gals" at $150 a month as "mothers' helpers and housekeepers," "German Gals" at $175 a month on one-year contracts, and "Haitian Gals" at $130 a month who are "French speaking." Moreover, in the "Situations Wanted" section of the newspaper, prospective female employees still were indicating their own race in January 1965.

The case of the help-wanted pages of the *New York Times* is of special note because New York was one of the states that had a state law against discrimination and a State Commission Against Discrimination in place, long prior to the passage of the federal Civil Rights Act of 1964. However, the toothlessness of New York's State Commission Against Discrimination is well-demonstrated by the fact that employers continued to indicate their racial preferences for new hires in help-wanted ads, as well as by descriptions of personal experience like that of John A. Williams in his semi-autobiographical novel, *The Angry Ones* (1960 [1996], pp. 30–1).

Help-wanted ads were only the tip of the iceberg of the process of racial exclusion in employment. After all, there is no reason to believe that the employers who did not indicate a racial preference were entirely open-minded about their applicant pool. How successful has the passage of federal antidiscrimination legislation in the 1960s been in producing an equal opportunity environment where job applicants are now evaluated on their qualifications? To give away the answer at the outset, our response is that discrimination by race has diminished somewhat, and discrimination by gender has diminished substantially. However, neither employment discrimination by race or by gender is close to ending. The Civil Rights Act of 1964 and subsequent related legislation has purged American society of the most overt forms of discrimination. However, discriminatory practices have continued in more covert and subtle forms. Furthermore, racial discrimination is masked and rationalized by widely-held presumptions of black inferiority.

Statistical Research on Employment Discrimination

Economic research on the presence of discrimination in employment has focused largely on black-white and male-female earnings and occupational disparities. The position typically taken by economists is that some part of the racial or gender gap in earnings or occupations is due to average group differences in productivity-linked characteristics (a human capital gap) and some part is due to average group differences in treatment (a discrimination gap). The more of the gap that can be explained by human capital differences, the easier it becomes to assert that labor markets function in a nondiscriminatory manner; any remaining racial or gender inequality in employment outcomes must be due to differences between blacks and whites or between men and women that arose outside the labor market. . . .

Regression Evidence on Racial Discrimination

When we consider economic disparities by race, a difference emerges by gender. Using a Blinder-Oaxaca approach in which women are compared by their various racial and ethnic subgroups, Darity, Guilkey and Winfrey (1996) find little systematic evidence of wage discrimination based on U.S. Census data for 1980 and 1990.[3] However, when males are examined using the same Census data a standard result emerges. A significant portion of the wage gap between black and white males in the United States cannot be explained by the variables included to control for productivity differences across members of the two racial groups.

Black women are likely to have the same school quality and omitted family background characteristics as black men (the same is true for white women and men). Hence, it strains credibility to argue that the black-white earnings gap for men is due to an omitted labor quality variable unless one also argues that black women are paid more than white women conditional on the unobservables. The findings of Darity, Guilkey and Winfrey (1996), Rodgers and Spriggs (1996) and Gottschalk (1997) indicate that in 1980 and 1990 black men in the United States were suffering a 12 to 15 percent loss in earnings due to labor market discrimination.

There is a growing body of evidence that uses color or "skin shade" as a natural experiment to detect discrimination. The approach of these studies has been to look at different skin shades within a particular ethnic group at a particular place and time, which should help to control for factors of culture and ethnicity other than pure skin color. Johnson, Bienenstock, and Stoloff (1995) looked at dark-skinned and light-skinned black males from the same neighborhoods in Los Angeles, and found that the combination of a black racial identity and a dark skin tone reduces an individual's odds of working by 52 percent, after controlling for education, age, and criminal record! Since both dark-skinned and light-skinned black males in the sample were from the same neighborhoods, the study *de facto* controlled for school quality. Further evidence that lighter-complexioned blacks tend to have superior incomes and life chances than darker-skinned blacks in the United States comes from studies by Ransford (1970), Keith and Herring (1991) and Johnson and Farrell (1995).

Similar results are found by looking at skin color among Hispanics. Research conducted by Arce, Murguia, and Frisbie (1987) utilizing the University of Michigan's 1979 National Chicano Survey involved partitioning the sample along two phenotypical dimensions: skin color, ranging from Very Light to Very Dark on a five-point scale; and physical features, ranging from Very European to Very Indian on a five-point scale. Chicanos with lighter skin color and more European features had higher socioeconomic status. Using the same data set, Telles and Murguia (1990) found that 79 percent of $1,262 of the earnings differences between the dark phenotypic group and other Mexican Americans was *not* explained by the traditional variables affecting income included in their earnings regression. Further support for this finding comes from Cotton (1993) and Darity, Guilkey, and Winfrey (1996) who find using 1980 and 1990 Census data that black Hispanics suffer close to ten times the proportionate income loss due to differential treatment of given characteristics than white Hispanics. Evidently, skin shade plays a critical role in structuring social class position and life chances in American society, even between comparable individuals within minority groups.

Cross-national evidence from Brazil also is relevant here. Despite conventional beliefs in Brazil that race is irrelevant and class is the primary index for social stratification, Silva (1985) found using the 1976 national household survey that blacks and mulattos (or "browns") shared closely in a relatively depressed economic condition relative to whites, with mulattos earning slightly more than blacks. Silva estimated that the cost of being nonwhite in Brazil in 1976 was about 566 cruzeiros per month (or $104 U.S.). But Silva found slightly greater unexplained income differences for mulattos, rather than blacks vis-à-vis whites, unexplained differences he viewed as evidence of discrimination. A new study by Telles and Lim (1997), based upon a random national survey of 5000 persons conducted by the Data Folha Institute des Pesquisas, compares economic outcomes based upon whether race is self-identified or interviewer-identified. Telles and Lim view interviewer-identification as more useful for establishing social classification and treatment. They find that self-identification underestimates white income and over-estimates brown and black incomes relative to interviewer-classification.

Despite the powerful results on skin shade, some continue to argue that the extent of discrimination is overestimated by regression techniques because of missing variables. After all, it seems likely that the general pattern of unobserved variables—for example, educational quality or labor force attachment—would tend to follow the observed variables in indicating reasons for the lower productivity of black males (Ruhm, 1989, p. 157). As a result, adjusting for these factors would reduce the remaining black-white earnings differential.[4]

As one might imagine, given the framework in which economists tackle the issue of discrimination, considerable effort has been made to find measures of all imaginable dimensions of human capital that could be used to test the presence of labor market discrimination. This effort has uncovered one variable in one data set which, if inserted in an earnings regression, produces the outcome that nearly all of the black-white male wage gap is explained by human capital and none by labor market discrimination. (However, thus far no one has suggested a reasonable missing variable for the skin shade effect.) The particular variable that eliminates evidence of discrimination in earnings against black men as a group is the Armed Forces Qualifying Test (AFQT) score in the National Longitudinal Survey of Youth (NLSY).

A number of researchers have confirmed with somewhat different sample sizes and methodologies that including AFQT scores in an earnings equation virtually will eliminate racial differences in wages. . . .

The conclusion of this body of work is that labor market discrimination against blacks is negligible or nonexistent. Using Neal and Johnson's (1996) language, the key to explaining differences in black and white labor market outcomes must instead rest with "premarket factors." These studies have led Abigail and Stephan Thernstrom (1997) in a prominent *Wall Street Journal* editorial to proclaim that "what may look like persistent employment discrimination is better described as employers rewarding workers with relatively strong cognitive skills."

But matters are not so straightforward. The essential problem is what the AFQT scores are actually measuring, and therefore what precisely is being controlled for. There is no consensus on this point. AFQT scores have been interpreted variously as providing information about school quality or academic achievement (O'Neill, 1990), about previously unmeasured skills (Ferguson, 1995; Maxwell, 1994; Neal and Johnson 1996), and even about intelligence (Herrnstein and Murray, 1994)—although the military did not design AFQT as an intelligence test (Rodgers and Spriggs, 1996).[5] The results obtained by O'Neill (1990), Maxwell (1994), Ferguson (1995), and Neal and Johnson (1996) after using the AFQT as an explanatory variable are, upon closer examination, not robust to alternative specifications and are quite difficult to interpret.

The lack of robustness can be illustrated by looking at how AFQT scores interact with other variables in the earnings equation. Neal and Johnson (1996), for example, adjust for age and AFQT score in an earnings equation, but not for years of schooling, presumably on the assumption that same-age individuals would have the same years of schooling, regardless of race. However, this assumption does not appear to be true. Rodgers, Spriggs and Waaler (1997) find that white youths had accumulated more schooling at a given age than black or Hispanic youths. When AFQT scores are both age and education-adjusted, a black-white wage gap reemerges, as the authors report (p. 3):[6]

> ... estimates from models that use our proposed age and education adjusted AFQT score [show] that sharp differences in racial and ethnic wage gaps exist. Instead of explaining three-quarters of the male black-white wage gap, the age and education adjusted score explains 40 percent of the gap. Instead of explaining the entire male Hispanic-white gap, the new score explains 50 percent of the gap . . . [B]lack women no longer earn more than white women do, and . . . Hispanic women's wage premium relative to white women is reduced by one-half.

Another specification problem arises when wage equations are estimated using both AFQT scores and the part of the NLSY sample that includes measures of psychological well-being (for "self-esteem" and "locus of control") as explanatory variables. The presence of the psychological variables restores a negative effect on wages of being African-American (Goldsmith, Veum and Darity, 1997).[7]

Yet another specification problem becomes relevant if one interprets AFQT scores as providing information about school quality. But since there is a school survey module of the NLSY which can be used to provide direct evidence on school quality, using variables like the books/pupil ratio, the percent of students classified as disadvantaged, and teacher salaries, it would surely be more helpful to use this direct data on school quality rather than the AFQT scores. In another method of controlling for school quality, Harrison (1972) compared employment and earnings outcomes for blacks and whites living in the same black ghetto communities, on grounds that school quality would not be very different between them. Harrison found sharp differences in earnings favoring whites.[8]

One severe difficulty in interpreting what differences in the AFQT actually mean is demonstrated by Rodgers and Spriggs (1996) who show that AFQT scores appear to be biased in a specific sense. . . . [They] create a hypothetical set of "unbiased" black scores by running the mean black characteristics through the equation with the white coefficients. When those scores replace the actual AFQT scores in a wage equation, then the adjusted AFQT scores no longer explain black-white wage differences. A similar result can be obtained if actual white scores are replaced by hypothetical scores produced by running white characteristics through the equation with black coefficients.[9] Apparently, the AFQT scores themselves are a consequence of bias in the underlying processes that generate AFQT scores for blacks and whites. Perhaps AFQT scores are a proxy for skills that do not capture all skills, and thus leave behind a bias of uncertain direction. Or there may be other predictors of the test that are correlated with race but which are left out of the AFQT explanatory equation.

To muddy the waters further, focusing on the math and verbal subcomponents of AFQT leads to inconsistent implications for discriminatory differentials. For example, while a higher performance on the verbal portion of the AFQT contributes to higher wages for black women versus black men, it apparently has little or no effect on the wages of white women versus white men (Currie and Thomas, 1995). However, white women gain in wages from higher scores on the math portion of the AFQT, but black women do not. Perhaps this says that white women are screened (directly or indirectly) for employment and pay on the basis of their math performance, while black women are screened based upon their verbal skills. Perhaps this is because white employers have a greater "comfort zone" with black women who have a greater verbal similarity to whites. Or perhaps something not fully understood and potentially quirky is going on with the link between these test results and wages.

Finally, since skill differentials have received such widespread discussion in recent years as an underlying cause of growing wage inequality in the U.S. economy—see, for example, the discussion in the Spring 1997 issue of *The Journal of Economic Perspectives*—it should be pointed out that growth in the rewards to skill does not mean that the effects of race have diminished. If the importance of race and skill increase simultaneously, then a rising skill premium will explain more of the changes in *intraracial* wage inequality, which may well leave a larger unexplained portion of interracial wage inequality. For example, when Murnane et al. (1995) ask whether test scores in math, reading, and vocabulary skills for respondents in the National Longitudinal Study of the High School Class of 1972 and High School and Beyond datasets have more explanatory power in wage equations for 1980 graduates than 1972 graduates, their answer is "yes"—the rate of return to cognitive skill (test scores) increased between 1978 and 1986. However, in these same regressions, the absolute value of the negative race coefficient is larger for the 1980 graduates than it is for the 1972 graduates! These results confirm that there are increasing returns to skills measured by standardized tests, but do not indicate that the rise in returns to skills can explain changes in the black-white earnings gap very well.

The upshot is the following. There is no doubt that blacks suffer reduced earnings in part due to inferior productivity-linked characteristics, like skill gaps or school quality gaps, relative to nonblack groups. However, evidence based on the AFQT should be treated with extreme caution. Given that this one variable in one particular data set is the only one that suggests racial discrimination is no longer operative in U.S. employment practices, it should be taken as far from convincing evidence. Blacks, especially black men, continue to suffer significantly reduced earnings due to discrimination and the extent of discrimination.

Direct Evidence on Discrimination: Court Cases and Audit Studies

One direct body of evidence of the persistence of employment discrimination, despite the presence of antidiscrimination laws, comes from the scope and dispensation of job discrimination lawsuits. A sampling of such cases from recent years ... reveals [that] discriminatory practices have occurred at highly visible U.S. corporations often having multinational operations. The suits reveal racial and gender discrimination in employment, training, promotion, tenure, layoff policies, and work environment, as well as occupational segregation.

Perhaps the most notorious recent case is the $176 million settlement reached between Texaco and black employees after disclosure of taped comments of white corporate officials making demeaning remarks about blacks, remarks that revealed an outlook that translated into corresponding antiblack employment practices. Clearly, neither federal antidiscrimination laws nor the pressures of competitive markets have prevented the occurrence of discriminatory practices that have resulted in significant awards or settlements for the plaintiffs.

Another important source of direct evidence are the audit studies of the type conducted in the early 1990s by the Urban Institute (Mincy, 1993). The Urban Institute audit studies sought to examine employment outcomes for young black, Hispanic, and white males, ages 19–25, looking for entry-level jobs. Pairs of black and white males and pairs of Hispanic and non-Hispanic white males were matched as testers and sent out to apply for jobs at businesses advertising openings. Prior to application for the positions, the testers were trained for interviews to minimize dissimilarity in the quality of their self-presentation, and they were given manufactured résumés designed to put their credentials on a par. The black/white tests were conducted in Chicago and in Washington, D.C., while the Hispanic/non Hispanic tests were conducted in Chicago and in San Diego.

A finding of discrimination was confirmed if one member of the pair was offered the position and the other was not. No discrimination was confirmed if both received an offer (sequentially, since both were instructed to turn the position down) or neither received an offer. This is a fairly stringent test for discrimination, since, in the case where no offer was made to either party, there is no way to determine whether employers were open to the prospect of hiring a black or an Hispanic male, what the overall applicant pool looked like, or who was actually hired. However, the Urban Institute audits found that black males were three times as likely to be turned down for a job as white males, and Hispanic males also were three times as likely as non-Hispanic white males to experience discrimination in employment (Fix, Galster and Struyk, 1993, pp. 21–22).

Bendick, Jackson and Reinoso (1994) also report on 149 race-based (black, white) and ethnicity-based (Hispanic, non-Hispanic) job audits conducted by the Fair Employment Council of Greater Washington, Inc. in the D.C. metropolitan area in 1990 and 1991. Testers were paired by gender. The audit findings are striking. White testers were close to 10 percent more likely to receive interviews than blacks. Among those interviewed, half of the white testers received job offers versus a mere 11 percent of the black testers. When both testers received the same job offers, white testers were offered 15 cents per hour more than black testers. Black testers also were disproportionately "steered" toward lower level positions after the job offer was made, and white testers were disproportionately considered for unadvertised positions at higher levels than the originally advertised job.

Overall, the Fair Employment Council study found rates of discrimination in excess of 20 percent against blacks (in the black/white tests) and against Hispanics (in the Hispanic/non-Hispanic tests). In the Hispanic/non-Hispanic tests, Hispanic male job seekers were three times as likely to experience discrimination as Hispanic females. But, surprisingly, in the black/white tests, black females were three times as likely to encounter discrimination as black males. The racial results for women in this particular audit stand in sharp contrast with the results in the statistical studies described above.

The most severe criticisms of the audit technique have come from Heckman and Siegelman (1993). At base, their central worry is that testers cannot be paired in such a way that they will not signal a difference that legitimately can be interpreted by the prospective employer as a difference in potential to perform the job, despite interview training and doctored résumés.[10] For example, what about intangibles like a person's ability to make a first impression or the fact that certain résumés may be unintentionally superior to others?

In an audit study consciously designed to address many of the Heckman and Siegelman (1993) methodological complaints, Neumark, Bank, and Van Nort (1995) examined sex discrimination in restaurant hiring practices. Four testers (all college students, two men and two women) applied for jobs waiting tables at 65 restaurants in Philadelphia. The restaurants were separated into high, medium, and low price, according to average cost of a meal. Waiters at the high price restaurants tend to receive greater wages and tips than their counterparts in low price restaurants; specifically, the authors find that average hourly earnings for waiters were 47 and 68 percent higher in the high price restaurant than the medium and low price restaurant, respectively. One man and one woman applied for a job at each restaurant, so there were 130 attempts to obtain employment. Thirty-nine job offers were received.

One interesting twist to this methodology is that three reasonably comparable résumés were constructed, and over a three-week period each tester used a different résumé for a period of one week. This résumé-switching mitigates any differences that may have occurred because one résumé was better than another. To reduce other sources of unobserved ability—for example, the ability to make a good first impression—the testers were instructed to give their applications to the first employee they encountered when visiting a restaurant. That employee was then asked to forward the résumé to the manager. In effect, personality and appearance were eliminated as relevant variables for the interview decision, if not for the job offer decision.

Neumark et al. (1995) find that in the low-priced restaurants, the man received an offer while the woman did not 29 percent of the time. A woman never received an offer when the man did not. In the high-priced restaurants, the man received an offer while the woman did not in 43 percent of the tests, while the woman received an offer while the man did not in just 4 percent of the tests. Also, at high-priced restaurants, women had roughly a 40 percent lower probability of being interviewed and 50 percent lower probability of obtaining a job offer, and this difference is statistically significant. Hence, this audit study shows that within-occupation employment discrimination may be a contributing source to wage discrimination between men and women. . . .

The Theoretical Backdrop

Standard neoclassical competitive models are forced by their own assumptions to the conclusion that discrimination only can be temporary. Perhaps the best-known statement of this position emerges from Becker's (1957) famous "taste for discrimination" model. If two groups share similar productivity profiles under competitive conditions where at least some employers prefer profits to prejudice, eventually all workers must be paid the same wage. The eventual result may involve segregated workforces—say, with some businesses hiring only white men and others hiring only black women—but as long as both groups have the same average productivity, they will receive the same pay. Thus, in this view, discrimination only can produce temporary racial or gender earnings gaps. Moreover, alternative forms of discrimination are separable processes; wage discrimination and employment segregation are unrelated in Becker's model.

Despite the theoretical implications of standard neoclassical competitive models, we have considerable evidence that it took the Civil Rights Act of 1964 to alter the discriminatory climate in America. It did not, by any means, eliminate either form of discrimination. Indeed, the impact of the law itself may have been temporary, since there is some evidence that the trend toward racial inequality came to a halt in the mid-1970s (even though interracial differences in human capital were continuing to close) and the momentum toward gender equality may have begun to lose steam in the early 1990s. Moreover, we believe that the forms of discrimination have altered in response to the act. Therefore, it is not useful to argue that either racial or gender discrimination is inconsistent with the operation of competitive markets, especially when it has taken antidiscrimination laws to reduce the impact of discrimination in the market. Instead, it is beneficial to uncover the market mechanisms which permit or encourage discriminatory practices.

Since Becker's work, orthodox microeconomics has been massaged in various ways to produce stories of how discrimination might sustain itself against pressures of the competitive market. The tacit assumption of these approaches has been to find a way in which discrimination can increase business profits, or to identify conditions where choosing not to discriminate might reduce profits.

In the customer discrimination story, for example, businesses discriminate not because they themselves are bigoted but because their clients are bigoted. This story works especially well where the product in question must be delivered via face-to-face contact, but it obviously does not work well when the hands that made the product are not visible to the customer possessing the "taste for discrimination." Moreover, as Madden (1975, p. 150) has pointed out, sex-typing of jobs can work in both directions: "While service occupations are more contact-oriented, sexual preference can work both ways: for example, women are preferred as Playboy bunnies, airline stewardesses, and lingerie salespeople, while men seem to be preferred as tire salespeople, stock-brokers, and truck drivers."

Obviously, group-typing of employment will lead to a different occupational distribution between group A and B, but will it lead to different earnings as well? Madden (1975, p. 150, emphasis in original) suggests not necessarily:

> . . . consumer discrimination causes occupational segregation rather than wage differentials. If the female wage decreases as the amount of consumer contact required by a job increases, women seek employment in jobs where consumer contact is minimal and wages are higher. Only if there are not enough non-consumer contact jobs for working women, forcing them to seek employment in consumer-contact jobs, would consumer discrimination be responsible for wage differentials. Since most jobs do not require consumer contact, consumer discrimination would segregate women into these jobs, but not *cause* wage differentials.

Perhaps the best attempt to explain how discrimination might persist in a neoclassical framework is the statistical discrimination story, which, at base, is a story about imperfect information. The notion is that potential employers cannot observe everything they wish to know about job candidates, and in this environment, they have an incentive to seize group membership as a signal that allows them to improve their predictions of a prospective candidate's ability to perform.

However, this model of prejudicial beliefs does not ultimately wash well as a theory of why discrimination should be long-lasting. If average group differences are perceived but not real, then employers should *learn* that their beliefs are mistaken. If average group differences are real, then in a world with antidiscrimination laws, employers are likely to find methods of predicting the future performance of potential employees with sufficient accuracy that there is no need to use the additional "signal" of race or gender. It seems implausible that with all the resources that corporations put into hiring decisions, the remaining differentials are due to an inability to come up with a suitable set of questions or qualifications for potential employees.

Moreover, models of imperfect competition as explanations of discrimination do not solve the problem completely either. The reason for the immutability of the imperfection is rarely satisfactorily explained—and often not addressed at all—in models of this type (Darity and Williams, 1985). Struggle as it may, orthodox microeconomics keeps returning to the position that sustained observed differences in economic outcomes between groups must be due to an induced or inherent deficiency in the group that experiences the inferior outcomes. In the jargon, this is referred to as a deficiency in human capital. Sometimes this deficiency is associated with poor schooling opportunities, other times with culture (Sowell, 1981).[11] But the thrust of the argument is to absolve market processes, at least in a putative long run, of a role in producing the differential outcome; the induced or inherent deficiency occurs in premarket or extra-market processes.

Certainly years of schooling, quality of education, years of work experiences and even culture can have a role in explaining racial and gender earnings differences. However, the evidence marshaled above indicates that these factors do not come close to explaining wage differentials and employment patterns observed in the economy. Instead, discrimination has been sustained both in the United States and elsewhere, for generations at a time. Such discrimination does not always even need direct legal support nor has it been eliminated by market pressures. Instead, changes in social and legal institutions have been needed to reduce it.

James Heckman (1997, p. 406) draws a similar conclusion in his examination of a specific sector of employment, the textile industry:

> . . . substantial growth in Southern manufacturing had little effect on the labor-market position of blacks in Southern textiles prior to 1965. Through tight and slack labor markets, the proportion of blacks was small and stable. After 1964, and in synchronization with the 1964 Civil Rights Act, black economic progress was rapid. Only South Carolina had a Jim Crow law prohibiting employment of blacks as textile workers, and the law was never used after the 1920s. Yet the pattern of exclusion of blacks was prevalent throughout Southern textiles, and the breakthrough in black employment in the industry came in all states at the same time. Informally enforced codes and private practices, and not formally enforced apartheid, kept segregation in place, and market forces did not break them down.

Nontraditional alternatives to orthodox microeconomic analysis can lead to a logically consistent basis for a persistent gap in wage outcomes. These alternatives typically break down the line between in-market and pre-market discrimination so often drawn in conventional economics. The first of these involves a self-fulfilling prophecy mechanism. Suppose employers believe that members of group A are more productive than members of group B on average. Suppose further that they act upon their beliefs, thereby exhibiting a stronger demand for A workers, hiring them more frequently and paying them more.

Next, suppose that members of group B become less motivated and less emotionally healthy as a consequence of the employment rebuff. Notice that the original decision not to hire may have been completely unjustified on productivity grounds; nonetheless, the decision made *in* the labor market—a decision not to hire or to hire at low pay—alters the human capital characteristics of the members of group B so that they become inferior candidates for jobs. The employers' initially held mistaken beliefs become realized over time as a consequence of the employers' initial discriminatory decisions. As Elmslie and Sedo (1996, p. 474) observe in their development of this argument, "One initial bout of unemployment that is not productivity based can lay the foundation for continued future unemployment and persistently lower job status even if no future discrimination occurs."

More broadly, depressed expectations of employment opportunities also can have an adverse effect on members of group B's inclination to acquire additional human capital—say, through additional schooling or training. The effects of the past could be passed along by the disadvantaged group from generation to generation, another possibility ignored by orthodox theory. For example, Borjas (1994) writes of the ethnic intergenerational transmission of economic advantage or disadvantage. He makes no mention of discrimination in his work but a potential interpretation is that the effects of past discrimination, both negative and positive, are passed on to subsequent generations. Other evidence along these lines includes Tyree's (1991) findings on the relationship between an ethnic group's status and performance in the past and the present, and Darity's (1989) development of "the lateral mobility" hypothesis based upon ethnic group case histories.

More narrowly, the group-typed beliefs held by employers/selectors also can have a strong effect on the performance of the candidate at the interview stage. In an experiment performed in the early 1970s, psychologists Word, Zanna and Cooper (1974, pp. 109–120) found that when interviewed by "naïve" whites, trained black applicants "received (a) less immediacy, (b) higher rates of speech error, and (c) shorter amounts of interview time" than white applicants. They then trained white interviewers to replicate the behavior received by the black applicants in the first phase of their experiment, and found that "naïve" white candidates performed poorly during interviews when they were "treated like blacks." Such self-fulfilling prophecies are familiar in the psychology literature (Sibicky and Dovidio, 1986).

A second nontraditional theory that can lead to a permanent gap in intergroup outcomes is the noncompeting groups hypothesis advanced by the late W. Arthur Lewis (1979). Related arguments emerge from Krueger's (1963) extension of the trade-based version of the Becker model, Swinton's (1978) "labor force competition" model for racial differences, and Madden's (1975) male monopoly model for gender differences, but Lewis's presentation is the most straightforward. Lewis starts with an intergroup rivalry for the preferred positions in a hierarchical occupational structure. Say that group A is able to control access to the preferred positions by influencing the required credentials, manipulating opportunities to obtain the credentials, and serving a gatekeeping function over entry and promotion along job ladders. Group B is then rendered "noncompeting."

One theoretical difficulty with this argument that its proponents rarely address is that it requires group A to maintain group solidarity even when it may have subgroups with differing interests. In Krueger's (1963) model, for example, white capitalists must value racial group solidarity sufficiently to accept a lower return on their capital as the price they pay for a generally higher level of income for all whites (and higher wages for white workers). In Madden's (1975) model, male capitalists must make a similar decision on behalf of male workers.

This noncompeting group hypothesis blurs the orthodox distinction between in-market and pre-market discrimination, by inserting matters of power and social control directly into the analysis. This approach then links discrimination to racism or sexism, rather than to simple bigotry or prejudice. It leads to the proposition that discrimination—in the sense of differential treatment of those members of each group with similar productivity-linked characteristics—is an endogenous phenomenon. "In-market" discrimination need only occur when all the earlier attempts to control access to jobs, credentials, and qualifications are quavering.

One interesting implication here is that growth in skills for what we have been calling group B, the disadvantaged group, may be accompanied by a surge of in-market discrimination, because that form of discrimination has become more necessary to preserve the position of group A. There are several instances of cross-national evidence to support this notion. Darity, Dietrich and Guilkey (1997) find that while black males were making dramatic strides in acquiring literacy between 1880 and 1910 in the United States, simultaneously they were suffering increasing proportionate losses in occupational status due to disadvantageous treatment of their measured characteristics. Geographer Peggy Lovell (1993) finds very little evidence of discrimination in earnings against blacks in northern Brazil, where blacks are more numerous, but substantial evidence of discrimination against them in southern Brazil. Northern Brazil is considerably poorer than southern Brazil and the educational levels of northern black Brazilians are more depressed than in the south.[12] It is easy to argue that the exercise of discrimination is not "needed" in the north, since blacks are not generally going to compete with whites for the same sets of jobs. Indeed, there is relatively more evidence of discrimination against mulattos than blacks, the former more likely to compete directly with whites for employment. A third example, in a study using data for males based upon a survey taken in Delhi in 1970, Desi and Singh (1989) find that the most dramatic instance of discriminatory differentials in earnings was evident for Sikh men vis-à-vis Hindu high caste men. On the other hand, most of the earnings gap for Hindu middle caste, lower caste and scheduled caste men was due to inferior observed characteristics. Since these latter groups could be excluded from preferred positions because of an inadequate educational background, it would not be necessary for the upper castes to exercise discrimination against them. Sikh males, on the other hand, possessed the types of credentials that would make them viable contestants for the positions desired by the Hindu higher castes.

A final alternative approach at construction of a consistent economic theory of persistent discrimination evolves from a reconsideration of the neoclassical theory of competition. Darity and Williams (1985) argued that replacement of neoclassical competition with either classical or Marxist approaches to competition—where competition is defined by a tendency toward equalization of rates of profit and where monopoly positions are the consequence of competition rather than the antithesis of competition—eliminates the anomalies associated with the orthodox approach (Botwinick, 1993; Mason, 1995, forthcoming-b). A labor market implication of this approach is that wage diversity, different pay across firms and industries for workers within the same occupation, is the norm for competitive labor markets. In these models, remuneration is a function of the characteristics of the individual and the job. The racial-gender composition of the job affects worker bargaining power and thereby wage differentials. In turn, race and gender exclusion are used to make some workers less competitive for the higher paying positions. This approach emphasizes that the major elements for the persistence of discrimination are racial or gender differences in the access to better paying jobs within and between occupations.

Whatever alternative approach is preferred, the strong evidence of the persistence of discrimination in labor markets calls into question any theoretical apparatus that implies that the discrimination must inevitably diminish or disappear.

Notes

1. The only significant exception to the help-wanted ads pattern of maintaining a fairly strict sexual division of labor that we could detect was evident in the *Los Angeles Times* employment section of early January 1945, where we found women being sought as aircraft riveters, assemblers, and army photographers. Of course, World War II was ongoing at that stage, and the comparative absence of men produced the "Rosie the Riveter" phenomenon. However, despite wartime conditions, even this temporary breakdown in gender-typing of occupations was not evident in the help-wanted ads for the *Chicago Tribune,* the *New York Times,* or the *Washington Post* at the same time. Moreover, racial preferences also remained strongly pronounced in wartime advertisements of each of the four newspapers.

2. The C.W. Agency, advertising in the *Los Angeles Times* on January, 1, 1950, wanted a "Girl Model 38 bust, 25 waist, 36 hips"; "Several Other Types" with physical characteristics unspecified in the advertisement apparently also were acceptable.

3. The 1980 and 1990 Censuses provide only self-reported information on interviewees' race and their ancestry, which makes it possible to partition the American population into 50 different detailed ethnic and racial groups, like Asian Indian ancestry women, Mexican ancestry women, Polish ancestry women, French Canadian ancestry women, and so on. The explanatory variables were years of school, years of college, number of children, married spouse present, years of work experience, years of work experience squared, very good or fluent English, disabled, born in the United States, assimilated (that is either married to a person with a different ethnicity or having claimed two different ethnic groups in the census), location, region, and occupation. Annual earnings was the dependent variable. There was no control for the difference between potential and actual experience; hence, to the extent that the gap between potential and actual experience and the rate of return to actual experience varies by race, the results for the female regressions may be less reliable than the results for the male regression.

4. For a view that unobservable factors might favor black male productivity, thereby meaning that the regression coefficients are underestimating the degree of discrimination, see Mason (forthcoming-a).

5. Indeed, if one uses a measure that, unlike the AFQT, was explicitly designed as a measure of intelligence, it does not explain the black-white gap in wages. Mason (forthcoming-b; 1996) demonstrates this by using in a wage equation an explanatory variable that comes from a sentence completion test given to 1972 respondents to the Panel Study of Income Dynamics (PSID)—a test which was designed to assess "g," so-called general intelligence. Mason finds that the significant, negative sign on the coefficient for the race variable is unaffected by inclusion of the PSID sentence completion test score as an explanatory variable. Indeed, Mason (1997) finds that although discrimination declined

during 1968 to 1973, discrimination grew by 2.0 percent annually during 1973–1991. On the other hand, the rate of return to cognitive skill (IQ) was relatively constant during 1968–1979, but had an annual growth rate of 1.6 percent during 1979–1991.

6. Mason (1997) finds a similar result when age and education-adjusted IQ scores are used.

7. Attention to the psychological measures also provides mild evidence that blacks put forth more effort than whites, a finding consistent with Mason's (forthcoming-a) speculation that there may be unobservables that favor black productivity. Mason argues that effort or motivation is a productivity-linked variable that favors blacks, based upon his finding that blacks acquire more schooling than whites for a comparable set of resources.

8. Card and Krueger (1992) also directly control for school quality. They find that there is still a substantial wage gap left after controlling for school quality.

9. Systematic racial differences in the structural equations for the determination of standardized test scores also are evident in the General Social Survey data. Fitting equations for Wordsum scores separately for blacks and whites also yields statistically distinct structures (White, 1997).

10. Although some of their criticisms along these lines frankly strike us as ridiculous; for example, concerns about facial hair on the Hispanic male testers used by the Urban Institute.

11. To address the effects of culture, following Woodbury (1993), Darity, Guilkey, and Winfrey (1996) held color constant and varied culture by examining outcomes among blacks of differing ancestries. Unlike Sowell's expectation, black males of West Indian and non-West Indian ancestry were being confronted with the same racial penalty in U.S. labor markets by 1990.

12. The portion of the gap that can be explained by discrimination is much lower in the high black region of Brazil, the Northeast, than the rest of Brazil. We know of no evidence which suggests that this is or is not true for the U.S. south.

James J. Heckman  **NO**

Detecting Discrimination

In the current atmosphere of race relations in America, the authors of the three main papers presented in this symposium are like persons crying "fire" in a crowded theater. They apparently vindicate the point of view that American society is riddled with racism and that discrimination by employers may account for much of the well-documented economic disparity between blacks and whites. In my judgement, this conclusion is not sustained by a careful reading of the evidence.

In this article, I make three major points. First, I want to distinguish market discrimination from the discrimination encountered by a randomly selected person or pair of persons at a randomly selected firm as identified from audit studies.

Second, I consider the evidence presented by the authors in the symposium, focusing for brevity and specificity on labor markets. It is far less decisive on the issue of market discrimination than it is claimed to be. Disparity in market outcomes does not prove discrimination in the market. A careful reading of the entire body of available evidence confirms that most of the disparity in earnings between blacks and whites in the labor market of the 1990s is due to the differences in skills they bring to the market, and not to discrimination within the labor market. This interpretation of the evidence has important consequences for social policy. While undoubtedly there are still employers and employees with discriminatory intentions, labor market discrimination is no longer a first-order quantitative problem in American society. At this time, the goal of achieving black economic progress is better served by policies that promote skill formation, like improving family environments, schools and neighborhoods, not by strengthening the content and enforcement of civil rights laws—the solution to the problem of an earlier era.

Third, I want to examine the logic and limitations of the audit pair method. All of the papers in this symposium use evidence from this version of pair matching. However, the evidence acquired from it is less compelling than is often assumed. Inferences from such studies are quite fragile to alternative assumptions about unobservable variables and the way labor markets work. The audit method can find discrimination when in fact none exists; it can also disguise discrimination when it is present. These findings are especially

From James J. Heckman, "Detecting Discrimination," *Journal of Economic Perspectives,* vol. 12, no. 2 (Spring 1998). Copyright © 1998 by The American Economic Association. Reprinted by permission.

troubling because the Equal Employment Opportunity Commission has recently authorized the use of audit pair methods to detect discrimination in labor markets (Seelye, 1997).

Discrimination Definition and Measurement

The authors of these papers focus on the question of whether society is color blind, not on the specific question of whether there is market discrimination in realized transactions. But discrimination at the individual level is different from discrimination at the group level, although these concepts are often confused in the literature on the economics of discrimination.

At the level of a potential worker or credit applicant dealing with a firm, racial discrimination is said to arise if an otherwise identical person is treated differently by virtue of that person's race or gender, and race and gender by themselves have no direct effect on productivity. Discrimination is a causal effect defined by a hypothetical *ceteris paribus* conceptual experiment—varying race but keeping all else constant. Audit studies attempt to identify racial and gender discrimination so defined for the set of firms sampled by the auditors by approximating the *ceteris paribus* condition.

It was Becker's (1957) insight to observe that finding a discriminatory effect of race or gender at a randomly selected firm does not provide an accurate measure of the discrimination that takes place in the market as a whole. At the level of the market, the causal effect of race is defined by the marginal firm or set of firms with which the marginal minority member deals. The impact of market discrimination is not determined by the most discriminatory participants in the market, or even by the average level of discrimination among firms, but rather by the level of discrimination at the firms where ethnic minorities or women actually end up buying, working and borrowing. It is at the margin that economic values are set. This point is largely ignored in the papers in this symposium.

This confusion between individual firm and market discrimination arises in particular in the audit studies. A well-designed audit study could uncover many individual firms that discriminate, while at the same time the marginal effect of discrimination on the wages of employed workers could be zero. . . . Purposive sorting within markets eliminates the worst forms of discrimination. There may be evil lurking in the hearts of firms that is never manifest in consummated market transactions.

Estimating the extent and degree of distribution, whether at the individual or the market level, is a difficult matter. In the labor market, for example, a worker's productivity is rarely observed directly, so the analyst must instead use available data as a proxy in controlling for the relevant productivity characteristics. The major controversies arise over whether relevant omitted characteristics differ between races and between genders, and whether certain included characteristics systematically capture productivity differences or instead are a proxy for race or gender.

How Substantial Is Labor Market Discrimination Against Blacks?

In their paper in this symposium, [William A.] Darity [Jr.] and [Patrick L.] Mason present a bleak picture of the labor market position of African-Americans in which market discrimination is ubiquitous. They present a quantitative estimate of the magnitude of estimated discrimination: 12 to 15 percent in both 1980 and 1990 using standard regressions fit on Current Population Survey and Census data. Similar regressions show that the black/white wage gap has diminished sharply over the last half century. Comparable estimates for 1940 show a black/white wage gap ranging from 30 percentage points, for men age 25–34 to 42 percentage points, men age 55–64. In 1960, the corresponding numbers would have been 21 percent and 32 percent, for the same two age groups; in 1970, 18 and 25 percent (U.S. Commission on Civil Rights, 1986, Table 6.1, p. 191). The progress was greatest in Southern states where a blatantly discriminatory system was successfully challenged by an external legal intervention (Donohue and Heckman, 1991; Heckman, 1990).

How should the residual wage gap be interpreted? As is typical of much of the literature on measuring racial wage gaps, Darity and Mason never precisely define the concept of discrimination they use. As is also typical of this literature, the phrase "human capital variable" is thrown around without a clear operational definition. The implicit definition of these terms varies across the studies they discuss. In practice, human capital in these studies has come to mean education and various combinations of age and education, based on the available Census and Current Population Survey (CPS) data. However, there is a staggering gap between the list of productivity characteristics available to economic analysts in standard data sources and what is available to personnel departments of firms. Regressions based on the Census and/or CPS data can typically explain 20 to 30 percent of the variation in wages. However, regressions based on personnel data can explain a substantially higher share of the variation in wages; 60–80 percent in professional labor markets (for example, see Abowd and Killingsworth, 1983). It is not idle speculation to claim that the standard data sets used to estimate discrimination omit many relevant characteristics actually used by firms in their hiring and promotion decisions. Nor is it idle speculation to conjecture that disparity in family, neighborhood and schooling environments may account for systematic differences in unmeasured characteristics between race groups.

Consider just one well-documented source of discrepancy between Census variables and the productivity concepts that they proxy: the measurement of high school credentials. The standard Census and CPS data sources equate recipients of a General Equivalence Degree, or GED, with high school graduates. However, black high school certificate holders are much more likely than whites to receive GEDs (Cameron and Heckman, 1993), and a substantial portion of the widely trumpeted "convergence" in measured black educational attainment has come through GED certification. Thus, in 1987 in the NLSY data that Darity and Mason discuss, and Neal and Johnson (1996) analyze,

79 percent of black males age 25 were high school certified, and 14 percent of the credential holders were GED recipients. Among white males, 88 percent were high school certified, and only 8 percent of the white credential holders were GED certified. Given the evidence from Cameron and Heckman that GED recipients earn the same as high school dropouts, it is plausible that standard Census-based studies that use high school credentials to control for "education" will find that the wages of black high school "graduates" are lower than those of whites.

Most of the empirical literature cited by Darity and Mason takes Census variables literally and ignores these issues. The GED factor alone accounts for 1–2 percentage points of the current 12–15 percent black-white hourly wage gap. An enormous body of solid evidence on inferior inner city schools and poor neighborhoods makes the ritual of the measurement of "discrimination" using the unadjusted Census or Current Population Survey data a questionable exercise.

Darity and Mason bolster their case for rampant discrimination by appealing to audit pair evidence. They do not point out that audit pair studies have primarily been conducted for hiring in entry level jobs in certain low skill occupations using overqualified college students during summer vacations. They do not sample subsequent promotion decisions. They fail to point out that the audits undersample the main avenues through which youth get jobs, since only job openings advertised in newspapers are audited, and not jobs found through networks and friends (Heckman and Siegelman, 1993, pp. 213–215). Auditors are sometimes instructed on the "problem of discrimination in American society" prior to sampling firms, so they may have been coached to find what the audit agencies wanted to find. I have already noted that audit evidence does not translate into actual employment experiences and wages obtained by actors who purposively search markets.

Putting these objections to the side, what do the audits actually show for this unrepresentative snapshot of the American labor market? Table 1 presents evidence from three major audits in Washington, D.C., Chicago and Denver. The most remarkable feature of this evidence is the a + b column which records the percentage of audit attempts where black and white auditors were treated symmetrically (both got a job; neither got a job). In Chicago and Denver this happened about 86 percent of the time. The evidence of disparity in hiring presented in the last two columns of the table suggests only a slight preference for whites over minorities; in several pairs, minorities are favored. Only a zealot can see evidence in these data of pervasive discrimination in the U.S. labor market. And, as I will show in the next section, even this evidence on disparity has to be taken with a grain of salt, because it is based on the implicit assumption that the distribution of unobserved productivity is the same in both race groups.

Darity and Mason go on to dismiss the research of Neal and Johnson (1996) who analyze a sample of males who took an achievement or ability test in their early teens—specifically, the Armed Forces Qualifications Test (AFQT)—and ask how much of the gap in black-white wages measured a decade or so after the test was taken can be explained by the differences in the

Table 1

Outcomes From Major Audit Studies for Blacks
(outcome: get job or not)

Number of Audits	Pair	(a) Both Get Job	(b) Neither Gets a Job	Equal Treatment a + b	White Yes, Black No	White No, Black Yes
Chicago*						
35	1	(5) 14.3%	(23) 65.7%	80.0%	(5) 14.3%	(2) 5.7%
40	2	(5) 12.5%	(25) 62.5%	75.0%	(4) 10.0%	(2) 15.0%
44	3	(3) 6.8%	(37) 84.1%	90.9%	(3) 6.8%	(1) 2.3%
36	4	(6) 16.7%	(24) 66.7%	83.4%	(6) 16.7%	(0) 0.0%
42	5	(3) 7.1%	(38) 90.5%	97.6%	(1) 2.4%	(2) 0.0%
197	Total	(22) 11.2%	(147) 74.6%	85.8%	(19) 9.6%	(9) 4.5%
Washington*						
46	1	(5) 10.9%	(26) 56.5%	67.4%	(12) 26.1%	(3) 6.5%
54	2	(11) 20.4%	(31) 57.4%	77.8%	(9) 16.7%	(3) 5.6%
62	3	(11) 17.7%	(36) 58.1%	75.8%	(11) 17.7%	(4) 6.5%
37	4	(6) 16.2%	(22) 59.5%	75.7%	(7) 18.9%	(2) 5.4%
42	5	(7) 16.7%	(26) 61.9%	77.6%	(7) 16.7%	(2) 4.8%
241	Total	(40) 16.6%	(141) 58.5%	75.1%	(46) 19.1%	(14) 5.8%
Denver**						
18	1	(2) 11.1%	(11) 61.1%	72.1%	(5) 27.8%	(0) 0.0%
53	2	(2) 3.8%	(41) 77.4%	81.2%	(0) 0.0%	(10) 18.9%
33	3	(7) 21.2%	(25) 75.8%	97.0%	(1) 3.0%	(0) 0.0%
15	4	(9) 60.0%	(3) 20.0%	80.0%	(2) 6.7%	(2) 13.3%
265	5	(3) 11.5%	(23) 88.5%	100.0%	(0) 0.0%	(0) 0.0%
145	Total	(23) 15.8%	(103) 71.1%	86.9%	(7) 4.8%	(12) 8.3%

Note: Results are percentages; figures in parentheses are the relevant number of audits.

*This study was conducted by the Urban Institute.

**Denver pair numbers are for both black and Hispanic audits. For the sake of brevity, I only consider the black audits. The Denver study was not conducted by the Urban Institute but it was conducted to conform to Urban Institute practice.

Sources: Heckman and Siegelman (1993).

test scores.[1] It is remarkable and important that this early "premarket" measure of ability plays such a strong role in explaining wages measured a decade after the test is taken. This is as true for studies of white outcomes taken in isolation as it is for black-white comparisons. Their findings are important for interpreting the sources of black-white disparity in labor market outcomes. . . .

The Neal-Johnson story is not about genetic determination. They demonstrate that schooling and environment can affect their measured test score. A huge body of evidence, to which the Neal-Johnson study contributes, documents that human abilities and motivations are formed early and have a decisive effect on lifetime outcomes; the evidence is summarized in Heckman (1995) and in Heckman, Lochner, Taber, and Smith (1997). Not only is early ability an important predictor of later success for blacks or whites, it can be manipulated. Early interventions are far more effective than late ones because early skills and motivation beget later skills and motivation. As Heckman, Lochner, Taber and Smith document, however, successful early interventions can be quite costly.

The objections raised by Darity and Mason against the Neal-Johnson study are largely specious. For example, Rodgers and Spriggs (1996) miss the point of the Neal-Johnson article by "adjusting" the test score by a later variable, such as schooling. But ability is known to be an important determinant of schooling (Cawley, Heckman and Vtylacil, 1998), so it should be no surprise that "adjusting" the score for later schooling eliminates an important component of ability and that adjusted scores play a much weaker role in explaining black-white differentials.[2]

Only one point raised by Darity and Mason concerning Neal and Johnson is potentially valid—and this is a point made by Neal and Johnson in their original article. Black achievement scores may be lower than white scores not because of the inferior environments encountered by many poor blacks, but because of expectations of discrimination in the market. If black children and their parents face a world in which they receive lower rewards for obtaining skills, they will invest less if they face the same tuition costs as whites. Poor performance in schools and low achievement test scores may thus be a proxy for discrimination to be experienced in the future.

There is solid empirical evidence that expectations about rewards in the labor market influence human capital investment decisions; for example, the reward to skills held by black workers increased following the passage of the 1964 Civil Rights Act, and a rapid rise in college enrollment of blacks followed (Donohue and Heckman, 1991). But the difficulty with the argument in this context is that it presumes that black parents and children operate under mistaken expectations about the present labor market. Although it was once true that the returns to college education were lower for blacks than for whites (Becker, 1957; U.S. Civil Rights Commission, 1986), the return to college education for blacks was higher than the return for whites by the mid-1970s, and continues to be higher today. Some parallel evidence presented by Johnson and Neal (1998) shows that the returns to (coefficient on) AFQT scores for black males in an earnings equation are now as high or higher than those for whites, although they used to be lower in the pre–Civil Rights era. Given the greater return for blacks to college education and ability, it seems implausible to argue that a rational fear of lower future returns is currently discouraging black formation of skills.

Ability as it crystallizes at an early age accounts for most of the measured gap in black and white labor market outcomes. Stricter enforcement of civil rights laws is a tenuous way to improve early childhood skills and ability.[3] The weight of the evidence suggests that this ability and early motivation is most easily influenced by enriching family and preschool learning environments and by improving the quality of the early years of schooling.

The Implicit Assumptions Behind the Audit Method

The method of audit pairs operates by controlling for systematic observed differences across pairs. It does this by attempting to create two candidates for jobs or loans who are "essentially" the same in their paper qualifications and personal characteristics, and then comparing their outcomes in their dealings with the same firm. Averaging over the outcomes at all firms for the same audit pair produces an estimate of the discrimination effect. An average is often taken over audit pairs as well to report an "overall" estimate of discrimination. More sophisticated versions of the method will allow for some heterogeneity in treatment among firms and workers or firms and applicants.

One set of difficulties arise, however, because there are sure to be many unobserved variables. As noted by Heckman and Siegelman (1993), given the current limited state of knowledge of the determinants of productivity within firms, and given the small pools of applicants from which matched pairs are constructed that are characteristic of most audit studies, it is unlikely that all characteristics that might affect productivity will be perfectly matched. Thus, the implicit assumption in the audit pair method is that controlling for some components of productivity and sending people to the same firm will reduce the bias below what it would be if random pairs of, say, whites and blacks were compared using, for example, Census data. The implicit assumption that justifies this method is that the effect of the unobserved characteristics averages out to zero across firms for the same audit pair.

However, the mean of the differences in the unobserved components need not be zero and assuming that it is begs the problem. Nowhere in the published literature on the audit pair method will you find a demonstration that matching one subset of observable variables necessarily implies that the resulting difference in audit-adjusted treatment between blacks and whites is an unbiased measure of discrimination—or indeed, that it is even necessarily a better measure of discrimination than comparing random pairs of whites and blacks applying at the same firm or even applying to different firms. . . .

Consider the following example. Suppose that the market productivity of persons is determined by the sum of two productivity components. These two productivity components are distributed independently in the population so their values are not correlated with each other. Both factors affect employer assessments of employee productivity.[4] Suppose further that average productivity of the sum is the same for both whites and blacks; however, blacks are more productive on average on one component while whites are more productive on average on the other. Now consider an audit pair study that equates only the first component of productivity and equates firm effects by sending the audit pair to the same firm. Under these conditions, the audit estimator is biased toward a finding of discrimination, since in this example, only the characteristic which makes black productivity look relatively high is being used to standardize the audit pair. The condition of zero mean of unobservable productivity differences across race groups is not especially compelling and requires a priori knowledge that is typically not available.

Now consider the case in which the observed and unobserved components of productivity are dependent. In this case, making the included components as alike as possible may accentuate the differences in the unobserved components. As a result, it can increase the bias over the case where the measured components are not aligned.

. . . [T]hink of pairing up black and white high jumpers to see if they can clear a bar set at a certain height. There is no discrimination, in the sense that they both use the same equipment and have the bar set at the same level. Suppose now that the chance of a jumper (of any race) clearing the bar depends on two additive factors: the person's height and their jumping technique. We can pair up black and white jumpers so that they have identical heights, but we can't directly observe their technique. Let us make the generous assumption, implicit in the entire audit literature, that the mean jumping technique is equal for the two groups. Then, if the variance of technique is also the same for white and black high-jumpers, we would find that the two racial groups are equally likely to clear the bar. On the other hand, if the variance differs, then whether the black or white pair is more likely to clear the bar will depend on how the bar is set, relative to their common height, and which racial group has a higher variance in jumping technique. If the bar is set at a low level so that most people of the given height are likely to clear the bar, then the group with the lower variance will be more likely to clear the bar. If the bar is set at a very high level relative to the given height, then the group with a higher variance in jumping technique will be more likely to clear the bar. A limitation of the audit method is readily apparent from this analogy: there is no discrimination, yet the two groups have different probabilities of clearing the bar.[5] And if there is discrimination—that is, the bar is being set higher for blacks—the differential dispersion in the unobserved component could still cause the minority group to clear the bar more often. The method could fail to detect discrimination when it does exist.

Thus, depending on the distribution of unobserved characteristics for each race group and the audit standardization level, the audit method can show reverse discrimination, or equal treatment, or discrimination, even though blacks and whites in this example are subject to the same cutoff and face no discrimination. The apparent bias depends on whether the level of qualifications set by the audit designer makes it more or less likely that the applicant will receive the job, and the distribution of variables that are unobservable to the audit design. The apparent disparity favoring Washington whites in Table 1 may be a consequence of differences in unobserved characteristics between blacks and whites when there is no discrimination.

Even more disturbing, suppose that there is discrimination against blacks, so the productivity cutoff used by firms is higher for blacks than whites. Depending on the audit designer's choice of what level of qualifications are given to the auditors, the audit study can find no discrimination at all. However, whether the qualifications make it relatively likely or unlikely to get the job is a fact rarely reported in audit studies. . . .

Making audit pairs as alike as possible may seem an obviously useful step, but it can greatly bias the inference about average discrimination or discrimination at the margin. Intuitively, by taking out the common components that are most easily measured, differences in hiring rates as monitored by audits arise from the idiosyncratic factors, and not the main factors, that drive actual labor markets. These examples highlight the fragility of the audit method to untested and unverifiable assumptions about the distributions of unobservables. Similar points arise in more general nonlinear models that characterize other employment decision rules.

The Becker Model

The papers in this symposium make the erroneous claim that in Becker's (1957) model, market discrimination disappears in the long run. It need not. Entrepreneurs can consume their income in any way they see fit. If a bigoted employer prefers whites, the employer can indulge that taste as long as income is received from entrepreneurial activity just as a person who favors an exotic ice cream can indulge that preference by being willing to pay the price. Only if the supply of entrepreneurship is perfectly elastic in the long run at a zero price, so entrepreneurs have no income to spend to indulge their tastes, or if there are enough nonprejudiced employers to hire all blacks, will discrimination disappear from Becker's model.

However, even if the common misinterpretation of Becker's model is accepted, it is far from clear that the prediction of no or little discrimination in the U.S. labor market in the long run is false. The substantial decline over the past 50 years in wage differentials between blacks and whites may well be a manifestation of the dynamics of the Becker model. It may take decades for the effects of past discrimination in employment and schooling as it affects current endowments of workers to fade out of the labor market. But the evidence from the current U.S. labor market is that discrimination by employers alone does *not* generate large economic disparities between blacks and whites.

Appendix

Implicit Identifying Assumptions in the Audit Method

Define the productivity of a person of race $r \in \{1, 0\}$ at firm f, with characteristics $\sim X = (X_1, X_2)$ as $P(\sim X, r, f)$. $r = 1$ corresponds to black; $r = 0$ corresponds to white. Assume that race does not affect productivity so we may write $P = P(\sim X, f)$. The treatment at the firm f for a person of race r and productivity P is $T(P(\sim X, f), r)$. Racial discrimination exists at firm f if

$$T(P(\sim X, f), r = 1) \neq T(P(\sim X, f), r = 0).$$

As noted in the text, audit methods monitor discrimination at randomly selected firms within the universe designated for sampling, not the firms where blacks are employed.

The most favorable case for auditing assumes that T (or some transformation of it) is linear in f and X. Assume for simplicity that $P = X_1 + X_2 + f$ and

$T(P, r) = P + \gamma r$. When $\gamma < 0$ there is discrimination against blacks. γ may vary among firms as in Heckman and Siegelman (1993). For simplicity suppose that all firms are alike. Audit methods pair racially dissimilar workers in the following way: they match some components of $\sim X$ and they sample the same firms. Let P_1^* be the standardized productivity for the black member of the pair; P_0^* is the standardized productivity for the white member. If $P_0^* = P_1^*$,

$$T(P_1^*, 1) - T(P_0^*, 0) = \gamma.$$

When averaged over firms, the average treatment estimates the average γ.

Suppose that standardization is incomplete. We can align the first coordinate of X at $\{X_1 = X_1^*\}$ but not the second coordinate, X_2, which is unobserved by the auditor but acted on by the firm. $P_1^* = X_1^* + X_2^1$ where X_2^1 is the value of X_2 for the $r = 1$ member and $P_0^* = X_1^* + X_2^1$. In this case

$$T(P_1^*, 1) - T(P_1^*, 0) = X_2^1 - X_2^0 + \gamma.$$

For averages over pairs to estimate γ without bias, it must be assumed that $E(X_2^1) = E(X_2^0)$; i.e., that the mean of the unobserved productivity traits is the same. This is the crucial identifying assumption in the conventional audit method. Suppose that this is true so $E(X_2^1) = E(X_2^0) = \mu$. Then the pair matching as in the audit method does not increase bias and in general reduces it over comparisons of two X_1-identical persons at two randomly selected firms. Under these conditions, bias is lower than if two randomly chosen auditors are selected at the same firm if $E(X_1^1) \neq E(X_1^0)$.

However, the decision rule to offer a job or extend credit often depends on whether or not the perceived productivity P exceeds a threshold c:

$$T = 1 \text{ if } P > T = c$$
$$T = 0 \text{ otherwise}$$

In this case, the audit pair method will still produce bias even when it does not when T is linear in $\sim X$ and f unless the *distributions* of the omitted characteristics are identical in the two race groups. Suppose that $P = X_1 + X_2$. X_2 is uncontrolled. Then assuming no discrimination ($\gamma = 0$)

$$T(P_1^*, 1) = 1 \text{ if } X_1^* + X_2^1 + f \geq c = 0 \text{ otherwise}$$
$$T(P_0^*, 0) = 1 \text{ if } X_1^* + X_2^0 + f \geq c = 0 \text{ otherwise.}$$

Even if the distributions of f are identical across pairs, and f is independent of X, unless the *distributions* of X_2^1 and X_2^0 are identical, $\Pr(T(P_1^*, 1) = 1) \neq \Pr(T(P_0^*) = 1)$ for most values of the standardization level X_1^*. The right tail area of the distribution governs the behavior of these probabilities. This implies that even if blacks and whites face the same cutoff value, and in this sense are treated without discrimination in the labor market, even if the means of the distributions of unobservables are the same across race group, if the distributions of the unobservables are different, their probabilities of being hired will differ and will depend on the level of standardization used in the audit study—something that is rarely reported. The pattern of racial disparity in Table 1 may simply be a consequence of the choice of the level of standardization in those audits, and not discrimination.

Worse yet, suppose that the cutoff $c = c_1$ for blacks is larger than the cutoff $c = c_0$ for whites so that blacks are held to a higher standard. Then depending on the right tail area of X_2^1 and X_2^0, the values of c_1 and c_0, and the level of standardization X_1^*,

$$\Pr(T(P_1^*) = 1) \gtrless P(T(P_0^*, 0) = 1).$$

In general, only if the *distributions* of X_2^1 and X_2^0 are the same for each race group, will the evidence reported in Table 1 be informative on the level of discrimination in the universe of sampled firms.

Figures 1 and 2 illustrate these two cases for X_2^1 and X_2^0 normally distributed (and independent of each other) where X_1^* is the level of audit standardization and firms are standardized to have $f = 0$. In Figure 1 there is no discrimination in the market. Yet the black hire rate falls short of the white rate if the standardization rate is $X_1^* < 0$, and the lower the value of X_1^*, the greater the shortfall. In Figure 2, which is constructed for a hypothetical economy where there is discrimination against blacks, for high standardization rates, audits would appear to reveal discrimination *in favor* of blacks when in fact blacks are being held to a higher standard. The evidence in Table 1 is intrinsically ambiguous about the extent of discrimination in the market. For further discussion, see Heckman and Siegelman (1993).

Figure 1

Relative Hiring Rate as a Function of the Level of Standardization. Blacks Have More Dispersion. Threshold Hiring Rule: No Discrimination Against Blacks Normally Distributed Unobservables

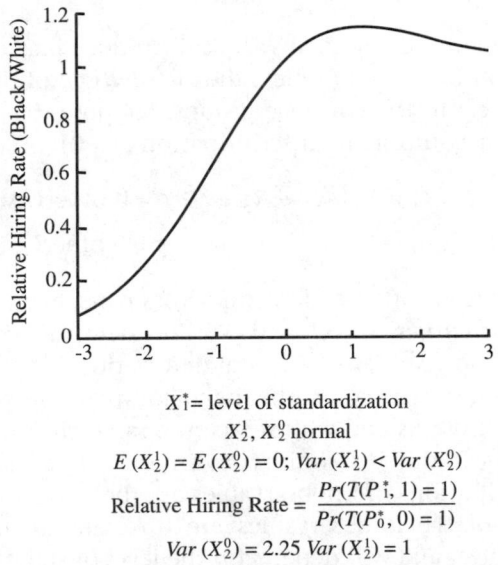

$X_1^* =$ level of standardization

X_2^1, X_2^0 normal

$E(X_2^1) = E(X_2^0) = 0;\ Var(X_2^1) < Var(X_2^0)$

Relative Hiring Rate $= \dfrac{Pr(T(P_1^*, 1) = 1)}{Pr(T(P_0^*, 0) = 1)}$

$Var(X_2^0) = 2.25\ Var(X_2^1) = 1$

$c_1 = c_0 = 0$

Figure 2

Relative Hiring Rate as a Function of the Level of Standardization. Blacks Held to Higher Standard; Blacks Have More Dispersion. Threshold Hiring Rule: No Discrimination Against Blacks Normally Distributed Unobservables

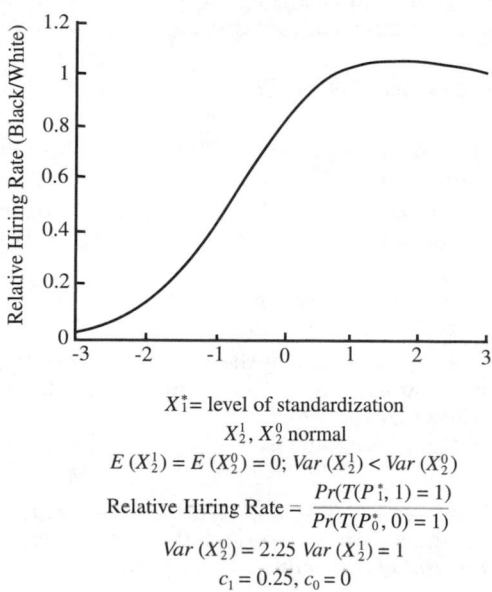

$X_1^* =$ level of standardization

X_2^1, X_2^0 normal

$E(X_2^1) = E(X_2^0) = 0; Var(X_2^1) < Var(X_2^0)$

Relative Hiring Rate $= \dfrac{Pr(T(P_1^*, 1) = 1)}{Pr(T(P_0^*, 0) = 1)}$

$Var(X_2^0) = 2.25 \ Var(X_2^1) = 1$

$c_1 = 0.25, c_0 = 0$

Notes

1. Specifically, Darity and Mason write: "This effort has uncovered one variable in one data set which, if inserted in an earnings regression, produces the outcome that nearly all of the black male-white male wage gap is explained by human capital and none by labor market discrimination."

2. The Rodgers and Spriggs comment (1997) on Neal-Johnson raises other red herrings. Their confused discussion of endogeneity of AFQT, and their "solution" to the problem end up with an "adjusted" AFQT measure that is poorly correlated with the measured AFQT, and so is a poor proxy for black ability.

3. However, nothing I have said vindicates abolishing these laws. They have important symbolic value and they addressed and solved an important problem of blatant discrimination in the American South.

4. They need not be perfectly observed by employers but may only be proxied. However, it is easiest to think of both components as fully observed by the employer, but that the observing economist has less information.

5. I owe this analogy to Alan Krueger. This analogy also shows how artificial the audit studies are because one would expect to find athletes choosing their sports based on their chances of success, as in the purposive search in the labor market discussed earlier.

6. For simplicity, assume that γ is the same across all firms. Alternatively, assume that it is distributed independently of $\sim X$ and f.

7. Allowing f to vary but assuming it is normal mean zero and variance σ_f^2 does not change the qualitative character of these calculations assuming that f is distributed independently of the characteristics.

References

Abowd, John, and Mark Killingsworth, "Sex, Discrimination, Atrophy, and the Male-Female Wage Differential," *Industrial And Labor Relations Review,* Fall 1983, *22*:3, 387–402.

Becker, Gary, *The Economics of Discrimination.* Chicago: University of Chicago Press, 1957.

Cameron, Stephen, and James Heckman, "The Nonequivalence of High School Equivalents," *Journal of Labor Economics, 1993, 11*:1, pt1, 1–47.

Cawley, John, James Heckman, and Edward Vytlacil, "Cognitive Ability and the Rising Return to Education," NBER working paper 6388, January 1998.

Donohue, John, and James Heckman, "Continuous vs. Episodic Change: The Impact of Affirmative Action and Civil Rights Policy on The Economic Status of Blacks," *Journal of Economic Literature,* December 1991. *29*:4, 1603–43.

Heckman, James, "The Central Role of the South in Accounting For The Economic Progress of Black Americans," Papers and Proceedings of The American Economic Association, May 1990.

Heckman, James, "Lessons From the Bell Curve," *Journal of Political Economy,* 1995, *103*:5, 1091–1120.

Heckman, James, and Peter Siegelman, "The Urban Institute Audit Studies: Their Methods and Findings." In M. Fix and R. Struyk, eds. *Clear and Convincing Evidence: Measurement of Discrimination in America.* Urban Institute, Fall 1993.

Heckman, James, Lance Lochner, Christopher Taber, and Jeffrey Smith, "The Effects of Government Policy on Human Capital Investment and Wage Inequality," *Chicago Policy Review,* Spring 1997, *1*:2, 1–40.

Johnson, William R., and Derek Neal, "Basic Skills and the Black-White Earnings Gaps." In Jencks, Christopher and Meredith Phillips, eds. *The Black-White Test Score Gap.* Washington, D.C. Brookings, 1998.

Neal, Derek, and William Johnson, "The Role of Premarket Factors in Black-White Wage Differences," *Journal of Political Economy, 1996, 104:5,* 869–95.

Rodgers III, William, and William Spriggs, "What Does AFQT Really Measure: Race, Wages, Schooling and the AFQT Score," *The Review of Black Political Economy,* Spring 1996, *24*:4, 13–46.

Rodgers III, William, William E. Spriggs, and Elizabeth Waaler, "The Role of Pre-market Factors in Black-White Differences: Comment," Unpublished Manuscript, College of William and Mary, May 25, 1997.

Seelye, Katherine, "Employment Panel To Send People Undercover to Detect Bias in Hiring," *New York Times,* Sunday, December 7, 1997, p. 22.

U.S. Commission on Civil Rights, *The Economic Progress of Black Men in America,* Clearinghouse Publication 91, 1986.

POSTSCRIPT

Is There Discrimination in U.S. Labor Markets?

Economists assume that markets are anonymous; that is, they assume that rational economic actors would not take race, sex, religious affiliation, or any other personal characteristic into consideration when buying or selling. Consumers are trying to maximize their consumer satisfaction, while producers are in the same marketplace trying to maximize their profits. Just as the often paraphrased axiom of Adam Smith suggests: Each acting for his or her own self-interest advances the well-being of the whole. In the world of neoclassical economics, there is simply no room for discrimination.

Yet the appearance of discrimination, if not the reality of discrimination, is all around us. Why are unemployment rates for African Americans twice those for white Americans? Why, on the average, do African American households earn 60 cents for every dollar earned by white households? Why do U.S. corporations, universities, courthouses, and even military officers' clubs have so many whites? And, more important, why do nearly 40 percent of African American children suffer the life-altering effects of poverty? Is this the product of market discrimination, or is it the consequence of deficient skill levels among African Americans?

In addition to Heckman's many contributions—he is perhaps the most prolific contributor to this debate from the neoclassical position—we suggest that you return to the source of his position, the work of Gary Becker, who in 1957 wrote *The Economics of Discrimination* (University of Chicago Press). Some of Heckman's other work is also highly recommended. See, for example, his essay "Lessons From the Bell Curve," *Journal of Political Economy* (vol. 103, 1995), pp. 1091–1120, and the book chapter he wrote with Peter Siegelman, "The Urban Institute Audit Studies: Their Methods," which appears in Michael Fix and Raymond Struyk, eds., *Clear and Convincing Evidence: Measurement of Discrimination in America* (Urban Institute Press, 1993). Finally, you might read Heckman's paper "The Value of Quantitative Evidence on the Effect of the Past on the Present," *American Economic Review* (May 1997).

Darity and Mason have also contributed extensively to this literature. See, for example, Mason's "Male Interracial Wage Differentials: Competing Explanations," *Cambridge Journal of Economics* (May 1999). You might also look for Darity and Samuel L. Myers, Jr.'s book *Persistent Disparity* (Edward Edgar, 1999). Lastly, we suggest a coauthored essay by Darity, Jason Dietrich, and David K. Guilkey, "Racial and Ethnic Inequality in the United States: A Secular Perspective," *American Economic Review* (May 1997).

ISSUE 4

Is the New Medicare Part D Drug Benefit Good Health Care Policy?

YES: Mark McClellan, from "Generic Drugs and the Medicare Prescription Drug Benefit," Testimony to the Senate Special Committee on Aging (September 21, 2006)

NO: Jagadeesh Gokhale, from "An Evaluation of Medicare's Prescription Drug Policy," Testimony to the Committee on Homeland Security and Government Affairs Subcommittee on Federal Financial Management, Government Information, and International Security (September 20, 2005)

ISSUE SUMMARY

YES: Health care administrator Mark McClellan believes that the Part D drug benefit is the most important new addition to Medicare in its history, providing millions of Americans with better benefits "at a significantly lower cost than originally estimated."

NO: Cato Institute senior fellow Jagadeesh Gokhale believes that Medicare's Part D drug benefit is a "bad and shortsighted economic policy." He believes this program will, among other things, increase private drug prices, impose higher fiscal burdens on future generations, and reduce national saving and investment.

$\mathbf{M}$edicare came into existence on July 30, 1965, when President Lyndon B. Johnson signed Public Law 98-97. This law amended the Social Security Act by adding Title XVIII, which created Medicare. Medicare can be described, very simply, as a program to provide medical care to the elderly. Generally speaking, persons over age 65 and getting Social Security benefits automatically qualify for Medicare. Public Law 98-97 also added Title XIX or Medicaid, a program designed to help the poor obtain medical care. Thus, this law, by extending the ability of elderly and the poor to obtain medical care, constituted a critical component of President Johnson's Great Society program.

At its creation, Medicare consisted of two major parts. Part A is an insurance program that covers inpatient hospital care, skilled nursing care, and other services. Part B is described as a medical services insurance program and covers physician services, outpatient hospital services, certain home health services, and durable medical equipment. At the end of 2003 Medicare covered 41 million people with annual costs of approximately $280 billion, or about 2.7 percent of U.S. gross domestic product.

On December 8, 2003, President George W. Bush signed the Medicare Prescription Drug Improvement and Modernization Act. This legislation has been described as the most significant change in Medicare since its creation. In particular, it established Part D of Medicare, which is intended to fill an important gap in Medicare's coverage by providing some assistance to seniors for their purchases of prescription drugs. The importance of prescription drugs in modern medicine can hardly be overstated. There are drugs to prevent conception, drugs to promote conception, drugs to battle HIV, drugs to lower cholesterol, and most recently drugs to prevent cancer. The drug industry is large with U.S. sales of approximately $235 billion in 2004, and growing rapidly with 2004 sales over 8 percent higher than 2003.

Part D was designed to relieve a problem for many seniors: the high cost of prescription drugs that are essential to living well, and in some cases, essential simply to living. Part D, or the Medicare Prescription Drug Coverage, began on January 1, 2006. The program, which covers both brand-name and generic drugs, is voluntary. The enrollee must select a drug insurance program from a number offered by a variety of different vendors (the number varies from state to state). The enrollee pays a monthly premium for a basic benefit package (one estimate of the average monthly premium in 2006 was about $35). In addition, the enrollee pays an annual deductible up to $250 (for 2006). There is coinsurance as well. For 2006 the coinsurance was set at 25 percent of the covered drugs between $251 and $2,250; 100 percent of the cost of the covered drugs between $2,251 and $5,100 (this is the so-called donut hole); and 5 percent of the covered drugs above $5,101. The U.S. Department of Health and Human Services estimates that about 53 percent of Medicare beneficiaries now have Part D coverage, 37 percent have some other type of drug coverage, but 10 percent remain without any coverage. Most recent estimates place the cost to the federal government of the program at $30 billion for 2006 and $48 billion for 2007.

This then provides some background on the issue. The debate as framed here considers the broad consequences of Part D. Mark McClellan emphasizes the large number of persons who benefit from the program, while Jagadeesh Gokhale raises concerns about those who do not have drug insurance and future costs.

YES

Mark McClellan

Generic Drugs and the Medicare Prescription Drug Benefit

Chairman Smith, Senator Kohl, distinguished committee members, thank you for the opportunity to provide you with information on how the new Medicare prescription drug benefit (Part D) is helping to encourage generic drug utilization and lower the cost of prescription drugs for people with Medicare, the Medicare program, and taxpayers. I appreciate your interest in this topic, but more importantly, Members of Congress from both parties have been a key part of this massive grassroots education effort put in place to help Medicare beneficiaries select a plan that best fits their needs. Members of Congress have supported and participated in enrollment events sponsored by CMS and our thousands of partners throughout the country, sent flyers to their constituents, and spoken extensively to the public about the value of this new benefit. With the recent launch of this fall's *My Health. My Medicare.* campaign, I expect that this partnership will continue as we begin to drive greater awareness and use of the enhanced preventive benefits and coverage options for 2007.

Improvements made to the drug benefit in 2007 will continue to help beneficiaries save money, in part by increasing awareness about the value of generic drugs. There are a number of tools available to consumers to help them evaluate their options for the new plan year, including enhancements for the Drug Plan Finder, the *Medicare & You Handbook,* and personalized assistance through our 1-800-Medicare call centers and the State Health Insurance Assistance Programs (SHIP). As we change our focus from that of a payer of health benefits to one that promotes steps to stay well and reduce health care costs, we will be educating beneficiaries and partners about the preventive benefits offered in Medicare.

The Part D benefit is the most important new coverage to be added to the Medicare program in its more than 40-year history. It is critical to preventing and managing chronic disease, treating illness, preserving quality of life, and delivering modern medical care in the 21st century. Comprehensive prescription drug coverage is also a key element of our ongoing efforts to transform the emphasis in Medicare from simply paying bills when people get sick to paying for high quality, prevention-oriented care that allows

Testimony for the Senate Special Committee on Aging, Mark McClellan, (September 21, 2006).

people with Medicare to live healthier lives while avoiding preventable healthcare costs.

Thanks to the enactment of the new Medicare prescription drug benefit, tens of millions of Americans are now getting better benefits from Medicare than ever before and at a significantly lower cost than originally projected. Strong competition in 2006 and well-informed beneficiary choices have resulted in significant savings over what had been previously estimated. Current estimates of the cost of the drug benefit indicate that beneficiaries and the Federal government will be saving tens of billions of dollars more, over the next five years, than had been anticipated just a year ago. Notably, the average Part D premium for 2006, now estimated to be less than $24, is about 35 percent lower than had been projected a year ago. Beneficiaries, the Federal government and the states are all benefiting from lower costs and will continue doing so next year. And even greater savings are ahead in 2007. Based in part on the strong competitive bids for 2007, average premiums will again be around $24 for beneficiaries, and the vast majority of beneficiaries will have access to Medicare drug plans that have lower premiums than those in 2006. In addition, costs to taxpayers may be even lower in 2007 than 2006 because lower bid amounts mean that the Federal government's costs will be commensurately lower.

The utilization of generic drugs has played an important role in the low costs and expected further cost reductions in the drug benefit. Due in part to increasing generic drug availability, strong competition in the prescription drug marketplace has led to slower rates of growth in overall prescription drug spending. Also, the availability of excellent coverage of generic drugs in the Part D drug benefit, as well as personalized information and support to help beneficiaries find out about how they can save using generics, have been important contributors to costs that are much lower than expected. Continuing to promote greater reliance on generics when available among Medicare beneficiaries is an important strategy to keep the new drug benefit affordable over the long term.

Generics Are Widely Available at Low Cost

With ever increasing generic drug availability, more and more Americans are seeing the value of generics and using them to help save money on their prescription drug costs. Roughly three-quarters of the drugs currently listed in the Food and Drug Administration's Orange Book currently have generic counterparts. According to the Generic Pharmaceutical Association (GPhA), U.S. generic pharmaceutical sales increased 10 percent between 2003 and 2004 and amounted to $22.3 billion in 2005; the generic share of the pharmaceutical market is expected to grow by roughly 13 percent in 2006. This growing availability of generics is well accounted for in Medicare Part D, with all stand-alone prescription drug plans and Medicare Advantage Prescription Drug plans (MA-PDs) offering comprehensive, low-cost access to generic pharmaceuticals in 2006. In addition, all Medicare beneficiaries eligible for Medicare Part D had access to at least one prescription drug plan with some coverage in the gap in 2006, including coverage of generics during the gap. And in 2007, even more plans will offer coverage of generics in the gap.

Equally important, and again as a result of strong competition, the cost of generic drugs in the United States is very low and they are relatively widely used. The FDA notes that generic drugs typically cost 50–70 percent less than their brand-name counterparts. Further, prices for generic drugs in the U.S. are much lower than in many other countries. For example, a study by the National Opinion Research Center at the University of Chicago reported that people living in Canada pay 37 percent more for generic drugs than people in the U.S.[1] In addition, generic drugs are more widely used in the U.S. than in other countries, providing further drug cost savings. For example, during 2005, in terms of value, generic drugs accounted for less than 10 percent of the market in Austria, Belgium, Finland, France, Ireland, Italy, Portugal and Spain.[2]

The Medicare prescription drug benefit is reinforcing these trends. Generic drug prices for people with Medicare can be even lower due to the excellent coverage available through Part D. Medicare plans encourage the use of generics with tiered formularies, under which generic drug co-pays are typically far lower than co-pays for brand alternatives. Some Part D plans even offer generics for a $0 copay. As a result of very low prices and information and support for beneficiaries on how they personally can save by using generic versions of their medicines, Medicare Part D has resulted in increased use of generic drugs by Medicare beneficiaries.

The benefits of generic drug use by the Medicare population is clear, and generic drug availability for Medicare beneficiaries will be increasing further, leading to additional savings. The GPhA has indicated that "blockbuster" name-brand pharmaceuticals coming off patent are valued at $22 billion in 2006, $27 billion in 2007, and $29 billion in 2008. For example, Zocor, a cholesterol lowering drug and one of the nation's top sellers, just recently came off patent. An anti-depressant, Zoloft, recently came off patent as well. The patent for a high blood pressure medicine, Norvasc, expires next year, and Advair, an asthma fighter, loses its patent protection in 2008. All told, between 2006 and 2009, there will be a significant number of patent expirations, opening the way for cheaper, generic alternatives.

Under the Medicare Part D program, prescription drug plans are able to add to their formularies at any time, making it simple to pass along to beneficiaries and taxpayers the savings offered by new generics as they become available. CMS takes its role as public health educator seriously; and we are committed to helping health care providers and people with Medicare to understand the value of generics.

Generic Utilization on the Rise

As more widely used branded prescription drugs go off patent and more generics become available, we expect to continue to see generic utilization rise. This will help provide additional savings on prescriptions for beneficiaries, as well as for the Medicare program. In fact, early evidence shows that CMS and its partners' efforts to promote generic utilization are paying off. There are early indications Medicare beneficiaries enrolled in Part D are relying on generics to a greater extent than the U.S. population as a whole. We would expect this utilization trend to continue, as more and more beneficiaries realize the significant savings available by switching to generic drugs.

Nationwide, among all payers, the proportion of generic usage by prescriptions dispensed stands at 51.9 percent. Data recently gathered by CMS show that generic usage among all types of Part D plans was 60.1 percent during the first two quarters of 2006. Notably, Medicare Advantage plans offering drug coverage have achieved an even higher generic utilization rate. We attribute this to their longer experience with providing low-cost drug coverage to the Medicare beneficiaries they serve, and greater experience and ability to help provide well-coordinated, low-cost care for beneficiaries. In addition, many Part D plans are increasing the growth rate of generic utilization at a faster rate than the overall market. One large plan sponsor's generic utilization rate has grown at three times that of the national market.

This is very good news for beneficiaries and for the program. It means that beneficiaries have access to and are using lower-cost alternatives offered by their plans. It also means that our efforts to educate beneficiaries about the cost-saving potential of therapeutic alternatives have been successful and that pharmacists and physicians have the information they need to help beneficiaries make choices about their medications.

The benefit of greater reliance on generics or, in many cases, less expensive brand-name drugs that are equally effective for the same condition and appropriate for the beneficiary is well documented. According to an ongoing CMS analysis of negotiated price discounts available to illustrative beneficiaries under Medicare Part D, when compared to retail prices, such beneficiaries would see savings of up to 74 percent if they joined one of a broad range of lower-cost Part D plans and then switched to generics.[3] When such beneficiaries, who are taking a brand name drug for which there are cheaper brand name drugs that treat the same condition and are clinically appropriate, switch to those cheaper alternatives, their savings increase to 82 percent for the lowest-cost plan and up to 75 percent for a range of low-cost plans. A number of external reports have comparable findings. For example, Consumers Union found that beneficiaries with common chronic conditions who switch to generic or other therapeutically equivalent medications can save between $2,300 and $5,300 a year.[4] These individual savings can add up to billions of dollars in savings across the beneficiary population as a whole.

Similarly, the Pharmaceutical Care Management Association (PCMA) released a study earlier this year indicating that Medicare drug plans offer significant price discounts compared to what beneficiaries would pay without coverage.[5] A recent follow-up PCMA study found that beneficiaries can maximize the already-significant savings noted above by switching to lower-cost medications, such as generics.[6]

Education Helps Beneficiaries Save

Beneficiary and partner education has been an essential component of our strategy to increase the utilization of generic drugs among Medicare beneficiaries, to help them get the most out of their prescription drug coverage. The personalized attention that people found so helpful in making decisions about the new drug benefit has become part of routine business for CMS, and we are going to continue to build on it to ensure that beneficiaries have what they need to make informed choices.

Immediately after the MMA was signed into law in 2003, CMS devised a comprehensive strategy for successful implementation of the Part D benefit by its January 1, 2006 effective date. Educating people with Medicare about the design and availability of the new drug benefit, and developing information and resources to assist them in evaluating numerous plan options were and continue to be among CMS' highest priorities.

Beginning in the fall of 2005, CMS launched a major initiative to educate beneficiaries about Part D, putting into place an outreach and education partnership comprised of more than 20,000 local and national organizations. Forty thousand volunteers staffed more than 50,000 Part D enrollment events across the country. Today, more than 38 million Medicare beneficiaries—over 90 percent of people with Medicare—have prescription drug coverage either through Part D directly, an employer plan that is supported through Part D, or another equivalent source, and satisfaction rates with the Part D prescription drug plans' coverage are very high—over 80 percent.

Improvements for 2007

CMS has a new and more comprehensive approach to beneficiary outreach called *My Health, My Medicare*, which exemplifies the transformation of CMS from an entity which simply pays the bills, to one that promotes quality health care, that provides personalized support to help each of our beneficiaries stay well and lower their health care costs. We have been working to transform our approach at the agency to assisting beneficiaries in achieving this goal over the past few years. As a part of this approach, CMS has developed and enhanced many tools available to provide beneficiaries enrolled in Part D the information they need to achieve maximum savings on their prescription drugs. One of these key tools is the *Medicare & You Handbook* that beneficiaries will receive in October. This year, the Handbook will highlight the preventive services available to people with Medicare, including a wide range of screening services. It has also been revised to enhance information on the benefits of using generic drugs, and to address potential beneficiary concerns about switching from brand name drugs to generics. Additionally, during our outreach events and through our extensive partner network, we are advising beneficiaries that asking their doctor or pharmacist about the generics or lower cost brand name alternatives available for their prescription drug needs can help them delay reaching the coverage gap. This strategy is supported by a recent PCMA study, which found that beneficiaries who use more generic drugs may be able to delay by an average of 74 days or even avoid the coverage gap.[7]

In addition to outreach through partners and special events, CMS developed and maintains a comprehensive resource that beneficiaries can use to find lower-cost drugs covered by their plan: the "Drug Plan Finder" available at . . . . Beneficiaries can use the Plan Finder to search for lower cost alternatives available under a specific plan. When beneficiaries enter their drug regimen in the Plan Finder, the system defaults to provide them information about lower cost generic drugs when they are available, including personalized information on the specific additional estimated savings. In addition, the Plan Finder provides a link to a page that highlights the benefits of generic alternatives. Millions of people have already accessed this site to find information on their options and to help make important choices about their drug coverage based on their preferences. Even beneficiaries who choose a plan with no coverage in the gap can use the Plan Finder to access and compare prices negotiated by their plan on both generics and branded drugs.

In an effort to improve our many resources for beneficiaries, we have made enhancements to the Medicare Drug Plan Finder for 2007. In addition to including call center performance, complaint information and other plan performance information, it will be tightly integrated with the updated Medicare Coverage Options tool, making it easy for people to get personalized comparisons of their health plan choices along with their drug plan options. Users will be able to get estimates for their total annual health costs, and month to month estimated costs, incorporating the latest information on discounted drugs.

Plans, Pharmacists and Physicians Help Beneficiaries Save

In a competitive Part D market with proactive consumers who receive the support they need, Medicare drug plans have shown that competition leads to attractive plan options at competitive prices. Promoting generic utilization through education or by offering coverage for generics through the coverage gap helps plans stay competitive and saves beneficiaries and taxpayers money. This increased availability of plans with some coverage in the gap is good news for beneficiaries, who in 2006 overwhelmingly opted for benefit packages offering predictable coverage this year through features such as gap coverage, fixed co-pays and zero deductibles.

Physicians and pharmacists are important partners in helping beneficiaries get the most from their prescription drug coverage, and CMS truly appreciates their leadership in assisting so many beneficiaries to use their coverage effectively. CMS, Part D plans, pharmacists and physicians are all helping beneficiaries achieve even greater cost savings by educating them about lower-cost alternatives and their money saving potential. CMS has worked closely with physicians to ensure they have the tools and knowledge they need to help their Medicare patients. Among these key tools is a feature on . . . . called the Formulary Finder that allows doctors to link directly to a plan's formulary through the Web. Additionally, it is possible for physicians to use handheld and web based clinical reference tools, to access all Medicare Part D formularies, which are being made available for free. This means that any physicians using this approach will have quick access to formulary information, enabling them to make a decision about the potential of a lower-cost prescription while a beneficiary is in their office.

As an important element of Part D implementation, CMS supported the launch of the Pharmacy Quality Alliance (PQA), in partnership with pharmacy organizations, health plans, employers, consumers and many others. This strong and extensive alliance will focus primarily on developing strategies for defining and measuring pharmacy performance. A key step that PQA has taken is to develop an initial set of metrics to measure quality based on available pharmacy claims data. Included in these metrics is an evaluation of generic efficiency and formulary management. More specifics on the results of these evaluations will be available in the fall, and will help CMS promote best practices in pharmacy care—including generic utilization—for the Medicare population and more broadly.

Looking Ahead

Notwithstanding the many successes and high satisfaction with the Part D benefit in 2006, we are confident that even better things are coming in 2007 as a result of strong competition and enhanced benefit choices. More plans will be offering coverage in the gap, and lower-cost options will be available for most beneficiaries everywhere. Additional enhanced plan options enable beneficiaries to obtain more stable monthly costs throughout the year. And, with the average bids for 2007 almost 10 percent lower than in 2006, Part D will have lower Federal costs, making the program more stable and affordable over time. These cost savings are due in no small part to tough plan negotiation for lower drug prices and effective use of generics that cost much less than the drugs seniors may have used in the past.

Conclusion

Chairman Smith and Senator Kohl, thank you again for inviting me to speak with you today about generic drug utilization and how we can work to continue providing a high quality, low cost prescription drug benefit for Medicare beneficiaries. The drug benefit provides important new coverage for people with Medicare, and generic alternatives serve as an important and safe way to save a lot of money for both beneficiaries and the Medicare program.

CMS is working hard to make sure that everyone with Medicare has the tools and knowledge to make the most of their Medicare coverage. This means receiving high quality benefits at the lowest possible cost. We will continue to work to meet the health needs of beneficiaries by building on the strong partnerships that are helping to make the Medicare prescription drug program a success.

Notes

1. Understanding Variations in International Drug Prices. National Opinion Research Center (NORC) at the University of Chicago and Georgetown University. July 2006.

2. See. . . .

3. CMS Office of Policy, Analysis of Savings Available Under Medicare Prescription Drug Plans, June 20, 2006.

4. "Helping Medicare Beneficiaries Lower Their Out-of-Pocket Costs Under the New Prescription Drug Benefit," Consumer's Union, December 14, 2005. As CMS has noted, beneficiaries should discuss any therapeutic changes with their physician and pharmacist, and the personalized information we provide can help inform those discussions.

5. "Medicare Drug Discounts Real & Holding Steady," Pharmaceutical Care Management Association, February 7, 2006.

6. "Potential Beneficiary Savings Associated with Generics & Mail-Service Pharmacies for Five Conditions Chronic to Seniors," Pharmaceutical Care Management Association, September 7, 2006.

7. Pharmaceutical Care Management Association, "Potential Beneficiary Savings Associated with Generics & Mail-Service Pharmacies For Five Conditions Common to Seniors," September 7, 2006.

An Evaluation of Medicare's Prescription Drug Policy

Chairman Coburn, Senator Carper, members of the Committee, thank you for the opportunity to testify on the Medicare Prescription Drug Program. I feel very honored by it.

I especially appreciate this opportunity because no policy issue appears more vital than how to preserve the efficient operation of health care markets to pay for our growing health care needs. It is well known that designing policies to improve health-care market efficiency is difficult. But it is not yet widely appreciated how huge Medicare's future financial shortfall is. The Medicare Prescription Drug Improvement And Modernization Act of 2003 (MMA) substantially increases that shortfall and is likely to worsen the operation of markets for prescription drugs and drug insurance. As such it deserves urgent reconsideration—a view that is shared by many health care experts and policymakers including, I suspect, by members of this Committee.

MMA offers prescription drug coverage to all retirees. The new law will benefit seniors on the whole but will exert several negative economic effects:

Five issues stand out:

- Government intervention is usually justified when private markets fail. With 75 percent of retirees already having prescription drug coverage and 90 percent having access to prescription drugs prior to MMA, this market did not exhibit the symptoms of "market failure." Indeed, passage of MMA is likely to cause market failure by displacing the private market's provision of drug insurance.
- MMA will improve access to prescription drugs for poorer retirees—both those who are and those who are not currently covered under Medicaid. Well-to-do retirees will also benefit in general but some may experience higher out-of-pocket costs if they lose their private drug coverage and are forced to enroll into Medicare Part D. This law, therefore, appears designed to first displace the private market followed by sustained pressure on Congress to liberalize the MMA's benefit formula over time.
- MMA will influence prescription drug prices in the private market as the share of government-subsidized purchasers expands. Theoretical reasoning and empirical studies suggest that private drug prices would increase with additional government-subsidized patients entering the

Testimony to the Committee on Homeland Security and Government Affairs Subcommittee on Federal Financial Management, Government Information, and International Security, Jagadeesh Gokhale (September 20, 2005).

market. Most of the burden of this increase will fall on workers by making employer-provided health insurance or private plans more expensive. That will reduce younger workers' likelihood of employment, cause lower wage growth, increase conversion from full- to part-time jobs, and reduce work effort.

- MMA makes a large addition to the already considerable financial shortfall in the rest of Medicare. Unresolved, this shortfall will grow larger and impose higher fiscal burdens on future generations, further eroding their productivity and work incentives.
- MMA will change workers' and younger generations' perceptions about the need to save for health-care expenses during retirement. Studies show that expansion in government entitlement obligations leads to higher consumption and reduces national saving and investment—delivering a further negative impact on future worker productivity and output.

MMA was hastily passed without a proper evaluation of its short- and long-term cost and it lacks appropriate measures to control spending escalations. That means future Congresses may be induced to regulate the actions of pharmacies, drug manufacturers, employers, and plan providers with regard to drug pricing and spending per person on prescription drugs. Such regulations would be counterproductive because they would restrict prescription drug supply, generate illegal prescription drug sales, and reduce the quality of prescription drug coverage for everyone—and not just for retirees.

If MMA cannot be repeated, a financially and economically sensible course would be to scale it back to a sustainable level by providing coverage only to those seniors who are under financial pressure on account of their prescription drug expenses. That effort needs to be combined with restoring the rest of Medicare to financial sustainability.

II. Pre-MMA Prescription Drug Coverage of Retirees

Prior to MMA's enactment, Medicare Parts A and B provided no limits on out-of-pocket costs and did not insure retirees against outpatient prescription drug expenses.

The vast majority of retirees (75 percent) had prescription drug coverage under private plans: Employer supplemental health coverage (33 percent), Medicaid and state drug programs (17 percent), Medicare + Choice Plans (15 percent), Medigap policies with prescription drug coverage (2 percent) or other sources (8 percent). New retirees were guaranteed access to 10 alternative Medigap plans, three of which covered prescription drugs.

Some retirees, however, faced financial pressure on account of their prescription drug costs: Estimates as of 2000 suggest that average out of pocket costs for retirees in poor health took up about 44 percent of their incomes. Low-income single women not covered under Medicaid spent about 52 percent of their incomes on health expenses, on average.

Enrollment into Medigap plans including prescription drug coverage has been quite low. Such plans impose spending caps and so do not cover catastrophic expenses. Their high premiums, deductibles and cost-sharing requirements make them expensive and their availability varies widely by geographic area. Premium inflation among plans with prescription drug coverages has been very rapid. The plans also provided first-dollar coverage that discouraged prudent use of services and prescription drugs.

These features made Medigap policies inferior to employer supplemental coverage, which generally had low co-insurance requirements, no separate spending caps for prescription drugs, and drug prices after negotiated discounts. Employer plans also do not provide first-dollar coverage, thus promoting prudent use of health services including prescription drugs.

III. MMA, the Drug Market, and Retiree Prescription Drug Coverage

Drug treatments are becoming standard practice treating chronic conditions. Greater intensity of use of existing drugs and the development of new and more effective, but also more expensive, drugs have increased the entire population's dependence on drugs therapies. Higher drug development costs and higher demand for drug treatments have caused drug prices to grow rapidly.

1. Is There "Market Failure" in the Prescription Drug Marketplace?

Data (cited earlier) show that a significant share of retirees already had access to prescription drugs and drug insurance. About 90 percent of seniors reported taking at least 1 prescription drug. Thus, MMA represents an increase in government intervention in prescription drug and drug insurance markets where there was no prior market failure.

Whether the provision of a good or service is financed by the government or through private markets makes a large difference to whether the economy's scarce resources are allocated efficiently. Efficient allocation of resources implies their use in meeting the most important needs first—as signaled by peoples' willingness to pay.

It is well known that government intervention replaces resource allocation through competitive forces by allocation through fiat. Because the government does not maximize profits, federal price setting and resource allocation decisions are not based on market signals of efficient resource use. The usual result is a loss in economic efficiency. That will happen to the prescription drug and drug insurance markets because of MMA.

That does not necessarily mean that market outcomes are fully acceptable. If there is considerable inequality of wealth or of needs among individuals, market operation will provide goods and services to the rich, whereas the poor will be unable to make their demands effective. Because such outcomes may be socially unacceptable, government intervention could be justified— but only at the margin—to assist those in need of subsidies because of economic misfortunes.

A study based on 2003 data indicates that only 25 percent of retirees reported forgoing medications due to high costs. The most vulnerable categories of retirees on account of prescription drug expenses are those without any drug insurance (50 percent spending $100 or more on prescription drugs), those in low-income groups (34 percent spending more than $100 per month) and those with three or more chronic conditions (42 percent spending more than $100 per month).

It is usually difficult to demarcate the appropriate extent of government intervention on account of wealth inequality. MMA clearly oversteps all reasonable limits, however, because it provides a broad drug subsidy to all retirees regardless of their economic status, previous access to prescription drug coverage, and prescription drug needs.

MMAs generosity will significantly worsen the economy's ability to allocate resources efficiently—directly by reducing the size of the private market, increasing drug prices, imposing larger than necessary tax burdens on current and future productive citizens, and indirectly by reducing their ability and willingness to save and invest for the future.

2. Who Will Benefit From MMA?

Dual eligible beneficiaries—those eligible for both Medicaid and Medicare coverage—will now receive drug coverage through Medicare. The lowest income beneficiaries among them will receive premium and cost-sharing subsidies as well—and would have to pay out-of-pocket only for nominal drug co-payments. Low-income cost-sharing support would be phased out for families with higher income and assets.

Dual beneficiaries will not lose the value of their coverage. Indeed, their drug coverage is likely to become more generous under Medicare Part D compared to Medicaid—especially as state budget problems increase the likelihood of stricter future cost containment measures under Medicaid. Several states already regulate the number of prescriptions filled per period, the number of allowable refills, size of dosages, and drug dispensing frequencies etc. These limitations will be disallowed when dual-eligible beneficiaries are shifted to Medicare Part D—making their prescription drug coverage more valuable.

Many states facing budget pressures are likely to increase their cost-sharing requirements in the future making Medicaid benefits less valuable. Hence, taxpayer costs of covering dual eligibles' drug insurance may be higher under Medicare Part D because Medicaid savings "clawed back" by the federal government are likely to be smaller than the actual costs saved.

In addition, MMA will benefit seniors with poor health and considerable dependence on costly prescription drugs—including those who purchase Medigap plans offering prescription drug coverage. As mentioned earlier, such plans' premiums, deductibles, and cost-sharing requirements can amount to thousands of dollars. In contrast, Medicare Part D's co-insurance rates are only 5 percent beyond expenditures exceeding $5,100. For example, under Medigap plan J, retirees must spend $6,250 out of pocket to attain the maximum benefit of $3,000 (implying total annual health care spending of $9,250). In contrast, Medicare Part D's cost-sharing formula would pick-up $5,059 of spending up to $9,250 leaving the beneficiary better off by $2,058 per year.

Medicare Part D will also benefit those retirees who choose to purchase Medigap plans without prescription drug coverage because they face restrictive choices among available plans. Such purchasers constitute the vast majority of Medigap clients.

3. Some Retirees May Pay More in the Long-Term

Generally, employer provided retiree health coverage is broad, includes comprehensive drug coverage, requires low co-pay and co-insurance rates, and does not impose separate caps on drug expenses. In contrast, Medicare Part D premium, deductible, and co-insurance costs will be substantial for those with drug expenses up to $5,100 per year. Hence, during the short-term many retirees may choose to remain under employer-provided prescription drug insurance.

Over the long-term, however, MMA is likely to induce employers and other private providers to restrict or eliminate retiree drug coverage. Those covered under such plans would then be forced to sign up for Medicare Part D and could face larger out-of-pocket costs—unless they qualify for additional low-income subsidies. This is likely to increase political pressure to shrink or eliminate the "donut-hole" in the benefit formula. That, in turn, could prompt yet more seniors to drop their private coverage and enroll into Medicare Part D, increasing the program's already high overall costs.

Thus, although retirees as a whole would gain considerably, on net, from the implementation of MMA, some retirees may become worse off over the long-term if employers cut costs by dropping retiree drug coverage. That means some of MMA's benefit won't stay with retirees but flow through to employers. Employers' overall gains could be limited, however, as prescription drug usage expands and drug prices increase. Those effects would increase the cost of providing health care insurance to workers.

IV. MMA's Impact On The Private Drug Market

The government already subsidizes prescription drug use by Medicaid patients. The federal subsidy is provided through the states' Medicaid programs. States possess set drug reimbursement rates within but must adhere to federally specified upper-payment limits. Drug reimbursement rates to providers, however, must be set to ensure drug provision consistent with the provision of other complementary medical services within each state. Rates must also ensure that comparable service levels [are] available to those eligible for Medicaid in all states.

Drug prices and federal and state drug spending under Medicaid has escalated recently because of increased drug use and availability of new, effective, but more expensive drugs for replacing traditional medical treatments. Because prices of established drugs are not allowed to rise by more that the Consumer Price Index, manufacturers have set high initial prices for drugs that are technically "new" but work very much like older versions already on the market.

The entry of sizable additional government-subsidized patients (retirees) in the drug market means either that drug manufacturers must ramp up drug production or substitute sales to Medicare in place of sales to private purchasers including drug exports.

Some studies have estimated that post-MMA increases in drug demand would be small. But they assume that those who already purchase prescription drugs will not change their use of prescription drugs. That assumption defies past experience.

Those who lack coverage today would increase their drug usage as they obtain insurance against out-of-pocket costs. So also would those with very high dependence on prescription drugs because MMA reduces their cost-sharing expenses. In addition, MMA is likely to reduce state restrictions on drug usage for dual-eligibles—whose drug costs would now be met through Medicare Part D. And doctors will hesitate less in prescribing drugs now that their retiree patients have acquired access to a new "third party" payer.

As mentioned earlier, drug usage intensity is likely to increase as MMA expands retiree budgets for prescription drugs. Consequently, the demand for drugs is likely to increase considerably and will likely cause higher-than-projected program outlays.

If manufacturers can increase drug production without significant additional costs it may be feasible to accommodate the additional demand without significant price increases. However, in a competitive marketplace where manufacturers must accept the highest price offers first, pharmacies and, in turn, the federal government may have to increase offer prices to manufacturers to obtain additional drug supplies for their new Medicare patients. In that case, prices charged in the private market must also increase and the size of the private drug market must become smaller. Thus, theoretically, an increase in the drug market share of government patients would increase drug prices and shrink the private drug market.

This theoretical expectation is supported by empirical evidence on the relationship between the government's share in particular drug markets and the private market prices of those drugs. A study covering 200 drugs during 1997 and 2001 found that government participation in the drug market through Medicaid significantly increased drug prices faced by non-government payers. An increase in the government's market share by 10 percent was found to be associated with a 10 percent increase in the drug's price. This finding remains true despite the addition of several controlling factors such as drug therapeutic classes, the existence of generics, the number of close substitutes, and the time since the drug's first introduction.

Considering Medicaid's market share in the top 200 drugs, the study suggests that private-market drug prices would have been lower by 13.3 percent, on average, in the absence of Medicaid. Greater intensity of drug use by retirees would, therefore, imply yet higher prescription drug prices. Thus, with federal drug insurance guaranteed to all retirees, the higher drug prices will negatively impact workers through employer-sponsored or privately provided health plans.

As a consequence, employers may seek to cut back on wages, reduce workers' health-care coverage, increase health-insurance premiums, or convert full-time jobs to part-time positions that do not provide health benefits.

Another recent study documents that higher health insurance costs are taking a heavy toll on workers. Each 10 percent hike in health insurance costs reduces the likelihood of being employed by 1.6 percent, and cuts hours worked by 1 percent. Workers whose health insurance is maintained are forced to accept smaller wage gains: A 10 percent increase in premiums is off-set by a 2.3 percent decrease in wages.

The prior study also demonstrates that the government's drug rebate program operated for Medicaid—that limits established drugs' price increases to no more than the Consumer Price Index—leads to larger manufacturer incentives to introduce new drugs with slight performance enhancements but with initial prices set at much higher levels to compensate for the federal drug rebate program.

V. MMA's Financial Implications for Workers and Future Generations

CMS estimates that Medicare Part D's unfunded obligation (future outlays less enrollee premiums and cost-sharing) is zero. However, CMS assumes that Congress will continue to authorize general revenue transfers to Medicare Part D as and when needed to bridge the gap between outlays and enrollee premiums. In present discounted value, total future general-revenue infusions required are estimated at $18.2 trillion. That is, Medicare Part D promises to provide net benefits to current and future generations of retirees to the tune of $18.2 trillion in excess of the premiums they will pay for enrollment into Medicare Part D.

According to CMS, Medicare's Parts A and B combined are estimated to require total financial infusions of almost $50 trillion in present value to meet benefit costs under current laws. MMA's enactment has, therefore, increased Medicare's fiscal burden on current and future taxpayers to $68.1 trillion. The additional charge on federal general revenues from the new drug program is significantly higher than Social Security's future financial shortfall—estimated by Social Security's Trustees to be $11.2 trillion.

An $18.2 trillion figure is better understood as a share of the present value of GDP from which it must be financed. According to CMS's projections, that share equals 1.9 percent. That is, MMA commits 1.9 percent of all future GDP to funding seniors' drug coverage.

Because, the entire GDP is not (and will never be) subject to taxes, it is more instructive to compare MMA's general revenue charge to the present value of the future income tax base from which all federal general receipts are drawn. Unfortunately, there is no official estimate of the present value of the income tax base. However, if future taxable (personal and corporate) income averages about 55 percent of GDP—its current ratio—Medicare Part D's

$18.2 trillion charge on general revenues would equal 3.5 percent of the present value of the income tax base.

Because Medicare Part D is not financed out of a dedicated revenue sources, it is impossible to know when the implied fiscal burden—either higher taxes or federal spending cuts—would be imposed. It is also impossible to know how this fiscal burden will be distributed across different income groups and across living and future generations.

The calculation of MMA's fiscal burden above involves a critical assumption: That GDP and the tax base will remain unchanged despite the imposition of higher taxes or spending cuts. However, higher taxes will adversely impact work incentives and spending cuts may degrade critical economic infrastructure, both of which would adversely affect productivity. Thus, financing the $18.2 trillion charge on general revenues is likely to require an income tax-rate increase exceeding 3.5 percentage points because the "feedback" effect of financing MMA benefits through higher taxes on national output would reduce future national output.

VI. The Impact of MMA on National Saving

The difference between what current generations earn by way of income each year and their annual consumption determines how many resources are saved and invested. The more current generations consume, the less is available for investment. The $18.2 trillion estimate of the present value of Part D benefit encompasses the entire future without a time limit. That is, it includes benefits that will accrue to future generations.

Unborn generations, obviously, do not consume out of current income. The impact of Medicare Part D's net benefit on current consumption depends on the share of it accruing to those alive today. The Medicare program's Trustees' have estimated that federal general revenue infusions into Medicare Part D will equal $8.7 trillion through the year 2079. Of this, $6.7 trillion will be on account of those alive today. That is, today's retirees and workers (those aged 15 and older) can, under MMA, expect to receive from the federal government $6.7 trillion dollars on net by way of prescription drug coverage.

As the drug law is implemented and as today's generations' expectations regarding their drug benefits become firmer, they will perceive an improvement in their total wealth position. Their natural response to higher perceived wealth would be to increase their consumption. As a consequence, national saving would decline.

Evidence from survey data confirms that retirees increase their consumption in response to receipt of additional entitlement benefits. Figure 1 [omitted] shows consumption indices by age derived from the Consumer Expenditure Surveys for four periods: 1960–61, 1972–73, 1984–87 and 1987–90. In each period, the consumption per capita of all age groups is shown relative to the consumption of a contemporaneous 30-year-old person—whose consumption index is set equal to 1 in each of the four periods.

The figure shows that consumption per capita of 70-year-olds in 1960–61 fell short of 30-year-olds' consumption per capita in the same period by

29 percent. However, by 1987–90, 70-year-olds consumed 18 percent more per capita than 30-year-olds in the same period. More recent data also show the same pattern of increasing consumption levels by retirees relative to the consumption of their younger contemporaries.

One of the most important elements driving the change in relative consumption patterns by age appears to be the change in the pattern of resource ownership by age. The expansion of federal benefits by way of growing Social Security and Medicare outlays have transferred resources from workers to retirees during the past four decades. That process is continuing today with liberalized Social Security benefits and the enactment of new entitlement benefits—such as Medicare Part D.

Those transfers have increased retirees' command over resources relative to those available to younger generations. Figure 2 [omitted] shows total resource indices by age for the same four periods, where total resources include current net worth per capita and present values per capita of life-time earnings, pensions, and government transfers from all programs.

Figure 2 shows that retirees' had more resources at their disposal compared to their younger counterparts' resources in 1987–90 than did retirees in 1961–62. The passage of MMA will continue the trend of increasing retiree resources relative to those of workers and younger generations. As a result, consumption by retirees is likely to increase and national saving will continue to decline.

How large would be the impact of MMA's cross-generation resource redistribution on saving? A Congressional Budget Office study reviewed academic literature on this question and concluded that for every $1 increase in federal unfunded entitlement obligations, current national saving declines by between 0 and 50 cents.

That range indicates the considerable uncertainty surrounding such estimates. However, it suggests that the best estimate of the MMA's impact on national saving is negative. Taking the mid-point of the range of estimates, national saving may be expected to cumulatively decline by $1.7 trillion by the time today's workers achieve retirement age. That is, by 2079, the national capital stock would erode by $1.7 trillion and future Americans' income and living standards would decline correspondingly.

MMA subsidizes retirees' prescription drug expenses but will probably lead to considerable economic inefficiency. It will improve prescription drug coverage for low-income seniors who were previously covered under Medicaid. It is also likely to benefit low-income seniors without Medicaid coverage and those with high drug expenses. It will also provide a substantial subsidy for those seniors previously covered against drug expenses under a Medigap policy. However, out-of-pocket costs of those seniors previously covered under an employer-provided prescription drug plan are likely to increase as employers increase their premiums to soak up the subsidy or reduce, possibly drop, their coverage completely leaving retirees to foot MMA's premiums and cost-sharing expenses.

MMA will increase the share of government-subsidized patients in the market for prescription drugs. That is likely to shrink the share of privately purchased drugs via higher drug prices. The adverse impact will mostly be on workers as the cost of employer provided health insurance plans increases. That will trigger lower employment, slower wage growth, reduced hours worked, and conversion of more full-time jobs to part-time jobs.

MMA's long-term costs represent a massive addition to the already steep fiscal burdens implicit in current Medicare Part A and Part B policies. This massive cost must eventually be met via tax increases or cuts in other federal spending such as defense, infrastructure, education, social welfare programs, R&D and so on. Meeting future health-care needs as projected under current policies through tax increases alone appears infeasible as higher tax burdens erode work incentives, lower employment, reduce national output and the tax base—requiring yet higher tax rates to draw the necessary revenues.

Past experience indicates that redistributing sizable amounts of resources from workers and future generations toward retirees will erode national saving and investment, and increase our dependence on foreign savings. Implementing MMA will induce a similar intergenerational redistribution of resources, causing higher consumption by retirees and reducing national saving. This is likely to further reduce worker productivity and exacerbate the output-reducing effects of higher taxes.

Overall, MMA is a bad and shortsighted economic policy. This program needs to be re-evaluated and recalibrated from its current focus on covering all retirees regardless of their health-care costs and ability to pay for prescription drugs. It should be refocused on those retirees who most need financial support against prescription drug expenses.

POSTSCRIPT

Is the New Medicare Part D Drug Benefit Good Health Care Policy?

Mark McClellan begins his testimony before the Senate Special Committee on Aging by asserting that Medicare's Part D is "critical to preventing and managing chronic disease, treating illness, preserving quality of life, and delivering modern medical care in the twenty-first century." He gives the new program high marks for at least three reasons. First, the costs of the program, including insurance premiums and cost to taxpayers, have been lower than expected; for example, premiums for 2006 were about 35 percent lower than initially expected. The reasons for the lower cost include greater use of generic drugs and strong competition within the drug marketplace. Second, drug coverage has been extended, either through Part D, an employer drug plan, or some equivalent source, to 90 percent of Medicare beneficiaries. Third, those participating in Part D are happy with their drug plans: "satisfaction rates with the Part D prescription drug plans' coverage are very high—over 80 percent." Although improvements can be made in the program, it is a high-quality, low-cost benefit for Medicare beneficiaries.

In his Senate testimony Jagadeesh Gokhale argues for the repeal of Medicare Prescription Drug Program (MMA) or at least a significant recalibration "from its current focus on covering all retirees." Gokhale rests his position on what he sees as five major negative effects of MMA. First, the new program is likely to displace the private market in the provision of drug insurance. Second, as the government program expands, there will be demands that Congress provide ever increasing benefits. Third, with government-subsidized patients entering the market, private drug prices will increase. Fourth, Part D will generate a significant increase in Medicare deficits. Fifth, there will be lower saving and investment because Part D will change worker and younger people's "perceptions about the need to save for health-care expenses during retirement." In short, MMA is bad policy.

The literature on MMA and Part D can be divided into two parts. One part of the literature tries to explain this complex piece of legislation and the various drug insurance plans that it has created. One place to start in looking for this information is the U.S. Department of Health and Human Resources Prescription Drug Coverage site: http://www.medicare.gove/pdphome.asp. Another site is provided by the U.S. Pharmacist at http://www.uspahramaist.com/index.asp?page=ce/105381/default.in. The second part of the literature concentrates on evaluations of MMA and Part D. The best single source of alternative assessments involves testimony given by several individuals before the House Committee on Ways and Means on June 14, 2006. This can be accessed at http://waysandmeans.house.gov/hearings.asp.

ISSUE 5

Are Health Savings Accounts the Right Medicine for the Ills of the Health Care Industry?

YES: Edward L. Langston, from Testimony to the Senate Special Committee on Aging on Health Savings Accounts and the New Medicare Law: The Face of Health Care's Future (May 19, 2004)

NO: Robert Greenstein, from Testimony to the Senate Special Committee on Aging on Health Savings Accounts and the New Medicare Law: The Face of Health Care's Future (May 19, 2004)

ISSUE SUMMARY

YES: Edward L. Langston, a medical doctor and a trustee of the American Medical Association, believes that Health Savings Accounts (HSAs) will create better conditions in the health care industry, including improvement of the patient-physician relationship and provision of "incentives to utilize health care in a cost-conscious manner."

NO: Robert Greenstein, founder and executive director of the Center for Budget and Policy Priorities, argues that HSAs have several negative consequences. In particular, he asserts these accounts will weaken "the existing comprehensive employer-based health insurance market," without, at the same time, providing any "significant cost containment."

Evaluations of the health care sector of the U.S. economy usually take one of two approaches. In one approach analysts and commentators point to the advances in health care produced by the U.S. economy: miracle drugs, path breaking surgical procedures, new diagnostic machinery, and so. This approach suggests that American medicine is the best in the world. The second approach takes a cost-benefit position and yields a less optimistic assessment. The analysts and commentators using this approach note that the United States spends more on health care than any other country in the world, an estimated 15 percent of gross domestic product. But the results are considered mediocre at best: 35 countries have lower infant mortality rates than the

United States and 37 countries have higher life expectancy (see Geography IQ at http://www.geographyiq.com/index.htm).

Even though the analysts and commentators may be undecided about the right approach for the evaluation of the health care sector, most would agree that the sector does not operate as efficiently as it should. In particular, they point to health insurance and the extensive use of third-party payment of health expenses, arguing that even with deductibles and coinsurance, there is little incentive for the typical health care consumer to "comparison shop." In short, there would be a bigger bang for the medical buck if health care consumers had more incentive to spend their health care dollars in the same way they spend their dollars on housing, on automobiles, and on computers—seeking out low-cost providers and using medical health care resources only when they are needed. The question then is how to create these incentives and induce great efficiency in the health care sector.

The Bush administration promotes one answer: Health Savings Accounts (HSAs). These accounts were created on December 8, 2003 when President Bush signed the Medicare Prescription Drug, Improvement, and Modernization Act. How do HSAs work? First, a consumer must purchase an inexpensive health insurance plan that has a high deductible. Then, the consumer can open an HSA account at a financial institution, contributing an amount to the account up to 100 percent of the insurance's deductible. This is done on a tax-preferred basis. Withdrawals from the account are tax-exempt if they are spent on out-of-pocket medical expenses, and unused funds can be rolled over from one year to the next. As described by the U.S. Treasury:

> You own and control the money in your HSA. Decisions on how to spend the money are made by you without relying on a third party or a health insurer. You will also decide what types of investments to make with the money in your account in order to make it grow.

The debate on HSAs did not end with their creation in 2003. Edward L. Langston, speaking for the American Medical Association, supports these accounts and offers suggestions for making them more attractive. Robert Greenstein objects to the HSAs for several reasons, but especially because he sees these accounts hurting older and less healthy workers.

YES

Edward L. Langston

Testimony on the Face of Health Care's Future

Thank you for the opportunity to share our views with the committee on health savings accounts, which are an expansion of their predecessor, medical savings accounts (MSAs).

The AMA has long been a champion of MSAs, a consumer-driven health care option. They provide affordable protection against high medical costs, greater patient control over use of health services, assistance with the patient-physician relationship, and incentives to utilize health care in a cost-conscious manner. We support the newly created HSAs.

A main element of AMA's proposal for expanding health insurance coverage is creating opportunities for individuals and families to access alternative markets for the purchase of individually owned health insurance. This hearing is an important step in exploring such consumer-driven health care options for our Nation.

AMA Supports HSAs

Both MSAs and HSAs are a form of health insurance coverage that includes a high-deductible insurance plan coupled with a tax-advantaged personal savings account to be used only for qualified medical expenses. Under the options, patients have incentives to utilize health care in a cost-conscious manner because they spend from their own accounts and/or out-of-pocket before meeting the deductible. Unspent account balances accumulate and accrue interest from year to year. High deductibles keep premiums low, making coverage more affordable than traditional insurance and freeing up monies to fund the accounts. Once the deductible has been met, coverage resembles conventional insurance. HSAs can result in administrative savings to the extent that services utilized before the deductible are not sent through claims processing. Account funds can finance long-term care with untaxed dollars and serve as retirement savings for nonmedical expenses, though subject to income tax upon withdrawal.

According to the Internal Revenue Service, nearly 75 percent of MSA enrollees had been previously uninsured. The AMA and other MSA supporters sought

From *Congressional Digest,* May 19, 2004. Published by Congressional Digest Corporation. Reprinted by permission.

to make MSAs permanent and eliminate restrictions hindering their growth. Legislation passed in 2001 and 2002 renewed the MSA demonstration through the end of 2003. In December 2003, the Medicare Prescription Drug, Improvement, and Modernization Act (P.L. 108-173) established HSAs as part of an overall trend toward consumer-directed health care, in which patients have greater control over health care decisionmaking and gain a better understanding of the financial consequences of their decisions.

Since the authorization of HSAs, employers, insurers, financial institutions, policymakers, and the media have shown intense interest in HSAs. We are hopeful that HSAs will assist with restraining health care utilization, exerting competitive pressure on prices, and forcing transparency of pricing. We are encouraged that HSAs possibly will cut the ranks of the uninsured, boost innovation in benefit design, and spur demand for cost-containing medical technology. Moreover, we anticipate that HSAs could reduce managed care interference in treatment decisions and restore the patient-physician relationship.

The AMA supports the permanent establishment of HSAs by the Medicare Prescription Drug, Improvement, and Modernization Act and subsequent regulatory guidance. We especially support the following elements of HSAs:

- Repealing the limit on the number of HSAs and removing the demonstration status of the project.
- Expanding eligibility to employees of any size employer and to any individual.
- Allowing both employees and employers to contribute to HSAs.
- Allowing annual HSA deposits up to 100 percent of the deductible, with no limit on the fraction that can be deposited at any time of the year.
- Reducing the permitted annual minimum deductibles and allowing higher annual maximum deductibles.
- Allowing HSAs to be offered in cafeteria plans provided by employers.
- Extending a "safe harbor" to high-deductible plans in all States to allow for the coverage of preventive services regardless of whether the deductible has been met.
- Making HSAs available from a variety of sources, including banks, brokerage houses, and health insurers.

HSAs Enhance the Patient-Physician Relationship

High-deductible health insurance policies provide patients and their physicians an incentive to avoid wasteful health spending. When spending comes from the patient's personal HSA, patients and their physicians have a strong incentive to balance the costs of medical procedures against the potential favorable impact on health. The same enticement can influence the choice among hospitals and among different prescription drugs. Because these cost incentives reduce the need for HMO [health maintenance organization] rules that limit the availability of care, individuals can have greater flexibility in choosing the care that they want. In short, the new HSA tax and insurance rules may be the beginning of successfully controlling medical spending and bringing it in line with the best interests of patients.

Effects of HSAs on Cost and Access

Demand for HSAs among individuals The loosening of eligibility restrictions vastly increases the potential market for HSAs. Eventually, demand for HSAs is likely to be particularly strong among workers whose employers do not offer health insurance benefits—the group that accounts for the majority of the uninsured. During the first week of 2004, one insurer received over 1,000 applications for HSAs, and during the first six weeks of the year, 30 percent of the new HSA enrollees were among the previously uninsured. HSAs also have the potential to expand coverage by funding premium payments for workers who lose their jobs.

The lowering of required deductibles also makes HSAs appeal to more people, especially given that there is already a trend toward higher deductibles. Given limits on out-of-pocket expenditures, even frequent utilizers of health care services could be attracted to HSAs as a means of wresting control over health care decisions from managed care insurers. The fact that HSA health plans are now permitted to exempt a wide array of preventive services from the high-deductible will also make HSAs more attractive to many individuals and families. It should be noted that some analysts worry that families might be deterred from purchasing an HSA because, in contrast with insurance industry norms, plans generally may not apply lower embedded individual deductibles to individual family members.

Individuals will be attracted to HSAs both for insurance coverage and as an investment vehicle, since HSA contributions and interest earnings are not taxed and individuals own and control the investment choices. Even if HSA funds are not rolled over the following year, the individual reaps a tax advantage by paying for out-of-pocket medical expenses with untaxed dollars. The tax advantages of HSAs, although generally greater for those in higher tax brackets, are substantial for anyone earning enough to pay income taxes.

Demand for HSAs among employers Employers seeking to rein in rapidly escalating health benefit costs—or simply offer health benefits—will be attracted to HSAs. In a 2003 survey of small business owners conducted by the National Small Business Association, 73 percent of respondents reported that HSAs would appeal to their employees. A recent survey of large employers indicates rapid growth in the number of firms offering employees a consumer-driven health care plan.

Because of the timing of the HSA regulatory guidance relative to open-enrollment periods, some employers were unable to offer HSAs in 2004; yet there is expected to be a large wave of employers offering HSAs in 2005. In April 2004, the Federal Office of Personnel Management announced that, starting in 2005, HSAs will be offered to the nearly 9 million Federal employees and their dependents covered through the Federal Employees Health Benefits Program. Employers offering HSAs alongside other health plan choices are likely to adjust premiums and benefits in order to mitigate any adverse selection across plans.

Supply of HSAs by the insurance and financial services industries In early 2004, demand for HSAs on the individual market seemed to outpace supply, with some individuals having difficulty finding knowledgeable, qualified banks or other institutions with which to establish accounts (hence, the Department of the Treasury granted transition relief guidance allowing extra time to establish HSAs). Many insurers planning to market HSA accounts along with their insurance plans will start by offering simple accounts and later offering more sophisticated investment options. At least one company already plans to issue debit cards for HSA, MSA, and flexible spending arrangements (FSAs) that would verify patient eligibility and track deductibles. Although some insurers are awaiting final regulatory guidance, most industry experts expect the availability of HSA plans and accounts to expand rapidly, as was the case following the liberalization of IRA eligibility restrictions in 1981.

In a recent survey of insurers serving employer groups, 42 percent of respondents reported having an HSA product either ready or under development, with another 25 percent considering entering the HSA market. The first insurers offering qualifying high-deductible health plans have been companies already offering MSAs or health reimbursement accounts (HRAs). The large carriers tend to offer plans with a wide range of benefit designs, some already complying with HSA requirements. Large carriers were already positioned to serve as HSA account custodians and to educate and mobilize brokers to market HSAs. Large carriers also are reportedly working with large employers to develop sophisticated benefits packages that integrate HSAs with HRAs and/or FSAs, to the extent that the Department of the Treasury Guidance permits such arrangements.

Criticisms of HSAs Appear to Be Unfounded

The major criticism of HSAs is that they are only for the "healthy and wealthy." Based on the limited available evidence to date from MSAs and HRAs, this concern has not been borne out. A simulation model developed by the RAND Corporation suggested that MSAs would not disproportionately attract younger, healthier individuals.

At a February 2004 Galen Institute forum on consumer-directed health care, six insurers presented data showing that HRA enrollees were older and of slightly poorer health status than those opting for other forms of coverage. Similarly, there is evidence that, despite chronic conditions or high medical expenses, some people are attracted to HRAs because they gain greater control over health care decisions than under conventional managed care plans.

Calculations conducted by the AMA show that the annual cost of an HSA compared to a PPO [preferred provider organization] plan depends on health plan premiums, deductibles, coinsurance, and out-of-pocket limits, as well as individual medical expenses and tax bracket. Not surprisingly, individuals with little or no medical expense generally save money with an HSA because of the premium difference. Individuals with moderate to high medical expenses are more likely to find the PPO less expensive. However, two factors in addition to low premiums could make an HSA more affordable than conventional coverage even for those with higher expenses.

First, although generally higher than PPO out-of-pocket limits, the HSA out-of-pocket limit serves as a powerful protection against catastrophic loss. Second, out-of-pocket expenses funded by an HSA are paid for with untaxed dollars. Because of this tax advantage, some individuals may find an HSA less expensive than the PPO, regardless of their medical expenses.

One must consider how an HSA compares to alternative health plans. People with high medical expenses will pay attention not only to their overall costs—which could be lower with an HSA than conventional coverage—but also to gaining greater choice and control over physicians and treatment decisions, an advantage of HSAs.

Future Congressional Actions

The AMA strongly supports the newly created HSAs. Additionally, AMA supports the following, which would make HSAs even more attractive to patients:

- Allowing early retirees and others who are unemployed but not receiving unemployment compensation to use account funds to pay for high-deductible health insurance premiums, without being taxed or penalized the 10 percent fee.
- Allowing patients to receive tax-free rollovers of unspent FSA funds to go into an FSA or an HSA. This would promote more prudent health care spending by curtailing the "use it or lose it" mentality promoted by current law.
- Allowing high-deductible health insurance plans issued to families in conjunction with HSAs to apply lower per-person deductibles to individual family members with: (1) the permitted levels for person-to-person deductibles being the same as permitted levels for individual deductibles; and (2) the annual HSA contribution limit being determined by the full family deductible or the dollar limit for family policies.

Testimony on the Face of Health Care's Future

Health savings accounts (HSAs) were established as part of last year's Medicare drug legislation. Under that law, any individual who enrolls in a high-deductible health insurance plan with a deductible of at least $1,000 for individuals and $2,000 for family coverage may establish a tax-favored savings account known as a health savings account.

An individual with an HSA may take a tax deduction for contributions to the account equal to 100 percent of the health insurance deductible so long as the contributions do not exceed an annual limit, which is set at $2,600 for individuals and $5,150 for family coverage in tax year 2004.

Both employers and employees may make deductible contributions to HSAs in the same year; the aggregate contributions are subject to the contribution limit. Funds held in these accounts may be placed in various investment vehicles such as stocks and bonds, with earnings accruing on a tax-free basis. Withdrawals from the account also are exempt from tax if they are used to pay for out-of-pocket medical costs such as deductibles, copayments, and other uncovered medical expenses. Withdrawals for non-medical purposes are subject to income tax and a financial penalty, but no penalty applies to non-medical withdrawals made after reaching age 65.

Risk to Comprehensive Employer-Based Health Insurance

Health savings accounts pose a significant risk of weakening the existing comprehensive employer-based health insurance market due to what economists and health analysts call "adverse selection," under which healthier, low-risk individuals abandon one type of health insurance for another. When this occurs, the people who remain in the initial type of insurance constitute a group that becomes less healthy, on average, and hence more expensive to insure, which pushes up premiums for that type of coverage.

The rise in premiums then induces still more of the healthier individuals to abandon that form of insurance. Over time, a so-called "death spiral" can result, whereby healthy individuals abandon such coverage in mounting numbers, causing premiums to climb to levels that are unaffordable.

From *Congressional Digest,* March 2006 (ref. May 19, 2004 hearings). Published by Congressional Digest Corporation. Reprinted by permission.

As discussed in greater detail below, due to the advent of HSAs, adverse selection is likely to occur as healthy individuals abandon comprehensive employer-based plans for high-deductible plans used in conjunction with HSAs.

Today, the employer-based health insurance system typically offers comprehensive health insurance coverage. Such coverage generally carries relatively modest deductibles and copayment charges and covers a wide array of benefits. It may be provided through a variety of administrative structures including health maintenance organizations (HMOs), preferred provider organizations (PPOs), and point-of-service (POS) plans. (These are also the types of plans through which many Members of Congress and their staffs obtain coverage, such as through the Blue-Cross-Blue-Shield Standard Option offered under the Federal Employee Health Benefits Program.)

Rapidly increasing health care costs and the current economic slump have encouraged some employers to increase the deductibles and copayments that workers must shoulder and have somewhat reduced the scope of benefits.

Nevertheless, high-deductible plans are still far from the norm in employer-based coverage. For example, among PPO plans in 2003, the average in-network deductible was $275 per individual, well below the minimum $1,000 deductible for individuals required under HSAs.

As a result, according to the Joint Committee on Taxation, only a "very small number" of employers currently offer high-deductible plans meeting the statutory requirements of HSAs.

With the advent of HSAs, however, many healthy workers are likely to find high-deductible plans considerably more attractive. Because of their excellent health, these workers would believe they will not require much health care and therefore will not need the greater financial protection that comprehensive coverage provides. Moreover, if they end up using little or no health care, healthy workers can accumulate funds in their HSAs on a tax-advantaged basis since earnings accrue tax-free in these accounts. In addition, as noted above, any funds that individuals deposit in HSAs are tax-deductible.

Healthy people who are affluent can find this particularly advantageous; higher-income workers can better afford the risk of high-deductible coverage if they do become sick, and they also secure the largest tax deductions for deposits into HSAs. That is because the value of a tax deduction rises with an individual's tax bracket. In addition, these workers' employers would be able to make deposits into their HSAs on their behalf. (Firms receive the full employer health insurance deduction for such deposits.) Moreover, withdrawals from the accounts used for out-of-pocket medical costs are tax-free. Finally, unlike traditional individual retirement accounts (IRAs), there are no income limits on who can participate in HSAs. As a result, these accounts can be quite lucrative as tax shelters for healthy and affluent individuals.

A recent survey of nearly 1,000 employers conducted by Mercer Human Resource Consulting appears to confirm the attractiveness of HSAs to healthy, higher-income workers. The survey found that a large majority of employers (61 percent) believed their higher-paid employees would be most likely to participate in HSAs. A plurality (44 percent) believed that their healthiest employees would be most likely to participate.

Similarly, evidence from a General Accounting Office survey of insurers that was conducted in conjunction with the medical savings account demonstration project, which preceded HSAs and included fewer tax benefits, found that "insurers expect relatively better health status and lower service utilization by enrollees selecting high deductible plans."

Older and sicker workers, on the other hand, would prefer to remain in the comprehensive coverage typically offered by employers today.

Early retirees would be one population that would tend to choose to remain in comprehensive coverage. A Commonwealth Fund study found that 26 percent of all adults ages 62 to 64 are in fair or poor health and require more health care services on average.

Older and sicker workers who have low incomes are particularly likely to prefer comprehensive plans, as they often would be unable to afford the greater out-of-pocket costs required under high-deductible plans. Moreover, low-income individuals derive little or no benefit from the tax benefits of HSAs, and they generally lack the income or resources to make substantial contributions to HSAs.

Would Widespread Use of HSAs Reduce Overall Health Care Costs?

Proponents of HSAs argue that high-deductible policies would discourage unnecessary utilization of health care services by requiring individuals to bear a greater portion of the costs of their care. As a result, supporters argue, HSAs would produce substantial reductions in overall health care spending in the United States over time.

It is unlikely, however, that HSAs would provide significant cost containment. According to recent research, 10 percent of the population accounts for 69 percent of total health care spending, and as Henry Aaron, a Senior Fellow at the Brookings Institution and a leading expert in the areas of health care and tax policy, explains in a recent *Tax Notes* article:

> . . . most medical spending occurs during high-cost episodes in which the total cost of care charged to patients greatly exceeds the limits of any plausible high-deductible plan. . . . Once patients enter the stop-loss range of their insurance, they would, by definition, be as free of financial discipline to attend to health care costs as they are under low-deductible insurance. The direct effects of high-deductible insurance on health care costs are therefore likely to be small.

Similarly, Linda Blumberg, a Senior Research Associate at the Urban Institute, has concluded:

> Because the majority of spending is attributable to the small share of individuals with very large medical expenses, increasing deductibles even to $1,000 or $2,000 from currently typical levels will not decrease premiums dollar for dollar. The vast majority of medical spending still will occur above even these higher deductibles.

It also should be noted that research indicates that increased cost-sharing requirements are a blunt instrument with which to try to control costs. Among low-income individuals, higher cost-sharing charges can discourage utilization of both necessary and unnecessary services. If a medical condition or illness goes untreated because individuals are unable to pay for appropriate care out-of-pocket, this can eventually lead to greater use of more expensive services like hospitalization. For some individuals, the high-deductible insurance policies required under HSAs thus might actually result in increases in health care costs over time.

With healthy, affluent workers moving to high-deductible plans in conjunction with HSAs while older and sicker workers remain in comprehensive coverage, premiums for comprehensive plans would necessarily rise. Research conducted in the mid-1990s on the likely effects of medical savings accounts by RAND, the Urban Institute, and the American Academy of Actuaries concluded that the risks of adverse selection were quite high and that premiums for comprehensive insurance could more than double if MSA use becomes widespread.

In the past, some have downplayed the risks of adverse selection on the grounds that HSAs are unlikely to proliferate in the employer-based health insurance market. It is increasingly clear that such a judgment is mistaken. To provide benefits that are attractive to their managers, firms generally must provide low-cost, comprehensive coverage to all of their workers.

With HSAs, however, employers can provide less costly, less generous high-deductible plans tied to HSAs without worrying as much that such plans might encourage executives to seek jobs elsewhere that offer better health benefits. High-income managers and executives could use their HSAs as tax shelters by making substantial contributions to the HSAs on a tax-deductible basis. Since these individuals would have the ability to accumulate significant amounts in their HSAs—and the value of the HSA tax break is greatest for those in the top tax brackets—these tax benefits could more than make up for the increases in deductibles and other reductions in covered benefits that the executives could face under the high-deductible plans their employers might substitute for more comprehensive coverage. With health insurance premium costs rising annually at double-digit rates in recent years, this could make HSAs particularly attractive to employers.

For rank-and-file lower-income workers, however—and especially for older, less healthy workers—such a change would generally be harmful. Those workers would lose the comprehensive low-deductible insurance that they need and receive in its place a tax break of little value to them.

In providing a cost estimate to accompany the Medicare prescription drug bill, the Joint Committee on Taxation (JCT) assumed that HSA would expand significantly, starting at one million participants in tax year 2004 and rising to three million by 2013. But most analysts now believe the JCT estimate dramatically understates likely HSA use, given the wide-spread attention that HSAs are receiving and the intention of various insurance and financial investment companies to offer HSAs and high-deductible policies and market them heavily.

The [George W. Bush] Administration now estimates that the HSA provisions of the new Medicare law will cost $16 billion over 10 years; two and a half times the $6.4 billion that Congress assumed when the law was enacted. In addition, the employer survey discussed above found that nearly three-quarters of employers (73 percent) are likely or somewhat likely to offer health savings accounts by 2006. A smaller employer survey conducted by Hewitt Associates found that 61 percent of employers are likely to offer HSAs in the near future.

If HSA use becomes widespread, as is likely, and premiums for the comprehensive coverage typically offered by employers today rise substantially (with some employers dropping comprehensive coverage entirely), many older and sicker workers, including early retirees, would suffer adverse consequences. Such individuals would either have to switch to a high-deductible plan or become uninsured.

Coverage through high-deductible plans would leave many such individuals underinsured; such plans are likely to provide inadequate coverage for these workers. A Commonwealth Fund study reported that older individuals ages 50 to 64 who have purchased high-deductible policies in the individual market similar to the plans required under HSAs are twice as likely as comparable individuals with comprehensive employer-based coverage to fail to see a doctor when a medical problem develops or to skip medical tests or follow-up treatment.

Another Commonwealth analysis determined that so-called bare-bone health plans—which may be comparable to some of the high-deductible plans provided with HSAs—can leave some lower-wage individuals and families with catastrophic costs well in excess of their annual incomes.

A study conducted by the Center for Studying Health System Change estimated that high-deductible, less comprehensive plans would expose many individuals to substantial out-of-pocket costs; nearly a third of individuals in poor health enrolled in hypothetical plans with high deductibles of $1,000 were projected to incur out-of-pocket costs in excess of 10 percent of their annual incomes. The study also estimated that more than half of such individuals would incur out-of-pocket costs of this magnitude if they were enrolled in hypothetical plans with deductibles of $2,500.

As Linda Blumberg of the Urban Institute recently warned, "the practical effect [of HSAs] . . . is that the most vulnerable populations (the sick and low-income) are left bearing a greater burden of their health expenses."

Such individuals will either have to spend more out of pocket or go without essential health care services they may need. A study from the Employee Benefit Research Institute concludes that "the loss of comprehensive coverage generally would leave many people who need significant amounts of health care, such as individuals with chronic conditions, little recourse but to become underinsured or uninsured."

Dangerous Precedent for Long-Term Fiscal Policy

Under the tax code, a basic principle governs: If contributions to a savings or retirement account are tax deductible and earnings on the account compound tax-free, then withdrawals from the account are taxed as ordinary income. This is how 401(k)s, traditional IRAs, and similar accounts long have worked. (There are several types of accounts from which withdrawals are tax-free, but contributions to those accounts are *not* tax deductible.)

Under health savings accounts, this fundamental principle is abrogated. Not only are deposits to HSAs tax deductible, with earnings then compounding on a tax-free basis, but withdrawals also are tax free so long as they are used for medical costs. Allowing an account to feature *both* tax-deductible contributions *and* tax-free withdrawals is unprecedented. (Note: This was a feature of medical savings accounts, which preceded HSAs, but MSAs operated only as a demonstration project on a very limited basis and were not available to most people. Unlike MSAs, HSAs are universally available and provide more extensive benefits as a tax shelter.)

The Congressional Budget Office projects that the Federal Government will collect several trillion dollars in revenue over the course of future decades as tens of millions of Americans retire and withdraw funds from 401(k)s and IRAs. These anticipated revenues are reflected in the long-term budget baseline. Even with these revenues, the long-term fiscal picture is bleak; budget deficits are expected to rise eventually to levels dangerous to the economy. Stern warnings about the fiscal dangers that lie ahead have been voiced recently by the International Monetary Fund (IMP), the Comptroller General of the United States (the head of the General Accounting Office), the Chairman of the Federal Reserve, the investment house Goldman Sachs, and such luminaries as former Treasury Secretary Robert Rubin, former Senator Warren Rudman, and former Congressional Budget Office director Robert Reischauer.

For example, the *New York Times* reported that an IMF report issued in January "sounded a loud alarm about the shaky fiscal foundation of the United States . . . warning that large budget deficits pose 'significant risks' not just for the United States but for the rest of the world."

In strong language usually reserved for developing countries struggling with international debt obligations, the IMF report disapprovingly noted that the "United States is on course to increase its next external liabilities to around 40 percent of GDP [gross domestic product] within the next few years—an unprecedented level of external debt for a large industrial country."

If the precedent that HSAs set is pursued—and policymakers begin allowing some of the funds deposited in retirement accounts into which contributions were made on a tax-deductible basis to be withdrawn tax free, so long as they are used for health care or some other designated purpose—an already grim long-term fiscal outlook will become considerably worse.

In a recent scholarly assessment of the Nation's long-term fiscal problems, Alan Auerbach of the University of California at Berkeley, one of the Nation's leading public finance experts, and Brookings economists William Gale and Peter Orszag warn that ". . . proposals to reduce the taxation of withdrawals from retirement accounts could significantly and adversely affect an already bleak fiscal outlook."

Conclusion

Use of health savings accounts is likely to become more widespread over time. Such a trend is likely to create a troubling system of winners and losers in the U.S. health care system. Individuals who are healthy and affluent would gain from the tax benefits that HSAs offer. Older and sicker workers, especially those with low incomes, would generally be made worse off by having to shoulder a greater percentage of the costs of their care than they do now. As a result, some of them likely will lose access to some important medical services they need.

POSTSCRIPT

Are Health Savings Accounts the Right Medicine for the Ills of the Health Care Industry?

Edward L. Langston, MD and American Medical Association (AMA) Trustee, states that the AMA strongly supports Health Savings Accounts (HSAs). This support stems from the presumed benefits of HSAs. One expressed benefit is affordable protection against high medical costs because the HSAs require the purchase of a high deductible, catastrophic health insurance policy. A second benefit is greater patient control over the use of health care services because the consumer can spend the funds in his/her HSA on the health care services they desire—not constrained by rules and regulations for an insurance company. A third benefit is an incentive to utilize health care in a cost-conscious manner. The benefit arises because unspent funds can be left to grow without taxation and then be spent in retirement without taxation. A fourth benefit involves "assistance with the patient-physician relationship." Here Langston argues that the cost incentives associated with HSAs reduce the need for health maintenance organization "rules that limit the availability of care." Langston and the AMA propose a number of changes in the program that would make HSAs more attractive.

Robert Greenstein, founder and executive director of the Center on Budget and Policy Priorities, identifies a number of problems with HSAs. First, he believes that healthier people will have an incentive to move from employer-based health insurance to the HSAs, forcing those who are less healthy and who remain in the employer-based plans to pay higher premiums. These shifts will weaken the current and widespread employer-based health insurance market. He then turns to the presumed reductions in overall health care costs that HSAs are suppose to generate. He rejects this prospective savings for several reasons including the reality that most health care spending is accounted for by a small portion of the population, and these persons do not consider costs after they reach the "stop-loss" range of their insurance. A third problem with HSAs involves their consequences for the federal government's budget. HSAs make projected deficits larger for several reasons that reduce government tax revenue: the contributions to the HSA accounts are tax deductible, any investment income in the account grows tax-free, and the withdrawals, as long as they are spent on medical costs or made after retirement, are also tax-free. All of these features will reduce tax revenue, and without offsetting tax increases or cuts in the spending on other government programs, will lead to even higher federal government budget deficits.

For more detail about the basic structure of HSAs, the U.S. Treasury provides ample information at its Web site, http://www.ustreas.gov/offices/public-affairs/hsa/. An alternative source of similar information is the "The Pocket Guide to Health Savings Accounts" by Liv S. Fine and Tanya E. Karwaki from the Washington Policy Center http://www.washingtonpolicy.org/HealthCare/HSAHowToGuidePocket2.pdf. For the position of the Bush administration, see: http://www.whitehouse.gov/news/releases/2006/04/20060405-6.html. For more background and a number of additional evaluations, see the March 2006 issue of the *Congressional Digest.*

ISSUE 6

Is It Time to Reform Medical Malpractice Litigation?

YES: U.S. Department of Health and Human Services, from "Confronting the New Health Care Crisis: Improving Health Care Quality and Lowering Costs by Fixing Our Medical Liability System" (July 24, 2002)

NO: Jackson Williams, from "Bush's Medical Malpractice Disinformation Campaign: A Rebuttal to the HHS Report on Medical Liability," A Report of Public Citizen's Congress Watch (January 2003)

ISSUE SUMMARY

YES: The U.S. Department of Health and Human Services (HHS) argues that although the United States has a health care system that "is the envy of the world," it is a system that is about to be brought to its knees by aggressive attorneys who force the medical community to practice costly "defensive medicine."

NO: Jackson Williams, legal counsel for the watchdog group Public Citizen, charges that the position taken by the HHS is factually "incorrect, incomplete, or misleading" and even contradicted by other governmental agencies.

The headline reads, "Princeton Senior Permanently Disabled." The newspaper story reveals that honor student John Francis slipped on the icy steps of the Harvey S. Firestone Memorial Library after the ice storm that swept through central New Jersey. Francis was rushed to Pokagon Hospital, where emergency surgery was required to repair his ruptured spleen. Unfortunately, Francis failed to recover his strength and vitality after the surgery. He visited the campus infirmary, where X-rays of the surgery site revealed a silhouette of a silver object in his abdominal cavity. When Francis took the X-rays to his surgeon, it was clear that a retractor had been left behind. That is not the end of this tragic story, however. During surgery to remove this foreign object, it was discovered that the retractor had caused the growth of flesh-eating bacteria: necrotizing faciitis. The damage was severe indeed; this once avid tennis player is now permanently disabled. He will be confined to a wheelchair for the rest of his life.

The question that this news article raises is the fundamental question addressed in this issue. Francis has been irreversibly damaged by a medical mistake. The liability seems clear: someone left the retractor behind, and the presence of this foreign object has caused flesh-eating bacteria to grow and invade an otherwise healthy body.

So what is owed to Francis? Few would challenge a demand to be compensated for the explicit costs he incurred: the additional medical expenditures, his wheelchair, and perhaps the costs associated with the extra semester he will spend earning his undergraduate degree. Then there is the "gray area." What of his future employment? Although Francis can be gainfully employed, are his options now limited? If his options are limited, should he be compensated for the fact that he cannot become the tennis pro he wanted to be but must now resign himself to being a stockbroker? Is he entitled to receive compensation for the pain and suffering he will endure for the rest of his life?

It is important to note that "medical misadventures" are few and far between, given the number of medical procedures that occur annually in the United States. The U.S. medical care industry is universally regarded as the best in the world. Thousands and thousands of individuals each year undergo medical procedures in the United States. Since physicians are human, however, mistakes are made. The number of people who suffer the consequences of these mistakes is a tiny fraction of those who seek medical relief, but that number is not inconsequential. Some estimate that in 2003 alone, nearly 100,000 will die of a medical misstep. A surprising number of other surgical procedures will result in some foreign object being left behind the sutures; in fact, it is estimated that in 2003, some 1,500 retractors, gauze pads, sponges, etc., will be left behind. Consequently, Francis is not alone in facing the life-long aftereffects of a surgery gone wrong.

In light of rapidly rising medical insurance rates, it is fair to ask what underlies those rate increases. The medical community and the medical insurance industry, backed by the George W. Bush administration, allege that jury awards for "pain and suffering" are excessive and unreasonable and that they undermine the foundations of the medical industry. Attorneys for those who are impacted by alleged medical misadventures respond that the skyrocketing medical insurance rates are not the result of jury awards and court settlements; rather, they can be traced to insurance companies that have been mismanaged and the recent decline in interest rates in the U.S. economy at large.

The following selections exhibit vastly different views as to why medical malpractice insurance rates are increasing. The U.S. Department of Health and Human Services points a finger at extreme jury awards in medical malpractice cases, arguing that these awards drive the price of malpractice insurance beyond the reach of some practitioners. As a result, these doctors must either increase their fees, which reduces accessibility, or they must begin to practice "defensive medicine"—prescribing redundant medicines, making unnecessary referrals to specialists, and recommending too many invasive procedures. Jackson Williams accuses the HHS of disinformation, concluding that medical malpractice insurance rates are rising not because of jury awards but because of poor management decisions on the part of insurance companies.

Confronting the New Health Care Crisis

American health care is the envy of the world, but with rapidly rising health care costs, reforms are needed to make high-quality, affordable health care more widely available. These include new approaches to making employer-provided coverage more affordable, new initiatives to help states expand Medicaid and S-CHIP [State Children's Health Insurance Program] coverage for lower-income persons, and new policies including health insurance credits for persons who do not have access to employer or public health insurance. A critical element for enabling all of these reforms to provide real relief, and to help all Americans get access to better and more affordable health care, is curbing excessive litigation.

Americans spend proportionately far more per person on the costs of litigation than any other country in the world. The excesses of the litigation system are an important contributor to "defensive medicine"—the costly use of medical treatments by a doctor for the purpose of avoiding litigation. As multimillion-dollar jury awards have become more commonplace in recent years, these problems have reached crisis proportions. Insurance premiums for malpractice are increasing at a rapid rate, particularly in states that have not taken steps to make their legal systems function more predictably and effectively. Doctors are facing much higher costs of insurance, and some cannot obtain insurance despite having never lost a single malpractice judgment or even faced a claim.

This is a threat to health care quality for all Americans. Increasingly, Americans are at risk of not being able to find a doctor when they most need one because the doctor has given up practice, limited the practice to patients without health conditions that would increase the litigation risk, or moved to a state with a fairer legal system where insurance can be obtained at a lower price.

This broken system of litigation is also raising the cost of health care that all Americans pay, through out-of-pocket payments, insurance premiums, and federal taxes. Excessive litigation is impeding efforts to improve quality of care. Hospitals, doctors, and nurses are reluctant to report problems and participate in joint efforts to improve care because they fear being dragged into lawsuits, even if they did nothing wrong.

From U.S. Department of Health and Human Services, Office of the Assistant Secretary for Planning and Evaluation, "Confronting the New Health Care Crisis: Improving Health Care Quality and Lowering Costs by Fixing Our Medical Liability System" (July 24, 2002). Notes omitted.

Increasingly extreme judgments in a small proportion of cases and the settlements they influence are driving this litigation crisis. At the same time, most injured patients receive no compensation. Some states have already taken action to squeeze the excesses out of the litigation system. But federal action, in conjunction with further action by states, is essential to help Americans get high-quality care when they need it, at a more affordable cost.

Access to Care Is Threatened

There are a number of obstacles that limit access to affordable health care in this country, including lack of affordable insurance and an outdated Medicare program. We now face another—the litigation crisis that has made insurance premiums unaffordable or even unavailable for many doctors, through no fault of their own. This is making it more difficult for many Americans to find care, and threatening access for many more.

- Nevada is facing unprecedented problems in assuring quick access to urgently needed care. The University of Nevada Medical Center closed its trauma center in Las Vegas for ten days earlier this month [July 2002]. Its surgeons had quit because they could no longer afford malpractice insurance. Their premiums had increased sharply, some from $40,000 to $200,000. The trauma center was able to re-open only because some of the surgeons agreed to become county government employees for a limited time, which capped their liability for non-economic damages if they were sued. This is obviously only a temporary solution. If the Las Vegas trauma center closes again, the most severely injured patients will have to be transported to the next nearest Level 1 trauma center, five hours away. Access to trauma care is only one problem Nevada faces; access to obstetrics and many other types of care is also threatened.
- Overall, more than 10% of all doctors in Las Vegas are expected to retire, or relocate their practices by this summer. For example, Dr. Cheryl Edwards, 41, closed her decade-old obstetrics and gynecology practice in Las Vegas because her insurance premium jumped from $37,000 to $150,000 a year. She moved her practice to West Los Angeles, leaving 30 pregnant women to find new doctors.
- Dr. Frank Jordan, a vascular surgeon, in Las Vegas, left practice. "I did the math. If I were to stay in business for three years, it would cost me $1.2 million for insurance. I obviously can't afford that. I'd be bankrupt after the first year, and I'd just be working for the insurance company. What's the point?"
- Other states are facing the same problem. A doctor in a small town in North Carolina decided to take early retirement when his premiums skyrocketed from $7,500 to $37,000 per year. His partner, unable to afford the practice expenses by himself, may now close the practice, and work at a teaching hospital.
- Pennsylvania physicians are also leaving their practices. About 44 doctors at the height of their careers in Delaware County outside Philadelphia left the state in 2001 or stopped practicing medicine because of high malpractice insurance costs. . . .

Patient Safety Is Jeopardized

Because the litigation system does not accurately judge whether an error was committed in the course of medical care, physicians adjust their behavior to avoid being sued. A recent survey of physicians revealed that one-third shied away from going into a particular specialty because they feared it would subject them to greater liability exposure. When in practice, they engage in defensive medicine to protect themselves against suit. They perform tests and provide treatments that they would not otherwise perform merely to protect themselves against the risk of possible litigation. The survey revealed that over 76% are concerned that malpractice litigation has hurt their ability to provide quality care to patients.

Because of the resulting legal fear:

- 79% said that they had ordered more tests than they would, based only on professional judgment of what is medically needed, and 91% have noticed other physicians ordering more tests;
- 74% have referred patients to specialists more often than they belived was medically necessary;
- 51% have recommended invasive procedures such as biopsies to confirm diagnoses more often than they believed was medically necessary; and
- 41% said that they had prescribed more medications, such as antibiotics, than they would based only on their professional judgment, and 73% have noticed other doctors similarly prescribing excessive medications.

Every test and every treatment poses a risk to the patient, and takes away funds that could better be used to provide health care to those who need it.

Physicians' understandable fear of unwarranted litigation threatens patient safety in another way. It impedes efforts of physicians and researchers to improve the quality of care. As medical care becomes increasingly complex, there are many opportunities for improving the quality and safety of medical care, and reducing its costs, through better medical practices. According to some experts, these quality improvement opportunities hold the promise of not only significant improvements in patient health outcomes, but also reductions in medical costs of as much as 30%. . . .

However, these efforts and other efforts are impeded and discouraged by the lack of clear and comprehensive protection for collaborative quality efforts. Doctors are reluctant to collect quality-related information and work together to act on it for fear that it will be used against them or their colleagues in a lawsuit. Perhaps as many as 95% of adverse events are believed to go unreported. To make quality improvements, doctors must be able to exchange information about patient care and how it can be improved—what is the effect of care not just in one particular institution or of the care provided by one doctor—but how the patient fares in the system across all providers. These quality efforts require enhancements to information and reporting systems.

In its recent report, "To Err is Human," the Institute of Medicine (IOM) observed that, "[R]eporting systems are an important part of improving patient safety and should be encouraged. These voluntary reporting systems [should] periodically assess whether additional efforts are needed to address gaps in information to improve patient safety and to encourage health care organizations to participate in . . . reporting, and track the development of new reporting systems as they form."

However, as the IOM emphasized, fear that information from these reporting systems will be used to prepare a lawsuit against them, even if they are not negligent, deters doctors and hospitals from making reports. This fear, which is understandable in the current litigation climate, impedes quality improvement efforts. According to many experts, the "#1 barrier" to more effective quality improvement systems in health care organizations is fear of creating new avenues of liability by conducting earnest analyses of how health care can be improved. Without protection, quality discussions to improve health care provide fodder for litigants to find ways to assert that the status quo is deficient. Doctors are busy, and they face many pressures. They will be reluctant to engage in health care improvement efforts if they think that reports they make and recommendations they make will be thrown back at them or others in litigation. Quality improvement efforts must be protected if we are to obtain the full benefit of doctors' experience in improving the quality of health care.

The IOM Report emphasized the importance of shifting the inquiry from individuals to the systems in which they work: "The focus must shift from blaming individuals for past errors to a focus on preventing future errors by designing safety into the system." But the litigation system impedes this progress—not only because fear of litigation deters reporting but also because the scope of the litigation system's view is restricted. The litigation system looks at the past, not the future, and focuses on the individual in an effort to assess blame rather than considering how improvements can be made in the system. "Tort law's overly emotional and individualized approach . . . has been a tragic failure."

Health Care Costs Are Increased

The litigation and malpractice insurance problem raids the wallet of every American. Money spent on malpractice premiums (and the litigation costs that largely determine premiums) raises health care costs. Doctors alone spent $6.3 billion last year to obtain coverage. Hospitals and nursing homes spent additional billions of dollars.

The litigation system also imposes large indirect costs on the health care system. Defensive medicine that is caused by unlimited and unpredictable liability awards not only increases patients' risk but it also adds costs. The leading study estimates that limiting unreasonable awards for non-economic damages could reduce health care costs by 5–9% without adversely affecting quality of care. This would save $60–108 billion in health care costs each year.

These savings would lower the cost of health insurance and permit an additional 2.4–4.3 million Americans to obtain insurance.

The costs of the runaway litigation system are paid by all Americans, through higher premiums for health insurance (which reduces workers' take home pay if the insurance is provided by an employer), higher out-of-pocket payments when they obtain care, and higher taxes.

The Federal Government—and thus every taxpayer who pays federal income and payroll taxes—also pays for health care, in a number of ways. It provides direct care, for instance, to members of the armed forces, veterans, and patients served by the Indian Health Service. It provides funding for the Medicare and Medicaid programs. It funds Community Health Centers. It also provides assistance, through the tax system, for workers who obtain insurance through their employment. The direct cost of malpractice coverage and the indirect cost of defensive medicine increases the amount the Federal Government must pay through these various channels, it is estimated, by $28.6–47.5 billion per year. If reasonable limits were placed on non-economic damages to reduce defensive medicine, it would reduce the amount of taxpayers' money the Federal Government spends by $25.3–44.3 billion per year. This is a very significant amount. It would more than fund a prescription drug benefit for Medicare beneficiaries *and* help uninsured Americans obtain coverage through a refundable health credit.

The Increasingly Unpredictable, Costly, and Slow Litigation System Is Responsible

Insurance premiums are largely determined by the expensive litigation system. The malpractice insurance system and the litigation system are inexorably linked. The litigation system is expensive, but, at the same time, it is slow and provides little benefit to patients who are injured by medical error. Its application is unpredictable, largely random, and standardless. It is traumatic for all involved.

Most victims of medical error do not file a claim—one comprehensive study found that only 1.53% of those who were injured by medical negligence even filed a claim. Most claims—57–70%—result in no payment to the patient. When a patient does decide to go into the litigation system, only a very small number recover anything. One study found that only 8–13% of cases filed went to trial; and only 1.2–1.9% resulted in a decision for the plaintiff.

Although most cases do not actually go to trial, it costs a significant amount of money to defend each claim—an average of $24,669. The most dramatic cost, however, is the cost of the few cases that result in huge jury awards. Even though few cases result in these awards, they encourage lawyers and plaintiffs in the hope that they can win this litigation lottery, and they influence every settlement that is entered into.

A large proportion of these awards is not to compensate injured patients for their economic loss—such as wage loss, health care costs, and replacing services the injured patient can longer perform (such as child care). Instead, much of the judgment (in some cases, particularly the largest judgments, perhaps 50% or more) is for non-economic damages. Awarded on top of compensation for the injured patient's actual economic loss, non-economic damages are said to be compensation for intangible losses, such as pain and suffering, loss of consortium, hedonic (loss of the enjoyment of life) damages, and various other theories that are imaginatively created by lawyers to increase the amount awarded.

Non-economic damages are an effort to compensate a plaintiff with money for what are in reality non-monetary considerations. The theories on which these awards are made however, are entirely subjective and without any standards. As one scholar has observed: "The perceived problem of pain and suffering awards is not simply the amount of money expended, but also the erratic nature of the process by which the size of the awards is determined. Juries are simply told to apply their 'enlightened conscience' in selecting a monetary figure they consider to be fair."

Unless a state has adopted limitations on non-economic damages, the system gives juries a blank check to award huge damages based on sympathy, attractiveness of the plaintiff, and the plaintiff's socio-economic status (educated, attractive patients recover more than others).

The cost of these awards for non-economic damages is paid by all other Americans through higher health care costs, higher health insurance premiums, higher taxes, reduced access to quality care, and threats to quality of care. The system permits a few plaintiffs and their lawyers to impose what is in effect a tax on the rest of the country to reward a very small number of patients who happen to win the litigation lottery. It is not a democratic process.

The number of mega-verdicts is increasing rapidly. The average award rose 76% from 1996–1999. The median award in 1999 was $800,000, a 6.7% increase over the 1998 figure of $750,000; and between 1999 and 2000, median malpractice awards increased nearly 43%. Specific physician specialties have seen disproportionate increases, especially those who deliver babies. In the small proportion of cases where damages were awarded, the median award in cases involving obstetricians and gynecologists jumped 43% in one year, from $700,000 in 1999 to $1,000,000 in 2000.

The number of million dollar plus awards has increased dramatically in recent years. In the period 1994–1996, 34% of all verdicts that specified damages assessed awards of $1 million or more. This increased by 50% in four years; in 1999–2000, 52% of all awards were in excess of $1 million. There have been 21 verdicts of $9 million or more in Mississippi since 1995—one of $100,000,000. Before 1995 there had been no awards in excess of $9,000,000.

These mega-awards for non-economic damages have occurred (as would be expected) in states that do not have limitations on the amounts that can be recovered. . . .

Mirroring the increase in jury awards, settlement payments have steadily risen over the last two decades. The average payment per paid claim increased from approximately $110,000 in 1987 to $250,000 in 1999. Defense expenses per paid claim increased by $24,000 over the same period.

The winning lottery ticket in litigation, however, is not as attractive as it may seem at first blush. A plaintiff who wins a judgment must pay the lawyer 30–40% of it, and sometimes even more. Lawyers, therefore, have an interest in finding the most attractive case. They develop a portfolio of cases and have an incentive to gamble on a big "win." If only one results in a huge verdict, they have had a good payday. Thus, they have incentives to pursue cases to the end in the hope of winning the lottery, even when their client would be satisfied by a settlement that would make them whole economically. The result of the contingency fee arrangement is that lawyers have few incentives to take on the more difficult cases or those of less attractive patients.

One prominent personal injury trial lawyer explained the secret of his success: "The appearance of the plaintiff [is] number one in attempting to evaluate a lawsuit because I think that a good healthy-appearing type, one who would be likeable and one that the jury is going to want to do something for, can make your case worth double at least for what it would be otherwise and a bad-appearing plaintiff could make the case worth perhaps half . . ."

For most injured patients, therefore, the litigation process, while offering the remote chance of a jackpot judgment, provides little real benefit, even for those who file claims and pursue them. Even successful claimants do not recover anything on average until five years after the injury, longer if the case goes to trial.

The friction generated by operating the system takes most of the money. When doctors and hospitals buy insurance (sometimes they are required to buy coverage that provides more "protection" than the total amount of their assets), it is intended to compensate victims of malpractice for their loss. However, only 28% of what they pay for insurance coverage actually goes to patients; 72% is spent on legal, administrative, and related costs. Less than half of the money that does go back to injured patients is used to compensate the patient for economic loss that is not compensated from other sources—the purpose of a compensation system. More than half of the amount the plaintiff receives duplicates other sources of compensation the patient may have (such as health insurance) and goes for subjective, non-economic damages (a large part of which, moreover, actually goes to the plaintiff's lawyer).

The malpractice system does not accurately identify negligence, deter bad conduct, or provide justice. The results it obtains are unpredictable, even random. The same study that found that only 1.53% of patients who were injured by medical error filed a claim also found, on the flip side, that most events for which claims were filed did not constitute negligence. Other studies show the same random results. "The evidence is growing that there is a poor correlation between injuries caused by negligent medical treatment and malpractice litigation."

Not surprisingly, most people involved in health care delivery on a day-to-day basis believe that the system does not accurately reflect the realities of health care or correctly identify malpractice. A recent survey indicated that 83% of physicians and 72% of hospital administrators do not believe the system achieves a reasonable result. . . .

Insurance Premiums Are Rising Rapidly

The cost of the excesses of the litigation system shows up in the cost of malpractice insurance coverage. Premiums have increased rapidly over the past several years. Experts believe we are seeing just the tip of what will happen this year and next. Rates have escalated rapidly for doctors who practice internal medicine, general surgery, and obstetrics/gynecology. The average increases ranged from 11% to 17% in 2000, were about 10% in 2001, but are accelerating rapidly. . . . A recent special report revealed that rate increases are averaging 20%.

However, these increases have varied widely across states, and some states have experienced increases of 30–75%, although there is no evidence that patient care had worsened. . . . [A] major contributing factor to the most enormous increases in liability premiums has been rapidly growing awards for non-economic damages in states that have not reformed their litigation system to put reasonable standards on these awards.

Among the states with the highest average medical malpractice insurance premiums are Florida, Illinois, Ohio, Nevada, New York, and West Virginia. These states have not reformed their litigation systems as others have. (Florida's caps apply only in limited circumstances. New York has prevented insurers from raising rates, and accordingly it is expected that substantial increases will be needed in 2003.) . . .

The effect of these premiums on what patients must pay for care can be seen from an example involving obstetrical care. The vast majority of awards against obstetricians involve poor outcomes at childbirth. As a result, payouts for poor infant outcomes account for the bulk of obstetricians' insurance costs. If an obstetrician delivers 100 babies per year (which is roughly the national average) and the malpractice premium is $200,000 annually (as it is in Florida), each mother (or the government or her employer who provides her health insurance) must pay approximately $2,000 merely to pay her share of her obstetrician's liability insurance. If a physician delivers 50 babies per year, the cost for malpractice premiums per baby is twice as high, about $4,000. It is not surprising that expectant mothers are finding their doctors have left states that support litigation systems imposing these costs.

In addition to premium increases for physicians, nursing home malpractice costs are rising rapidly because of dramatic increases in both the number of lawsuits and the size of awards. Nursing homes are a new target of the litigation system. Between 1995 and 2001, the national average of insurance costs increased from $240 per occupied skilled nursing bed per year to $2,360. From 1990 to 2001, the average size of claims tripled, and the number of claims increased from 3.6 to 11 per 1,000 beds.

These costs vary widely across states, again in relation to whether a state has implemented reforms that improve the predictability of the legal system. Florida ($11,000) had one of the highest per bed costs in 2001. Nursing homes in Mississippi have been faced with increases as great as 900% in the past two years. It has been recently reported that "nearly all companies that used to write nursing home liability [insurance] are getting out of the business." Since the costs of nursing home care are mainly paid by Medicaid and Medicare, these increased costs are borne by taxpayers, and consume resources that could otherwise be used to expand health (or other) programs.

Insurers Are Leaving the Market

The litigation crisis is affecting patients' ability to get care not only because many doctors find the increased premiums unaffordable but also because liability insurance is increasingly difficult to obtain at any price, particularly in nonreform states. Demonstrating and exacerbating the problem, several major carriers have stopped selling malpractice insurance.

- St. Paul Companies, which was the largest malpractice carrier in the United States, covering 9% of doctors, announced in December 2001 that it would no longer offer coverage to any doctor in the country.
- MIXX pulled out of every state; it will reorganize and sell only in New Jersey.
- PHICO and Frontier Insurance Group have also left the medical malpractice market.
- Doctors Insurance Reciprocal stopped writing group specialty coverage at the beginning of 2002.

States that had not enacted meaningful reforms (such as Nevada, Georgia, Oregon, Mississippi, Ohio, Pennsylvania, and Washington) were particularly affected. Fifteen insurers have left the Mississippi market in the past five years.

States With Realistic Limits on Non-Economic Damages Are Faring Better

The insurance crisis is less acute in states that have reformed their litigation systems. States with limits of $250,000 or $350,000 on non-economic damages have average combined highest premium increases of 12–15%, compared to 44% in states without caps on non-economic damages. . . .

As Table 1 shows, there is a substantial difference in the level of medical malpractice premiums in states with meaningful caps, such as California, Wisconsin, Montana, Utah and Hawaii, and states without meaningful caps.

In the early 1970s, California faced an access crisis like that facing many states now and threatening others. With bi-partisan support, including leadership from then Governor Jerry Brown and now Congressman Henry Waxman, then chairman of the Assembly's Select Committee on Medical Malpractice, California enacted comprehensive changes to make its medical liability system more predictable and rational. The Medical Injury Compensation Reform Act of 1975 (MICRA) made a number of reforms, including:

- Placing a $250,000 limit on non-economic damages while continuing unlimited compensation for economic damages.
- Shortening the time in which lawsuits could be brought to three years (thus ensuring that memories would still be fresh and providing some

Table 1

Malpractice Liability Rate Ranges by Specialty by Geography as of July 2001

	Cap in Non-Economic Damages	Low	High
INTERNISTS			
State Wide Data			
Wisconsin	$350,000	$5,000	$6,000
Montana	$250,000	5,300	7,000
Utah	$250,000	5,900	5,900
Hawaii	$350,000	6,800	6,800
Connecticut	No cap	6,200	15,800
Washington	No cap	7,100	9,000
Metropolitan Area Data			
California (Los Angeles area)	$250,000	$7,900	$13,000
Pennsylvania (Urban Philadelphia area)	No cap	10,700	11,800
Nevada (Las Vegas area)	No cap	11,600	15,800
Illinois (Chicagoland area)	No cap	16,500	28,100
Florida (Miami and Ft. Lauderdale areas)*	No cap	17,600	50,700
GENERAL SURGEONS			
State Wide Data			
Wisconsin (state wide)	$350,000	$16,000	$17,500
Montana (state wide)	$250,000	23,300	27,000
Utah (state wide)	$250,000	26,200	26,200
Hawaii (state wide)	$350,000	24,500	24,500
Connecticut (state wide)	No cap	26,200	45,800
Washington (state wide)	No cap	20,100	32,600
Metropolitan Area Data			
California (Los Angeles area)	$250,000	$23,700	$42,200
Pennsylvania (Urban Philadelphia area)	No cap	31,500	35,800
Nevada (Las Vegas area)	No cap	40,300	56,900
Illinois (Chicagoland area)	No cap	50,000	70,200
Florida (Miami and Ft. Lauderdale areas)*	No cap	63,200	126,600
OBSTETRICIANS/GYNECOLOGISTS			
State Wide Data			
Wisconsin (state wide)	$350,000	$23,800	$27,500
Montana (state wide)	$250,000	36,000	38,600
Hawaii (state wide)	$350,000	40,900	40,900
Utah (state wide)	$250,000	44,300	44,300
Connecticut (state wide)	No cap	45,400	64,800
Washington (state wide)	No cap	34,100	59,300

(continued)

Table 1 (Continued)

	Cap in Non-Economic Damages	Low	High
Metropolitan Area Data			
California (Los Angeles area)	$250,000	$46,900	$57,700
Pennsylvania (Urban Philadelphia area)	No cap	45,900	66,300
Nevada (Las Vegas area)	No cap	71,100	94,800
Illinois (Chicagoland area)	No cap	72,500	110,100
Florida (Miami and Ft. Lauderdale areas)*	No cap	108,000	208,900

Source: Medical Liability Monitor, Vol. 26, No. 10, October 2001: Shook, Hardy, Bacon, L.L.P., October 9, 2001.

*Florida imposes caps of $250,000–350,000 unless neither party demands binding arbitration or the defendant refuses to arbitrate.

> assurance to doctors that they would not be sued years after an event that they may well have forgotten).
> • Providing for periodic payment of damages to ensure the money is available to the patient in the future.

California has more than 25 years of experience with this reform. It has been a success. Doctors are not leaving California. Insurance premiums have risen much more slowly than in the rest of the country without any effect on the quality of care received by residents of California. Insurance premiums in California have risen by 167% over this period while those in the rest of the country have increased 505%. This has saved California residents billions of dollars in health care costs and saved federal taxpayers billions of dollars in the Medicare and Medicaid programs.

The President's Framework for Improving the Medical Liability System

Federal and state action is needed to address the impact of the medical liability crisis on health care costs and the quality of care.

Achieving a Fair, Predictable, and Timely Medical Liability Process

As years of experience in many states have proven, reasonable limits on the amount of non-economic damages that are awarded significantly restrain increases in the cost of malpractice premiums. These reforms improve the predictability of the medical liability system, reducing incentives for filing frivolous suits and for prolonged litigation. Greater predictability and more timely resolution of cases means patients who are injured can get fair compensation more quickly. They also reduce health care costs, enabling Americans to get more from their health care spending and enabling federal health programs to provide more relief. They improve access to care, by making insurance more affordable and available. They also improve the quality of health care, by avoiding unnecessary "defensive" treatments and enabling doctors to spend significantly more time focusing on patient care. Congress needs to enact legislation that would give all Americans the benefit of these reforms, eliminate the excesses of the litigation system, and protect patients' ability to get care.

The President [George W. Bush] supports federal reforms in medical liability law that would implement these proven steps for improving our health care system:

- Improve the ability of all patients who are injured by negligence to get quicker, unlimited compensation for their "economic losses," including the loss of the ability to provide valuable unpaid services like care for children or a parent.
- Ensure that recoveries for non-economic damages could not exceed a reasonable amount ($250,000).
- Reserve punitive damages for cases that justify them—where there is clear and convincing proof that the defendant acted with malicious intent or deliberately failed to avoid unnecessary injury to the patient—and avoid unreasonable awards (anything in excess of the greater of two times economic damages or $250,000).
- Provide for payment of a judgment over time rather than in one lump sum—and thus ensure that the money is there for the injured patient when needed.
- Ensure that old cases cannot be brought years after an event when medical standards may have changed or witnesses' memories have faded, by providing that a case may not be brought more than three years following the date or injury or one year after the claimant discovers or, with reasonable diligence, should have discovered the injury.
- Informing the jury if a plaintiff also has another source of payment for the injury, such as health insurance.
- Provide that defendants pay any judgment in proportion to their fault, not on the basis of how deep their pockets are.

The success of the states that have adopted reforms like these shows that malpractice premiums could be reduced by 34% by adopting these reforms. The savings to the Federal Government resulting from reduced malpractice premiums would be $1.68 billion.

Legislation such as H.R. 4600—a bill introduced by Congressman Jim Greenwood [R-Pennsylvania] with almost 100 bipartisan cosponsors—is now pending in Congress. Enactment of this legislation with improvements to ensure that its meaningful standards will apply nationally, will be a significant step toward the goals of affordable, high-quality health care for all Americans, and a fair and predictable liability system for compensating injured patients.

In addition, there are other promising approaches for compensating patients injured by negligence fairly and without requiring them to go through full-scale, time-consuming, and expensive litigation. Just as states like California have demonstrated the effectiveness of litigation reforms, they should also adopt and evaluate the impact of alternatives to litigation.

Early Offers is one innovative approach. This would provide a new set of balanced incentives to encourage doctors to make offers, quickly after an injury, to compensate the patient for economic loss, and for patients to accept. It would make it possible for injured patients to receive fair compensation quickly, and over time if any further losses are incurred, without having to enter into the litigation fray. Because doctors and hospitals would have an incentive to discover adverse events quickly in order to make a qualifying offer, it would lead to prompt identification of quality problems. The money that otherwise would be spent in conducting litigation would be recycled so that more patients get additional recovery, more quickly, with savings left over to the benefit of all Americans. It may also be possible to implement an administrative form of Early Offers as an option for care provided under federal health programs.

A second innovative approach involves strengthening medical review boards. Boards with special expertise in the technical intricacies of health care can streamline the fact-gathering and hearing process, make decisions more accurately, and provide compensation more quickly and predictably than the current litigation process. As with Early Offers, incentives are necessary for patients and health care providers to submit cases to the boards and to accept their decisions.

The Administration intends to work with states on developing and implementing these alternatives to litigation, so that injured patients can be fairly compensated quickly and without the trauma and expense that litigation entails.

Bush's Medical Malpractice Disinformation Campaign

Introduction

The medical community continues to tout a report, *Confronting the New Health Care Crisis: Improving Health Care Quality and Lowering Costs by Fixing Our Medical Liability System*, issued by the Department of Health and Human Services [HHS] last summer [2002] as making an overwhelming case for medical liability "reform." In truth, a cursory examination of the report finds it to be a classic "clip job"—a collection of anecdotes, reports, and propaganda provided by lobbyists and stamped with the government's official imprimatur. The report cites such sources as Fox News Channel, Congressman Chip Pickering, and the Physician Insurers Association of America, the trade group leading the lobbying campaign. *It contains no new research nor any data generated by government health care experts or economists.*

A more intensive examination of the report shows that most of the "facts" it provides are incorrect, incomplete, or misleading; and that its conclusions are contradicted by those of other government agencies. . . .

The Bush Administration Says: "Access to Care Is Threatened"

> *"There are a number of obstacles that limit access to affordable health care in this country, including lack of affordable insurance and an outdated Medicare program. We now face another—the litigation crisis that has made insurance premiums unaffordable or even unavailable for many doctors, through no fault of their own. This is making it more difficult for many Americans to find care, and threatening access for many more. Dr. Cheryl Edwards, 41, closed her decade-old obstetrics and gynecology practice in Las Vegas because her insurance premium jumped from $37,000 to $150,000 a year. She moved her practice to West Los Angeles, leaving 30 pregnant women to find new doctors."*

> *The Facts: Malpractice insurance costs are a miniscule part of a doctor's expenses and don't affect decisions about where to practice medicine.*

- *There is a greater likelihood of doctors withdrawing from practice due to increases in their office rents or payroll costs than due to increases in malpractice insurance costs.* While there is a temporary spike in medical malpractice insurance rates due to insurance industry economics, it is necessary to look at the larger and longer-term picture. Specifically, while physicians spend about 3.2 percent of their gross income on medical malpractice costs, they spend 17 percent on payroll costs and 5.8 percent on office rent. According to the Medicare Payment Advisory Commission (MedPAC), the average increase in medical malpractice insurance rates last year was 4.4 percent. A doctor who stops practicing because of a malpractice insurance increase would be just as likely to retire due to increased health insurance costs for office staff, or because of increased rent for office space. If increased costs to doctors justify legislative action, they could also justify repeal of wages and hours laws or enactment of rent control laws.

- *Liability laws have no effect on a doctor's decision where to practice.* Even though damage awards are higher in more affluent states, those states still have more doctors. The District of Columbia has the highest average damage award and the most doctors. Idaho, with the fewest doctors, has the third lowest median damage award. While five of the states with the lowest per capita number of doctors have enacted caps on noneconomic damages, only three of the states with the highest number of doctors per capita have enacted them. According to the U.S. Chamber of Commerce, Iowa, Utah, and South Dakota rank 5th, 8th and 9th for "reasonable litigation environment," yet those states rank in the bottom ten in number of doctors. Only one state in the Chamber's legal climate top ten, Connecticut, also ranks in the top ten for doctors. California, whose damage caps supposedly drew Dr. Edwards from Las Vegas, did not add one additional doctor per 100,000 residents between 1990 and 1999, but the number of doctors per 100,000 residents increased in Nevada from 136 to 162 during that period.

- *Two factors explain almost all the variation in the number of doctors in a state: income level and urbanization.* Like anyone else, doctors want to live in places where they can earn high incomes, enjoy cultural and leisure activities, and send their children to good schools. Seven of the top ten states for doctors also rank in the top ten states in percentage of households earning $200,000 or more. Doctors want to live in areas with lots of affluent people—such areas are more likely to have the leafy suburbs, premium housing, clubs, and other amenities that doctors want. For every $1,000 increase in a state's median income for a four-person family, a state will have 2.3 more doctors per 100,000 residents. Doctors migrate to states on lists of "Best Places to Live": Forty of the top 100 cities with "strong arts, cultural programs, and higher education" were in the ten states with the highest per capita number of doctors, while there were none in the ten states with the lowest per capita number of doctors. Polled by the U.S. Chamber of Commerce, 41 percent of West Virginia doctors said that the inability of the state's poor resident to pay fees was responsible for the state's shortage of doctors, and 27 percent said that quality of life in the state was responsible.

- *There is no relationship between the level of increase in liability insurance premiums and the likelihood of discontinuing obstetric practice.* A recent study examined whether New York obstetricians facing higher premiums for obstetric liability insurance were more likely to discontinue practicing than physicians experiencing lower increases in premiums. The study found that the decrease in doctors practicing obstetrics was associated with the length of time since receiving a medical license in New York. This relationship "very likely represents the phenomenon of physicians retiring from practice or curtailing obstetrics as they age."

The Bush Administration Says: "Patient Safety Is Jeopardized"

"In its recent report, 'To Err is Human,' the Institute of Medicine (IOM) observed that, '[R]eporting systems are an important part of improving patient safety and should be encouraged. These voluntary reporting systems [should] periodically assess whether additional efforts are needed to address gaps in information to improve patient safety . . .' However, as the IOM emphasized, fear that information from these reporting systems will be used to prepare a lawsuit against them, even if they are not negligent, deters doctors and hospitals from making reports."

The Facts: Patient safety is enhanced by the tort system; it would be further enhanced by increased regulation of doctors.

- *The Administration's own Council of Economic Advisors said the opposite last year—the tort system increases patient safety.* Even the conservative appointees to the President's Council of Economic Advisors admit, "a patient purchasing a medical procedure, for example, may be unlikely to fully understand the complex risks, costs and benefits of that procedure relative to others. Such a patient must turn to a physician who serves as a 'learned intermediary,' though there remains the problem that the patient may also not be able to judge the skill of the physician from whom the procedure is 'purchased.' In such a case, the ability of the individual to pursue a liability lawsuit in the event of an improper treatment, for example, provides an additional incentive for the physician to follow good medical practice. Indeed, from a broad social perspective, this may be the least costly way to proceed—less costly than trying to educate every consumer fully. In a textbook example, recognition of the expected costs from the liability system causes the provider to undertake the extra effort or care that matches the customer's desire to avoid the risk of harm. This process is what economists refer to as 'internalizing externalities.' In other words, the liability system makes persons who injure others aware of their actions, and provides incentives for them to act appropriately."
- *Patient safety is at risk from medical providers' failure to commit to reducing medical errors.* In 1999 the Institute of Medicine released its report on patient safety in the U.S. The report estimated that between 44,000 and 98,000 Americans die annually as a result of preventable medical errors. The IOM recommended creation of a nationwide *mandatory*

reporting system of serious errors—those that result in death or serious harm—for hospitals, other institutional providers and ambulatory care systems. The IOM argued that such a system is necessary to hold providers accountable for maintaining safety and to implement safety systems that reduce the likelihood of such events occurring. IOM also recommended that health professional licensing conduct periodic re-examinations and re-licensing of doctors, nurses, and other key providers, based on both competence and knowledge of safety practices. Neither of these recommendations has been implemented, due to opposition from the medical community; nor are they mentioned in the HHS report.

• *Patient safety is also at risk from incompetent doctors.* Five percent of doctors are responsible for 54 percent of malpractice in the U.S., according to records in the National Practitioner Data Bank, maintained by HHS. An inquiry to this database, which covers malpractice judgments and settlements since September 1990, found that 5.1 percent of doctors (35,009) have paid two or more malpractice awards to patients. These doctors are responsible for 54 percent of all payouts reported to the Data Bank. Of these, only 7.6 percent have ever been disciplined by state medical boards. Even physicians who have made 5 payouts have been disciplined at only a 13.3 percent rate.

The Bush Administration Says: "Health Care Costs Are Increased"

"The litigation and malpractice insurance problem raids the wallet of every American. Money spent on malpractice premiums (and the litigation costs that largely determine premiums) raises health care costs. The litigation system also imposes large indirect costs on the health care system. Defensive medicine that is caused by unlimited and unpredictable liability awards not only increases patients' risk but it also adds cost . . . The leading study estimates that limiting unreasonable awards for noneconomic damages could reduce health care costs by 5–9% without adversely affecting quality of care. This would save $60–108 billion in health care costs each year."

The Facts: The Congressional Budget Office (CBO) says that limiting liability would have a negligible impact on health care costs.

• *In evaluating the impact of H.R. 4600, which would have severely limited the ability of patients to recover damages, the Congressional Budget Office projected only minimal savings.* This bill, which contained very stringent restrictions on patients' ability to recover damages, passed the U.S. House in 2002. CBO said: "The percentage effect of H.R. 4600 on overall health insurance premiums would be far smaller than the percentage impact on medical malpractice insurance premiums. Malpractice costs account for a very small fraction of total health care spending; even a very large reduction in malpractice costs would have a relatively small effect on total health plan premiums. In addition, some of the savings leading to lower medical malpractice premiums—those savings arising from changes in the treatment of collateral-source benefits—would represent a shift in costs from medical malpractice insurance to health insurance. Because providers of collateral-source benefits would be prevented from recovering their costs arising from the malpractice injury, some of the costs that would be borne by malpractice insurance under current law would instead be borne by the providers of collateral-source benefits. Most such providers are health insurers."

- *The Congressional Budget Office has rejected the "defensive medicine" theory.* CBO was asked to quantify the savings from reduced "defensive medicine" if Congress passed H.R. 4600. CBO declined, saying:

Estimating the amount of health care spending attributable to defensive medicine is difficult. Most estimates are speculative in nature, relying, for the most part, on surveys of physicians' responses to hypothetical clinical situations, and clinical studies of the effectiveness of certain intensive treatments. Compounding the uncertainty about the magnitude of spending for defensive medicine, there is little empirical evidence on the effect of medical malpractice tort controls on spending for defensive medicine and, more generally, on overall health care spending.

A small number of studies have observed reductions in health care spending correlated with changes in tort law, but that research was based largely on a narrow part of the population and considered only hospital spending for a small number of ailments that are disproportionately likely to experience malpractice claims. Using broader measures of spending, CBO's initial analysis could find no statistically significant connection between malpractice tort limits and overall health care spending. Although the provisions of H.R. 4600 could result in the initiation of fewer lawsuits, the economic incentives for individual physicians or hospitals to practice defensive medicine would appear to be little changed.

- *Overall tort expenditures are less than the cost of medical injuries.* Because so few medical injuries result in compensation to patients, the overall expenditures made for medical liability are far below the projected injury costs. The Institute of Medicine estimated the costs of preventable medical injuries in hospitals alone at between $17 billion and $29 billion a year. The Utah Colorado Medical Practice study estimated it at $20 billion. By contrast, the National Association of Insurance Commissioners reports that the total amount spent on medical malpractice insurance in 2000 was $6.4 billion. This is at least three to five times less than the cost of malpractice to society.

- *A leading actuary says the HHS report's numbers are "rubbish."* According to Robert Hunter, Director of Insurance for Consumer Federation of America, "The total cost of medical malpractice premiums is $6.4 billion (not just for doctors, as the report says, but for doctors, hospitals and other facilities). This represents about one-half of a percent of total health care expenses. In other words, if an outright ban were placed on medical malpractice lawsuits the total savings would be about $6 billion. The idea that a cap of any kind can save $60 to $108 billion is pure rubbish. How in the world could 'defensive medicine' possibly be more than equal to the total risk measured in premiums, much less 10 to 20 times the risk, as HHS assumes? This makes no economic sense at all."

The Bush Administration Says: "The Increasingly Unpredictable, Costly, and Slow Litigation System Is Responsible"

"Insurance premiums are largely determined by the expensive litigation system . . . Its application is unpredictable, largely random, and standardless . . . Although most cases do not actually go to trial, it costs a significant amount of money to defend each claim—an average of $24,669 . . . Awarded on top of compensation for the injured patient's actual economic loss, non-economic damages are said to be compensation for intangible losses, such as pain and suffering, loss of consortium, hedonic (loss of the enjoyment of life) damages, and various other theories that are imaginatively created by lawyers to increase the amount awarded . . . The average award rose 76% from 1996–1999. The median award in 1999 was $800,000, a 6.7% increase over the 1998 figure of $750,000; and between 1999 and 2000, median malpractice awards increased nearly 43%."

The Facts: The medical malpractice litigation process is logical, and awards are explained by income, cost of health care, and injury severity.

- *Government data show that medical malpractice awards have increased at a much slower pace than claimed by Jury Verdict Research.* According to the federal government's National Practitioner Data Bank (NPDB), the median medical malpractice payment by a physician to a patient rose 35 percent from 1997 to 2001, from $100,000 to $135,000. By contrast, data from Jury Verdict Research (JVR), a private research firm, which was cited in the HHS report shows that awards rose 100 percent from 1997 to 2000, from $503,000 to $1 million. The reason for the huge difference, which is explained in more detail below: JVR collects only jury *verdict* information that is reported to it by attorneys, court clerks and stringers. The NPDB is the most comprehensive source of information that exists because it includes both verdicts *and* settlements. Ninety-six percent of all medical malpractice cases are settled, as opposed to decided by a jury, and settlements result in much lower awards than jury verdicts. Jury verdicts are higher than the average settlement because cases involving severe injuries are more likely to go to trial, and the defendant has usually rejected a settlement offer for a much smaller amount. JVR reported that the median final plaintiff demand in 2000 was $562,000, and the median final settlement offer from the doctor was $80,000. Thus, in the twenty percent of trials that doctors lost, a conscious decision was made to risk a much higher jury verdict. The plaintiffs were usually willing to settle for about half of what the jury awarded. According to NPDB's database of all medical malpractice settlements and judgments, the median payment in a settlement in 2000 was $125,000, same as the median for all payments; but the median payment for a judgment was $235,000. This figure is lower than the jury verdict figure because the ultimate payment received by a successful plaintiff reflects remittiturs ordered by judges, and discounts agreed to by plaintiffs in order to avert appeals.
- *Government data show that medical malpractice awards have increased at a slower pace than health insurance premiums.* While NPDB data show

that the median medical malpractice payment rose 35 percent from 1997 to 2001 (an average of 8.5 percent a year), the average premium for single health insurance coverage increased 39 percent over that time period (9.5 percent a year). Payments for health care costs, which directly affect health insurance premiums, make up the lion's share of most medical malpractice awards.

- *"Non-economic" damages are not as easy to quantify as lost wages or medical bills, but they compensate real injuries.* So-called "non-economic" damages are awarded for the pain and suffering that accompany any loss of normal functions (e.g. blindness, paralysis, sexual dysfunction, lost bowel and bladder control) and inability to engage in daily activities or to pursue hobbies, such as hunting and fishing. This category also encompasses damages for disfigurement and loss of fertility. The fact that Americans spend a great deal of money to remedy these conditions (e.g. on pain relief medication, reconstructive surgery, etc.) belies any notion that such damages are "non-economic." According to Physician Insurer Association of America (PIAA), the average payment between 1985 and 2001 for a "grave injury," which encompasses paralysis, was only $454,454.

- *No evidence supports the claim that jury verdicts are random "jackpots."* Studies conducted in California, Florida, North Carolina, New York, and Ohio have found that jury verdicts bear a reasonable relationship to the severity of the harm suffered. In total the studies examined more than 3,500 medical malpractice jury verdicts and found a consistent relationship between the severity of the injury and the size of the verdict. Uniformly the authors concluded that their findings did not support the contention that jury verdicts are frequently unpredictable and irrational.

- *The insurance industry's own numbers demonstrate that awards are proportionate to injuries.* PIAA's Data Sharing Report also demonstrates the relationship between the severity of the injury and the size of the settlement or verdict. PIAA, as do most researchers, measures severity of injury according to the National Association of Insurance Commissioners' classifications. The average indemnity paid per file was $49,947 for the least severe category of injury and increased with severity, to $454,454 for grave injuries. All researchers found that the amount of jury verdicts fell off in cases of death, for which the average indemnity was $195,723. This is not surprising, as the costs of medical treatment for a grave injury are likely to be greater and pain and suffering would be experienced over a longer time period than in the case of death.

- *The contingency fee system discourages attorneys from bringing frivolous claims.* Medical malpractice cases are brought on a contingency fee basis, meaning the attorney receives payment only in the event there is a settlement or verdict. If the claim is closed without payment, the attorney does not receive a fee. Since attorneys must earn money to stay in business, it follows that they would not intentionally take on a non-meritorious case.

- *The high cost of preparing a medical malpractice case discourages frivolous claims—and meritorious claims as well.* Medical malpractice cases are very expensive for plaintiffs' attorneys to bring, with out-of-pocket costs for cases settled at or near the time of trial (when most cases are settled) ranging from $15,000 to $25,000. If the case goes to trial, the costs can easily be doubled. These costs do not include the plaintiff's attorney's time, and an attorney pursuing a frivolous case incurs opportunity costs in not pursuing other cases. An attorney incurs expenses beginning with the determination of whether a case has merit. First, the attorney is required to obtain copies of the patient's medical records from all the providers for analysis by a competent medically trained person. If that initial consultation reveals a likelihood of medical negligence, the records must then be submitted to medical specialists, qualified to testify in court, for final review. Typically, the records must be sent to experts outside of the plaintiff's state, as physicians within the state will refuse to testify against local colleagues. As a result, the experts who agree to review records and testify can and do charge substantial fees. Fees from $1,000 per hour to several thousand dollars are not uncommon. Discovery involves taking the sworn testimony of witnesses and experts. Such depositions cost $300 and up, depending upon their length and complexity. If an expert witness is deposed, the plaintiff's attorney is charged for the witness' preparation time and time attending the deposition.

- *Plaintiffs drop 10 times more claims than they pursue.* PIAA reports that between 1985 and 2001 a total of 108,300 claims were "dropped, withdrawn or dismissed." This is 63 percent of the total number of claims (172,474) closed during the study period. It is unclear what portion constitutes involuntarily dismissed cases (dismissed after a motion was filed by the defendant) rather than cases voluntarily dismissed by plaintiffs. According to researchers at the University of Washington School of Medicine, about nine percent of claims files are closed after the defendant wins a contested motion. Based on this figure, Public Citizen estimates that about 54 percent of claims are being abandoned by patients. An attorney may send a statutorily-required notice of intent to claim or file a lawsuit in order to meet the requirements of the statute of limitations but, after collecting medical records and consulting with experts, decide not to pursue the claim. We estimate that the number of cases withdrawn voluntarily by plaintiffs was 92,621, *10 times* the number of cases that were taken to trial and lost during that period (9,293). The percentage of claims pursued by plaintiffs to final rejection by a jury is only *five percent.*

- *The small number of claims pursued to a defense verdict are not frivolous.* Researchers at the American Society of Anesthesiologists arranged for pairs of doctors to review 103 randomly selected medical negligence claims files. The doctors were asked to judge whether the anesthesiologist in question had acted reasonably and prudently. The doctors only agreed on the appropriateness of care in 62 percent of the cases; they disagreed in 38 percent of cases. The researchers concluded, "These observations indicate that neutral experts (the reviews were conducted in a situation that did not involve advocacy or financial compensation) commonly disagree in their assessments when using the accepted standard of reasonable and prudent care." The percentage of all medical malpractice claims that go to trial is only 6.6 percent, according to PIAA, meaning that the parties and their attorneys ultimately reach agreement about liability five times more often than neutral doctors do. If truly frivolous lawsuits were being pursued, the proportion of claims going to trial would exceed the 38 percent of claims on which even doctors will disagree.

- *The costs of defending claims that are ultimately dropped are not unreasonable.* Medical liability insurers have complained about the costs of defending cases that are ultimately dropped. But the professional obligation of lawyers to exercise due diligence is essentially identical to the duty of physicians. The lawyer must rule out the possibility of proving medical negligence before terminating a claim, just as doctors must rule out the possibility of illnesses suggested by their patients' symptoms. The doctor performs his duty by administering tests; the lawyer performs hers by using discovery procedures. Both processes can lead to dead ends. But plaintiffs' lawyers have no financial incentive to abuse the litigation process: they are using their own time and money to pursue discovery activities, and are only paid for work on behalf of clients whose cases are successful.
- *Award amounts correlate to plaintiff's income and the cost of living in the plaintiff's home state.* Median malpractice awards vary from state to state. Much of the variation is explained by two factors—median family income and urbanization. Public Citizen's analysis of NPDB and census data found that for every $1,000 increase in a state's median family income, the median award amount increases by about $1,100. Our analysis also found that awards increase in relation to state population density—logical, since urbanized areas have a higher cost of living than rural areas.

The Bush Administration Says: "Insurance Premiums Are Rising Rapidly"

"The cost of the excesses of the litigation system shows up in the cost of malpractice insurance coverage. Premiums have increased rapidly over the past several years."

The Facts: The spike in medical liability premiums was caused by the insurance cycle, not by an "explosion" of lawsuits or "skyrocketing" jury verdicts.

- *There is no growth in the number of new medical malpractice claims.* According to the National Association of Insurance Commissioners (NAIC), the number of new medical malpractice claims declined by about four percent between 1995 and 2000. There were 90,212 claims filed in 1995; 84,741 in 1996; 85,613 in 1997; 86,211 in 1998; 89,311 in 1999; and 86,480 in 2000.
- *For much of the 1990s, doctors benefited from artificially lower premiums.* According to the International Risk Management Institute (IRMI), one of the leading analysts of commercial insurance issues, "What is happening to the market for medical malpractice insurance in 2001 is a direct result of trends and events present since the mid to late 1990s. Throughout the 1990s, and reaching a peak around 1997 and 1998,

insurers were on a quest for market share, that is, they were driven more by the amount of premium they could book rather than the adequacy of premiums to pay losses. In large part this emphasis on market share was driven by a desire to accumulate large amounts of capital with which to turn into investment income." IRMI also noted: "Clearly a business cannot continue operating in that fashion indefinitely."

- *West Virginia Insurance Commissioner blames the market.* According to the Office of the West Virginia Insurance Commission (one of the states in the throes of a medical malpractice "crisis"), "[T]he insurance industry is cyclical and necessarily competitive. We have witnessed these cycles in the Medical Malpractice line in the mid-'70's, the mid-'80's and the present situation. This particular cycle is, perhaps, worse than previous cycles as it was delayed by a booming economy in the '90's and is now experiencing not just a shortfall in rates due to competition, but a subdued economy, lower interest rates and investment yields, the withdrawal of a major medical malpractice writer and a strong hardening of the reinsurance market. Rates will, at some point, reach an acceptable level to insurers and capital will once again flow into the Medical Malpractice market."

- *Medical liability premiums track investment results.* J. Robert Hunter, one of the country's most knowledgeable insurance actuaries and director of insurance for the Consumer Federation of America, recently analyzed the growth in medical liability premiums. He found that premiums charged do not track losses paid, but instead rise and fall in concert with the state of the economy. When the economy is booming and investment returns are high, companies maintain premiums at modest levels; however, when the economy falters and interest rates fall, companies increase premiums in response.

- *The same trends are present in other lines of insurance.* Property/casualty refers to a large group of liability lines of insurance (30 in total) including medical malpractice, homeowners, commercial, and automobile. The property/casualty insurance industry has exhibited cyclical behavior for many years, as far back as the 1920s. These cycles are characterized by periods of rising rates leading to increased profitability. Following a period of solid but not spectacular rates of return, the industry enters a down phase where prices soften, supply of the insurance product becomes plentiful, and, eventually, profitability diminishes, or vanishes completely. In the down phase of the cycle, as results deteriorate, the basic ability of insurance companies to underwrite new business or, for some companies even to renew some existing policies, can be impaired. This is because the capital needed to support the underwriting of risk has been depleted through losses. The current market began to harden in 2001, following an unusually prolonged period of soft market conditions in the property-casualty section in the 1990s. The current hard market is unusual in that many lines of insurance are affected at the same time, including medical malpractice. As a result, premiums are rising for most types of insurance. The increases have taken policyholders by surprise given that they came after several years of relatively flat to decreasing prices.

- *Insurer mismanagement compounded the problems.* Compounding the impact of the cycle has been misleading accounting practices. As the

Wall Street Journal found in a front page investigative story on June 24, 2002, "[A] price war that began in the early 1990s led insurers to sell malpractice coverage to obstetrician-gynecologists at rates that proved inadequate to cover claims. Some of these carriers had rushed into malpractice coverage because an accounting practice widely used in the industry made the area seem more profitable in the early 1990s than it really was. A decade of short-sighted price slashing led to industry losses of nearly $3 billion last year." Moreover, "In at least one case, aggressive pricing allegedly crossed the line into fraud." According to Donald J. Zuk, chief executive of SCPIE Holdings Inc., a leading malpractice insurer in California, "Regardless of the level of . . . tort reform, the fact remains that if insurance policies are consistently under-priced, the insurer will lose money."

The Bush Administration Says: "Insurers Are Leaving the Market"

"The litigation crisis is affecting patients' ability to get care not only because many doctors find the increased premiums unaffordable but also because liability insurance is increasingly difficult to obtain at any price, particularly in non-reform states. Demonstrating and exacerbating the problem, several major carriers have stopped selling malpractice insurance."

The Facts: At least three of the four insurance companies identified by HHS as leaving the market had serious management problems during the past two years.

- *PHICO had been placed under the supervision of insurance regulators and was later sued by the state's Insurance Department.* The lawsuit alleged that PHICO directors ignored signs of financial trouble at the company and pressured the board to pay dividends at a time when the insurer's surplus "was declining drastically and significant strengthening of loss reserves was required."
- *St. Paul exited other insurance markets as well.* St. Paul Companies reported in December 2001 that it had $85 million in exposure as related to the Enron Corporation and that it held approximately $23 million in Enron Corporation senior unsecured debt. At the same time St. Paul announced it would exit its medical malpractice business, it also announced it would add reserves for claims related to the September 11 terrorist attacks, "exit certain reinsurance lines, exit countries where the company is not likely to achieve competitive scale, and reduce corporate overhead expenses, including staff reductions."
- *MIIX was found by Weiss Ratings to be the hardest hit by the property and casualty insurance industry's overall $6.6 billion decline in investment gains during the first half of 2002.* MIIX reported the largest capital losses. Weiss, a leading independent provider of ratings and analyses of financial services companies, downgraded MIIX from D- to E+, E being the lowest score possible. A former MIIX official has alleged conflicts of interest on the company's board that may have affected the situation.

The Bush Administration Says: "States With Realistic Limits on Non-Economic Damages Are Faring Better"

"The insurance crisis is less acute in states that have reformed their litigation systems. States with limits of $250,000 or $350,000 on non-economic damages have average combined highest premium increases of 12–15%, compared to 44% in states without caps on non-economic damages . . ."

The Facts: Neither the HHS report nor anyone else has presented a factual case that caps lower premiums; Public Citizen's analysis found that premiums are higher in states with caps.

- *The HHS report's "comparison" of premiums in ten states with caps to just ten states without caps is pure baloney.* HHS omitted data from other states without damage caps that did not have high premium increases. The Pennsylvania Medical Society . . . released a critique of another premium comparison, concluding that "Multivariate modeling must be used to control for outside influences . . . An issue as important as liability insurance reform deserves no less than a careful scientific approach to assessment of the impact of policy changes." While they did not prepare a multivariate model, Public Citizen did.
- *Public Citizen's analysis finds that, controlling for other factors, premiums are higher in states with caps than in states without caps.* Public Citizen entered U.S. Census, NPDB, and Medical Liability Monitor data into a multiple regression model to determine the effect that damage caps have on awards and on doctors' liability insurance premiums. Our preliminary finding is that a damage cap lowers the median payment made by doctors to plaintiffs by $29,000, in turn lowering a doctor's premium by about $11,000. Nevertheless, controlling for this and the rate of lawsuits against doctors in each state, states with caps still have premiums that are $14,000 higher than in states without caps, a $3,000 net increase. We believe that the cap encourages doctors to take more cases to trial, and the resulting higher defense attorney costs more than offset the lower indemnity payments.

POSTSCRIPT

Is It Time to Reform Medical Malpractice Litigation?

The question of medical malpractice litigation must be placed in context. No one disputes the fact that doctors make mistakes. Physicians are human and are therefore subject to human fallibilities. It should be noted that the large majority of these medical errors never result in legal action. But since the United States does not have in place a nationally mandated reporting system for medical mishaps and near mishaps, the public does not have certain knowledge of just how many medical mistakes are made annually. Doctors and their insurance carriers would have people believe that every medical mistake is litigated and that many other lawsuits are brought to the courts when there are no grounds for them. Lawyers, for their part, argue that they file lawsuits for only a small fraction of the medical mistakes that are made annually in the United States. Indeed, they contend that if it were not for the cases they did bring to light, the public would naively believe that doctors are infallible.

The truth of the matter may lie somewhere in the middle. Outside observers generally assume that about one out of every six "medical misadventures" results in a lawsuit. Of those who do seek legal redress, about half of these malpractice lawsuits are settled out of court or withdrawn before they go to trial. It is those that find their way through the court system and result in large financial settlements that are political lightning rods.

Those who litigate medical malpractice cases contend that their jury and settlement awards have little impact on medical malpractice insurance rates. They contend that the appearance of high insurance premiums can be traced to poor management decisions. When times were good and interest rates were high, these companies engaged in excessive competition, which drove the insurance rates down too far in the most competitive markets. When times were not as good and interest rates were low, insurance companies had no choice but to increase their rates. The increase, of course, was most severe in markets where the rates had been driven to the lowest levels.

This issue has been hotly debated in recent months; consequently, you might look to the press for background reading. The *New York Times* is a good source. The March 16, 2003, issue of the *New York Times Magazine* carried an article concerning four individuals who had foreign objects left in their bodies after surgeries. "The Biggest Mistake of Their Lives" discusses the case of Dan Jennings. If the miseries suffered by John Francis, as described in the introduction to this issue, seem remarkably like those of Jennings, that is because Francis is a fictional character based on Jennings.

Those who would limit malpractice awards have written widely. See, for example, "The Tort Mess," by Michael Freeman, *Forbes* (May 13, 2002). The

American Medical Association has many such references, including "Medical Liability Reform Background and Talking Points." This summary, which was updated on May 8, 2002, incorporates many of the points found in the HHS report. To see how the medical community interprets history in this area, see James C. Mohr, "American Medical Malpractice Litigation in Historical Perspective," *JAMA* (April 3, 2000). Finally, to read firsthand how the insurance industry feels, see Doctor's Company chairman Richard E. Anderson's July 17, 2002, testimony before the Subcommittee on Health, Committee on Energy and Commerce, in "Harming Patient Access to Care: The Impact of Excessive Litigation."

For a good summary of President George W. Bush's statement on the medical malpractice issue and a panel discussion, see the January 16, 2003, segment of *The News Hour With Jim Lehrer*, which includes Larry Smarr, president of the Physicians Insurers Association of America; Ken Suggs, secretary to the Association of American Trial Lawyers; Donald Palmisano, president-elect of the American Medical Association; and Joanne Doroshow, executive director of the Center for Justice and Democracy.

Internet References . . .

Board of Governors of the Federal Reserve System

The home page for the Board of Governors of the Federal Reserve System provides a number of useful links to information about monetary policy and the financial industry.

http://www.federalreserve.gov/

Bureau of Economic Analysis

The home page of the Bureau of Economic Analysis of the U.S. Department of Commerce provides access to a wealth of economic information on a national, regional, international, and industry basis.

http://www.bea.gov/

Joint Economic Committee

This site describes the work of the Joint Economic Committee of the U.S. Congress. It includes the research reports of the committee on many topics including tax reform and government spending, monetary policy, and international economic policy.

http://www.house.gov/jec/

National Bureau of Economic Research (NBER)

The NBER is "a private, nonprofit, nonpartisan, research organization dedicated to promoting a greater understanding of how the economy works." Its home page provides a number of useful links; of special importance is the information about the business cycle.

http://www.nber.org/

The Public Debt Online

This site, maintained by the Bureau of the Public Debt of the U.S. Department of the Treasury, provides "to the penny" information on the current debt of the U.S. federal government. It also provides historical information on the dollar size of the debt, on ownership of the debt, and on the interest expense associated with the debt.

http://www.publicdebt.treas.gov/opd/opd/htm

U.S. Macroeconomic and Regional Data

Hosted by the State University of New York, Oswego, Department of Economics, this site contains the full text of recent *Economic Reports of the President* and links to various global and regional economic indicators.

http://www.oswego.edu/~economic/mac-data.htm

UNIT 2

Macroeconomic Issues

*T*he *economy incorporates the behavior of different groups including consumers, businesses, and the government. The actions of very large businesses like the world's largest retailer and credit card companies affect almost everyone, but it is consumers who ultimately decide where they shop and whether to use credit cards. Government policies in the areas of Social Security, taxation, the minimum wage, and immigration have consequences across the economy. But consumers, when they act as voting citizens, select the political officials who pass the laws. These interactions are reflected in each of the issues and help underscore the importance of the issues.*

- Is Wal-Mart Good for the Economy?

- Should Social Security Be Changed to Include Personal Retirement Accounts?

- Should the Double Taxation of Corporate Dividends Be Eliminated?

- Are Credit Card Companies Exploiting American Consumers?

- Should Minimum Wage and Living Wage Laws Be Eliminated?

- Do Unskilled Immigrants Hurt the Economy?

ISSUE 7

Is Wal-Mart Good for the Economy?

YES: Los Angeles County Economic Development Corporation, from "Wal-Mart Supercenters: What's in Store for Southern California?" http://www.laedc.info/data/documents.asp (January 2004)

NO: Democratic Staff of the House Committee on Education and the Workforce, from "Everyday Low Wages: The Hidden Price We All Pay for Wal-Mart," http://www.mindfully.org/Industry/2004/wal-mart-labor-record16feb04.htm (February 16, 2004)

ISSUE SUMMARY

YES: The Los Angeles County Economic Development Corporation believes that the introduction of Wal-Mart supercenter stores into the Southern California market will generate significant savings for consumers on their grocery, apparel, and general merchandise spending, and the redirected spending from the savings will create over 35,000 new jobs.

NO: The Democratic Staff of the House Committee on Education and the Workforce believes that Wal-Mart, in its efforts to achieve and maintain low prices, has "come to represent the lowest common denominator in the treatment of working people."

Given the company's ubiquitous presence across the country, it would come as a great surprise to find an American who did not recognize the name "Wal-Mart" or find someone who had not shopped at a Wal-Mart store. Many people are familiar with the yellow smiley face that appears in Wal-Mart television ads, in its newspapers ads, and on its in-store promotions. While many people might not know of the persons who created other major retailers like Target, Home Depot, and Kmart, a fair number would be able to identify Sam Walton as Wal-Mart's founder. And, some of these would even be able to tell a short story about the company's history.

Such a short story would begin in 1962; this is the year Sam Walton opened the first Wal-Mart store in Rogers, Arkansas. Interestingly enough, 1962 also marked the first year of operations for Kmart and Target. All three retailers are similar in their devotion to discount retailing. Indeed, Sam Walton began his venture into discount retailing, in part because his chain of

Arkansas and Kansas variety stores (what used to be called five- and ten-cent stores) had experienced competition from regional discount retailers. It was 1968 when Wal-Mart first ventured outside of Arkansas, establishing outlets in Missouri and Oklahoma.

By 1970 there were 38 Wal-Mart stores with annual sales of $44.2 million and 1,500 employees. By the end of the decade, sales had grown to $1.2 billion with 276 stores in 11 states and 21,000 employees. By its twenty-fifth anniversary in 1987, Wal-Mart had reached sales of $15.9 billion with 1,198 stores, and some 200,000 employees. Today, Wal-Mart stands as a "global colossus" with $256 billion in global revenue, 5,000 stores in 10 countries, and 1.3 million employees. It is said to be the largest private or non-government employer in the world.

What explains Wal-Mart's business success? According to the company's founder, "The secret of successful retailing is to give your customers what they want." And what do customers want? Sam Walton thought they wanted everything: "a wide assortment of good quality merchandise; the lowest possible prices; guaranteed satisfaction with what you buy; friendly, knowledgeable service; convenient hours; free parking; a pleasant shopping experience." Based on Wal-Mart's business success, Sam Walton's creation appears to give consumers what they want. And many, based on the growth figures previously cited, consider Wal-Mart to be the ultimate business success story.

But not everyone admires this business success. Rather, there are those who believe that Wal-Mart's business success has been built upon a series of abuses, with most of the abuses related to the company's goal of offering the lowest possible prices. These critics charge that in its drive to achieve its goal of lowest prices, Wal-Mart is driven to be anti-union, to pay low wages, to discriminates against women, to refuse to pay workers for some of their work, and to break child labor laws.

This issue examines the role of Wal-Mart in the economy. The first reading is a segment of an economic impact study prepared by the Los Angeles County Economic Development Corporation (LAEDC). In this study, paid for by Wal-Mart, the non-profit organization assesses what would happen if Wal-Mart began to open a series of so-called Supercenter stores in Southern California. The report concludes that Wal-Mart's entry into the Southern California market would be of major benefit to consumers and create a significant number of new jobs. The second reading, prepared by the Democratic Staff of the House Committee on Education and the Workforce, summarizes a series of reports prepared by others as well as a series of legal actions taken against Wal-Mart. The staff's conclusion from this summary is that Wal-Mart's business success has only been achieved at a very high social cost.

Wal-Mart Supercenters: What's in Store for Southern California?

Executive Summary

Wal-Mart Stores, Inc. is now the largest grocery retailer in the country based on sales. It is preparing to introduce its Supercenters, which combine a large general merchandise store with a full service market, into Southern California. The City of Los Angeles, in particular, with its 3.61 million people, 1.28 million households, and annual food store spending of approximately $5.65 billion, is a very attractive market. Wal-Mart's planned expansion into the local grocery business creates both a challenge to the major grocery store chains in the region, and an opportunity for cities to encourage strategic reinvestment in underserved neighborhoods.

The LAEDC [Los Angeles County Economic Development Corporation] agreed to assess the economic implications of Wal-Mart's entry into the Southern California grocery market because existing studies, which tend to tally only the negative impacts of Wal-Mart's operations, miss half the story. Here we aim to provide a fair and balanced assessment of both the good and not so good impacts of Supercenters in Southern California. Thus, we include not only the potential effects on existing grocery chains and their employees, but also the potential savings to consumers, and the potential job creation outside the grocery industry.

Costs and Savings

Wal-Mart Supercenters have a substantial cost advantage relative to traditional supermarkets, based on careful supply chain and inventory management, volume discounts, and lower labor costs. Much of this can be attributed to Wal-Mart's willingness to invest in technology and business practices which make its operations more efficient. Wal-Mart passes the savings on to consumers, offering lower prices on groceries than traditional grocery market chains. If Wal-Mart Supercenters are introduced in Los Angeles, food prices should fall.

Wal-Mart shoppers would immediately save an estimated average of 15 percent relative to what they would have paid under the current status quo. The savings could be higher, particularly in portions of the City of Los Angeles such as South Los Angeles and the northeast San Fernando Valley, which are underserved by traditional grocery stores. The corner stores where much of the food purchases in these areas take place offer uncompetitive prices relative to existing grocery stores, never mind Supercenters. As Wal-Mart gradually builds market share, major competitors will lower their prices as well, thus bringing additional savings to some consumers who will never set foot in a Wal-Mart store. Smaller stores will adjust by emphasizing specific market niches and specialty products which Wal-Mart does not provide.

The LAEDC conservatively calculated the potential savings to consumers in the City of Los Angeles to be *at least* $668 million, or $524 per household, annually, once Wal-Mart reaches 20 percent market share. The savings could be much higher, though the savings will not materialize overnight. They will increase gradually over many years in step with Wal-Mart's market share. These savings add to a household's discretionary *after tax dollars*—the portion of the income actually available for spending. This "found" money will be redirected to other items, including housing, savings, health, entertainment, and transportation. As households redeploy their savings, their spending will create jobs outside the grocery industry. In the City of Los Angeles, redirected grocery savings will create 6,500 additional jobs. The new jobs will be in a wide variety of occupations, reflecting the diverse spending patterns of Los Angeles households and the breadth of the regional economy.

The LAEDC also looked at the potential impact of Wal-Mart Supercenters on the entire Southern California market. In Los Angeles County, the aggregate annual savings to consumers would be at least $1.78 billion. When the savings are redirected to other purchases, the county-wide job creation will total 17,300 jobs. For consumers in Imperial, Los Angeles, Orange, Riverside, San Bernardino, San Diego and Riverside counties, the combined total annual savings will be at least $3.76 billion. The seven-county Southern California job creation total is 36,400 jobs.

Wal-Mart compensation, while lower than for the best-paid unionized grocery employees, is better than most people realize, particularly in its food business. Wal-Mart benefits include health care, a stakeholders' bonus, which is paid to employees at stores that perform well, profit-sharing, company contributions to 401(k) plans, which are the most common form of defined contribution retirement plan, a 15 percent discount on company stock, and a 10 percent discount on purchases of general merchandise. Wal-Mart's health-care plan requires employees to share the upfront costs (Wal-Mart pays 2/3rd; the associates pay 1/3rd), but in return does not have single incident or lifetime caps on coverage.

Two important factors make Wal-Mart's wages appear lower than they might otherwise. First, Supercenters are a relatively new phenomenon. Most Supercenters have simply not been open long enough to have accumulated many employees with lengthy service records, and thus higher rates of pay. Second, and perhaps most important, Wal-Mart's pay among its front line grocery workers is skewed downwards because it promotes from within. Wal-Mart recruits its management primarily from within the ranks of its own employees. This opens up career opportunities for associates, and crucially for wage comparisons, removes some of the most experienced and best paid Wal-Mart employees from the pool of workers typically being compared. In contrast to unionized grocery stores, where some of the most senior employees are cashiers, at Wal-Mart cashier is an entry level position.

Unionized grocery workers earn $2.50–$3.50 per hour more, on average, than Supercenter employees in Southern California could expect. Some union grocery workers are very well compensated, but the wages of the most highly compensated among them are frequently mistaken for *average* union wages, which are lower. The widely-cited Orange County Business Council (OCBC) study calculated the potential wage loss if all union workers in the Southern California grocery industry were to earn the same wages as Wal-Mart employees. Using more realistic assumptions of Wal-Mart Supercenter employee pay (and hence a narrower wage gap), we find the potential cumulative wage loss in Los Angeles County is $150 million to $258 million annually. For the 7-county Southern California region (including Los Angeles), the range is $307 million to $529 million. If all current unionized grocery employees were to eventually earn the equivalent of Wal-Mart Supercenter employees, the lost spending due to eroded household income could cost Los Angeles County alone 1,500 to 2,500 jobs and the 7-county region 3,000 to 5,100 jobs. Should these losses materialize, they would be offset by region-wide gains of 36,400 jobs, meaning that outside the grocery sector at least seven jobs would be added for every one lost.

Timing

Timing will be critical in determining the potential impact of Supercenters. Experience in other regions suggests that existing stores will have time to adjust. The potential benefits as well as the costs of Wal-Mart entering the Southern California grocery market described in this report assume that Wal-Mart will eventually gain a market share of 20 percent. Yet, gaining share will take a long time.

Wal-Mart will struggle to find suitable locations for its stores in many areas of heavily urbanized, built-out Southern California, including most of the City of Los Angeles. By comparison, in Fort Worth, Texas, it took Wal-Mart six years to achieve a 6.5 percent share in a market where stores can be built quickly. Unlike California, permitting, environmental regulation, and community opposition are not generally a factor in Texas, where growth has nonetheless proceeded at only a modest pace. Wal-Mart appears to be proceeding cautiously in California, with plans to build just 40 Supercenters in the state over the next three to five years. This represents just 4 percent of the 1,000 new Supercenters that will be added nationwide during the same period. Based solely on the state's share of the national population and the potential size of its market, the expected number of new Supercenters in California should be in the range of 100 to 150. If the distribution of existing Supercenters were factored in, the California number would be higher still. Again, by comparison, Texas, which is the nation's second most populous state, already has many Supercenters while California, the most populous state, has none.

The slow roll out of Supercenters in Southern California, compared to other regions, will delay the arrival of benefits for consumers, but it will also give Wal-Mart's competitors more time to adapt. With Southern California's rapidly growing population, Wal-Mart is likely to increase its presence by taking a greater share of overall market growth, rather than by luring existing customers from large supermarket chains. While a scenario in which Wal-Mart captures most of this growth may constitute a challenge for the major supermarket chains, their situation—aside from fierce price competition, which benefits consumers, and increased pressure on their balance sheets—is not likely to be significantly different than it is now.

Conclusion

All indicators suggest that Wal-Mart will gradually enter the grocery market in Southern California. A 20 percent market share may be achievable over time, but not in the near future. Unlike what has occurred in other parts of the country, Supercenters will be rolled out slowly here, delaying the arrival of benefits. Conversely, any negative impacts will also be delayed, and lessened, since competitors will have more time to adapt. Over the long term, Wal-Mart is likely to increase its market share by absorbing a larger share of overall market growth, rather than by attracting existing customers from the large grocery chains.

The real choice facing the City of Los Angeles is whether Wal-Mart will serve residents from within the city's boundaries or from without. If Wal-Mart decides to open Supercenters to serve demand in the region, the stores could conveniently serve customers residing in the City of Los Angeles from within the city, or from neighboring jurisdictions. In the former case, the city government would have the opportunity to influence Wal-Mart's presence. The City of Los Angeles could guide Wal-Mart and other large scale retailers to sites where their presence and spending would be a boon for local redevelopment. If, however, Wal-Mart builds in neighboring jurisdictions, the City of Los Angeles will have no control over the development. Wal-Mart customers in Los Angeles would leave the city to shop, taking their taxable spending (and any resulting local sales tax revenues) with them.

Study Highlights

Savings for Consumers and New Jobs Outside the Grocery Industry

- Supercenter customers will save an average of 15 percent on their groceries.
- Price competition will lead to reduced prices at existing grocery chains, providing customers who shop at stores other than Wal-Mart average savings of 10 percent.
- Increased competition in non-grocery items will lead to price reductions averaging 3 percent at general merchandise and apparel competitors.

- Money that people save on groceries will be redirected to other items, including housing, savings, health, entertainment, and transportation. This new spending will, in turn, create jobs outside the grocery industry.

Savings in the City of Los Angeles

- Consumers in the City of Los Angeles are conservatively estimated to save at least $668 million annually, or $524 per household, per year.
- Redirected grocery savings will create 6,500 additional full-time-equivalent jobs.

Savings in Los Angeles County

- Consumers in Los Angeles County are conservatively estimated to save at least $1.78 billion annually, or $569 per household, per year.
- Redirected grocery savings will create 17,300 new jobs County-wide.

Savings in Southern California

- Consumers in Imperial, Los Angeles, Orange, Riverside, San Bernardino, San Diego, and Ventura Counties are conservatively estimated to save at least $3.76 billion annually, or $589 per household, per year.
- In these seven counties, 36,400 new jobs will be created.

Potential Impacts to Major Grocery Chains

- Major grocery companies have used fear of intense competition to seek wage concessions from unionized employees, most likely by lowering the wages of new hires.
- Future foregone wages of unionized grocery employees in Los Angeles County could equal $150 million to $258 million annually, and could reach $307 to $529 million annually across the entire 7-county Southern California region.
- These foregone wages would reduce overall household spending, potentially costing Los Angeles County 1,500 to 2,500 jobs and the 7-county region (including Los Angeles) 3,000 to 5,100 jobs.
- These losses will be offset by region-wide gains of 36,400 jobs outside the grocery business, or a net gain of at least seven new jobs for every one lost.

Catalyst for Redevelopment

- Wal-Mart can be used as a catalyst for redevelopment, particularly in areas saddled with struggling (or failed) retail centers. In Panorama City, Wal-Mart replaced the Broadway department store, creating new jobs and revitalizing the mall and the surrounding neighborhood. Wal-Mart will open stores in an abandoned K-Mart in Canoga Park and in an abandoned AutoNation site in Harbor Gateway.
- Wal-Mart has demonstrated a willingness to enter communities that other businesses appear uninterested in serving. In Baldwin Hills, WalMart brought jobs and retail opportunities to an underserved community by opening a store in a former Macy's, which had sat vacant for five years.

- There are many parts of Los Angeles that are underserved by retail. The need is acute in the grocery sector and these communities stand to gain the most if Wal-Mart were to enter the market and offer lower prices.

Sales Tax Leakage

- Jurisdictions without Supercenters will lose taxable sales when their residents shop elsewhere. Supercenters have become an issue because they sell groceries, which are non-taxable. Sixty to seventy percent of the sales at Supercenters, however, are taxable. The appeal of Supercenters, for both Wal-Mart and the consumer, is that they allow shoppers to combine trips and do all of their purchasing in one location. If city residents choose to buy their groceries at Supercenters outside of the city, the City of L.A. will lose out on the local share of any taxable purchases shoppers make on those trips.
- Cities without Supercenters will also lose out on sales tax revenue when their residents combine trips to Wal-Mart with shopping at nearby stores.
- Overall sales taxes will increase to the extent that customers spend their savings generated from lower-priced groceries (which are not taxable) on goods which are taxable.
- The modest increase in overall taxable sales should not obscure the key issue—the distribution of taxable sales (and hence tax revenues) among Southern California jurisdictions based on where consumers choose to shop.

Everyday Low Wages: The Hidden Price We All Pay for Wal-Mart

Introduction

The retail giant Wal-Mart has become the nation's largest private sector employer with an estimated 1.2 million employees.[1] The company's annual revenues now amount to 2 percent of the U.S. Gross Domestic Product.[2] Wal-Mart's success is attributed to its ability to charge low prices in mega-stores offering everything from toys and furniture to groceries. While charging low prices obviously has some consumer benefits, mounting evidence from across the country indicates that these benefits come at a steep price for American workers, U.S. labor laws, and community living standards.

Wal-Mart is undercutting labor standards at home and abroad, while those federal officials charged with protecting labor standards have been largely indifferent. Public outcry against Wal-Mart's labor practices has been answered by the company with a cosmetic response. Wal-Mart has attempted to offset its labor record with advertising campaigns utilizing employees (who are euphemistically called "associates") to attest to Wal-Mart's employment benefits and support of local communities. Nevertheless—whether the issue is basic organizing rights of workers, or wages, or health benefits, or working conditions, or trade policy—Wal-Mart has come to represent the lowest common denominator in the treatment of working people.

This report reviews Wal-Mart's labor practices across the country and around the world and provides an overview of how working Americans and their allies in Congress are seeking to address the gamut of issues raised by this new standard-bearer of American retail.

Wal-Mart's Labor Practices

Workers' Organizing Rights

The United States recognizes workers' right to organize unions. Government employers generally may not interfere with public sector employees' freedom

From the Democratic Staff of the House Committee on Education and the Workforce, February 16, 2004.

of association. In the private sector, workers' right to organize is protected by the National Labor Relations Act.[3] Internationally, this right is recognized as a core labor standard and a basic human right.[4]

Wal-Mart's record on the right to organize recently achieved international notoriety. On January 14, 2004, the International Confederation of Free Trade Unions (ICFTU), an organization representing 151 million workers in 233 affiliated unions around the world, issued a report on U.S. labor standards.[5] Wal-Mart's rampant violations of workers' rights figured prominently. In the last few years, well over 100 unfair labor practice charges have been lodged against Wal-Mart throughout the country, with 43 charges filed in 2002 alone. Since 1995, the U.S. government has been forced to issue at least 60 complaints against Wal-Mart at the National Labor Relations Board.[6] Wal-Mart's labor law violations range from illegally firing workers who attempt to organize a union to unlawful surveillance, threats, and intimidation of employees who dare to speak out.

With not a single Wal-Mart store in the United States represented by a union, the company takes a pro-active role in maintaining its union-free status. Wal-Mart has issued "A Manager's Toolbox to Remaining Union Free," which provides managers with lists of warning signs that workers might be organizing, including "frequent meetings at associates' homes" and "associates who are never seen together start talking or associating with each other."[7] The "Toolbox" gives managers a hotline to call so that company specialists can respond rapidly and head off any attempt by employees to organize.

When employees have managed to obtain a union election and vote for a union, Wal-Mart has taken sweeping action in response. In 2000, when a small meatcutting department successfully organized a union at a Wal-Mart store in Texas, Wal-Mart responded a week later by announcing the phase-out of its meatcutting departments entirely. Because of deficient labor laws, it took the meatcutters in Texas three years to win their jobs back with an order that Wal-Mart bargain with their union.[8] Rather than comply, Wal-Mart is appealing this decision.[9]

Wal-Mart's aggressive anti-union activity, along with the nation's weak labor laws, have kept the largest private sector employer in the U.S. union-free. Breaking the law that guarantees workers' right to organize has material consequences for both the workers and the company. According to data released by the Bureau of Labor Statistics in January 2004, union workers earn median weekly salaries of $760, compared to non-union workers' median weekly salaries of $599—a difference of over 26 percent.[10] In the supermarket industry, the union difference is even more pronounced, with union members making 30 percent more than non-union workers. Union representation also correlates with higher benefits.[11] For instance, 72 percent of union workers have guaranteed pensions with defined benefits, while only 15 percent of non-union workers enjoy such retirement security.[12] On the health care front, which will be explored in more detail later, 60 percent of union workers have medical care benefits on the job, compared to only 44 percent of non-union workers.[13] For companies like Wal-Mart seeking to maintain low labor costs, these statistics obviously provide an incentive to remain union-free.

Unfortunately, U.S. labor laws fail to provide a sufficient disincentive against violating workers' rights.

Low Wages

By keeping unions at bay, Wal-Mart keeps its wages low—even by general industry standards. The average supermarket employee makes $10.35 per hour.[14] Sales clerks at Wal-Mart, on the other hand, made only $8.23 per hour on average, or $13,861 per year, in 2001.[15] Some estimate that average "associate" salaries range from $7.50 to $8.50 per hour.[16] With an average on-the-clock workweek of 32 hours, many workers take home less than $1,000 per month.[17] Even the higher estimate of a $13,861 annual salary fell below the 2001 federal poverty line of $14,630 for a family of three.[18] About one-third of Wal-Mart's employees are part-time, restricting their access to benefits.[19] These low wages, to say the least, complicate employees' ability to obtain essential benefits, such as health care coverage, which will be explored in a later section.

The low pay stands in stark contrast to Wal-Mart's slogan, "Our people make the difference." Now-retired Senior Vice President Don Soderquist has explained: "'Our people make the difference' is not a meaningless slogan—it's a reality at Wal-Mart. We are a group of dedicated, hardworking, ordinary people who have teamed together to accomplish extraordinary things."[20] With 2002 company profits hitting $6.6 billion, Wal-Mart employees do indeed "accomplish extraordinary things."[21] But at poverty level wages, these workers are not sharing in the company's success.

Unequal Pay and Treatment

Title VII of the Civil Rights Act prohibits discrimination in employment based on employees' race, color, religion, sex, or national origin.[22] Additionally, the Equal Pay Act, an amendment to the Fair Labor Standards Act, prohibits unequal pay for equal work on the basis of sex.[23] These basic labor and civil rights laws have become an issue at Wal-Mart.

In 2001, six women sued Wal-Mart in California claiming the company discriminated against women by systematically denying them promotions and paying them less than men. The lawsuit has expanded to potentially the largest class action in U.S. history—on behalf of more than 1 million current and former female employees. While two-thirds of the company's hourly workers are female, women hold only one-third of managerial positions and constitute less than 15 percent of store managers.[24] The suit also claims that women are pushed into "female" departments and are demoted if they complain about unequal treatment. One plaintiff, a single mother of four, started at Wal-Mart in 1990 at a mere $3.85 an hour. Even with her persistent requests for training and promotions, it took her eight years to reach $7.32 an hour and seven years to reach management, while her male counterparts were given raises and promotions much more quickly. For this plaintiff, annual pay increases were as little as 10 cents and never more than 35 cents per hour.[25]

Off-the-Clock Work

While wages are low at Wal-Mart, too often employees are not paid at all. The Fair Labor Standards Act (FLSA), along with state wage and hour laws, requires hourly employees to be paid for all time actually worked at no less than a minimum wage and at time-and-a-half for all hours worked over 40 in a week.[26] These labor laws have posed a particular obstacle for Wal-Mart. As of December 2002, there were thirty-nine class-action lawsuits against the company in thirty states, claiming tens of millions of dollars in back pay for hundreds of thousands of Wal-Mart employees.[27]

In 2001, Wal-Mart forked over $50 million in unpaid wages to 69,000 workers in Colorado. These wages were paid only after the workers filed a class action lawsuit. Wal-Mart had been working the employees off-the-clock. The company also paid $500,000 to 120 workers in Gallup, New Mexico, who filed a lawsuit over unpaid work.[28]

In a Texas class-action certified in 2002 on behalf of 200,000 former and current Wal-Mart employees, statisticians estimated that the company short-changed its workers $150 million over four years—just based on the frequency of employees working through their daily 15 minute breaks.[29]

In Oregon, 400 employees in 27 stores sued the company for unpaid, off-the-clock overtime. In their suit, the workers explained that managers would delete hours from their time records and tell employees to clean the store after they clocked out. In December 2002, a jury found in favor of the workers.[30] One personnel manager claimed that, for six years, she was forced to delete hours from employee time sheets.[31]

In the latest class-action, filed in November 2003, noting evidence of systematic violations of the wage-and-hour law, a judge certified a lawsuit for 65,000 Wal-Mart employees in Minnesota. Reacting to the certification, a Wal-Mart spokesperson told the Minneapolis *Star Tribune:* "We have no reason to believe these isolated situations . . . represent a widespread problem with off-the clock work."[32]

Many observers blame the wage-and-hour problems at Wal-Mart on pressure placed on managers to keep labor costs down. In 2002, operating costs for Wal-Mart were just 16.6 percent of total sales, compared to a 20.7 percent average for the retail industry as a whole.[33] Wal-Mart reportedly awards bonuses to its employees based on earnings. With other operating and inventory costs set by higher level management, store managers must turn to wages to increase profits. While Wal-Mart expects those managers to increase sales each year, it expects the labor costs to be cut by two-tenths of a percentage point each year as well.[34]

Reports from former Wal-Mart managers seem to corroborate this dynamic. Joyce Moody, a former manager in Alabama and Mississippi, told the *New York Times* that Wal-Mart "threatened to write up managers if they didn't bring the payroll in low enough." Depositions in wage and hour lawsuits reveal that company headquarters leaned on management to keep their labor costs at 8 percent of sales or less, and managers in turn leaned on assistant managers to work their employees off-the-clock or simply delete time from employee time sheets.[35]

Child Labor and Work Breaks Violations

The Fair Labor Standards Act and state wage and hour laws also govern child labor and work breaks. These work time regulations have likewise posed a problem at Wal-Mart stores.

In January 2004, the *New York Times* reported on an internal Wal-Mart audit which found "extensive violations of child-labor laws and state regulations requiring time for breaks and meals."[36] One week of time records from 25,000 employees in July 2000 found 1,371 instances of minors working too late, during school hours, or for too many hours in a day. There were 60,767 missed breaks and 15,705 lost meal times.[37]

According to the *New York Times* report: "Verette Richardson, a former Wal-Mart cashier in Kansas City, Mo., said it was sometimes so hard to get a break that some cashiers urinated on themselves. Bella Blaubergs, a diabetic who worked at a Wal-Mart in Washington State, said she sometimes nearly fainted from low blood sugar because managers often would not give breaks."[38]

A store manager in Kentucky told the *New York Times* that, after the audit was issued, he received no word from company executives to try harder to cut down on violations: "There was no follow-up to that audit, there was nothing sent out I was aware of saying, 'We're bad. We screwed up. This is the remedy we're going to follow to correct the situation.'"[39]

Unaffordable or Unavailable Health Care

In 2002, 43 million non-elderly Americans lacked health insurance coverage—an increase of almost 2.5 million from the previous year. Most Americans receive their health insurance coverage through their employers. At the same time, most of the uninsured are working Americans and their families, with low to moderate incomes. Their employers, however, either do not offer health insurance at all or the health insurance offered is simply unaffordable.[40]

Among these uninsured working families are a significant number of Wal-Mart employees, many of whom instead secure their health care from publicly subsidized programs. Fewer than half—between 41 and 46 percent—of Wal-Mart's employees are insured by the company's health care plan, compared nationally to 66 percent of employees at large firms like Wal-Mart who receive health benefits from their employer.[41] In recent years, the company increased obstacles for its workers to access its health care plan.

In 2002, Wal-Mart increased the waiting period for enrollment eligibility from 90 days to 6 months for full-time employees. Part-time employees must wait 2 years before they may enroll in the plan, and they may not purchase coverage for their spouses or children. The definition of part-time was changed from 28 hours or less per week to less than 34 hours per week. At the time, approximately one-third of Wal-Mart's workforce was part-time. By comparison, nationally, the average waiting period for health coverage for employees at large firms like Wal-Mart was 1.3 months.[42]

The Wal-Mart plan itself shifts much of the health care costs onto employees. In 1999, employees paid 36 percent of the costs. In 2001, the employee burden rose to 42 percent. Nationally, large-firm employees pay on average 16 percent of the premium for health insurance. Unionized grocery workers typically pay nothing.[43] Studies show that much of the decline in employer-based health coverage is due to shifts of premium costs from employers to employees.[44]

Moreover, Wal-Mart employees who utilize their health care confront high deductibles and co-payments. A single worker could end up spending around $6,400 out-of-pocket—about 45 percent of her annual full-time salary—before seeing a single benefit from the health plan.[45]

According to an AFL-CIO report issued in October 2003, the employees' low wages and Wal-Mart's cost-shifting render health insurance unaffordable, particularly for those employees with families. Even under the Wal-Mart plan with the highest deductible ($1,000)—and therefore with the lowest employee premium contribution—it would take an $8 per hour employee, working 34 hours per week, almost one-and-a-half months of pre-tax earnings to pay for one year of family coverage.[46]

Wal-Mart's spending on health care for its employees falls well below industry and national employer-spending averages. A Harvard Business School case study on Wal-Mart found that, in 2002, Wal-Mart spent an average of $3,500 per employee. By comparison, the average spending per employee in the wholesale/retailing sector was $4,800. For U.S. employers in general, the average was $5,600 per employee.[47]

In the end, because they cannot afford the company health plan, many Wal-Mart workers must turn to public assistance for health care or forego their health care needs altogether. Effectively, Wal-Mart forces taxpayers to subsidize what should be a company-funded health plan. According to a study by the Institute for Labor and Employment at the University of California Berkeley, **California taxpayers subsidized $20.5 million worth of medical care for Wal-Mart in that state alone.**[48] In fact, Wal-Mart personnel offices, knowing employees cannot afford the company health plan, actually encourage employees to apply for charitable and public assistance, according to a recent report by the PBS news program *Now With Bill Moyers.*[49]

When a giant like Wal-Mart shifts health insurance costs to employees, its competitors invariably come under pressure to do the same. Currently engaged in the largest ongoing labor dispute in the nation, unionized grocery workers in southern California have refused to accept higher health care costs resulting from cost-shifting on health insurance premiums by their grocery chain employers—cost-shifting, the grocers say, inspired by the threat of Wal-Mart competition. Beginning on October 11, 2003, 70,000 grocery employees of Vons, Pavilions, Ralphs, and Albertsons have either been on strike or locked out. The companies want to dramatically increase workers' share of health costs, claiming that the change is necessary in order to compete with Wal-Mart's incursion in the southern California market. E. Richard Brown, the director of the Center for Health Policy at the University of California, Los Angeles, told the *Sacramento Bee* that, if the grocery chains drastically reduce health benefits, the trends toward cost shifting and elimination of health coverage will accelerate. Following the grocers' lead, more employers would offer fewer benefits, would require their workers to pay more, and may even drop health benefits altogether.[50] Whether the current pressure from Wal-Mart is real or imagined or merely a convenient excuse for the grocers' cost-cutting bargaining position, Wal-Mart has sparked a new race to the bottom among American retail employers. Undeniably, such a race threatens to undermine the employer-based health insurance system.

Low Wages Mean High Costs to Taxpayers

Because Wal-Mart wages are generally not living wages, the company uses taxpayers to subsidize its labor costs. While the California study showed how much taxpayers were subsidizing Wal-Mart on health care alone, the total costs to taxpayers for Wal-Mart's labor policies are much greater.

The Democratic Staff of the Committee on Education and the Workforce estimates that one 200-person Wal-Mart store may result in a cost to federal taxpayers of $420,750 per year—about $2,103 per employee. Specifically, the low wages result in the following additional public costs being passed along to taxpayers:

- $36,000 a year for free and reduced lunches for just 50 qualifying Wal-Mart families.
- $42,000 a year for Section 8 housing assistance, assuming 3 percent of the store employees qualify for such assistance, at $6,700 per family.
- $125,000 a year for federal tax credits and deductions for low-income families, assuming 50 employees are heads of household with a child and 50 are married with two children.
- $100,000 a year for the additional Title I expenses, assuming 50 Wal-Mart families qualify with an average of 2 children.
- $108,000 a year for the additional federal health care costs of moving into state children's health insurance programs (S-CHIP), assuming 30 employees with an average of two children qualify.
- $9,750 a year for the additional costs for low income energy assistance.

Among Wal-Mart employees, some single workers may be able to make ends meet. Others may be forced to take on two or three jobs. Others may have a spouse with a better job. And others simply cannot make ends meet. Because Wal-Mart fails to pay sufficient wages, U.S. taxpayers are forced to pick up the tab. In this sense, Wal-Mart's profits are not made only on the backs of its employees—but on the backs of every U.S. taxpayer.

The ultimate costs are not limited to subsidies for underpaid Wal-Mart workers. When a Wal-Mart comes to town, the new competition has a ripple effect throughout the community. Other stores are forced out of business or forced to cut employees' wages and benefits in order to compete with Wal-Mart. The Los Angeles City Council commissioned a report in 2003 on the effects of allowing Wal-Mart Supercenters into their communities. The report, prepared by consulting firm Rodino and Associates, found that Supercenters drive down wages in the local retail industry, place a strain on public services, and damage small businesses. It recommended that the City Council refuse to allow any Supercenters to be built in Los Angeles without a promise from Wal-Mart to increase wages and benefits for its employees.[51]

The findings of the Rodino report are alarming. The labor impacts of a Wal-Mart Supercenter on low-income communities include:

- "Big box retailers and superstores may negatively impact the labor market in an area by the conversion of higher paying retail jobs to a fewer number of lower paying retail jobs. The difference in overall compensation (wages and benefits) may be as much as $8.00."
- "Lack of health care benefits of many big box and superstore employees can result in a greater public financial burden as workers utilize emergency rooms as a major component of their health care."
- "A study conducted by the San Diego Taxpayers Association (SDCTA), a nonprofit, nonpartisan organization, found that an influx of big-box stores into San Diego would result in an annual decline in wages and benefits between $105 million and $221 million, and an increase of $9 million in public health costs. SDCTA also estimated that the region would lose pensions and retirement benefits valued between $89 million and $170 million per year and that even increased sales and property tax revenues would not cover the extra costs of necessary public services."
- "[The threat of Wal-Mart's incursion into the southern California grocery market] is already triggering a dynamic in which the grocery stores are negotiating with workers for lowered compensation, in an attempt to re-level the 'playing field.'"
- "One study of superstores and their potential impact on grocery industry employees found that the entry of such stores into the Southern California regional grocery business was expected to depress industry wages and benefits at an estimated range from a low of $500 million to a high of almost $1.4 billion annually, potentially affecting 250,000 grocery industry employees ... [T]he full impact of lost wages and benefits throughout Southern California could approach $2.8 billion per year."[52]

Reports such as these have provided supporting evidence to localities which seek to pass ordinances restricting "big box" or supercenter stores. Such ordinances were recently passed in Alameda and Contra Costa counties in California. Wal-Mart, however, has moved to overturn those ordinances. In Contra Costa, Wal-Mart launched a petition drive to challenge that county's ordinance in a referendum in March 2004. In Alameda, the company has filed a lawsuit to void an ordinance passed by the Board of Supervisors in January 2004.[53]

One of the most cited studies on Wal-Mart's impact on local communities was performed by economist Kenneth Stone at Iowa State University in 1993. Stone looked at the impact of Wal-Mart on small towns in Iowa. He found a 3 percent spike in total retail sales in communities immediately after a Wal-Mart opened. But the longer term effects of Wal-Mart were disastrous for nearby independent businesses. Over the course of the next several years, retailers' sales of mens' and boys' apparel dropped 44 percent on average, hardware sales fell by 31 percent, and lawn and garden sales fell by 26 percent. Likewise, a Congressional Research Service report in 1994 explained that Wal-Mart uses a saturation strategy with store development. In other words, it builds stores in nearby connected markets in order to stifle any competition in the targeted area by the size of its presence.[54]

By all accounts, Wal-Mart's development strategy has been working. Currently, Wal-Mart operates around 3,000 total stores and close to 1,400 Supercenters. It is the largest grocer in the U.S., with a 19 percent market share, and the third-largest pharmacy, with a 16 percent market share. According to Retail Forward, a global management consulting and research firm, for every one Supercenter that will open, two supermarkets will close.[55] Since 1992, the supermarket industry has experienced a net loss of 13,500 stores.[56] Over the next five years, Wal-Mart plans to open 1,000 more Supercenters in the U.S.[57] By 2007, Wal-Mart is expected to control 35 percent of food and drug sales in the U.S.[58]

Illegal Use of Undocumented Workers

Among the lowest paid workers in the U.S. economy are undocumented immigrants. As was reported in the fall of 2003, these workers are not foreign to the floors of Wal-Mart stores. On October 23, 2003, federal agents raided 61 Wal-Mart stores in 21 states. When they left, the agents had arrested 250 nightshift janitors who were undocumented workers.[59]

Following the arrests, a grand jury convened to consider charging Wal-Mart executives with labor racketeering crimes for knowingly allowing undocumented workers to work at their stores. The workers themselves were employed by agencies Wal-Mart contracted with for cheap cleaning services. While Wal-Mart executives have tried to lay the blame squarely with the contractors, federal investigators point to wiretapped conversations showing that executives knew the workers were undocumented.[60]

Additionally, some of the janitors have filed a class-action lawsuit against Wal-Mart alleging both racketeering and wage-and-hour violations. According to the janitors, Wal-Mart and its contractors failed to pay them overtime totaling, along with other damages, $200,000. One of the plaintiffs told the *New York Times* that he worked seven days per week for eight months, earning $325 for 60-hour weeks, and he never received overtime.[61] A legal question now being raised is whether these undocumented workers even have the right to sue their employers.[62]

Not surprisingly, this recent raid was not the first time Wal-Mart was caught using undocumented workers. In 1998 and 2001, federal agents arrested 102 undocumented workers at Wal-Marts around the country.[63]

President Bush's newly proposed temporary foreign worker plan would legalize such undocumented workers without granting them an opportunity for citizenship, creating a new class of indentured servants and a safer source of cheap labor for companies like Wal-Mart.

Trading Away Jobs

Since the recession began in March 2001, the United States has lost 2.4 million jobs. In every recession, since the Great Depression, jobs were recovered within the first 31 months after the recession began—until now. The latest recession began 34 months ago and officially ended in November 2001, but the jobs have not been recovered. For American working families, by all accounts, the "jobless recovery" has been of little benefit to them. While GDP growth was strong or solid in the third and fourth quarters of 2003, real wages for workers remained stagnant and even declined.[64]

Indeed, of the jobs that remain, the pay is low. The country has seen a dramatic shift from high-paying jobs to low-paying jobs. For instance, in New Hampshire, which still has not recovered the number of jobs it lost in the recession, new jobs pay 35 percent lower wages than lost jobs. In Delaware, those wages are 43 percent lower; in Colorado, 35 percent lower; in West Virginia, 33 percent lower. In fact, the low-pay shift has hit all but two of the fifty states.[65]

Moreover, these changes in the labor market reveal themselves in a marked decline in living standards for low- and middle-income workers. The real weekly earnings for full-time workers age 25 and older fell for the bottom half of the workforce between the fourth quarters of 2002 and 2003. In particular, workers in the 10th percentile saw their weekly earnings fall 1.2 percent; in the 20th percentile, by 0.5 percent, in the 50th percentile, by 0.1 percent.[66] Conversely, earners in the top percentiles of income experienced growth. The 90th percentile, for instance, saw a 1.1 percent increase in weekly earnings. As the Economic Policy Institute points out: "This pattern of earnings growth suggests that while the economy is expanding, the benefits of growth are flowing to those at the top of the wage scale."[67]

These lower-paying jobs are largely service sector jobs, like retail, replacing traditionally higher-paying and unionized manufacturing jobs. Between January 1998 and August 2003, the nation experienced a net loss of 3 million manufacturing jobs.[68] During the "recovery," 1.3 million manufacturing jobs disappeared.[69] American manufacturers find it increasingly difficult to keep jobs in the U.S., given the availability of cheap labor abroad. In 2003, the U.S. trade deficit hit a record high of $551 billion, increasing 15 percent from 2002 and exceeding 5 percent of GDP.[70]

Wal-Mart plays a curiously illustrative role in this jobs phenomenon—not just in the creation of low-paying jobs and the downward pressure on wages and benefits, but also in the export of existing manufacturing jobs to foreign countries offering cheap labor. Wal-Mart markets itself with a patriotic, small-town, red-white-and-blue advertising motif. But Wal-Mart's trade practices are anything but small-town. Indeed, Wal-Mart conducts international trade in manufactured goods on a scale that can bring down entire nations' economies.

While the red-white-and-blue banners remain, long-gone are the days when Wal-Mart abided by the mottos of "Buy American" and "Bring It Home to the USA." In 1995, Wal-Mart claimed only 6 percent of its merchandise was imported. Today an estimated 50–60 percent of its products come from overseas.[71] In the past five years, Wal-Mart has doubled its imports from China. In 2002, the company bought 14 percent of the $1.9 billion of clothes exported by Bangladesh to the United States. Also in 2002, the company purchased $12 billion in merchandise from China, or 10 percent of China's total U.S.-bound exports, a 20 percent increase from the previous year. In 2003, these Chinese purchases jumped to $15 billion, or almost one-eighth of all Chinese exports to the United States.[72] Today, more than 3,000 supplier factories in China produce for Wal-Mart.[73]

Wal-Mart maintains an extensive global network of 10,000 suppliers.[74] Whether American, Bangladeshi, Chinese, or Honduran, Wal-Mart plays these producers against one another in search of lower and lower prices. American suppliers have been forced to relocate their businesses overseas to maintain Wal-Mart contracts.[75] Overseas manufacturers are forced to engage in cut-throat competition that further erodes wages and working conditions of what often already are sweatshops. To keep up with the pressure to produce ever cheaper goods, factories force employees to work overtime or work for weeks without a day off. A Bangladeshi factory worker told the *Los Angeles Times* that employees at her factory worked from 8 a.m. to 3 a.m. for 10 and 15 day stretches just to meet Wal-Mart price demands. And still, Wal-Mart's general manager for Bangladesh complained of his country's factories, telling the *Los Angeles Times,* "I think they need to improve. When I entered a factory in China, it seemed they are very fast."[76]

While low-wage jobs displace higher-paid manufacturing jobs in the United States, undercutting living standards at home, living standards abroad are not reaping the benefits one might expect. Reports indicate that Wal-Mart's bargaining power is able to maintain low wages and poor working conditions among its foreign suppliers. The *Washington Post* has explained: "As capital scours the globe for cheaper and more malleable workers, and as poor countries seek multinational companies to provide jobs, lift production, and open export markets, Wal-Mart and China have forged themselves into the ultimate joint venture, their symbiosis influencing the terms of labor and consumption the world over."[77] Thanks to a ban on independent trade unions and a lack of other basic human rights, China offers Wal-Mart a highly-disciplined and cheap workforce. A Chinese labor official who asked to remain anonymous for fear of punishment told the *Washington Post* that "Wal-Mart pressures the factory to cut its price, and the factory responds with longer hours or lower pay. And the workers have no options."[78]

One employee of a Chinese supplier described the difficulties of surviving on $75 per month. She could rarely afford to buy meat, and her family largely subsisted on vegetables. Over four years, she had not received a single salary increase.[79]

Wal-Mart has countered that it insists that its suppliers enforce labor standards and comply with Chinese law. One-hundred Wal-Mart auditors inspect Chinese plants, and the company has suspended contracts with about 400 suppliers, mainly for violating overtime limits. An additional 72 factories were permanently blacklisted in 2003 for violating child labor standards. Still, critics point out that the Wal-Mart does not regularly inspect smaller factories that use middlemen to sell to the company. Nor does it inspect the factories of subcontractors. A Chinese labor organizer explained that the inspections are "ineffective," since Wal-Mart usually notifies the factories in advance. The factories "often prepare by cleaning up, creating fake time sheets and briefing workers on what to say."[80]

The factories themselves complain that, because Wal-Mart demands such low prices, they have slim profit margins—if any. A manager of one Chinese supplier told the *Washington Post,* "In the beginning, we made money . . . But when Wal-Mart started to launch nationwide distribution, they pressured us for a special price below our cost. Now, we're losing money on every box, while Wal-Mart is making more money."[81] Obviously, one way to regain a profit for such suppliers would be to begin cutting back on labor costs.

Finally, as testament to Wal-Mart's stalwart anti-union policy, none of its 31 stores in China are unionized, despite the fact that the Communist Party-controlled official union has told the company that it would not help workers fight for higher pay.[82] Oddly enough, Article 10 of China's Trade Union Law requires that any establishment with 25 or more workers must have a union. Wal-Mart, however, claims that it has received assurances from the central government that it need not allow unions in any of its stores.[83] As one reporter has explained, "The explanation for the apparent contradiction may be that the government's desire for foreign investment and jobs trumps any concern for workers' rights. That wouldn't be surprising in the Chinese environment, where strikes are forbidden and the official labor grouping actively supports the government's efforts to block the rise of independent unions."[84] With China, any company in search of pliant and cheap labor has found a perfect mix of cooperative government officials and workers made submissive through fear.

Disability Discrimination

The Americans with Disabilities Act (ADA) prohibits discrimination against persons with disabilities in employment matters. In particular, an employer may not discriminate against an employee or prospective employee who is otherwise qualified to perform the job if given reasonable accommodations.[85]

In addition to lawsuits over lost wages or unequal pay, Wal-Mart has faced a barrage of lawsuits alleging that the company discriminates against workers with disabilities. In 2001, Wal-Mart paid over $6 million to settle 13 such lawsuits. These cases were brought by the U.S. Equal Employment Opportunity Commission (EEOC) on behalf of disabled persons whom Wal-Mart failed to hire. The settlement also required Wal-Mart to change its procedures in dealing with disabled job applicants and provide more training for its employees on anti-discrimination laws.[86]

Yet, on January 20, 2004, the EEOC filed another lawsuit against the retail giant on behalf of a job applicant who claims he was not hired because he needed a wheelchair. The lawsuit was filed in Kansas City after the EEOC failed to obtain a settlement with Wal-Mart.[87]

Worker Safety

The Occupational Safety and Health Act (OSHA) is designed to protect workers from workplace injuries and illnesses.[88] OSHA is enforced by the

Department of Labor's Occupational Safety and Health Administration. Regulations issued by that agency lay out clear rules for such safety matters as the provision of exits for employees.[89]

The latest Wal-Mart scandal to hit the news is its reported lockdown of its nighttime shift various stores around the country. According to a January 18, 2004, *New York Times* report, the company institutes a "lock-in" policy at some of its Wal-Mart and Sam's Club stores.[90] The stores lock their doors at night so that no one can enter or leave the building, leaving workers inside trapped. Some workers are then threatened that, if they ever use the fire exit to leave the building, they will be fired. Instead, a manager is supposed to have a key that will unlock doors to allow employees to escape. Many workers have found themselves locked in without a manager who has a key, as the *New York Times* story detailed.[91]

The company has claimed that the policy is designed to protect stores and employees from crime. Former store managers, however, have claimed the real reason behind the lockdown is to prevent "shrinkage"—i.e., theft by either employees or outsiders. It is also designed to eliminate unauthorized cigarette breaks or quick trips home.[92]

Locked-in workers have had to wait for hours off-the-clock for a manager to show up to let them go home after they completed their shift. One worker claims to have broken his foot on the job and had to wait four hours for someone to open the door. Another worker alleges she cut her hand with box cutters one night and was forced to wait until morning to go to the hospital, where she received thirteen stitches.[93]

In the history of American worker safety, some of the worst tragedies have involved employees locked in their workplaces in an emergency, including the Triangle Waist Company fire of 1911 in which 146 women died in a fire because the garment factory's doors were locked. As recently as 1991, 25 workers perished in a fire at a chicken processing plant in North Carolina. The plant's owner had locked the doors for fear of employee theft and unauthorized breaks. According to recent reports, ten percent of Wal-Mart's stores are subjected to the nighttime lockdown.[94]

In 2002, in a telling junction of alleged labor law violations, the National Labor Relations Board (NLRB) issued a complaint against a Wal-Mart in Texas regarding health and safety threats made by management against employees. According to the complaint, a company official told workers that, after a worker filed complaints regarding unsafe conditions with the Occupational Safety and Health Administration (OSHA), any fines imposed upon the company would come out of employee bonuses.[95] . . .

Conclusion

Wal-Mart's success has meant downward pressures on wages and benefits, rampant violations of basic workers' rights, and threats to the standard of living in communities across the country. The success of a business need not come at the expense of workers and their families. Such short-sighted profit-making strategies ultimately undermine our economy.

In the past few years, Wal-Mart has been subjected to dozens of class-action suits seeking backpay for hundreds of thousands of shortchanged workers, dozens of unfair labor practice complaints by the U.S. government for violations of workers' right to organize, and other legal actions stemming from the company's employment practices. At the same time, it has managed to keep its wages low and put suppliers on a downward spiral to cut their own wages. To keep up with Wal-Mart's low-cost demands, U.S. manufacturers have found it increasingly difficult to remain in the U.S. Cuts in health care benefits to Wal-Mart employees are pushing other U.S. grocers to do the same.

Wal-Mart's current behavior must not be allowed to set the standard for American labor practices. Standing together, America's working families, including Wal-Mart employees, and their allies in Congress can reverse this race to the bottom in the fast-expanding service industry. The promise that every American can work an honest day's work, receive an honest day's wages, raise a family, own a home, have decent health care, and send their children to college is a promise that is not easily abandoned. It is, in short, the American Dream.

Notes

1. Anthony Bianco and Wendy Zellner, "Is Wal-Mart Too Powerful?" *Business Week* 100 (October 6, 2003).

2. Charles Stein, "Wal-Mart Finds Success, Image Breed Contempt," *Boston Globe* H1 (November 30, 2003).

3. 29 U.S.C. § 141 *et seq.*

4. International Labor Organization, Convention No. 87, Freedom of Association and Protection of the Right to Organize (1948), and No. 98, Right to Organize and Collective Bargaining (1949).

5. International Confederation of Free Trade Unions (ICFTU), *Internationally Recognised Core Labour Standards in the United States: Report for the WTO General Council Review of the Trade Policies of the United States* (Geneva, January 14-16, 2004).

6. *Id.* at 3-4.

7. Wal-Mart, *A Manager's Toolbox to Remaining Union Free* at 20-21 (no date). Available online at. . . .

8. Pan Demetrakakes, "Is Wal-Mart Wrapped in Union Phobia?" *Food & Packaging* 76 (August 1, 2003).

9. Dan Kasler, "Labor Dispute Has Historical Precedent," *Scripps Howard News Service* (November 3, 2003).

10. Bureau of Labor Statistics, Department of Labor, "Union Members in 2003," Table 1 (January 21, 2004).

11. Stephen Franklin and Delroy Alexander, "Grocery Walkouts Have Broad Reach," *Chicago Tribune* C1 (November 12, 2003).

12. Bureau of Labor Statistics, Department of Labor, "Employee Benefits in Private Industry, 2003," Table 1 (September 17, 2003).

13. *Id.*

14. Charles Williams, "Supermarket Sweepstakes: Traditional Grocery Chains Mull Responses to Wal-Mart's Growing Dominance," *The Post and Courier* (Charleston, SC) 16E (November 10, 2003).

15. *Id.*

16. "Unaffordable Health Care, Low Wages, Sexual Discrimination—the Wal-Mart Way of Life," . . . (January 26, 2004).

17. Doug Dority, "The People's Campaign: Justice@Wal-Mart," *Air Line Pilot* 55 (February 2003).

18. Bianco and Zellner, *supra* note 1.

19. PBS, "Store Wars: When Wal-Mart Comes to Town," . . . (February 2, 2004). This percentage of part-time employees was based on the earlier Wal-Mart definition of part-time as working 28 hours or less per week. In 2002, Wal-Mart changed the definition to less than 34 hours per week, which likely increased the company's number of part-time workers.

20. Wal-Mart.com, "3 Basic Beliefs," . . . (January 26, 2004).

21. Karen Olsson, "Up Against Wal-Mart," *Mother Jones* 54 (March/April 2003).

22. 42 U.S.C. § 2000e *et seq.*

23. 29 U.S.C. § 206.

24. Neil Buckley and Caroline Daniel, "Wal-Mart vs. the Workers: Labour Grievances Are Stacking Up Against the World's Biggest Company," *Financial Times* 11 (November 20, 2003).

25. Sheryl McCarthy, "Wal-Mart—Always Low Wages for Women!" *Newsday* (May 1, 2003).

26. 29 U.S.C. § 201 *et seq.*

27. Associated Press, "Federal Jury Finds Wal-Mart Guilty in Overtime Pay Case," *Chicago Tribune*, Business 3 (December 20, 2003).

28. *Id.*

29. Steven Greenhouse, "Suits Say Wal-Mart Forces Workers to Toil Off the Clock," *New York Times* A1 (June 25, 2002).

30. Associated press, *supra* note 27.

31. Kristian Foden-Vencil, "Multiple Lawsuits Accuse Wal-Mart of Violating Workplace Regulations," *NPR Morning Edition* (January 14, 2004).

32. Gwendolyn Freed and John Reenan, "Wal-Mart Suit Gets Class Status," *Star Tribune* 1D (November 6, 2003).

33. Greenhouse, *supra* note 29.

34. United Food & Commercial Workers (UFCW), "Wal-Mart's War on Workers' Wages and Overtime Pay," . . . (January 26, 2004).

35. Greenhouse, *supra* note 29.

36. Steven Greenhouse, "In-House Audit Says Wal-Mart Violated Labor Laws," *New York Times* 16A (January 13, 2004).

37. *Id.*

38. *Id.*

39. *Id.*

40. Kaiser Family Foundation, *The Uninsured: A Primer—Key Facts About Americans Without Health Insurance,* at 1 (December 2003).

41. AFL-CIO, *Wal-Mart: An Example of Why Workers Remain Uninsured and Underinsured,* at 1 (October 2003).

42. *Id.* at 11.

43. *Id.*

44. John Holahan, "Changes in Employer-Sponsored Health Insurance Coverage," *Snapshots of America's Families III,* Urban Institute (September 17, 2003).

45. AFL-CIO, *supra* note 41, at 16.

46.   *Id*. at 12.

47.   Panjak Ghemawat, Ken Mark, and Stephen Bradley, "Wal-Mart Stores in 2003," case study, Harvard Business School (revised January 30, 2004).

48.   Sylvia Chase, "The True Cost of Shopping at Wal-Mart," *Now with Bill Moyers,* Transcript (December 19, 2003).

49.   *Id.*

50.   Laura Mecoy, "Health Benefits Fight Heats Up: South State Grocery Strike Spotlights a Contentious Trend in Contract Talks," *Sacramento Bee* A1 (January 19, 2004).

51.   Nancy Cleeland, "City Report is Critical of Wal-Mart Supercenters," *Los Angeles Times* C1 (December 6, 2003).

52.   Rodino Associates, *Final Report on Research for Big Box Retail/Superstore Ordinance,* prepared for Industrial and Commercial Development Division, Community Development Department, at 18–20 (October 28, 2003).

53.   Michelle Maitre, "Wal-Mart is Suing Alameda County: Retail Giant Challenges Law that Bars Supercenters in Unincorporated Areas," *Alameda Times-Star* (Alameda, CA) at More Local News (January 27, 2004).

54.   Jessica Hall and Jim Troy, "Wal-Mart Go Home! Wal-Mart's Expansion Juggernaut Stumbles as Towns Turn Thumbs Down and Noses Up," *Warfield's Business Record* 1 (July 22, 1994).

55.   Bianco and Zellner, *supra* note 1.

56.   Matthew Swibel, "How to Outsmart Wal-Mart," . . . (November 24, 2003).

57.   Bianco and Zellner, *supra* note 1.

58.   Williams, supra note 14.

59.   Steven Greenhouse, "Suit by Wal-Mart Cleaners Asserts Rackets Violation," *New York Times,* 12A (November 11, 2003).

60.   Greg Schneider and Dina ElBoghdady, "Wal-Mart Confirms Probe of Hiring," *Washington Post* E1 (November 5, 2003).

61.   Greenhouse, *supra* note 59.

62.   Sarah Paoletti, "Q: Should illegal aliens be able to sue U.S. employers for labor racketeering?; Yes: Employees who have suffered discrimination or exploitation in the workplace are entitled to sue, regardless of their immigration status," *Insight Magazine* 46 (January 19, 2004).

63.   Steven Greenhouse, "Illegally in the U.S., and Never a Day Off at Wal-Mart," *International Herald Tribune* 2 (November 6, 2003).

64.   Jobwatch.org, Economic Policy Institute, . . . (January 26, 2004).

65.   Economic Policy Institute, "Jobs Shift from Higher-Paying to Lower-Paying Industries," *Economic Snapshots* (January 21, 2004).

66.   Economic Policy Institute, "Economic Growth Not Reaching Middle- and Lower Wage Earners," *Economic Snapshots* (January 28, 2004).

67.   *Id.*

68.   Josh Bivens, Robert Scott, and Christian Weller, "Mending Manufacturing: Reversing poor policy decisions is the only way to end current crisis," *EPI Briefing Paper #44* (September 2003).

69.   Economic Policy Institute, "Job Growth Up, Job Quality Down," *Economic Snapshots* (December 17, 2003).

70.   Economic Policy Institute, "Souring Trade Deficit Threatens to Destabilize U.S. Financial Markets," *Economic Snapshots* (January 7, 2004).

71.   Nancy Cleeland, Evelyn Iritani, and Tyler Marshall, "The Wal-Mart Effect: Scouring the Globe to Give Shoppers an $8.63 Polo Shirt," *Los Angeles Times* A1 (November 24, 2003).

72. Peter S. Goodman and Philip P. Pan, "Chinese Workers Pay for Wal-Mart's Low Prices," *Washington Post* A1 (February 8, 2004).

73. Cleeland, Iritani, and Marshall, *supra* note 71.

74. *Id.*

75. Abigail Goodman and Nancy Cleeland, "The Wal-Mart Effect: An Empire Built on Bargains Remakes the Working World," *L.A. Times* 1 (November 23, 2003); Charles Fishman, "The Wal-Mart You Don't Know," *Fast Company* 68 (December 2003).

76. Cleeland, Iritani, and Marshall, *supra* note 71.

77. Goodman and Pan, *supra* note 72.

78. *Id.*

79. *Id.*

80. *Id.*

81. *Id.*

82. *Id.*

83. Carl Goldstein, "Wal-Mart in China," *The Nation* (November 20, 2003).

84. *Id.*

85. 29 U.S.C. § 706 *et seq.*

86. "Disabled Man Sues Wal-Mart," *Business Journal* (Kansas City) (January 20, 2004).

87. *Id.*

88. 29 U.S.C. § 651 *et seq.*

89. 29 C.F.R. 1910.35 *et seq.*

90. Steven Greenhouse, "Workers Assail Lock-Ins by Wal-Mart," *New York Times* 1 (January 18, 2004).

91. *Id.*

92. *Id.*

93. *Id.*

94. *Id.*

95. Walmartwatch.org, "Wal-Mart's War on Workers: Frontline Report from Texas and California," . . . (May 2, 2002).

POSTSCRIPT

Is Wal-Mart Good for the Economy?

LAEDC believes that the entry of Wal-Mart Supercenter stores into Southern California would lead to lower prices for consumers on their grocery, general merchandise, and apparel purchases. The magnitude of the savings is estimated for the City of Los Angeles, for Los Angeles County, and for Southern California. For the latter, the establishment of Wal-Mart Supercenters would eventually lead to savings amounting to $3.76 billion per year. LAEDC believes that consumers would take these savings and spend them on other things and thereby create new jobs. For the City of Los Angeles, the redirected grocery savings alone would create some 6,500 new jobs.

The Democratic Staff of the House Committee on Education and the Workforce cites a number of deficiencies in Wal-Mart's behavior. It charges that Wal-Mart has violated workers' right to organize, maintained low wages, discriminated against women and the disabled, failed to pay employees for all the hours they worked, violated child labor laws, provided inadequate health care insurance, used undocumented workers, and traded away jobs. When all these deficiencies are considered, the Democratic Staff concludes that the costs of Wal-Mart's low prices are just too high.

Perhaps the best place to start with additional readings on this issue is the complete versions of the LAEDC and the Democratic Staff reports. The former can be found at http://www.google.com/search?q=cache:k2x3GeYdFOgJ: www.mayocommunications.com/2003LAEDCIMAGES/WaMart%2520Supercenters% 2520%2520What's%2520in%2520store%2520for%2520Southern%2520California.pdf +Wal-mart+ecoomic+impact+study&hl=en&ie=UTF-8, while the latter can be found at http://edworkforce.house.gov/demcrats/WALMARTREPORT.pdf. There are a number of additional studies on the effects of Wal-Mart, including "The New Colossus" by Jay Nordlinger in the *National Review* (April 19, 2004); *The Case Against Wal-Mart* by Al Norman in *Raphel Marketing* (2004); "The Case for Wal-Mart" by Karen DeCoster and Brad Edmonds (January 31, 2003), http:// www.mises.org/fullstory.aspx?control=1151; "Declaring War on Wal-Mart" by Aaron Bernstein in *Business Week* (February 7, 2005); "Rejuvenating Wal-Mart's Reputation" by Thomas A. Hemphill in *Business Horizons* (January/February 2005); "Just Say No" by Julian E. Barnes and Tim Appenzeller in *U.S., News & World Report* (April 19, 2004); and "Up Against Wal-Mart" by Karen Olsson in *Mother Jones* (March/April 2003).

ISSUE 8

Should Social Security Be Changed to Include Personal Retirement Accounts?

YES: The White House, from "Strengthening Social Security for the 21st Century," http://www.whitehouse.gov/infocus/socialsecurity/200501/strengtheningsocialsecurity.html (February 2005)

NO: Dean Baker, from "Bush's Numbers Racket: Why Social Security Privatization Is a Phony Solution to a Phony Problem," *The American Prospect Online Edition* (February 1, 2005)

ISSUE SUMMARY

YES: The White House identifies a number of problems with the present structure of the Social Security system and proposes personal retirement accounts as a way of resolving these problems, and "dramatically reduce the costs of permanently fixing the system."

NO: Dean Baker, co-director of the Center for Economic and Policy Research, argues that President Bush's plan for personal retirement accounts would not fix Social Security; instead, it would "undermine a system that has provided security for ten of millions of workers, and their families, for seven decades, and which can continue to do so long into the future if it is just left alone."

In retrospect, it is not surprising that an event as catastrophic as the Great Depression of the 1930s would produce fundamental change in the American economy. The reality of the human suffering generated by the collapse of one-third of the nation's banks, an unemployment rate of 25 percent, and a 30 percent decline in the production of goods and services as well as household net worth led to a rush of legislation. The legislation, in general terms, was intended to achieve two objectives: to restore confidence in the economy and to provide greater economic security. Today the institutions and programs created by this legislative avalanche are familiar to almost all Americans, including the Federal Deposit Insurance Corporation, the Securities and Exchange Commission, and Social Security.

Social Security, more formally the Old Age, Survivors, and Disability Insurance Program (OASDI), was signed into law on August 14, 1935, by President Franklin D. Roosevelt. As originally designed, OASDI provided three types of benefits: retirement benefits to the elderly who were no longer working, survivor benefits to the spouses and children of persons who had died, and disability benefits to persons who experienced nonwork-related illness or injury. The Medicare portion of Social Security, which provides benefits for hospital, doctor, and medical expenses, was created in 1965 (see Issue 4).

There are many terms used to describe OASDI. It is an entitlement program in the sense that everyone who satisfies the eligibility requirements receives benefits. Eligibility is established by employment and contributions to the system (in the form of payroll taxes) for a minimum period of time. It is also a defined benefits program; that is, the level of benefits is determined by legislation. The opposite of a defined benefits program is a defined contributions program, where benefits are determined by contributions and whatever investment income is generated by those contributions. OASDI is also described as a pay-as-you-go system; this means that payments received by recipients are financed primarily by the contributions of current workers. Still another description of OASDI is that it is an income security program. In this context, the reference is to a whole set of government programs designed to provide minimum levels of income to various persons. Finally, OASDI is described as a social insurance program to distinguish it from private insurance programs. The insurance feature rests on the fact that OASDI protects against certain unforeseen events like disability or early death. The social feature arises from the fact that contributions and the level of benefits are determined by legislation as well as the fact that the contributions are mandatory (payroll taxes that must be paid). In a private insurance program, the beneficiary and the insurance issuer voluntarily negotiate the level of contributions and the level of benefits.

The Social Security "crisis" refers to the fact that with the currently legislated structure of revenues and benefits, the system will eventually be unable to meet its financial obligations. Presently revenues are greater than out-payments, and the excess is accumulated in a trust fund. Around the year 2019, out-payments will exceed revenues, and drawing down the trust fund will cover the difference. Eventually the trust fund will be exhausted, and revenues will only be sufficient to cover a portion of scheduled benefits. According to the most recent report from the Social Security Trustees, that year is 2042, and at that point revenues will be equal to 73 percent of scheduled benefits.

Strengthening Social Security for the 21st Century

The Problems Facing Social Security

- **A Social Security System designed for a 1935 world does not fit the needs of the 21st Century.** Social Security was designed in 1935 for a world that is very different from today. In 1935, most women did not work outside the home. Today, about 60% of women work outside the home. In 1935, the average American did not live long enough to collect retirement benefits. Today, life expectancy is 77 years. . . .
- **Social Security will not be changed for those 55 or older (born before 1950).** Today, more than 45 million Americans receive Social Security benefits and millions more are nearing retirement. For these Americans, Social Security benefits are secure and will not change in any way.
- **Social Security is making empty promises to our children and grandchildren.** For our younger workers, Social Security has serious problems that will grow worse over time. Social Security cannot afford to pay promised benefits to future generations because it was designed for a 1935 world in which benefits were much lower, life-spans were shorter, there were more workers per retiree, and fewer retirees were drawing from the system.
- **With each passing year, there are fewer workers paying ever-higher benefits to an ever-larger number of retirees.** Social Security is a pay-as-you-go system, which means taxes on today's workers pay the benefits for today's retirees. A worker's payroll taxes are not saved in an account with his or her name on it for the worker's retirement.
  - **There are fewer workers to support our retirees.** When Social Security was first created, there were 40 workers to support every one retiree, and most workers did not live long enough to collect retirement benefits from the system. Since then, the demographics of our society have changed dramatically. People are living longer and having fewer children. As a result we have seen a dramatic change in the number of workers supporting each retiree's benefits. According to the 2004 Report of the Social Security Trustees (page 47):

From Strengthening Social Security for the 21st Century, February 2005. http://www.whitehouse.gov/infocus/socialsecurity/200501/strengtheningsocialsecurity.html. References omitted.

- In 1950, there were 16 workers to support every one beneficiary of Social Security.
- Today, there are only 3.3 workers supporting every Social Security beneficiary.
- And, by the time our youngest workers turn 65, there will be only 2 workers supporting each beneficiary.
- **Benefits are scheduled to rise dramatically over the next few decades.** Because benefits are tied to wage growth rather than inflation, benefits are growing faster than the rest of the economy. This benefit formula was established in 1977. As a result, today's 20-year old is promised benefits that are 40% higher, in real terms, than are paid to seniors who retire this year. But the current system does not have the money to pay these promised benefits.
- **The retirement of the Baby Boomers will accelerate the problem.** In just 3 years, the first of the Baby Boom generation will begin to retire, putting added strain on a system that was not designed to meet the needs of the 21st century. By 2031, there will be almost twice as many older Americans as today—from 37 million today to 71 million. . . .
- **Social Security is heading toward bankruptcy.** According to the Social Security Trustees, thirteen years from now, in 2018, Social Security will be paying out more than it takes in and every year afterward will bring a new shortfall, bigger than the year before. And, when today's young workers begin to retire in 2042, the system will be exhausted and bankrupt. . . . If we do not act now to save it, the only solution will be drastically higher taxes, massive new borrowing, or sudden and severe cuts in Social Security benefits or other government programs.
- **As of 2004, the cost of doing nothing to fix our Social Security system had hit an estimated $10.4 trillion, according to the Social Security Trustees.** . . . The longer we wait to take action, the more difficult and expensive the changes will be.
  - $10.4 trillion is almost twice the combined wages and salaries of every working American in 2004.
  - Every year we wait costs an additional $600 billion. . . .
  - Today's 30-year-old worker can expect a 27% benefit cut from the current system when he or she reaches normal retirement age. . . . And, without action, these benefit cuts will only get worse.

Personal Retirement Accounts

- **The President believes personal retirement accounts must be part of a comprehensive solution to strengthen Social Security for the 21st century.**
- **Under the President's plan, personal retirement accounts would start gradually. Yearly contribution limits would be raised over time, eventually permitting all workers to set aside 4 percentage points of their payroll taxes in their accounts.** Annual contributions to personal retirement accounts initially would be capped, at $1,000 per year in 2009. The cap would rise gradually over time, growing $100 per year, plus growth in average wages.

- Personal retirement accounts offer younger workers the opportunity to build a "nest egg" for retirement that the government cannot take away.
  - **Personal retirement accounts provide ownership and control.** Personal retirement accounts give younger workers the opportunity to own an asset and watch it grow over time.
  - **Personal retirement accounts could be passed on to children and grandchildren.** The money in these accounts would be available for retirement expenses. Any unused portion could be passed on to loved ones. Permitting individuals to pass on their personal retirement accounts to loved ones will be particularly beneficial to widows, widowers, and other survivors. According to the non-partisan analysis by the Social Security Administration's Office of Retirement Policy, the ability to inherit personal accounts provides the largest gains to widows and other survivors.
  - **Personal retirement accounts help make Social Security better for younger workers.** A personal retirement account gives a younger worker the chance to save a portion of his or her money in an account and watch it grow over time at a greater rate than anything the current system can deliver. The account will provide money for the worker's retirement in addition to the check he or she receives from Social Security. Personal retirement accounts give younger workers the chance to receive a higher rate of return from sound, long-term investing of a portion of their payroll taxes than they receive under the current system.
- **Personal retirement accounts would be voluntary.** At any time, a worker could "opt in" by making a *one-time* election to put a portion of his or her payroll taxes into a personal retirement account.
  - Workers would have the flexibility to choose from several different low-cost, broad-based investment funds and would have the opportunity to adjust investment allocations periodically, but would not be allowed to move back and forth between personal retirement accounts and the traditional system. If, after workers choose the account, they decide they want only the benefits the current system would give them, they can leave their money invested in government bonds like those the Social Security system invests in now.
  - Those workers who do not elect to create a personal retirement account would continue to draw benefits from the traditional Social Security system, reformed to be permanently sustainable.
- **Personal retirement account options and management would be similar to that of the Federal employee retirement program, known as the Thrift Savings Plan (TSP).** A centralized administrative structure would be created to collect personal retirement account contributions, manage investments, maintain records, and facilitate withdrawals at retirement. The structure would be designed to facilitate low costs, ease of use for new investors, and timely crediting of contributions. This centralized investment structure would help minimize compliance costs for employers.
  - Contributions would be collected and records maintained by a central administrator. Similar to the TSP, private investment managers

would be chosen through a competitive bidding process to manage the pooled account contributions.

- The central administrator would answer questions from account participants and distribute periodic account statements.
- The central administrator would also facilitate withdrawals and the purchase of annuities with account balances.
- Like TSP, we expect participants to have easy access to investment information and to their accounts. Participants could easily check account balances and adjust investment allocations.

- **Personal retirement accounts would be invested in a mix of conservative bonds and stock funds.** Guidelines and restrictions would be put in place to provide sound investment choices and prevent individuals from spending the money in these accounts on the lottery or at the race track. Workers would be permitted to allocate their personal retirement account contributions among a small number of very broadly diversified index funds patterned after the current TSP funds.

  - Like TSP, personal retirement accounts could be invested in a safe government securities fund; an investment-grade corporate bond index fund; a small-cap stock index fund; a large-cap stock index fund; and an international stock index fund.
  - In addition to these TSP-type funds, workers could choose a government bond fund with a guaranteed rate of return above inflation.
  - Workers could also choose a "life cycle portfolio" that would automatically adjust the level of risk of the investments as the worker aged. The life cycle fund would automatically and gradually shift the allocation of investment funds as the individual neared retirement age so that it was weighted more heavily toward secure bonds.

- **Personal retirement accounts would be protected from sudden market swings on the eve of retirement.** To protect near-retirees from sudden market swings on the eve of retirement, personal retirement accounts would be automatically invested in the "life cycle portfolio" when a worker reaches age 47, unless the worker and his or her spouse specifically opted out by signing a waiver form stating they are aware of the risks involved. The waiver form would explain in clear, easily understandable terms the benefits of the life cycle portfolio and the risks of opting out. By shifting investment allocations from high growth funds to secure bonds as the individual nears retirement, the life cycle portfolio would provide greater protections from sudden market swings.

- **Personal retirement accounts would not be eaten up by hidden Wall Street fees.** Personal retirement accounts would be low-cost. The Social Security Administration's actuaries project that the ongoing administrative costs for a TSP-style personal account structure would be roughly 30 basis points or 0.3 percentage points, compared to an average of 125 basis points for investments in stock mutual funds and 88 basis points in bond mutual funds in 2003. . . .

  - The low costs are made possible by the economies of scale of a centralized administrative structure, as well as limiting investment options to a small number of prudent, broadly diversified funds.

- Most of these administrative costs are for recordkeeping which would be done by the government, not investment management done by Wall Street. . . .
- **Personal retirement accounts would not be accessible prior to retirement.** American workers who choose personal retirement accounts would not be allowed to make withdrawals from, take loans from, or borrow against their accounts prior to retirement.
- **Personal retirement accounts would not be emptied out all at once, but rather paid out over time, as an addition to traditional Social Security benefits.** Under a system of personal retirement accounts, procedures would be established to govern how account balances would be withdrawn at retirement. This would involve some combination of annuities to ensure a stream of monthly income over the worker's life expectancy, phased withdrawals indexed to life expectancy, and lump sum withdrawals. Individuals would not be permitted to withdraw funds from their personal retirement accounts as lump sums, if doing so would result in their moving below the poverty line. Account balances in excess of the poverty-protection threshold requirement could be withdrawn as a lump sum for any purpose or left in the account to accumulate interest. Any unused portion of the account could be passed on to loved ones.
- **Personal retirement accounts would be phased in.** To ease the transition to a personal retirement account system, participation would be phased in according to the age of the worker. In the first year of implementation, workers currently between age 40 and 54 (born 1950 through 1965 inclusive) would have the option of establishing personal retirement accounts. In the second year, workers currently between age 26 and 54 (born 1950 through 1978 inclusive) would be given the option and by the end of the third year, all workers born in 1950 or later who want to participate in personal retirement accounts would be able to do so.
- **The President's personal retirement account proposal is fiscally responsible.** The President's proposal is consistent with his overall goal of cutting the deficit in half by 2009. Based on analysis by the Social Security Administration Actuary, the Office of Management and Budget estimates that the President's personal retirement account proposal will require transition financing of $664 billion over the next ten years ($754 billion including interest). This transition financing will not have the same effect on national savings, and thus the economy, as traditional government borrowing. Personal retirement accounts will not reduce the pool of savings available to the markets because every dollar borrowed by the Federal government to fund the transition is fully offset by an increase in savings represented by the accounts themselves. Moreover, the transition financing for personal retirement accounts should be viewed as part of a comprehensive plan to make the Social Security system permanently sustainable. Publicly released analysis by the Social Security Administration has found that several comprehensive proposals including personal accounts would dramatically reduce the costs of permanently fixing the system. . . .
- **Establishing personal retirement accounts does not add to the total costs that Social Security faces.** Personal retirement accounts

effectively pre-fund Social Security benefits already promised to today's workers and do not represent a net increase in Federal obligations. The obligation to pay Social Security benefits is already there. While personal retirement accounts affect the timing of these costs, they do not add to the total amount obligated through Social Security.

 **NO**

Bush's Numbers Racket: Why Social Security Privatization Is a Phony Solution to a Phony Problem

The word from President Bush and his minions is that Social Security is on its last legs, facing imminent danger of bankruptcy. Fortunately, Bush is prepared to rescue this antiquated program by offering workers the opportunity to invest a portion of their Social Security taxes in private accounts. He would like us to believe that this plan will both get the government out from under a crushing debt burden, in the form of future Social Security obligations, and provide younger workers with a more secure retirement.

Almost every part of this story is untrue. First, Social Security does not face any crisis in the normal meaning of the term. Second, private accounts would not give workers a more secure retirement; they reduce security. And third, the basic logic of the story is faulty; it is impossible to both reduce government spending on Social Security and increase benefits, unless the plan somehow increases growth. And no economist seriously contends that putting Social Security money in the stock market will increase growth.

The Basic Numbers

Starting with the crisis story, the first place to look is the Social Security trustees' projections, the standard basis for analysis of the program. The most recent projections show that the program, with no changes whatsoever, can pay all benefits through the year 2042. Even after 2042, Social Security would always be able to pay a higher benefit (adjusted for inflation) than what current retirees receive, although the payment would only be about 73 percent of scheduled benefits.

The Social Security trustees' projections are based on extremely pessimistic assumptions about the future. (Four of the six trustees are political appointees of President Bush: the treasury, labor, and health and human services secretaries, plus the Social Security commissioner.) For example, the trustees assume that economic growth over the 75-year planning period will be less than half as fast as over the last 75 years. While most of this difference is due to the assumption of slower labor-force growth following the retirement of the baby-boomer generation, the trustees also assume that productivity growth will revert back to the rate of productivity growth during the slowdown years of 1973–95. Even so, the trustees themselves have begun using slightly more realistic assumptions. In 1997, they placed the year that Social Security would begin facing a shortfall at 2029. By 2003, they had revised that projection to 2042. Any system that gains 13 years of health in six years is hardly bankrupt.

The nonpartisan Congressional Budget Office (CBO) did its own analysis of the program last summer. Using only slightly more optimistic assumptions, the CBO found that the program, with no changes at all, could pay all benefits through the year 2052 and more than 80 percent of scheduled benefits in subsequent years.

On the face of it, the fact that Social Security may face a shortfall in just under 40 years (according to the trustees' report) or 50 years (according to the CBO) hardly sounds like a crisis. After all, the program faced projected shortfalls in the 1950s, '60s, '70s, and '80s. Each of these shortfalls was dealt with—usually with modest tax increases, and in the case of the '80s shortfall, a phased increase in the retirement age beginning in 2003. In the past, no one seemed to feel the need to begin whining about a looming crisis 40 or 50 years ahead of time.

But the proponents of the crisis story have been largely successful in spreading fear. Part of this success is due to the use of deceptive language in framing the issue. The promoters of the crisis routinely speak of an $11 trillion "unfunded liability" for Social Security. But most of the people who hear the $11 trillion figure or use it (including reporters) probably have no idea what it means.

The $11 trillion is obtained by projecting Social Security taxes and spending for the infinite future. The gap between projected spending and taxes for all time is then summed up (using a 3-percent real-discount rate) to get a projection of $11 trillion of debt.

However, more than two-thirds of this projected debt is due to spending beyond the 75-year planning period for Social Security. This means that the debt is not something that we are imposing on our children or grandchildren. Rather, it is a debt that we are projecting that our great-grandchildren would impose on their grandchildren—assuming pessimistic economic projections.

The basic story is that life expectancies are projected to increase through time. This raises the cost of the program through time. If taxes are never raised and benefits are never reduced, the shortfall would eventually be very large.

But serious people don't worry about designing Social Security for the 22nd century. (The secret here is that we don't actually get to design Social Security for the 22nd century anyhow—the people who are alive in 50, 60, and 70 years will design the program in a way that makes sense to them. They will not care at all about what we thought was a good system in 2005.)

If we just confine ourselves to the already lengthy 75-year planning period, the projected shortfall comes to $3 trillion. This may still sound very large. However, the Social Security trustees calculate that this shortfall is 0.7 percent of national income over the planning period. The CBO projects an even smaller number, just 0.4 percent of income over the next 75 years.

By comparison, the increase in annual defense spending since 2001 has been more than 1 percent of the gross domestic product, twice the size of the Social Security shortfall projected by the CBO. And Bush's tax increases equal about 2 percent of the GDP. In fact, rolling back Bush's tax cuts on the very wealthiest would raise sufficient revenue to cover the shortfall for 75 years.

The Trust-Fund Scare Stories

The promoters of privatization have one other standard trick to promote fear about Social Security's future: They point out that, beginning in 2018, Social Security will be forced to rely on income from the trust fund to pay benefits. But this was deliberate. The 1983 Social Security Commission, chaired by Alan Greenspan, deliberately designed a system that would build up a surplus—taxing more than was necessary to pay benefits—so that the income from this surplus could be used help pay the costs of the baby boomers' retirement. Drawing on the trust fund is no more of a problem for Social Security than it is for any pension fund to use some of its accumulated assets to pay benefits to retirees. Indeed, that is exactly what is supposed to happen.

Some conservatives have even derided the Social Security trust fund as an "accounting fiction." Like most claims to wealth in a modern economy, it exists primarily as an accounting entry (how much gold does Bill Gates have in his basement?), but it is hardly fiction. Under the law, the federal government is obligated to repay the government bonds held by the Social Security trust fund, just as it is obligated to repay other government bonds. While tax revenue will be needed to repay these bonds, it is slated to come from personal and corporate income taxes, both very progressive forms of taxation. By contrast, the Social Security tax is a highly regressive wage tax. The meaning of the trust fund is that workers effectively prepaid their Social Security taxes. Now, the government is obligated to tax the Bill Gates and Pete Petersons of the world to repay this debt.

Funny Numbers on Private Accounts

After telling people that Social Security poses the risk of economic disaster, the privatizers promise that individual accounts would provide everyone with a secure retirement. The basic argument is that high returns in the stock market would allow workers to get more money from their Social Security taxes than what they can get through the current system.

There is a simple and obvious problem with this logic. When they project rates of return in the stock market, the privatizers routinely assume that the returns in the future will be equal to the returns in the past, 6.5 percent to 7 percent above the rate of inflation. But the whole basis for projecting a Social Security shortfall is the assumption that the future will have far slower growth than in the past.

Given the much slower projected rate of profit growth, and the fact that price-to-earnings ratios in the stock market continue to be far higher than the historic average, it will be impossible for stock returns to be as high in the future as they were in the past. Projections of stock returns that are consistent with projections of profit growth and current price-to-earnings ratios are approximately 5 percent above the rate of inflation. Because most projections assume a 50-50 mix of stocks and bonds, the implied return on private accounts, after deducting administrative costs, would be about 3.5 percent. This is not much different than the 3-percent return projected for the government bonds held by the trust fund.

In short, there is no untapped bonanza to be claimed by putting Social Security money in the stock market. This step would add little, if anything, to average returns. It would simply add risk. Individual workers may do worse than the average because they make bad investment choices or they happen to retire during a downturn in the stock market. Going in this direction makes sense if the purpose is to increase fees for the financial industry, but it is not a step toward increasing workers' retirement security. Moreover, with individual accounts, retirees would have to worry about living too long, whereas Social Security is guaranteed for life.

Even with individual accounts, most workers would still see large benefit cuts under the second plan produced by President Bush's Social Security Commission, the one that Bush indicated would be the model for his proposal. An average wage earner who is age 20 at the time the plan is implemented could expect his or her basic Social Security benefit to be cut by $200,000, or more than 30 percent, over the course of his or her retirement. He or she could expect to make back less than $70,000, or about one-third of this cut, through his or her private account.

But it is not just the retirement security of individual workers that would be threatened by privatization. President Bush's plan would also lead to transition costs that could be as high as $200 billion a year (almost 2 percent of the GDP) for more than 30 years. The transition problem stems from the fact that workers would begin placing their money in private accounts immediately, leading to large losses of revenue to the government. However, the commission's plan proposes phasing in cuts to new retirees, beginning five years after the plan takes effect. These cuts would not get large enough to offset the lost revenue (and resulting interest burden) for more than three decades, which would lead to a substantial deficit increase in the intervening years.

In order to avoid the appearance that his plan would lead to record-breaking deficits (measured as a share of the GDP), President Bush wants to take this transition by not counting this borrowing as part of the budget. The argument is that we would pay this money back (with benefit cuts) 40 or 50 years in the future, so the current borrowing should not be viewed as adding to the deficit.

The question of whether the transition borrowing could be taken off the books is a political one, but politics won't determine the impact of this borrowing on the nation's economy. There is little evidence that financial markets look 40 and 50 years into the future (and it's not clear what they would see if they did). But every other country that has privatized its Social Security system has felt the need to offset the immediate loss of tax revenue with some spending cuts and/or tax increases. And none of them started with deficits that are as large as those the United States is currently running.

There were already grounds for believing that the Bush deficits were too large and would lead to a substantial increase in interest rates if not reduced quickly. Adding $200 billion a year to these deficits makes it far more likely that the country would face considerably higher interest rates in the near future.

There is also a good example of what can happen when a country tries the Bush approach to Social Security privatization (even if it didn't go quite as far). In 1994, Argentina partially privatized its social-security system. While there were some cuts included in this package, it cost the government an amount of tax revenue equal to approximately 0.9 percent of the GDP, equivalent to $100 billion a year in the United States. In 2001, Argentina went into bankruptcy and defaulted on its debt. If the social-security revenue had still been coming to the government over the period between 1994 and the default, Argentina would have been running a balanced budget in 2001.

The United States is obviously very different from Argentina, but this example is not encouraging for proponents of privatization. The financial markets were not impressed with the fact that Argentina's social-security payments would be lower 20 years in the future. The markets focused on the deficits the country was running in the present. It is likely that they would also focus on the $600 billion (plus deficits) that would result from President Bush's Social Security plan.

In short, Bush's plan would undermine a system that has provided security for tens of millions of workers, and their families, for seven decades, and which can continue to do so long into the future if it is just left alone. His private accounts would provide far less security, while hugely raising costs in the form of fees to the financial industry. Finally, the cost of transitioning to this new system could throw the country into an economic crisis. It's small wonder that Bush is facing increasing skepticism.

POSTSCRIPT

Should Social Security Be Changed to Include Personal Retirement Accounts?

The White House begins by describing what it believes are the problems facing Social Security. One central problem is that there are "fewer workers paying ever-higher benefits to an ever-larger number of retirees." Consequently, Social Security is facing critical financing problems; it is heading toward "bankruptcy." The White House refers to an estimate from the Social Security Trustees: "As of 2004 the cost of doing nothing to fix our Social Security system had hit an estimated $10.4 trillion." The White House lists the advantages of personal retirement accounts. One advantage is that ownership and control of the account would rest with the individual. Another advantage is that an individual could pass the account on to his or her children and grandchildren. Perhaps most importantly, the White House believes that the creation of these accounts "would dramatically reduce the costs of permanently fixing the system."

Baker begins his analysis by denying the claims that he says the Bush administration makes about Social Security and personal retirement accounts. Baker argues (1) there is no Social Security "crisis," (2) the retirement accounts would not make retirement "more secure," and (3) "it is impossible to both reduce government spending on Social Security and increase benefits, unless the plan somehow increases growth." Baker then turns to the numbers that are used to support the claims of those who believe that there is a Social Security crisis. He finds fault with these numbers on a variety of criteria. For example, he disputes the forecast by the Social Security Trustees that by 2042 The Social Security trust fund will be exhausted; he believes this prediction is based on "extremely pessimistic assumptions about the future." He cites an alternative forecast by the nonpartisan Congressional Budget Office that sets 2052 as the corresponding date. He then proceeds to discuss the Social Security trust fund in more detail; in particular, he disputes the charge that it is an "accounting fiction." In the last part of his analysis, Baker discusses the numbers associated with private accounts. He asserts that these accounts would add little to average returns but would add risk. He concludes that the burdens of moving to the system proposed by the Bush administration "could throw the country into an economic crisis."

The Social Security "crisis" has been a major concern to economists and policymakers for at least the last 10 years. As a consequence, a vast amount of information is available about the "crisis" and personal retirement accounts, and there are several Web sites devoted exclusively to the issue. They include The

Social Security Network, available at http://www.socsec.org/, and the Cato Institute Project on Social Security Choice, available at http://www.socialsecurity.org/. A visit to the Social Security Administration's official Web site at http://www.ssa.gov/ provides access to an array of useful information including the latest Trustees Report. Another batch of studies regarding Social Security can be found at the research center of the American Association of Retired Persons (AARP) at http://search.aarp.org/cgi-bin/htsearch?config=htdig_research_aarp_org& method=and&restrict=research.aarp.org%2Fecon&words=social+security. Several additional readings on Social Security are available from the Century Foundation at http://www.tcf.org/about.asp. Several specific plans for Social Security reform been developed. For example, see the description of The Ryan-Sununu Social Security reform bill by Peter Ferrara: "Personal Social Security Accounts that Work" Policy Report 185 Institute for Policy Innovation (November 2004). Another plan is offered by Michael Tanner, "The 6.2 Percent Solution: A Plan for Reforming Social Security," Cato Project on Social Security Choice SSP No. 32 (February 17, 2004). A third plan is offered by Peter A. Diamond and Peter R. Orszag in *Saving Social Security: A Balanced Approach* (Brookings Institution Press, 2003).

ISSUE 9

Should the Double Taxation of Corporate Dividends Be Eliminated?

YES: Norbert J. Michel, Alfredo Goyburu, and Ralph A. Rector, from "The Economic and Fiscal Effects of Ending the Federal Double Taxation of Dividends," A Working Paper of the Heritage Center for Data Analysis (January 27, 2003)

NO: Joel Friedman and Robert Greenstein, from "Exempting Corporate Dividends From Individual Income Taxes," A Report of the Center on Budget and Policy Priorities (January 11, 2003)

ISSUE SUMMARY

YES: Free-market economists Norbert J. Michel, Alfredo Goyburu, and Ralph A. Rector applaud the George W. Bush administration's initiative to eliminate the double taxation of corporate dividends. They assert that this action will improve economic efficiency and that, in the long run, this tax cut will pay for itself because it will stimulate economic growth.

NO: Economic policy analysts Joel Friedman and Robert Greenstein argue that there are no valid economic justifications to propose the elimination of the tax on dividends. All that cutting dividend taxes will really do, they say, is reduce the tax burden of high-income individuals.

The U.S. federal government engages in a wide variety of economic and noneconomic activities. In the United States these activities range from the provision of national and domestic security to the construction and maintenance of public and private transportation systems. Additionally, the government provides economic security in the form of income transfers to the elderly, the unemployed, and the poor. Finally, it creates institutions that allow markets to flourish, since markets are the engines that drive the economic system. All of these efforts are taken for granted, are costly, and must be paid for. To finance these activities, governments have three options: they can create money, they can tax, or they can borrow. The United States does not create money, but the government certainly does tax and borrow.

Consider, for example, federal government total outlays and receipts for fiscal year 2002. That year alone the federal government spent $2.01 trillion. This was financed by $1.85 trillion in receipts or taxes, and since taxes were less than expenditures, America incurred $160 billion in new federal debt. The bulk of this tax revenue came from income-related taxes: the individual income tax raised $858 billion; payroll taxes—largely social security contributions—generated $701 billion; and last, as well as a distant third, corporate income taxes accounted for another $148 billion. All the other federal taxes combined—federal excise taxes, customs duties, estate/gift taxes, and a dozen or so miscellaneous taxes—summed to a total of $146 billion in tax revenue.

The unvarnished truth is that no one likes to pay taxes. However, making deep cuts in the tax system is not always practical, given that there is a widespread belief that all or most of the expenditures and transfers that are generally taken for granted are demanded by a majority of taxpayers. Although "taxes, like death" are inevitable, the displeasure with taxes can be minimized if the tax system meets two basic criteria: equity and efficiency.

The first criterion of equity, or fairness, from the economist's perspective, requires looking horizontally and vertically. That is, for a tax to be horizontally equitable, that tax must treat individuals in identical circumstances identically. In this case, those with the same economic characteristics should pay the same amount in taxes. Vertical equity is a bit more complicated. It assumes that unlike individuals will be treated unequally; that is, a person with greater tax-paying capacity should not pay the same amount of taxes as someone with a lower income. At a minimum, those with higher incomes should pay proportionally the same as those with lower incomes and, in some cases, share a larger percentage of the tax burden than those of more moderate means.

Besides being equitable, a tax system needs to satisfy a second general criterion. Taxes should not interfere significantly with the efficient operation of a market economy. Consider the case of an extreme tax that took all of an individual's income. Economists would argue that this tax is inefficient because it would undermine work incentives. In technical terms, since work and leisure are substitutes for one another, a 100 percent tax would make the price of an additional hour of leisure equal to zero. Why work if you are not going to be better off from working? In this case one would expect folks to work far less and therefore increase their consumption of leisure. If no one works, the size of the economic pie has to decline because resources are wasted.

Most would conclude that taxes are necessary and that policymakers should do all they can to impose taxes that take into account equitable and efficient consequences of these taxes. Unfortunately, sometimes in order to get equity, one must sacrifice efficiency. In other cases, in order to get efficiency, one has to sacrifice equity. The importance that is placed on one or the other of these two considerations helps shape which taxes we support and which we take issue with. In the following selections, Norbert J. Michel, Alfredo Goyburu, and Ralph A. Rector argue that, above all, policymakers should maximize efficiency. Joel Friedman and Robert Greenstein, on the other hand, plead the case for equity.

YES

Norbert J. Michel, Alfredo Goyburu, and Ralph A. Rector

The Economic and Fiscal Effects of Ending the Federal Double Taxation of Dividends

On January 7, 2003, President George W. Bush unveiled a multi-faceted proposal to improve the nation's economic growth. One of the most important features of his plan calls for abolition of the current federal double taxation of corporate dividends paid to individual shareholders. Economic analysts at the Center for Data Analysis (CDA) at The Heritage Foundation found, in a study of a dividend reform proposal similar to President Bush's, that ending the double taxation of dividends would improve the nation's economic growth, employment level, and other economic indicators over the next 10 years.

For example, CDA estimates indicate that the employment level would average 285,000 additional jobs from 2003 to 2012. In addition, CDA analysis has found that ending this double taxation would reduce federal revenue by $64 billion over ten years, or 79 percent less than an estimate that does not account for the effects of greater economic activity following the proposal's implementation. The CDA's $64 billion estimate is slightly more than one-fifth of the $364 billion cost estimated by the United States Department of the Treasury for President Bush's proposal.[1] The CDA and Treasury analyses consider slightly different proposals, but this cost difference is largely due to the more realistic estimation method used by the CDA.

The Treasury Department employs an erroneous "static" approach to estimate the revenue effect of tax law changes, while the CDA uses dynamic simulation, a method that accounts for the impact that federal tax policy may exert on economic growth.[2] Figure 1 shows that the estimation method chosen can make a large difference in the projected revenue loss. The figure compares the CDA's own static and dynamic projections of the federal revenue change resulting from a particular plan to end the double taxation of dividends.

This double taxation[3] has two stages. The first stage occurs when the federal government taxes shareholders on corporate income through corporate taxes. The second occurs after the corporation has distributed part of the post-tax profits to the shareholders in the form of dividends. In this second stage, the federal government taxes shareholders on their dividend income through the personal income tax.

Figure 1

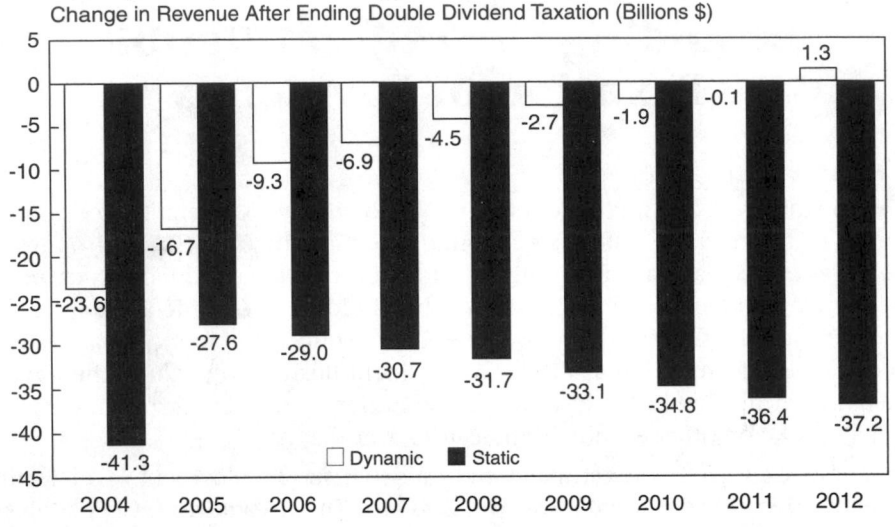

Dynamic vs. Erroneous Static Revenue Cost Estimates of Ending Double Dividend Taxation

Note: Assumes legislative enactment on September 30, 2003.

Source: Estimates by the Center for Data Analysis at The Heritage Foundation, using August 2002 Congressional Budget Office projections and the DRI–WEFA U.S. Macroeconomic Model.

Economists have long argued that the double taxation of dividends reduces the after-tax return on capital in the nation's economy and thus discourages investment—in other words, purchases of new business equipment and machinery.[4] This reduced investment in turn weakens economic growth. Consequently, eliminating the double taxation would spur investment and improve the economy's long-term growth. Recognizing these economic benefits, several nations, including Australia, France, Italy, Canada, Germany, Japan, and the United Kingdom, have abolished or reduced their double taxation of corporate dividends.[5]

One recent legislative proposal to abolish this double taxation in the United States was sponsored by Representative Christopher Cox (R–CA).[6] The Heritage Foundation's CDA used this proposal to illustrate the economic and federal fiscal effects of ending the double taxation of dividends.[7] To estimate these effects, Heritage analysts employed the DRI–WEFA U.S. Macroeconomic Model and the Center's own Individual Income Tax Model. Assuming the reform becomes law in September 2003, the investigation found that:[8]

- *GDP increases.* During the period from 2003 through 2012, the Cox proposal would increase the nation's gross domestic product (GDP) by an inflation-adjusted[9] $32 billion per year on average, compared to what it would otherwise have been. GDP would be at least $22 billion

Figure 2

Ending Double Taxation of Dividends Bolsters Economic Growth, Gross Domestic Product Compared to Baseline

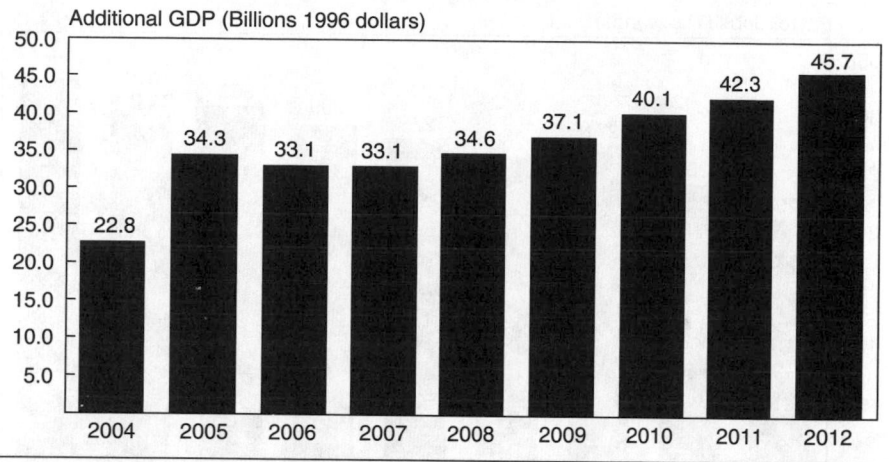

Additional GDP (Billions 1996 dollars)

Year	Value
2004	22.8
2005	34.3
2006	33.1
2007	33.1
2008	34.6
2009	37.1
2010	40.1
2011	42.3
2012	45.7

Note: Assumes legislative enactment on September 30, 2003.

Source: Estimates by the Center for Data Analysis at The Heritage Foundation, using August 2002 Congressional Budget Office projections and the DRI–WEFA U.S. Macroeconomic Model.

higher in 2004 and no less than $45 billion higher in 2012 if the proposal were to be implemented. (See Figure 2.)

- *Employment grows.* The provisions in the Cox bill would enable the economy to support 325,000 more jobs by 2012. (See Figure 3.) With these additional jobs in the economy, the unemployment rate would be 0.2 percent lower throughout the period 2005–2012 than current projections indicate.

- *Investment strengthens.* Over the 10-year period from 2003 through 2012, the proposal would result in an aggregate increase of at least $253 billion (adjusted for inflation) in non-residential investment. Because of this higher level of investment, the nation's non-residential capital stock would be $175 billion higher in 2012. (See Figure 4.)

- *Disposable income picks up.* Under the Cox legislation, disposable personal income would average an inflation-adjusted $56 billion higher from 2003 through 2012. (See Figure 5.) This higher level would raise annual disposable personal income by $192 per person on average during the period. For a family of four, this increase would correspond to $768 more in disposable income on average each year.

- *Personal savings increases.* The proposal would increase personal savings by an inflation-adjusted average of $18 billion per year from 2003 through 2012.

- *Higher economic growth reduces the "cost" to the Treasury by over 70 percent.* The CDA's own static estimates suggest the proposal would reduce federal revenue by about $300 billion from 2003 through 2012. However, the CDA's more realistic dynamic estimates show that

Figure 3

Ending Double Taxation of Dividends Strengthens Job Growth Compared to Baseline

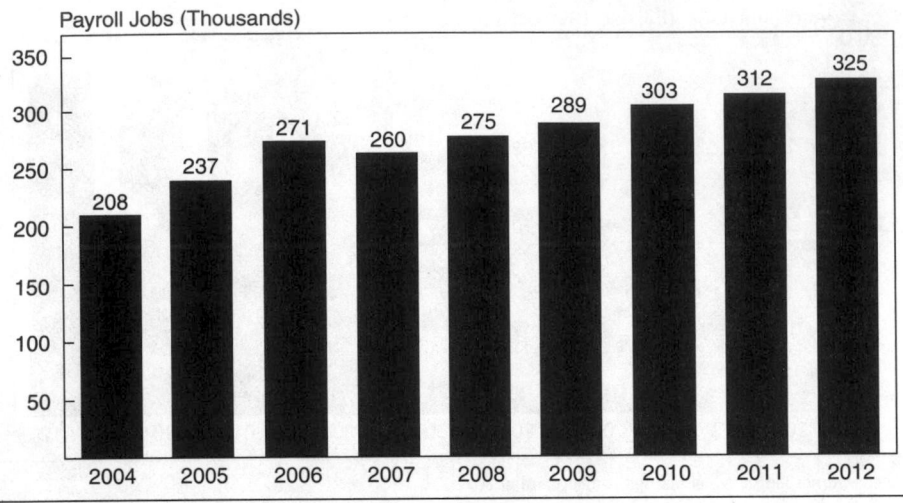

Note: Assumes legislative enactment on September 30, 2003.

Source: Estimates by the Center for Data Analysis at The Heritage Foundation, using August 2002 Congressional Budget Office projections and the DRI–WEFA U.S. Macroeconomic Model.

Figure 4

Ending Double Taxation of Dividends Raises Net Capital Stock Compared to Baseline

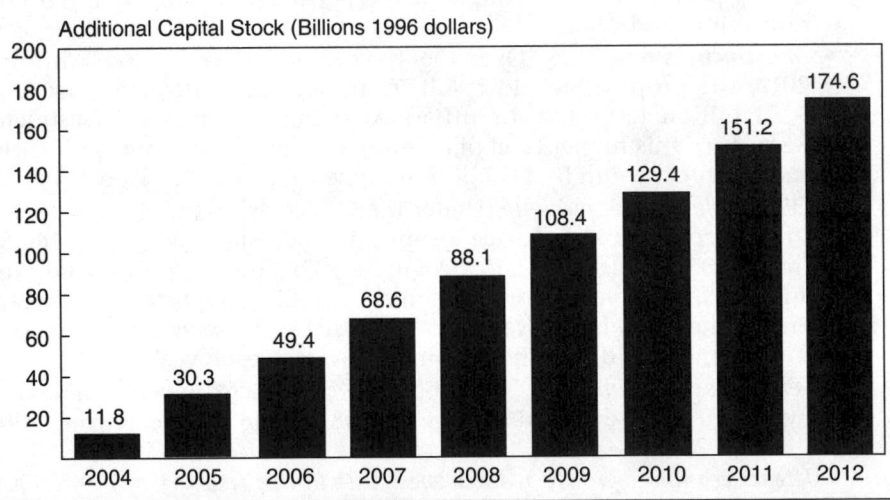

Note: Assumes legislative enactment on September 30, 2003.

Source: Estimates by the Center for Data Analysis at The Heritage Foundation, using August 2002 Congressional Budget Office projections and the DRI–WEFA U.S. Macroeconomic Model.

Figure 5

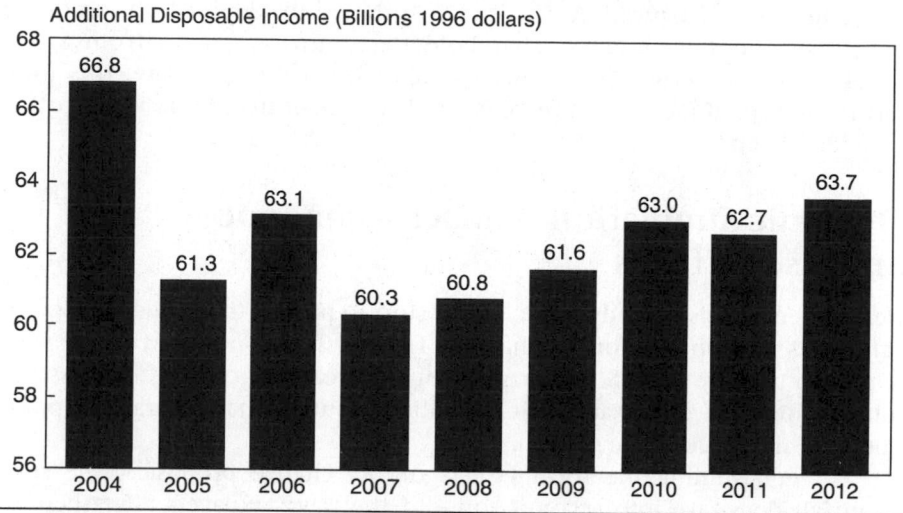

Ending Double Taxation of Dividends Boosts Disposable Income Compared to Baseline

Additional Disposable Income (Billions 1996 dollars)

Year	Value
2004	66.8
2005	61.3
2006	63.1
2007	60.3
2008	60.8
2009	61.6
2010	63.0
2011	62.7
2012	63.7

Note: Assumes legislative enactment on September 30, 2003.

Source: Estimates by the Center for Data Analysis at The Heritage Foundation, using August 2002 Congressional Budget Office projections and the DRI–WEFA U.S. Macroeconomic Model.

the proposal would reduce federal revenue during the period by a total of $64 billion. (See Figure 1.) During the last five years, the proposal would be nearly revenue neutral, since the improved economic growth caused by the legislation would, in turn, increase tax collections. For reasons discussed below, these estimates do not take into account the way in which the proposal's effect on capital gains tax collections would change federal tax revenue.

How the Double Taxation of Dividends Works

The double taxation of dividends[10] is one of the clearest examples of the way the nation's current tax law reduces the return on capital and, therefore, the incentive to invest. The following example illustrates the effect of this double taxation.

Consider $100 in pre-tax profit earned by a corporation in the flat 35 percent bracket. Suppose that, after paying the $35 in federal corporate taxes, the firm distributed the remaining $65 to a shareholder. Suppose, further, that this individual was in the 27 percent personal income tax bracket. This shareholder would pay $17.55 in personal income taxes on these dividends. This second round of taxation would leave only $47.45 of the original $100 in corporate profits. In other words, for every $100 in pre-tax profits, the federal government would absorb approximately $52.55 in taxes.

In contrast, consider the taxes the shareholder might have paid if that person could have received the dividend before the firm paid corporate taxes. In this case, the corporation would have paid the shareholder all $100 in the form of a dividend. The shareholder would then have paid $27 in personal income taxes on the dividends, leaving that investor with $73 out of the $100 in pre-tax corporate profit. As this example shows, the double taxation of corporate dividends reduced the shareholder's return on capital from $73 to $47.45—a reduction of 35 percent (or $25.55). In the aggregate, this lower return on capital means that there is less investment than there would otherwise have been.

Dynamic Simulation of Macroeconomic and Fiscal Effects

Heritage economists use dynamic simulation to project the economic and fiscal effects of proposals for tax changes. This method contrasts with the static approach used by the U.S. Department of the Treasury and the Congressional Joint Committee on Taxation (JCT), which assumes that federal tax policy does not affect economic growth.

In determining the fiscal effects of tax change proposals, the static approach does take into account some of the ways taxpayers alter their tax reporting and filing in response to changes in tax law. For example, the static approach takes into account that taxpayers could increase their itemized deductions or shift compensation from taxable to tax-exempt (or tax-deferred) forms in response to certain changes in the tax laws. However, the static approach does not take into account the way investors and workers alter their consumption, investment, saving, and work effort in response to changes in tax policy. This is a major shortcoming of the static approach because economic theory suggests that tax policy changes bring about such alterations.[11]

Such changes in taxpayers' behavior could affect important macroeconomic variables, including employment, personal income, and GDP. Thus, changes in tax law often exert an impact on the nation's economy. The static approach necessarily ignores these impacts, leading to systematic inaccuracies in the estimates of the fiscal effects of tax policy changes.

In contrast, The Heritage Foundation uses dynamic simulation in evaluating the fiscal and economic effects of tax policy proposals. Dynamic simulation takes into account the impact that tax policy legislation can exert on taxpayers' economic decisions, such as consumption, investment, saving, and work effort. Dynamic simulation, therefore, can reflect changes in macroeconomic variables that new tax policies can cause.

For example, if a tax rate reduction were to strengthen national economic growth and therefore increase the tax base, a resultant increase in tax collections could partially offset the federal revenue losses caused by the rate reduction. Static analysis would not take such an offset into account and therefore would overestimate the net decline in federal tax collections resulting from the tax rate reduction. Dynamic analysis would include this offset because it would take full account of the economic benefits that the tax rate reduction could cause. It would also capture the ways in which these benefits could strengthen the economy, bolster the tax base, and ameliorate the reduction in tax collections.

In analyzing the economic and fiscal impact of the Cox proposal, CDA analysts made a number of assumptions regarding the alternative minimum tax, capital gains taxation, federal spending, and the date the bill would be enacted. These assumptions were as follows.

- *Alternative minimum tax.* The form of the bill submitted for consideration in the 107th Congress does not clearly state how the dividend tax credit should be handled under those parts of the tax code that establish the alternative minimum tax (AMT). Heritage Foundation analysts assumed that taxpayers required to file under the AMT rules would be able to take advantage of the dividend tax credit. If this were not the case, the dividend tax relief for those taxpayers would be negated.
- *Capital gains tax.* The Cox proposal would be expected to cause an increase in equity prices. This increase would likely cause investors to adjust their portfolios, perhaps triggering increased capital gains tax liability. Estimating the total increase in capital gains tax collections would require both distributional and basis data that are not readily available to Heritage economists. Therefore, CDA analysts assumed that such collections would remain unchanged relative to the baseline forecast.
- *Federal spending.* Heritage Foundation analysts assumed that Congress would make no government program spending reductions to offset federal revenue cuts expected with the Cox proposal. As a result, any changes in federal spending observed in the simulation are attributable solely to the Cox proposal's effect on the national economy and, in turn, the economy's effect on federal spending.
- *Dividend increase.* Heritage analysts assumed that ending the double taxation of dividends would increase dividend payouts by 10 percent. A portion of this increase would be caused by higher shareholder demand for dividends. In response to this higher demand, corporations would increase their payouts of dividends out of after-tax profits. The remainder of this 10 percent increase would be explained by a reduction in the user cost of capital and a corresponding increase in profits. Some of these higher profits would then be returned to shareholders as higher dividends. The combined result of these two effects was assumed to be a 10 percent increase in dividends.[12]
- *Date of enactment.* Heritage economists assumed that the tax reform would become law on September 30, 2003, and apply retroactively to dividends received after January 1, 2003. Assuming an earlier date of enactment would have resulted in the proposal's benefits being realized sooner.

Macroeconomic and Fiscal Effects of the Cox Proposal

Heritage economists used a modified version of the DRI–WEFA U.S. Macroeconomic Model to conduct a dynamic simulation of the effects of Representative Cox's bill.[13] Specifically, Heritage economists developed a baseline by adapting the DRI–WEFA macroeconomic forecast from September 2002 to yield the same economic and budget projections as those of the Congressional Budget Office (CBO) in August 2002.[14] Thus, the economic baseline employed in this analysis should be comparable to baselines used by the CBO and JCT in analyzing this legislation. . . .

Specifically, the dynamic analysis projects that the Cox proposal would:

- *Increase economic growth.* GDP would increase by an average of at least $32 billion per year (adjusted for inflation) within the period from 2003 through 2012. GDP would be an inflation-adjusted $22 billion higher in 2004 and $45 billion higher in 2012. (See Figure 2.)
- *Create more job opportunities.* The proposal would increase the number of jobs by at least 325,000 in 2012. (See Figure 3.) This increase in jobs would correspond to a decline in the unemployment rate of no less than 0.2 percent per year over the next 10 years. (See Figure 3.)
- *Increase investment.* Non-residential investment would average nearly $25 billion per year (adjusted for inflation) higher between 2003 and 2012. By the end of fiscal year 2012, the net capital stock would be at least an inflation-adjusted $174 billion higher. (See Figure 4.) The user cost of capital would be about 5.4 percent lower in 2012.
- *Increase disposable personal income.* Disposable personal income would increase by an inflation-adjusted average of $56 billion or more per year from 2003 through 2012. For a family of four, this increase in disposable income would correspond to an average of at least $768 per year. (See Figure 5.)
- *Increase personal savings and personal consumption.* Personal savings would average an inflation-adjusted $18 billion higher during the 10 year period. Personal consumption expenditures would average an inflation-adjusted $36 billion higher than current projections.
- *Slightly increase consumer prices.* Under the Cox proposal, growth in the consumer price index would average 0.1 percent higher from 2004 through 2008. Over the final four years of the forecast period, increases in the price level would be virtually unchanged in comparison with those of the baseline.
- *Decrease federal tax revenue.* The Cox dividend proposal would reduce total federal tax revenues by a total of $64 billion during its first 10 years. Close to $56 billion of this reduction would take place during the first five years, for an average of $11 billion per year. During the final five years of the simulation period, the tax cut would be virtually revenue neutral, reducing federal revenue by an average of less then $2 billion per year. During this latter five-year period, increases mostly in corporate and Social Security tax collections would offset expected declines in personal income taxes. Corporate tax collections would rise because of higher pre-tax corporate profits. Payroll taxes would increase because of higher employment levels.
- *Increase federal spending.* If Congress were not to reduce federal program spending to offset the tax revenue reductions caused by this proposal, overall federal spending would rise. Spending would average about $13 billion higher after ending the double taxation of dividends. About two-thirds of this increase would result from additional federal interest payments. The rest would be caused by increases in federal

expenditures on income-maintenance programs for federal and Social Security retirees. These increases in federal income maintenance spending would be caused mainly by higher consumer prices observed during the years from 2004 through 2008.

Conclusion

President Bush has proposed reforming the U.S. tax code to abolish the federal double taxation on corporate dividends. Economists have long argued that this double taxation exerts a harmful effect on the nation's economy because it increases the user cost of capital and therefore reduces investment in the United States. Last fall [2002], Representative Christopher Cox introduced legislation that would end this double taxation.

This Heritage Foundation working paper investigates the 10-year economic and fiscal impact of Representative Cox's proposal to abolish this double taxation. It finds that the proposal would, by the year 2012, improve growth in the nation's GDP, add hundreds of thousands of jobs to the economy, increase investment, strengthen growth in disposable income, and add to the nation's capital stock.

Notes

1. United States Department of the Treasury, Office of Public Affairs, "Tax Provisions of the President's Growth Package," at. . . .

2. Forthcoming sections of this paper further discuss the differences between static and dynamic analysis.

3. The term "double taxation" refers only to the federal taxation of dividends. When state and local taxes and estate taxes are considered, there are more than two layers of taxation on dividend income. However, this working paper limits its discussion to federal tax policy, so its language refers only to federal double taxation. Consequently, the examples discussed herein set aside the effect of state and local taxation on corporate shareholder return and the user cost of capital.

4. For more on the economic effects of federal double taxation of dividends, see James M. Poterba, "Tax Policy and Corporate Saving," *Brookings Papers on Economic Activity* No. 2, 1987, pp. 455–515; Peter Birch Sorensen, "Changing Views of the Corporate Income Tax," *National Tax Journal,* Vol. 48, Issue 2 (June 1995), pp. 279–294; James M. Poterba and Lawrence H. Summers, "The Economic Effects of Dividend Taxation," National Bureau of Economic Research *Working Paper* No. 1353, 1984; and James M. Poterba and Lawrence H. Summers, "New Evidence that Taxes Affect the Valuation of Dividends," *The Journal of Finance,* Vol. 39, Issue 5 (December 1984), pp. 1397–1415.

5. Deborah Thomas and Keith Sellers, "Eliminate the Double Tax on Dividends," *Journal of Accountancy,* November 1994, and Ervin L. Black, Joseph Legoria, and Keith F. Sellers, "Capital Investment Effects of Dividend Imputation," *The Journal of the American Taxation Association,* Vol. 22, Issue 2 (2000), pp. 40–59.

6. H.R. 5323, 107th Congress.

7. The Center for Data Analysis was asked to evaluate this proposal in September 2002 and plans to evaluate the "exclusion method" in President Bush's proposal in a forthcoming study.

8. CDA analysts assumed that the reform would be enacted on September 30, 2003, and applicable retroactively to dividends paid after January 1, 2003.

9. All dollar values listed as "inflation-adjusted" are indexed to the general 1996 price level.

10. The Bureau of Economic Analysis (BEA) and the Internal Revenue Service (IRS) define the word "dividend" differently. This paper uses the BEA definition. There are at least two major differences between the BEA and IRS definitions. For example, the IRS defines as "dividend income" interest earned by mutual funds on the funds' non-equity holdings, while the BEA does not count this as dividend income. In contrast, the BEA counts as dividend income flows from S-Corporations, while the IRS does not. The numerical differences between the two definitions can be quite large. For example, during calendar year 2000, IRS dividends were $142.2 billion, while BEA dividends were $375.7 billion. See Thae S. Park, "Comparison of BEA Estimates of Personal Income and IRS Estimates of Adjusted Gross Income," Bureau of Economic Analysis, *Survey of Current Business,* November 2002, Table 2, at. . . .

11. For a discussion of the shortcomings of static analysis of the effects of tax policy changes, see Daniel J. Mitchell, "The Correct Way to Measure the Revenue Impact of Changes in Tax Rates," Heritage Foundation *Backgrounder* No. 1544, May 3, 2002, at 45524i. See also "The Argument for Reality-Based Scoring," Heritage Foundation *Web Memo* No. 92, March 29, 2002, at . . ., and Daniel R. Burton, "Reforming the Federal Tax Policy Process," Cato Institute, *Cato Policy Analysis* No. 463, December 17, 2002, at. . . .

12. Based on empirical evidence, this 10 percent increase in dividends appears to be a low-end estimate. See Martin Feldstein, "Corporate Taxation and Dividend Behavior," *The Review of Economic Studies,* Vol. 37, Issue 1 (January 1970), pp. 57–72, and Poterba, "Tax Policy and Corporate Saving." Assuming a larger increase in dividends would have resulted in a higher estimated growth in GDP.

13. The Center for Data Analysis used the Mark 11 U.S. Macroeconomic Model of DRI–WEFA, Inc., to conduct this analysis. The model was developed in the late 1960s by Nobel Prize–winning economist Lawrence Klein and several colleagues at the University of Pennsylvania. It is widely used by *Fortune* 500 companies, prominent federal agencies, and economic forecasting departments. The methodologies, assumptions, conclusions, and opinions herein are entirely the work of Heritage Foundation analysts. They have not been endorsed by, and do not necessarily reflect the views of, the owners of the model.

14. Congressional Budget Office, "The Budget and Economic Outlook: An Update," August 2002, at. . . .

15. To maintain comparability with published CBO long-term projections, projections of changes in federal spending and revenue are not adjusted for inflation in this paper.

**Joel Friedman and
Robert Greenstein**

 **NO**

Exempting Corporate Dividends
From Individual Income Taxes

As the centerpiece of its "growth package," the [George W.] Bush Administration proposes a large reduction in the taxes that individuals pay on dividend payments they receive from corporations. According to Administration
estimates, this tax cut reduces revenues by $364 billion, representing more
than half of the package's $674 billion cost through 2013. This proposal to
eliminate the taxes on dividends raises a number of questions. It would do little to stimulate the economy in the near term. In addition, its high cost over
the next decade and beyond would result in further damage to the federal
budget, increasing deficits and thereby reducing national savings and imposing longterm costs on the economy. . . .

Proposal Likely to Have Little Effect
as Economic Stimulus

Even though the current weakness in the economy is used as justification for
the proposal, reducing or eliminating the taxation of dividends would be ineffective at stimulating the economy now while it is weak. Indeed, most investors would not receive a tax cut from this proposal until *well over one year
from now,* when they file their 2003 taxes in early 2004.

According to the Administration's estimates, exempting certain dividends from individual income taxes would cost $364 billion over the next
decade. About 95 percent of this hefty cost would not occur until after 2003,
by which time the economy is expected to have recovered from the current
downturn.

Adding to the proposal's inefficiency as a stimulus mechanism is the
fact that it would put cash primarily into the hands of high-income individuals, a group that is likely to save rather than spend a larger portion of any
additional funds it receives than middle- and lower-income families. Yet only
if funds are spent will they have the desired effect of stimulating the economy
now. The Congressional Research Service found that "dividends are concentrated among higher income individuals who tend to save more" and that

overall "using dividend tax reductions to stimulate the economy is unlikely to be very effective."[1]

Benefits Would Be Heavily Concentrated at the Top

It should also be noted that any claims that the benefits of this tax cut would be spread broadly across a growing "investor class" would be misleading. Many middle-income families are more likely to do their investing in the context of tax-deferred retirement accounts, such as 401(k)s and Individual Retirement Accounts. Yet only dividends paid from stocks held in taxable accounts would be affected by this proposal.

According to estimates by the Urban Institute-Brookings Institution Tax Policy Center:

- Nearly two-thirds of the benefits of exempting corporate dividends from the individual income tax would flow to the top five percent of the population, because these taxpayers own the lion's share of stocks. (The top five percent includes tax filers with incomes over $140,000; these filers have average income of $350,000.)
- The top one percent of tax filers—a group whose incomes start at $330,000 and that has average income of about $1 million—would receive 42 percent of the benefits.
- Those with incomes over $1 million—the top 0.2 percent of tax filers, with an average income that exceeds $3 million—would receive nearly one-quarter of the tax-cut benefits.
- In fact, the group with incomes over $1 million—which consists of about 226,000 tax filers in 2003—would receive roughly as much in benefits as the 120 million tax filers with incomes below $100,000. Stated another way, the top 0.2 percent of tax filers would receive nearly as much from this tax cut as the bottom 90 percent of filers combined.

The dollar value of the benefits of this tax cut for different income groups is also illustrative. Exempting corporate dividends from the individual income tax would yield an average annual tax savings of $27,100 for tax filers with incomes over $1 million, according to preliminary Tax Policy Center estimates. In contrast, those with incomes between $30,000 and $40,000 would see an average annual benefit of $42. Those with incomes between $40,000 and $50,000 would see an average annual benefit of $84.

The high-income taxpayers who would reap the vast majority of these tax-cut benefits have experienced far more substantial income gains over the past two decades than families lower down on the economic spectrum. Moreover, this high-income group is also the primary beneficiary of the tax-cut package enacted in 2001. Those with incomes over $1 million can expect an annual tax cut of *over $130,000* when all of the income-tax changes enacted in 2001 are fully in effect, and this figure does not even include the benefits this group would receive from repeal of the estate tax. The benefits of a dividend tax cut would come on top of this amount.

State Budget Deficits Would Be Enlarged

Exempting dividends from the individual income tax also would undercut other federal efforts to bolster the economy by worsening the dire fiscal situation in the states, which are facing a $60 billion to $85 billion budget gap in the next fiscal year, the largest shortfall in the last half-century. As states cut spending and raise taxes to meet their balanced budget requirements, they are placing a drag on the economy. Cutting the individual tax on dividends would reduce state revenues, because of the linkages between state and federal tax codes. Eliminating the tax could reduce state revenues by approximately $4 billion a year.[2] In general, states will have to raise taxes or cut expenditures by one dollar for each dollar of revenue loss, further undermining the proposal's effectiveness as economic stimulus.

IMPACT OF A DIVIDEND EXEMPTION
ON THE ELDERLY

Supporters of exempting dividends from individual taxation are stressing the impact of this tax cut on the elderly. And indeed, preliminary Tax Policy Center estimates indicate that about 41 percent of the benefits of a dividend exemption would go to those over age 65. But while the elderly as a group would receive a large relative share of the tax cut, these benefits would flow predominately to those elderly individuals who have high incomes.

- Nearly 40 percent of the benefits of the dividend exemption that would accrue to elderly individuals would flow to the 2.5 percent of elderly people with incomes exceeding $200,000.
- Nearly three-quarters of the benefits that would go to the elderly from this tax cut would flow to the 19 percent of elderly with incomes above $75,000.
- Elderly people with incomes below $50,000—a group that represents two-thirds of all of the elderly in the nation—would receive only 13 percent of the tax cut going to the elderly and *less than 6 percent* of the total tax cut.

By citing a statistic showing that a large share of the benefits from the dividend exemption would go to the elderly, some proponents of this tax cut appear to be trying to foster the impression that it would benefit the average or typical elderly person. This is not the case. Most elderly have fairly low incomes and would receive little or nothing from this tax cut.

The benefits of the proposal would flow predominately to a small group of individuals with high incomes, and a disproportionate share of these high-income taxpayers happen to be elderly. That this is so does not alter the fact that most elderly people would not benefit significantly from it. In fact, many elderly could be adversely affected if the tax cut resulted in fewer resources being available for programs upon which ordinary elderly people rely.

States would also be hard hit by the anticipated increase in interest rates expected to result from this proposal. The proposal will draw funds away from the bond market, as corporate stocks become more attractive investments following the tax cut. To compete for investor dollars with stocks paying dividends that are fully or partially exempt from taxation, entities that issue bonds—including state and local governments—would have to offer higher interest rates. In addition, the cost of reducing or eliminating taxes on dividends for individuals would enlarge the deficit and increase government borrowing. As government borrowing needs crowd out other borrowers, interest rates can rise. Overall, higher interest rates increase the cost of borrowing for states, putting further strain on their budgets.

Positive Effects on the Stock Market Appear to Be Exaggerated

Claims that this tax cut, by making stocks more valuable, would significantly buoy the stock market and thereby bolster consumer confidence and help the economy are likely to be exaggerated. A more muted response seems more likely than a strong reaction when one considers that over half of dividends would not be directly affected by the proposal (because they are paid to tax-exempt accounts, such as pension funds). Moreover, corporate investments would be negatively affected by the higher interest rates that would likely result from this tax cut.

Furthermore, trying to induce an increase in the stock market is an indirect and rather inefficient way to encourage consumers to spend more and thus stimulate the economy. The Congressional Research Service concluded that the link between a stock market increase and consumer spending "is weaker, more uncertain, and perhaps more delayed, than a direct stimulus to the economy via spending increases or cuts in taxes aimed at lower income individuals."[3] In addition, cutting dividends taxes to manipulate the market in an effort to aid investors hurt by the recent downturn is questionable public policy. As Brookings Institution economists Gale and Orszag have noted, "having the government bail out investors who voluntarily accepted risks by investing in the stock market would set a dangerous precedent."[4]

Potential Negative Impact on Certain Sectors of the Economy, Including Small Businesses

As the economy adjusted to lower taxes for corporate dividends, some sectors of the economy would likely be disadvantaged, at least in the short run. This tax cut would make stocks a more attractive investment in terms of their after-tax returns, prompting investors to pull funds out of some other investments and shift these dollars to corporate stocks.

As noted above, the tax cut would draw funds away from the bond market, which would result in higher interest rates. These higher rates not only raise costs for state and local governments and business investment but also for home mortgages and car loans. Similarly, one would also expect the noncorporate sector, which is comprised primarily of small businesses, to be affected adversely, as investment dollars shift into corporate stocks.

Effect on Economy Over the Long Run

The high cost of ending the taxation of dividends would likely mitigate any beneficial long-term impact the proposal might have on the economy. Supporters tout the positive effects of cutting dividend taxes on encouraging more investment in corporations. They often ignore the negative effects associated with the tax cut's long-term cost, however, and the resulting increase in the federal deficit. Although a one-time increase in the current deficit to pay for stimulus can be good economic medicine, permanently increasing future deficits as this proposal would do would have a corrosive effect on the economy. The preponderance of economic research indicates that sustained budget deficits reduce national savings, which results in less investment and ultimately lowers the nation's income in the future. So while the proposal may improve the efficiency of the allocation of investment dollars, it would also shrink the pool of investment dollars available by increasing the deficit. In the end, it is the combination of these positive and negative effects that will determine the overall impact on the economy.

Other Proposals Would Be More Effective Stimulus and Do Less Fiscal Damage Over the Long Run

Other proposals would be far more effective at providing immediate economic stimulus by directing funds to individuals and businesses that would spend the money—and thereby bolster the economy now when it is weak. A generous extension of unemployment benefits, for instance, would put money into the hands of families who are out of work and likely facing cash-flow constraints. Similarly, fiscal assistance to the states would pump money directly into the economy by helping states avoid making deep program cuts or increasing taxes, which would otherwise place a drag on the economy. A tax cut aimed at lower- and moderate-income working families would also offer considerably more stimulus for each dollar of cost in the ten-year budget window—than a cut in taxes on dividends.

Although a temporary increase in the deficit can be justified as providing economic stimulus in the short run, a permanent increase in the deficit is much harder to defend given the deterioration in the fiscal outlook and the knowledge that, just over the horizon, the retirement of the baby boomers will place a huge burden on the federal budget. Despite the need to begin to take steps now to reduce, or certainly not to worsen, future deficits—as well as the need to pay for the ongoing fight against terrorism at home and abroad and the generally agreed-upon need for a prescription drug benefit for seniors—this proposal would produce a substantial drain on the Treasury. These revenue losses would come on top of the massive revenue losses the 2001 tax cut will cause when it is fully in effect. Overall, a costly proposal to eliminate or reduce sharply individual taxes on corporate dividends seems particularly inappropriate.

Supporters of this tax cut are pushing for it to be part of an economic stimulus package, despite its being ineffective and inefficient as stimulus. By doing so, they may seek to create a belief that its high, permanent cost does not have to be offset. Including this proposal in a stimulus package that is said to warrant rapid congressional action avoids linking the proposal to broader consideration of corporate tax reforms that would address the "zero taxation" of much corporate income resulting from the proliferation of corporate tax avoidance and tax sheltering schemes. Any proposal to lighten the tax burden on corporate dividends should be considered, however, only in the context of a deficit-neutral package of corporate reforms, where the range of issues related to corporate taxation can be addressed together.

This analysis is divided into three sections. The first section looks at the cost and distribution of proposals to reduce or eliminate the tax on corporate dividends. The second assesses the impact on the economy of such a tax change. The final section examines the concept of the "double taxation" of corporate dividends and its relevance to the current debate.

Reducing or Eliminating the Tax on Corporate Dividends

A corporation can use dividends as a way to distribute earnings to its share-holders, with dividends being paid out of its after-tax income.[5] In other words, a corporation makes dividend payments to its shareholders out of the earnings that remain after corporate income taxes have been paid. Share-holders include these dividend payments in their income for tax purposes. To the extent that shareholders are subject to the individual income tax, they pay tax on their dividend income.

The Urban Institute-Brookings Institution Tax Policy Center estimates that in 2000, corporations paid $201 billion in dividends out of their after-tax incomes. More than half of these dividends were paid to tax-exempt entities—such as pension funds, individual retirement accounts, and non-profit foundations—or to individuals that owed no income tax. As a result, only about 46 percent of the dividends paid by corporations to individuals (or $93 billion in dividends) were subject to the individual income tax in 2000.[6]

Over the years, various options to eliminate the taxation of corporate dividends have been proposed. Some proposals would exempt from the *corporate* income tax all earnings paid out in dividends. Such proposals would be more costly than making dividends tax free for individuals, because of the large share of dividends flowing to tax-exempt accounts not currently subject to individual income taxes. . . .

Economic Impact of Eliminating the Individual Taxation of Dividends

The Treasury Department released a comprehensive report on various options to reduce the taxation of dividends in 1992.[7] Although the different options had varying effects, the Treasury Department concluded that all of the options—including ending taxes on dividends at the individual level—would have a positive impact on the economy. It concluded such a tax change "will encourage capital to shift into the corporate sector" and "stimulate improvements in overall economic well-being." But the Treasury report was able to reach these positive conclusions in large part because *it assumed that the cost of the tax cuts would be fully offset.* That is, the Treasury options were assessed assuming they had no net impact on the deficit. This assumption is in sharp contrast to the Bush Administration's tax-cut proposal, which is not expected to be offset and would result in higher deficits. These different assumptions are crucial to understanding the long-term effects of the proposals on the economy, because of the negative impact of budget deficits on future economic growth.

The Long-Term Effect—More Efficient Investments but Less Invested

Brookings Institution economists William Gale and Peter Orszag recently undertook an exhaustive review of the available economics literature on the impact of budget deficits on the economy.[8] They found a broad consensus among economists that "declines in budget surpluses (or increases in budget deficits) reduce national savings and thus reduce future national income." They also found that a wide variety of perspectives, from empirical research and leading macroeconomic models to the views of numerous leading academics and policy institutions, "all indicate that increases in expected future deficits raise long-term interest rates." Although the link between future deficits and long-term interest rates has received the most attention in the media, their paper makes the important point that because sustained budget deficits reduce national savings, they have a negative impact on the economy regardless of their effect on interest rates.[9]

As Gale and Orszag point out in their paper, an increase in the budget deficit and the resulting reduction in national savings mean the nation has less to invest. Lower investment leads to a smaller stock of capital assets and lower economic growth in the future. Exempting dividends from individual taxation may encourage a more efficient allocation of resources—that is, it may encourage more investments in those areas that will yield the highest returns for economic growth. But if the revenue losses generated by the tax cut are not offset and result in larger deficits, there will be lower national savings and thus less to invest. So even though the proposal may promote more efficient investment of the capital that is available, there will be a lower level of investment overall. It is the combined effect of these factors—more efficient investments, but less invested—that ultimately will determine the long-term impact of the proposal on the economy.

In Short Run, Tax Cut Offers Little to Boost Economy

Although the long-term impact of the proposal would be modest at best, its effects in the short term are clearer. The proposal is particularly ineffective economic stimulus, offering little "bang for the buck."

- The benefits of eliminating individual taxes on corporate dividends would flow primarily to those with higher incomes. This higher-income group, however, is likely to save more and spend less of any additional funds it receives than low- and moderate-income families would. Funds must be spent if they are to stimulate the economy in the near term.
- Despite the hefty ten-year cost of the proposal, only a small portion of the revenue losses would result in an immediate increase in spending. This undermines the proposal's effectiveness as a mechanism to deliver immediate stimulus to the economy. More than 90 percent of the revenue losses over the next ten years would occur after 2003, in years when the economy is expected to have recovered.
- The tax cut also is poorly designed to put money into the hands of consumers quickly, because most tax-cut recipients would not begin receiving the bulk of their annual tax-cut benefits until they filed their 2003 tax returns in early 2004. To receive the benefits earlier, taxpayers would have to adjust their withholding or estimated payments for the remainder of this year, a step that few—particularly those with only modest levels of dividends—would be likely to take, given the difficulty individuals would have estimating the impact of the tax cut and their fear of penalties in the event of underpayment.
- A tax cut for dividends would reduce state revenues because of the linkages between state and federal tax codes, worsening the state fiscal crisis that is imposing a drag on the economy. Preliminary estimates by the Center on Budget and Policy Priorities indicate that exempting dividends from individual income tax could cost states about $4 billion a year. Given the large budget deficits that states face and the requirements that they balance their budgets, states would be forced to make up for these revenue losses with dollar-for-dollar expenditure reductions or tax increases. Such actions by the states counteract federal efforts to stimulate the economy.[10]
- The proposal also could have a negative impact on the economy in the near-term because of its effects on long-term interest rates. As Gale and Orszag explain in their analysis, financial markets are forward looking and take into account today changes that are expected to occur in the future. Thus, a costly proposal to eliminate or substantially reduce the taxation of dividends would create the expectation of higher future deficits, which in turn could exert upward pressure on long-term interest rates today. These higher long-term rates could dampen prospects for current economic growth, because individuals and businesses make fewer large purchases when the long-term interest rates they pay on the funds they borrow to make the purchases rise to higher levels.

It also is worth noting that in the short run, a proposal to eliminate or reduce substantially the individual taxation of corporate dividends would create winners and losers—that is, it would benefit some sectors of the economy and some firms at the expense of others.

- With a tax cut for corporate stocks that pay dividends, the after-tax returns of this type of investment would rise. While more money would flow to these stocks, these funds would be drawn away from other sectors.

- Funds would likely flow out of the non-corporate sector and into corporate stocks. In the analysis it conducted in 1992, the Treasury Department concluded that the proposal would result in "the reallocation of physical capital (and other real resources) from the rest of the economy into the corporate sector." Thus, the non-corporate sector—typically comprised of small businesses, including sole proprietors—would likely experience a loss of investment funds.

- Similarly, by making equities a more attractive investment, the proposal would make bonds relatively less attractive. Interest rates on bonds would rise under these circumstances, as the bond market would have to offer higher interest rates to attract investors. This result, plus the effect on interest rates stemming from the increase in the deficit the tax cut would engender, could place significant upward pressure on rates. Higher interest rates would not only affect business investment and borrowing by state and local governments, but would also impact consumers by increasing rates on home mortgages and car loans, for instance.

Positive Impact on the Stock Market Likely Exaggerated

Eliminating individual taxes on dividends would make dividend-paying stocks more valuable in terms of their after-tax return. Supporters of this tax cut maintain that investors would seek out these higher returns, thereby bidding up the price of these stocks and boosting the stock market as a whole. This improvement in the stock market would, in turn, have a salutary effect on the economy, they argue, as consumers, heartened by the increase in their portfolios, would react by increasing their spending. This analysis is flawed in a number of respects.

It is far from clear that the proposal would lead to a significant rise in the stock market. As noted previously, about half of all dividends are not subject to individual income tax, primarily because they flow to tax-exempt pension funds, retirement accounts, and non-profit foundations. None of the investment decisions made by these groups would be directly affected by the elimination of the individual tax on corporate dividends, because they are not subject to the tax. Further, corporate investments would be negatively affected by the higher interest rates that likely would follow from this deficit-increasing tax cut.

While one might expect to see stock prices rise modestly in reaction to the proposed tax cut, it would likely be a one-time increase that primarily yielded a windfall for current holders of dividend-paying stocks, who purchased their stocks at prices that reflected the current tax treatment of dividends. University of Michigan tax expert Reuven Avi-Yonah recently wrote that "it is doubtful that cutting the tax on dividends will have a significant impact on the stock market. And even if it did, current holders of the stock, wealthy individuals who bought the stock at a discounted price anticipating that they would be taxed on future dividends, would get an unjustified windfall."[11]

Similarly, the *Daily Tax Report* issued by the Bureau of National Affairs cites economists from the investment firm Credit Suisse First Boston as predicting that cutting dividend taxes would have only a "mildly positive" effect on stock prices.[12]

The key question in assessing the stimulative effect of such changes in stock prices is whether a modest increase in the market would be sufficient to increase consumer spending enough to have a meaningful impact on the economy; most estimates—including those of the Federal Reserve—indicate that consumers boost their spending by only a few cents for each dollar increase in their wealth. If the goal is to get consumers to spend more, encouraging such spending through a rise in the stock market consequently is an indirect and inefficient method of achieving that goal. Other proposals, such as extending and strengthening unemployment benefits and providing fiscal assistance for states, would have far more "bang for the buck" in terms of stimulating the economy. As the Congressional Research Service recently concluded, the link between higher stock prices and increased consumer spending "is weaker, more uncertain, and perhaps more delayed, than a direct stimulus to the economy via increases in spending or cuts in taxes aimed at lower income individuals."[13]

"Double Taxation" of Corporate Dividends

Supporters of eliminating the taxation of corporate dividends typically argue that such a change is necessary to end the "double taxation" of these dividends. Double taxation arises because, in theory, corporations pay dividends out of their after-tax earnings, and these payments are subsequently taxed as part of the shareholders' income. Thus, these corporate earnings are taxed twice—once at the corporate level and again at the individual level.

In reality, not all corporate dividends are taxed twice; some are only taxed once and some not at all. As noted above, on the individual side, more than half of all corporate dividends flow to entities, such as tax-exempt retirement funds, that are not subject to individual income tax. Further, some corporate earnings distributed to shareholders are not subject to the corporate income tax, as corporations make use of available tax preferences and other less scrupulous tax avoidance techniques to lower or eliminate their tax bills.

Significant Corporate Profits Escape
Corporate Income Tax

To be taxed twice, corporate profits first have to be subjected to the corporate income tax. Yet there is significant evidence that corporations are aggressively employing tax avoidance strategies that have resulted in a growing share of corporate profits escaping corporate taxation altogether. In recent years, the Treasury Department, the congressional tax-writing committees, academics and journalists have raised concerns over the rise in corporate tax sheltering activities.

As evidence of this trend, recent studies have shown a growing divergence in the amount of profits that corporations report to their shareholders (known as book income) and the amounts that these companies report to the Internal Revenue Service for purposes of paying corporate income taxes.[14] Harvard economist Mihir Desai concludes that the traditional link between these two measures of corporate profits has "broken down" and that "the patterns of the deteriorating link between tax and book income are consistent with increased levels of sheltering over the decade." For instance, Desai found that $154 billion, or more than half of the gap between corporate book and tax income in 1998, the latest year covered in his study, could not be explained by the traditional accounting differences between these two measures.

On a related front, the Institute on Taxation and Economic Policy examined the books of 250 large companies between 1996 and 1998.[15] Together these companies pay about 30 percent of all federal corporate income taxes.

- Over that three-year period, ITEP found that 41 companies—or about one in six of the total sample—paid "less than zero" in federal corporate taxes in at least one year. Despite reporting nearly $26 billion in profits to their shareholders over the period, these companies not only paid no corporate income tax but actually received rebate checks from the federal government totaling $3 billion. This list includes companies such as General Motors, ChevronTexaco, Goodyear and CSX.
- Building on these findings, Citizens for Tax Justice currently estimates that in 2002, less than half of corporate profits were subject to the corporate income tax. As [a] result, CTJ concludes that only a little more than half of corporate profits were subject to tax at any level, corporate or individual.[16]

In a *New York Times* article on January 5, 2003, *Times* business columnist Gretchen Morgenson concluded that "companies are paying less and less in taxes each year, making the 35 percent corporate tax rate a fiction."[17] Morgenson reported, for example, that Bristol-Myers Squibb's effective tax rate fell to 15.4 percent in 2001 from 25.2 percent in the previous year. (A firm's effective tax rate is the percentage of the firm's profits paid in taxes.) Similarly, in a recent article, Robert McIntyre, executive director of Citizens for Tax Justice and an expert in corporate tax avoidance, points out that CSX, despite having U.S. profits of more than $930 million over the past four years, paid no federal corporate income taxes over the period and instead received refunds totaling $164 million.[18]

Taxing Dividends Twice Not Relevant Equity Issue

The moniker "double taxation" tends to raise the specter of some group—in this case, individuals who receive dividends—being treated unfairly by the tax system, because part of their income is being taxed twice. On its editorial page, for example, the *Wall Street Journal* has argued that the policy of taxing dividend income twice should be ended as a matter of equity.[19]

But for economists, whether this income is taxed once or twice is not the relevant equity issue. As McIntyre aptly noted, "Who wouldn't feel better, for instance, about paying two taxes of 10 percent each rather than a single tax of

40 percent?"[20] Moreover, many forms of income are taxed more than once. An obvious example is wages. While corporate dividends are theoretically double taxed first at the corporate level and then at the individual level, an individual's wages are immediately subject to both payroll and income taxes.

Equity, in the context of taxes, is about whether taxpayers in similar circumstance pay similar amounts of tax and about how the burden of taxes is borne by different income groups, not about the number of times a particular type of income is taxed. The current federal tax system as a whole (including the taxation of dividends, and also including payroll and excise taxes) is modestly progressive.[21] The most significant equity issue related to the taxation of dividends is whether eliminating the tax on dividends and thereby reducing the level of progressivity in the tax system is a desirable step.

Concerns That Dividend Taxation Distorts Investment Decisions

The more significant concern raised by many economists is that the current tax treatment of corporate dividends may interfere with the efficient allocation of the nation's resources by directing investments into less productive, but more lightly taxed, areas. In a dynamic market economy, such as in the United States, investment funds flow to those areas that yield the highest *after-tax* return—other factors, such as risk, being equal. Consequently, investors may be deterred from investing in the corporate sector because the after-tax return of a corporate investment would be lower than the after-tax return of a non-corporate investment that is taxed only as part of an individual's income tax return.[22] Although it might offer a higher after-tax return, the non-corporate investment could be a less productive use of investment dollars (as measured by its *pre-tax* return) and thus be less beneficial for overall economic growth.

Furthermore, within the corporate sector, some economists believe the current tax treatment of dividends can distort corporate financing decisions. Corporations raise funds to finance capital investment through essentially three methods: debt (i.e., issuing bonds); equity (i.e., issuing new shares of stock); and retained earnings (i.e., reinvesting after-tax earnings rather than distributing them to shareholders in the form of dividends). The concern is that current tax law biases corporate investment decisions against issuing new equity and toward debt financing and retaining earnings, which are both more lightly taxed than dividends.[23] As a result, corporations may not be using an optimal mix of these three financing mechanisms, which would ultimately be less efficient for the economy.

There is a large body of academic work examining the impact on the economy of having separate corporate and individual income taxes. Many of these studies conclude that, for the efficiency reasons discussed above, the economy would benefit if the corporate and individual taxes were integrated. The 1992 Treasury study reached this conclusion and, to that end, proposed *a deficit-neutral* dividend exclusion at the individual level. There is not unanimous agreement on this issue among economists, however, particularly when international economic issues are taken into account. As University of Michigan international tax expert Reuven Avi-Yonah recently wrote, the case for corporate tax integration in a globalizing world "is much shakier than is commonly thought," with many of our trading partners now moving away from the full exclusion of dividends from taxation.[24]

Conclusion

As short-term stimulus, exempting all or a portion of corporate dividends from individual income taxes is ill-conceived. It fails to meet the basic requirements of any stimulus proposal, which are that such a proposal be temporary and be targeted in a way that encourages as much new spending as possible in the short term. The proposal to reduce or eliminate the taxation of dividends is clearly intended to be permanent, and its benefits would flow primarily to those with the highest incomes, a group likely to save more of a tax cut than moderate- and lower-income families would.

Despite its shortcomings as stimulus, reducing or eliminating individual taxes on corporate dividends is expected to be the centerpiece of the Bush Administration's economic growth package. The Administration likely will use the continued uncertainty surrounding the state of the economy both to push for rapid consideration of its package and to argue that the package's large long-term costs need not be offset. This, however, is the wrong context for debating the dividend proposal, since it precludes consideration of other relevant corporate tax issues and thus virtually ensures this costly tax cut will impose a permanent drain on the Treasury.

Consideration of measures to reduce or eliminate the so-called "double taxation" of corporate dividends should be accompanied by consideration of measures to curb the "zero taxation" of a rising share of corporate profits as a result of the increasingly aggressive use of corporate tax shelters and other tax-avoidance techniques. A tax cut for dividends should be considered only as part of a more comprehensive, deficit-neutral package of corporate tax reforms.

Notes

1. Gregg A. Esenwein and Jane G. Gravelle, "The Taxation of Dividend Income: An Overview and Economic Analysis of the Issues," Congressional Research Service, October 7, 2002.

2. Iris J. Lav, "Bush 'Growth Plan' Would Worsen State Budget Crises," Center on Budget and Policy Priorities, January 9, 2002.

3. Esenwein and Gravelle.

4. William Gale and Peter Orszag, "A New Round of Tax Cuts," Center on Budget and Policy Priorities, August 23, 2002.

5. Dividend-paying firms tend to be large, well-established companies. For example, many of the highest-yielding stocks (i.e., pay the highest dividends relative to their share prices) tend to be familiar companies, such as Philip Morris, J.P. Morgan Chase, General Motors, Eastman-Kodak, Dow Chemical, Bristol-Myers Squibb, ConAgra Foods, Ford Motor, and ChevronTexaco. See

Greg Bartalos, "New Tax Plan May Yield Sweet Dividends," *Barron's Online*, December 12, 2002.

6. William G. Gale, "About Half of Dividend Payments Do Not Face Double Taxation," *Tax Notes*, November 11, 2002.

7. "Integration of the Individual and Corporate Tax Systems: Taxing Business Income Once," U.S. Department of the Treasury, January 1992.

8. William G. Gale and Peter R. Orszag, "The Economic Effects of Long-Term Fiscal Discipline," Urban-Brookings Tax Policy Center Discussion Paper, December 17, 2002.

9. Gale and Orszag point out that if lower national savings leads to increased foreign borrowing, interest rates may not rise. But if foreign borrowing increases, then America's indebtedness to rest of the world increases. The returns to these investments flow overseas, rather than raising the future incomes of Americans. As a result, higher deficits lower the nation's income in the future, regardless of whether interest rates increase.

10. States would also be negatively affected by the proposal because it would likely result in higher interest rates and thus increase their cost of borrowing.

11. Reuven S. Avi-Yonah, "Back to the 1930s? The Shaky Case for Exempting Dividends," *Tax Notes*, December 23, 2002.

12. Brett Ferguson, "Treasury Renews Push for Higher Debt Limit, Warns Ceiling Could be Hit in late February," *BNA Daily Tax Report*, December 27, 2002.

13. Esenwein and Gravelle.

14. See Mihir Desai, "The Corporate Profit Base, Tax Sheltering Activity, and the Changing Nature of Employee Compensation," NBER Working Paper 8866, April 2002, and George A. Plesko, "Reconciling Corporation Book and Tax Net Income, Tax Years 1996–1998," *Statistics of Income Bulletin*, Spring 2002.

15. Robert S. McIntyre and T.D. Coo Nguyen, "Corporate Income Taxes in the 1990s," Institute on Taxation and Economic Policy, October 2000.

16. Robert McIntyre, "New Gang, Old Myths," *The American Prospect*, January 13, 2003.

17. Gretchen Morgenson, "Waiting for the President to Pass the Tax-Cut Gravy," *The New York Times*, January 5, 2003.

18. McIntyre, "New Gang, Old Myths."

19. "Ending Double Tax Trouble," *The Wall Street Journal*, December 26, 2002.

20. McIntyre, "New Gang, Old Myths."

21. Joel Friedman and Isaac Shapiro, "Are Taxes Too Concentrated at the Top? Rapidly Rising Income at the Top Lie Behind Increase in Share of Taxes Paid by High-Income Taxpayers," Center on Budget and Policy Priorities, December 18, 2002.

22. Earnings in a non-corporate business are taxed only at the individual income tax rates. The majority of non-corporate businesses are sole proprietorships, earnings from which are taxed at the owner's individual income tax rates. Other non-corporate enterprises such as partnerships are often referred to as "passthrough" companies because the earnings pass through to the partners and shareholders and are taxed at their individual rates. See Jack H. Taylor, "Passthrough Organizations Not Taxed As Corporations," Congressional Research Service, August 20, 2002.

23. Of these three methods, debt receives the most favorable tax treatment. Although interest payments to bondholders are treated as income to the bondholder, just as dividend payments are treated as income to shareholders, interest payments are a deductible expense for a corporation. As a deductible expense, interest payments reduce the amount of corporate profits subject to

tax; in contrast, dividends are paid out of after-tax funds. Thus, interest payments are taxed at most only once, at the individual level, and are more lightly taxed than dividends, which can face both corporate and individual taxes.

Retained earnings can also be subject to double taxation, but to a much lesser degree than dividends. When a corporation retains its earnings for investment purposes, it tends to push the firm's share prices higher. Thus, shareholders become subject to higher capital gains taxes when (or if) they decide to sell their shares. But capital gains are taxed at a lower rate than regular income taxes, and shareholders can control when they will sell shares, potentially deferring capital gains taxes indefinitely. As a result, retained earnings generate lower taxes at the individual level than dividend payments, which are subject to tax in the year in which the payment is made at individual income tax rates.

24.   Avi-Yohan.

POSTSCRIPT

Should the Double Taxation
of Corporate Dividends
Be Eliminated?

Ignore for the moment whether or not eliminating the tax on dividend income will stimulate the economy, and focus on the issue of "double taxation." If one concludes that the efficiency concerns raised by Michel, Goyburu, and Rector outweigh the equity issues raised by Friedman and Greenstein, one should ask whether or not there really is double taxation in the first place.

Before considering that discussion, it is important to understand how double taxation allegedly comes into being. Those who favor the repeal of the dividend tax argue that every time a corporation has an excess profit of one dollar that they plan to distribute as a dividend, 35 cents of that potential dividend goes to the U.S. Treasury, assuming that the corporation is in the highest corporate income tax bracket of 35 percent. As the corporation "distributes" its excess profits to its shareholders, those 65 pennies are now subject to personal income taxes. Again, assuming the highest tax bracket, this time of the personal income tax, the 65 cents that is distributed would be taxed at 38.6 percent. That represents another 24 cents in taxes for a total of 59 cents for every dollar earned and distributed to shareholders.

There are some very big assumptions here that should be underscored. One could ask, for example, just how much of a corporation's net income is subject to the corporate income tax? The taxation of corporate income is too complex to detail, but it is important to note that over the past 40 years, the amount of corporate taxes paid as a percentage of all federal taxes from all sources has steadily decreased. On the other hand, in the 1960s corporate taxes were a close second to personal income taxes as a percentage of federal tax revenue; now corporate taxes are a distant third to social security taxes. This is the result of accelerated depreciation allowances and other tax preferences that have been granted to the corporate sector. Thus, a significant amount of corporate net income never passes through the corporate tax mill. That portion of corporate net income that is distributed in the form of dividends is only taxed once—as personal income.

One could also note the consequences of corporations' having two options for their net income: they can distribute their net earnings as dividends, or they can "retain" these corporate earnings and invest them in the corporate enterprise. Over time this should increase the value of the corporation, but that increased valuation is not fully taxed as personal income. This is because any asset that is held for more than one year and that appreciates in value is subject to special rates. The maximum tax that an individual must pay on these capital gains is 20 percent, and that is not paid until the gain is realized—that is, there is no capital gain income to tax until the appreciated asset is sold. In this extreme case, the total tax is 48 percent (35 cents of corporate taxes and another 13 cents of capital gains taxes). This is not an insignificant amount, even though it is not the 60 percent that is often cited.

Much has been written in support of eliminating the tax on corporate dividends. Alan Greenspan offered an interesting view on this topic in his February 12, 2003, testimony before the House Financial Services Committee. Greenspan concluded that, in the long run, "virtually everyone" benefits from the elimination of this tax. Greenspan is not alone in this view, particularly in the conservative "think tanks." See, for example, the March 6, 2003, testimony before the House Ways and Means Committee by John H. Makin, a resident scholar of the American Enterprise Institute, which can be found on the Internet at http://www.aei.org/news/newsID.16393/news_detail.asp, and "How the Tax Code Contributed to the Corporate Scandals and Bankruptcies," by Lawrence H. Whitman, *Heritage Backgrounder No. 1578* (August 27, 2002).

Many others take exception to the tax code. Their concerns take several forms. William G. Gale and Peter R. Orszag, for example, question the growth consequences of eliminating the dividend tax in "The Economic Effects of Long Term Fiscal Discipline," Urban-Brookings Tax Policy Center Discussion Paper (December 17, 2002), which can be found at http://www.som.yale.edu/faculty/pks4/files/macro_readings/inv_gale_orszag_brookings_021217.pdf. Avrum D. Lank agrees in "Forget the Plan to Stop Taxing Dividends," *JSOnline/Milwaukee Journal Sentinel*, http://www.Jsonline.com/bym/your/jan03/113334.asp. In this essay, Lank raises the issue of the complexities that this will introduce into the tax code. Many agree, including Gregg A. Esenwein and Jane G. Gravelle in "The Taxation of Dividends: An Overview and Economic Analysis of the Issues," Congressional Research Service (October 7, 2002) and Dean Baker in "The Dividend Tax Break: Taxing Logic," Center for Economic and Policy Research Issue Brief (January 6, 2003).

ISSUE 10

Are Credit Card Companies Exploiting American Consumers?

YES: Robert D. Manning, from "Perpetual Debt, Predatory Plastic," *Southern Exposure* (Summer 2003)

NO: Michael F. McEneney, from "Written Statement of Michael F. McEneney on Behalf of the Consumer Bankers Association," Testimony before the House Subcommittee on Financial Institutions and Consumer Credit (September 15, 2004)

ISSUE SUMMARY

YES: Professor Robert D. Manning lists a number of problems with credit cards, including high interest rates, misrepresentation of the cost of debt consolidation loans, use of double billing cycles, use of "bait and switch" techniques, improper use of personal consumer credit information, and the proliferation of a number of practices that are of little or no benefit to consumers.

NO: Lawyer Michael F. McEneney stresses the benefits that consumers experience because of the "ever-expanding choices available to consumers," and he supports his claims by reporting that a Federal Reserve study found that "91% of credit card holders are satisfied with their credit card issuers."

When a consumer makes a purchase, he or she can "pay" for the item in a variety of ways. There is the old-fashioned way of paying with cash—exchanging Federal Reserve Notes and treasury currency for the item. A second option, also of fairly long standing, involves paying by check. The options then evolve to more recent creations—credit cards, debit cards, and even stored-value cards. There is even something called a smart card.

Concentrating on credit cards, the statistics regarding their use are almost mind-boggling. According to one account:

- There are over 641 million credit cards in circulation.
- Credit cards in circulation support some $1.5 trillion in consumer spending.

- Some 115 million Americans carry monthly credit card debt.
- The average household has a credit card balance of about $8,000.

Of course, credit cards are issued by profit-seeking financial institutions, and it appears to be a lucrative business; in 2003 the before-tax profits of the credit card industry exceeded $30 billion.

These numbers become more impressive when one realizes that the ubiquitous credit card has only been around for a little more than 50 years. The creation of the credit card is usually attributed to Frank X. McNamara. Legend has it that he conceived of the notion of a credit card when he had insufficient cash to pay for a "power lunch" at Major's Cabin Grill in New York. So in 1951 Diners Club credit cards were issued to some 200 customers who were then able to charge their meals at 27 participating New York restaurants.

Today, people are most familiar with what are called general-purpose credit cards: Visa, MasterCard, Discover, and American Express. Other credit cards carry the name of a particular retailer (for example, the credit cards issued by oil companies, large department stores, and so on). Bank of America usually gets the credit for creating the first general-purpose credit card in 1958; back then it was called BankAmericard. In 1965 Bank of America began licensing other banks to issue BankAmericards. In 1977 BankAmericard became Visa. MasterCard, on the other hand, traces its origins to 1967 when four California banks introduced MasterCharge to compete with BankAmericard. MasterCharge became MasterCard in 1979.

Besides the distinction between general-purpose and other kinds of credit cards, there are also several types of general-purpose credit cards. A secured credit card is one that requires a security deposit. These cards are typically issued to individuals with a troubled credit history or who are just starting out. There are also premium cards (gold, platinum, etc.); these cards have higher borrowing limits and frequently have extra features.

Visa and MasterCard credit cards can be obtained from any number of financial institutions. Each issuer is free to set whatever terms it wishes; that is, a bank issuing a Visa card or MasterCard is free to set its own conditions. These conditions include the APR (annual percentage rate) that applies to unpaid credit card balances, various fees (annual membership fee, cash advance fee, late payment fee, etc.) and incentives (rebates, frequent flier miles, car rental insurance, etc.). Making matters even more complex, a single credit card may have multiple APRs: one for purchases, another for cash advances, and a third for balance transfers. There may also be a special penalty APR, an introductory APR, and a delayed APR.

But something else is associated with credit cards: controversy. This issue takes us to the heart of that controversy. No one denies that the general-purpose card was a marvelous invention, conferring all kinds of benefits to their holders. But, the argument goes, the costs that consumers pay for these advantages are too high. Indeed, credit card issuers have taken advantages of unsuspecting and naïve consumers.

YES

Robert D. Manning

Perpetual Debt, Predatory Plastic

Last year John, a 55-year-old African American living on public assistance in Takoma Park, Maryland, a Washington, D.C., suburb, received an invitation in the mail promising him a chance to join millions of other Americans who enjoy the convenience and status of credit-card membership. In its direct mail solicitation, United Credit National Bank Visa declared, "ACE VISA GUARANTEED ISSUE or we'll send you $100.00! (See inside for details.)" For the unsuspecting, it might have sounded like a terrific opportunity to enter the credit mainstream. But a closer look inside showed that the primary beneficiary was the credit-card company:

> Initial credit line will be at least $400.00. By accepting this offer, you agree to subscribe to the American Credit Educator Financial and Credit Education Program. The ACE program costs $289.00 plus $11.95 for shipping and handling plus $19.00 Processing Fee, a small price to pay compared to the high cost of bad credit! The Annual Card Fee [is] $49.00. . . . For your convenience, we will charge these costs to your new ACE Affinity VISA card.

In other words, getting the card would cost John $369, leaving a net credit line of as little as $31—all financed at an annual percentage rate (APR) of 19.8 percent. As a poor, minority consumer, John's been gouged often enough to recognize a come-on: "Man, they just want to rip me off." He didn't go for the offer.

The credit card industry tries to whitewash such usurious and predatory practices by arguing that it is "democratizing" access to credit through its offers to households previously limited to "second-tier" lenders such as pawnshops and rent-to-own stores.

But not everyone has John's hard-earned savvy. Many impoverished consumers are blinded by financial desperation, low literacy skills, and a desire to part of what the TV commercials tell them is an exclusive club: the fellowship of consumers lucky enough to have earned bank credit cards. After all, exclaim the well-dressed actors, "You work hard for your money. Don't you deserve some credit?"

Not surprisingly, they sign up and become willing subjects of America's new credit economy, a brave new world where technology, marketing innovations, and deregulation have transformed old ways of lending and borrowing. The only thing that hasn't changed is this time-honored principle: The most

From *Southern Exposure,* Summer 2003, pp. 49–53, published by The Institute for Southern Studies. Reprinted by permission of Robert D. Manning.

profitable way to make money off the vulnerable is to keep them in debt at the highest rates for as long as possible.

~◆~

In the 1940s, when folksinger Merle Travis was memorializing the harsh life of Southern coal miners in his famous ballad "Sixteen Tons," consumer debt served as an effective management tool for lowering both wages and worker turnover. Coal miners became indebted to the company store through high prices and excessive finance charges in an era when *"saving for a rainy day"* reflected the vagaries of the business cycle (unemployment) and the physical risks of the job (accidents). As a result, company scrip often replaced government currency, and miners' household debts bound them to their employers in a form of debt servitude.

> *You load sixteen tons what do you get*
> *Another day older and deeper in debt*
> *Saint Peter don't you call me 'cause I can't go*
> *I owe my soul to the company store*

As mail order retailers like Sears Roebuck expanded into the hamlets of the American South in the early 20th century, the growth of working class consumer markets became intertwined with access to credit. Unlike the company stores of Appalachia, where extending credit was a profitable business practice, the "open book" credit policies of local merchants (usually interest free), as well as credit lines at retail chains, were designed primarily to promote sales volume and customer loyalty. Although household incomes rose throughout the 1950s and 60s, the popular Sears credit card—the largest proprietary consumer credit system in the post-World War II era—featured an onerous finance charge of 1.5 percent per month on outstanding balances. Even so, the high costs of administering these low volume "revolving" accounts typically resulted in annual losses to the company; retail profits were made from selling rather than financing consumption in the golden age of U.S. manufacturing.

The recent revolution in consumer financial services dates to the 1970s and the increasingly successful assaults against Depression-era banking regulations. For example, the 1933 McFadden Act limited national banks from crossing state boundaries and competing with state-chartered banks. Until the 1980s, these restrictions protected the community banking system and its conservative installment lending policies. Significantly, the best customers of these local banks were those with the lowest outstanding debts—the borrowers who were most likely to repay their loans within an agreed period.

By the late 1970s, high inflation and declining real wages encouraged families to embrace debt as a strategy for coping with financial hardship. State usury laws and interstate banking restrictions, however, limited the growth of the "all-purpose" or "universal" national bank credit card until 1978, when the U.S. Supreme Court ruled that nationally chartered banks could charge the highest interest rate permitted by their "home" states and export these rates to their out-of-state credit card clients. Banks quickly relocated their "brick and mortar" offices to states without usury ceilings—Citibank, for example, moved from New York to South Dakota. In this way, the universal credit card (led by Visa and MasterCard) was transformed into a high profit product that could hurdle state banking regulatory barriers.

The universal bank credit card played a major role in the deregulation of the U.S. banking industry in the 1980s. National "money center" banks faced mounting losses on Third World, residential, and commercial real estate loans following the 1981–82 recession. Credit cards became the banks' means of profit salvation. Although Citibank's credit card division bled over $500 million in red ink between 1979 and 1981, the sharp reduction in inflation and advances in computer technology sparked a dramatic shift toward consumer financial services over the next two decades.

In the 1980s, an average of one million blue-collar workers lost their jobs each year, swelling the pool of families struggling to make ends meet and increasing the demand for quick, unsecured consumers loans. The consumer services revolution shifted into high gear. Soaring bank profits fueled unprecedented consolidation. In 1977, the top 50 banks accounted for about half of the credit card market. Twenty-five years later, the top ten banks controlled over 80 percent of the market. In the process, "net" revolving credit card debt climbed from about $51 billion in 1980 to over $610 billion in 2002. At the same time, more than half of all outstanding credit card debt is resold in the secondary financial markets as securitized bonds, at a typical premium of 15 to 18 percent in 2001. Many institutional investors such as pension funds purchase these bonds for their portfolios.

Today, the ascendance of credit cards marks the shift from installment lending to revolving loans, where the "best" bank customers will never repay their high interest credit card balances. In this new world of consumer finance, the most disadvantage (debtors) subsidize the low cost of credit for the most advantaged (convenience users). It is this moral divide that leads banks to refer to those clients who pay their charges in full each month (39 percent of all customers in 2002) as "deadbeats."

The other 61 percent are the ones who fuel the banks' profits, and for them the price is growing ever higher. The true cost of borrowing on bank credit cards has more than doubled since the advent of banking deregulation in 1980, thanks to painful interest rates and escalating penalty and user fees. The upward spiral began in 1996, when the U.S. Supreme Court invalidated state limits on credit card fees by ruling that fees are part of the cost of borrowing. This decision produced a striking change in the way card issuers do business, along with some striking numbers:

- The average late fee jumped from $13 in 1996 to $30 in 2002.
- Penalty fee revenue climbed from $1.7 billion in 1996 to $7.3 billion in 2001.
- Total fee income rose more than five times faster than overall credit card profits between 1995 and 2001.
- Together penalty ($7.3 billion) and cash advance ($3.8 billion) fees equaled the after-tax profits of the entire credit card industry ($11.1 billion) in 2001.

- Three out of five families (61%) now carry a balance on their credit cards each month. Their average card debt has risen from over $10,000 in 1998 to over $12,000 in 2002.

In response, banks argue that they provide an efficient service to consumers in urgent need of cash or a necessary purchase. Also, they emphasize the payment flexibility credit cards give their clients, many of whom face increasing financial demands and prefer to carry balances from month to month.

꙳

As profits have climbed, corporate retailers have become increasingly dependent on finance revenues to make up for shrinking margins on consumer sales. In 2001, for instance, Sears and Circuit City reported that more than half of their profits were due to finance-related revenues. This is not surprising since credit cards are the most profitable product of the financial services industry. Even during the current recession, pre-tax profits of the credit card industry (measured by Return on Assets) jumped 20 percent from 2000 to 2001. The industry pulled in record pre-tax profits of nearly $18 billion in 2001, or a whopping 4 percent of assets—three times greater than the average of the banking industry.

Not incidentally, the growing burden of high-cost credit card debt is borne by middle-income and working poor families. The current recession, which elicited President Bush's patriotic exhortations to spend more time and money in the malls, has highlighted the critical role of consumer spending to the vitality of the corporate economy. Although government policy-makers have encouraged household spending by reducing interest rates (the Federal Funds rate was cut from 6.5 percent in 2000 to 1.75 percent at end of 2001), the sharp decline in the cost of borrowing by banks has not been passed on to consumers. For the major credit card companies, the Federal Reserve's low-interest rate policy has produced a windfall, given that they had reduced their rates only modestly—from an average of 18 percent in 2000 to about 16 percent in 2001.

The industry, meanwhile, has fought to stop or hinder any state regulation of credit card interest rate ceilings and fees—or requirements that consumers be given meaningful notice of rate hikes or other changes in their contract provisions. For example, Maryland-based Chevy Chase Bank promised its credit card clients not to raise the top interest rate above 24 percent. In 1996, however, it moved its credit card headquarters to Virginia and raised its interest rate to a high of 28.8 percent. It also changed the terms of its contract to include higher late fees, a new overlimit fee, and a more costly "daily" calculation of finance charges—all without the sort of effective notification that would give customers a chance to reject these unfavorable amendments to their existing contracts.

Real disclosure would cut into profits, so the industry has fought to keep customers in the dark. If credit card clients understood the long-term cost of their accounts, they might make higher monthly payments—something banks don't want. The American Bankers Association has sued to prevent the enactment of a 2002 California law that requires banks to use clients' monthly statements to inform them of the number of years necessary to pay off the outstanding balance, assuming there are no additional charges and only the minimum payment is remitted.

Although banks emphasize the availability of low-interest balance transfers, the most indebted rarely qualify for these promotional programs or benefit for only a short period of time (two to six months). More frequently, heavily indebted households encounter "bait and switch" offers, where low-interest promises are quickly replaced with high-interest realities. Furthermore, credit card companies have adopted a stringent policy of imposing penalties on promotional interest rates for minor payment infractions or simply due to high outstanding balances on other consumer loan accounts.

In Houston, Texas, for example, Doug received an enticing six-month, 1.9 percent balance transfer offer from Chase MasterCard and shifted $5,000 from his MBNA credit card account. Unfortunately, Doug's wife mistakenly sent $80 instead of the required $97 for the first month's minimum payment. Even though it was received two weeks before the due date, his next statement reported $17 past due plus a $35 late fee. More striking was the increase in the interest rate, from 1.9 percent to 22.99 percent, even though he had not had a late payment in over two years. A Chase customer service representative informed Doug he would have to document six months of on-time payments before the bank would consider his request for a lower interest rate. This followed a previous "bait and switch" from Chase on the same card in 2001, where the 4.9 percent promotional rate was raised without warning—simply because the bank had decided that the balances on his other credit cards were "too high."

The passage of the Financial Services Modernization Act of 1997, which authorized the Citibank and Traveler's Group merger, marks the end of Depression-era regulation of retail banking as separate from commercial banking/insurance services. Moreover, the ability to acquire companies across financial services sectors and share client information with corporate subsidiaries underlies the rise of "cross-selling" financial products such as investment services to credit card clients. This explains Citibank's 1997 purchase, at a substantial premium, of AT&T's unprofitable credit card company (eighth largest), with its disproportionate number of high-income customers. For Citigroup, this corporate synergy produces multiple revenue flows by originating high interest loans through credit card and subprime lending, which are then resold through its Salomon Smith Barney division to individual and institutional investors.

Not incidentally, access to personal consumer credit information enables predatory lenders to identify highly indebted households that are susceptible to slippery solicitations for "debt consolidation." According to a 2002 California lawsuit, Household Finance obtained lists of prospective clients from Best Buy, K-Mart, Costco, and other retailers. Homeowners with high debts were identified from these lists and contacted by account executives at nearby branches. Household promised these potential customers that their debt consolidation loans would save them money after the refinancing of their credit card, consumer loan, and mortgage debts into a single monthly payment. In the process, the lawsuit alleged, Household deliberately sought to "upsell," or persuade their clients to accept consolidated loans in amounts so high in relation to the value of their homes that it would be nearly impossible to sell or refinance in the future.

By misrepresenting the total cost of these debt consolidation loans (origination fees, mandatory insurance, high interest rates), the suit claims, Household Finance Corporation generates high profits from the initiation of these loans as well as from their resale in secondary mortgage and securitized bond markets.

Today, high credit card interest rates are no longer sufficient to satisfy the financial services industry's voracious appetite for profits. Penalty and transaction fees continue to rise while new fees are imposed, such as overdraft transactions, foreign currency conversion, and "double billing" cycles which reduce the payment "grace" period. In addition, banks have begun aggressively marketing financial-related services that offer little practical benefits for their clients. These include credit protection programs ($9.99 per month from Citibank) that cannot prevent identity fraud, and unemployment and injury insurance (typically 0.5 percent of outstanding monthly balance) with premium costs that usually exceed the minimum credit card payments provided by the insurance. The proliferation of these products yields big profits for the banks and only modest benefits for consumers.

For American families and consumer advocates, fighting back isn't easy. The industry has thwarted state and local attempts to create better consumer protections by invoking the principle of federal preemption—the U.S. Constitution's provision that public efforts to regulate the national banking system can be legislated only by Congress. The influence of the banking industry on both the U.S. Congress and the executive branch (MBNA was the largest contributor to George Bush's Presidential campaign) seemingly ensures that no significant pro-consumer bills will see the light of day in the next couple of years. At the same time, the industry has reduced its vulnerability to class-action lawsuits by specifying arbitration agreements in their credit card contracts that deny consumers their right to a day in court.

Now, with the threat of regulation and litigation diminished, the credit card industry is focusing its efforts on passing the Bankruptcy Reform Act. President Clinton vetoed the measure at the end of 2000, but other versions of this industry-written bill were passed by both houses of Congress in 2002, and again by the U.S. House of Representatives in April 2003. The aim of the bill is to increase the amount of unsecured consumer loans (especially credit card debts) that must be repaid before the approval of a bankruptcy petition. If this bill is enacted into law, it will expand the U.S. government's role as a *de facto* debt collector and increase the costs assumed by the public in extending consumer credit to the most risky credit card clients. In doing so, it will provide banks even greater incentive to push high-cost credit to their most marginal clients. For an industry whose motto is "Greed is Good," this legislative distortion of the free market system could enable it to top even its current record profits and spiraling executive bonuses.

Written Statement of Michael F. McEneney on Behalf of the Consumer Bankers Association

Before the Subcommittee on Financial Institutions and Consumer Credit

Good morning Chairman Bachus, Ranking Member Sanders, and Members of the Subcommittee. My name is Michael F. McEneney. I am a partner in the law firm of Sidley Austin Brown & Wood LLP. It is my pleasure to appear before you this morning on behalf of the Consumer Bankers Association ("CBA"). The CBA is the recognized voice on retail banking issues in the nation's capital. Member institutions are the leaders in consumer financial services, including auto finance, home equity lending, card products, education loans, small business services, community development, investments, deposits, and delivery. CBA was founded in 1919 and provides leadership, education, research, and federal representation on retail banking issues such as privacy, fair lending, consumer protection legislation, and regulation. CBA members include most of the nation's largest bank holding companies, as well as regional and super community banks that collectively hold two-thirds of the industry's total assets.

Today's hearing is focused on financial products and services from the consumer's perspective. There is no doubt that today's financial marketplace looks quite good from the consumer's perspective. The financial services marketplace offers consumers a wider variety of financial products and services than ever before. This includes loans, deposit products, checking accounts, investment options and a growing variety of payment and remittance services. Not only consumers choose from a wide range of products, but they can obtain them over the phone, using the Internet, or through personal interaction at the financial institutions' offices.

Our financial marketplace is truly a success story. However, the success did not develop overnight, or by accident. There was a time when consumers did not enjoy all of the conveniences they are offered today. In fact, it was not too long ago when retail banking services looked much different than they do today. Back then many people had to carry cash or checks at all times because

From Testimony before the House Subcommittee on Financial Institute of Consumer Credit, September 15, 2004.

credit cards as we know them did not exist. And to get that cash people had to spend time going to the bank branch and standing in line for a teller. Why? There was no such thing as an ATM. Visiting the bank branch in person was also necessary to get a loan, and, in many instances, you had to have an account with the bank. The opportunities to shop around for a loan that are available today really did not exist. Most people were just happy if their bank approved them and accepted the rate the bank was offering at the time. The approval process could last weeks, and fewer people qualified for loans than would qualify today.

There are obviously a number of reasons for the spectacular evolution of the financial services industry and the ever-expanding choices available to consumers. However, I believe that most of these reasons relate to providing financial institutions with the flexibility to compete fiercely with one another to provide a better product to consumers at lower costs. I would like to use a few examples to illustrate my point.

First, the process by which consumers obtain home mortgages has been simplified and made more efficient through increased competition in the marketplace. Hopeful homebuyers at one time submitted their mortgage application to their bank and waited on pins and needles for several days, or even a few weeks, while their application was considered. Those who did not have a relationship with a bank, or those who did not have many local banks from which to choose, obviously had a more challenging time obtaining a mortgage. However, today, consumers benefit from lenders across the country competing with one another to provide consumers with home loan opportunities wherever they may reside. Decisions are oftentimes made almost instantaneously, and lenders are able to offer loans that meet a variety of consumer needs. Given the number of lenders and types of mortgages available, credit-worthy borrowers are likely to have several choices when choosing how to finance their homeownership.

Second, we take for granted that a consumer today can obtain a credit card that suits his or her individual needs. The credit card may offer frequent flyer miles, or the logo of the consumer's charity. It may offer the consumer a rebate on some or all purchases the consumer makes with the credit card. The consumer can also shop for low interest rates, and credit cards that do not have any annual fees. I believe that all of these benefits can be traced in great part to the ease with which credit card issuers can compete with one another through a variety of mechanisms, including a process known as "prescreening."

It is hard to imagine, but there once was a time when annual fees were common and consumers obtained few "fringe" benefits for using their credit cards. Today, most people can find an offer for a card without an annual fee or that offers other benefits simply by reading their mail. Before large numbers of card issuers engaged in prescreening, a consumer obtained a credit card from his or her local bank. Although local banks competed with one another to provide retail banking services to consumers, including credit card products, the competition was nothing like we see today. Some time ago, credit card issuers began to prescreen consumers in order to offer them credit cards. This process, combined with uniform rules for interest rates and fees, allowed banks in any location to offer credit cards to consumers *nationwide* through the mail. Basically, prescreening allows a creditor to obtain a limited amount of credit information in order to offer consumers a "firm offer of credit." With the advent of prescreening, suddenly the consumer did not need to be satisfied with the credit card from his or her local bank—a card that likely had an annual fee and comparatively higher interest rates. In fact, as more card issuers made more credit card offers to consumers, consumers could pick from a variety of credit cards. Naturally, this competition fostered lower prices and improved features on credit cards. Perhaps these developments help explain why the staff of the Federal Reserve Board recently found that 91% of cardholders are satisfied with their credit card issuers.

Third, the ability of financial institutions to price their products in a more precise manner has resulted in enormous benefits to all consumers—most notably the extraordinary homeownership rate. This Subcommittee has gathered large amounts of information pertaining to our national credit system as part of its deliberations on the FACT Act just last year. However, a few of the key points are worth repeating today. The consumer reporting process has developed into a very sophisticated information delivery mechanism that allows lenders to evaluate large amounts of objective and accurate information about consumers. Successful lenders have used this information to evaluate and manage risk in a way that allows them to lower the costs of credit to those consumers who have good credit histories. Yet, consumers with good credit histories are not the only primary beneficiaries of the benefits resulting from the developments fostered by our national credit system. In fact, as lenders obtain more information about potential borrowers through applications and credit reports, for example, they can offer credit to consumers who at one time could not qualify for credit. Now, instead of a bank offering a "one size fits all" loan product to only those consumers with above average credit histories, the bank can use risk-based pricing to offer more consumers access to credit at a variety of risk-based prices. Indeed, many reputable lenders have developed successful lines of business making prudent loans to lower- and moderate-income families that have been traditionally underserved. The more competition there is from reputable lenders making responsible lending decisions to consumers, the less opportunity there will be for bad actors to prey on the vulnerable. That means more home mortgages, more college education loans, and more auto loans for safe transportation for consumers of all walks of life—not just the wealthy or those with perfect credit histories.

Competition in the market place also means an expanding pie where those who have been traditionally underserved can enter the mainstream of our economy. For example, CBA's members continue to develop and expand product offerings to satisfy the demands of an increasingly diverse market. This includes efforts to bank the so-called "unbanked" through use of payroll cards, stored value products, and remittance services in addition to offering low-cost traditional banking products, such as checking accounts. For example, CBA is hosting a Hispanic Banking Forum later this month to highlight bank activities in this area and provide an opportunity for banks to share their knowledge and experience.

Mr. Chairman, current law ensures that consumers receive valuable information with respect to financial products. Laws such as the Truth in Lending Act, the Truth in Savings Act, the Electronic Fund Transfer Act, and the Real Estate Settlement Procedures Act establish frameworks under which consumers are provided important disclosures with respect to the price of financial services, and the terms on which they are offered. Consumers receive a variety of disclosures in other contexts, such as under the Equal Credit Opportunity Act and the Fair Credit Reporting Act. In short, it is clear that consumers do not lack for disclosures of information in connection with financial transactions.

It is also important to note that our financial marketplace is a complex system that relies on providing consumers with choice. Any system that offers choices requires consumers to understand the relative benefits and costs of those choices. Disclosure laws like Truth in Lending are important, but they can only do so much in the absence of fundamental financial literacy on the part of consumers. Banks have long understood that the most innovative and beneficial financial products in the world are likely of no use to the consumer who lacks basic knowledge of how to participate in our financial system, and unsophisticated consumers are more easily targeted by the unscrupulous. That is why banks have been in the forefront of efforts to expand financial education.

In April 2004, CBA published a survey regarding the progress made in the financial literacy of consumers as a result of banks' educational efforts. The report focuses on eight areas including credit counseling, mortgage and homeownership, predatory lending, public school programs, college programs and small business training. The results of the survey evidence an increase in banks that participate in consumer financial literacy education. Of those that responded, 100% of the institutions participate in at least one of the eight areas of concentration. Most notably, approximately 89% of the 54 responding institutions offer public school financial literacy programs (this is a 16% increase from the survey conducted one year ago), and financial literacy efforts of banks in colleges almost doubled. A portion of CBA's 2004 Survey of Bank Sponsored Financial Literacy Programs has been submitted with this testimony. The entire survey may be found at. . . .

In conclusion Mr. Chairman, I would like to highlight that consumers of all income levels in the United States have financial opportunities that are the envy of the world. Virtually any creditworthy consumer can obtain credit when they need it. Retail banking and other financial services are widely available and can be obtained by walking down the street to the local financial institution, or by using phone, mail or the Internet. Continued improvements in technology and risk control allow more financial institutions to improve their financial products, to offer them to broader groups of consumers, and to develop new financial products altogether. Naturally, we face the challenge of ensuring that consumers understand the opportunities they have available to them. But I can assure you that CBA's members are committed to ensuring that consumers receive the information they need, including through information disclosures and financial education materials and opportunities.

Thank you again for inviting me to appear before you today. I would be pleased to answer any questions.

POSTSCRIPT

Are Credit Card Companies Exploiting American Consumers?

Manning begins his critique of the credit card industry by relating the story of John, who was offered an effective credit line of $31 at a cost of $369. Manning believes that the new credit economy embodies what he calls a time-honored principle: "The most profitable way to make money off the vulnerable is to keep them in debt at the highest interest rate for as long as possible." Manning describes a number of changes that have led to the new credit economy, including two U.S. Supreme Court decisions. One was in 1978, allowing national banks to "charge the highest interest rate permitted by their 'home' states and export these rates to their out-of state-credit card clients." The second was in 1996, eliminating state-imposed limits on credit card fees. He proceeds to review a number of credit card company practices that produce "big profits for the banks and only modest benefits for consumers." Manning concludes by stating his opposition to a reform of bankruptcy law, supported by the credit card industry, that would allow the industry to "top even its current record profits and spiraling executive bonuses."

McEneney begins by identifying himself: He is appearing before the subcommittee on behalf of the Consumer Bankers Association, an organization that includes "most of the nation's largest bank holding companies, as well as regional and super community banks that collectively hold two-thirds of the industry's total assets." His assessment of the market for consumer financial products and services is positive; from the consumer perspective, it is "quite good." This assessment is based on the fact that consumers have lots of products that can be accessed in a variety of ways. McEneney believes this positive environment was created because financial institutions had the flexibility to compete with one another. He offers several examples. With respect to credit cards, he states "most people can find an offer for a card without an annual fee or that offers other benefits simply by reading their mail." This is the case because the competition for credit cards is national, and this national competition became possible because of prescreening. That is, before prescreening, consumers could only get a credit card from their local bank. McEneney cites a recent Federal Reserve survey that reported that 91 percent of credit card holders were "satisfied with their credit card issuers." He concludes his testimony by asserting, "consumers of all income levels in the United States have financial opportunities that are the envy of the world."

A good place to start for additional perspective on this issue is additional testimony before the House Subcommittee on Financial Institutions and Consumer Credit. During the September 15, 2004, hearings, Jean Ann Fox of the Consumer Federation of America and Tamara Draut of Demos offer more criticism of the credit card industry while Randy Lively of the American Financial Services Association extols the positives associated with credit cards: http://financialservices.house.gov/hearings.asp?formmode=detail&hearing=333. Manning has two books related to this issue: *Credit Card Nation: The Consequences of America's Addiction to Credit* (Basic Book, 2000) and *Give Yourself Credit!* (Alta Mira, 2004). General information on credit cards is available from the Federal Reserve at http://www.federalreserve.gov/pubs/shop/. The Federal Reserve also makes information available from its survey of banks that issue credit cards; the information includes, among other things, the name of the bank, the types of credit cards it issues, the APRs, annual fees, and other features: http://www.federalreserve.gov/pubs/shop/survey.htm. To find more information regarding Visa and MasterCard, visit their home sites.

ISSUE 11

Should Minimum Wage and Living Wage Laws Be Eliminated?

YES: D. W. MacKenzie, from "Mythology of the Minimum Wage," Ludwig von Mises Institute, http://www.mises.org/story/2130 (May 3, 2006)

NO: Jeannette Wicks-Lim, from "Measuring the Full Impact of Minimum and Living Wage Laws," *Dollars & Sense* (May/June 2006)

ISSUE SUMMARY

YES: Economics instructor D. W. MacKenzie believes that eliminating minimum wage laws would "reduce unemployment and improve the efficiency of markets for low productivity labor." He also believes that the "economic case for a living wage is unfounded."

NO: Economist Jeannette Wicks-Lim stresses the ripple effects of minimum and living wage laws; these effects increase the "effectiveness" of minimum and living wage laws as "antipoverty strategies."

$\mathbf{C}$ongress passed the Fair Labor Standards Act (FLSA) of 1938 in the midst of the Great Depression. In one bold stroke, it established a minimum wage rate of \$.25 an hour, placed controls on the use of child labor, designated 44 hours as the normal workweek, and mandated that time-and-a-half be paid to anyone working longer than the normal workweek. Sixty-eight years later the debates concerning child labor, length of the workweek, and overtime pay have long subsided, but the debate over the minimum wage rages on.

The immediate and continued concern over the minimum wage component of the FLSA should surprise few people. Although \$.25 an hour is a paltry sum compared to today's wage rates, in 1938 it was a princely reward for work. It must be remembered that jobs were hard to come by and unemployment rates at times reached as high as 25 percent of the workforce. When work was found, any wage seemed acceptable to those who roamed the streets with no safety net to protect their families. Indeed, consider the fact that \$.25 an hour was 40.3 percent of the average manufacturing wage rate for 1938.

Little wonder, then, that the business community in the 1930s was up in arms. Business leaders argued that if wages went up, prices would rise. This would choke off the little demand for goods and services that existed in the marketplace, and the demand for workers would be sure to fall. The end result would be a return to the depths of the depression, where there was little or no hope of employment for the very people who were supposed to benefit from the Fair Labor Standards Act.

Simple supply-and-demand analysis supports this view. As modern-day introductory textbooks in economics invariably show, unemployment occurs when a minimum wage greater than the equilibrium wage is mandated by law. The simplistic analysis, which assumes competitive conditions in both the product and factor markets, is predicated upon the assumptions that as wages are pushed above the equilibrium level, the quantity of labor demanded will fall and the quantity of labor supplied will increase. Wage rigidity prevents the market from clearing. The end result is an excess in the quantity of labor supplied relative to the quantity of labor demanded. The same would be true for the imposition of a living wage above the equilibrium wage.

The question that should be addressed in this debate is whether or not a simple supply-and-demand analysis is capable of adequately predicting what happens in real-world labor markets when a minimum wage or living wage is introduced or an existing minimum/living wage is raised. The significance of this is not based on idle curiosity. The minimum wage has been increased numerous times since its introduction in 1938. The current federal minimum wage of $5.15 was set in 1997. Did this minimum wage increase, and other increases before it, do irreparable harm to those who are least able to defend themselves in the labor market, the marginal worker? That is, if a minimum wage of $5.15 is imposed, what happens to all those marginal workers whose value to the firm is something less than $5.15? Are these workers fired? Do firms simply absorb this cost increase in the form of reduced corporate profits? What happens to productivity?

D. W. Mackenzie argues that eliminating the minimum wage would increase economic efficiency in the labor market for teenagers and ethnic minorities, lowering their unemployment rates. Imposition of living wages would make their unemployment rates rise higher than they are already. Jeannette Wicks-Lim focuses on the ripple effects of minimum wages and living wages, that is, how much would the wages of *other* workers increase as a result of an increase in the minimum wage? The larger the ripple effects, the stronger is the case for higher wage minimums to improve the lives of the working poor.

D. W. MacKenzie

Mythology of the Minimum Wage

Once again politicians and pundits are calling for increases in the legal minimum wage. Their reasons are familiar. Market wages are supposedly immoral. People need to earn a "living wage." If the minimum wage went up at least to $7, or better still to near $10 an hour, millions would be lifted out of poverty.[1]

The economic case against minimum wage laws is simple. Employers pay a wage no higher than the value of an additional hour's work. Raising minimum wages forces employers to dismiss low productivity workers. This policy has the largest affect on those with the least education, job experience, and maturity. Consequently, we should expect minimum wage laws to affect teenagers and those with less education. Eliminating minimum wage laws would reduce unemployment and improve the efficiency of markets for low productivity labor.

There are a few economists who have been leading the charge for higher minimum wages. Some of these economists have obvious ideological leanings. Economists connected with the Left-orientated Economic Policy Institute and the Clinton Administration have concocted a rational for minimum wage increases. According to these economists higher wages make employees more content with their jobs, and this leads to higher worker productivity. Thus workers will be worth paying a minimum wage once their employers are forced to pay these wages. Of course, if this were true—if employers could get higher productivity out of less educated and experienced workers by paying higher wages—they would be willing to do this without minimum wage legislation. But the economists who make this case claim to have empirical evidence that proves them right. Economists David Card and Alan Krueger have published studies of the fast food industry indicated that small increases in the minimum wage would cause only minor job losses, and might even increase employment slightly in some instances. These studies by Card and Krueger show only that a small increase in minimum wage rates might not cause much of an increase in unemployment. Such studies ignore the fact that the current level of minimum wages are already causing significant unemployment for some workers.

The economic case for minimum wage increases has gained some ground with public and even professional opinion. Even some free market leaning economists, like Steven Landsburg, have conceded that minimum wage increases do not affect employment significantly.[2] Landsburg notes that critics of minimum wage laws emphasize that they have a disproportionate effect on teens and blacks. But he dismisses these critics because "minimum wages have at most a tiny impact on employment . . . The minimum wage kills very few jobs, and the jobs it kills were lousy jobs anyway. It is almost impossible to maintain the old argument that minimum wages are bad for minimum-wage workers."

Real statistics indicate that the critics of minimum wage laws were right all along. While it is true that minimum wages do not drive the national unemployment rate up to astronomical levels, it does adversely affect teenagers and ethnic minorities. According to the Bureau of Labor Statistics the unemployment rate for everyone over the age of 16 was 5.6% in 2005. Yet unemployment was 17.3% for those aged 16–19 years. For those aged 16–17 unemployment was 19.7%. In the 18–19 age group unemployment was 15.8%. Minimum wage laws do affect ethnic minorities more so than others.[3] The unemployment rate for white teens in the 16–17 age group was 17.3% in 2005. The same figures for Hispanic and black teens were 25% and 40.9% respectively. Of course, these figures decrease for older minorities. Blacks aged 18–19 and 20–24 had 25.7% and 19.9% unemployment in 2005. For Hispanics unemployment was slightly lower—17.8% at age 18–19 and 9.6% at age 20–24.

Landsburg might maintain that most of these lost jobs are lousy jobs that teens will not miss. DeLong thinks that minimum wage laws can help to avert poverty—workers who keep their jobs at the minimum wage gain much, while unemployed workers lose little. Part of the problem with this argument is that it involves arbitrary value judgments. According to mainstream economic theory, we achieve economic efficiency when markets clear because this is how we realize all gains from trade. With teen unemployment in double digits—running as high as 40.9%—it is obvious that some labor markets are not clearing. If labor market imperfections led to such levels of unemployment, economists like DeLong, Card, and Krueger would call for government intervention to correct these "market failures." Yet they find double digit teen unemployment acceptable when it derives from government intervention. Why? Because they want to use such policies to redistribute income.[4]

Mainstream economic theory lacks any basis for judging the effects of income redistribution. According to textbook economics we attain the highest level of economic efficiency when markets clear, when we realize the maximum gains from mutually advantageous trade. Income transfers benefit some at the expense of others. Economists have no scientific methods for comparing gains and losses through income transfers.[5] Once economists depart from discussing efficiency conditions and begin to speak about income redistribution, they become advocates of a political agenda, rather than objective scientists. The jobs lost to minimum wage laws might not seem worthwhile to DeLong or Landsburg, but they obviously are worthwhile to the workers and employers whom these laws affect. Why should the value judgments of a few armchair economists matter more than the interests of would be employees and employers? These jobs may be "lousy jobs," but one could also argue that these jobs are quite important because they are a first step in gaining job experience and learning adult responsibility.

A second problem with the case against minimum wages is that they affect older workers too. As already noted, workers in the 20–24 age group appear to be affected by minimum wage laws. Unemployment rates in the 25–34 age group are higher than for the 35–44 age group. The unemployment rate for blacks and Hispanics aged 25–34 were 11.1% and 5.8% in 2005. Unemployment for whites and Asians in this age group were 4.4% and 3.5%. In the 35–44 age group the unemployment rates for these four ethnicities were 7.2%., 5.1%, 4.4%, and 2.7%. A comparison of black to Asian unemployment is revealing. In the United States, Asians tend to attain higher levels of education than blacks. Thus minimum wage laws are relatively unimportant to Asian Americans. Consequently, Asians are able to attain unemployment as low as the 2–3% range. For Asians aged 16+ the unemployment rate was only 3.3% in 2005. For Asians in the 20–24 age group unemployment was 5.1%. These figures are only a fraction of the unemployment rates experienced by blacks in 2005. There is no reason why white, Hispanic, and black Americans cannot also reach the 2–3% range of unemployment.

Supporters of minimum wage laws do not realize that prior to minimum wage laws the national unemployment rate did fall well below 5%. According to the US Census, national unemployment rates were 3.3% in 1927, 1.8% in 1926, 3.2% in 1925, 2.4% in 1923, 1.4% in 1919 and 1918, 2.8% in 1907, 1.7% in 1906, and 3.7% in 1902.[6] Even today, some states have unemployment rates as low as 3%. Virginia now has an unemployment rate of 3.1%. Wyoming has an unemployment rate of 2.9%. Hawaii has an unemployment rate of 2.6%. National unemployment rates seldom drop below 5% because some categories of workers are stuck with double digit unemployment. Given these figures, it is quite arguable that minimum wage laws keep the national unemployment rate 3 percentage points higher than would otherwise be the case.

Economist Arthur Okun estimated that for every 1% increase in unemployment GDP falls by 2.5–3%. If minimum wage laws are responsible for keeping the national unemployment rate 3 percentage points above where it would otherwise be, then the losses to minimum wage unemployment are substantial. Since Okun's law is an empirical proposition it is certainly not constant. Eliminating minimum wages might not increase GDP as much as this "law" indicates. However, the elimination of minimum wage laws would surely have a positive effect on GDP. In any case, economic theory and available data indicate that minimum wage laws do result in economic inefficiency. The implementation of a "living wage" would only increase these losses. Do proponents of living wages really want to see unemployment rates among ethnic minorities and teens climb even higher?

The economic case for a living wage is unfounded. Current minimum wage rates do create high levels of unemployment among low productivity workers. Higher "living wages" would only make these problems worse. The alleged moral case for a living wage ignores the fact that minimum wage increases adversely affect the very people whom advocates of living wages intend to help. If politicians wish to pursue sound policies, they should consider repealing minimum wage laws, especially where teens are concerned. Unfortunately, most politicians care more about political expediencies than sound economic policy. This being the case, minimum wages will increase unless public opinion changes significantly.

Notes

1. See Dreier and Candeale *A Moral Minimum Wage*, April 27 2006 and Cauchon *States Say 5.15 too little*, April 27 2006.
2. See *"The Sin of Wages"* by Steven Landsburg and *"The Minimum Wage and the EITC"* by J. Bradford DeLong.
3. This is likely due to the poor quality of many inner city public schools.
4. It is worth noting that Landsburg opposes redistribution via minimum wage laws.
5. This would require interpersonal comparisons of welfare. Robbins (1933) proved that such comparisons are unscientific.
6. US Bureau of the Census *Historical Statistics*, p. 135.

Jeannette Wicks-Lim  **NO**

Measuring the Full Impact of
Minimum and Living Wage Laws

Raising the minimum wage is quickly becoming a key political issue for this fall's midterm elections. In the past, Democratic politicians have shied away from the issue while Republicans have openly opposed a higher minimum wage. But this year is different. Community activists are forcing the issue by campaigning to put state minimum-wage proposals before the voters this fall in Arizona, Colorado, Ohio, and Missouri. No doubt inspired by the 100-plus successful local living-wage campaigns of the past ten years, these activists are also motivated by a federal minimum wage that has stagnated for the past nine years. The $5.15 federal minimum is at its lowest value in purchasing-power terms in more than 50 years; a single parent with two children, working full-time at the current minimum wage, would fall $2,000 below the poverty line.

Given all the political activity on the ground, the Democrats have decided to make the minimum wage a central plank in their party platform. Former presidential candidate John Edwards has teamed up with Sen. Edward Kennedy (D-Mass.) and ACORN, a leading advocacy group for living wage laws, to push for a $7.25 federal minimum. Even some Republicans are supporting minimum wage increases. In fact, a bipartisan legislative coalition unexpectedly passed a state minimum wage hike in Michigan this March.

Minimum-wage and living-wage laws have always caused an uproar in the business community. Employers sound the alarm about the dire consequences of a higher minimum wage both for themselves and for the low-wage workers these laws are intended to benefit: Minimum wage mandates, they claim, will cause small-business owners to close shop and lay off their low-wage workers. A spokesperson for the National Federation of Independent Business (NFIB), commenting on a proposal to raise Pennsylvania's minimum wage in an interview with the Philadelphia Inquirer, put it this way: "That employer may as well be handing out pink slips along with the pay raise."

What lies behind these bleak predictions? Mark Shaffer, owner of Shaffer's Park Supper Club in Crivitz, Wisc., provided one explanation to the Wisconsin State Journal: ". . . increasing the minimum wage would create a chain reaction. Every worker would want a raise to keep pace, forcing up prices and driving away customers." In other words, employers will not only

From *Dollars & Sense*, May/June 2006. Reprinted by permission of Dollars & Sense, a progressive economics magazine. www.dollarsandsense.org.

be forced to raise the wages of those workers earning below the new minimum wage, but also the wages of their co-workers who earn somewhat more. The legally required wage raises are difficult enough for employers to absorb, they claim; these other raises—referred to as ripple effect raises—aggravate the situation. The result? "That ripple effect is going to lay off people."

Ripple effects represent a double-edged sword for minimum-wage and living-wage proponents. Their extent determines how much low-wage workers will benefit from such laws. If the ripple effects are small, then a higher minimum (or living) wage would benefit only a small class of workers, and boosting the minimum wage might be dismissed as an ineffective antipoverty strategy. If the ripple effects are large, then setting higher wage minimums may be seen as a potent policy tool to improve the lives of the working poor. But at the same time, evidence of large ripple effects provides ammunition to employers who claim they cannot afford the costs of a higher wage floor.

So what is the evidence on ripple effects? Do they bloat wage bills and overwhelm employers? Do they expand the number of workers who get raises a little or a lot? It's difficult to say because the research on ripple effects has been thin. But getting a clear picture of the full impact of minimum and living wage laws on workers' wages is critical to evaluating the impact of these laws. New research provides estimates of the scope and magnitude of the ripple effects of both minimum-wage and living-wage laws. This evidence is crucial for analyzing both the full impact of this increasingly visible policy tool and the political struggles surrounding it.

Why Do Employers Give Ripple-Effect Raises?

Marge Thomas, CEO of Goodwill Industries in Maryland, explains in an interview with The Gazette (Md.): "There will be a ripple effect [in response to Maryland's recent minimum wage increase to $6.15], since it wouldn't be fair to pay people now making above the minimum wage at the same level as those making the new minimum wage." That is, without ripple effects, an increase in the wage floor will worsen the relative wage position of workers just above it. If there are no ripple effects, workers earning $6.15 before Maryland's increase would not only see their wages fall to the bottom of the wage scale, but also to the same level as workers who had previously earned inferior wages (i.e., workers who earned between $5.15 and $6.15).

Employers worry that these workers would view such a relative decline in their wages as unfair, damaging their morale—and their productivity. Without ripple effect raises, employers fear, their disgruntled staff will cut back on hard-to-measure aspects of their work such as responding to others cheerfully and taking initiative in assisting customers.

So employers feel compelled to preserve some consistency in their wage scales. Workers earning $6.15 before the minimum increase, for example, may receive a quarter raise, to $6.40, to keep their wages just above the new $6.15 minimum. That employers feel compelled to give non-mandated raises to some of their lowest-paid workers because it is the "fair" thing to do may appear to be a dubious claim. Perhaps so, but employers commonly express anxiety about the costs of minimum-wage and living-wage laws for this very reason.

The Politics of Ripple Effects

Inevitably, then, ripple effects come into play in the political battles around minimum-wage and living-wage laws—but in contradictory ways for both opponents and supporters. Opponents raise the specter of large ripple effects bankrupting small businesses. At the same time, though, they argue that minimum-wage laws are not effective in fighting poverty because they do not cover many workers—and worse, because those who are covered are largely teens or young-adult students just working for spending money. If ripple effects are small, this shores up opponents' assertions that minimum-wage laws have a limited impact on poverty. Evidence of larger ripple effects, on the other hand, would mean that the benefits of minimum-wage laws are larger than previously understood, and that these laws have an even greater potential to reduce poverty among the working poor.

The political implications are complicated further in the context of living-wage laws, which typically call for much higher wage floors than state and federal minimum-wage laws do. The living-wage movement calls for wage floors to be set at rates that provide a "livable income," such as the federal poverty level for a family of four, rather than at the arbitrary—and very low—level current minimum-wage laws set. The difference is dramatic: the living-wage ordinances that have been passed in a number of municipalities typically set a wage floor twice the level of federal and state minimum wages.

So the mandated raises under living-wage laws are already much higher than under even the highest state minimum-wage laws. If living-wage laws have significant ripple effects, opponents have all the more ammunition for their argument that the costs of these laws are unsustainable for employers.

How Big are Ripple Effects?

My answer is a typical economists' response: it depends. In a nutshell, it depends on how high the wage minimum is set. The reason for this is simple. Evidence from the past 20 years of changes to state and federal minimum wages suggests that while there is a ripple effect, it doesn't extend very far beyond the new minimum. So, if the wage minimum is set high, then a large number of workers are legally due raises and, relatively speaking, the number of workers who get ripple-effect raises is small. Conversely, if the wage minimum is set low, then a small number of workers are legally due raises and, relatively speaking, the number of workers who get ripple-effect raises is large.

In the case of minimum-wage laws, the evidence suggests that ripple effects do dramatically expand their impact. Minimum wages are generally set low relative to the wage distribution. Because so many more workers earn wages just above the minimum wage compared to those earning the minimum, even a small ripple effect increases considerably the number of workers who benefit from a rise in the minimum wage. And even though the size of these raises quickly shrinks the higher the worker's wage rate, the much greater number of affected workers translates into a significantly larger increase in the wage bills of employers.

For example, my research shows that the impact of the most recent federal minimum-wage increase, from $4.75 to $5.15 in 1997, extended to workers earning wages around $5.75. Workers earning between the old and new minimums generally received raises to bring their wages in line with the new minimum—an 8% raise for those who started at the old minimum. Workers earning around $5.20 (right above the new minimum of $5.15) received raises of around 2%, bringing their wages up to about $5.30. Finally, those workers earning wages around $5.75 received raises on the order of 1%, bringing their wages up to about $5.80.

This narrow range of small raises translates into a big overall impact. Roughly 4 million workers (those earning between $4.75 and $5.15) received mandated raises in response to the 1997 federal minimum wage increase. Taking into account the typical work schedules of these workers, these raises translated into a $741 million increase to employers' annual wage bills. Now add in ripple effects: Approximately 11 million workers received ripple-effect raises, adding another $1.3 billion to employers' wage bills. In other words, ripple-effect raises almost quadrupled the number of workers who benefited from the minimum-wage increase and almost tripled the over-all costs associated with it.

Dramatic as these ripple effects are, the real impact on employers can only be gauged in relation to their capacity to absorb the higher wage costs. Here, there is evidence that businesses are not overwhelmed by the costs of a higher minimum wage, even including ripple effects. For example, in a study I co-authored with University of Massachusetts economists Robert Pollin and Mark Brenner on the Florida ballot measure to establish a $6.15 state minimum wage (which passed overwhelmingly in 2004), we accounted for ripple-effect costs of roughly this same magnitude. Despite almost tripling the number of affected workers (from almost 300,000 to over 850,000) and more than doubling the costs associated with the new minimum wage (from $155 million to $410 million), the ripple effects, combined with the mandated wage increases, imposed an average cost increase on employers amounting to less than one-half of 1% of their sales revenue. Even for employers in the hotel and restaurant industry, where low-wage workers tend to be concentrated, the average cost increase was less than 1% of their sales revenue. In other words, a 1% increase in prices for hotel rooms or restaurant meals could cover the increased costs associated with both legally mandated raises and ripple-effect raises.

The small fraction of revenue that these raises represent goes a long way toward explaining why economists generally agree that minimum-wage laws are not "job killers," as opponents claim. According to a 1998 survey of economists, a consensus seems to have been reached that there is minimal job loss, if any, associated with minimum-wage increases in the ranges that we've seen.

Just as important, this new research revises our understanding of who benefits from minimum wage laws. Including ripple-effect raises expands the circle of minimum-wage beneficiaries to include more adult workers and fewer teenage or student workers. In fact, accounting for ripple effects decreases the prevalence of teenagers and traditional-age students (age 16 to 24) among workers likely to be affected by a federal minimum-wage increase from four out of ten to three out of ten. In other words, adult workers make up an even larger majority of likely minimum-wage beneficiaries when ripple effects are added to the picture.

The Case of Living-Wage Laws

With living-wage laws, the ripple effect story appears to be quite different, however—primarily because living wage laws set much higher wage minimums.

To understand why living-wage laws might generate far less of a ripple effect than minimum-wage hikes, it is instructive to look at the impact of raising the minimum wage on the retail trade industry. About 15% of retail trade workers earn wages at or very close to the minimum wage, compared to 5% of all workers. As a result, a large fraction of the retail trade industry workforce receives legally mandated raises when the minimum wage is raised, which is just what occurs across a broader group of industries and occupations when a living-wage ordinance is passed.

My research shows that the relative impact of the ripple effect that accompanies a minimum-wage hike is much smaller within retail trade than across all industries. Because a much larger share of workers in retail receive legally required raises when the minimum wage is raised, this reduces the relative number of workers receiving ripple effect raises, and, in turn, the relative size of the costs associated with ripple effects. This analysis suggests that the ripple effects of living wage laws will likewise be smaller than those found with minimum-wage laws.

To be sure, the ripple effect in the retail trade sector may underestimate the ripple effect of living-wage laws for a couple of reasons. First, unlike minimum-wage hikes, living-wage laws may have ripple effects that extend across firms as well as up the wage structure within firms. Employers who do not fall under a living-wage law's mandate but who are competing for workers within the same local labor market as those that do may be compelled to raise their own wages in order to retain their workers. Second, workers just above living-wage levels are typically higher on the job ladder and may have more bargaining power than workers with wages just above minimum-wage levels and, as a result, may be able to demand more significant raises when living-wage laws are enacted.

However, case studies of living-wage ordinances in Los Angeles and San Francisco do suggest that the ripple effect plays a smaller role in the case of living-wage laws than in the case of minimum-wage laws. These studies find that ripple effects add less than half again to the costs of mandated raises— dramatically less than the almost tripling of costs by ripple effects associated with the 1997 federal minimum-wage increase. In other words, the much higher wage floors set by living-wage laws appear to reverse the importance of legally required raises versus ripple-effect raises.

Do the costs associated with living-wage laws—with their higher wage floors—overwhelm employers, even if their ripple effects are small? To date, estimates suggest that within the range of existing living-wage laws, businesses are generally able to absorb the cost increases they face. For example, Pollin and Brenner studied a 2000 proposal to raise the wage floor from $5.75 to $10.75 in Santa Monica, Calif. They estimated that the cost increase faced by a typical business would be small, on the order of 2% of sales revenue, even accounting for both mandated and ripple-effect raises. Their estimates also showed that some hotel and restaurant businesses might face cost increases amounting to up to 10% of their sales revenue—not a negligible sum. However, after examining the local economy, Pollin and Brenner concluded that even these cost increases would not be likely to force these businesses to close their doors. Moreover, higher productivity and lower turnover rates among workers paid a living wage would also reduce the impact of these costs.

Ultimately, the impact of ripple-effect raises appears to depend crucially on the level of the new wage floor. The lower the wage floor, as in the case of minimum-wage laws, the more important the role of ripple-effect raises. The higher the wage floor, as in the case of living-wage laws, the less important the role of ripple-effect raises.

Making the Case

The results of this new research are generally good news for proponents of living- and minimum-wage laws. Ripple effects do not portend dire consequences for employers from minimum and living wage laws; at the same time, ripple-effect raises heighten the effectiveness of these laws as antipoverty strategies.

In the case of minimum-wage laws, because the cost of legally mandated raises relative to employer revenues is small, even ripple effects large enough to triple the cost of a minimum-wage increase do not represent a large burden for employers. Moreover, ripple effects enhance the somewhat anemic minimum-wage laws to make them more effective as policy tools for improving the lot of the working poor. Accounting for ripple effects nearly quadruples the number of beneficiaries of a minimum-wage hike and expands the majority of those beneficiaries who are adults—in many instances, family breadwinners.

However, ripple effects do not appear to overwhelm employers in the case of the more ambitious living-wage laws. The strongest impact from living-wage laws appears to come from legally required raises rather than from ripple-effect raises. This reinforces advocates' claims that paying a living wage is a reasonable, as well as potent, way to fight poverty.

POSTSCRIPT

Should Minimum Wage and Living Wage Laws Be Eliminated?

The impact of the minimum wage can be expressed in many ways. Two important ways of looking at such legislative initiatives are to examine minimum wages over time in real dollars and as a percentage of manufacturing wages. In real terms the 1965–1970 period saw the highest level of the minimum wage. In constant 1982–1984 dollars, the minimum wage for these years was approximately $4.00 an hour, reaching nearly 50 percent of the prevailing manufacturing wage. For the next 20 years, however, the value of the minimum wage in real terms and as a percentage of the manufacturing wage fell. This is especially true for the last nine years when the minimum wage has not changed in nominal terms.

The renewed interest in the minimum wage can be traced in part to the research findings of David Card and Alan Krueger. They found that moderate increases in the minimum wage have few negative effects on employment patterns and in some cases are associated with increases in employment. Their work was published in professional journals: *Industrial and Labor Relations Review* (October 1992 and April 1994) and the *American Economic Review* (September 1994 and May 1995). They also detailed their findings in a book entitled *Myth and Measurement: The New Economics of the Minimum Wage* (Princeton University Press, 1995).

D. W. MacKenzie claims that studies by Card and Krueger do not recognize that the current level of minimum wages is already causing significant unemployment for some workers. Here, he cites the high unemployment rates for Hispanic and black teens (and even for older age groups). He also suggests that minimum wage laws keep the national unemployment rate 3 percentage points higher than it otherwise would be, and that elimination of minimum wage laws might have a positive effect on GDP.

While Mackenzie dismisses the "moral case" for a living wage, Jeannette Wicks-Lim estimates that the ripple effect associated with the increase in the minimum wage from $4.75 to $5.15 in 1997 quadrupled the number of workers who benefited from the increase. Moreover, there is evidence that businesses are not overwhelmed by the higher wage costs—in one study, legally mandated raises and the ripple effect raises amounted to less than half of 1 percent of business sales revenue. Ripple effects of living wage laws also do not appear to overwhelm employers, making living wages "a reasonable, as well as potent, way to fight poverty."

Two vocal critics of Card and Krueger's research are David Neumark and William Wascher. Their empirical studies are supportive of the traditional neoclassical findings that the minimum wage causes unemployment, particularly among teenagers and young adults. See their work published in *Industrial and Labor Relations Review* (September 1992 and April 1994); NBER Working Paper No. 4617 (1994); *Journal of Business and Economic Statistics* (April 1995); and *American Economic Review Papers and Proceedings* (May 1995). Still considered the best anti-minimum wage statement, however, is George J. Stigler's 1946 essay "The Economics of Minimum Wage Legislation," *American Economic Review*.

ISSUE 12

Do Unskilled Immigrants Hurt the American Economy?

YES: Steven Malanga, from "How Unskilled Immigrants Hurt Our Economy," *City Journal* (Summer 2006)

NO: Diana Furchtgott-Roth, from "The Case for Immigration," *The New York Sun* (September 22, 2006)

ISSUE SUMMARY

YES: Columnist Steven Malanga believes the influx of unskilled immigrants into the U.S. economy has imposed large costs on the larger society, including job loss by native workers and lower investment in labor-saving technology. More importantly, he argues that this immigration has increased utilization of the "vast U.S. welfare and social-services apparatus."

NO: Diana Furchtgott-Roth, senior fellow at the Hudson Institute and director of Hudson's Center for Employment Policy, and a former chief economist at the U.S. Department of Labor, observes that annual immigration is "a tiny fraction of our labor force," and immigrant laborers are "complements, rather than substitutes for native born Americans." She also cites a National Academy of Sciences study that concluded that foreign-born households are no more likely to use "welfare" than native-born households.

Between 700,000 and 900,000 legal immigrants enter the United States each year. There were 34 million immigrants (defined as naturalized American citizens, permanent residents, temporary residents, and undocumented immigrants) in the United States in 2003, amounting to 12 percent of the population (*Economic Report of the President, 2005*). Over half are from Latin America, and over a fifth have less than nine years of education. Between 1996 and 2003, foreign-born workers accounted for 58 percent of the net increase in employment and 41 percent of the increase in population growth. Undocumented immigrants are estimated at 10 million (half from Mexico).

In May 2006, President Bush offered a strategy for "comprehensive" immigration reform consisting of securing the U.S. border (signing the

Secure Fence Act into law in October 2006), enforcement of immigration laws, and creating a lawful path for foreign workers to enter on a temporary basis—"a rational middle ground" between amnesty and deportation.

The economic impact of immigrants is a fundamental consideration in the current discourse on immigration in the United States. There are questions about their effect on efficiency and distribution. Debate on issues such as the fiscal (and broader economic) costs and benefits of immigrants, illegal immigration, whether immigrants displace natives, lower natives' wages, and contribute to income inequality, has intensified over the last two decades. The issues are complex and emotionally and politically charged, and empirical evidence is not definitive.

Testimonies to Congress in July 2006 reflect the disagreement on costs and benefits of immigrants today. Some, like Michael Fix (vice president and director of studies, Migration Policy Institute), argue that social welfare use by immigrants is declining since the 1996 welfare reforms, and "fears that welfare systems will be swamped by increased legal immigration and by a legalization program are overstated." Others, like Steven A. Camarota (director of research, Center for Immigration Studies), argue that large-scale immigration of less-educated immigrants creates significant funding problems for social programs, citing the National Research Council's 1997 report showing the net lifetime fiscal burden of an immigrant without a high school diploma ($89,000), with only a high school education ($31,000), and with an education beyond high school (fiscal benefit of $105,000).

The papers by Steven Malanga and Diana Furchtgott-Roth are part of the ongoing debate on the impact of immigrants on the U.S. economy. Malanga argues that today's immigrants are unlike earlier immigrants and that supporters of today's immigration are wrong on many counts and zeroes in on unskilled immigrants particularly Mexican (legal and illegal) immigrants. Furchtgott-Roth offers a point-for-point rebuttal.

YES

Steven Malanga

How Unskilled Immigrants Hurt Our Economy

The day after Librado Velasquez arrived on Staten Island after a long, surreptitious journey from his Chiapas, Mexico, home, he headed out to a street corner to wait with other illegal immigrants looking for work. Velasquez, who had supported his wife, seven kids, and his in-laws as a *campesino*, or peasant farmer, until a 1998 hurricane devastated his farm, eventually got work, off the books, loading trucks at a small New Jersey factory, which hired illegals for jobs that required few special skills. The arrangement suited both, until a work injury sent Velasquez to the local emergency room, where federal law required that he be treated, though he could not afford to pay for his care. After five operations, he is now permanently disabled and has remained in the United States to pursue compensation claims. . . .

Velasquez's story illustrates some of the fault lines in the nation's current, highly charged, debate on immigration. Since the mid-1960s, America has welcomed nearly 30 million legal immigrants and received perhaps another 15 million illegals, numbers unprecedented in our history. These immigrants have picked our fruit, cleaned our homes, cut our grass, worked in our factories, and washed our cars. But they have also crowded into our hospital emergency rooms, schools, and government-subsidized aid programs, sparking a fierce debate about their contributions to our society and the costs they impose on it.

Advocates of open immigration argue that welcoming the Librado Velasquezes of the world is essential for our American economy: our businesses need workers like him, because we have a shortage of people willing to do low-wage work. Moreover, the free movement of labor in a global economy pays off for the United States, because immigrants bring skills and capital that expand our economy and offset immigration's costs. Like tax cuts, supporters argue, immigration pays for itself.

But the tale of Librado Velasquez helps show why supporters are wrong about today's immigration, as many Americans sense and so much research has demonstrated. America does not have a vast labor shortage that requires waves of low-wage immigrants to alleviate; in fact, unemployment among unskilled workers is high—about 30 percent. Moreover, many of the unskilled, uneducated workers now journeying here labor, like Velasquez, in shrinking industries, where they force out native workers, and many others work in industries where the availability of cheap workers has led businesses to suspend investment in new technologies that would make them less labor-intensive.

Yet while these workers add little to our economy, they come at great cost, because they are not economic abstractions but human beings, with their own culture and ideas—often at odds with our own. Increasing numbers of them arrive with little education and none of the skills necessary to succeed in a modern economy. Many may wind up stuck on our lowest economic rungs, where they will rely on something that immigrants of other generations didn't have: a vast U.S. welfare and social-services apparatus that has enormously amplified the cost of immigration. Just as welfare reform and other policies are helping to shrink America's underclass by weaning people off such social programs, we are importing a new, foreign-born underclass. As famed free-market economist Milton Friedman puts it: "It's just obvious that you can't have free immigration and a welfare state."

Immigration can only pay off again for America if we reshape our policy, organizing it around what's good for the economy by welcoming workers we truly need and excluding those who, because they have so little to offer, are likely to cost us more than they contribute, and who will struggle for years to find their place here.

Hampering today's immigration debate are our misconceptions about the so-called first great migration some 100 years ago, with which today's immigration is often compared. . . . If America could assimilate 24 million mostly desperate immigrants from that great migration—people one unsympathetic economist at the turn of the twentieth century described as "the unlucky, the thriftless, the worthless"—surely, so the story goes, today's much bigger and richer country can absorb the millions of Librado Velasquezes now venturing here.

But that argument distorts the realities of the first great migration. . . . Those waves of immigrants—many of them urban dwellers who crossed a continent and an ocean to get here—helped supercharge the workforce at a time when the country was going through a transformative economic expansion that craved new workers, especially in its cities. A 1998 National Research Council report noted "that the newly arriving immigrant nonagricultural work force . . . was (slightly) more skilled than the resident American labor force": 27 percent of them were skilled laborers, compared with only 17 percent of that era's native-born workforce.

Many of these immigrants quickly found a place in our economy, participating in the workforce at a higher rate even than the native population. Their success at finding work sent many of them quickly up the economic ladder: those who stayed in America for at least 15 years, for instance, were just as likely to own their own business as native-born workers of the same age, one study found. . . .

What the newcomers of the great migration did not find here was a vast social-services and welfare state. They had to rely on their own resources or those of friends, relatives, or private, often ethnic, charities if things did not go well. That's why about 70 percent of those who came were men in their prime. It's also why many of them left when the economy sputtered several times during the period. . . .

Today's immigration has turned out so differently in part because it emerged out of the 1960s civil rights and Great Society mentality. In 1965, a new immigration act eliminated the old system of national quotas, which critics saw as racist because it greatly favored European nations. Lawmakers created a set of broader immigration quotas for each hemisphere, and they added a new visa preference category for family members to join their relatives here. Senate immigration subcommittee chairman Edward Kennedy reassured the country that, "contrary to the charges in some quarters, [the bill] will not inundate America with immigrants," and "it will not cause American workers to lose their jobs."

But, in fact, the law had an immediate, dramatic effect, increasing immigration by 60 percent in its first ten years. Sojourners from poorer countries around the rest of the world arrived in ever-greater numbers, so that whereas half of immigrants in the 1950s had originated from Europe, 75 percent by the 1970s were from Asia and Latin America. And as the influx of immigrants grew, the special-preferences rule for family unification intensified it further, as the pool of eligible family members around the world also increased. Legal immigration to the U.S. soared from 2.5 million in the 1950s to 4.5 million in the 1970s to 7.3 million in the 1980s to about 10 million in the 1990s.

As the floodgates of legal immigration opened, the widening economic gap between the United States and many of its neighbors also pushed illegal immigration to levels that America had never seen. In particular, when Mexico's move to a more centralized, state-run economy in the 1970s produced hyper-inflation, the disparity between its stagnant economy and U.S. prosperity yawned wide. Mexico's per-capita gross domestic product, 37 percent of the United States' in the early 1980s, was only 27 percent of it by the end of the decade—and is now just 25 percent of it. With Mexican farmworkers able to earn seven to ten times as much in the United States as at home, by the 1980s illegals were pouring across our border at the rate of about 225,000 a year, and U.S. sentiment rose for slowing the flow.

But an unusual coalition of business groups, unions, civil rights activists, and church leaders thwarted the call for restrictions with passage of the inaptly named 1986 Immigration Reform and Control Act, which legalized some 2.7 million unauthorized aliens already here, supposedly in exchange for tougher penalties and controls against employers who hired illegals. The law proved no deterrent, however, because supporters, in subsequent legislation and court cases argued on civil rights grounds, weakened the employer sanctions. Meanwhile, more illegals flooded here in the hope of future amnesties from Congress, while the newly legalized sneaked their wives and children into the country rather than have them wait for family-preference visas. The flow of illegals into the country rose to between 300,000 and 500,000 per year in the 1990s, so that a decade after the legislation that had supposedly solved the undocumented alien problem by reclassifying them as legal, the number of illegals living in the United States was back up to about 5 million, while today it's estimated at between 9 million and 13 million.

The flood of immigrants, both legal and illegal, from countries with poor, ill-educated populations, has yielded a mismatch between today's immigrants and the American economy and has left many workers poorly positioned to succeed for the long term. . . . Nearly two-thirds of Mexican immigrants, for instance, are high school dropouts, and most wind up doing either unskilled factory work or small-scale construction projects, or they work in service industries, where they compete for entry-level jobs against one another, against the adult children of other immigrants, and against native-born high school dropouts. Of the 15 industries employing the greatest percentage of foreign-born workers, half are low-wage service industries, including gardening, domestic household work, car washes, shoe repair, and janitorial work. . . .

Although open-borders advocates say that these workers are simply taking jobs Americans don't want, studies show that the immigrants drive down wages of native-born workers and squeeze them out of certain industries. Harvard economists George Borjas and Lawrence Katz, for instance, estimate that low-wage immigration cuts the wages for the average native-born high school dropout by some 8 percent, or more than $1,200 a year. . . .

Consequently, as the waves of immigration continue, the sheer number of those competing for low-skilled service jobs makes economic progress difficult. A study of the impact of immigration on New York City's restaurant business, for instance, found that 60 percent of immigrant workers do not receive regular raises, while 70 percent had never been promoted. . . .

Similarly, immigration is also pushing some native-born workers out of jobs, as Kenyon College economists showed in the California nail-salon workforce. Over a 16-year period starting in the late 1980s, some 35,600 mostly Vietnamese immigrant women flooded into the industry, a mass migration that equaled the total number of jobs in the industry before the immigrants arrived. Though the new workers created a labor surplus that led to lower prices, new services, and somewhat more demand, the economists estimate that as a result, 10,000 native-born workers either left the industry or never bothered entering it.

In many American industries, waves of low-wage workers have also retarded investments that might lead to modernization and efficiency. Farming, which employs a million immigrant laborers in California alone, is the prime case in point. Faced with a labor shortage in the early 1960s, when President Kennedy ended a 22-year-old guest-worker program that allowed 45,000 Mexican farmhands to cross over the border and harvest 2.2 million tons of California tomatoes for processed foods, farmers complained but swiftly automated, adopting a mechanical tomato-picking technology created more than a decade earlier. Today, just 5,000 better-paid workers—one-ninth the original workforce—harvest 12 million tons of tomatoes using the machines.

The savings prompted by low-wage migrants may even be minimal in crops not easily mechanized. Agricultural economists Wallace Huffman and Alan McCunn of Iowa State University have estimated that without illegal workers, the retail cost of fresh produce would increase only about 3 percent in the summer-fall season and less than 2 percent in the winter-spring season, because labor represents only a tiny percent of the retail price of produce and because without migrant workers, America would probably import more foreign fruits and vegetables. . . .

As foreign competition and mechanization shrink manufacturing and farmworker jobs, low-skilled immigrants are likely to wind up farther on the margins of our economy, where many already operate. For example, although only about 12 percent of construction workers are foreign-born, 100,000 to 300,000 illegal immigrants have carved a place for themselves as temporary workers on the fringes of the industry. In urban areas like New York and Los Angeles, these mostly male illegal immigrants gather on street corners, in empty lots, or in Home Depot parking lots to sell their labor by the hour or the day, for $7 to $11 an hour. . . .

Because so much of our legal and illegal immigrant labor is concentrated in such fringe, low-wage employment, its overall impact on our economy is extremely small. A 1997 National Academy of Sciences study estimated that immigration's net benefit to the American economy raises the average income of the native-born by only some $10 billion a year—about $120 per household. And that meager contribution is not the result of immigrants helping to build our essential industries or making us more competitive globally but instead merely delivering our pizzas and cutting our grass. Estimates by pro-immigration forces that foreign workers contribute much more to the economy, boosting annual gross domestic product by hundreds of billions of dollars, generally just tally what immigrants earn here, while ignoring the offsetting effect they have on the wages of native-born workers.

If the benefits of the current generation of migrants are small, the costs are large and growing because of America's vast range of social programs and the wide advocacy network that strives to hook low-earning legal and illegal immigrants into these programs. A 1998 National Academy of Sciences study found that more than 30 percent of California's foreign-born were on Medicaid— including 37 percent of all Hispanic households—compared with 14 percent of native-born households. The foreign-born were more than twice as likely as the native-born to be on welfare, and their children were nearly five times as likely to be in means-tested government lunch programs. Native-born house-holds pay for much of this, the study found, because they earn more and pay higher taxes—and are more likely to comply with tax laws. Recent immigrants, by contrast, have much lower levels of income and tax compliance (another study estimated that only 56 percent of illegals in California have taxes deducted from their earnings, for instance). The study's conclusion: immi-grant families cost each native-born household in California an additional $1,200 a year in taxes.

Immigration's bottom line has shifted so sharply that in a high-immigration state like California, native-born residents are paying up to ten times more in state and local taxes than immigrants generate in economic benefits. Moreover, the cost is only likely to grow as the foreign-born population—which has already mushroomed from about 9 percent of the U.S. population when the NAS studies were done in the late 1990s to about 12 per-cent today—keeps growing. . . . This sharp turnaround since the 1970s, when immigrants were less likely to be using the social programs of the Great Society than the native-born population, says Harvard economist Borjas, suggests that welfare and other social programs are a magnet drawing certain types of immigrants—nonworking women, children, and the elderly—and keeping them here when they run into difficulty.

Not only have the formal and informal networks helping immigrants tap into our social spending grown, but they also get plenty of assistance from advocacy groups financed by tax dollars, working to ensure that immigrants get their share of social spending. Thus, the Newark-based New Jersey Immigration Policy Network receives several hundred thousand government dollars annually to help doctors and hospitals increase immigrant enrollment in Jersey's subsidized health-care programs. Casa Maryland, operating in the greater Washington area, gets funding from nearly 20 federal, state, and local government agencies to run programs that "empower" immigrants to demand benefits and care from government and to "refer clients to government and private social service programs for which they and their families may be eligible." . . .

Almost certainly, immigrants' participation in our social welfare programs will increase over time, because so many are destined to struggle in our workforce. Despite our cherished view of immigrants as rapidly climbing the economic ladder, more and more of the new arrivals and their children face a lifetime of economic disadvantage, because they arrive here with low levels of education and with few work skills—shortcomings not easily overcome. Mexican immigrants, who are up to six times more likely to be high school dropouts than native-born Americans, not only earn substantially less than the native-born median, but the wage gap persists for decades after they've arrived. A study of the 2000 census data, for instance, shows that the cohort of Mexican immigrants between 25 and 34 who entered the United States in the late 1970s were earning 40 to 50 percent less than similarly aged native-born Americans in 1980, but 20 years later they had fallen even further behind their native-born counterparts. Today's Mexican immigrants between 25 and 34 have an even larger wage gap relative to the native-born population. Adjusting for other socioeconomic factors, Harvard's Borjas and Katz estimate that virtually this entire wage gap is attributable to low levels of education. . . .

One reason some ethnic groups make up so little ground concerns the transmission of what economists call "ethnic capital," or what we might call the influence of culture. More than previous generations, immigrants today tend to live concentrated in ethnic enclaves, and their children find their role models among their own group. Thus the children of today's Mexican immigrants are likely to live in a neighborhood where about 60 percent of men dropped out of high school and now do low-wage work, and where less than half of the population speak English fluently, which might explain why high school dropout rates among Americans of Mexican ancestry are two and a half times higher than dropout rates for all other native-born Americans, and why first-generation Mexican Americans do not move up the economic ladder nearly as quickly as the children of other immigrant groups.

In sharp contrast is the cultural capital transmitted by Asian immigrants to children growing up in predominantly Asian-American neighborhoods.

More than 75 percent of Chinese immigrants and 98 percent of South Asian immigrants to the U.S. speak English fluently, while a mid-1990s study of immigrant households in California found that 37 percent of Asian immigrants were college graduates, compared with only 3.4 percent of Mexican immigrants. Thus, even an Asian-American child whose parents are high school dropouts is more likely to grow up in an environment that encourages him to stay in school and learn to speak English well, attributes that will serve him well in the job market. Not surprisingly, several studies have shown that Asian immigrants and their children earn substantially more than Mexican immigrants and their children.

Given these realities, several of the major immigration reforms now under consideration simply don't make economic sense—especially the guest-worker program favored by President Bush and the U.S. Senate. Careful economic research tells us that there is no significant shortfall of workers in essential American industries, desperately needing supplement from a massive guest-worker program. Those few industries now relying on cheap labor must focus more quickly on mechanization where possible. Meanwhile, the cost of paying legal workers already here a bit more to entice them to do such low-wage work as is needed will have a minimal impact on our economy.

The potential woes of a guest-worker program, moreover, far overshadow any economic benefit, given what we know about the long, troubled history of temporary-worker programs in developed countries. They have never stemmed illegal immigration, and the guest workers inevitably become permanent residents, competing with the native-born and forcing down wages. Our last guest-worker program with Mexico, begun during World War II to boost wartime manpower, grew larger in the postwar era, because employers who liked the cheap labor lobbied hard to keep it. By the mid-1950s, the number of guest workers reached seven times the annual limit during the war itself, while illegal immigration doubled, as the availability of cheap labor prompted employers to search for ever more of it rather than invest in mechanization or other productivity gains.

The economic and cultural consequences of guest-worker programs have been devastating in Europe, and we risk similar problems. When post–World War II Germany permitted its manufacturers to import workers from Turkey to man the assembly lines, industry's investment in productivity declined relative to such countries as Japan, which lacked ready access to cheap labor. When Germany finally ended the guest-worker program once it became economically unviable, most of the guest workers stayed on, having attained permanent-resident status. Since then, the descendants of these workers have been chronically underemployed and now have a crime rate double that of German youth. . . .

"Importing labor is far more complicated than importing other factors of production, such as commodities," write University of California at Davis prof Philip Martin, an expert on guest-worker programs, and Michael Teitelbaum, a former member of the U.S. Commission on Immigration Reform. "Migration involves human beings, with their own beliefs, politics, cultures, languages, loves, hates, histories, and families."

If low-wage immigration doesn't pay off for the United States, legalizing illegals already here makes as little sense as importing new rounds of guest workers. The Senate and President Bush, however, aim to start two-thirds of the 11 million undocumented aliens already in the country on a path to legalization, on the grounds that only thus can America assimilate them, and only through assimilation can they hope for economic success in the United States. But such arguments ignore the already poor economic performance of increasingly large segments of the *legal* immigrant population in the United States. Merely granting illegal aliens legal status won't suddenly catapult them up our mobility ladder, because it won't give them the skills and education to compete. . . .

If we do not legalize them, what can we do with 11 million illegals? Ship them back home? Their presence here is a fait accompli, the argument goes, and only legalization can bring them above ground, where they can assimilate. But that argument assumes that we have only two choices: to decriminalize or deport. But what happened after the first great migration suggests a third way: to end the economic incentives that keep them here. We could prompt a great remigration home if, first off, state and local governments in jurisdictions like New York and California would stop using their vast resources to aid illegal immigrants. Second, the federal government can take the tougher approach that it failed to take after the 1986 act. It can require employers to verify Social Security numbers and immigration status before hiring, so that we bar illegals from many jobs. It can deport those caught here. And it can refuse to give those who remain the same benefits as U.S. citizens. Such tough measures do work: as a recent Center for Immigration Studies report points out, when the federal government began deporting illegal Muslims after 9/11, many more illegals who knew they were likely to face more scrutiny voluntarily returned home.

If America is ever to make immigration work for our economy again, it must reject policies shaped by advocacy groups trying to turn immigration into the next civil rights cause or by a tiny minority of businesses seeking cheap labor subsidized by the taxpayers. Instead, we must look to other developed nations that have focused on luring workers who have skills that are in demand and who have the best chance of assimilating. Australia, for instance, gives preferences to workers grouped into four skilled categories: managers, professionals, associates of professionals, and skilled laborers. Using a straightforward "points calculator" to determine who gets in, Australia favors immigrants between the ages of 18 and 45 who speak English, have a post–high school degree or training in a trade, and have at least six months' work experience as everything from laboratory technicians to architects and surveyors to information-technology workers. Such an immigration policy goes far beyond America's employment-based immigration categories, like the H1-B visas, which account for about 10 percent of our legal immigration and essentially serve the needs of a few Silicon Valley industries.

Immigration reform must also tackle our family-preference visa program, which today accounts for two-thirds of all legal immigration and has helped create a 40-year waiting list. Lawmakers should narrow the family-preference visa program down to spouses and minor children of U.S. citizens and should exclude adult siblings and parents.

America benefits even today from many of its immigrants, from the Asian entrepreneurs who have helped revive inner-city Los Angeles business districts to Haitians and Jamaicans who have stabilized neighborhoods in Queens and Brooklyn to Indian programmers who have spurred so much innovation in places like Silicon Valley and Boston's Route 128. But increasingly over the last 25 years, such immigration has become the exception. It needs once again to become the rule.

Diana Furchtgott-Roth  **NO**

The Case for Immigration

It was raining in Washington last week, and vendors selling $5 and $10 umbrellas appeared on the streets. They had Hispanic accents, and were undoubtedly some of the unskilled immigrants that Steven Malanga referred to in his recent City Journal article, "How Unskilled Immigrants Hurt Our Economy."

I already had an umbrella. But the many purchasers of the umbrellas did not seem to notice that the economy was being hurt. Rather, they were glad of the opportunity to stay dry before their important meetings.

The City Journal article is worth a look because it reflects an attitude becoming more common these days in the debate. The article speaks approvingly of immigrants from Portugal, Asia, China, India, Haiti, and Jamaica. But it also makes it clear that we have too many Mexicans, a "flood of immigrants" who cause high unemployment rates among the unskilled. They work in shrinking industries, drive down wages of native-born Americans, cost millions in welfare, and retard America's technology.

These are serious charges indeed. Similar charges, that immigrants have caused native-born Americans to quit the labor market, have been made by Steven Camarota of the Center for Immigration Studies. But are they true?

Annual immigration is a tiny fraction of our labor force. The Pew Hispanic Center Report shows that annual immigration from all countries as a percent of the labor force has been declining since its recent peak in 1999.

Annual immigration in 1999 equaled 1% of the labor force—by 2005 it had declined to 0.8%. Hispanics, including undocumented workers, peaked in 2000 as a percent of the labor force at 0.5%, and by 2004 accounted for only 0.4% (0.3% for Mexicans) of the labor force.

Looking at unskilled workers, Hispanic immigration as a percent of the American unskilled labor force (defined as those without a high school diploma) peaked in 2000 at 6%, and was 5% in 2004 (4% for Mexicans). Five percent is not "floods of immigrants."

Mr. Malanga writes that America does not have a vast labor shortage because "unemployment among unskilled workers is high—about 30%." It isn't. In 2005, according to Bureau of Labor Statistics data, the unemployment rate for adults without a high school diploma was 7.6%. Last month it stood at 6.9%.

Data from a recent study by senior economist Pia Orrenius of the Dallas Federal Reserve Bank show that foreign-born Americans are more likely to work than native-born Americans. Leaving their countries by choice, they are naturally more risk-taking and entrepreneurial.

In 2005 the unemployment rate for native-born Americans was 5.2%, but for foreign-born it was more than half a percentage point lower, at 4.6%. For unskilled workers, although the total unemployment rate was 7.6%, the native-born rate was 9.1% and the foreign-born was much lower, at 5.7%.

According to Mr. Malanga, unskilled immigrants "work in shrinking industries where they force out native workers." However, data show otherwise. Low-skilled immigrants are disproportionately represented in the expanding service and construction sectors, with occupations such as janitors, gardeners, tailors, plasterers, and stucco masons. Manufacturing, the declining sector, employs few immigrants.

One myth repeated often is that immigrants depress wages of native-born Americans. As Professor Giovanni Peri of the University of California at Davis describes in a new National Bureau of Economic Analysis paper last month, immigrants are complements, rather than substitutes, for native-born workers. As such, they are not competing with native-born workers, but providing our economy with different skills.

Education levels of working immigrants form a U-shaped curve, with unusually high representation among adult low- and high-skilled. In contrast, the skills of native-born Americans form a bellshaped curve, with many B.A.s and high school diplomas but relatively few adult high school drop-outs or Ph.D.s

Low-skill immigrants come to be janitors and housekeepers, jobs native-born Americans typically don't want, but they aren't found as crossing guards and funeral service workers, low-skill jobs preferred by Americans. Similarly, high-skilled immigrants also take jobs Americans don't want. They are research scientists, dentists, and computer hardware and software engineers, but not lawyers, judges, or education administrators.

Because immigrants are complements to native-born workers, rather than substitutes, they help reduce economic bottlenecks, resulting in income gains. Mr. Peri's new study shows that immigrants raised the wages of the 90% of native-born Americans with at least a high school degree by 1% to 3% between 1990 and 2004. Those without a high school diploma lost about 1%, an amount that could be compensated from the gains of the others.

If immigrants affect any wages, it's those of prior immigrants, who compete for the same jobs. But we don't see immigrants protesting in the streets to keep others out, as we see homeowners in scenic locations demonstrating against additional development. Rather, some of the biggest proponents of greater immigration are the established immigrants themselves, who see America's boundless opportunities as outweighing negative wage effects.

Mr. Malanga cites a 1998 National Academy of Sciences study to say, "The foreign-born were more than twice as likely as the native-born to be on welfare." Yet this study contains estimates from 1995, more than a decade ago, and mentions programs such as Aid to Families with Dependent Children that no longer exist. Even so, the NAS study says that foreign-born households "are not more likely to use AFDC, SSI, or housing benefits."

The NAS study concludes that, since the foreign-born have more children, the "difference in education benefits accounts for nearly all of the relative deficit . . . at the local government level." Mr. Malanga, writing about how unskilled immigrants hurt the economy, would likely be in favor of these immigrants trying to educate their children, especially since these children will be contributing to his Social Security benefits.

Mr. Malanga suggests that the availability of low-wage immigrants retards investments in American technology. He cites agriculture as an example where machines to pick produce could be invented if labor were not available. Or, Mr. Malanga says, we could import produce from abroad at little additional cost.

Although consumers don't care where their food comes from, farmers certainly do. Farms provide income to farmers as well as to other native-born Americans employed in the industry as well as in trucking and distribution, just as immigrants in the construction industry have helped fuel the boom that sent employment of native-born construction workers to record levels. It makes little sense to send a whole economic sector to other countries just to avoid employing immigrants.

If unskilled immigrants don't hurt our economy, do they hurt our culture? City Journal editor Myron Magnet writes that Hispanics have "a group culture that devalues education and assimilation." Similar concerns about assimilation were made about Jews, Italians, Irish, Germans, Poles, and even Norwegians when they first came to America. All eventually assimilated.

Moreover, for those who are concerned with Spanish-speaking enclaves, a September 2006 paper by a professor at Princeton, Douglas Massey, shows that within two generations Mexican immigrants in California stop speaking Spanish at home, and within three generations they cease to know the language altogether. He concludes, "Like taxes and biological death, linguistic death seems to be a sure thing in the United States, even for Mexicans living in Los Angeles, a city with one of the largest Spanish-speaking urban populations in the world."

Legalizing the status of the illegal immigrants in America by providing a guest-worker program with a path to citizenship would produce additional gains to our economy. This is not the same as temporary worker programs in Germany, which did not have a path to citizenship, and so resulted in a disenfranchised class of workers.

With legal status, workers could move from the informal to the formal sector, and would pay more taxes. It would be easier to keep track of illegal financial transactions, reducing the potential for helping terrorists.

For over 200 years, American intellectual thought has included a small but influential literature advocating reduced immigration. The literature has spawned political parties such as the Know-Nothing Party in the mid-19th century and periodically led to the enactment of anti-immigrant laws. Immigrants, so the story goes, are bad for our economy and for our culture.

The greatness of America is not merely that we stand for freedom and economic prosperity for ourselves, but that we have consistently overcome arguments that would deny these same benefits to others.

POSTSCRIPT

Do Unskilled Immigrants Hurt the American Economy?

Steven Malanga contrasts today's immigrants unfavorably with immigrants who came a hundred years ago. Today's flood of legal and illegal immigrants are less educated, unskilled, and from poorer countries. Two-thirds of Mexican immigrants are high school dropouts doing unskilled factory work, small-scale construction, or work in entry-level jobs in service industries for low wages. They compete for these jobs with other immigrants and with native-born high school dropouts. Malanga selectively cites from diverse studies on the effects of the unskilled workers on the economy to show that (i) "immigrants drive down the wages of native-born workers and squeeze them out of certain industries"; (ii) the "waves of low-wage workers have also retarded investments that might lead to modernization"; (iii) without illegal workers, the retail cost of farm produce would be "only" 2 to 3 percent higher because labor is a "tiny percent of the retail price," and because the United States would probably import more fruit and vegetables; and (iv) the overall impact of legal and illegal immigration on the U.S. economy is to raise "the average income of the native-born by only some $10 billion a year." Malanga then turns to the costs associated with the current generation of migrants, which he claims are large and growing. Again he draws from several studies including one that concludes immigrant families cost each native-born household in California as additional $1,200 a year in taxes. He believes that a guest-worker program doesn't make economic sense since "economic research tells us that there is no significant shortfall of workers in essential American industries." He also notes that unemployment among unskilled workers is about 30 percent. Further, legalizing the illegal immigrants "won't suddenly catapult them up our mobility ladder because it won't give them the skills and education to compete."

Diana Furchtgott-Roth begins by refuting Malanga's "flood of immigrants" charge: Annual immigration declined from 1 percent (1999) to 0.8 percent (2005) of the labor force and undocumented workers accounted for only 0.4 percent of the labor force (0.3 percent for Mexicans) based on the Pew Hispanic Center Report. Next, she disputes Malanga's figure of 30 percent unemployment among the unskilled by referring to the government's unemployment rate of 7.6 percent for adults without a high school diploma in 2005. Third, Furchtgott-Roth cites a recent study showing that foreign-born Americans are more likely to work than native-born Americans. Fourth, unskilled workers are employed in *expanding*, not shrinking, industries where they force out native workers. Fifth, Furchtgott-Roth dispels the myth that immigrants depress wages of natives, refering to a 2006 study showing immigrants are complements, providing our economy with different skills. Sixth, low-skilled immigrants take jobs that natives do not want and do not take low-skill jobs that natives prefer. Sixth, Furchtgott-Roth questions the relevancy of Malanga's citation of a study showing the foreign-born were twice as likely to be on welfare as it uses decade-old data and some programs mentioned in the study no longer exist. Seventh, she defends the use of immigrant labor on farms (rather than importing food) because they provide income and employment to truckers and distributors as well as to farmers. Eighth, Furchtgott-Roth notes that concerns that Mexicans may not assimilate are not well-founded: All other groups eventually assimilated. She concludes her analysis by endorsing the guest-worker program.

There is a large and growing body of literature on the economic impact of immigration. Recent papers include testimonies before the House Committee on Ways and Means on July 26, 2006 by Michael Fix, vice president and director of studies, Migration Policy Institute, available at http://waysandmeans.house.gov/hearings.asp?formmode=view&id=5175, and by Steven A. Camarota, director of research, Center for Immigration Studies, available at http://www.cis.org/articles/2006/sactestimony072606.html. "Immigration Nation" by Tamar Jacoby in *Foreign Affairs*, November/December 2006, considers the need for unskilled and skilled immigrants. It is available at http://www.foreignaffairs.org. Her other papers on the subject are available at http://www.manhattan-institute.org/html/jacoby.htm. *The Economic Consequences of Migration* by Julian L. Simon (Cambridge, MA: Basil Blackwell, 1989) is an early study with a favorable view of immigration. For a more critical early view, see *Friends or Strangers: The Impact of Immigrants on the U.S. Economy* by George J. Borjas (New York: Basic Books, 1990). The reader should also refer to the studies cited in both the Malanga and Furchtgott-Roth arguments.

Internet References . . .

European Central Bank (ECB)

The home page for the ECB provides a number of useful links that provide information regarding ECB's monetary policy, the structure of the ECB, and economic conditions in the European Union countries.

http://www.ecb.int/home/html/index.en.html

European Union: Delegation of the European Commission to the U.S.A.

This site provides access to information regarding EU membership and its basic organization and structure, to lists of EU publications, and to overviews of EU law and policy.

http://www.eurunion.org

Geography IQ

This site provides, among other things, rankings of countries on a variety of characteristics ranging from the number of radios to the growth rates of gross domestic product.

http://www.geographyiq.com/index.htm

International Monetary Fund

The home page of the International Monetary fund provides links to information about its purposes and activities, its news releases, and its publications including the most recent *World Economic Outlook*.

http://www.imf.org

International Trade Administration (ITA)

The U.S. Department of Commerce's ITA is dedicated to helping U.S. businesses compete in the global marketplace. This site offers assistance through many Web links under such headings as Trade Statistics, Tariffs and Taxes, Market Research, and Export Documentation. It also provides information regarding recent actions taken to promote trade.

http://www.ita.doc.gov

Social Science Information Gateway (SOSIG)

The SOSIG catalogs 17 subjects and lists more URL addresses from European and developing countries than many U.S. sources do.

http://sosig.esrc.bris.ac.uk

The World Bank

The home page of the World Bank offers links to a vast array of information regarding developing countries. Of special interest is the link to *World Development Indicators*.

http://www.worldbank.org

The World Around Us

*T*he issues explored in this unit are more diverse than those of Units 1 and 2. Three of the issues have an international theme; one addresses federal government deficits and debt; one spotlights the environment and humankind's ability to sustain the ecosystem in the face of both population and economic growth; another explores the effectiveness of a recent and ongoing attempt to improve public education; and the final issue looks at a general effort to improve the economy's efficiency as well as its fairness.

- Are Protectionist Policies Bad for America?

- Should We Sweat About Sweatshops?

- Are the Costs of Global Warming Too High to Ignore?

- Are Spending Cuts the Right Way to Balance the Federal Government's Budget?

- Has the North American Free Trade Agreement Benefited the Economies of Canada, Mexico, and the United States?

- Is the No Child Left Behind Act Working?

- Will the Creation of an Ownership Society Make the American Economy More Efficient and More Equitable?

ISSUE 13

Are Protectionist Policies Bad for America?

YES: Murray N. Rothbard, from "Protectionism and the Destruction of Prosperity," Ludwig von Mises Institute, http://mises.org/fullarticle.asp?title=Protectionism&month=1 (July 13, 1998)

NO: Patrick J. Buchanan, from "Free Trade Is Not Free," Address to the Chicago Council on Foreign Relations (November 18, 1998)

ISSUE SUMMARY

YES: Free-trade economist Murray N. Rothbard objects to the prospect of protectionism, which he sees as an attempt by the few who make up special interest groups "to repress and loot the rest of us" who make up the many.

NO: Social critic and three-time presidential hopeful Patrick J. Buchanan argues that America's "new corporate elite" is willing to sacrifice the country's best interests on "the altar of that golden calf, the global economy."

The economic logic that supports international trade has changed little since David Ricardo provided us with his basic insight that the patterns and the gains of trade depend on relative factor prices. More correctly stated, Ricardo argued nearly 200 years ago that if there were differences in the "opportunity costs" of producing goods and services, trade will occur between countries and that, more important, the countries that engage in trade will all benefit.

Although the large majority of economists accept the logic and the policy conclusions of Ricardo's theory, the debate rages on. The debate between "free traders" and those who plead for protection is timeless. The basic logic of international trade is indistinguishable from the basic logic of purely domestic trade. That is, both domestic and international trade must answer the fundamental economic questions: *what* to produce, *how* to produce it, and *for whom* to produce it. The distinction is that the international trade questions are posed in an international arena. This is an arena filled with producers and consumers who speak different languages, use different currencies, and are often suspicious of the actions and reactions of foreigners.

If markets work the way they are expected to work, free trade simply increases the size or the extent of a purely domestic market and, therefore, increases the advantages of specialization. Market participants should be able to buy and consume a greater variety of inexpensive goods and services after the establishment of free trade than they could before free trade. One might ask, then, why some wish to close U.S. borders and deny Americans the benefits of free trade. The answer to this question is straightforward—these benefits do not come without a cost.

There are two sets of winners and two sets of losers in the game of free trade. The most obvious winners are the consumers of the less expensive imported goods. These consumers are able to buy the low-priced color television sets, automobiles, or steel that is made abroad. Another set of winners is the producers of the exported goods. All the factors in the export industry, as well as those in industries that supply the export industry, experience an increase in market demand. Therefore, their income increases. In the United States, agriculture is one such export industry. As new foreign markets are opened, farmers' incomes increase, as do the incomes of those who supply the farmers with fertilizer, farm equipment, gasoline, and other basic inputs.

On the other side of this coin are the losers. The obvious losers are those who own the factors of production that are employed in the import-competing industries. These factors include the land, labor, and capital that are devoted to the production of such U.S.-made items as color television sets, automobiles, and steel. The less expensive foreign imports displace the demand for these products. The consumers of exported goods are also the losers. For example, as U.S. farmers sell more of their products abroad, less of this output is available domestically. As a result, the domestic prices of these farm products and other export goods and services rise.

The bottom line is that there is nothing really "free" in a market system. Competition—whether it is domestic or foreign—creates winners and losers. Historically, we have sympathized with the losers when they suffer at the hands of foreign competitors. However, we have not let our sympathies seriously curtail free trade.

The "free" that Murray N. Rothbard and Patrick J. Buchanan debate in the following selections goes beyond the notion of winners and losers in a marketplace. Rothbard asserts that protectionism is a restraint of trade, which imposes severe losses on foreign and domestic consumers alike. Buchanan argues that we have to think of "America first, and not only first, but also second and third as well" when considering international trade issues.

YES

Murray N. Rothbard

Protectionism and the Destruction of Prosperity

Protectionism, often refuted and seemingly abandoned, has returned, and with a vengeance. The Japanese, who bounced back from grievous losses in World War II to astound the world by producing innovative, high-quality products at low prices, are serving as the convenient butt of protectionist propaganda. Memories of wartime myths prove a heady brew, as protectionists warn about this new "Japanese imperialism," even "worse than Pearl Harbor." This "imperialism" turns out to consist of selling Americans wonderful TV sets, autos, microchips, etc., at prices more than competitive with American firms.

Is this "flood" of Japanese products really a menace, to be combated by the U.S. government? Or is the new Japan a godsend to American consumers?

In taking our stand on this issue, we should recognize that all government action means coercion, so that calling upon the U.S. government to intervene means urging it to use force and violence to restrain peaceful trade. One trusts that the protectionists are not willing to pursue their logic of force to the ultimate in the form of another Hiroshima and Nagasaki [Japanese cities destroyed by the first atomic bombs used in warfare].

Keep Your Eye on the Consumer

As we unravel the tangled web of protectionist argument, we should keep our eye on two essential points: (1) protectionism means force in restraint of trade; and (2) the key is what happens to the consumer. Invariably, we will find that the protectionists are out to cripple, exploit, and impose severe losses not only on foreign consumers but especially on Americans. And since each and every one of us is a consumer, this means that protectionism is out to mulct [swindle] all of us for the benefit of a specially privileged, subsidized few—and an inefficient few at that: people who cannot make it in a free and unhampered market.

Take, for example, the alleged Japanese menace. All trade is mutually beneficial to both parties—in this case Japanese producers and American consumers—otherwise they would not engage in the exchange. In trying to stop this trade, protectionists are trying to stop American consumers from enjoying high living standards by buying cheap and high-quality Japanese products. Instead, we are to be forced by government to return to the inefficient, higher-priced products we have already rejected. In short, inefficient producers are trying to deprive all of us of products we desire so that we will have to turn to inefficient firms. American consumers are to be plundered.

How to Look at Tariffs and Quotas

The best way to look at tariffs or import quotas or other protectionist restraints is to forget about political boundaries. Political boundaries of nations may be important for other reasons, but they have no economic meaning whatever. Suppose, for example, that each of the United States were a separate nation. Then we would hear a lot of protectionist bellyaching that we are now fortunately spared. Think of the howls by high-priced New York or Rhode Island textile manufacturers who would then be complaining about the "unfair," "cheap labor" competition from various low-type "foreigners" from Tennessee or North Carolina, or vice versa.

Fortunately, the absurdity of worrying about the balance of payments is made evident by focusing on inter-state trade. For nobody worries about the balance of payments between New York and New Jersey, or, for that matter, between Manhattan and Brooklyn, because there are no customs officials recording such trade and such balances.

If we think about it, it is clear that a call by New York firms for a tariff against North Carolina is a pure ripoff of New York (as well as North Carolina) consumers, a naked grab for coerced special privilege by less efficient business firms. If the 50 states were separate nations, the protectionists would then be able to use the trappings of patriotism, and distrust of foreigners, to camouflage and get away with their looting the consumers of their own region.

Fortunately, inter-state tariffs are unconstitutional. But even with this clear barrier, and even without being able to wrap themselves in the cloak of nationalism, protectionists have been able to impose inter-state tariffs in another guise. Part of the drive for continuing increases in the federal minimum-wage law is to impose a protectionist devise against lower-wage, lower-labor-cost competition from North Carolina and other southern states against their New England and New York competitors.

During the 1966 Congressional battle over a higher federal minimum wage, for example, the late Senator Jacob Javits (R-NY) freely admitted that one of his main reasons for supporting the bill was to cripple the southern competitors of New York textile firms. Since southern wages are generally lower than in the north, the business firms hardest hit by an increased minimum wage (and the workers struck by unemployment) will be located in the south.

Another way in which interstate trade restrictions have been imposed has been in the fashionable name of "safety." Government-organized state milk cartels in New York, for example, have prevented importation of milk from nearby New Jersey under the patently spurious grounds that the trip across the Hudson would render New Jersey milk "unsafe."

If tariffs and restraints on trade are good for a country, then why not indeed for a state or region? The principle is precisely the same. In America's first great depression, the Panic of 1819, Detroit was a tiny frontier town of only a few hundred people. Yet protectionist cries arose—fortunately not fulfilled—to prohibit all "imports" from outside of Detroit, and citizens were exhorted to buy only Detroit. If this nonsense had been put into effect, general starvation and death would have ended all other economic problems for Detroiters.

So why not restrict and even prohibit trade, i.e., "imports," into a city, or a neighborhood, or even on a block, or, to boil it down to its logical conclusion, to one family? Why shouldn't the Jones family issue a decree that from now on, no member of the family can buy any goods or services produced outside the family house? Starvation would quickly wipe out this ludicrous drive for self-sufficiency.

And yet we must realize that this absurdity is inherent in the logic of protectionism. Standard protectionism is just as preposterous, but the rhetoric of nationalism and national boundaries has been able to obscure this vital fact.

The upshot is that protectionism is not only nonsense, but dangerous nonsense, destructive of all economic prosperity. We are not, if we were ever, a world of self-sufficient farmers. The market economy is one vast latticework throughout the world, in which each individual, each region, each country, produces what he or it is best at, most relatively efficient in, and exchanges that product for the goods and services of others. Without the division of labor and the trade based upon that division, the entire world would starve. Coerced restraints on trade—such as protectionism—cripple, hobble, and destroy trade, the source of life and prosperity. Protectionism is simply a plea that consumers, as well as general prosperity, be hurt so as to confer permanent special privilege upon groups of less efficient producers, at the expense of more competent firms and of consumers. But it is a peculiarly destructive kind of bailout, because it permanently shackles trade under the cloak of patriotism.

The Negative Railroad

Protectionism is also peculiarly destructive because it acts as a coerced and artificial increase in the cost of transportation between regions. One of the great features of the Industrial Revolution, one of the ways in which it brought prosperity to the starving masses, was by reducing drastically the cost of transportation. The development of railroads in the early 19th century, for example, meant that for the first time in the history of the human race, goods could be transported cheaply over land. Before that, water—rivers and oceans—was the only economically viable means of transport. By making land transport accessible and cheap, railroads allowed interregional land transportation to break up expensive inefficient local monopolies. The result was an enormous improvement in living standards for all consumers. And what the protectionists want to do is lay an axe to this wondrous principle of progress.

It is no wonder that Frederic Bastiat, the great French laissez-faire economist of the mid-19th century, called a tariff a "negative railroad." Protectionists are just as economically destructive as if they were physically chopping up railroads, or planes, or ships, and forcing us to revert to the costly transport of the past—mountain trails, rafts, or sailing ships.

"Fair" Trade

Let us now turn to some of the leading protectionist arguments. Take, for example, the standard complaint that while the protectionist "welcomes competition," this competition must be "fair." Whenever someone starts talking about "fair competition" or indeed, about "fairness" in general, it is time to keep a sharp eye on your wallet, for it is about to be picked. For the genuinely "fair" is simply the voluntary terms of exchange, mutually agreed upon by buyer and seller. As most of the medieval scholastics were able to figure out, there is no "just" (or "fair") price outside of the market price.

So what could be "unfair" about the free-market price? One common protectionist charge is that it is "unfair" for an American firm to compete with, say, a Taiwanese firm which needs to pay only one-half the wages of the American competitor. The U.S. government is called upon to step in and "equalize" the wage rates by imposing an equivalent tariff upon the Taiwanese. But does this mean that consumers can never patronize low-cost firms because it is "unfair" for them to have lower costs than inefficient competitors? This is the same argument that would be used by a New York firm trying to cripple its North Carolina competitor.

What the protectionists don't bother to explain is why U.S. wage rates are so much higher than Taiwan. They are not imposed by Providence. Wage rates are high in the U.S. because American employers have bid these rates up. Like all other prices on the market, wage rates are determined by supply and demand, and the increased demand by U.S. employers has bid wages up. What determines this demand? The "marginal productivity" of labor.

The demand for any factor of production, including labor, is constituted by the productivity of that factor, the amount of revenue that the worker, or the pound of cement or acre of land, is expected to bring to the brim. The more productive the factory, the greater the demand by employers, and the higher its price or wage rate. American labor is more costly than Taiwanese because it is far more productive. What makes it productive? To some extent, the comparative qualities of labor, skill, and education. But most of the difference is not due to the personal qualities of the laborers themselves, but to the fact that the American laborer, on the whole, is equipped with more and better capital equipment than his Taiwanese counterparts. The more and better the capital investment per worker, the greater the worker's productivity, and therefore the higher the wage rate.

In short, if the American wage rate is twice that of the Taiwanese, it is because the American laborer is more heavily capitalized, is equipped with more and better tools, and is therefore, on the average, twice as productive. In a sense, I suppose, it is not "fair" for the American worker to make more than the Taiwanese, not because of his personal qualities, but because savers and investors have supplied him with more tools. But a wage rate is determined not just by personal quality but also by relative scarcity, and in the United States the worker is far scarcer compared to capital than he is in Taiwan.

Putting it another way, the fact that American wage rates are on the average twice that of the Taiwanese, does not make the cost of labor in the U.S. twice that of Taiwan. Since U.S. labor is twice as productive, this means that the double wage rate in the U.S. is offset by the double productivity, so that the cost of labor per unit product in the U.S. and Taiwan tends, on the average, to be the same. One of the major protectionist fallacies is to confuse the price of labor (wage rates) with its cost, which also depends on its relative productivity.

Thus, the problem faced by American employers is not really with the "cheap labor" in Taiwan, because "expensive labor" in the U.S. is precisely the result of the bidding for scarce labor by U.S. employers. The problem faced by less efficient U.S. textile or auto firms is not so much cheap labor in Taiwan or Japan, but the fact that other U.S. industries are efficient enough to afford it, because they bid wages that high in the first place.

So, by imposing protective tariffs and quotas to save, bail out, and keep in place less efficient U.S. textile or auto or microchip firms, the protectionists are not only injuring the American consumer. They are also harming efficient U.S. firms and industries, which are prevented from employing resources now locked into incompetent firms, and who could otherwise be able to expand and sell their efficient products at home and abroad.

"Dumping"

Another contradictory line of protectionist assault on the free market asserts that the problem is not so much the low costs enjoyed by foreign firms, as the "unfairness" of selling their products "below costs" to American consumers, and thereby engaging in the pernicious and sinful practice of "dumping." By such dumping they are able to exert unfair advantage over American firms who presumably never engage in such practices and make sure that their prices are always high enough to cover costs. But if selling below costs is such a powerful weapon, why isn't it ever pursued by business firms within a country?

Our first response to this charge is, once again, to keep our eye on consumers in general and on American consumers in particular. Why should it be a matter of complaint when consumers so clearly benefit? Suppose, for example, that Sony is willing to injure American competitors by selling TV sets to Americans for a penny apiece. Shouldn't we rejoice at such an absurd policy of suffering severe losses by subsidizing us, the American consumers? And shouldn't our response be: "Come on, Sony, subsidize us some more!" As far as consumers are concerned, the more "dumping" that takes place, the better.

But what of the poor American TV firms, whose sales will suffer so long as Sony is willing to virtually give their sets away? Well, surely, the sensible policy for RCA, Zenith, etc. would be to hold back production and sales until Sony drives itself into bankruptcy. But suppose that the worst happens, and RCA, Zenith, etc. are themselves driven into bankruptcy by the Sony price war? Well, in that case, we the consumers will still be better off, since the plants of the bankrupt firms, which would still be in existence, would be picked up for a song at auction, and the American buyers at auction would be able to enter the TV business and outcompete Sony because they now enjoy far lower capital costs.

For decades, indeed, opponents of the free market have claimed that many businesses gained their powerful status on the market by what is called "predatory price-cutting," that is, by driving their smaller competitors into bankruptcy by selling their goods below cost, and then reaping the reward of their unfair methods by raising their prices and thereby charging "monopoly prices" to the consumers. The claim is that while consumers may gain in the short run by price wars, "dumping," and selling below costs, they lose in the long run from the alleged monopoly. But, as we have seen, economic theory shows that this would be a mug's [fool's] game, losing money for the "dumping" firms, and never really achieving a monopoly price. And sure enough, historical investigation has not turned up a single case where predatory pricing, when tried, was successful, and there are actually very few cases where it has even been tried.

Another charge claims that Japanese or other foreign firms can afford to engage in dumping because their governments are willing to subsidize their losses. But again, we should still welcome such an absurd policy. If the Japanese government is really willing to waste scarce resources subsidizing American purchases of Sony's, so much the better! Their policy would be just as self-defeating as if the losses were private.

There is yet another problem with the charge of "dumping," even when it is made by economists or other alleged "experts" sitting on impartial tariff commissions and government bureaus. There is no way whatever that outside observers, be they economists, businessmen, or other experts, can decide what some other firm's "costs" may be. "Costs" are not objective entities that can be gauged or measured. Costs are subjective to the businessman himself, and they vary continually, depending on the businessman's time horizon or the stage of production or selling process he happens to be dealing with at any given time.

Suppose, for example, a fruit dealer has purchased a case of pears for $20, amounting to $1 a pound. He hopes and expects to sell those pears for $1.50 a pound. But something has happened to the pear market, and he finds it impossible to sell most of the pears at anything near that price. In fact, he finds that he must sell the pears at whatever price he can get before they become overripe. Suppose he finds that he can only sell his stock of pears at 70 cents a pound. The outside observer might say that the fruit dealer has, perhaps "unfairly," sold his pears "below costs," figuring that the dealer's costs were $1 a pound.

"Infant" Industries

Another protectionist fallacy held that the government should provide a temporary protective tariff to aid, or to bring into being, an "infant industry." Then, when the industry was well-established, the government would and should remove the tariff and toss the now "mature" industry into the competitive swim.

The theory is fallacious, and the policy has proved disastrous in practice. For there is no more need for government to protect a new, young, industry from foreign competition than there is to protect it from domestic competition.

In the last few decades, the "infant" plastics, television, and computer industries made out very well without such protection. Any government subsidizing of a new industry will funnel too many resources into that industry as compared to older firms, and will also inaugurate distortions that may persist and render the firm or industry permanently inefficient and vulnerable to competition. As a result, "infant-industry" tariffs have tended to become permanent, regardless of the "maturity" of the industry. The proponents were carried away by a misleading biological analogy to "infants" who need adult care. But a business firm is not a person, young or old.

Older Industries

Indeed, in recent years, older industries that are notoriously inefficient have been using what might be called a "senile-industry" argument for protectionism. Steel, auto, and other outcompeted industries have been complaining that they "need a breathing space" to retool and become competitive with foreign rivals, and that this breather could be provided by several years of tariffs or import quotas. This argument is just as full of holes as the hoary infant-industry approach, except that it will be even more difficult to figure out when the "senile" industry will have become magically rejuvenated. In fact, the steel industry has been inefficient ever since its inception, and its chronological age seems to make no difference. The first protectionist movement in the U.S. was launched in 1820, headed by the Pennsylvania iron (later iron and steel) industry, artificially force-fed by the War of 1812 and already in grave danger from far more efficient foreign competitors.

The Non-Problem of the Balance of Payments

A final set of arguments, or rather alarms, center on the mysteries of the balance of payments. Protectionists focus on the horrors of imports being greater than exports, implying that if market forces continued unchecked, Americans might wind up buying everything from abroad, while selling foreigners nothing, so that American consumers will have engorged themselves to the permanent ruin of American business firms. But if the exports really fell to somewhere near zero, where in the world would Americans still find the money to purchase foreign products? The balance of payments, as we said earlier, is a pseudo-problem created by the existence of customs statistics.

During the day of the gold standard, a deficit in the national balance of payments was a problem, but only because of the nature of the fractional-reserve banking system. If U.S. banks, spurred on by the Fed or previous forms of central banks, inflated money and credit, the American inflation would lead to higher prices in the U.S., and this would discourage exports and encourage imports. The resulting deficit had to be paid for in some way, and during the gold standard era this meant being paid for in gold, the international money. So as bank credit expanded, gold began to flow out of the country, which put the fractional-reserve banks in even shakier shape. To meet the threat to their solvency posed by the gold outflow, the banks eventually were forced to contract credit, precipitating a recession and reversing the balance of payment deficits, thus bringing gold back into the country.

But now, in the fiat-money era, balance of payments deficits are truly meaningless. For gold is no longer a "balancing item." In effect, there is no deficit in the balance of payments. It is true that in the last few years, imports have been greater than exports by $150 billion or so per year. But no gold flowed out of the country. Neither did dollars "leak" out. The alleged "deficit" was paid for by foreigners investing the equivalent amount of money in American dollars: in real estate, capital goods, U.S. securities, and bank accounts.

In effect, in the last couple of years, foreigners have been investing enough of their own funds in dollars to keep the dollar high, enabling us to purchase cheap imports. Instead of worrying and complaining about this development, we should rejoice that foreign investors are willing to finance our cheap imports. The only problem is that this bonanza is already coming to an end, with the dollar becoming cheaper and exports more expensive.

We conclude that the sheaf of protectionist arguments, many plausible at first glance, are really a tissue of egregious fallacies. They betray a complete ignorance of the most basic economic analysis. Indeed, some of the arguments are almost embarrassing replicas of the most ridiculous claims of 17th-century mercantilism: for example, that it is somehow a calamitous problem that the U.S. has a balance of trade deficit, not overall, but merely with one specific country, e.g., Japan.

Must we even relearn the rebuttals of the more sophisticated mercantilists of the 18th century: namely, that balances with individual countries will cancel each other out, and therefore that we should only concern ourselves with the overall balance? (Let alone realize that the overall balance is no problem either.) But we need not reread the economic literature to realize that the impetus for protectionism comes not from preposterous theories, but from the quest for coerced special privilege and restraint of trade at the expense of efficient competitors and consumers. In the host of special interests using the political process to repress and loot the rest of us, the protectionists are among the most venerable. It is high time that we get them, once and for all, off our backs, and treat them with the righteous indignation they so richly deserve.

Patrick J. Buchanan

Free Trade Is Not Free

This is a prestigious forum; and I appreciate the opportunity to address it. As my subject, I have chosen what I believe is the coming and irrepressible conflict between the claims of a new American nationalism and the commands of the Global Economy.

As you may have heard in my last [presidential] campaign, I am called by many names. "Protectionist" is one of the nicer ones; but it is inexact. I am an economic nationalist. To me, the country comes before the economy; and the economy exists for the people. I believe in free markets, but I do not worship them. In the proper hierarchy of things, it is the market that must be harnessed to work for man—and not the other way around.

As for the Global Economy, like the unicorn, it is a mythical beast that exists only in the imagination. In the real world, there are only national economies—Japan's that has lost its animal spirits, South Korea's that is deep in recession, China's which is headed for trouble, Brazil's which is falling, Indonesia and Russia's which are in collapse.

In these unique national economies, critical decisions are based on what is best for the nation. Only in America do leaders sacrifice the interests of their own country on the altar of that golden calf, the Global Economy.

What is Economic Nationalism? Is it some right-wing or radical idea? By no means. Economic nationalism was the idea and cause that brought [George] Washington, [Alexander] Hamilton and [James] Madison to Philadelphia. These men dreamed of creating here in America the greatest free market on earth, by elimination all internal barriers to trade among the 13 states, and taxing imports to finance the turnpikes and canals of the new nation and end America's dependence on Europe. It was called the American System.

The ideology of free trade is the alien import, an invention of European academics and scribblers, not one of whom ever built a great nation, and all of whom were repudiated by America's greatest statesmen, including all four presidents on Mount Rushmore.

The second bill that Washington signed into law was the Tariff Act of 1789. Madison saved the nation's infant industries from being buried by the dumping of British manufactures, with the first truly protective tariff, the Tariff Act of 1816. "Give me a tariff and I will give you the greatest nation on earth," said

[Abraham] Lincoln. "I thank God I am not a free trader," Theodore Roosevelt wrote to Henry Cabot Lodge.

Under economic nationalism, there was no income tax in the United States, except during the Civil War and Reconstruction. Tariffs produced fifty to ninety percent of federal revenue. And how did America prosper? From 1865 to 1913, U.S. growth averaged 4% a year. We began the era with half Britain's production, but ended with twice Britain's production.

Yet, this era is now disparaged in history books and public schools as the time of the Robber Barons, a Gilded Age best forgotten.

Not only did America rise to greatness through the economic nationalism so did every other first-rank power in history—from Britain in the 18th century, to [Otto von] Bismarck's Germany in the 19th, to post-war Japan. Economic nationalism has been the policy of rising nations, free trade the practice of nations that have commenced their historic decline. Today, this idea may be mocked by the talking heads, but it is going to prevail again in America, for it alone comports with the national interests of the United States. And this is the subject of my remarks.

. . . These are good times in America. . . .

Is this our reward for free trade? My answer is no. Though these are good times in America, our growth today is anemic, compared to what it was in the Protectionist Era, and the Roaring Twenties, when growth rates hit seven percent. Free trade does not explain our prosperity; free trade explains the economic insecurity that is the worm in the apple of our prosperity.

The great free-market economist Milton Friedman is credited with the line, "there is no free lunch." Let me amend to Friedman's Law with Buchanan's Corollary: Free trade is no free lunch.

And it is time its costs were calculated.

Back in 1848, another economist wrote that if free trade were ever adopted, societies would be torn apart. His name was Karl Marx, and he wrote: ". . . the Free Trade system works destructively. It breaks up old nationalities and carries antagonism of proletariat and bourgeoisie to the uttermost point . . . the Free trade system hastens the Social Revolution. In this revolutionary sense alone . . . I am in favor of Free Trade."

Marx was right. Here, then, is the first cost of open-borders free trade. It exacerbates the divisions between capital and labor. It separates societies into contending classes, and deepens the division between rich and poor. Under free trade, economic and social elites, whose jobs and incomes are not adversely impacted by imports or immigration, do well. For them, these have been the best of times. Since 1990, the stock market has tripled in value; corporate profits have doubled since 1992; there has been a population explosion among millionaires. America's richest one percent controlled 21 percent of the national wealth in 1949; in 1997 it was 40 percent. Top CEO salaries were 44 times the average wage of their workers in 1965; by 1996 they were 212 times an average worker's pay.

How has Middle America fared? Between 1972 and 1994, the real wages of working Americans fell 19 percent. In 1970, the price of a new house was twice a young couple's income; it is now four times. In 1960, 18 percent of women with children under six were in the work force; by 1995 it had risen 63 percent. The U.S. has a larger percentage of women in its work force than any industrial nation, yet median family income fell 6 percent in the first six years of the 1990s.

Something is wrong when wage earners work harder and longer just to stay in the same place. Under the free trade regime, economic insecurity has become a preexisting condition of life.

A second cost of global free trade is a loss of independence and national sovereignty. America was once a self-reliant nation; trade amounted to only 10 percent of GNP [gross national product]; imports only 4 percent. Now, trade is equal to 25% of GNP; and the trade surpluses we ran every year from 1900–1970 have turned into trade deficits for all of the last 27 years.

Since 1980 our total merchandise trade deficit adds up to $2 trillion. This year's [1998's] trade deficit is approaching $300 billion. Year in and year out, we consume more than we produce. This cannot last.

Look at what this is doing to an industrial plant that once produced 40 percent of all that the world produced. In 1965, 31 percent of the U.S. labor force had manufacturing equivalent jobs. By 1997, it was down to 15 percent, smallest share in 100 years.

More Americans now work in government than in manufacturing. We Americans no longer make our own cameras, shoes, radios, TV's, toys. A fourth of our steel, a third of our autos, half our machine tools, two-thirds of our textiles are foreign made. We used to be the world's greatest creditor nation; now, we are its greatest debtor.

Friends, this is the read-out of the electrocardiogram of a nation in decline. Writes author-economist Pat Choate, "a peek behind the glitter of record stock prices and high corporate profits reveals a deepening economic dry rot—a nation that is eating its seed corn and squandering its economic leadership position, here and abroad."

And American sovereignty is being eroded. In 1994, for the first time, the U.S. joined a global institution, the World Trade Organization, where America has no veto power and the one-nation, one-vote rule applies. Where are we headed? Look at the nations of Europe that are today surrendering control of their money, their immigration policy, their environmental policy, even defense policy—to a giant socialist superstate called the EU [European Union].

For America to continue down this road of global interdependence is a betrayal of our history and our heritage of liberty. What does it profit a man if he gain the whole world, and suffer the loss of his own country?

A third cost of the Global Economy is America's vulnerability to a financial collapse caused by events beyond our control. Never has this country been so exposed. When Mexico, with an economy no larger than Illinois', threatened a default in 1994, the U.S. cobbled together a $50 billion bailout, lest Mexico's default bring on what Michel Camdessus of the IMF [International Monetary Fund] called "global financial catastrophe."

When tiny Asian dominoes began to fall [in 1997], the IMF had to put together $117 billion in bailouts of Thailand, Indonesia, South Korea, lest the Asian crisis bring down all of Latin America and the rest of the world with it.

In the Global Economy, the world is always just one default away from disaster. What in heaven's name does the vaunted Global Economy give us— besides all that made-in-China junk down at the mall—to justify having the U.S. financial system at permanent risk of collapse—if some incompetent foreign regime decides to walk on its debts?

A fourth cost of this Global Economy is the de-industrialization of America and the de-Americanization of our industries. Many of our Fortune 500 corporations have already shed their American identity.

When Gilbert Williamson, then president of NCR [National Cash Register Company, now known as NCR Corporation], was asked about U.S. workers being unable to compete in a global economy, he dismissed the question with this remark: "I was asked the other day about U.S. competitiveness, and I replied that I don't think about it at all. We at NCR think of ourselves as a globally competitive company that happens to be headquartered in the United States."

Many companies still carry fine old American names, but their work forces are becoming less and less American. In 1985, GE employed 243,000 Americans; ten years later, it was down to 150,000. IBM has lopped off half of its U.S. workers in the past decade. Here is author William Greider:

"By 1995, Big Blue had become a truly global firm—with more employees abroad than at home . . . Intel . . . shrank U.S. employment last year from 22,000 to 17,000. Motorola's . . . work force is now only 56 percent American. . . . Ma Bell once made all its home telephones in the U.S. and now makes none here."

Boeing's Philip Condit says he would be happy if, twenty years from now, no one thought of Boeing as an American company.

Here is Carl A. Gerstacker of Dow Chemical: "I have long dreamed of buying an island owned by no nation and of establishing the World Headquarters of the Dow Company on the truly neutral ground of such an island, beholden to no nation or society." A Union Carbide spokesman agreed: "It is not proper for an international corporation to put the welfare of any country in which it does business above that of any other."

To this new corporate elite, putting America first betrays a lack of loyalty to the company. Some among our political elite share this view. Here is Strobe Talbott, [Bill] Clinton's roommate at Oxford and architect of his Russian policy: "All countries," said Talbott in 1991, "are basically social arrangements . . . No matter how permanent and even sacred they may seem at any one time, in fact they are all artificial and temporary . . . within the next hundred years . . . nationhood as we know it will be obsolete; all states will recognize a single, global authority."

This is the transnational elite, our new Masters of the Universe.

The Cold War has been succeeded by a new struggle. "The real divisions of our time," writes scholar Christisan Kopff, "are not between left and right, but between nations and the globalist delusion." That struggle will shape the politics of the new century; and a familiar question is being asked again across America: When the commands of the Global Economy conflict with call of patriotism, whose side are you on?

If you would see the consequences of free trade ideology, go to Detroit. In the 1950s this was the forge and furnace of the Arsenal of Democracy, with 2 million of the most productive people on earth. Compare Detroit then to Detroit now. Free trade is not free.

Forty years ago, Japan exported 6000 cars. Today, Japan has as large a share of the U.S. auto and truck market as GM.

How did Japan do it? Yes, they built fine cars; but the Japanese did not leave the outcome of this struggle for dominance in the world's first industry to the vagaries of the market place. The Japanese fixed the game.

Japan virtually sealed off its market to U.S. auto imports, subsidized its auto industry and exports, and paid its workers 15% of U.S. wages in factories that would have had to be shut down in the United States. Tokyo's political and industrial elite did not let [economist] Adam Smith [1723–1790] dictate how they would play the game.

In short, Tokyo in the 1970s and 1980s looked on our auto market the way their grandfathers looked on China in the 1920s and 30s—as an inviting target for conquest. They did not read Richard Cobden on free trade; they read Alexander Hamilton, who would never have allowed Japan to overrun our auto industry, our radio industry, or our television industry.

Remember NAFTA. This treaty was going to open Mexico to U.S. auto exports. Well, in 1996, we shipped 46,000 cars to Mexico; and Mexico sent 550,000 cars back to us. Where did Mexico get its booming auto industry? From Michigan, Ohio, and Missouri.

In the 1950s, "Engine Charlie" Wilson immortalized himself with the remark, "What's good for America is good for General Motors, and vice versa." What Engine Charlie said was true, when he said it. We see that now as we watch GM closing factories here and opening up abroad. GM's four newest plants are going up in Argentina, Poland, China, and Thailand. "GM's days of building new plants in North America may be over," says the *Wall Street Journal.*

GM used to be the largest employer in the United States; today, it is the largest employer in Mexico where it has built 50 plants in 20 years. In Juarez alone, there are 18 plants of Delphi Automotive, a GM subsidiary. Across from Juarez, El Paso is becoming a glorified truck stop, as Texans watch their manufacturing jobs go south.

Volkswagen has closed its U.S. plant in the Mon Valley and moved production of its new Beetle into Mexico, where it will produce 450,000 vehicles this year. Wages at Volkswagen's plant in Puebla average $1.69 an hour, one-third of the U.S. minimum wage.

Let me make a simple point here. If you remove all trade barriers between a Third World economy like Mexico and a First World country like the United States, First World manufacturers will head south, to the advantage of the lower wages, and the Third World workers will head north, to the advantage of the higher wages. Economics 101.

Since the free-trade era began, 4000 new factories have been built in northern Mexico, and 35 million immigrants, most of them poor, have come into the United States—among them five million illegal aliens, mostly from Mexico. Free trade is not free.

But the free traders respond: Who cares who makes what, where? What's important is that consumers get the best buy at the cheapest price. But this is Grasshopper Economics. Americans are not only consumers; we are producers and citizens. We have obligations to one another and to our country; and one of those obligations is not to behave like wastrel children squandering a family estate built up over generations. A family estate is something you can sell off—only once.

What is the wealth of nations? Is it stocks, bonds, derivatives—the pieces of paper traded on Wall Street that can be gone with in the wind? No, the true wealth of a nation lies in its factories, farms, fisheries, and mines, in the genius and capacities of its people. Industrial power is at the heart of economic power, and economic power is at the heart of strategic power. America won two world wars and the Cold War because our industrial power and technology proved beyond the ability of our enemies to match.

Is this steady attrition of America's independence in sovereignty irreversible? My answer is no. For the balance of power in America has begun to shift. In 1997, on the vote to give the president a blank check to negotiate trade treaties without Congressional amendment—so-called Fast Track authority, it went down to defeat. When Newt [Gingrich] brought up "fast track" this year [1998], it was crushed again, by 63 votes.

A majority of Americans no longer believe these trade deals are good for America, and a majority of the House now agrees with them. The force is with us. Neither NAFTA [North American Free Trade Agreement] nor GATT [General Agreement on Tariffs and Trade] would pass today.

The day is not too distant when economic nationalism will triumph. Several events will hasten that day. The first is the tidal wave of imports from Asia about to hit these shores. When all those manufactured goods pour in, taking down industries and killing jobs, there will arise a clamor from industry and labor for protection. If that cry goes unheeded, those who turn a stone face to the American workers will be turned out of power.

In the Democratic Party or the Republican Party or the Reform Party or some new party, economic nationalism will find its vehicle and its voice. Rely upon it.

It is already happening—with the crisis in the steel industry.

Here is a perfect example of the folly of free trade. Since the mid-1980s, fifty billion dollars was invested in modernization; a steel worker today is three times as productive as his father; and the industry has only a third as many workers as twenty-five years ago.

Yet, Russia, Japan, South Korea, Brazil and Indonesia—four of them being bailed out with our tax dollars—are dumping steel into our market, taking down our steel industry to save their own. Why do we allow subsidized foreign steel to be dumped into the U.S. to destroy the greatest private steel industry on earth?

Well, says the free trader: If we can get it cheaper, let our industry go, just as we let our televisions go, our textiles go, radios go, and the shoe industry go. Besides, these countries need to sell steel here to get the dollars to pay back their IMF loans. Thus, the United Steelworkers of America are being sacrificed—to make the world safe for Goldman Sachs.

There is another reason the free trade era is coming to a close. One day soon, Americans will wake up and discover that other nations do not believe in free trade, and do not practice our particular faith. China and Japan each run $60 billion in annual trade surpluses at America's expense, but each cordons off its own market to U.S. goods.

We must start looking out for America first. As Andrew Jackson once declared: "We have been too long subject to the policy of [foreign] merchants. We need to become more Americanized, and instead of feeding the paupers and laborers of Europe . . . feed our own, or in a short time . . . we shall all be rendered paupers ourselves."

America First, and not only first, but second and third as well.

POSTSCRIPT

Are Protectionist Policies Bad for America?

The desirability of free trade is an issue on which a large majority of professional economists agree. Survey after survey confirms this. Although economists are ardent supporters of free trade, they must grapple with the reality that the world that Ricardo modeled in 1807 is starkly different from the world we know in this new millennium.

The concern that Ricardo could ignore is the modern ability of capital and technology to cross national boundaries almost at will. This mobility of capital and technology suggests that a country's comparative advantages can radically change in a relatively short period of time. This is a far cry from Ricardo's world. In his world, comparative advantages were stable and predictable. Consider the example that Ricardo used to illustrate comparative advantage: the trade between England and Portugal in cloth and wine. In the nineteenth century, it was highly unlikely that agrarian Portugal would seriously challenge the manufacturing base of England and equally unlikely that dreary English weather would ever produce a wine to compete with the vineyards of sun-drenched Portugal. This kind of trade stability is rarely found in the modern world. Examples abound of comparative advantages won or lost overnight, as dollars and technology chase one another around the globe. Japan provides an interesting case study. Consider how quickly this country moved from dominance among Pacific Rim countries to fighting for its economic life as Korea, Malaysia, and their other Asian neighbors stole market after market from them.

The bottom line is clear. Comparative advantage does lead to economic efficiency, but, as with any market adjustment, there can be serious dislocations as less efficient producers must make way for more efficient producers. In the modern world this occurs quickly and sometimes quite unexpectedly. This does not mean that there is a shortage of advocates of free trade. Conservative "think tanks" provide ample support for Rothbard's position. For example, see the Reason Foundation, which sponsors *Reason Online* (http://reason.com). On October 25, 1999, it posted an article entitled "Buchanomics Rebuked," which is a frontal attack on Buchanan. To place the free trade argument in its historic context, see John V. C. Nye's essay "The Myth of Free-Trade Britain," The Library of Economics and Liberty, http://www.econlib.org/library/Columns/y2003/Nyefreetrade.html (March 3, 2003).

For more on Buchanan's position, see his book *The Great Betrayal: How American Sovereignty and Social Justice Are Being Sacrificed to the Gods of the Global Economy* (Little, Brown, 1998). Also read John Gray's *False Dawn: The Delusions of Global Capitalism* (New Press, 1999).

ISSUE 14

Should We Sweat About Sweatshops?

YES: Richard Appelbaum and Peter Dreier, from "The Campus Anti-Sweatshop Movement," *The American Prospect* (September–October 1999)

NO: Nicholas D. Kristof and Sheryl WuDunn, from "Two Cheers for Sweatshops," *The New York Times Magazine* (September 24, 2000)

ISSUE SUMMARY

YES: Sociologist Richard Appelbaum and political scientist Peter Dreier chronicle the rise of student activism on American campuses over the issue of sweatshops abroad. Students demand that firms be held responsible for "sweatshop conditions" and warn that if conditions do not improve, American consumers will not "leave their consciences at home when they shop for clothes."

NO: News correspondents Nicholas D. Kristof and Sheryl WuDunn agree that the working conditions in many offshore plant sites "seem brutal from the vantage point of an American sitting in his living room." But they argue that these work opportunities are far superior to the alternatives that are currently available in many parts of the world and that what is needed are more sweatshops, not fewer sweatshops.

The sleeping giant of student activism awoke in the late 1990s. This giant slumbered for nearly three decades. It was last heard from in the late 1960s and the early 1970s, when students on college campuses across the United States caused so much disruption that public awareness of the war in Vietnam slowly but surely came into focus. Prior to the antiwar activism, students were at the forefront of the civil rights movement. As in the case of the antiwar activists, the civil rights activists rebelled. They confronted their parents and grandparents but with less violent, less confrontational means than the antiwar activists.

Many argue that in both of these cases public policy might have eventually changed, but if it did change it would have taken much longer for that change to occur. In essence, these social historians maintain that without the idealism of college-aged students, society has a tendency to become inflexible and rigid. It is slower to change and more likely to assume that what exists today should always exist. The lack of student activism and the resulting return to more traditional values was the pattern throughout the late 1970s, the 1980s, and most of the 1990s. That peaceful atmosphere was shattered in the late 1990s.

It all began rather quietly on a talk show cohosted by Kathie Lee Gifford. In 1996 Charles Kernaghan, who is executive director of the National Labor Committee for Worker and Human Rights, charged that the Walmart apparel that bears Gifford's name was produced in offshore sweatshops that employed child labor. On air she roundly denied that charge. Kernaghan persisted. The media eventually covered the charges and the countercharges, and the more the story was denied, the more the media investigated. Kernaghan's allegations turned out to be true. Because of Gifford's high profile and the extensive coverage that this story received, college students soon learned of the widespread use of sweatshops to produce a wide range of items that they habitually wore.

Students were outraged; they wanted action immediately. Just as many of their uncles, aunts, fathers, and mothers had done 30 years earlier, the students staged sit-ins. University presidents could not duck the issue by simply assigning the problem to a study committee. Student activism had returned to college campuses. If university administrators did not want the situation to erupt into the widespread disruption and possible violence that marked the antiwar period, they had to act.

But how could these colleges and universities respond? More important, *should* they respond? They do not purchase their T-shirts and football jerseys directly from factories in China or Brazil; rather, they license firms who request the use of that university's logo to be sewn onto football jerseys or printed on T-shirts. Should colleges and universities require their licensees to guarantee that neither they nor their subcontractors will produce any items bearing the university's logo under sweatshop conditions? Is this wise? College T-shirts and football jerseys are cheap because they are produced in low-wage countries. If the same items were produced in the United States or another high-wage country, their prices would be substantially higher. Should universities deny their students the chance to buy these items at a low cost? If the answer is yes, what happens to the workers in El Salvador and other poor countries who will lose their jobs if the sweatshops are closed down? Is that what student activists want?

These and other questions are raised in the following selections. Richard Appelbaum and Peter Dreier detail the horrors of working in the sweatshops that allow Americans to pay less for their apparel and the student activism that has brought this issue to the attention of the public. Nicholas D. Kristof and Sheryl WuDunn argue that workers in sweatshops do not want to see them closed because they offer the best jobs many workers in poor countries have ever had.

YES

**Richard Appelbaum and
Peter Dreier**

The Campus Anti-Sweatshop Movement

If University of Arizona activist Arne Ekstrom was aware of today's widely reported student apathy, he certainly was not deterred when he helped lead his campus anti-sweatshop sit-in. Nor, for that matter, were any of the other thousands of students across the United States who participated in anti-sweatshop activities during the past academic year, coordinating their activities on the United Students Against Sweatshops (USAS) listserv (a listserv is an online mailing list for the purpose of group discussion) and Web site.

Last year's student anti-sweatshop movement gained momentum as it swept westward, eventually encompassing more than 100 campuses across the country. Sparked by a sit-in at Duke University, students organized teach-ins, led demonstrations, and occupied buildings—first at Georgetown, then northeast to the Ivy League, then west to the Big Ten. After militant actions at Notre Dame, Wisconsin, and Michigan made the *New York Times, Business Week, Time,* National Public Radio, and almost every major daily newspaper, the growing student movement reached California, where schools from tiny Occidental College to the giant ten-campus University of California system agreed to limit the use of their names and logos to sweatshop-free apparel. Now the practical challenge is to devise a regime of monitoring and compliance.

⋙◉⋘

The anti-sweatshop movement is the largest wave of student activism to hit campuses since students rallied to free Nelson Mandela by calling for a halt to university investments in South Africa more than a decade ago. This time around, the movement is electronically connected. Student activists bring their laptops and cell phones with them when they occupy administration buildings, sharing ideas and strategies with fellow activists from Boston to Berkeley. On the USAS listserv, victorious students from Wisconsin counsel neophytes from Arizona and Kentucky, and professors at Berkeley and Harvard explain how to calculate a living wage and guarantee independent monitoring in Honduras.

The target of this renewed activism is the $2.5 billion collegiate licensing industry—led by major companies like Nike, Gear, Champion, and Fruit of the Loom—which pays colleges and universities sizable royalties in exchange for the right to use the campus logo on caps, sweatshirts, jackets, and other items. Students are demanding that the workers who make these goods be paid a living wage, no matter where in the world industry operates. Students are also calling for an end to discrimination against women workers, public disclosure of the names and addresses of all factories involved in production, and independent monitoring in order to verify compliance.

These demands are opposed by the apparel industry, the White House, and most universities. Yet so far students have made significant progress in putting the industry on the defensive. A growing number of colleges and clothing companies have adopted "codes of conduct"—something unthinkable a decade ago—although student activists consider many of these standards inadequate.

In a world economy increasingly dominated by giant retailers and manufacturers who control global networks of independently owned factories, organizing consumers may prove to be a precondition for organizing production workers. And students are a potent group of consumers. If students next year succeed in building on this year's momentum, the collegiate licensing industry will be forced to change the way it does business. These changes, in turn, could affect the organization of the world's most globalized and exploitative industry—apparel manufacturing—along with the growing number of industries that, like apparel, outsource production in order to lower labor costs and blunt worker organizing.

The Global Sweatshop

In the apparel industry, so-called manufacturers—in reality, design and marketing firms—outsource the fabrication of clothing to independent contractors around the world. In this labor-intensive industry where capital requirements are minimal, it is relatively easy to open a clothing factory. This has contributed to a global race to the bottom, in which there is always someplace, somewhere, where clothing can be made still more cheaply. Low wages reflect not low productivity, but low bargaining power. A recent analysis in *Business Week* found that although Mexican apparel workers are 70 percent as productive as U.S. workers, they earn only 11 percent as much as their U.S. counterparts; Indonesian workers, who are 50 percent as productive, earn less than 2 percent as much.

The explosion of imports has proven devastating to once well-paid, unionized U.S. garment workers. The number of American garment workers has declined from peak levels of 1.4 million in the early 1970s to 800,000 today. The one exception to these trends is the expansion of garment employment, largely among immigrant and undocumented workers, in Los Angeles, which has more than 160,000 sweatshop workers. Recent U.S. Department of Labor surveys found that more than nine out of ten such firms violate legal health and safety standards, with more than half troubled by serious violations that could lead to severe injuries or death. Working conditions in New York City, the other major domestic garment center, are similar.

The very word "sweatshop" comes from the apparel industry, where profits were "sweated" out of workers by forcing them to work longer and faster at their sewing machines. Although significant advances have been made in such aspects of production as computer-assisted design, computerized marking, and computerized cutting, the industry still remains low-tech in its core production process, the sewing of garments. The basic unit of production continues to be a worker, usually a woman, sitting or standing at a sewing machine and sewing together pieces of limp cloth.

The structure of the garment industry fosters sweatshop production. During the past decade, retailing in the United States has become increasingly concentrated. Today, the four largest U.S. retailers—Wal-Mart, Kmart, Sears, and Dayton Hudson (owner of Target and Mervyns)—account for nearly two-thirds of U.S. retail sales. Retailers squeeze manufacturers, who in turn squeeze the contractors who actually make their products. Retailers and manufacturers preserve the fiction of being completely separate from contractors because they do not want to be held legally responsible for workplace violations of labor, health, and safety laws. Retailers and manufacturers alike insist that what happens in contractor factories is not their responsibility—even though their production managers and quality control officers are constantly checking up on the sewing shops that make their clothing.

The contracting system also allows retailers and manufacturers to eliminate much uncertainty and risk. When business is slow, the contract is simply not renewed; manufacturers need not worry about paying unemployment benefits or dealing with idle workers who might go on strike or otherwise make trouble. If a particular contractor becomes a problem, there are countless others to be found who will be only too happy to get their business. Workers, however, experience the flip side of the enormous flexibility enjoyed by retailers and manufacturers. They become contingent labor, employed and paid only when their work is needed.

Since profits are taken out at each level of the supply chain, labor costs are reduced to a tiny fraction of the retail price. Consider the economics of a dress that is sewn in Los Angeles and retails for $100. Half goes to the department store and half to the manufacturer, who keeps $12.50 to cover expenses and profit, spends $22.50 on textiles, and pays $15 to the contractor. The contractor keeps $9 to cover expenses and profits. That leaves just $6 of the $100 retail price for the workers who actually make the dress. Even if the cost of direct production labor were to increase by half, the dress would still only cost $103—a small increment that would make a world of difference to the seamstress in Los Angeles, whose $7,000 to $8,000 in annual wages are roughly two-thirds of the poverty level. A garment worker in Mexico would be lucky to earn $1,000 during a year of 48 to 60 hour workweeks; in China, $500.

At the other end of the apparel production chain, the heads of the 60 publicly traded U.S. apparel retailers earn an average $1.5 million a year. The heads of the 35 publicly traded apparel manufacturers average $2 million. In 1997, according to the *Los Angeles Business Journal,* five of the six highest-paid apparel executives in Los Angeles all came from a single firm: Guess?, Inc. They took home nearly $12.6 million—enough to double the yearly wages of 1,700 L.A. apparel workers.

Organizing workers at the point of production, the century-old strategy that built the power of labor in Europe and North America, is best suited to production processes where most of the work goes on in-house. In industries whose production can easily be shifted almost anywhere on the planet, organizing is extremely difficult. Someday, perhaps, a truly international labor movement will confront global manufacturers. But in the meantime, organized consumers may well be labor's best ally. Consumers, after all, are not as readily moved as factories. And among American consumers, college students represent an especially potent force.

Kathie Lee and Robert Reich

During the early 1990s, American human rights and labor groups protested the proliferation of sweatshops at home and abroad—with major campaigns focusing on Nike and Gap. These efforts largely fizzled. But then two exposés of sweatshop conditions captured public attention. In August 1995, state and federal officials raided a garment factory in El Monte, California—a Los Angeles suburb—where 71 Thai immigrants had been held for several years in virtual slavery in an apartment complex ringed with barbed wire and spiked fences. They worked an average of 84 hours a week for $1.60 an hour, living eight to ten persons in a room. The garments they sewed ended up in major retail chains, including Macy's, Filene's and Robinsons-May, and for brand-name labels like B.U.M., Tomato, and High Sierra. Major daily papers and TV networks picked up on the story, leading to a flood of outraged editorials and columns calling for a clamp-down on domestic sweatshops. Then in April 1996, TV celebrity Kathie Lee Gifford tearfully acknowledged on national television that the Wal-Mart line of clothing that bore her name was made by children in Honduran sweatshops, even though tags on the garments promised that part of the profits would go to help children. Embarrassed by the publicity, Gifford soon became a crusader against sweatshop abuses.

For several years, then—Labor Secretary Robert Reich (now the *Prospect*'s senior editor) had been trying to inject the sweatshop issue onto the nation's agenda. The mounting publicity surrounding the El Monte and Kathie Lee scandals gave Reich new leverage. After all, what the apparel industry primarily sells is image, and the image of some of its major labels was getting a drubbing. He began pressing apparel executives, threatening to issue a report card on firms' behavior unless they agreed to help establish industry-wide standards.

In August 1996, the Clinton administration brought together representatives from the garment industry, labor unions, and consumer and human rights groups to grapple with sweatshops. The members of what they called the White House Apparel Industry Partnership (AIP) included apparel firms (Liz Claiborne, Reebok, L.L. Bean, Nike, Patagonia, Phillips-Van Heusen, Wal-Mart's Kathie Lee Gifford brand, and Nicole Miller), several nonprofit organizations (including the National Consumers League, Interfaith Center on Corporate Responsibility, International Labor Rights Fund, Lawyers Committee for Human Rights, Robert F. Kennedy Memorial Center for Human Rights, and Business for Social Responsibility), as well as the Union of Needletrades, Industrial and Textile Employees (UNITE), the Retail, Wholesale, and Department Store Union, and the AFL-CIO.

After intense negotiations, the Department of Labor issued an interim AIP report in April 1997 and the White House released the final 40-page report in November 1998, which included a proposed workplace code of conduct and a set of monitoring guidelines. By then, Reich had left the Clinton administration, replaced by Alexis Herman. The two labor representatives on the AIP, as well as the Interfaith Center on Corporate Responsibility, quit the group to protest the feeble recommendations, which had been crafted primarily by the garment industry delegates and which called, essentially, for the industry to police itself. This maneuvering would not have generated much attention except that a new factor—college activism—had been added to the equation.

A "Sweat-Free" Campus

The campus movement began in the fall of 1997 at Duke when a group called Students Against Sweatshops persuaded the university to require manufacturers of items with the Duke label to sign a pledge that they would not use sweatshop labor. Duke has 700 licensees (including Nike and other major labels) that make apparel at hundreds of plants in the U.S. and in more than 10 other countries, generating almost $25 million annually in sales. Following months of negotiations, in March 1998 Duke President Nannerl Keohane and the student activists jointly announced a detailed "code of conduct" that bars Duke licensees from using child labor, requires them to maintain safe workplaces, to pay the minimum wage, to recognize the right of workers to unionize, to disclose the locations of all factories making products with Duke's name, and to allow visits by independent monitors to inspect the factories.

The Duke victory quickly inspired students on other campuses. The level of activity on campuses accelerated, with students finding creative ways to dramatize the issue. At Yale, student activists staged a "knit-in" to draw attention to sweatshop abuses. At Holy Cross and the University of California at Santa Barbara, students sponsored mock fashion shows where they discussed the working conditions under which the garments were manufactured. Duke students published a coloring book explaining how (and where) the campus mascot, the Blue Devil, is stitched onto clothing by workers in sweatshops. Activists at the University of Wisconsin infiltrated a homecoming parade and, dressed like sweatshop workers in Indonesia, carried a giant Reebok shoe. They also held a press conference in front of the chancellor's office and presented him with an oversized check for 16 cents—the hourly wage paid to workers in China making Nike athletic shoes. At Georgetown, Wisconsin, Michigan, Arizona, and Duke, students occupied administration buildings to pressure their institutions to adopt (or, in Duke's case, strengthen) anti-sweatshop codes.

⋅◆⋅

In the summer of 1998, disparate campus groups formed United Students Against Sweatshops (USAS). The USAS has weekly conference calls to discuss their negotiations with Nike, the Department of Labor, and others. It has sponsored training sessions for student leaders and conferences at several campuses where the sweatshop issue is only part of an agenda that also includes helping to build the labor movement, NAFTA, the World Trade Organization, women's rights, and other issues.

Last year, anti-sweatshop activists employed the USAS listserv to exchange ideas on negotiating tactics, discuss media strategies, swap songs to sing during rallies, and debate the technicalities of defining a "living wage" to incorporate in their campus codes of conduct. In May, the USAS listserv heated up after the popular Fox television series *Party of Five* included a scene in which one of the show's characters, Sarah (played by Jennifer Love Hewitt), helps organize a Students Against Sweatshops sit-in on her campus. A few real-life activists worried that the mainstream media was trivializing the movement by skirting the key issues ("the importance of unionized labor, the globalization of the economy, etc.") as well as focusing most of that episode on the characters' love life. University of Michigan student Rachel Paster responded:

> Let's not forget that we ARE a student movement, and students do complain about boyfriends and fashion problems. One of the biggest reasons why USAS and local student groups opposing sweatshops have been as successful as we have been is that opposition to sweatshops ISN'T that radical. Although I'm sure lots of us are all for overthrowing the corporate power structure, the human rights issues involved are what make a lot of people get involved and put their energies into rallies, sit-ins, et cetera. If we were a 'radical' group, university administrations would have brushed us off. . . . The fact that they don't is testament to the fact that we have support, not just from students on the far left, but from students in the middle ground who don't consider themselves radicals. Without those people we would NEVER have gotten as far as we have.

Indeed, the anti-sweatshop movement has been able to mobilize wide support because it strikes several nerves among today's college students, including women's rights (most sweatshop workers are women and some factories have required women to use birth control pills as a condition of employment), immigrant rights, environmental concerns, and human rights. After University of Wisconsin administrators brushed aside anti-sweatshop protestors, claiming they didn't represent student opinion, the activists ran a slate of candidates for student government. Eric Brakken, a sociology major and anti-sweatshop leader, was elected student body president and last year used the organization's substantial resources to promote the activists' agenda. And Duke's student government unanimously passed a resolution supporting the anti-sweatshop group, calling for full public disclosure of the locations of companies that manufacture Duke clothing.

The Labor Connection

At the core of the movement is a strong bond with organized labor. The movement is an important by-product of the labor movement's recent efforts, under President John Sweeney, to repair the rift between students and unions that dates to the Vietnam War. Since 1996, the AFL-CIO's Union Summer has placed almost 2,000 college students in internships with local unions around the country, most of whom work on grassroots organizing campaigns with low-wage workers in hotels, agriculture, food processing, janitorial service, and other industries. The program has its own staff, mostly young organizers only a few years out of college themselves, who actively recruit on campuses, looking for the next generation of union organizers and researchers, particularly minorities, immigrants, and women. Union Summer graduates are among the key leadership of the campus anti-sweatshop movement.

UNITE has one full-time staff person assigned to work on sweatshop issues, which includes helping student groups. A number of small human rights watchdog organizations that operate on shoestring budgets—Global Exchange, Sweatshop Watch, and the National Labor Committee [NLC]—give student activists technical advice. (It was NLC's Charles Kernaghan, an energetic researcher and publicist, who exposed the Kathie Lee Gifford connection to sweatshops in testimony before Congress.) These groups have helped bring sweatshop workers on speaking tours of American campuses, and have organized delegations of student activists to investigate firsthand the conditions in Honduras, Guatemala, El Salvador, Mexico, and elsewhere under which workers produce their college's clothing.

Unions and several liberal foundations have provided modest funding for student anti-sweatshop groups. Until this summer USAS had no staff, nor did any of its local campus affiliates. In contrast, corporate-sponsored conservative foundations have, over the past two decades, funded dozens of conservative student publications, subsidized student organizations and conferences, and recruited conservative students for internships and jobs in right-wing think tanks and publications as well as positions in the Reagan and Bush administrations and Congress, seeking to groom the next generation of conservative activists. The Intercollegiate Studies Institute, the leading right-wing campus umbrella group, has an annual budget over $5 million. In comparison, the Center for Campus Organizing, a Boston-based group that works closely with anti-sweatshop groups and other progressive campus organizations, operates on a budget under $200,000.

This student movement even has some sympathizers among university administrators. "Thank God students are getting passionate about something other than basketball and bonfires," John Burness, a Duke administrator who helped negotiate the end of the 31-hour sit-in, told the *Boston Globe*. "But the tone is definitely different. In the old days, we used to have to scramble to cut off phone lines when they took over the president's office, but we didn't have to worry about that here. They just bring their laptops and they do work."

At every university where students organized a sit-in (Duke, Georgetown, Arizona, Michigan, and Wisconsin) they have wrested agreements to require licensees to disclose the specific location of their factory sites, which is necessary for independent monitoring. Students elsewhere (including Harvard, Illinois, Brown, the University of California, Princeton, Middlebury, and Occidental) won a public disclosure requirement without resorting to civil disobedience. A few institutions have agreed to require manufacturers to pay their employees a "living wage." Wisconsin agreed to organize an academic conference this fall to discuss how to calculate living-wage formulas for countries with widely disparate costs of living, and then to implement its own policy recommendations. [See Richard Rothstein, "The Global Hiring Hall: Why We Need Worldwide Labor Standards," *TAP,* Spring 1994.]

The Industry's New Clothes

Last November, the White House-initiated Apparel Industry Partnership created a monitoring arm, the Fair Labor Association (FLA), and a few months later invited universities to join. Colleges, however, have just one seat on FLA's 14-member board. Under the group's bylaws the garment firms control the board's decisionmaking. The bylaws require a "supermajority" to approve all key questions, thus any three companies can veto a proposal they don't like.

At this writing, FLA member companies agree to ban child and prison labor, to prohibit physical abuse by supervisors, and to allow workers the freedom to organize unions in their foreign factories, though independent enforcement has not yet been specified. FLA wants to assign this monitoring task to corporate accounting firms like PricewaterhouseCoopers and Ernst & Young, to allow companies to select which facilities will be inspected, and to keep factory locations and the monitoring reports secret. Student activists want human rights and labor groups to do the monitoring.

This is only a bare beginning, but it establishes the crucial moral precedent of companies taking responsibility for labor conditions beyond their shores. Seeing this foot in the door, several companies have bowed out because they consider these standards too tough. The FLA expects that by 2001, after its monitoring program has been in place for a year, participating firms will be able to use the FLA logo on their labels and advertising as evidence of their ethical corporate practices. [See Richard Rothstein, "The Starbucks Solution: Can Voluntary Codes Raise Global Living Standards?" *TAP,* July-August 1996.]

The original list of 17 FLA-affiliated universities grew to more than 100 by mid-summer of this year. And yet, some campus groups have dissuaded college administrations (including the Universities of Michigan, Minnesota, Oregon, Toronto, and California, as well as Oberlin, Bucknell, and Earlham Colleges) from joining FLA, while others have persuaded their institutions (including Brown, Wisconsin, North Carolina, and Georgetown) to join only if the FLA adopts stronger standards. While FLA members are supposed to abide by each country's minimum-wage standards, these are typically far below the poverty level. In fact, no company has made a commitment to pay a living wage.

The campus movement has succeeded in raising awareness (both on campus and among the general public) about sweatshops as well as the global economy. It has contributed to industry acceptance of extraterritorial labor standards, something hitherto considered utopian. It has also given thousands of students experience in the nuts and bolts of social activism, many of whom are likely to carry their idealism and organizing experiences with them into jobs with unions, community and environmental groups, and other public interest crusades.

So far, however, the movement has had only minimal impact on the daily lives of sweatshop workers at home and abroad. Nike and Reebok, largely because of student protests, have raised wages and benefits in their Indonesian footwear factories—which employ more than 100,000 workers—to 43 percent above the minimum wage. But this translates to only 20 cents an hour in U.S. dollars, far below a "living wage" to raise a family and even below the 27 cents Nike paid before Indonesia's currency devaluation. Last spring Nike announced its willingness to disclose the location of its overseas plants that produce clothing for universities. This created an important split in industry ranks, since industry leaders have argued that disclosure would undermine each firm's competitive position. But Nike has opened itself up to the charge of having a double standard, since it still refuses to disclose the location of its non-university production sites.

Within a year, when FLA's monitoring system is fully operational, students at several large schools with major licensing contracts—including Duke, Wisconsin, Michigan, North Carolina, and Georgetown—will have lists of factories in the U.S. and overseas that produce university clothing and equipment. This information will be very useful to civic and labor organizations at home and abroad, providing more opportunities to expose working conditions. Student activists at each university will be able to visit these sites—bringing media and public officials with them—to expose working conditions (and, if necessary, challenge the findings of the FLA's own monitors) and support organizing efforts by local unions and women's groups.

If the student activists can help force a small but visible "ethical" niche of the apparel industry to adopt higher standards, it will divide the industry and give unions and consumer groups more leverage to challenge the sweatshop practices of the rest of the industry. The campus anti-sweatshop crusade is part of what might be called a "conscience constituency" among consumers who are willing to incorporate ethical principles into their buying habits, even if it means slightly higher prices. Environmentalists have done the same thing with the "buy green" campaign, as have various "socially responsible" investment firms.

Beyond Consumer Awareness

In a global production system characterized by powerful retailers and invisible contractors, consumer action has an important role to play. But ultimately it must be combined with worker organizing and legislative and regulatory remedies. Unionizing the global apparel industry is an organizer's nightmare. With globalization and the contracting system, any apparel factory with a union risks losing its business.

Domestically, UNITE represents fewer than 300,000 textile and garment industry workers, down from the 800,000 represented by its two predecessor unions in the late 1960s. In the low-income countries where most U.S. apparel is now made, the prospects for unionization are dimmer still. In Mexico, labor unions are controlled by the government. China outlaws independent unions, punishing organizers with prison terms. Building the capacity for unfettered union organizing must necessarily be a long-term strategy for union organizers throughout the world. Here, the student anti-sweatshop movement can help. The independent verification of anti-sweatshop standards that students want can also serve the goal of union organizing.

Public policy could also help. As part of our trade policy, Congress could require public disclosure of manufacturing sites and independent monitoring of firms that sell goods in the American market. It could enact legislation that requires U.S. companies to follow U.S. health and safety standards globally and to bar the import of clothing made in sweatshops or made by workers who are denied the basic right to organize unions. In addition, legislation sponsored by Representative William Clay could make retailers and manufacturers legally liable for the working conditions behind the goods they design and sell, thereby ending the fiction that contractors are completely independent of the manufacturers and retailers that hire them. Last spring the California Assembly passed a state version of this legislation. Student and union activists hope that the Democrat-controlled state senate and Democratic Governor Gray Davis—whose lopsided victory last November was largely attributed to organized labor's get-out-the-vote effort—will support the bill.

Thanks to the student movement, public opinion may be changing. And last spring, speaking both to the International Labor Organization in Geneva and at the commencement ceremonies at the University of Chicago (an institution founded by John D. Rockefeller and a stronghold of free market economics, but also a center of student anti-sweatshop activism), President Clinton called for an international campaign against child labor, including restrictions on government purchases of goods made by children.

A shift of much apparel production to developing countries may well be inevitable in a global economy. But when companies do move their production abroad, student activists are warning "you can run but you can't hide," demanding that they be held responsible for conditions in contractor factories no matter where they are. Students can't accomplish this on their own, but in a very short period of time they have made many Americans aware that they don't have to leave their consciences at home when they shop for clothes.

**Nicholas D. Kristof and
Sheryl WuDunn**

 **NO**

Two Cheers for Sweatshops

It was breakfast time, and the food stand in the village in northeastern Thailand was crowded. Maesubin Sisoipha, the middle-aged woman cooking the food, was friendly, her portions large and the price right. For the equivalent of about 5 cents, she offered a huge green mango leaf filled with rice, fish paste and fried beetles. It was a hearty breakfast, if one didn't mind the odd antenna left sticking in one's teeth.

One of the half-dozen men and women sitting on a bench eating was a sinewy, bare-chested laborer in his late 30's named Mongkol Latlakorn. It was a hot, lazy day, and so we started chatting idly about the food and, eventually, our families. Mongkol mentioned that his daughter, Darin, was 15, and his voice softened as he spoke of her. She was beautiful and smart, and her father's hopes rested on her.

"Is she in school?" we asked.

"Oh, no," Mongkol said, his eyes sparkling with amusement. "She's working in a factory in Bangkok. She's making clothing for export to America." He explained that she was paid $2 a day for a nine-hour shift, six days a week.

"It's dangerous work," Mongkol added. "Twice the needles went right through her hands. But the managers bandaged up her hands, and both times she got better again and went back to work."

"How terrible," we murmured sympathetically.

Mongkol looked up, puzzled. "It's good pay," he said. "I hope she can keep that job. There's all this talk about factories closing now, and she said there are rumors that her factory might close. I hope that doesn't happen. I don't know what she would do then."

He was not, of course, indifferent to his daughter's suffering; he simply had a different perspective from ours—not only when it came to food but also when it came to what constituted desirable work.

Nothing captures the difference in mind-set between East and West more than attitudes toward sweatshops. Nike and other American companies have been hammered in the Western press over the last decade for producing shoes, toys and other products in grim little factories with dismal conditions. Protests against sweatshops and the dark forces of globalization that they seem to represent have become common at meetings of the World Bank and the World Trade Organization and, this month, at a World Economic Forum in

Australia, livening up the scene for Olympic athletes arriving for the competition. Yet sweatshops that seem brutal from the vantage point of an American sitting in his living room can appear tantalizing to a Thai laborer getting by on beetles.

Fourteen years ago, we moved to Asia and began reporting there. Like most Westerners, we arrived in the region outraged at sweatshops. In time, though, we came to accept the view supported by most Asians: that the campaign against sweatshops risks harming the very people it is intended to help. For beneath their grime, sweatshops are a clear sign of the industrial revolution that is beginning to reshape Asia.

This is not to praise sweatshops. Some managers are brutal in the way they house workers in firetraps, expose children to dangerous chemicals, deny bathroom breaks, demand sexual favors, force people to work double shifts or dismiss anyone who tries to organize a union. Agitation for improved safety conditions can be helpful, just as it was in 19th-century Europe. But Asian workers would be aghast at the idea of American consumers boycotting certain toys or clothing in protest. The simplest way to help the poorest Asians would be to buy more from sweatshops, not less.

On our first extended trip to China, in 1987, we traveled to the Pearl River delta in the south of the country. There we visited several factories, including one in the boomtown of Dongguan, where about 100 female workers sat at workbenches stitching together bits of leather to make purses for a Hong Kong company. We chatted with several women as their fingers flew over their work and asked about their hours.

"I start at about 6:30, after breakfast, and go until about 7 p.m.," explained one shy teenage girl. "We break for lunch, and I take half an hour off then."

"You do this six days a week?"

"Oh, no. Every day."

"Seven days a week?"

"Yes." She laughed at our surprise. "But then I take a week or two off at Chinese New Year to go back to my village."

The others we talked to all seemed to regard it as a plus that the factory allowed them to work long hours. Indeed, some had sought out this factory precisely because it offered them the chance to earn more.

"It's actually pretty annoying how hard they want to work," said the factory manager, a Hong Kong man. "It means we have to worry about security and have a supervisor around almost constantly."

It sounded pretty dreadful, and it was. We and other journalists wrote about the problems of child labor and oppressive conditions in both China and South Korea. But, looking back, our worries were excessive. Those sweatshops tended to generate the wealth to solve the problems they created. If Americans had reacted to the horror stories in the 1980's by curbing imports of those sweatshop products, then neither southern China nor South Korea would have registered as much progress as they have today.

The truth is, those grim factories in Dongguan and the rest of southern China contributed to a remarkable explosion of wealth. In the years since our first conversations there, we've returned many times to Dongguan and the surrounding towns and seen the transformation. Wages have risen from about $50 a month to $250 a month or more today. Factory conditions have improved as businesses have scrambled to attract and keep the best laborers. A private housing market has emerged, and video arcades and computer schools have opened to cater to workers with rising incomes. A hint of a middle class has appeared—as has China's closest thing to a Western-style independent newspaper, Southern Weekend.

Partly because of these tens of thousands of sweatshops, China's economy has become one of the hottest in the world. Indeed, if China's 30 provinces were counted as individual countries, then the 20 fastest-growing countries in the world between 1978 and 1995 would all have been Chinese. When Britain launched the Industrial Revolution in the late 18th century, it took 58 years for per capita output to double. In China, per capita output has been doubling every 10 years.

In fact, the most vibrant parts of Asia are nearly all in what might be called the Sweatshop Belt, from China and South Korea to Malaysia, Indonesia and even Bangladesh and India. Today these sweatshop countries control about one-quarter of the global economy. As the industrial revolution spreads through China and India, there are good reasons to think that Asia will continue to pick up speed. Some World Bank forecasts show Asia's share of global gross domestic product rising to 55 to 60 percent by about 2025—roughly the West's share at its peak half a century ago. The sweatshops have helped lay the groundwork for a historic economic realignment that is putting Asia back on its feet. Countries are rebounding from the economic crisis of 1997–98 and the sweatshops—seen by Westerners as evidence of moribund economies—actually reflect an industrial revolution that is raising living standards in the East.

✦

Of course, it may sound silly to say that sweatshops offer a route to prosperity, when wages in the poorest countries are sometimes less than $1 a day. Still, for an impoverished Indonesian or Bangladeshi woman with a handful of kids who would otherwise drop out of school and risk dying of mundane diseases like diarrhea, $1 or $2 a day can be a life-transforming wage.

This was made abundantly clear in Cambodia, when we met a 40-year-old woman named Nhem Yen, who told us why she moved to an area with particularly lethal malaria. "We needed to eat," she said. "And here there is wood, so we thought we could cut it and sell it."

But then Nhem Yen's daughter and son-in-law both died of malaria, leaving her with two grandchildren and five children of her own. With just one mosquito net, she had to choose which children would sleep protected and which would sleep exposed.

In Cambodia, a large mosquito net costs $5. If there had been a sweatshop in the area, however harsh or dangerous, Nhem Yen would have leapt at the chance to work in it, to earn enough to buy a net big enough to cover all her children.

For all the misery they can engender, sweatshops at least offer a precarious escape from the poverty that is the developing world's greatest problem. Over the past 50 years, countries like India resisted foreign exploitation, while countries that started at a similar economic level—like Taiwan and South Korea—accepted sweatshops as the price of development. Today there can be no doubt about which approach worked better. Taiwan and South Korea are modern countries with low rates of infant mortality and high levels of education; in contrast, every year 3.1 million Indian children die before the age of 5, mostly from diseases of poverty like diarrhea.

The effect of American pressure on sweatshops is complicated. While it clearly improves conditions at factories that produce branded merchandise for companies like Nike, it also raises labor costs across the board. That encourages less well established companies to mechanize and to reduce the number of employees needed. The upshot is to help people who currently have jobs in Nike plants but to risk jobs for others. The only thing a country like Cambodia has to offer is terribly cheap wages; if companies are scolded for paying those wages, they will shift their manufacturing to marginally richer areas like Malaysia or Mexico.

Sweatshop monitors do have a useful role. They can compel factories to improve safety. They can also call attention to the impact of sweatshops on the environment. The greatest downside of industrialization is not exploitation of workers but toxic air and water. In Asia each year, three million people die from the effects of pollution. The factories springing up throughout the region are far more likely to kill people through the chemicals they expel than through terrible working conditions.

By focusing on these issues, by working closely with organizations and news media in foreign countries, sweatshops can be improved. But refusing to buy sweatshop products risks making Americans feel good while harming those we are trying to help. As a Chinese proverb goes, "First comes the bitterness, then there is sweetness and wealth and honor for 10,000 years."

POSTSCRIPT

Should We Sweat About Sweatshops?

Economists have not remained mute as this debate has raged across college campuses. In a letter circulated across American campuses in September 2000, 90 academics, mostly economists, urged college and university presidents not to yield to student pressure demanding the adoption of strict codes of conduct for the manufacturers of university apparel that is produced in poor countries. There were many distinguished signers, including Nobel Laureate Robert Lucas, several former presidents of the American Economic Association, several former presidents of the Econometric Society, and Paul McCracken, former chairman of the President's Council of Economic Advisers. These market-oriented economists warned against codes of conduct that required offshore plants to pay wages that are above the prevailing wage rates. They asserted that these higher wages might result "in shifts in employment that will worsen the collective welfare of the very workers in poor countries who are supposed to be helped." This group is supported by the Academic Consortium on International Trade (ACIT), an organization of economists and lawyers dedicated to the establishment of free trade on a worldwide basis. Their Web site is at http://www.spp.umich.edu/rsie/acit/.

In "White Hats or Don Quixotes? Human Rights Vigilantes in the Global Economy," NBER Working Paper No. W8102 (January 2001), published by the National Bureau of Economic Research, Kimberly Ann Elliott and Richard Freeman examine the pros and cons of codes of conduct for multinationals working in poor countries. They analyze the incentives for corporations to respond to the demand for more equitable treatment of the workforce in these offshore facilities. They conclude that the pressure applied by student activist groups and others who are concerned about sweatshop conditions may be one of those cases "when 'doing good' actually does good." Elliott and Freeman also suggest that a counterpetition to the Academic Consortium on International Trade is being prepared by Robert Pollin of the University of Massachusetts at Amherst and James K. Galbraith of the University of Texas at Austin. As of April 2001 that petition had not appeared.

There is a wealth of antisweatshop literature to examine, much of which is produced by organized labor. The National Labor Committee, for example, provides a wellspring of data on this topic. They can be found on the Internet at http://www.nlcnet.org. In addition, there is an article on sweatshop abuses in nearly every issue of *Working USA,* a journal sponsored by organized labor. In addition to various organized labor groups, you might also check out the Global Alliance for Workers and Communities. This is an initiative of the International Youth Foundation in partnership with the John

D. and Catherine T. MacArthur Foundation. Their Web site is http://www.the-globalalliance.org. Other pro-worker rights organizations are the Campaign for Labor Rights, the Clean Clothes Campaign, the Collegiate Living Wage Association, the Ethical Trading Initiative, the Global Exchange, the International Labour Organisation, the International Labor Rights Fund, the Investor Responsibility Research Center, Sweatshop Watch, and the UNITE! Stop Sweatshops Campaign.

On the other side you will have no difficulty finding material to support globalization. Start with the National Retail Federation (NRF), which is the largest retail trade organization in the world. It represents 1.4 million U.S. retail establishments, which employ nearly 1 in every 5 American workers—about 20 million workers in all. See the NRF's Web site at http://www.nrf.com. The ACIT also provides an up-to-date list of articles that support globalization, which often entails acceptance of sweatshop use. Some of these articles are Daniel W. Drezner, "Bottom Feeders," *Foreign Policy* (November/December 2000); Michael Barkey, "Globalization, Social Justice and the Plight of the Poor," Acton Commentary, http://www.acton.org/ppolicy/comment/article.php?id=22 (August 2000); Philip Knight, "A Forum for Improving Globalisation," *Financial Times* (August 1, 2000); Thomas Friedman, "Knight Is Right," *The New York Times* (June 20, 2000); "Assessing Globalization," World Bank Briefing Papers (April 2000); "Globalization: Threat or Opportunity?" IMF Issues Brief (April 12, 2000); and "Trade and Poverty: Is There a Connection?" WTO Special Study No. 5 (March 2000).

ISSUE 15

Are the Costs of Global Warming Too High to Ignore?

YES: Lester R. Brown, from *Eco-Economy: Building an Economy for the Earth* (W. W. Norton, 2001)

NO: Lenny Bernstein, from "Climate Change and Ecosystems," A Report of the George C. Marshall Institute (August 2002)

ISSUE SUMMARY

YES: Lester R. Brown, founder and president of the Earth Policy Institute, describes his vision of an environmentally sustainable economy, which includes food supplies, population growth issues, water availability, climatic changes, and renewable energy.

NO: Lenny Bernstein, head of L. S. Bernstein & Associates, which advises companies and trade associations on political and scientific developments on global environmental issues, acknowledges that ecosystems are sensitive to climate change, but he argues that the change that we have seen repeated again and again over the course of history can lead to benefits for our children and our children's children.

The severe weather that has plagued much of the United States from the late 1980s to the present has offered some memorable events for Americans. National forests have burst into wildfires; electric bills have skyrocketed as air conditioners in homes and businesses have been run at full strength day and night; and local officials have banned car washing and lawn sprinkling to conserve precious water as lakes, streams, and reservoirs have fallen to critically low levels. Citizens and public policymakers alike have increasingly come to believe that the world has entered the long-predicted and much-feared period of global warming, which many associate with the "greenhouse effect."

In the past decade or so, stretching back to the 1992 United Nations Earth Summit in Rio de Janeiro, there have been a series of international agreements or attempted agreements to limit the amount of greenhouse gas emissions. The 1992 summit is worth noting in that regard. That summit produced a landmark treaty that suggested that stabilizing the world environment must be undertaken irrespective of costs. More than 180 countries, including the United States, ratified this treaty. It set the stage for a decade of international negotiations all aimed at rolling back toxic emissions—primarily in the industrialized world—to 1990 levels. In spite of these good intentions, there is little evidence that any measurable success was achieved. This might be attributed to the fact that the U.S. Senate has not ratified the implementing instrument—the 1997 Kyoto Protocol—which failed by a 95-0 vote in July 1997.

The Senate's concerns were that the treaty exempted developing countries and posed serious problems for the U.S. economy at large. Both of these problems can be traced to the fact that the only way to reduce greenhouse gas emissions, which are essentially carbon dioxide gases, would be to stop burning fossil fuels: coal, oil, natural gas, wood, and peat. Eliminating these emissions by taxing them or by imposing regulations comes at a high price. Poor countries cannot afford to do this, and the United States is unwilling to pay the high price. President George W. Bush, for his part, put the final coup de grace to the Kyoto Protocol in March 2001. He rejected the protocol, saying that it was "fatally flawed in fundamental ways." He went on to note that since climate change was a serious concern, he would ask the National Academy of Sciences to review the state of our understanding of global warming and to issue a report. That 2001 report is entitled *Climate Change Science: An Analysis of Some Key Questions* and can be accessed online at http://www.nap.edu/books/0309075742/html/.

This report and the debate over the Kyoto Protocol continue to be controversial. Most acknowledge that social and economic development has impacted the concentration levels of greenhouse gases in our atmosphere, but some people do challenge this widely held belief. Whatever the cause of the accumulated greenhouse gases in our atmosphere, what experts do know is that since the beginning of the Industrial Revolution, concentrations of these gases have increased by 30 percent. More worrisome, perhaps, is the fact that each year the world adds another 6 billion tons of carbon dioxide to the atmosphere.

At the crux of this debate are the consequences of the toxic wastes that we are dumping into the air—air that we depend upon for our very existence. No one seems to know for certain just how the environment will respond to these accumulated greenhouse gases. Many contend that in a very short period of time there will be a sharp rise in surface temperatures. If that turns out to be the case, modern civilization and the ecosystem will be in for dire consequences. Others believe that there might be a more gradual and more modest increase in global warming. This increase might be relatively easy to adjust to and perhaps even lead to benefits for the ecosystem and humankind.

In the following selections, Lester R. Brown argues that economic growth is generally incompatible with the environment but that by basing the economy in an ecological framework, environmentally sustainable economic development can be achieved. Lenny Bernstein maintains that human activities will not have a severe impact on ecosystems and that, in fact, ecosystems that adapt appropriately will benefit from human-induced climate change.

YES

Lester R. Brown

The Economy and the Earth

In 1543, Polish astronomer Nicolaus Copernicus published "On the Revolutions of the Celestial Spheres," in which he challenged the view that the Sun revolved around the earth, arguing instead that the earth revolved around the Sun. With his new model of the solar system, he began a wide-ranging debate among scientists, theologians, and others. His alternative to the earlier Ptolemaic model, which had the earth at the center of the universe, led to a revolution in thinking, to a new worldview.

Today we need a similar shift in our worldview, in how we think about the relationship between the earth and the economy. The issue now is not which celestial sphere revolves around the other but whether the environment is part of the economy or the economy is part of the environment. Economists see the environment as a subset of the economy. Ecologists, on the other hand, see the economy as a subset of the environment.

Like Ptolemy's view of the solar system, the economists' view is confusing efforts to understand our modern world. It has created an economy that is out of sync with the ecosystem on which it depends.

Economic theory and economic indicators do not explain how the economy is disrupting and destroying the earth's natural systems. Economic theory does not explain why Arctic Sea ice is melting. It does not explain why grasslands are turning into desert in northwestern China, why coral reefs are dying in the South Pacific, or why the Newfoundland cod fishery collapsed. Nor does it explain why we are in the early stages of the greatest extinction of plants and animals since the dinosaurs disappeared 65 million years ago. Yet economics is essential to measuring the cost to society of these excesses.

Evidence that the economy is in conflict with the earth's natural systems can be seen in the daily news reports of collapsing fisheries, shrinking forests, eroding soils, deteriorating rangelands, expanding deserts, rising carbon dioxide (CO_2) levels, falling water tables, rising temperatures, more destructive storms, melting glaciers, rising sea level, dying coral reefs, and disappearing species. These trends, which mark an increasingly stressed relationship between the economy and the earth's ecosystem, are taking a growing economic toll. At some point, this could overwhelm the worldwide forces of progress, leading to economic decline. The challenge for our generation is to reverse these trends before environmental deterioration leads to long-term economic decline, as it did for so many earlier civilizations.

These increasingly visible trends indicate that if the operation of the subsystem, the economy, is not compatible with the behavior of the larger system—the earth's ecosystem—both will eventually suffer. The larger the economy becomes relative to the ecosystem, and the more it presses against the earth's natural limits, the more destructive this incompatibility will be.

An environmentally sustainable economy—an eco-economy—requires that the principles of ecology establish the framework for the formulation of economic policy and that economists and ecologists work together to fashion the new economy. Ecologists understand that all economic activity, indeed all life, depends on the earth's ecosystem—the complex of individual species living together, interacting with each other and their physical habitat. These millions of species exist in an intricate balance, woven together by food chains, nutrient cycles, the hydrological cycle, and the climate system. Economists know how to translate goals into policy. Economists and ecologists working together can design and build an eco-economy, one that can sustain progress. . . .

Economists rely on the market to guide their decisionmaking. They respect the market because it can allocate resources with an efficiency that a central planner can never match (as the Soviets learned at great expense). Ecologists view the market with less reverence because they see a market that is not telling the truth. For example, when buying a gallon of gasoline, customers in effect pay to get the oil out of the ground, refine it into gasoline, and deliver it to the local service station. But they do not pay the health care costs of treating respiratory illness from air pollution or the costs of climate disruption.

Ecologists see the record economic growth of recent decades, but they also see an economy that is increasingly in conflict with its support systems, one that is fast depleting the earth's natural capital, moving the global economy onto an environmental path that will inevitably lead to economic decline. They see the need for a wholesale restructuring of the economy so that it meshes with the ecosystem. They know that a stable relationship between the economy and the earth's ecosystem is essential if economic progress is to be sustained.

We have created an economy that cannot sustain economic progress, an economy that cannot take us where we want to go. Just as Copernicus had to formulate a new astronomical worldview after several decades of celestial observations and mathematical calculations, we too must formulate a new economic worldview based on several decades of environmental observations and analyses.

Although the idea that economics must be integrated into ecology may seem radical to many, evidence is mounting that it is the only approach that reflects reality. When observations no longer support theory, it is time to change the theory—what science historian Thomas Kuhn calls a paradigm shift. If the economy is a subset of the earth's ecosystem, as [I contend], the only formulation of economic policy that will succeed is one that respects the principles of ecology.

The good news is that economists are becoming more ecologically aware, recognizing the inherent dependence of the economy on the earth's ecosystem. For example, some 2,500 economists—including eight Nobel laureates—have endorsed the introduction of a carbon tax to stabilize climate. More and more economists are looking for ways to get the market to tell the ecological truth. This spreading awareness is evident in the rapid growth of the International Society of Ecological Economics, which has 1,200 members and chapters in Australia/New Zealand, Brazil, Canada, India, Russia, China, and throughout Europe. Its goal is to integrate the thinking of ecologists and economists into a transdiscipline aimed at building a sustainable world.

Economy Self-Destructing

The economic indicators for the last half-century show remarkable progress. . . . [T]he economy expanded sevenfold between 1950 and 2000. International trade grew even more rapidly. The Dow Jones Index, a widely used indicator of the value of stocks traded on the New York Stock Exchange, climbed from 3,000 in 1990 to 11,000 in 2000. It was difficult not to be bullish about the long-term economic prospect as the new century began.

Difficult, that is, unless you look at the ecological indicators. Here, virtually every global indicator was headed in the wrong direction. The economic policies that have yielded the extraordinary growth in the world economy are the same ones that are destroying its support systems. By an conceivable ecological yardstick, these are failed policies. Mismanagement is destroying forests, rangelands, fisheries, and croplands—the four ecosystems that supply our food and, except for minerals, all our raw materials as well. Although many of us live in a high-tech urbanized society, we are as dependent on the earth's natural systems as our hunter-gatherer forebears were.

To put ecosystems in economic terms, a natural system, such as a fishery, functions like an endowment. The interest income from an endowment will continue in perpetuity as long as the endowment is maintained. If the endowment is drawn down, income declines. If the endowment is eventually depleted, the interest income disappears. And so it is with natural systems. If the sustainable yield of a fishery is exceeded, fish stocks begin to shrink. Eventually stocks are depleted and the fishery collapses. The cash flow from this endowment disappears as well.

As we begin the twenty-first century, our economy is slowly destroying its support systems, consuming its endowment of natural capital. Demands of the expanding economy, *as now structured,* are surpassing the sustainable yield of ecosystems. Easily a third of the world's cropland is losing topsoil at a rate that is undermining its long-term productivity. Fully 50 percent of the world's rangeland is overgrazed and deteriorating into desert. The world's forests have shrunk by about half since the dawn of agriculture and are still shrinking. Two thirds of oceanic fisheries are now being fished at or beyond their capacity; overfishing is now the rule, not the exception. And overpumping of underground water is common in key food-producing regions.

Over large areas of the world, the loss of topsoil from wind and water erosion now exceeds the natural formation of new soil, gradually draining the land of its fertility. In an effort to curb this, the United States is retiring highly erodible cropland that was earlier plowed in overly enthusiastic efforts to expand food production. This process began in 1985 with the Conservation Reserve Program that paid farmers to retire 15 million hectacres, roughly one tenth of U.S. cropland, converting it back to grassland or forest before it became wasteland.

In countries that lack such programs, farmers are being forced to abandon highly erodible land that has lost much of its topsoil. Nigeria is losing over 500 square kilometers of productive land to desert each year. In Kazakhstan, site of the 1950s Soviet Virgin Lands project, half the cropland has been abandoned since 1980 as soil erosion lowered its productivity. This has dropped Kazakhstan's wheat harvest from roughly 13 million tons in 1980 to 8 million tons in 2000—an economic loss of $900 million per year.

The rangelands that supply much of the world's animal protein are also under excessive pressure. As human populations grow, so do livestock numbers. With 180 million people worldwide now trying to make a living raising 3.3 billion cattle, sheep, and goats, grasslands are simply collapsing under the demand. As a result of overstocking, grasslands are now deteriorating in much of Africa, the Middle East, Central Asia, the northern part of the Indian subcontinent, and much of northwestern China. Overgrazing is now the principal cause of desertification, the conversion of productive land into desert. In Africa, the annual loss of livestock production from the cumulative degradation of rangeland is estimated at $7 billion, a sum almost equal to the gross domestic product of Ethiopia.

In China, the combination of overplowing and overgrazing to satisfy rapidly expanding food needs is creating a dust bowl reminiscent of the U.S. Dust Bowl of the 1930s—but much larger. In a desperate effort to maintain grain self-sufficiency, China has plowed large areas of the northwest, much of it land that is highly erodible and should never have been plowed.

As the country's demand for livestock products—meat, leather, and wool—has climbed, so have the numbers of livestock, far exceeding those of the United States, a country with comparable grazing capacity. In addition to the direct damage from overplowing and overgrazing, the northern half of China is literally drying out as aquifers are depleted by overpumping.

These trends are converging to form some of the largest dust storms ever recorded. The huge dust plumes, traveling eastward, affect the cities of northeast China—blotting out the sun and reducing visibility. Eastward-moving winds also carry soil from China's northwest to the Korean Peninsula and Japan, where people regularly complain about the dust clouds that filter out the sunlight and blanket everything with dust. Unless China can reverse the overplowing and overgrazing trends that are creating the dust bowl, these trends could spur massive migration into the already crowded cities of the northeast and undermine the country's economic future.

The world is also running up a water deficit. The overpumping of aquifers, now commonplace on every continent, has led to falling water tables as pumping exceeds aquifer recharge from precipitation. Irrigation problems are as old as irrigation itself, but this is a new threat, one that has evolved over the last half-century with the advent of diesel pumps and powerful electrically driven pumps.

Water tables are falling under large expanses of the three leading food-producing countries—China, India, and the United States. Under the North China Plan, which accounts for 25 percent of China's grain harvest, the water table is falling by roughly 1.5 meters (5 feet) per year. The same thing is happening under much of India, particularly the Punjab, the country's breadbasket. In the United States, water tables are falling under the grain-growing states of the southern Great Plains, shrinking the irrigated area. . . .

Economic demands on forests are also excessive. Trees are being cut or burned faster than they can regenerate or be planted. Overharvesting is common in many regions, including Southeast Asia, West Africa, and the Brazilian Amazon. Worldwide, forests are shrinking by over 9 million hectacres per year, an area equal to Portugal.

In addition to being overharvested, some rainforests are now being destroyed by fire. Healthy rainforests do not burn, but logging and the settlements that occur along logging roads have fragmented and dried out tropical rainforests to the point where they often will burn easily, ignited by a lightning strike or set afire by opportunistic plantation owners, farmers, and ranchers desiring more land.

In the late summer of 1997, during an El Niño–induced drought, tropical rainforests in Borneo and Sumatra burned out of control. This conflagration made the news because the smoke drifting over hundreds of kilometers affected people not only in Indonesia but also in Malaysia, Singapore, Viet Nam, Thailand, and the Philippines. A reported 1,100 airline flights in the region were canceled due to the smoke. Motorists drove with their headlights on during the day, trying to make their way through the thick haze. Millions of people became physically sick.

Deforestation can be costly. Record flooding in the Yangtze River basin during the summer of 1998 drove 120 million people from their homes. Although initially referred to as a "natural disaster," the removal of 85 percent of the original tree cover in the basin had left little vegetative cover to hold the heavy rainfall.

Deforestation also diminishes the recycling of water inland, thus reducing rainfall in the interior of continents. When rain falls on a healthy stand of dense forest, roughly one fourth runs off, returning to the sea, while three fourths evaporates, either directly or through transpiration. When land is cleared for farming or grazing or is clearcut by loggers, this ratio is reversed—three fourths of the water returns to the sea and one fourth evaporates to be carried further inland. As deforestation progresses, nature's mechanism for watering the interior of large continents such as Africa and Asia is weakening.

Evidence of excessive human demands can also be seen in the oceans. As the human demand for animal protein has climbed over the last several decades, it has begun to exceed the sustainable yield of oceanic fisheries. As a result, two thirds of oceanic fisheries are now being fished at their sustainable yield or beyond. Many are collapsing. In 1992, the rich Newfoundland cod fishery that had been supplying fish for several centuries collapsed abruptly, costing 40,000 Canadians their jobs. Despite a subsequent ban on fishing, nearly a decade later the fishery has yet to recover.

Farther to the south, the U.S. Chesapeake Bay has experienced a similar decline. A century ago, this extraordinarily productive estuary produced over 100 million pounds of oysters a year. In 1999, it produced barely 3 million pounds. The Gulf of Thailand fishery has suffered a similarly dramatic decline: depleted by overfishing, the catch has dropped by over 80 percent since 1963, prompting the Thai Fisheries Department to ban fishing in large areas.

The world is also losing its biological diversity as plant and animal species are destroyed faster than new species evolve. This biological impoverishment of the earth is the result of habitat destruction, pollution, climate alteration, and hunting. With each update of its *Red List of Threatened Species,* the World Conservation Union (IUCN) shows us moving farther into a period of mass extinction. In the latest assessment, released in 2000, IUCN reports that one out of eight of the world's 9,946 bird species is in danger of extinction, as is one in four of the 4,763 mammal species and nearly one third of all 25,000 fish species.

Some countries have already suffered extensive losses. Australia, for example, has lost 16 of 140 mammal species over the last two centuries. In the Colorado River system of the southwestern United States, 29 of 50 native species of fish have disappeared partly because their river habitats were drained dry. Species lost cannot be regained. As a popular bumper sticker aptly points out, "Extinction is forever."

The economic benefits of the earth's diverse array of life are countless. They include not only the role of each species in maintaining the particular ecosystem of which it is a part, but economic roles as well, such as providing drugs and germplasm. As diversity diminishes, nature's pharmacy shrinks, depriving future generations of new discoveries.

Even as expanding economic activity has been creating biological deficits, it has been upsetting some of nature's basic balances in other areas: With the huge growth in burning of fossil fuels since 1950, carbon emissions have overwhelmed the capacity of the earth's ecosystem to fix carbon dioxide. The resulting rise in atmospheric CO_2 levels is widely believed by atmospheric scientists to be responsible for the earth's rising temperature. The 14 warmest years since recordkeeping began in 1866 have all occurred since 1980.

One consequence of higher temperatures is more energy driving storm systems. Three powerful winter storms in France in December 1999 destroyed millions of trees, some of which had been standing for centuries. Thousands of buildings were demolished. These storms, the most violent on record in France, wreaked more than $10 billion worth of damage—$170 for each French citizen. Nature was levying a tax of its own on fossil fuel burning.

In October 1998, Hurricane Mitch—one of the most powerful storms ever to come out of the Atlantic—moved through the Caribbean and stalled for several days on the coast of Central America. While there, it acted as a huge pump pulling water from the ocean and dropping it over the land. Parts of Honduras received 2 meters of rainfall within a few days. So powerful was this storm and so vast the amount of water it dropped on Central America that it altered the topography, converting mountains and hills into vast mud flows that simply inundated whole villages, claiming an estimated 10,000 lives. Four fifths of the crops were destroyed. The huge flow of rushing water removed all the topsoil in many areas, ensuring that this land will not be farmed again during our lifetimes.

The overall economic effect of the storm was devastating. The wholesale destruction of roads, bridges, buildings, and other infrastructure set back the development of Honduras and Nicaragua by decades. The estimated $8.5 billion worth of damage in the region approached the gross domestic product of both countries combined. . . .

Perhaps the most disturbing consequence of rising temperature is ice melting. Over the last 35 years, the ice covering the Arctic Sea has thinned by 42 percent. A study by two Norwegian scientists projects that within 50 years there will be no summer ice left in the Arctic Sea. The discovery of open water at the North Pole by an ice breaker cruise ship in mid-August 2000 stunned many in the scientific community.

This particular thawing does not affect sea level because the ice that is melting is already in the ocean. But the Greenland ice sheet is also starting to melt. Greenland is three times the size of Texas and the ice sheet is up to 2 kilometers (1.2 miles) thick in some areas. An article in *Science* notes that if the entire ice sheet were to melt, it would raise sea level by some 7 meters (23 feet), inundating the world's coastal cities and Asia's rice-growing river floodplains. Even a 1-meter rise would cover half of Bangladesh's riceland, dropping food production below the survival level for millions of people.

As the twenty-first century begins, humanity is being squeezed between deserts expanding outward and rising seas encroaching inward. Civilization is being forced to retreat by forces it has created. Even as population continues to grow, the habitable portion of the planet is shrinking.

Aside from climate change, the economic effects of environmental destruction and disruption have been mostly local—collapsing fisheries, abandoned cropland, and shrinking forests. But if local damage keeps accumulating, it will eventually affect global economic trends. In an increasingly integrated global economy, local ecosystem collapse can have global economic consequences.

Lessons From the Past

In *The Collapse of Complex Civilizations*, Joseph Tainter describes the decline of early civilizations and speculates about the causes. Was it because of the degradation of their environment, climate change, civil conflict, foreign invaders? Or, he asks, "is there some mysterious internal dynamic to the rise and fall of civilizations?"

As he ponders the contrast between civilizations that once flourished and the desolation of the sites they occupied, he quotes archeologist Robert McAdams, who described the site of the ancient Sumerian civilization located on the central floodplain of the Euphrates River, an empty, desolate area now outside the frontiers of cultivation. Adams described how the "tangled dunes, long disused canal levees, and the rubble-strewn mounds of former settlement contribute only low, featureless relief. Vegetation is sparse, and in many areas it is almost wholly absent. . . . Yet at one time, here lay the core, the heartland, the oldest urban, literate civilization in the world."

The early Sumerian civilization of the fourth millennium BC was remarkable, advancing far beyond any that had existed before. Its irrigation system, based on sophisticated engineering concepts, created a highly productive agriculture, one that enabled farmers to produce a surplus of food that supported the formation of the first cities. Managing the irrigation system required a complex social organization, one that may have been more sophisticated than any that had gone before. The Sumerians had the first cities and the first written language, the cuneiform script. They were probably as excited about it as we are today about the Internet.

It was an extraordinary civilization, but there was an environmental flaw in the design of the irrigation system, one that would eventually undermine its agricultural economy. Water from behind dams was diverted onto the land, raising crop yields. Some of the water was used by the crops, some evaporated into the atmosphere, and some percolated downward. Over time, this percolation slowly raised the water table until eventually it approached the surface of the land. When it reached a few feet from the surface it began to restrict the growth of deep-rooted crops. Somewhat later, as the water climbed to within inches of the surface, it began to evaporate into the atmosphere. As this happened, the salt in the water was left behind. Over time, the accumulation of salt reduced the productivity of the land. The environmental flaw was that there was no provision for draining the water that percolated downward.

The initial response of the Sumerians to declining wheat yields was to shift to barley, a more salt-tolerant plant. But eventually the yields of barley also declined. The resultant shrinkage of the food supply undermined the economic foundation of this great civilization. . . .

One unanswerable question about these earlier civilizations was whether they knew what was causing their decline. Did the Sumerians understand that rising salt content in the soil was reducing their wheat yields? If they knew, were they simply unable to muster the political support needed to lower water tables, just as we today are struggling unsuccessfully to lower carbon emissions?

Learning From China

The flow of startling information from China helps us understand why our economy cannot take us where we want to go. Not only is China the world's most populous country, with nearly 1.3 billion people, but since 1980 it has been the world's fastest-growing economy—expanding more than fourfold. In effect, China is telescoping history, demonstrating what happens when large numbers of poor people rapidly become more affluent.

As incomes have climbed in China, so has consumption. The Chinese have already caught up with Americans in pork consumption per person and they are now concentrating their energies on increasing beef production. Raising per capita beef consumption in China to that of the average American would take 49 million additional tons of beef. If all this were to come from putting cattle in feedlots, American-style, it would require 343 million tons of grain a year, an amount equal to the entire U.S. grain harvest.

In Japan, as population pressures on the land mounted during a comparable stage of its economic development, the Japanese turned to the sea for their animal protein. Last year, Japan consumed nearly 10 million tons of seafood. If China, with 10 times as many people as Japan, were to try to move down this same path, it would need 100 million tons of seafood—the entire world fish catch.

In 1994, the Chinese government decided that the country would develop an automobile-centered transportation system and that the automobile industry would be one of the engines of future economic growth. Beijing invited major automobile manufacturers, such as Volkswagen, General Motors, and Toyota, to invest in China. But if Beijing's goal of an auto-centered transportation system were to materialize and the Chinese were to have one or two cars in every garage and were to consume oil at the U.S. rate, China would need over 80 million barrels of oil a day—slightly more than the 74 million barrels per day the world now produces. To provide the required roads and parking lots, it would also need to pave some 16 million hectacres of land, and area equal to half the size of the 31 million hectacres of land currently used to produce the country's 132-million-ton annual harvest of rice, its leading food staple.

Similarly, consider paper. As China modernizes, its paper consumption is rising. If annual paper use in China of 35 kilograms per person were to climb to the U.S. level of 342 kilograms, China would need more paper than the world currently produces. There go the world's forests.

We are learning that the western industrial development model is not viable for China, simply because there are not enough resources for it to work. Global land and water resources are not sufficient to satisfy the growing grain needs in China if it continues along the current economic development path. Nor will the existing fossil-fuel-based energy economy supply the needed energy, simply because world oil production is not projected to rise much above current levels in the years ahead. Apart from the availability of oil, if carbon emissions per person in China ever reach the U.S. level, this alone would roughly double global emissions, accelerating the rise in the atmospheric CO_2 level.

China faces a formidable challenge in fashioning a development strategy simply because of the density of its population. Although it has almost exactly the same amount of land as the United States, most of China's 1.3 billion people live in a 1,500-kilometer strip on the eastern and southern coasts. Reaching the equivalent population density in the United States would require squeezing the entire U.S. population into the area east of the Mississippi and then multiplying it by four.

Interestingly, the adoption of the western economic model for China is being challenged from within. A group of prominent scientists, including many in the Chinese Academy of Sciences, wrote a white paper questioning the government's decision to develop an automobile-centered transportation system. They pointed out that China does not have enough land both to feed its people and to provide the roads, highways, and parking lots needed to accommodate the automobile. They also noted the heavy dependence on imported oil that would be required and the potential air pollution and traffic congestion that would result if they followed the U.S. path.

If the fossil-fuel-based, automobile-centered, throwaway economy will not work for China, then it will not work for India with its 1 billion people, or for the other 2 billion people in the developing world. In a world with a shared ecosystem and an increasingly integrated global economy, it will ultimately not work for the industrial economies either.

China is showing that the world cannot remain for long on the current economic path. It is underlining the urgency of restructuring the global economy, of building a new economy—an economy designed for the earth.

The Acceleration of History

. . . Until recently, population growth was so slow that it aroused little concern. But since 1950 we have added more people to world population than during the preceding 4 million years since our early ancestors first stood upright. Economic expansion in earlier times was similarly slow. To illustrate, growth in the world economy during the year 2000 exceeded that during the entire nineteenth century.

Throughout most of human history, the growth of population, the rise in income, and the development of new technologies were so slow as to be imperceptible during an individual life span. For example, the climb in grainland productivity from 1.1 tons per hectare in 1950 to 2.8 tons per hectacre in 2000 exceeds that during the 11,000 years from the beginning of agriculture until 1950.

The population growth of today has no precedent. Throughout most of our existence as a species, our numbers were measured in the thousands. Today, they measure in the billions. Our evolution has prepared us to deal with many threats, but perhaps not with the threat we pose to ourselves with the uncontrolled growth in our own numbers.

The world economy is growing even faster. The sevenfold growth in global output of goods and services since 1950 dwarfs anything in history. In the earlier stages of the Industrial Revolution, economic expansion rarely exceeded 1 or 2 percent a year. Developing countries that are industrializing now are doing so much faster than their predecessors simply because they do not have to invent the technologies needed by a modern industrial society, such as power plants, automobiles, and refrigerators. They can simply draw on the experiences and technology of those that preceded them. . . .

The pace of history is also accelerating as soaring human demands collide with the earth's natural limits. National political leaders are spending more time dealing with the consequences of the collisions described earlier—collapsing fisheries, falling water tables, food shortages, and increasingly destructive storms—along with a steadily swelling international flow of environmental refugees and the many other effects of overshooting natural limits. As change has accelerated, the situation has evolved from one where individuals and societies change only rarely to one where they change continuously. They are changing not only in response to growth itself, but also to the consequences of growth.

The central question is whether the accelerating change that is an integral part of the modern landscape is beginning to exceed the capacity of our social institutions to cope with change. Change is particularly difficult for institutions dealing with international or global issues that require a concerted, cooperative effort by many countries with contrasting cultures if they are to succeed. For example, sustaining the existing oceanic fish catch may be possible only if numerous agreements are reached among countries on the limits to fishing in individual oceanic fisheries. And can governments, working together at the global level, move fast enough to stabilize climate before it disrupts economic progress?

The issue is not whether we know what needs to be done or whether we have the technologies to do it. The issue is whether our social institutions are capable of bringing about the change in the time available. As H.G. Wells wrote in *The Outline of History,* "Human history becomes more and more a race between education and catastrophe."

The Option: Restructure or Decline

Whether we study the environmental undermining of earlier civilizations or look at how adoption of the western industrial model by China would affect the earth's ecosystem, it is evident that the existing industrial economic model cannot sustain economic progress. In our shortsighted efforts to sustain the global economy, as currently structured, we are depleting the earth's natural capital. We spend a lot of time worrying about our economic deficits, but it is the ecological deficits that threaten our long-term economic future. Economic deficits are what we borrow from each other; ecological deficits are what we take from future generations.

Herman Daly, the intellectual pioneer of the fast-growing field of ecological economics, notes that the world "has passed from an era in which manmade capital represented the limiting factor in economic development (an 'empty' world) to an era in which increasingly scarce natural capital has taken its place (a 'full' world)." When our numbers were small relative to the size of the planet, it was humanmade capital that was scarce. Natural capital was abundant. Now that has changed. As the human enterprise continues to expand, the products and services provided by the earth's ecosystem are increasingly scarce, and natural capital is fast becoming the limiting factor while humanmade capital is increasingly abundant.

Transforming our environmentally destructive economy into one that can sustain progress depends on a Copernican shift in our economic mindset, a recognition that the economy is part of the earth's ecosystem and can sustain progress only if it is restructured so that it is compatible with it. The preeminent challenge for our generation is to design an eco-economy, one that respects the principles of ecology. A redesigned economy can be integrated into the ecosystem in a way that will stabilize the relationship between the two, enabling economic progress to continue.

Unfortunately, present-day economics does not provide the conceptual framework needed to build such an economy. It will have to be designed with an understanding of basic ecological concepts such as sustainable yield, carrying capacity, nutrient cycles, the hydrological cycle, and the climate system. Designers must also know that natural systems provide not only goods, but also services—services that are often more valuable than the goods.

We know the kind of restructuring that is needed. In simplest terms, our fossil-fuel-based, automobile-centered, throwaway economy is not a viable model for the world. The alternative is a solar/hydrogen energy economy, an urban transport system that is centered on advanced-design public rail systems and that relies more on the bicycle and less on the automobile, and a comprehensive reuse/recycle economy. And we need to stabilize population as soon as possible.

How do we achieve this economic transformation when all economic decisionmakers—whether political leaders, corporate planners, investment bankers, or individual consumers—are guided by market signals, not the principles of ecological sustainability? How do we integrate ecological awareness into economic decisionmaking? Is it possible for all of us who are making economic decisions to "think like ecologists," to understand the ecological consequences of our decisions? The answer is probably not. It simply may not be possible.

But there may be another approach, a simpler way of achieving our goal. Everyone making economic decisions relies on market signals for guidance. The problem is that the market often fails to tell the ecological truth. It regularly underprices products and services by failing to incorporate the environmental costs of providing them.

Compare, for example, the cost of wind-generated electricity with that from a coal-fired power plant. The cost of the wind-generated electricity reflects the costs of manufacturing the turbine, installing it, maintaining it, and delivering the electricity to consumers. The cost of the coal-fired electricity includes building the power plant, mining the coal, transporting it to the power plant, and distributing the electricity to consumers. What it does not include is the cost of climate disruption caused by carbon emissions from coal burning—whether it be more destructive storms, melting ice caps, rising sea level, or record heat waves. Nor does it include the damage to freshwater lakes and forests from acid rain, or the health care costs of treating respiratory illnesses caused by air pollution. Thus the market price of coal-fired electricity greatly understates its cost to society.

One way to remedy this situation would be to have environmental scientists and economists work together to calculate the cost of climate disruption, acid rain, and air pollution. This figure could then be incorporated as a tax on coal-fired electricity that, when added to the current price, would give the full cost of coal use. This procedure, followed across the board, would mean that all economic decisionmakers—governments and individual consumers—would have the information needed to make more intelligent, ecologically responsible decisions.

We can now see how to restructure the global economy so as to restore stability between the economy and the ecosystem on which it rests. When I helped to pioneer the concept of environmentally sustainable economic development some 27 years ago, at the newly formed Worldwatch Institute, I had a broad sense of what the new economy would look like. Now we can see much more of the detail. We can build an eco-economy with existing technologies. It is economically feasible if we can get the market to tell us the full cost of the products and services that we buy.

The question is not how much will it cost to make this transformation but how much it will cost if we fail to do it. Øystein Dahle, retired Vice President of Esso for Norway and the North Sea, observes, "Socialism collapsed because it did not allow prices to tell the economic truth. Capitalism may collapse because it does not allow prices to tell the ecological truth."

Lenny Bernstein  **NO**

Climate Change and Ecosystems

Introduction

This report examines the basis for claims that projected human-induced climate change will have a severe impact on ecosystems. Past Marshall Institute Reports, most recently *Climate Science and Policy: Making the Connection,* have questioned the basis for projections that human activities will have a severe impact on the climate of the 21st century. This report does not repeat those arguments, but discusses the possible impact on ecosystems of different levels of climate change, as indicated by temperature rise, independent of time frame or cause.

There are many definitions of ecosystem. This report will use one developed by the Intergovernmental Panel on Climate Change (IPCC):

> A distinct system of interacting living organisms, together with their physical environment. The boundaries of what could be called an ecosystem are somewhat arbitrary, depending on the focus of interest or study. Thus the extent of an ecosystem may range from very small spatial scales to, ultimately, the entire Earth.

The ecosystems we discuss typically cover many thousand square miles, for example, the habitat of a bird species or a river's watershed.

Before considering specific claims of potential ecosystem damage, it is important to recognize that climate has always impacted on ecosystems and that human activities have been impacting on ecosystems for tens of thousands of years.

All of the plants and animals, including humans, that live on Earth are sensitive to climate and will respond to climate change. Climate is a key determinant of what crops can be grown in a particular area. Paleontologists argue that past climate changes were a factor, perhaps the major factor, in the extinction of the dinosaurs and many other species.

Human activities have had impacts on ecosystems since indigenous people, such as the Australian Aborigines, first used fire to clear underbrush to improve their hunting. Both primitive and modern people have caused the extinction of species, e.g. the moa in New Zealand and the passenger pigeon in North America.

The overwhelming majority of the Earth's ecosystems have been affected by human activities. Some of these activities have been planned, e.g., the conversion of forest to farmland. Others activities have been unplanned. For example, as documented in a recent issue of *Audubon*, the removal of wolves and other predators, and bans on hunting, have led to a dramatic increase in the U.S. deer population. This, in turn, has reduced the population of the plants deer like to eat, while increasing in the population of plants deer do not like to eat, thus changing the ecosystem.

Given the pervasive nature of human impacts, ecosystems can be divided into two categories:

- intensively-managed; farmland, managed forests and grasslands, and to a lesser extent, fisheries; and
- lightly-impacted; essentially unmanaged, natural wildlife areas and the oceans.

Concerns about intensely-managed ecosystems focus on the potential impact that climate change will have on the ability of these systems to produce the food and fiber they have traditionally supplied to the global economy. Concerns about lightly-impacted ecosystems focus on the potential for climate change to cause widespread species extinction.

This report examines the question: How sensitive are intensively-managed and lightly-impacted ecosystems to different levels of climate change? In the course of answering this question, it is necessary to consider the relative importance of climate change compared with other human impacts, such as habitat disruption and local or regional pollution, in determining the rate of species extinction.

Three climate changes are discussed in this report: higher atmospheric concentrations of CO_2, warmer temperatures, and increased precipitation. All IPCC projections are for higher CO_2. Based on projection of higher CO_2, climate models project increases in temperature for all parts of the world. They also project increases in average precipitation, but are less consistent in the projections of the regional distribution of precipitation. Most areas of the world are projected to get more precipitation than they now do, a few are projected to get less.

The IPCC Third Assessment Report includes projections of precipitation based on nine climate models using two emissions scenarios: high emissions and low emissions. The results were evaluated for 23 regions of the world, and for two seasons: winter and summer. This resulted in 92 comparisons (23 regions × 2 emissions scenarios × 2 seasons). IPCC reported that in a third (32) of the comparisons, the models gave inconsistent results. In 9 other comparisons they showed no significant change in precipitation. In 40 comparisons, they showed increases in precipitation, and in 11 comparisons they showed decreases. While these comparisons represent the best available modeling results, they hide large differences in the predictions of individual models. As the IPCC reports:

> The magnitude of regional precipitation changes varies considerably amongst models, with the typical range being around 0 to 50% where the direction of change is strongly indicated and around −30 to +30% where it is not.

Given the physical basis for assuming a wetter world, and the preponderance of modeling results, we will assume that most ecosystems will experience wetter conditions in the future.

Intensively-Managed Ecosystems

Society depends on ecosystems for a wide range of goods. Most of the food we eat, the wood we use for construction, and the natural fibers we use for clothing, are products of intensively-managed ecosystems. We also depend on both intensively-managed and lightly-impacted ecosystems for a wide variety of services including water purification and recreational opportunities. Since these ecosystems are sensitive to climate change, it is reasonable to ask whether changes in climate will diminish the ability of ecosystems to continue supplying these goods and services. The debate on the validity of this concern centers on the ability of human society to adapt intensively-managed ecosystems to climate change.

As climate changes, which it has and will in the future, human society will have to adapt to that change; adaptation is a necessity, not an option. But humanity's need to adapt to climate change is not a new phenomena, and both sides of the debate are succinctly captured by Brian Fagan, Professor of Archeology at the University of California, Santa Barbara, in his book, *The Little Ice Age:*

> Humanity has been at the mercy of climate change for its entire existence. Infinitely ingenious, we have lived through eight, perhaps nine, glacial episodes in the past 730,000 years. Our ancestors adapted to the universal but irregular global warming since the end of the Ice Age with dazzling opportunism. They developed strategies for surviving harsh drought cycles, decades of heavy rainfall or unaccustomed cold; adopted agriculture and stock-raising, which revolutionized human life; founded the world's first preindustrial civilization in Egypt, Mesopotamia, and the Americas. The price of sudden climate change, in famine, disease, and suffering, was often high.

Optimists point to the infinite ingenuity and dazzling opportunism Prof. Fagan refers to as evidence that humanity will be able to respond to any future climate change. Pessimists point to the high human costs of past climate changes. Which of these will shape the future?

The majority of studies of the impacts of climate change on intensively-managed ecosystems have the following characteristics:

- they assume today's technology with either no or limited adaptation;
- they use the impacts of severe weather events as predictors of the impacts of climate change; and
- they invariably show high negative impacts.

These studies are misleading. Severe weather events occur in the short-term, offering no opportunity for adaptation. But climate is the long-term average of weather, and climate change, whether natural or human-induced, will take decades to centuries to occur. During that time human society will continue to benefit from advances in knowledge and technology, and hence become more capable of adapting to different climate conditions.

The benefits of adaptation have been clearly demonstrated in the evolution of thinking about the potential impacts of climate change on agriculture. Early studies did not consider adaptation. They assumed no change in the behavior of farmers in response to changing climate. This was known as the "dumb farmer" hypothesis, and was at odds with all of human experience, which indicates that farmers and others whose livelihood is sensitive to climate are very attuned to climate change and adapt to it on a continuous basis.

Later studies considered adaptation by the individual farmer, i.e., planting species that were better matched to climate conditions. For example, wheat farmers have a wide variety of species to choose from, some of which are better adapted than others to the warmer, wetter conditions that are projected by climate models. Choosing these better adapted species would minimize the potential adverse impacts of climate change, and in many cases provide a net benefit. Still more sophisticated studies consider both farmer adaptation and marketplace adaptation. If climate changed sufficiently, wheat farmers might become corn farmers, and corn farmers might grow fruit and vegetables. Using a "smart farmer" assumption led to very different results, often showing that climate change yielded net benefits.

Benefits of Adaptation

The limited number of studies which take growth in adaptive capacity into account often show benefits for climate change. One such study by Adams *et al.* considers the impacts of climate change on U.S. agriculture in 2060, taking into account projected changes in the agricultural market to that time and allowing for the full range of adaptation. The authors considered the effects of changes in temperature, precipitation and atmospheric carbon dioxide (CO_2) content on agricultural yields. Photosynthesis, the process by which atmospheric CO_2 and water vapor are converted into plant matter, is enhanced by higher levels of atmospheric CO_2, though plants respond to increased CO_2 at different rates.

Adams, *et al.* looked at a series of cases in which atmospheric CO_2 concentration was increased from its 1999 level of about 365 ppm to 530 ppm, temperature increased by as much as 5°C, and precipitation increased by as much as 15%. These climate changes are larger than those typically projected by climate models for 2060. Farmers were allowed to adapt by either optimizing their current crops or by switching crops.

The authors found that for all cases studied, the U.S. benefited from improvements in the agricultural sector, with the benefits being split between consumers, who enjoyed lower food prices because of higher agricultural productivity, and the farmers who benefited from higher income. Not all cases resulted in benefits to both sides, nor were the benefits spread equally across all agricultural areas in the country, but the net effect for the U.S. economy was positive.

The physical basis for these benefits is fairly easy to understand. The benefits of higher CO_2 concentration have already been discussed. Warmer climates mean longer growing seasons and less chance of crop damage from frost. Much of the U.S. agricultural area suffers from periodic droughts, so increased precipitation also provides benefits.

A similar study by [Brent L.] Sohngen and [Robert] Mendelsohn for the U.S. timber industry projects benefits under the same range of climate change conditions. The authors conclude:

> Overall, the timber market is likely to adapt to climate change, thereby ameliorating the potential problem associated with ecological change. This work shows how harvest schedules will adjust from region to region and from moment to moment so as to use timber stocks efficiently during the transition period (to equilibrium climate change). These adjustments occur regardless of the specific climate and ecological scenario. This chapter also shows how timberland owners will adjust their replanting behavior by responding to future ecological and economic conditions. Despite the apparent severity of some ecological effects, market behavior offsets the potential damages through adaptation.

Overall, Mendelsohn and Neumann project that the benefits to managed ecosystems would result in a modest (+0.2%) benefit to the U.S. economy in 2060 for their moderate climate change case (+2.5°C, +7% precipitation). This result was generalized by the IPCC. In assessing these results, the IPCC concluded that there was medium confidence that small increases in temperature would have a net positive effect on the economies of developed nations.

The IPCC defines "small increases in temperature," as 0–2°C. This literature also indicates that most, if not all, of the benefit comes from gains in intensively-managed ecosystems.

While the IPCC agrees that moderate climate change would be beneficial to managed ecosystems in the developed world, it raises two concerns: first, that more than 2°C warming would have adverse effects, even in the developed world, and second, that even small amounts of climate change would have adverse effects in the developing world. Again, much of the basis for these concerns is the projected impact of climate change on intensely-managed ecosystems. The [following] paragraphs examine the validity of these concerns.

The basis for the IPCC's concerns about the inability of intensively-manage decosystems to adapt to large amounts of climate change appears to lie in the fact that the studies collected by Mendelsohn and Neumann, and other similar exercises, show declining benefits at large amounts of climate change. The extent to which these results are a function of model limitation or represent real limitations in the ability of intensively-managed ecosystems to adapt is unknown. As Mendelsohn and Neumann state:

> . . . it is important to recognize the significant limitations involved in projecting climate, biophysical, and economic conditions over the next century. Although this book seeks to improve the arsenal of methodologies

to measure the economic impact of climate change, none of the existing methods are perfect replicas of the experience that society will face if climate gradually warms over the next century.

. . . For the US, which has been subjected to more analysis than any other part of the world, the benefits extend out to double the temperature level considered by the IPCC (5°C vs. 2.5°C). More scientific study and modeling will be needed to determine the extent to which this result can be generalized to other countries and regions. However, there is clearly room for more optimism than exhibited by the IPCC.

Adaptation in the Developing World

The question of whether adaptation can provide benefits for intensively-managed ecosystems in the developing world is more complex. The benefits of higher CO_2 concentration are equally applicable in developed and developing countries. However, most developing countries are in the tropics, and would see no benefit, but potential adverse effects, from rising temperature. The IPCC points out many cases in which extremely high temperatures will inhibit critical stages of plant growth for existing crop species. These studies often do not consider the potential for developing more heat resistant crops or opportunities for adaptation through crop switching. Also, it should be noted that climate models typically project less than global average warming in the tropics.

In many developing countries, the growing season is 365 days of the year and frost does not exist. Thus longer growing season and less potential frost damage are not considerations. Some of these countries also have generous rainfall, so additional rainfall will provide little additional benefit. Others are either arid or desert countries, in which case, additional rainfall is a major benefit. No single description fits all cases.

The IPCC recognizes that there is considerable opportunity for the agriculture and forestry sectors to adapt to climate change, and that there is evidence that they have done so in the past. But it then raises concerns that the poorest and most vulnerable countries will not have the ability to adapt. This conclusion overlooks two factors.

First, there is little reason to believe that developing nations cannot take advantage of improvements in agricultural technology and use them to adapt to any changes in climate. Some of the poorest countries in the world were the ones that benefited most in the 1950s and '60s from adopting the suite of agricultural technologies (improved plant varieties, increased used of fertilizer and irrigation) known as the "Green Revolution," which dramatically raised food production in much of the developing world. Countries with relatively stable governments benefited most. Democratic countries, such as India, were able to take quick advantage of these developments, but even dictatorships, such as Syria, which became self-sufficient in grain in 1991, saw improvements in food production. In today's world, despite a growing population, famine is a problem only in those countries which are at war or have unstable governments. . . .

Second, CO_2 emissions are the result of economic activity, which generates wealth, which in turn results in adaptive capacity. Since projected climate change and the ability to adapt to it are both the result of economic activity, we need to consider the future level of economic activity in developing nations.

The IPCC Special Report on Emissions Scenarios (SRES), published in 2000, provides a wide range of scenarios of the changes in CO_2 emissions and per capita income for both developed and developing nations from 1990 to 2100. As the IPCC is careful to point out, scenarios are not predictions, they are alternate images of how the future might unfold. This report does not address the analytical basis for these scenarios or whether any of them are likely. They are used solely as a basis for assessing the potential growth in the adaptive capacity of developing nations.

The IPCC scenarios all show a faster rate of economic growth in developing nations than in developed nations, resulting in a narrowing of the economic gap between the developed and developing worlds. This higher rate of economic growth also results in developing nations emitting a higher fraction of the world's CO_2 emissions in 2100 than they currently do. The emissions scenarios that lead to the highest level of projected temperature rise to 2100 are the scenarios that have the highest level of economic growth in the developing world.

The SRES does not give country-by-county projections but divides the world into four regions:

1. The countries that were OECD members in 1990,
2. Russia and Eastern Europe,
3. Asia, and
4. Africa and Latin America.

The first two regions are developed nations, the last two, the developing nations.

The SRES authors developed 40 baseline scenarios; none of these scenarios include overt actions to control greenhouse gas emissions. . . .

[Table 1] summarizes the SRES projections for population, total CO_2 emissions, CO_2 emissions per capita, and GDP [gross domestic product] per capita for 1990 and 2100 for the illustrative scenarios with the highest (A1FI) and lowest (B1) global CO_2 emissions.

What the numbers in Table 1 show is a dramatic narrowing of current differences between developed and developing nation per capita CO_2 emissions and GDP during the 21st century. Even in the IPCC's lowest economic growth illustrative scenario, A2 (not shown), developing nation GDP per capita increases more than ten-fold (2.3%/yr.) during the 21st century, and the ratio of developed nation to developing nation GDP per capita decreases to 4.2. It is reasonable to assume that this growth in the wealth of developing nations will be accompanied by a growth in their ability to adapt food production to climate variability and change. At a minimum, the adaptive capacity of

Table 1

SRES Projections: CO_2 Emissions and GDP per Capita

	1990	2100	
		Highest Emissions	Lowest Emissions
Population, Billions			
Developed Nations	1.3	1.4	1.4
Developing Nations	4.0	5.7	5.7
Total CO_2 Emissions (GtC)*			
Developed Nations	4.1	10.0	1.1
Developing Nations	3.1	18.2	3.1
% Developing Nations	43	65	74
CO_2 per Capita (Tonnes C)			
Developed Nations	3.2	7.1	0.79
Developing Nations	0.78	3.2	0.54
Ratio	4.1	2.2	1.5
GDP per Capita (1990 US$)			
Developed Nations	13,800	109,500	71,700
Developing Nations	850	69,800	40,000
Ratio	16.1	1.6	1.8

*GtC = billion metric tonnes carbon

developing nations should be roughly equivalent to that of developed nations today. In many cases it should exceed that level.

Pessimists argue that these broad averages hide pockets of poverty that will be resistant to economic growth. The evidence is overwhelming that poverty is caused by government corruption and the lack of rule of law, property rights and individual freedom. These problems dwarf the potential impacts of climate change and need to be addressed on an urgent basis, independent of concerns about potential climate change.

Lightly-Impacted Ecosystems

. . . Before discussing the potential impact of climate change on species extinction, we will consider the extent to which humans are and have been responsible for the extinction of other species. The most dramatic and well-known cases involve over-hunting, which led to the extinction of such species as the dodo, moa, and passenger pigeon, and almost led to the extinction of the American buffalo. But, habitat destruction has also been a major cause of species extinction. Conversion of natural habitats to intensive-managed farms and forests has caused the extinction of both plant and animal species.

More recently, the introduction of invasive species, non-native plants or animals that have no natural enemies, has been another factor contributing to the stress on endangered species. Some of these species have been purposely introduced (e.g. kudzu, which was introduced in the southeastern U.S. for erosion control), while the introduction of others was inadvertent (e.g. zebra mussels, which entered the Great Lakes in the ballast water of ships).

While there is no debate that humans have been, and continue to be, responsible for the extinction of some species, there is an active debate as to how serious the problem is. We do not know how many species there are, nor what the background rate of species extinction is, nor how many species are becoming extinct as the result of human activities.

The current best estimate of the number of species on the Earth is between 10 and 80 million, of which only some 1.6 million have been identified. Such a wide range indicates deficiencies in the current estimating methodologies. Systematic studies invariably discover new species, even in intensively studied areas. For example, in 1998, about 12,000 species were known to exist in the Great Smoky Mountains National Park. In that year, the All Taxa (Species) Biodiversity Inventory project was started with the goal of raising the total number of species identified in the park to 100,000. Thus far, 1,480 new species have been identified in the park, 144 of which are new to science.

Background rates of extinction are similarly unknown. Fossil records indicate massive extinctions in the past, the most famous being the extinction of the dinosaurs 65,000,000 years ago. This extinction is now believed to have been caused when a massive asteroid hit the Earth creating a large, sudden change in climate. Fossil records also indicate that most of the species that existed over the Earth's history are now extinct. However, there is no accepted estimate for the number of species that would become extinct as the result of natural evolutionary processes during a "normal" year.

Estimates of the number of species becoming extinct because of human activities vary widely. One widely-quoted number is 40,000 per year, but as has been documented by Bjorn Lomborg in his book *The Skeptical Environmentalist,* this number can be traced to a speculation by Norman Myers, a well known environmentalist. Even critics of Lomborg's approach, such as Thomas Lovejoy, Chief Biodiversity Advisor to the President of the World Bank and a former Director of the World Wildlife Fund–US, agree that Myers provided no basis for his estimate. At the other extreme of the estimates for human-induced species extinction, documentary evidence exists for the extinction of only 1,033 species since 1600. Even those who believe that humans are not causing large-scale species extinction agree that this number is highly likely to be low, since undocumented extinctions as the result of human activities are certain to have occurred. . . .

Climate Change and Species Extinction

The starting point for concerns about the potential impacts of climate change on endangered species is indisputable: all plants and animals living on the Earth are sensitive to climate. All, with the possible exception of humans, have a preferred climate. These preferences are often shown as a plot of the type of ecosystem that will be prevalent as a function of average temperature and rainfall. Any change in climate will put stress on some plant or animal species. However, translating these generalities into threats to specific species is far from easy. The IPCC summarizes the problems involved as follows:

> Modeling changes in biodiversity in response to climate change presents some significant challenges. It requires projections of climate change at high spatial and temporal resolution and often depends on the balance between variables that are poorly handled by climate models (e.g., local precipitation and evaporative demand). It also requires an understanding of how species interact with each other and how these interactions affect the communities and ecosystems of which they are a part. In addition, the focus of attention in the results is often particular species that may be rare or show unusual biological behavior.

To address these knowledge gaps, the IPCC calls for:

> Improvement of regional scale models coupled with transient ecosystem models that deal with multiple pressures with appropriate spatial and temporal resolution and include spatial interactions between ecosystems within landscapes.

The term "landscape" refers to "groups of ecosystems (e.g., forests, rivers, lakes, etc.) that form a visible entity to humans.

Elsewhere the IPCC documents the huge difficulties involved in developing regional climate models. The challenges in developing transient ecosystem models are just as large, and coupling the two would be still another difficult task. Yet, the IPCC is correct in its conclusion that this is what would be needed for a predictive model of the effect of climate change on plant and animal species. Faced with the difficulty of developing predictive models and quantitative assessment tools, any discussion of the impacts of climate change on species is limited to qualitative statements. . . .

Any discussion of the role of climate change in future rates of species extinction must also consider the relative threats posed by climate change vs. habitat disruption and other human activities. Given the high level of uncertainty about both current and future rates of species extinction, we can only speculate about the relative importance of climate change vs. habitat disruption or other human activities.

One study has attempted such speculation and concluded that the dominant factors determining biodiversity decline will be climate change in polar regions and land-use change (habitat disruption) in the tropics. Temperate ecosystems were estimated to experience the least biodiversity change because major land-use changes have already occurred. There are far more plant and animal species, and apparently a far higher number of species becoming extinct, in the tropics than in polar regions. Therefore on a global basis, habitat disruption will continue to be the major impact on animal and plant species.

Not all of the impacts on ecosystems of projected climate change will be negative. As in the case of agriculture, a warmer, wetter, higher CO_2 world will be beneficial for uncultivated plants. Global ecosystem models project higher net biomass production, and observations of a variety of tree species indicate that they are already responding to higher atmospheric concentrations of CO_2 and higher temperatures with increased growth rates. Warmer, wetter conditions, and increased biomass production, also could be expected to benefit some animal species.

Animal and Plant Responses to Climate Change

There is agreement among experts that animals that are capable of moving will attempt to migrate in response to climate change. The movements of commercially important species, such as cod, in response to changes in ocean temperature, have been documented for centuries. More recent studies show that a variety of animal species have moved in response to the warming of the 20th century.

Individual plants cannot migrate, but plant species can and do migrate in response to changes in climate. All plants have seed dispersal mechanisms and therefore are constantly trying to establish seedlings in new areas. Seedlings thrive in a more desirable climate, but fail in a less desirable climate, moving the range of the plant as climate changes. The total change in range can be dramatic. Fossil evidence indicate that since the end of the last Ice Age, the balsam fir migrated from the southeastern U.S. to northern Canada, while the black spruce migrated from the central plains to Alaska.

While it is agreed that plants and animals could migrate in response to climate change, at least four further concerns are raised about the likelihood that this will occur to a sufficient degree to prevent large scale species extinction:

1. human activities, particularly habitat disruption, will block potential migration routes;
2. even if they can migrate, the members of a given ecosystem will migrate at different rates leading to imbalances that will result in species extinctions;
3. plants may not be able to migrate fast enough to keep up with projected rates of climate change; and
4. plants and animals that live in restricted niches, e.g., near mountain tops, will have no place to migrate.

These concerns assume no human intervention to help wild species to adapt to climate change. In light of the growing and successful effort to reintroduce species such as beaver and wolf to their former habitats, to replant native plants, and to remove invasive plant species, this assumption is overly conservative.

Can Species Migrate Given Habitat Disruption and Other Human Activities?

Human activities have fragmented the areas in which many plants and animals can thrive. The remaining habitats are often pictured as "islands," which climate change could make unattractive to the species that live there. Migration to other "islands" could be difficult or impossible because the paths for that migration would be blocked by farms, cities, etc. However, recent studies raise questions about this conceptual model. Many species have been shown to either make use of fairly limited habitats or use multiple habitats to provide the area they need.

A recent *New York Times* article quoted Dr. John Wiens, a professor of ecology at Colorado State University, as follows:

> "We need to shift our thinking away from isolated areas in the midst of inhospitable human development," he said. "They're not oceanic islands." Only if biologists think of fragments in the context of an overall landscape, he went on, can they help manage, conserve and restore these habitats.

The *New York Times* article went on to cite the work of Dr. Diane Debinski, a professor of animal ecology at Iowa State University. She found that even "habitat sensitive" species, which tend to stay in the interior of a particular "island," were present in greater number when those habitats were replicated in an attempt to provide a larger area of suitable habitat for these species. These results show that species are able to make use of all available suitable habitats, even if they are fragmented.

As noted above, habitat disruption is projected to be the largest contributor to human-induced species extinction in the 21st century. The steps that society will need to take to reverse this trend should also make it possible for plant and animal species to migrate in face of whatever climate change may occur in the future. . . .

Can Plants Migrate Fast Enough?

The IPCC summarizes the knowledge about the rate of plant species migration as follows:

> Many studies of past changes have estimated natural rates of migration of trees ranging from 40 to 500 meters per year. . . . Gear and Huntly calculated from several sites in Britain migration rates of Scot's pine of only 40–80 meters per year. However, for other species, such as white spruce, much faster dispersal rates of 1–2 kilometers per year have also been reported. It is not always clear whether observed past rates were maximal rates of migration or whether they were limited by the rate at which the climate changed.

The IPCC concludes that these rates of migration are slower than the 1.5–5.5 kilometers per year that trees would have to migrate to keep up with projected rates of warming. However, this analysis assumes that a tree's habitat is a fixed point. Viable trees have ranges that cover many kilometers. Climate change might reduce that range in the short-term, but climate change alone should not lead to significant rates of extinction. Adaptation, for example, by transplanting tree species, could be beneficial in speeding migration.

Can Species With Already Limited Habitats Survive?

If climate warms, the migration path for plants and animals that live on mountains will be upward. This option is limited, since the plant or animal will soon run out of mountain. Since soil conditions typically become poorer with increasing altitude, other factors may limit migration long before the top of the mountain is reached. For species that have very limited habitats, in the extreme, a single mountain, this could lead to extinction. No doubt some of the past climate-related extinctions occurred for this reason. However, most alpine species have broader habitats than a single mountain and would survive, albeit with a changed habitat.

Summary: Can Plants and Animals Adapt to Climate Change?

The answer to this question has to be yes, since plants and animals have been adapting to climate change for billions of years. However, not all plant and animal species will be successful in adapting. If biologists are correct that natural climate change has been a major factor in past species extinctions, any change in climate, whether natural or human-induced, will increase the risk that some marginal species will become extinct.

Despite the concern about climate change, habitat disruption will continue to be the largest threat posed by human activities to the survival of plant and animal species. Many innovative programs are being undertaken to help plants and animals counter the adverse effects of habitat disruption, and these programs will help make these species more resilient to climate change. However, understanding of ecosystem interactions and the potential impacts of climate change on those interactions is simply inadequate.

Migration is the major response that plants and animals can make to climate change. Many concerns have been raised about the ability of plants and animals to migrate given habitat disruption, scenarios involving high rates of climate change during the 21st century, etc. Societal efforts to counter adverse effects by relocating endangered plant and animal species to more favorable habitats could reduce the impact of these changes. . . .

Conclusions

The destruction of ecosystems and species extinction as a consequence of projected climate change have been reported widely by the media and drive much of the perception of the global warming debate. This study examined available scientific evidence to fairly evaluate the claim that anticipated changes in the Earth's climate will result in unacceptable ecosystem impacts.

There is no question that ecosystems are sensitive to climate change and that any significant change is likely to have detrimental consequences for some ecosystems and some species. However, the scope of these consequences is limited by the ability to adapt to an evolving climate.

With continued adaptation, intensively-managed ecosystems, such [as] farms and commercial forests, can benefit from the levels of climate change projected by the IPCC for the 21st century. Developed countries already have the necessary adaptive capacity, and developing countries will acquire the necessary adaptive capacity as their wealth increases.

Ecosystems, such as wildlife areas, which are currently lightly impacted by human activities, would also benefit from adaptation, but the understanding necessary to plan that adaptation is currently inadequate.

To address these questions in a manner that will provide information and analysis needed to evaluate risks and consequences, decision makers need better tools and better information. These include better models, more robust data collection, and better techniques for estimating species and effects on them.

POSTSCRIPT

Are the Costs of Global Warming Too High to Ignore?

It is reasonable to ask how the scientific community attempts to measure changes in the Earth's surface temperature. Certainly, written records only shed light on a tiny fraction of the Earth's long history, and even in the record books that we do have, written temperature records of more than 100 years ago are not available for large parts of the world.

In place of that written history the scientific community has turned to the physical records left by climatic changes. These appear in the growth rates of trees, sea sediment bore holes, pollen counts, the remains of coral colonies, ice cores, and mountain glacier deposits. They tell us that our world has undergone remarkable changes in the 10,000 years since the end of the last major ice age, which closed the Pleistocene epoch. It is important to examine two major climatic disturbances, which appear in more recent times—the past 1,000 years. Scientists call one of these disturbances the "Little Ice Age," which occurred approximately 1300–1900 A.D. The other anomaly occurred around 1000–1300 A.D. This relatively mild climatic period is called the Medieval Warm Period. It is remarkable in that in some regions radical increases in temperatures occurred. Some suggest that it may help explain the population explosion during the medieval period in Europe. This warm weather may also help explain why this period was marked by the construction of many European cathedrals. See H. H. Lamb, *Climate, History and the Modern World,* 2d ed. (Routledge, 1995).

An apparent conclusion is that global warming is not as clear-cut as some suggest. Simply because we can measure an increase in surface temperatures over a significant period of time may not in and of itself mean that we are experiencing global warming that can be traced to human activity. Rather, this warming may be the natural course of events—events that the world has experienced repeatedly over its long history. For more on that view, read Patrick J. Michaels and Robert Balling, Jr., *Satanic Gases: Clearing the Air About Global Warming* (Cato Institute, 2000). In it, the authors argue that those who warn of global warming have blown the issue all out of proportion and in the process have ignored all the evidence that suggests the contrary.

The other side is not mute on this issue. Indeed, there are many Web sites devoted to the issue of global warming. To read about the Kyoto Protocol, see http://unfccc.int/resource/convkp.html . Alternatively, visit the United Nations Industrial Development Organization's (UNIDO) Web site at http://www.unido.org/doc/ 3941. For a scholarly, balanced view, turn to Warwick J. McKibbin and Peter Wilcoxen's *Climate Change Policy After Kyoto: A Blueprint for a Realistic Approach* (Brookings Institution Press, 2002).

ISSUE 16

Are Spending Cuts the Right Way to Balance the Federal Government's Budget?

YES: Chris Edwards, from "Statement," Senate Committee on Finance, Subcommittee on Long-Term Growth and Debt Reduction (September 28, 2006)

NO: Charlie Stenholm, from "Testimony," Senate Committee on Finance, Subcommittee on Long-Term Growth and Debt Reduction (September 28, 2006)

ISSUE SUMMARY

YES: Chris Edwards, director of tax policy studies at the Cato Institute, believes that federal government overspending is the cause of its current fiscal problems. Higher taxes are not the solution because they "would result in greater tax avoidance, slower growth, less reported income, and thus less than expected tax revenue, perhaps prompting policymakers to jack up tax rates even higher."

NO: Former congressman Charlie Stenholm argues that in addressing deficit and debt problems, everything should be on the table. He stresses that addressing long-term fiscal challenges will require "some combination of stronger economic growth, restraining health care costs, scaling back benefit promises of entitlement programs, increasing the eligibility age for Social Security and Medicare, increasing revenues, and other tough choices."

$\mathbf{T}$he Full Employment and Balanced Growth Act of 1978 lists a number of economic goals for the federal government. Besides the familiar objectives of full employment, price stability, and increased real income, the act specifically mentions the goal of a balanced federal budget. This means that the government is to collect in taxes an amount equal to its expenditures. Despite this legislative call to action, the federal government has, with few exceptions, failed to balance its budget, and recent deficits have been large. For example, between 1940 and 1975 there were only two instances when the deficit was in excess of $50 billion. For the years 1980 through 1990, the federal government deficit averaged about $140 billion. Budget deficits continued until fiscal year 1998: Budget surpluses were recorded in that fiscal year and in each of the next three fiscal years. But the budget then returned to deficit and the estimates are for deficits of $423 billion and $354 billion for fiscal years 2006 and 2007 (*Economic Report of the President, 2006*).

When the federal government runs a deficit, it sells treasury bills, notes, and bonds. In this respect, the government is just like a business firm that sells securities to raise funds. The total of outstanding government securities is called the public or national debt. Thus, when the federal government runs a deficit, the public debt increases by the amount of the deficit. Thus, the public debt at any point in time is a summary of all prior deficits (offset by the retirement of securities if the government chooses to repurchase its securities when it has a budget surplus). By December 2006 the gross federal debt was approximately $8.6 trillion.

But why do deficits arise? One possibility is that the government spends more than it collects in revenues because it does not exercise fiscal restraint: It may be easy for politicians to spend money, but it is difficult for them to increase taxes to fund additional spending. The budget position of the government is also influenced by the state of the economy. The deficit is likely to increase if the economy enters a recession. A downturn in economic activity will decrease tax revenues (lower incomes mean less tax revenue) and will increase government spending (more expenditures for programs such as unemployment compensation). Because a deficit can arise for different reasons, it is important to understand exactly what forces create a deficit.

Another major question about deficits concerns their economic consequences. Some people perceive the deficits as harmful. With a deficit, the government borrows funds that otherwise would be have been available to business firms who might have built new factories or purchased new machinery with the borrowed funds. This is referred to as *crowding out*, since government borrowing to finance deficits presumably reduces the funds available for private investment. The reduction in investment slows the growth of productivity, and this means that the ability of the economy to produce goods and services is also reduced.

Both of the selected views agree that budget deficits must be slashed and the public debt kept from rising, but they disagree on how to achieve this. Chris Edwards, who views the problem primarily as one of overspending, recommends controlling spending, particularly on social programs, and tighter budget rules. Charlie Stenholm agrees that tighter rules are necessary; but he also believes that some tax cuts that are about to expire should be allowed to expire because this will increase government revenues.

YES

Chris Edwards

America's Public Debt: How Do We Keep It from Rising?

Mr. Chairman and members of the committee, thank you for inviting me to testify today on the topic of controlling growth in the federal public debt. Federal debt continues to rise as spending growth keeps running ahead of the increased tax revenues the government is enjoying as a result of the strong economy. I will discuss some of the relationships between federal debt, spending, and taxation in light of recent budget developments.

Background: The Cost of Federal Spending

To support its large budget, the federal government will extract $2.4 trillion in taxes and about $300 billion in borrowed funds from families, businesses, and investors in fiscal 2006. That extraction transfers resources from the more productive private sector to the generally less productive government sector of the economy. Many studies have shown that, all else equal, the larger the government's share of the economy, the slower economic growth will be.[1] That is true regardless of whether higher spending is financed by increased taxes or higher deficits, which can be considered deferred taxes on future generations.

It is clear that a larger federal budget results in slower growth when you consider that a big share of spending is aimed at "social" goals, not at spurring growth. Indeed, 50 percent of the federal budget goes to transfers, which are typically justified on "fairness" grounds, not economic grounds.[2] For example, the largest federal program, Social Security, has a negative impact on growth the way it is currently structured. People may support the current Social Security system for non-economic reasons, but economists believe that its pay-as-you-go structure reduces national savings and economic growth.

An additional problem is that extracting the current and future taxes needed to support federal spending is a complex and economically damaging process. As a result, substantially more than one dollar of private activities are displaced for every added dollar of spending. Those added costs are called "deadweight losses," which are inefficiencies created by distortions to working, investment, and entrepreneurship. Those distortions reduce the nation's standard of living.

From Senate Committee on Finance, Subcommittee on Long-Term Growth and Debt Reduction, Chris Edwards (September 28, 2006).

The Congressional Budget Office found that "typical estimates of the economic [deadweight] cost of a dollar of tax revenue range from 20 cents to 60 cents over and above the revenue raised."[3] Studies by Harvard's Martin Feldstein have found that deadweight losses are even larger. He noted that "the deadweight burden caused by incremental taxation . . . may exceed one dollar per dollar of revenue raised, making the cost of incremental governmental spending more than two dollars for each dollar of government spending."[4]

What this means is that the large increases in federal spending of recent years will create a substantial toll on the economy because current or future taxes will be higher than otherwise to fund the expansion. There is no free lunch on the spending side of the federal budget, but we can minimize the damage of raising federal funds by continuing to reform the most distortionary aspects of the income tax system.

Deficits and Tax Cuts

Policymakers opposed to recent tax cuts have argued that tax cuts that are "financed by deficits" don't do much good for the economy. It is true that recent tax cuts have not benefited the economy as much as they would have if they had been matched by spending cuts.[5] To the extent that recent tax cuts have added to federal deficits, a burden is imposed on future taxpayers (assuming that federal spending is not affected).[6]

However, there is a crucial point to consider with regard to the debate over recent tax cuts and budget deficits—*not all tax cuts are created equal*. "Supply-side" tax cuts that reduce distortions in the tax code will spur economic growth and will not create as large a revenue loss as static calculations suggest. Any added debt from such tax cuts can be compared against the larger gross domestic product that will be generated. Supply-side tax cuts that represent long-term reforms of the federal fiscal system should be implemented regardless of the current budget balance. By contrast, further "social policy" tax cuts that do not simplify the tax code or make it more efficient should be avoided, or at least not considered unless they are matched by equal spending cuts.

Numerous studies have found that supply-side tax cuts on capital income are particularly beneficial to the economy. A 2005 Joint Committee on Taxation study presented the results of a macroeconomic simulation of hypothetical personal and corporate income tax cuts.[7] They found that a corporate tax rate cut (matched by spending cuts) boosted U.S. output twice as much in the long run as an individual rate cut of the same dollar magnitude. The JCT also found that there are much larger positive growth effects when tax cuts are offset by spending cuts to prevent the deficit from increasing.

Federal tax legislation since 2001 has been a mix of supply-side and social policy cuts. About 55 percent of recent tax cuts have been supply-side tax cuts, including the reductions in individual rates, the dividend and capital gains tax cuts, small business expensing, and the liberalization of savings accounts.[8] The other 45 percent of recent tax cuts have been social policy tax cuts, including the new 10 percent income tax bracket, the expansion of the child tax credit, and various education tax benefits.

The economic impact of social policy tax cuts, if combined with higher deficits, is mixed at best because those cuts generally do not reduce the dead-weight losses of the tax system. By contrast, supply-side tax cuts boost long-term economic growth.[9] The dividend and capital gains tax cuts of 2003, for example, have helped to reduce long-recognized distortions caused by the double taxation of corporate equity. The markets have responded strongly to the dividend and capital gains cuts, indicating that the prior high rates were creating substantial distortions.

Spending Increases, Not Tax Cuts, Are the Problem

Have tax cuts or spending increases caused today's large budget deficits? Federal outlays have increased from $1.9 trillion in fiscal 2001 to $2.7 trillion by fiscal 2006, an increase of $800 billion. By contrast, the tax cuts enacted in 2001 and 2003 have reduced federal revenues by roughly $200 billion this year.[10] Thus, recent spending increases are four times more important in explaining the current budget deficit than are recent tax cuts.[11]

Another way to think about recent tax cuts is that they have helped reverse the large tax increases of 1990 and 1993. CBO data shows that those tax increases increased federal revenues by a combined 1.1 percent of GDP over the first five years after each was enacted. The 2001 and 2003 tax cuts reduced revenues by a similar magnitude of 1.2 percent of GDP over the first five years after each was enacted.[12]

Regardless of whether or not one supports recent tax cuts, it is clear that there are gigantic long-term fiscal problems on the spending side of the budget. The Government Accountability Office has projected a long-range business-as-usual scenario for the budget.[13] The projections assume that entitlement programs are not reformed, and that other programs and taxes stay at the same size as today relative to GDP. Under that scenario, federal spending would grow from 20 percent of GDP today to a staggering 45 percent of GDP by 2040. Such a European-sized government would bring with it slow growth, lower wages, a lack of opportunities, and many other pathologies.

Unfortunately, the long-term fiscal situation could be even worse than that. The GAO's "static" estimates ignore the economic death spiral that would occur if taxes were raised in an attempt to fund higher spending. Higher taxes would result in greater tax avoidance, slower growth, less reported income, and thus less than expected tax revenue, perhaps prompting policymakers to jack up tax rates even higher.

Consider Social Security and Medicare Part A, which are funded by the federal payroll tax. On a static basis, the cost of these two programs as a share of taxable wages is projected to rise from 14 percent in 2005 to 25 percent in 2040.[14] But as tax rates rise, the tax base will shrink. To get the money it would need to pay for rising benefits, and taking into account this dynamic effect, the government would have to hike the payroll tax rate to about 30 percent by 2040.[15] That would be a crushing blow to working Americans, who would have to pay this tax in addition to all the other federal and state taxes they pay.

Note that on top of these federal costs, state and local governments are also imposing large and unfunded obligations on future generations. State and local governments have rapidly rising levels of bond debt, and they have unfunded costs for their workers' pension and health plans that could total more than $2 trillion.[16]

Reform Options

These figures suggest a bleak fiscal future awaiting young Americans and taxpayers without major reforms. There are many actions that should be taken right away to reduce deficits and unfunded obligations.

- Social Security should be cut by indexing future initial benefits to the growth in prices rather than wages.
- Medicare deductibles and premiums should be increased. Those changes could be phased-in over time, but it is important to get the needed cuts signed into law to reduce the exposure of taxpayers.
- Medicaid should be block-granted and the federal contribution to the program restrained or cut. This was the successful strategy behind the 1996 welfare reform.
- Federalism should be revived and federal aid to the states cut sharply. Aid to the states does not make any economic sense. It has been a bastion of "pork" spending, and it has created massive bureaucracies at all three levels of government. With the coming entitlement crunch, the federal government simply cannot afford to be Santa Claus to the states any longer.

Of course, such cuts are politically difficult for Congress to make. That is why new budgeting structures are needed to get a handle on rising spending and deficits. Considering that federal outlays have increased 45 percent in the last five years and the government has run deficits in 33 of the last 37 years, it is obvious that current budget rules are not working very well.

That is why budget reform proposals, such Senator Gregg's "Stop Over Spending Act of 2006" (S. 3521) are important.[17] The Act contains new rules to control deficits, restrain entitlement spending, cap discretionary spending, limit "emergency" spending, and create a commission to eliminate waste in federal programs.

Some people argue that such new budget restrictions are not needed because Congress has the power to restrain spending anytime it wants. But political scientists have long recognized that the self-interested actions of individual policymakers often lead to overall legislative outcomes that undermine the general welfare. Indeed, frequent statements by many policymakers make it clear that their top priority is to target spending to interests in their states, not to legislate in the national interest. If left to their own devices, many members become activists for narrow causes, while broader concerns such as the size of the federal debt are ignored.

New and improved federal budget rules are needed to channel the energies of members into reforms that are in the interests of average citizens and taxpayers. Without tight budget rules, Capitol Hill descends into an "every man for himself" spending stampede—a budget anarchy that creates unsustainable budget expansion and soaring deficits. That is why there have been numerous, and often bipartisan, efforts to create new budget procedures, such the 1974 Budget Act, the 1985 Gramm-Rudman-Hollings Act, and the 1990 Budget Enforcement Act.

Consider also that the 50 states generally have much tighter budget rules than does the federal government.[18] Virtually all the states have statutory or constitutional requirements to balance their budgets. Governors in 42 states have line-item veto authority. Most state constitutions include limitations on government debt. More than half the states have some form of overall tax and expenditure limitation (TEL).[19] Also, the states are fiscally constrained by the need to prevent their bond ratings from falling.

Capping Total Federal Spending

Senator Gregg's proposals are a good starting point for discussing budget reforms, but Congress should also consider a more comprehensive budget control idea. That is to impose a statutory cap on the annual growth in total federal outlays, including discretionary and entitlement spending.[20] Deficits are a byproduct of the overspending problem, and such a cap would target that core problem directly. The basic principle of a budget growth cap is that the government should live within constraints, as average families do, and not consume an increasing share of the nation's output.

Prior budget control efforts have imposed caps on discretionary spending, but not entitlement spending. Yet the rapid growth in entitlement spending may cause a major budget crisis, and thus should be included under any cap. There has been interest in capping entitlements in the past. In 1992, the bipartisan Strengthening of America Commission, headed by Sens. Sam Nunn (D-GA) and Pete Domenici (R-NM), proposed capping all non-Social Security entitlement spending at the growth rate of inflation plus the number of beneficiaries in programs.[21] The Entitlement Control Act of 1994 (H.R. 4593) introduced by Rep. Charles Stenholm (D-TX) would have capped the growth in all entitlement programs to inflation plus one percent plus the number of beneficiaries. Both of those proposals included procedures for sequestering entitlement spending with broad cuts if the caps were breached.

A simple way to structure a cap is to limit annual spending growth to the growth in an economic indicator such as personal income. Another possible cap is the sum of population growth plus inflation. In that case, if population grew at 1 percent and inflation was 3 percent, then federal spending could grow at most by 4 percent. That is the limit used in Colorado's successful "TABOR" budget law. Whichever indicator is used should be smoothed by averaging it over about five years.

An interesting alternative would be to simply cap total federal spending growth at a fixed percentage, such as four percent. That would make it easy for

Congress to plan ahead in budgeting, and would prevent efforts to change caps by fudging estimates of economic indicators. Another interesting advantage of a fixed percentage cap is that it would provide an incentive for Congress to support a low inflation policy by the Federal Reserve Board.

With a spending cap in place, Congress would pass annual budget resolutions making sure that discretionary and entitlement spending was projected to fit under the cap for upcoming years. Reconciliation instructions could be included to reduce entitlement spending to fit under the cap for the current budget year and to reduce out-year spending to fit under projected future caps.

The Office of Management and Budget would provide regular updates regarding whether spending is likely to breach the annual cap, and Congress could take corrective actions as needed. If a session ended and the OMB determined that outlays were still above the cap, the president would be required to cut, or sequester, spending across the board by the amount needed. The GRH and the BEA included sequester mechanisms that covered only portions of the defense, nondefense, and entitlement budgets, but a sequester on the overall budget would be a better approach.

A shortcoming of a statutory spending cap and other budget rules is that Congress would always have the option of rewriting the law if it didn't want to comply. But a cap on overall spending would be a very simple and high-profile symbol of restraint for supporters in Congress and the public to rally around and defend. An overall cap on spending growth of, say, four percent is easy to understand, and watchdog groups would keep the public informed about any cheating by policymakers. Over time, public awareness and budgetary tradition would aid in the enforcement of a cap.

Conclusion

Federal policymakers need a change in mindset and tougher budget rules to ward off large tax hikes and rising debt as entitlement costs soar in future years. Policymakers need to scour the budget for programs and agencies to cut.[22] A cap on total federal spending should be part of the solution to get the budget under control. Clearly, current budget rules have not worked very well, and we should experiment with new rules to try and get a grip on the overspending problem.

Thank you for holding these important hearings. I look forward to working with the committee on its agenda for federal budget reform.

Notes

1. See James Gwartney and Robert Lawson, "Economic Freedom of the World: 2004 Annual Report," Fraser Institute, 2004, and see James Gwartney and Robert Lawson, "Economic Freedom of the World: 2005 Annual Report," Fraser Institute, 2005. For a summary of academic studies, see Daniel J. Mitchell, "The Impact of Government Spending on Economic Growth," Heritage Foundation, March 15, 2005. To state this relationship more precisely, if the government

increases its share of the economy beyond a certain modest level of about 15 percent, then growth begins to suffer.

2. Transfers are 50 percent of total program outlays (outlays excluding interest). See Chris Edwards "How to Spend $2.8 Trillion," Cato Institute Tax & Budget Bulletin no. 39, August 2006.

3. Congressional Budget Office, "Budget Options," February 2001, p. 381. For a general discussion, see Chris Edwards, "Economic Benefits of Personal Income Tax Rate Reductions," U.S. Congress, Joint Economic Committee, April 2001. See also William Niskanen, "The Economic Burden of Taxation," presented at a conference at the Federal Reserve Bank of Dallas, Texas, October 22–23, 2003.

4. Martin Feldstein, "How Big Should Government Be?" *National Tax Journal*, Volume 50, no. 2, June 1997, pp. 197–213.

5. Tax cuts matched by spending cuts produce much stronger growth effects in the long run. See the various simulations in Joint Committee on Taxation, "Macroeconomic Analysis of Various Proposals to Provide $500 Billion in Tax Relief," JCX-4-05, March 1, 2005.

6. If higher deficits create a "starve the beast" effect resulting in lower spending, then tax cuts now will not lead to equally large tax increases later.

7. Joint Committee on Taxation, "Macroeconomic Analysis of Various Proposals to Provide $500 Billion in Tax Relief," JCX-4-05, March 1, 2005.

8. Based on the dollar values of extending the cuts between 2012 and 2016. See Office of Management and Budget, *Midsession Review Fiscal Year 2007*, July 11, 2006, Table S-6. The estate tax is not included.

9. For example, see Joint Committee on Taxation, "Macroeconomic Analysis of Various Proposals to Provide $500 Billion in Tax Relief," JCX-4-05, March 1, 2005.

10. Based on CBO's estimate of the revenue loss from EGTRRA and JGTRRA in fiscal 2012 as a share of GDP, then applied to GDP in fiscal 2006. I have not included the alternative minimum tax.

11. Note that this estimate of federal revenue losses is on a static basis. The actual loss is likely to be smaller because of the positive economic effects of the cuts.

12. Chris Edwards, "Social Policy, Supply-Side, and Fundamental Reform: Republican Tax Policy, 1994 to 2004," *Tax Notes*, November 1, 2004, p. 691.

13. Government Accountability Office, "21st Century Challenges: Reexamining the Base of the Federal Government," GAO-05-325SP, February 2005, Figure 2, p. 8.

14. *The 2005 Annual Report of the Board of Trustees of the Federal Old-Age and Survivors Insurance and the Federal Disability Insurance Trust Funds* (Washington: Government Printing Office, April 5, 2005), p. 166. These are the intermediate assumptions.

15. Estimate based on Martin Feldstein, "Prefunding Medicare," National Bureau of Economic Research, Working Paper no. 6917, January 1999, p. 4.

16. Chris Edwards and Jagadeesh Gokhale, "Unfunded State and Local Health Costs: $1.4 Trillion," Cato Institute Tax & Budget Bulletin, September 2006.

17. U.S. Senate, Committee on the Budget, "The Stop Over Spending Act of 2006," Senate Report 109–283, July 14, 2006.

18. For background on state budget processes, see National Association of State Budget Officers, "Budget Processes in the States," January 2002.

19. Michael New, "Limiting Government through Direct Democracy," Cato Institute Policy Analysis no. 420, December 13, 2001.

20. For background, see Chris Edwards, "Capping Federal Spending," Cato Institute Tax & Budget Bulletin no. 32, March 2006. Also see Brian Riedl, "Restrain Runaway Spending with a Federal Taxpayers' Bill of Rights," Heritage Foundation, August 27, 2004.

21. The commission was sponsored by the Center for Strategic and International Studies.

22. For detailed discussion of federal programs that should be cut, see Chris Edwards, *Downsizing the Federal Government* (Washington: Cato Institute, 2005).

 **NO**

America's Public Debt: How Do We Keep It from Rising

Mr. Chairman, Senator Kerry and Members of the Committee. I am Charlie Stenholm, former Member of Congress from the 17th District of Texas and currently a Senior Policy Affairs Affairs Advisor at Olsson, Frank and Weeda. I am also a member of the Board of Directors of the Committee for a Responsible Federal Budget and the Concord Coalition. This testimony is my own and does not represent any position or conclusion of any of these organizations.

In my twenty six years in Congress, I worked with many members on both sides of the aisle, including several members of this committee, fighting to leave a better future for our children and grandchildren. We spent many years working extremely hard and casting many tough votes to eliminate the deficit and put us in a position to begin paying down the debt. It has been extremely frustrating to see the fruits of that labor squandered by the "deficit's don't matter" mentality that took hold in recent years. I am hopeful that this hearing and similar discussions about the dangers of continued deficits and the need to take action are a sign that the tide is shifting back to the bipartisan balanced budget consensus we had in the 1990s.

I have been asked to share my thoughts about how to deal with our nation's rising public debt. My testimony can be summarized in three recommendations based on West Texas Tractor Seat Common Sense:

- First, acknowledge that we face a problem. Policymakers need to take to heart the message of The Concord Coalition's Fiscal Wake Up Tour that Bob Bixby described—our nation is on a fiscally unsustainable course and difficult choices must be confronted.
- Second, stop digging the hole deeper through debt financed tax cuts or spending programs.
- Third, begin a bipartisan process in which both parties put everything on the table and honestly negotiate the tradeoffs. . . .

Deficits Do Matter

Some defenders of our current economic and fiscal policies have argued that deficits don't matter. The reality is that deficits do matter, both for our

From Senate Committee on Finance, Subcommittee on Long-Term Growth and Debt Reduction, Charlie Stenholm (September 28, 2006).

economic security today as well as the future we leave for our children and grandchildren.

The United States has been able to sustain large budget deficits without an increase in domestic interest rates because the increased demand for borrowing has been offset by an increased inflow of capital from global markets. Our increased reliance on foreign capital to finance our deficits places our economic security at the mercy of global bankers and foreign governments. If foreign investors stop buying US bonds we would face higher inflation and higher interest rates, putting our economy at risk of a large scale recession.

Large deficits financed by borrowing from foreign investors are also a major factor contributing to the trade deficits which are exporting jobs overseas. We need to keep the value of the dollar high in order to attract the foreign capital we need to finance our debt. If the value of the dollar declines, US bonds will be less valuable to foreign investors. But the strong dollar we need to help Treasury finance our budget deficits hurts our businesses by making US exports more expensive.

Our current borrow and spend policies are worse than the tax and spend policies of the past, because they will leave a crushing debt tax burden for future generations who don't have any say in what we are doing and don't benefit from the tax cuts and spending programs for current generations. Our grandchildren will face ever higher tax burdens simply to cover increasing interest payments instead of addressing other needs such as keeping our military the strongest in the world, protecting our domestic security, providing health care, strengthening Social Security and Medicare, and investing in our education system.

A German philosopher named Dietrich Bonhoeffer once said that the ultimate test of a moral society is the kind of world that it leaves to its children. We cannot leave it to our grandchildren to shoulder the enormous burden of our debt. Our grandchildren do not have a vote. That is why it is so easy for us to say here today we can fight two wars, we can fund homeland security, we can fight the war on terrorism, we can rebuild the Gulf Coast and we can keep cutting taxes, because we are going to send the bill to our grandchildren. . . .

The First Step Toward Getting Out of the Deficit Hole: Quit Digging

My philosophy on budget issues has always begun with some simple West Texas Tractor Seat Common Sense—When you find yourself in a hole, the first rule is to quit digging. Unfortunately, the legislative agenda is filled with items that would dig the hole deeper through tax cuts and increased spending. The most notable example was the so-called trifecta bill which combined a temporary extension of business tax breaks, a permanent reduction in the estate tax and a new mandatory spending program for mine reclamation along with an increase in the minimum wage. . . .

Dealing with our budget deficit must begin with reinstatement of budget enforcement rules to take away the shovels from Congress and the administration by restricting the ability of Congress and the President to enact legislation that would increase the deficit. The pay as you go budget enforcement rules and discretionary spending limits, which Congress and the President enacted in 1990 and extended in 1997 with bipartisan support, were an important part of getting a handle on the deficits in the early 1990s and getting the budget back into balance.

Reinstating paygo rules and discretionary spending limits would not balance the budget by themselves, but would represent an important first step in bringing discipline to the budget process by prohibiting policy changes that would further enlarge the deficit. They have been tested, and they worked. They didn't always work perfectly, but there is no question that they significantly improved the responsibility and accountability of the budget process.

The principle of paygo—if we want to reduce our revenues or increase our spending, we need to say how we would pay for it within our budget—is something all families understand. If we want to reduce our revenues, we need to say what spending we will do without. If we want to increase spending, we need to say where we will come up with the revenues for the new spending or what other spending we will do without.

The concept of applying PAYGO rules to all legislation—spending and revenues—has received support from both sides of the aisle since it was originally enacted. "Two-sided" PAYGO was originally enacted in the bipartisan budget agreement of 1990 and extended in the bipartisan balanced budget agreement of 1997. Furthermore, it was included in the budget passed by the Republican Congress in 1995. Applying pay-as-you-go rules to tax cuts does not prevent Congress from passing more tax cuts. All it requires is that Congress must identify another source of revenue or spending reduction if it wants to enact or extend a tax cut.

Those who want to extend expiring tax cuts or make the tax cuts permanent should be willing to put forward the spending cuts or other offsets necessary to pay for them. Similarly, those who want to spend more in certain areas need to be willing to say where they would cut or how they would raise revenues to pay for their proposals.

I would say with all due respect to my Republican friends that if you are sincere in what say about controlling spending, you should not have a problem with reinstating pay as you go for taxes as well as spending because it would force Congress to actually cut spending to accompany tax cuts instead of just promising to cut spending in the future. The problem is that the actions of the majority in Congress haven't matched the rhetoric. Congress and the administration have cut taxes without cutting spending, and have charged the difference to our children and grandchildren by increasing the deficit.

The pay-as-you-go principle is not simply a matter of bookkeeping, but a key element of sound economic policymaking. A recent report issued by the Treasury Department providing a dynamic analysis of proposals to permanently extend the 2001 and 2003 tax cuts illustrate the importance of offsetting the revenue loss from tax cuts. Although the report cited economic models which found that certain tax cuts can result in higher savings and increasing capital stock the report noted that "when lower taxes on capital income are financed initially by issuing government debt, private investment is crowded out by an increase in government borrowing," limiting the economic benefit from the tax cuts. The report went on to say that in some instances the benefits from tax relief that increases the deficit are more than offset by the financing of government debt.

No reputable analyst believes that cutting taxes will result in higher revenues than would have occurred without the tax cut. While some tax cuts may result in economic growth that produces some revenue feedback, there is no credible analysis that claims those potential benefits would offset the revenue loss. Analyses from the Congressional Budget Office, the Joint Committee on Taxation, the Federal Reserve Board, and the President's own Council of Economic Advisors have all concluded that the tax cuts enacted over the last four years will have little or no impact on long term economic growth and cause deficits to be larger than they otherwise would have been.

Put Everything on the Table

A serious discussion about balancing the budget will require both parties to make sacrifices. All areas of the budget must be on the table and the burden of deficit reduction should be distributed fairly across the budget. I have always said that those of us in agriculture are willing to accept our fair share of reductions if all other areas of the budget are asked to sacrifice as well, but we aren't willing to shoulder an undue burden of cuts so that other areas of the budget can avoid budget discipline. I believe that this view is shared by advocates of other areas of the budget as well.

The Promise to Our Children and Grandchildren being circulated by For Our Grandchildren, a bipartisan Social Security education organization which has retained me as a spokesman, embodies this approach. The promise asks candidates to seek an honest, bipartisan debate about Social Security and find responsible solutions to meet these challenges that the system will face in the years ahead. It doesn't commit candidates to any specific policy proposals. Rather, it calls on policymakers to put all options on the table to develop a solution which honestly addresses the pressure that the unfunded obligations that the current system will place on taxpayers and other budgetary priorities in a way that is fair to all generations, protects current retirees and strengthens the safety net for the most vulnerable. If all candidates from both parties conduct themselves in this spirit in the debate over Social Security and our other fiscal challenges it will be much easier to reach bipartisan agreement on responsible solutions.

The renewed public focus on the need to address the long-term problems facing entitlement programs has been encouraging. However, rhetoric about the need to make tough choices with regard to entitlement programs is undercut when it is not matched by a willingness to make similarly tough choices on the revenue side of the ledger. It is fiscally irresponsible and politically unrealistic to call for reforms of entitlement programs in the name of fiscal discipline while simultaneously advocating tax cuts that will make the short term deficit and long term fiscal imbalance worse. It is neither fiscally responsible nor politically viable to make cutbacks in some areas of the budget in the name of deficit reduction while exempting other areas of the budget from budget discipline. That is particularly true when deficit reduction efforts focus on the most vulnerable in society, while benefits for those in a better position to accept sacrifices are left untouched. It will take everyone pulling to get the wagon out of the ditch; we won't be able to get it out if some people are riding.

One specific proposal that would provide a substantial source of savings in a way that spreads the burden of deficit reduction broadly is utilizing a more accurate measure for indexing government programs as well as tax brackets and other provisions in the tax code. There is broad agreement among economists that the Consumer Price Index currently used for indexation of government programs overstates inflation. The Bureau of Labor Statistics has begun to publish a new "Chained Consumer Price Index" to provide a more accurate measure of inflation. Using the Chained CPI for indexation of government programs represents sound policy that reflects years of work by economists and other technical experts. Just as importantly, this proposal would achieve substantial budgetary savings—approximately $50 billion over the next five years—in a way which would spread the burden of deficit reduction fairly across the entire span of government.

Increasing the Debt Limit

This Committee has been called on to raise the debt limit four times in the last five years to finance our deficit problem, and probably will need to be asked to do so again next year. While raising the debt limit is something that Congress must do, increasing the debt limit should be accompanied by a full and open debate about the fiscal policies that have made the increase necessary and a discussion about what should be done to stem the tide of red ink. In addition, I believe that any long-term increase in the debt limit should be accompanied by a plan to restore fiscal discipline. I would propose that when Treasury indicates that it is nearing the debt limit Congress approve a short term increase in the debt limit to avert the imminent crisis and provide for a longer increase in the debt limit contingent upon Congress taking action to reinstate paygo rules and other budget enforcement mechanisms.

Addressing Long-Term Fiscal Problems

Although our near term budget deficits are cause for concern in their own right, what makes them particularly worrisome is the looming financial pressures we will face when the baby boom generation begins to retire in 2008. We need to bring more attention to the long-term liabilities facing our nation as part of the budget process.

I had hoped that last year would be the year that Congress and the President would take action to address the financial challenges facing Social Security, but neither party seemed interested in a serious discussion about the tough choices that will be necessary. These challenges will continue to get worse and become harder to address the longer we wait.

According to projections by the Government Accountability Office (GAO), the combination of allowing the growth of entitlement programs to continue unchecked and making tax cuts permanent while keeping discretionary spending constant as a percentage of GDP will result in a deficit of 10 percent of GDP by 2024. By 2030, the costs of Social Security, Medicare, Medicaid and interest on the debt would consume nearly 22 percent of GDP and the debt to GDP ratio would be 150%.

While the higher revenues from allowing the tax cuts to expire would fall far short of closing this long-term fiscal imbalance, it makes no sense to make the gap worse by locking in permanently lower revenues *before* restraining the growth of entitlement spending. Unless Congress enacts major reforms slowing the growth of entitlement spending, revenues will need to increase well above current levels to meet these obligations and keep up with the growth in spending associated with the baby boomers' retirement and health care costs. Congress should defer action on any tax cuts or entitlement spending increases with long term costs—including extension of the tax cuts which expire in 2010 or expansion of Medicare prescription drug benefit—until Congress has addressed the existing long-term fiscal challenges.

There is no magic bullet that will solve our long term fiscal challenges by itself. While stronger economic growth will help meet the burden of an aging population, higher economic growth alone will not be enough. GAO has estimated that we would need double-digit real economic growth for many decades to grow our way out of the fiscal problems. Slowing the rapid growth of health care spending will need to be part of the solution, but a substantial gap would remain even if we were somehow able to eliminate all excess health care cost growth. Proposals that have been put forward to raise revenues to finance the growing costs of entitlement programs should be considered, but it is unrealistic to expect that it is politically feasible or economically desirable to raise taxes enough to close the gap. Although I personally believe that individual accounts can be an important component of a comprehensive reform plan by providing a higher returns on worker contributions and a more reliable method of pre-funding benefit promises than government trust funds, they do not provide a painless solution to the financial challenges facing Social Security as some have claimed.

A serious solution to our long term fiscal challenges will likely require some combination of stronger economic growth, restraining the growth of health care costs, scaling back benefit promises of entitlement programs, increasing the eligibility age for Social Security and Medicare, increasing revenues, and other tough choices. There is plenty of room for debate over the exact mix of options that should be included in a plan, but policymakers need to begin by acknowledging that the solution will require tough choices and difficult tradeoffs.

Fiscal Commission

The experience of last year in which neither party in Congress was willing to take action on the financial challenges facing Social Security convinced me that we need to establish a bipartisan commission to objectively review the fiscal challenges facing our nation and make recommendations to Congress and the President about how to put the nation back on a fiscally sustainable course.

Senator George Voinovich and Congressman Frank Wolf have introduced legislation, the Securing America's Future Economy (SAFE) Act which would establish such a commission. The commission would solicit input from the public and develop proposals to address four key concerns:

1. The unsustainable gap between projected spending and revenue,
2. The need to increase national savings,
3. The implications of foreign ownership of U.S. government debt, and
4. The lack of emphasis on long-term planning in the budget process.

Congress and the president would be required to act on the proposal developed by the Commission under a fast track procedure. . . .

There is justifiably cynicism in Washington about proposals to establish a commission to study an issue. There are bookshelves filled with dust-covered reports from commissions that went nowhere. A commission isn't a silver bullet that will solve our problems. It will still take action by Members of Congress and the administration to make the tough choices. But a commission that reflects the principles I have outlined could provide the leadership necessary to get the process started in a constructive fashion, especially if the President follows through on his pledge to address the issue in a bipartisan manner and continues to make addressing the long-term challenges facing entitlement programs a priority.

Conclusion

Reaching consensus on a balanced package that will prevent the publicly held debt from growing to unsustainable levels will require all of us to accept sacrifices. As long as everyone advocates balancing the budget by cutting someone else's priorities, talk about deficit reduction will remain just that. As a farmer, I choose to be an optimist and believe that all sides will be willing to put aside their individual political interests to find a solution that is in the best interests of our nation and our children's future.

POSTSCRIPT

Are Spending Cuts the Right Way to Balance the Federal Government's Budget?

Chris Edwards defends supply-side tax cuts because they reduce distortions and increase economic efficiency by increasing the incentive to work, save, and invest. For example, corporate tax rate cuts benefit the economy, and there is evidence that if they are matched by spending cuts, there are large positive growth effects. He argues that an increase in federal spending on "social goals" causes slower economic growth. Higher taxes would result in more tax avoidance and slower growth, and would not solve the deficit problem. He recommends cutting Social Security by indexing future initial benefits to the inflation rate instead of wages, making changes to Medicare (increasing premiums and deductibles) and Medicaid (which should be block-granted), and cutting federal aid to states. New budgeting restrictions are needed to overcome the political difficulty of making the cuts. These include a cap on discretionary and entitlement spending. For example, annual spending growth could be limited to the growth in personal income or some other economic indicator such as the rates of growth of population and inflation combined, or even to a fixed percentage.

Charlie Stenholm condemns current "borrow-and-spend policies" as worse than past tax-and-spend policies because they impose a large burden on future generations. He recommends pay-as-you-go rules and limits on discretionary spending as an important first step towards fiscal discipline. He maintains there is no credible analysis showing that potential benefits of tax cuts would offset revenue losses. Extension of tax cuts must be deferred as must entitlement spending increases, at least until Congress addresses the long-term fiscal challenges.

Data on deficits and debt can be found in the yearly *Economic Report of the President.* Even more detail can be found in *Budget of the United States Government: Citizen's Guide to the Federal Budget* (Congressional Budget Office). Additional testimony was presented at the Senate subcommittee hearings from which the Edwards and Stenholm statements are taken: See the statement by Robert L. Bixby on behalf of The Concord Coalition and "Long-term Growth, Government Debt, and Family Incomes" by Joseph A. Peckman of the Brookings Institution. The Concord Coalition is a nonpartisan organization concerned with prudent fiscal policies. Useful material can be found at their Web site http://www.concordcoalition.org/. Another nonpartisan organization that focuses on the budget is the Center on Budget and Policy Priorities, and their Web site is http://www.cbpp.org/.

ISSUE 17

Has the North American Free Trade Agreement Benefited the Economies of Canada, Mexico, and the United States?

YES: John M. Melle, from "Statement," Senate Subcommittee on International Trade of the Committee on Finance of the United States Senate (September 11, 2006)

NO: Sandra Polaski, from "The Employment Consequences of NAFTA," Senate Subcommittee on International Trade of the Committee on Finance of the United States Senate (September 11, 2006)

ISSUE SUMMARY

YES: Deputy Assistant U.S. Trade Representative Melle outlines the benefits of NAFTA and concludes that the three NAFTA countries "have not only become better customers for each other but better neighbors, more committed partners, and effective colleagues in a wide range of trade-related international organizations."

NO: Sandra Polaski, director of the Trade, Equity and Development Project, argues that NAFTA has produced negative effects in all three countries, including contributing to wage inequality in the United States. But the largest negative effects have been felt by the rural poor in Mexico: They "have borne the brunt of the adjustment to NAFTA and been forced to adapt without adequate government support."

The North American Free Trade Agreement (NAFTA) was signed into law in the fall of 1993. The passage of NAFTA was no simple matter. Although the basic agreement was negotiated by the Republican George H.W. Bush administration during the late 1980s and early 1990s, the Democratic Bill Clinton administration faced the challenge of convincing Congress and the American people that NAFTA would work to the benefit of the United States as well as Mexico and Canada. In meeting this challenge, President Clinton did not hesitate to use a bit of drama to press the case for NAFTA. He arranged for all former, then-living U.S. presidents (Bush, Ronald Reagan, Jimmy Carter, Gerald Ford, and Richard Nixon) to gather together and speak out in support of NAFTA. The public debate probably reached its zenith with a face-to-face confrontation between H. Ross Perot, a successful businessman who ran for president and was perhaps the most visible and outspoken opponent of NAFTA, and then-vice president Al Gore on the *Larry King Live* television show. The vote on NAFTA in the House of Representatives reflected the sharpness of the debate; it passed by only a slim margin.

In pressing the case for NAFTA, proponents in the United States raised two major arguments. The first argument was economic: NAFTA would produce real economic benefits. These benefits were purported to include increased employment in the United States and increased productivity. Note that these arguments are based on the economic notions of specialization and comparative advantage. The second argument was political: NAFTA would support the political and economic reforms being made in Mexico and promote further progress in these two domains. These reforms had made Mexico a "better" neighbor—that is, Mexico had taken steps to become more like the United States—and NAFTA would support greater economic freedom and increased political freedom as well as greater economic stability and incrreased political stability.

In opposing NAFTA, critics in the United States countered both of these arguments, focusing mostly on U.S.–Mexican relations. They argued that freer trade between the United States and Mexico would mean a loss of jobs in the United States—Perot's reference to a "giant sucking sound" was the transfer of work and jobs from the United States to Mexico. They also argued that NAFTA did not do enough to protect the environment or to improve working conditions in Mexico. They felt that the notion of passing NAFTA as a reward to the Mexican government was premature; the government had not done enough to improve economic and political conditions in Mexico.

Implementation of NAFTA began in 1994, and evaluation was undertaken at the point of its 10-year anniversary, and again at its 12-year anniversary when almost all of its implementation periods were completed—the few remaining tariffs are planned to be eliminated on January 1, 2008. In assessing the impact of NAFTA, there are any number of different perspectives that can be employed. Should the focus be economic, political, or both? Should the evaluation concentrate on the benefits and costs to the United States, to Mexico, to Canada, or to all three countries? How much of the history that follows NAFTA can be attributed to NAFTA, and how much can be attributed to other factors? When is the appropriate time for an evaluation? In short, evaluation is no easy task.

But evaluation of NAFTA is important not only for its own sake. President George W. Bush supports an expansion of NAFTA to 34 countries in North, Central, and South America. This expansion is called the Free Trade Agreement of the Americas (FTAA). Clearly, whether or not a person is willing to support FTAA depends in part on whether that person believes that NAFTA has helped or hurt the three countries. John M. Melle believes that NAFTA has benefited all three countries. Sandra Polaski claims that NAFTA has hurt all three countries, especially Mexico's rural poor.

YES

John M. Melle

Statement

Mr. Chairman, Members of the Committee:

Thank you for the opportunity to appear before the Committee today. I am pleased to represent the Office of the United States Trade Representative and provide an overview of our trade and investment relationship with our NAFTA partners, Canada and Mexico.

The North American Free Trade Agreement (NAFTA) has defined our commercial relationship with Canada and Mexico since its entry into force on January 1, 1994. The NAFTA is a comprehensive trade agreement, covering trade in goods, services and investment, as well as government procurement, intellectual property rights, standards, and dispute settlement. Twelve years after implementation of the NAFTA began, essentially all of the agreement's transitional implementation periods are now complete with the exception of a handful of tariffs that fall to zero on January 1, 2008.

In evaluating the impact of the NAFTA on both the United States and its partners, the appropriate place to start is with trade and investment flows.

- For goods, our total trade (imports plus exports) with Canada and Mexico has more than doubled from pre-NAFTA levels. Growth in trade with our NAFTA partners exceeds growth with the world as a whole. Mexico has passed Japan to become our second largest trading partner and export market, trailing only Canada.
- There has also been a qualitative transformation in goods trade; in the 1980s, 80 percent of Mexico's exports were oil and raw materials. Today, value-added manufactured goods account for 90 percent of Mexico's exports, an indicator that Mexico has joined the United States and Canada as part of a continent-wide market of producers and consumers.
- Much of the recent concern about NAFTA is with agriculture. In fact, growth in agricultural trade has paralleled growth in total trade since 1994. U.S. agricultural exports to Canada and Mexico have grown by 98 percent since 1994, nearly matching the 101 percent total growth in U.S. total exports to those countries over the same period. Canada and Mexico are our top two agricultural export markets.
- Many of the most impressive export successes for the United States are also agricultural. Mexico is our largest market for a wide range of products—beef, dairy, swine, rice, turkey, apples, soymeal, sorghum,

From Senate Subcommittee on International Trade of the Committee on Finance of the United States Senate, John M. Melle (September 11, 2006).

and dry beans among them. Our share of Mexico's imports is above 90 percent, due in part to the preferential access we have under the NAFTA for five of these seven products. In 2005, Mexico was also our second largest market for corn, port, poultry meats, soybeans, wheat, and pears.

- NAFTA has solidified Canada's position as our largest trading partner. More trade crosses the Ambassador Bridge between Detroit and Windsor than moves between Spain and France.[1]
- U.S. exports of services to Canada and Mexico have grown by 75 percent since 1993. In 2004, the last year for which we have complete data, the United States exported $47.7 billion in private commercial services to our NAFTA partners, and maintained a trade surplus of $14.2 billion.

As a result of the NAFTA and the earlier bilateral free trade agreement, the phase-out of tariffs between the United States and Canada was completed on January 1, 1998, except for tariff-rate quotas which Canada maintains on certain supply-managed agricultural products. Nearly all of the NAFTA tariff cuts with Mexico have been implemented, except for the handful of remaining items whose tariffs will be eliminated in 2008. Since 1994, the average U.S. duty on Mexican goods has fallen to about 0.1 percent in 2005. Mexico's duties on U.S. goods are even smaller—0.003%.

By establishing a framework to promote a secure and predictable environment, investment in each of the NAFTA countries have grown. The NAFTA partners are investing more in each others' economies, and the rest of the world is also investing more in our economies.

- This change is especially important for Mexico. Since 1994, annual Foreign Direct Investment (FDI) inflows have averaged $14 billion, compared to less than $3 billion in the 1980s. Mexico's outward FDI flows have increased fourteen-fold since 1990, and it is now one of the largest developing country overseas investors.
- The United States accounts for approximately two-thirds of total foreign direct investment in Canada. U.S. investment is concentrated in the manufacturing, finance, and mining sectors.
- Investment growth in Canada and Mexico has not come at U.S. expense. Even excluding housing, U.S. business investment has risen by 104% since 1993, compared to a 37% rise between 1981 and 1993.

How much the NAFTA affected the changing trends in goods and services trade and investment cannot be measured precisely. This is especially true when looking at broader measures of economic performance since the NAFTA entered into force. However, there are a wide range of economic indicators that have grown more rapidly since the NAFTA was implemented.

- For the United States, job creation, industrial production, real compensation for manufacturing workers, business productivity and investment have all increased by higher rates in the period since 1993 compared with prior years.

- U.S. employment rose from 112.2 million in December 1993 to 134.4 million in December 2005, an increase of 22.2 million jobs, or nearly 20 percent. The average unemployment rate was 5.1 percent in the period 1994–2005, compared to 7.1 percent during the period 1982–1993.
- U.S. industrial production—78 percent of which is manufacturing—rose by 49 percent between 1993 and 2005, exceeding the 28 percent increase achieved between 1981 and 1993.
- Growth in real compensation for manufacturing workers improved dramatically. Average real compensation grew at an average annual rate of 2.3 percent from 1993 to 2005, compared to just 0.4 percent annually between 1987 (earliest data available) and 1993.
- U.S. business sector productivity rose by 2.6 percent year between 1993 and 2005, or by a total of 36.2 percent over the full period. Between 1981 and 1993 the annual rate of productivity growth was 1.8 percent, or 24.3 percent over the full 12 year period.
- Mexico has seen consistent GDP growth—40 percent since 1993—and annual real wage growth since 1995. This has been accompanied by much lower interest rates and rapid development of consumer finance services, such as home mortgages that have created a boom in consumer lending and home purchases.
- Real GDP in Canada grew from C$773.5 (1997 Canadian dollars) in 1993 to C$1,157.7 in 2005, an increase of nearly 50 percent. Real Canadian GDP per capita surged by 33 percent over the same period. Canadian unemployment fell from 11.2 percent in 1993 to 6.7 percent last year.[2]

NAFTA's Ability to Respond to Changes

The NAFTA remains a vibrant agreement, one that has been able to respond to changes in production methods and sourcing arrangements. For example, the NAFTA establishes schedules for the elimination of tariffs, but the agreement also allows the Parties to accelerate the elimination of tariffs. Since the entry into force in 1994, the NAFTA partners have accelerated the elimination of tariffs four times, in 1997, 1998, 2000 and 2001. The total value of trilateral trade covered by these four rounds of tariff cuts is approximately $28 billion.

Over time, manufacturers often change the way they design and build products. They choose new suppliers, change the materials used in the production of a good, or improve their products by using new parts. Since 2002, the NAFTA partners have worked to update the NAFTA rules of origin, the regulations that specify which goods are eligible for preferential treatment under the agreement. These changes have allowed U.S. companies to export their products duty-free to our NAFTA partners, saving thousands, sometimes millions of dollars in duties. The NAFTA partners have implemented three sets of changes to the rules of origin, in 2002, 2004 and 2006. The total value of trade covered by these changes exceeds $39 billion. We are working to implement a fourth set of changes in 2007.

Recent Successes

In 2006, the United States has resolved a number of our thorniest trade issues with Canada and Mexico.

- In January, the United States and Mexico signed a bilateral agreement on trade in tequila, which will ensure that U.S. bottlers can continue to import tequila in bulk form. The agreement imposes no obligations on the United States beyond current practice.
- In March, the United States and Mexico signed an agreement to promote bilateral trade in cement. The agreement will allow for additional supply of cement at a time of strong domestic demand following the devastation of Hurricanes Katrina and Rita. The agreement also ends all NAFTA and WTO litigation on cement from Mexico, which had stretched back 16 years.
- In July, the United States and Canada reached final agreement on softwood lumber, a dispute that has dogged trade relations for 20 years.
- In August, the United States and Mexico reached an agreement on trade in sweeteners, which puts the two countries on a glide path towards full implementation of the NAFTA sugar provisions in 2008. Mexico agreed to remove its beverage tax and duties on drinks sweetened with high fructose corn syrup and other non-sugar sweeteners, and the United States agreed to an increase in the amount of duty-free sugar that Mexico is allowed to export to the United States. Mexico is providing duty-free access for an equivalent volume of high fructose corn syrup (HFCS).

Current Challenges

To address the challenges the NAFTA framework faces today and in the future, there are three circumstances to consider.

The first is implementation of the remaining NAFTA commitments by January 1, 2008.

As I mentioned earlier, all tariff cuts between the United States and Canada have already been implemented, and the remaining tariffs between the United States and Mexico will be eliminated on January 1, 2008. While less than one percent of our NAFTA trade with Mexico remains subject to duties, final removal of these duties has raised concerns in some sectors. As the three NAFTA trade ministers made clear at their annual oversight meetings in Mexico this past March, they are committed to full implementation of the NAFTA and will not consider any reduction to our NAFTA obligations.

A second set of challenges must take into account the changes in global trade since the NAFTA entered into force. Simply put, each of the NAFTA partners have been reducing trade barriers with other countries, meaning the margins of preference provided by the NAFTA are shrinking.

- In 1993, for example, the average United States duty on imports from all countries in was 3.2 percent. By 2005, it had fallen to 1.4 percent.

Mexico still has a larger margin of preferential access today than it did before NAFTA implementation began, but it has begun to fall.

- The United States also faces more competition in the Mexican and Canadian markets: Mexico has free trade agreements with 42 other countries today, compared with one (Chile) in 1994. Canada has concluded three additional FTAs since 1994, and is currently engaged in negotiations with the Republic of Korea.
- And, of course, all three countries face the challenge of increased competition with economies such as China and India.

A third set of challenges is how to best address today's security concerns while not creating trade barriers. This is the fundamental challenge of the Security and Prosperity Partnership of North America, a trilateral initiative launched in March 2005. The SPP seeks to enhance the security, prosperity, and quality of life for the citizens of all three countries while respecting the sovereignty and unique cultural and legal heritage of each country. The SPP builds on and complements the NAFTA, and we can use both processes to advance common strategic North American goals. For example, under both the NAFTA and the SPP, USTR is soliciting proposals from U.S. industries to liberalize and simplify NAFTA Rules of Origin, making it easier to use the benefits of the duty-free access that the NAFTA provides.

To conclude, with the NAFTA firmly in place, the United States and its NAFTA partners have not only become better customers for each other but better neighbors, more committed partners, and effective colleagues in a wide range of trade-related international organizations.

I am pleased to answer any questions you may have.

Notes

1. Derived from GAO report 02-595R, page 1 and the CIA World Factbook.
2. See "Economic Indicators," on the website of the Department of Foreign Affairs and International Trade. . . .

Sandra Polaski  **NO**

The Employment
Consequences of NAFTA

Conclusion: Learning from the NAFTA Experience

At twelve years, the long-term effects of NAFTA on employment, wages, and incomes in the countries of North America cannot be judged definitively. However, short- and medium-term impacts can now be assessed on the basis of substantial, accumulating data, as presented above. That assessment also provides some potentially useful guidance for measures that might improve the employment and distributive outcomes of future trade agreements.

Employment

The most salient result of the NAFTA experience and the one most at odds with predictions of political advocates is that the trade agreement has produced disappointingly small net gains in employment in the countries of North America. In Mexico, employment destruction in domestic manufacturing and agriculture has all but swamped job creation in export manufacturing. In the United States, NAFTA has had either a neutral or very small net positive effect on employment. Meanwhile, in Canada, CUFTA led first to a significant net decrease in jobs in traded sectors, followed by a slow recovery of employment to pre-CUFTA levels after ten years, then a continued increase in subsequent years. The political and rhetorical claims for trade as an engine of net job growth are not borne out by experience, at least in the medium term.

Such claims have always been at odds with the predictions of trade theory. In theory, if an economy is at full employment before opening to trade, the shifting of resources into different productive activities based on comparative advantage will not result in a net gain or loss of jobs, but rather in a different mix of industries and employment. The gains from trade in a full-employment economy would be seen in rising wages and incomes, according to basic trade theory. The United States and, arguably, Canada have been at full employment during most of the NAFTA period. Thus, the lack of any significant job growth due to NAFTA in Canada and the United States is not at odds with the predictions of economic theory, although it certainly contradicts the claims of NAFTA boosters. What is surprising, even from the perspective of economic theory, is the weak job

From Senate Subcommittee on International Trade of the Committee on Finance of the United States Senate, Sandra Polaski (September 11, 2006).

creation in Mexico, which is far from full employment. As noted earlier, it is impossible to determine with certainty the precise share of agricultural job losses and manufacturing job gains in Mexico that resulted directly from NAFTA. However, the trade pact has been the single most important factor in Mexico's changing pattern of trade, and the overall growth of jobs in all traded sectors since 1993 has been very weak. It is thus evident that NAFTA has not been a robust job creator for the low-wage, labor-abundant trading partner.

In developing economies with surplus labor, such as Mexico, the NAFTA experience demonstrates that trade pacts cannot be counted on to produce much, if any, net employment growth in the absence of other targeted policies. Policies to maximize employment gains from trade would include measures to promote domestic supplier and support industries and terms in the trade agreement that reward rather than discourage the use of domestic inputs in the production of exported goods.

The experience of Mexico also suggests that a developing country with a high proportion of its labor force in low-productivity agriculture should negotiate very long transition periods for the phase-out of tariffs on basic crops. The negative situation currently faced by Mexico also demonstrates that a developing country must use that transition time aggressively to prepare the rural population for the wrenching adjustment it will face. Policies should be adopted to shift farmers to competitive crops, to develop alternative sources of employment in rural areas, and to invest heavily in education to prepare the population for more modern occupations. Another important factor for Mexico was that some of its most important basic crops, such as maize, were exposed to competition from subsidized U.S. crops that are sold at artificially low prices, sometimes below the cost of production. Further, U.S. policy on agricultural subsidies changed significantly in ways that were not foreseen during the NAFTA negotiations, most notably in the passage of the farm bill in 2002 that increased subsidies. Successful competition will be impossible for the developing country under those circumstances.

The transition times negotiated by Mexico were too short, and the government did not adopt sufficiently vigorous rural adjustment policies to help subsistence farmers adapt to the new trade conditions. In trade negotiations with developing countries with significant employment in subsistence agriculture, the US and its partners should carefully consider the sequencing of liberalization, to allow the absorption of rural workers into other sectors that expand due to liberalized access to foreign markets, before basic crops are liberalized. Developing countries will also need special safeguard mechanisms to protect the incomes of their rural households during the long transitional period.

The experience of Mexico also suggests that the government relied too heavily on export-led growth, adopting policies that repressed wages in order to pursue global competitiveness. These wage policies had the effect of depressing domestic demand in Mexico, which made the economy even more dependent on export sectors for job creation, in a vicious circle. A more balanced strategy of stimulating domestic demand through wage increases (commensurate with productivity gains) and support to rural households would likely produce better overall employment results.

Productivity

The one employment area where a clear positive impact has been seen during the NAFTA period is the growth of productivity in all three North American countries. At least in Mexico and Canada, which cut tariffs deeply and were exposed to competition from their giant neighbor, NAFTA likely played a significant role in the observed productivity growth. In Canada, increased productivity may have contributed to a medium-term revival and perhaps even long-term survival of the manufacturing sector.

However, the strong productivity growth in the United States and somewhat weaker growth in Mexico and Canada may have had the unwelcome side effect of reducing the pace of job creation in the three countries, as workers produced more and fewer new jobs were created.

Throughout North America, there has been a decoupling of productivity growth from wage growth over the last decade.

Wages

During the NAFTA period, productivity growth in Mexico has not translated into wage growth, as it did in earlier periods. Mexican wages are also diverging from, rather than converging toward, U.S. wages, as trade theory would suggest.

Because the net impact of NAFTA on U.S. employment is small, the impact on overall wages is also likely to be small. But a widening gap between the wages of skilled and unskilled workers is partly attributable to trade, and NAFTA probably accounts for a small portion of the observed growth in wage disparity within the United States.

Overall real wages in Canada were only slightly higher in 2002 than when CUFTA took effect in 1989, but manufacturing earnings had fared somewhat better. This suggests that NAFTA and CUFTA did not have a negative impact on wages, since earnings in non-traded sectors increased more slowly than in manufacturing. As in the case of Mexico, productivity increases in Canada significantly outstripped wage increases.

In all three countries, the evolution of wages and household incomes since NAFTA took effect has been toward greater inequality, with most gains going to the upper 20 percent of households and higher-skilled workers. While this trend is clearly compounded of many factors, more open trade appears to be one element—along with continental and global competition over the location of production—that restrains wage growth.

Whether productivity gains lead to higher wages also depends on the nature and quality of the institutions that determine the distribution of productivity gains within a society between the return to workers as higher wages and the return to investors as higher profits. Institutions that govern the ability of workers to organize unions and bargain collectively over wages are important determinants of distribution, as are government mechanisms such as minimum wage policies. If productivity gains are to be shared with workers in the form of rising wages, the institutions and public policies that affect wage outcomes will need to be strengthened. Weak laws and institutions related to freedom of association and collective bargaining should be addressed in conjunction with trade liberalization. Minimum wage policies need to be reconsidered; dispute resolution mechanisms, such as arbitration, could also be strengthened.

Income Distribution

Income inequality has been on the rise in Mexico since NAFTA took effect, reversing a brief downward trend in the early 1990s. Compared to the period before NAFTA, the top 10 percent of households have increased their share of national income, while the other 90 percent have lost income share or seen no change. Regional inequality within Mexico has also increased, reversing a long-term trend toward convergence in regional incomes.

In a trend that predates NAFTA, income inequality in the United States has been increasing for most of the last two decades. The growing wage gap between high-skilled and low-skilled workers is one of the causes, and to the extent that trade is a factor in the wage gap, it is also implicated in growing inequality.

Incomes in Canada are relatively more equal than in either Mexico or the United States, but inequality has been on a marked upward trend since CUFTA's entry into force in 1989. Because manufacturing wages have performed better than wages in most other sectors, it seems clear that trade-induced wage changes are not the cause of the observed increase in inequality. Rather, a reduction in transfer payments from government, which play an important role in the incomes of the bottom 40 percent of households, accounts for most of the change. The weakening of the Canadian social safety net, which generates these transfer payments, was a concern of CUFTA opponents, but there is currently no clear evidence to support a causal relationship.

If the gains from trade are to be shared widely throughout a country, the institutional mechanisms that govern how costs and benefits of economic change are distributed may need to be strengthened. Government measures that affect income distribution, such as tax and transfer mechanisms, should be reviewed and fortified to deal with the impact of trade opening.

The experience of each of the NAFTA countries confirms the prediction of trade theory that there will always be winners and losers from trade. The number of losers may equal or even surpass the number of winners, especially in the short-to-medium term. In Canada, it took a decade for manufacturing employment to recover from the initial displacements caused by CUFTA. In Mexico, rural farmers are still struggling to adapt to NAFTA-induced changes. The short-to-medium term adjustment costs faced by the losers from trade can be severe, and the losers are often those segments of society least able to cope with adjustment, due to low skills, low savings, and low mobility. It must also be recognized that there may be permanent losers from trade, due to limitations of education, skills, geographic isolation, and other factors.

Because the impacts of trade are uneven, governments should establish mechanisms that help offset the losses suffered by those in declining sectors. Trade adjustment assistance should provide income support to workers and small farmers during transitional periods, as well as funds for training for new occupations. Such policies are highly desirable complements to trade pacts. The existing trade adjustment assistance program in the United States and the broader social safety net in Canada serve these ends, although both countries' plans have critical gaps that should be addressed. In Mexico, budget constraints and policy choices have precluded the establishment of even the most basic unemployment insurance and social safety net. The harsh impact of agricultural trade liberalization on subsistence farmers there has not been offset by appropriate government policies. Developing countries negotiating with wealthier trading partners will likely need financial assistance from those countries, as part of the trade package, for transitional adjustment programs.

POSTSCRIPT

Has the North American Free Trade Agreement Benefited the Economies of Canada, Mexico, and the United States?

To evaluate the impact of NAFTA on the three partners, Melle points to the larger growth of the United States' trade with Canada and Mexico (compared with U.S. trade with the world), who are now the United States' second and third largest trading partners; to the changing composition of Mexico's exports, 90 percent of which are now manufactured goods (oil and raw materials comprised 80 percent of Mexican exports in 1980); to the near-doubling of U.S. agricultural exports to Canada and Mexico since NAFTA's implementation; to the surplus on U.S. trade in services with its NAFTA partners; and to the fall in average U.S. tariffs on Mexican goods (to about 0.5 percent in 2005), and Mexico's tariffs on American goods (0.003 percent). He also notes the more rapid growth in many of the United States' economic indicators since NAFTA's implementation. In Mexico, there has been consistent GDP growth, and annual real wage growth since 1995. In Canada there has been a 33 percent increase in real GDP per capita and a drop in unemployment from 11.2 percent in 1993 to 6.7 percent in 2005. In addition, the NAFTA partners have accelerated the elimination of tariffs four times and have been flexible in updating and regulations.

Sandra Polaski is critical of NAFTA's achievements. NAFTA has had at best a very small effect on employment in all three countries. Job creation in Mexico's export manufacturing sector is outweighed by job destruction in its domestic manufacturing sector and in agriculture. Moreover, Mexico's most basic crops were exposed to competition from subsidized U.S. crops sold at artificially low prices. Further, income inequality in Mexico has risen since NAFTA was implemented, and so has regional inequality (reversing its long-term trend). Also, Mexican wages are diverging from U.S. wages, and "NAFTA probably accounts for a small portion of the observed growth in wage disparity within the United States."

There is a large amount of literature relating to NAFTA. Robert Scott, "NAFTA's Hidden Costs: Trade Agreement Results in Job Losses, Growing Inequality, and Wage Suppression for the United States," ERP Briefing Paper (April 2001), and Daniel T. Griswold, "NAFTA at 10: An Economic and Foreign Policy Success," Free Trade Bulletin (December 2003) offer additional analyses of NAFTA's costs. For a more political critique of NAFTA, see *The Selling of "Free Trade": NAFTA, Washington, and the Subversion of American Democracy* by John

R. MacArthur (Hill & Wang, 2000). Besides controversy on the macro effects of NAFTA, there is significant debate on various elements within the NAFTA agreement. One good example is NAFTA's Chapter 11, the so-called investor-to-state protections: see William T. Warren, "NAFTA and State Sovereignty: A Pandora's Box of Property Rights," *Spectrum: The Journal of State Government* (Spring 2002) and "Update on NAFTA Chapter 11 Claim re Methanex," GreenYes Archives, <http://greeneyes.grrn.org/2002/11/msg00069.html>http://greeneyes. grrn.org/2002/11/msg00069.html (March 2003). For more about FTAA, see the section entitled "Trade Promotion Authority" in Chapter 6 of the *Economic Report of the President, 2003.*

ISSUE 18

Is the No Child Left Behind Act Working?

YES: House Education and the Workforce Committee, from Fact Sheet: No Child Left Behind Is Working (updated October 7, 2004)

NO: Gerald W. Bracey, from "The Perfect Law: No Child Left Behind and the Assault on Public Schools," *Dissent* (Fall 2004)

ISSUE SUMMARY

YES: The House Education and the Workforce Committee lists a number of positive results for the No Child Left Behind Act, including higher reading and math test scores in several states as well as improved data and information for teachers and parents.

NO: Professor Gerald W. Bracey believes that the No Child Left Behind Act is, from the perspective of the Republican party, a perfect law because it will ultimately transfer billions from the public sector to the private sector, because it will reduce the size of government, and because it will "wound or kill" a large Democratic party power base.

Elementary and secondary education in the United States is a massive undertaking. First, there is the public school component: during the 2002–03 school year, there were 95,615 public schools with over 48 million students. There is a significant private component as well; the most recent statistics list 27,223 private schools in 1999–00 and over 6 million students in 2003–04. Finally, there is a growing home-school component: 850,000 children in 1999 and about 1.1 million children in 2003.

But the focus in this issue is on public schools. The combined federal, state, and local government spending on elementary and secondary education is currently estimated at slightly more than $500 billion. This is more than the United States spends on national defense. The bulk of this spending is financed by state and local taxes, but there has been an important federal component since the passage of the Elementary and Secondary Education Act (ESEA) in 1965.

Americans are concerned about public education for a variety of reasons. One reason, as just indicated, is that public education absorbs a significant number of tax dollars. But Americans are also concerned because the results of all the spending are less than impressive. This dissatisfaction goes back to at least 1983 when the National Commission on Excellence in Education released its report, entitled *A Nation at Risk*. This report identified a variety of problems in public education. In spite of a number of "reforms" that have been put in place since then, the dissatisfaction with public education continued into the twenty-first century. For example, the U.S. Department of Education reported that in 2003, "Even after four years of public schooling, most students perform below proficiency in both reading and mathematics." And for the year 2000, the Department reported: "Upon graduating from high school, few students have acquired the math and science skills necessary to compete in the knowledge-based economy."

In his presidential campaign in 2000, candidate George W. Bush emphasized education reform. After taking office, he continued to push for educational reform, and the No Child Left Behind Act (NCLBA) was signed into law on January 8, 2002. This is not to say that NCLBA was strictly a Republican effort. In reality, it was a bipartisan effort; it passed the House by a 381–41 margin and the Senate with an 87–10 vote. A leading Democrat, Senator Ted Kennedy (D-MA), was a chief sponsor of the legislation in the Senate.

At this point, it is useful to provide some information regarding the content of NCLBA. As for the broad objectives of the legislation, former Education Secretary Rod Page states that NCLBA "ensures accountability and flexibility as well as increased federal support for education," and that it "continues the legacy of the *Brown v. Board* decision by creating an education system that is more inclusive, responsive, and fair." Turning to more specific provisions, NCLBA mandates that every state set standards for grade-level achievement and develop a system to see if students are reaching those standards. NCLBA rededicates the country to the goal of having a "highly qualified teacher" in every classroom where "highly qualified" means the teacher holds a bachelor's degree, holds a certification or licensure to teach in the state of his or her employment, and has proven knowledge of the subjects he or she teaches.

But just 3 years after its passage, the NCLBA has generated a good deal of controversy. There are those like the House Education and the Workforce Committee who believes the legislation is already beginning to generate positive results. At the same time, there is a significant vocal opposition, represented by critics like Bracey, who believe NCLBA has actually weakened public education.

Fact Sheet: No Child Left Behind Is Working

As a result of the bipartisan No Child Left Behind education reform law (NCLB) signed two years ago by President George W. Bush, America's public education system is focusing on improving academic achievement for all students like never before.

A short overview of the progress being made under NCLB:

- In exchange for billions in federal education funds, states and local school districts are being held accountable for ensuring every child learns—regardless of race, parents' income, disability, geography, or English proficiency.
- Millions of disadvantaged children who would once have been written off as unteachable are now getting the focus and attention they deserve.
- Reading and math scores in America's large urban schools have improved, and a number of states have reported promising improvement in student achievement.
- Parents and teachers are being empowered with new information to hold schools accountable.
- Parents of children in struggling schools have powerful new options, and they're using them.

Following are a few examples of how NCLB is already making a positive difference for America.

States Are Reporting Increased Reading and Math Test Scores

New test results recently released by several states for 2003–2004 show students are posting high math and reading scores on states tests. Even though No Child Left Behind's reforms have not been completely implemented, parents are already seeing positive results from its call for accountability and high standards for all students.

From the House Education and the Workforce Committee, October 7, 2004.

- **Delaware.** Student test scores in Delaware improved in three out of four grade levels in all three subjects tested—reading, writing and math. Fifth grade reading performance in Delaware climbed to 85 percent, a seven percentage point increase from last year.
- **Ohio.** Fourth grade math scores in Ohio improved dramatically, from 58 percent last year to 66 percent this year. Fourth grade reading test scores in the Dayton increased by 9 percentage points—from 25 percent passing last year to 34 percent passing this year. In math, Dayton fourth graders showed another 9 point gain—going from 22 percent passing on last year's test to 31 percent this year.
- **Maryland.** Seventy-one percent of Maryland's third graders passed the reading exam this year, as compared to 58 percent in 2003. Limited English Proficient (LEP) students posted an impressive 27 point increase in reading scores this year. In Anne Arundel County, 63.8 percent of their third graders scored proficient and advanced on state reading assessments. This year, 78.5 percent of third graders scored proficient and advanced.
- **Illinois.** According to the Chicago Tribune, students in every grade level posted increased scores on statewide reading and math tests in the 2003–2004 school year. In large part, these gains were fueled by increased test scores among Hispanic students. On the math test, Hispanic fifth-grade student scores jumped by 11.7 percentage points. Similarly, Hispanic fourth-graders improved by 10.7 percentage points on the reading test.

Teachers Applaud Early Success of No Child Left Behind

More than 3,000 teachers applauded the early success of President Bush's landmark Reading First literacy initiative at a July 2004 national education conference in Minnesota. The conference was the first of its type to bring together teachers who are implementing Reading First in their respective schools, allow them to discuss the program's early successes in raising student achievement and share strategies for continued student success.

Reading First, a cornerstone of the No Child Left Behind Act, is a scientifically based literacy program designed to ensure children have the knowledge base and essential skills needed to learn how to read. States have received more than $3 billion in Reading First grants over the last three years, helping every state ensure all students can read by the time they enter the third grade.

Substantial Gains in Reading and Math in America's Big City Schools

A major new report released in March 2004 concludes America's big city schools are making considerable progress in elevating student achievement, and the No Child Left Behind education law is helping to drive those scores. The report, released by the Council of Great City Schools—a national coalition representing more than 60 of the nation's largest urban school districts—shows students in the nation's major urban schools have posted substantial gains in statewide math and reading assessments since NCLB was enacted. A copy of the report is available online at. . . .

- **Reading and math scores have climbed in urban schools since NCLB was enacted.** The Great City Schools report shows improvement of fourth and eighth grade public school students in state-developed reading and math tests under NCLB. According to the report, 47.8 percent of urban school students performed at or above proficient in fourth grade reading and 51 percent scored at or above proficient in fourth grade math, a 4.9 and 6.8 percentage point increase respectively compared to 2002 scores. Eighth grade reading and math scores showed increases as well from 2002 to 2003. When compared to 2002, eighth grade reading and math scores increased by 1.1 and 3 percentage points in 2003.
- **Urban school officials credit NCLB with helping teachers and school officials raise student achievement.** "Our most recent report attempted to answer the question, 'Have urban schools improved student achievement since *No Child Left Behind* was enacted?' "The answer appears to be 'yes,'" testified Dr. Michael Casserly before the Education & the Workforce Committee on June 23, 2004. Casserly is the executive director of the Council of the Great City Schools.
- **High standards help teachers succeed.** The Great City Schools report credits the academic standards movement—which culminated in the NCLB law—with sparking real change and improvement in the nation's urban schools. The high standards at the heart of NCLB have helped teachers—not hindered them, as claimed by the National Education Association (NEA) and other reform opponents.

New Independent Report Shows States Are Making Progress in Implementing No Child Left Behind; Better Progress Needed to Ensure There Is a Highly Qualified Teacher in Every Public Classroom

A new independent report by the nonpartisan Education Commission of the States suggests states are making progress in implementing the education reforms included in the No Child Left Behind Act. However, the report's authors say states still have hard work remaining to ensure every classroom has a highly qualified teacher by the 2005–2006 deadline.

According to a recent *Associated Press* article ("Study: States show progress under new school law, but work ahead," Ben Feller, The Associated Press; July 14, 2004), the report's findings include:

- **98% of states are on track to define what constitutes a persistently dangerous school,** a classification which would immediately give parents the option to transfer their children to safer schools.
- **92% of states are on track to publicly report disaggregated student achievement data,** ensuring parents know how all student subgroups

are performing, including minority students, poor children, students with disabilities, and English-language learners.

- **53% of states are on track to identify which schools are in need of improvement** before the next school year begins, ensuring parents have time to make knowledgeable decisions on the options available to them to improve their children's educational opportunities.
- **22% of states are on track to place a highly qualified teacher in every classroom.**

A copy of the Education Commission of the States' report, "ECS Report to the Nation: State Implementation of the No Child Left Behind Act," can be found at. . . .

Black & Hispanic School Superintendents Say Weakening NCLB Would 'Turn Back the Clock' on Educating Disadvantaged Students

More than 100 African American and Latino school district superintendents from across the country recently sent a letter to federal leaders—including Sen. John Kerry (D-MA)—expressing their strong support for the No Child Left Behind Act signed by President Bush and warning that weakening the law, as proposed by the NEA and other opponents, would "turn back the clock." These pro-NCLB superintendents are collectively responsible for the education of more than 3 million American students.

- **Weakening NCLB would "pull the rug out from under" dedicated teachers and principals, reform advocates warn.** "Closing achievement gaps is never going to be easy. But it would be next to impossible without the demands and expectations in the federal law," said former urban school principal Paul Ruiz, now an official with the Education Trust (November 18, 2003). "These folks don't have the luxury of thinking they can implement all the changes they need to without the cover of the law. We can't pull the rug out from under them just as they are beginning to get some real traction."

A copy of the "Don't Turn Back the Clock" letter, including a list of signers, is available at:. . . .

Parents & Teachers Have Powerful New Data & Information

No Child Left Behind promised to empower parents and teachers with better information about the education children are receiving, and the law is delivering on that promise in a major way.

- **Report cards for parents and teachers on school performance.** All 50 states are moving to implement accountability plans that include providing report cards for parents on school performance. The light of public scrutiny—"sunshine"—is the primary enforcement mechanism behind the bipartisan NCLB reforms. Contrary to the claims made by the NEA and other education reform opponents, NCLB does not "punish" struggling schools; rather, schools identified by their states as needing improvement qualify for extra help, including additional federal funding and/or technical assistance.

- **Accountability goes online—at no cost to taxpayers.** A nonpartisan website launched by the School Information Partnership . . . is providing parents and teachers with up-to-date school, district, and state student achievement data. The website, made possible by the generosity of the Broad Foundation and endorsed by the U.S. Department of Education, is currently up and running for six pilot states— Delaware, Florida, Minnesota, Pennsylvania, Virginia, and Washington. Information from all 50 states, Puerto Rico, and the District of Columbia will be posted in summer 2004 as all of the available and relevant NCLB data is released.
- **New diagnostic tools for teachers, parents, and school leaders.** The new SchoolResults website is giving parents and teachers immediate access to information about the performance of their local schools, neighboring schools and districts, and the entire state. Teachers will be able to use this information as a diagnostic tool to identify areas in need of improvement, as well as identify the methods used by other schools to improve academic achievement. The website will also provide valuable comparative tools and benchmarks to monitor relative progress of local schools and districts within the state.

Parents Have Powerful New Options—and They Like Them

NCLB not only empowers parents with information, but also with choices. If parents are not satisfied with the quality of the education their children are receiving, they can do something about it under NCLB. Millions of children in schools identified by their states as needing improvement have qualified to receive free private tutoring and other supplemental educational services under NCLB. Parents have also been given the right to transfer their children to a higher-achieving or safer public or charter school.

- **Children in struggling schools are getting extra help.** "I'm better with it because I like this school better." That was what nine-year-old Nicole Brittle, a third grade student in southeast Virginia, told a reporter recently to explain the dramatic turnaround in her math scores since her grandmother and guardian exercised her rights under No Child Left Behind and transferred her to a new school. (Kristen King, "Extra Help in New School Turning Things Around for Third Grader," *Virginian-Pilot & Ledger-Star,* 27 May 2003.) "At her old school, Mount Hermon Elementary, she brought home C's and D's," the *Virginian-Pilot* noted. "Now, at Westhaven Elementary, she's earning mostly B's—and math has become her favorite subject."
- **Parents like their new options.** "It felt like a new beginning," said a Pittsburgh-area parent who talked to the *Pittsburgh Post-Gazette* last fall about her decision to transfer her third-grader and kindergartener

under NCLB. "I knew they must be doing something up there [at her daughter's new school]. I wanted my kid to get a piece of it. I don't want to wait until she gets to middle school." (Eleanor Chute, "Students not fleeing troubled schools," *Pittsburgh Post-Gazette,* November 24, 2003.)

- **More than 1600 supplemental service providers have been approved.** According to the U.S. Department of Education, more than 1600 supplemental service providers have been approved by the states since NCLB was enacted. With this option, parents can ensure their children get extra help to supplement the education being provided in the schools those children attend.
- **Parents can choose faith-based organizations to help educate their children.** To ensure parents have a wide range of choices, more than $1.7 billion has been made available to faith-based and community-based organizations through NCLB to help these groups provide quality supplemental educational services, according to the Education Department. Such organizations can participate in the Title I supplemental services program, the Early Reading First initiative, and other initiatives authorized under NCLB.

Gerald W. Bracey

The Perfect Law: No Child Left Behind and the Assault on Public Schools

Imagine a law that would transfer hundreds of billions of dollars a year from the public sector to the private sector, reduce the size of government, and wound or kill a large Democratic power base. Impossible, you say. But the law exists. It is Title I of the Elementary and Secondary Education Act of 2001, better known as the No Child Left Behind law (NCLB).

The Bush administration has often been accused of Orwellian double-speak in naming its programs, and NCLB is a masterpiece of a law to accomplish the opposite of what it apparently intends. While claiming to be the law that—finally!—improves public education, NCLB sets up public schools to fail, setting the stage for private education companies to move in on the $400 billion spent annually on K–12 education ($500 billion according to recent statements by Secretary of Education Rod Paige). The consequent destruction or reduction of public education would shrink government and cripple or eliminate the teachers' unions, nearly five million mostly Democratic voters. It's a law to drool over if you're Karl Rove or Grover Norquist. The Perfect Law, in fact, as in The Perfect Storm.

It doesn't look that way at first glance. Indeed, NCLB appears to fly in the face of all that the Bush administration stands for. That administration has tried to deregulate and outsource virtually everything it touches. Yet from this most deregulatory of administrations comes NCLB laying 1,100 pages of law and reams of regulations on public schools. On closer inspection, those pages are just the law's shiny surface to blind and confuse onlookers.

The principal means to accomplish this amazing end is called Adequate Yearly Progress or AYP. All schools that accept Title I money from the federal government are compelled by the law to show AYP. If they don't, they are labeled "failing schools." The official tag is "in need of improvement" but no one outside of the U.S. Department of Education uses that term.

The concept of AYP in Title I is not new, but NCLB yokes it to sanctions that become increasingly punitive with each consecutive year of failure. These sanctions alone should have been a clue to Democrats that the law was not what it said it was, for punishment is not an effective means to achieve either individual or institutional change.

NCLB requires not only that each school make AYP, but that each of many subgroups make AYP. For many schools, once test scores are disaggregated by gender, ethnicity, socio-economic status, special education, and English Language Learners, there are thirty-seven separate categories. All categories must make AYP. If one fails, the school fails. Not surprisingly, a study found that more diverse schools were more likely to fail—the odds that one group doesn't make it are against them. Even if all subgroups make AYP, it counts only if 95 percent of the kids in each group showed up on test day. If not, the school fails.

Here's how it works: all schools must test all students every year in grades three through eight in reading and math (and in a couple of years, science as well) and test one high school grade. For these tests, each state establishes a baseline of achievement. Its plan for AYP must be such that by the year 2014, 100 percent of the state's children achieve at the "proficient" level. At the moment, each state defines "proficient," but that will likely change. For some states, the progress from baseline to end state is a straight line. Other states have an accelerating curve with little required initially but a great deal of improvement required as the witching year of 2014 approaches.

How realistic is a goal of 100 percent proficiency? Well, at the 2004 convention of the American Educational Research Association (AERA), the California Department of Education presented projections indicating that by 2014, under AYP, 99 percent of its schools would be failing. In fact, this projection appears to be optimistic. It was predicated on assumptions about how fast test scores will improve. So far, these assumptions are not being met.

A reader might say, "Yes, but that is California. California is so educationally awful that it inspired a John Merrow PBS special, 'From First to Worst: The Rise and Fall of California's Public Schools.'" And it is true that in the National Assessment of Educational Progress's 2003 reading assessment California was at the bottom: forty-ninth at the fourth-grade level and tied with Hawaii for fiftieth at the eighth-grade level.

But consider a 2004 headline in the *St. Paul Pioneer Press:* "All Minnesota Left Behind?" The article beneath the headline described a report from the state's legislative auditor projecting that by 2014 some 80 percent of Minnesota's schools would be failing and that many of them would have failed for five consecutive years, a condition that unleashes the most draconian of NCLB's sanctions.

Academically, Minnesota is not California. In the Third International Mathematics and Science Study (TIMSS), twenty-five of forty-one participating nations outscored California in mathematics and only four (Iran, Kuwait, Colombia, and South Africa) scored lower (the remaining twelve scored about the same). In science, twenty scored higher and six scored lower. For Minnesota, the numbers are quite different. Only six of the forty-one nations outscored Minnesota in math, and only one outscored it in science.

This means that in a few years 80 percent of the schools in a state that outscores virtually the entire world will be labeled as failures.

Why would anyone foist such a no-win system on the public schools? To answer this question we must go back to the original legislation and note that it contained Bush-backed voucher amendments. If passed in this form, students would have been able to use these vouchers at any school that would accept them.

Congress struck the voucher provisions from the law. In the 2000 elections, voucher referenda in California and Michigan had suffered more than two-to-one defeats. The defeats were unusually decisive and not just because of the margins. Milton Friedman had argued that voucher efforts lose because, although the voucher proposals are "well thought out and initially warmly received, the educational establishment—administrators and teachers' unions—then launches an attack that is notable for its mendacity but is backed by much larger financial resources than the proponents can command and succeeds in killing the proposals."

In the 2000 referenda, though, advocates outspent opponents—in California by two to one—and the outcome was still not close. The public at large decisively rejected the concept of vouchers in one liberal and one conservative state. After these referenda, even ardent voucher advocates such as Harvard's Paul Peterson opined that vouchers would be of interest only to a small proportion—perhaps 5 percent—of parents, mostly those with kids in inner-city schools. Congress decided that they had no place in NCLB.

⁓⊙⁓

If Bush succeeds in his reelection campaign, vouchers will be back. Actually, they already are. Bush proposed a $75 million voucher program for a half-dozen cities. Congress trimmed it to a $15 million program for only the District of Columbia. The proposal passed the House by a single vote but was repeatedly rejected by the Senate until it was attached to a $328 billion omnibus spending bill. Even Democrats who opposed vouchers thought that law too important to kill just to keep vouchers out of the District. The bill passed sixty-five to twenty-eight. A second-term Bush would no doubt broaden the scope of voucher proposals.

Vouchers, of course, send money to private schools and remove money from public schools. At present, the principal beneficiaries of vouchers are religious schools, especially Catholic schools. In Cleveland, one of two cities with ongoing, tax-funded voucher programs, 96 percent of voucher-using students attend church-affiliated schools and 67 percent attend Catholic schools.

The D.C. program will offer a child up to $7,500 per year, but the elite privates in the D.C. area charge more than $20,000 tuition per year. Independent private schools have also shown no interest in vouchers out of fear that government money will lead to government control.

Catholic schools, on the other hand, charge much less and have been hemorrhaging students. In 1960, Catholic schools accounted for 12.4 percent of all students. In 2000, 4.7 percent. The Catholic connection was made clear when Bush made his strongest pitch for the D.C. voucher proposal in the East Room of the White House to 250 members of the National Catholic Education

Association, in town to mark their 100th anniversary. It could be seen as a cynical ploy to buy the Catholic vote in November. (Democratic presidential nominee John Kerry opposes vouchers. As a presidential candidate, John Edwards voiced similar opposition. Both expressed the position that vouchers help only the few, draw resources away from public schools, and inappropriately send taxpayer dollars to private institutions.)

✎☙✍

Thus, after the 2000 elections, even voucher proponents concluded that the middle classes were pretty much satisfied with their schools. To make vouchers attractive to the middle classes, some way would have to be found to drive a wedge between the parents and their public schools and shatter that satisfaction. AYP's impossible standards provide the way. At the AERA convention mentioned earlier, representatives from the Boulder Valley School District, the district that surrounds the University of Colorado at Boulder, reported that parents were surprised when some of their "good" schools failed. It causes, the researchers said, "dissonance" in the parents. One can only wonder how much louder the dissonance will clang as the number of failing schools grows. Already the law appears to be taking its toll. A June 2004 survey by Educational Testing Service found that in 2001, 8 percent of parents gave public schools an "A" and 35 percent gave them a "B." In 2004, the figures had fallen to 2 percent and 20 percent, respectively.

Currently, there are few non-religious schools to receive vouchers, but if the vouchers are there, one can expect the for-profit Educational Management Organizations to expand (currently, there are 53 such companies managing 461 schools). Indeed, the first overbearingly ambitious plan from the largest such company, Edison Schools, Inc., depended on Bush's father and his father's secretary of education, Lamar Alexander. Alexander was once a paid consultant to and board member of Edison's then-parent company, Whittle Communications. Edison's founder, Chris Whittle, had planned to have one thousand private schools by 2000, and that plan hinged on Bush *père* and Alexander's pushing vouchers through Congress (though it was never mentioned in any Edison press releases). When Bush lost to Clinton, the plan came a cropper and left Whittle managing a few schools, not owning a thousand. But Chris Whittle is an ambitious man, and if the vouchers are there, he will come.

One can get some sense of where people think NCLB will lead by looking at what is being said about it by organizations that should, ideologically, oppose it. In 1996, for example, the Heritage Foundation, whose mission statement says it promotes free enterprise and limited government, condemned federal intrusion into education as a "liberal solution." Yet, this organization, once dubbed by *Slate* editor Michael Kinsley as "a right-wing propaganda machine," not only endorses NCLB but also brags that one of its policy analysts, Krista Kafer, "produced two papers that helped define the lines of debate" over NCLB.

The most ardent voucher proponent in academia is Harvard's Paul Peterson, also a senior fellow at the Hoover Institution. Hoover proudly announced that Peterson, along with Erik Hanushek, another senior fellow, had been named to a Bush-sponsored National Education Panel to evaluate NCLB.

The Eagle Forum's Phyllis Schlafly contended "the tests mandated by NCLB had ripped back the curtain and exposed a major national problem." But, she went on NCLB wouldn't do much about that problem. We need "innovative solutions to introduce competition into the monopoly system." Vouchers, in other words.

With the voucher-touting right solidly lined up in favor of NCLB, shouldn't the center and the left be just a bit suspicious of it?

&⊙❦

Even with each state having a unique definition of proficient, most schools fail. The situation will likely get worse. If each state has a unique definition, no two states can be compared. Lack of comparability alone would make some people uncomfortable, but some of the early results seemed, well, anomalous. In the first estimate of how many schools would fail, Michigan projected fifteen hundred, while Arkansas foresaw none. This finding did not produce, so far as is known, a stampede of Michigan parents seeking to educate their children in the Razorback state.

There will be pressure to seek a common yardstick that, in this most normative of nations, will let people compare the states. It exists. It is called the National Assessment of Educational Progress (NAEP). NAEP reports results two ways: in terms of scores on the tests and in terms of what percentage of the students attained its three "achievement levels": basic, proficient (the magic word), and advanced. Secretary Paige has already said that he will use the discrepancy between NAEP and state test results to shame the states into better performance (ironically, the biggest discrepancy turned up in Texas, where Paige had been superintendent of Houston public schools. Texas said 91 percent of its eighth-graders were proficient in math, NAEP said 24 percent).

The result from Texas gives some idea of the problem. The NAEP achievement levels are ridiculously high. In the 2003 math assessment, for instance, only 32 percent of the nation's fourth graders reached the proficient level. Even in high-scoring Minnesota, only 42 percent were designated proficient (for some minorities, nationally, the percentage proficient fell as low as 5 percent). American fourth-graders were well above average on the TIMSS math test and third in the world in science. But only about a third showed up as proficient on NAEP math and science tests administered the same year. Kids who are virtually on top of the world are not proficient? It makes no sense.

And it gets worse. The NAEP levels are not only ridiculously high, they are "fundamentally flawed," to use the words of the National Academy of Sciences. The NAEP achievement levels have been examined and found wanting by the National Center for Research on Evaluation, Standards, and Student Testing; the National Academy of Education; the National Academy of Sciences; the General Accounting Office; and individual psychometricians. The reports say that the process is confusing, internally inconsistent, and lacking in evidence for validity. These conclusions would condemn any proposed commercial test to the trash bin. But NAEP chugs along ignoring the flaws. Having many students score low has political uses.

If NAEP comes to be the common yardstick, the dissonance in people's minds will only increase because the NAEP standards ensure that no one will ever attain 100 percent proficiency for any group. Asian American students score considerably higher than other ethnic groups in math, but on the 2003 NAEP math assessment, their best performance was 48 percent proficient at the eighth grade. In his AERA presidential address in 2003, Robert Linn of the University of Colorado estimated that we could have all twelfth graders proficient in math in 166 years.

Many other problems with NCLB are smaller and of a more technical nature. For instance, the role of summer loss in poor students but not middle class or affluent students, meaning that some schools that do well during the school year will not make AYP because of what happens when they are closed. Then there is the impact of the "choice option." Students in schools that have failed for two consecutive years must be offered the option of choosing another school. This requirement leads to logistical nightmares—currently Chicago must offer the option to two hundred thousand students but has only five hundred spaces—and to peculiar alterations in the schools' test scores. Purportedly, the choice option must be offered first to the "neediest" students, namely those with the lowest test scores. But if these kids leave, the sending school's average score goes up through no merit of its own. At the other end, the receiving school will find it harder to maintain AYP with these incoming hard-core non-achievers.

And no one seems to have thought much about mobility. In some schools, the kids in the building in May are not the kids who were there in September. How, then, can the school be held accountable for their performance?

Although private companies are not yet taking over schools, they are already cashing in on the law. The law makes provisions for "secondary providers"—private firms—to tutor low-scoring students and provide other services. The *Wall Street Journal* estimated that there are some 24.3 billion dollars for companies to lust after in aid to high-poverty schools, reading programs, technology improvements, and building and running charter schools. Educational Testing Service vice president Sharon Robinson is said to have called NCLB a full employment act for test publishers.

The big problem with NCLB, though, remains that its intent is the opposite of what it claims. Former assistant secretary of education, Chester E. Finn, Jr., once said, "The public education system as we know it has proved that it cannot reform itself. It is an ossified government monopoly." As the preordained casualties from NCLB mount, the Chester Finns, George W. Bushes, and the think tanks on the right will intensify their attacks on the "government monopoly" while holding vouchers as the solution. If their attacks on public schools are successful, NCLB will indeed have proved to be The Perfect Law.

POSTSCRIPT

Is the No Child Left Behind Act Working?

The House Education and Workforce Committee claims that NCLBA is working. The Committee divides the arguments and evidence in support of this claim into seven major parts. One part involves reading and math test scores from four states. For example, the Committee attributes a 7 percentage point increase in fifth grade reading performance in Delaware to NCLBA. Another major part concerns progress in big-city schools. Here the Committee relies on data from the Council of Great City Schools, a coalition of more than 60 of the largest urban school districts in the nation. According to the Committee, the Council reports a 4.9 percentage point increase in fourth grade reading and a 6.8 percentage point increase in fourth grade math for urban school students between 2002 and 2003. A third major part involves support for NCLBA from minority school superintendents. Here the Committee reports that more than 100 African and Latino school district superintendents sent a letter to "federal leaders" in which they expressed "strong support" for NCLBA.

Bracey begins his essay by clarifying what he means when he describes NCLBA as a perfect law. From the perspective of Republicans, NCLBA will ultimately achieve three objectives: transfer many dollars from public education to private education, reduce the size of government, and "cripple or eliminate" teachers unions that historically aligned themselves with the Democratic party. Thus the perfect law from the Republican perspective is the perfect storm for Democrats. Bracey states that this is the reason why the Bush administration, which "has tried to deregulate and outsource virtually everything it touches" fought for the NCLBA, legislation that lays "1,100 pages of law and reams of regulations on public schools." Bracey makes his case in terms of the Adequate Yearly Provision of NCLBA. He argues that this provision is such that "in a few years 80 percent of the schools in a state (Minnesota) that outscores virtually the entire world will be labeled as failures." Parents will react to this by demanding a voucher system, something that was supported in the original Bush version of NCLBA but excluded in the final version. The resurrection of a revamped and expanded voucher system becomes the vehicle by which funds get transferred from the public sector to the private sector, reducing the effectiveness of teacher unions and reducing the size of the public sector. Thus, Bracey concludes, the key problem with NCLBA "remains that its intent is the opposite of what it claims"; that is, instead of helping public schools, NCLBA represents an attack on public schools.

The reading from the House Education and the Workforce Committee references a number of Web sites that provide additional information on NCLBA. A wide variety of data on both public and private education is available in *Digest of Education Statistics* from the National Center for Education Statistics of the U.S. Department of Education at http://nces.ed.gov/programs/digest/. *A Guide to Education and No Child Left Behind* is available from the U.S. Department of Education (October 2004); it provides an overview of NCLBA. More information on private education can be obtained from the Council for American Private Education at http://www.capenet.org/. Also of interest are *No Child Left Behind? The Politics and Practice of School Accountability*, edited by Paul E. Peterson and Martin R. West (Brookings Institution, 2004); *Many Children Left Behind: How the No Child Left Behind Act Is Damaging Our Children and Our Schools*, edited by Deborah Meier and George Wood (Beacon, 2004); "U.S. Schools: Underperforming," by William C. Symonds in the January 10, 2005 issue of *Business Week*; "On Leaving No Child Behind," by Chester E. Finn, Jr. and Frederick M. Hess in *Public Interest* (Fall 2004); and "Damage Control for 'No Child Left Behind'" in *National Journal* (June 5, 2004).

ISSUE 19

Will the Creation of an Ownership Society Make the American Economy More Efficient and More Equitable?

YES: The White House, from "Fact Sheet: America's Ownership Society: Expanding Economic Opportunity," http://www.whitehouse.gov/news/releases/2004/08/20040809-9.html (August 2004)

NO: Paul Glastris, from "Bush's Ownership Society: Why No One's Buying," *Washington Monthly* (December 2005)

ISSUE SUMMARY

YES: The George W. Bush White House is promoting a plan to increase "ownership" in American society. The plan consists of a series of initiatives in health care, in home ownership, in small business, and in Social Security. These initiatives, if adopted, will create more ownership and more vitality and give more people "a vital stake in the future of this country."

NO: Paul Glastris argues that people have rejected the president's initiatives to give them more choice because they "feel quickly overwhelmed when they lack the information or expertise to decide confidently, and turn downright negative when the choices themselves seem to put what they already have at risk."

"If you break it, you own it." We all have seen signs like this in retail outlets of one sort or another. We take these signs as a rather blunt admonition to customers to handle the store's merchandise with care. The retail outlet hopes that the threat will make people treat the merchandise as their own and, in this fashion, be more careful.

But these kinds of signs belie a fundamental institution of capitalist market economies: private property or private ownership. The opposite to private ownership is public or social ownership. Even though we are all quite familiar with private ownership, there are any number of examples of public ownership in the U.S. government property, assets ranging from highways to office buildings to schools to books in the library representing collective ownership—we are the government, government owns these assets, so we own the assets.

Economic systems are distinguished on the basis of the ownership especially the ownership of the means of production. Socialist states are based on extensive ownership of the means of production—the factories, the machinery in those factories, the office buildings, the equipment in those office buildings. Capitalism, on the other hand, involves extensive private ownership of the means of production. One reason for the greater efficiency associated with capitalism stems from the private ownership of the means of production. Because individuals own the means of production they will take better care of it—like the merchandise in the retail outlet. But now taking better care of the means of production means more than just not breaking it, but directing capital to its most productive uses, earning the owner the greatest possible returns.

The right of private ownership is something that most Americans take for granted; it is embodied in the very fabric of our society. And it extends well beyond the private ownership of the means of production and includes the private ownership of homes, cars, clothes, cell phones, DVDs, etc. The private ownership of these consumer goods like the private ownership of the production goods promotes efficiency: We will arrange our spending on consumer goods and services in such a way as to maximize our well-being. Private ownership is also thought to support other desirable outcomes as well. Some believe that it promotes better citizenship: the more people own the more they will be concerned with the world around them, making sure that society moves in directions that are compatible with their desires and their goals. This rather vague concept can be made a bit more concrete by recalling the notion of the American dream: It is to own one's home.

Because of the presumed benefits of private ownership, the Bush administration has promoted the concept of "the ownership society." He seeks to create this society with a series of actions in the areas of health care, homeownership, small business, and retirement financing. Expanding ownership will promote "more vitality" in America and make it a better place. Paul Glastris supports the notion of more choice, but he believes it will take more rather than less government involvement.

Fact Sheet: America's Ownership Society: Expanding Opportunities

". . . if you own something, you have a vital stake in the future of our country. The more ownership there is in America, the more vitality there is in America, and the more people have a vital stake in the future of this country."

—President George W. Bush, June 17, 2004

The Challenge: America's Changing Society

Life in America is changing dramatically, and President Bush believes that the Federal government should change too to help meet the challenges of our times. American families should have choices and access they need to affordable health care and homeownership; Americans should have the option of managing their own retirement; and small businesses, which employ over half of all workers, need lower taxes and fewer government mandates so they can grow.

President Bush's Policies Promoting the Ownership Society

- *More Access and More Choices in Health Care.* The President's goal is to ensure that Americans can choose and afford private health care coverage that best fits their individual needs. The U.S. health care system can provide the best care in the world, but rising costs and loss of control to government and health plan bureaucrats threaten to keep patients from getting state-of-the-art care. The President's agenda includes:
  - *Health Savings Accounts (HSAs),* which combine low-cost, high-deductible health insurance with tax-free savings accounts to pay for health care expenses. The President has also proposed to make insurance premiums associated with HSAs tax deductible.
  - *Association Health Plans (AHPs)* to give America's working families greater access to affordable health insurance. By allowing small

businesses to band together and negotiate on behalf of their employees and their families, AHPs would help small businesses and employees obtain health insurance at an affordable price, much like large employers and unions.

- *Strengthening Medicare.* President Bush signed legislation in 2003 to establish a prescription drug benefit under Medicare. Under this plan, private health plans will compete for seniors' business by providing better coverage at affordable prices—helping to control the costs of Medicare by using market-place competition, not government price-setting. And seniors will be able to choose the health care plan that best fits their needs—instead of having that choice made by the government.

- *Expanding Homeownership.* The President believes that homeownership is the cornerstone of America's vibrant communities and benefits individual families by building stability and long-term financial security. In June 2002, President Bush issued *America's Homeownership Challenge* to the real estate and mortgage finance industries to encourage them to join the effort to close the gap that exists between the homeownership rates of minorities and non-minorities. The President also announced the goal of increasing the number of minority homeowners by at least 5.5 million families before the end of the decade. Under his leadership, the overall **U.S. homeownership rate** in the second quarter of 2004 was at an all time high of 69.2 percent. **Minority homeownership** set a new record of 51 percent in the second quarter, up 0.2 percentage point from the first quarter and up 2.1 percentage points from a year ago. President Bush's initiative to dismantle the barriers to homeownership includes:

  - *American Dream Downpayment Initiative,* which provides down payment assistance to approximately 40,000 low-income families;
  - *Affordable Housing.* The President has proposed the Single-Family Affordable Housing Tax Credit, which would increase the supply of affordable homes;
  - *Helping Families Help Themselves.* The President has proposed increasing support for the Self-Help Homeownership Opportunities Program; and
  - *Simplifying Homebuying and Increasing Education.* The President and HUD want to empower homebuyers by simplifying the home buying process so consumers can better understand and benefit from cost savings. The President also wants to expand financial education efforts so that families can understand what they need to do to become homeowners.

- *The Entrepreneurial Spirit of America: Providing Tax Relief to American Families and Small Businesses.* President Bush acted promptly to help America's workers by providing tax relief to put more money in families' pockets and encourage businesses to grow and invest. Tax relief brought substantial savings to families and helped fight back the effects of the recession. America's families and small businesses have more money to spend, save, and invest because of the President's 2001 and 2003 tax cuts. This year, 111 million taxpayers will receive, on average, a tax cut of $1,586 and 25 million small business owners will receive $75 billion in total tax relief.

- The Jobs and Growth Tax Relief Reconciliation Act of 2003 accelerated the tax relief signed into law by the President in 2001, including marriage penalty relief, an increase in the child tax credit, and tax rate reductions for every family that pays income taxes.
- The President's 2001 and 2003 tax cuts also provided new incentives for businesses, especially small businesses, to invest in plants and equipment and create new jobs.
- *President Bush has called on Congress to extend his tax relief plan set to expire next year.* If Congress does not act, American families and businesses would see a tax increase starting next year, thereby hurting economic recovery and future job creation. Unless Congress takes action:
  - In 2006, the small business expensing limit will shrink from $100,000 to just $25,000, increasing the cost of capital investments for America's small businesses;
  - In 2009, the top tax rate on dividends will increase from 15 to 35 percent, while the tax on capital gains will climb from 15 to 20 percent, raising the tax burden on retirees and families investing for their future; and
  - In 2011, the tax rate relief, new 10-percent tax bracket, death tax repeal, marriage penalty relief, small business expensing, and all the remaining tax relief enacted over the past three years will sunset, resulting in tax increases for every individual American man or woman who pays income taxes.
- *Securing America's Retirement Future and Strengthening Social Security:* President Bush is committed to ensuring that Social Security benefits are protected for all seniors, and allowing younger workers the option of investing in safe personal retirement accounts. Americans can also help secure their own future by saving, and President Bush has acted on policies that promote and protect saving.
- *Strengthening Social Security:* Social Security has to be fixed for our children and grandchildren. Fifty years ago there were fifty workers paying into Social Security for every one person receiving benefits. Today there are 3.3 workers supporting each person on Social Security. By the time today's young workers retire, there will be only two. Young workers need the option to invest in retirement accounts that they will own and control. The President's plan to strengthen retirement security includes:
  - The President has proposed voluntary personal accounts for younger workers that would allow them to build a nest egg for retirement that they would own and control, and could pass on to their families. The President's vision for Social Security includes a permanently strengthened Social Security system, without changing benefits for those now in or near retirement, and without raising payroll taxes on workers. Inheritance rights in personal accounts would especially help widows who depend on Social Security.
  - The President appointed a bipartisan Commission that authored a report of recommendations to permanently fix Social Security according to the President's reform principles. Since the report of the President's Commission, six fully detailed proposals have been introduced in Congress to permanently fix Social Security, many of

which adapt elements of the Commission recommendations. The President wants to work with Congress to build a consensus on the best elements of the many proposals that have been put forward. This will require leadership, bipartisanship, and public education.

- Successfully fixing Social Security means that Americans who retire in 2035 will not have to use a system that was built for the world of 1935, but a system that has been modernized to meet the realities of the 21st Century.

- ***Expanding Ownership of Retirement Assets:*** The tax relief legislation signed into law by the President provided almost $50 billion dollars of tax relief over the next ten years to strengthen retirement security. This landmark legislation raised the contribution limits for IRA and 401(k) accounts, allowed for additional "catch up" contributions for workers aged 50 and over, and speeded up the vesting process for employer contributions to 401(k) accounts.

- ***New Savings Opportunities:*** The President has proposed to expand savings opportunities through the creation of Retirement Savings Accounts (RSAs) and Lifetime Savings Accounts (LSAs). RSAs would provide all Americans with an easy, tax-preferred way to prepare for retirement. LSAs would give all Americans the opportunity to save tax free to pay for job training, college tuition, the down-payment on a first home, a car to drive to work, or their retirement.

- ***Ensuring Freedom of Choice:*** The President's proposal would ensure that workers who have participated in 401(k) plans for three years are given the freedom to choose where to invest their retirement savings. The President has also proposed that choice be a feature of Social Security itself, allowing individuals to voluntarily invest a portion of their Social Security taxes in personal retirement accounts.

Paul Glastris

Bush's Ownership Society: Why No One's Buying

.Conservatives have a knack for taking good ideas—say, patriotism or faith—to the sort of ideologized extreme that brands the ideas as theirs and leads liberals to abandon them. We're seeing that now with the issue of choice and individual empowerment. Those very concepts used to be associated with liberal causes like abortion and voting rights. But over the last couple of decades, conservative intellectuals have roped them to a larger agenda to revolutionize government.

And they're perfectly open about it. Talk to scholars at the Cato Institute or the Heritage Foundation or to movement organizers like Grover Norquist, and they'll walk you through the strategy. Big government and individual freedom, they'll explain, are opposed to each other; more of one means less of the other. The three big areas of non-defense-related government spending are retirement (mainly Social Security), health care (mainly Medicare and Medicaid), and education (mainly K–12 public schools). For political reasons, it is practically impossible to cut spending in these areas. But it is possible to dismantle the government bureaucracies that administer them in a way that enhances personal freedom and makes possible big cuts down the road: privatize the benefits.

The father of this line of thinking is Milton Friedman. In the 1950s and 1960s, the conservative economist dreamed up the notions of education vouchers and private accounts for Social Security. Republican operatives and think tankers seized on Friedman's ideas in the 1970s, expanded them into areas like health care, and fleshed out their philosophic and political logic. Vesting individuals with more choice, control, and ownership of their government benefits, they argued, would not only enhance virtues like personal responsibility, but over time, it would also result in the shift of hundreds of billions of tax dollars from the custodial care of government to the corporations that would help manage people's private accounts. Best of all, from the conservative point of view, it would transform the electorate's political identity. Instead of government-dependent supporters of the Democratic Party, voters would become self-reliant followers of the GOP.

These ideas are the intellectual fuel of the conservative movement that has swept across the country in recent decades. They were well understood in the Reagan administration, and the Gipper's speeches are suffused with them. But it has only been in the last few years, with both Congress and the White House in conservative Republican hands, that the ideas have truly debuted.

Now, the reviews are in—and they are not good.

Consider President Bush's effort to sell the public on private Social-Security accounts. Last September, when he first began talking about the idea on the campaign trail, it looked like a winner, with 58 percent support in the polls. By December, only 54 percent favored his proposal. By February, following his detailed explanation of private accounts in his State of the Union address, support fell to 46 percent. And by June, when informed that private accounts would be paired with cuts in benefits for future retirees—as the president himself admitted they would have to be to have any impact on Social Security's long-run finances—27 percent of voters gave their approval, a level of support below that for legalizing marijuana and gay marriage.

Or consider another high-profile element of what Bush calls the "ownership society": giving individuals more control over their government health-care benefits. In 2003, the president signed a landmark measure providing prescription drug coverage to Medicare recipients, with massive subsidies to lure beneficiaries into private plans. Prior to the law's passage, 90 percent of the public supported the idea of government helping seniors with drug costs. Today, a scant 31 percent of Americans have a favorable impression of the new program. It's possible that, once the benefit actually goes into effect beginning next year, seniors will flock to it gratefully. But an interim effort offering seniors a choice of drug discount cards doesn't inspire confidence. Only 6.4 million seniors wound up getting the drug discount cards, a million fewer than the government predicted. Low-income seniors who signed up for the card were given an extra $600 subsidy to help defray the cost of co-pays—a benefit the government estimated would lure 4.7 million low-income seniors into the program. Only 1.9 million lower-income seniors actually did sign up.

Finally, consider the president's efforts to give parents more choice over the schools their children attend. Under Bush's No Child Left Behind Act, millions of students in failing schools can now transfer to other schools in their district. It is the grandest experiment in public-school choice ever attempted, and polls show overwhelming support for it. In practice, however, only about 1 percent of students in failing schools annually have taken advantage of the opportunity. That could mean that districts aren't eagerly publicizing the choice provisions, or that parents aren't impressed with the array of often-dysfunctional public schools they have to choose from. That's why conservatives say the federal government should go the next step and provide students with vouchers for private schools. Yet a two-year-old federal voucher experiment in D.C. that provides low-income students a hefty $7,500 to attend private schools has garnered only modestly more interest. Only 7 percent of families with children eligible for the vouchers have applied for them.

You can begin to see a pattern here. Americans love the idea of choice— in the abstract. But when faced with the actual choices conservatives present, they aren't buying. The reason is that conservatives have constructed choices that fail to take human nature into account. People like to have choices but feel quickly overwhelmed when they lack the information or expertise to decide confidently, and they turn downright negative when the choices themselves seem to put what they already have at risk. Conservatives were bound to make these mistakes because their very aim has been to transfer more risks from government to individuals so that government's size and expenditures can be cut. That's not a bargain most Americans will accept. They like choice just fine, but they won't trade security to get it.

That's not to say individual choice and control can't be applied intelligently to government. In fact, doing so may be key to achieving important progressive aims like universal health care. But designing policies that use choice and that Americans would actually embrace won't make government weaker. Rather, it will require government to be stronger.

Dozen Card Monte

It's understandable that conservatives would think that giving individuals more choice and control over government services would be an easy sell. After all, consumers increasingly enjoy these things in the marketplace. Everything, from cars to computers to pastas, now comes in an astonishing array of styles, colors, and configurations. Consumers today have access to new tools that shift control to them, and the younger they are, the more comfortable they are with that control. No one under 30 these days calls a travel agent; they use Orbitz.

But as choices and individual control have expanded, economists and behavioral psychologists have begun to document some unexpected ways people actually react to these new marketplace choices. Swarthmore social theorist Barry Schwartz explored their findings in his book *The Paradox of Choice*. On the one hand, notes Schwartz, having control and choice clearly benefits us. People who peruse a variety of options before choosing tend to make objectively better decisions. There are important psychological benefits as well. The ability to express one's identity via the choices one makes—in everything from the clothes we wear to the charities we contribute to—greatly increases human happiness.

On the other hand, having an ever-expanding number of choices doesn't necessarily make us happier, just as bigger and bigger food portions don't make us healthier. Indeed, too many choices tend to stress us out. Even trivial choices often require expenditures of time and energy to make informed decisions. When the variables are too numerous, people often decide that the effort isn't worth it. In one study, individuals were offered tastes of six different exotic jams and given a coupon worth a dollar off any of the jams. Another group was offered a choice of 24 jams and a coupon. Those in the first group were more likely to buy jam than those in the second.

As choices have proliferated, we feel overwhelmed, as if we're losing control—the very opposite of the feeling choice is supposed to bring. These anxieties, plus the natural human tendency to procrastinate, means that most people, most of the time, respond to choices by doing nothing. They choose not to choose.

The prescription-drug discount-card program is a classic example. The program seemed designed to give seniors more stress than savings. There were dozens of cards to choose from. Each card was good at only certain pharmacies. Each covered only certain drugs. And the amount of discount for each medicine varied by card. With so many possible permutations, figuring out which card was the best deal was largely guesswork. According to surveys conducted for the government by Apt Associates Inc, seniors complained that they "found the multiplicity of choices to be overwhelming." Those who did sign up for the cards generally liked them—though many said they found better prices at Costco without using the cards. Yet more than half of card users didn't shop around. They just accepted the first card they heard about (usually from their pharmacist). And the few seniors who did comparison-shop for cards reported only slightly higher levels of satisfaction than those who didn't.

The big flaw in the drug discount-card program was the complexity and incomparability of the choices it provided seniors. Had the GOP lawmakers and administration appointees who designed the program been less enamored of market principles and corporate lobbying agendas and been willing to impose stricter guidelines on the participating companies, so that the different features of the cards could be more easily compared, more seniors might have participated. After all, the program did offer Medicare recipients something they wanted and didn't have: financial help paying for prescription drugs.

The more intractable problem with the president's ownership society is its effort to inject choice and control into benefits people already have. Here, the culprit is not complexity but risk. Behavioral economists have described what's known as an "endowment effect": People are psychologically prone to be exceptionally risk-averse with benefits they already have. With his Social-Security private-accounts proposal, the president was in essence offering voters a variety of ways to have less retirement security. The reaction should not have been a surprise. Surveys by the Pew Research Center found that 60 percent of those who opposed private Social-Security accounts said they worried about the risk—to themselves, to others, and to the system as a whole.

Conservatives may have been blindsided by the public's rejection of the president's plan because they assumed that most Americans share their fundamental assumptions about government: that more of it is bad, less of it is good. On an abstract level, many people do feel that way. The line in the president's stump speech, that the American people can be trusted to spend their own money better than the government, usually gets an applause. But when forced to consider concrete alternatives, Americans often wind up putting their trust in the collective efforts of government to protect their security rather than in themselves. Though the president succeeded in convincing the public that Social Security has long-term financial problems, he did not convince them that shifting control and choice to individuals was the solution. Rather, polls showed huge majorities favor such measures as raising the income cap on payroll taxes to inject more money into the current system—in other words, making government bigger, not smaller.

The same dichotomy, between the choice people say they want in the abstract and what they actually want in practice, exists in other realms. For instance, conservatives have looked at polls and focus groups and convinced themselves that individuals are willing to accept more responsibility for their own health care. That's why so many on the right who detested the high cost of the prescription drug law are excited by one of its provisions, that would set up Health Savings Accounts. These are tax-favored 401(k)-like devises that allow individuals to "own" their own health care and make their own health care decisions. But in the end, will the public really welcome more individual responsibility over health care? Consider this: sixty-five percent of people polled say that if they got cancer they would want to choose their treatment options. But 88 percent of people who actually have cancer say they don't want to choose their treatment, preferring instead that their doctors do so. "Having the opportunity to choose," writes Schwartz, "is no blessing if we feel we do not have the wherewithal to choose wisely."

Forcing a Decision

It would be easy and natural for liberals to react to the failure of Bush's Ownership Society with a "Phew, that was close. Now, we don't have to think about choice anymore." That would be a mistake, for two reasons.

First, it's not like the right is suddenly going to stop pushing these ideas just because Bush himself failed to sell them. The voucherizing of government is part of the guiding vision of modern conservatism. Entire organizations are funded primarily to achieving it. The problem with Social-Security private accounts, Grover Norquist recently told me, is "nothing that can't be solved with 60 Republican votes in the Senate."

Second, as reform-minded progressives from author and speechwriter Andrei Cherny to British Prime Minister Tony Blair have been at pains to argue, the public's aspirations are changing. People want and receive more choice and individual control in the marketplace, and for all its frustrations, they rather like it, and will naturally expect more individual choice and control from government, too. Conservatives have tapped into a real yearning. What they've failed to do, for ideological reasons, is apply these concepts in ways that actually solve problems. Liberals are in a much better ideological position to actually deliver on the demand for more individual control and choice. The only obstacle is realizing that liberal policy goals can be advanced by smart proposals that let citizens make their own decisions.

An instructive example is public housing. Back in the early 1990s, Jack Kemp, George H.W. Bush's charismatic Housing and Urban Development secretary, was pushing the idea of selling off public housing to tenants and letting those tenants manage their own buildings. It was a classic early example of "ownership-society" thinking—Kemp called it "empowerment"—and it was, when you think about it, highly dubious. Is it really a favor to saddle the responsibility for maintaining decrepit high-rise buildings in terrible neighborhoods on the tenants who are stuck there, many of whom have trouble managing their own personal lives? Kemp wanted to fix the places up first, but the cost would have run $100,000 per unit in 1990 dollars—enough, noted OMB Director and Kemp nemesis Richard Darman, to buy each tenant a condo.

Kemp's ideas, well-meaning as they were, went nowhere. It took his successor in the Bill Clinton administration, Henry Cisneros, to figure out an "empowerment" strategy that actually worked.

Cisneros and his advisers—including Chief of Staff Bruce Katz and Assistant Secretary (and later secretary) Andrew Cuomo—figured out two important truths. First, they understood what urban experts had been saying for years: that the heart of the problem of public housing was the way it concentrated poverty in one place. Second, they grasped that to address this problem would require using certain choice-enhancing, market-based tools long favored by Republicans and disparaged by Democrats—namely, housing vouchers and tax credits for developers.

And so, with the backing of the president and GOP moderates in Congress, Cisneros and his team implemented a sweeping plan to break up that concentrated poverty. The department forced local housing authorities to tear down broken-down, crime-ridden public-housing complexes. It encouraged the building of low-rise replacement public housing or gave departing residents Section 8 housing vouchers to help find private apartments in better neighborhoods. It also provided private and non-profit developers tax credits to build or rehab apartment buildings with rules requiring that they rent to a mix of both poor and working-class tenants.

These largely unsung efforts helped drive the renewal of many urban centers that took place in the 1990s. Not enough time has passed to know how effective they were in improving the lives of HUD's poor. But surveys by the Urban Institute show that those who left public housing did wind up in somewhat better neighborhoods, and that former residents "generally perceive themselves as being better off," with better housing conditions and fewer mental-health problems.

Notice how Cisneros's reforms were structured. They utilized policies that empowered individuals (housing vouchers, tax credits). But they relied on strict government regulation to guide the process towards a goal (breaking up concentrated poverty) that public officials determined was in the best interests of tenants and the nation. And they understood that most people, most of the time, will choose not to choose, and so they forced the issue. Individuals could move to other public housing or to temporary housing until the new low-rise developments were finished, or take a Section 8 voucher, but staying in condemned public housing wasn't an option.

Libertarian Paternalism

Choice, then, can be a powerful tool to advance public ends as long as one ironic truth is recognized: People like having choice but often don't like to choose.

This concept is at the center of a brewing movement within public-policy circles, one that Cass Sunstein and Richard H. Thaler of the University of Chicago have affectionately, if cheekily, dubbed "libertarian paternalism." The idea is for government to shape the choices people have so that the natural human tendency to avoid making a decision works to the individuals' and society's advantage.

For instance, many private-sector employees don't participate in company-sponsored 401(k) programs, even though participation is hugely in their financial interest (employees can invest pre-tax dollars and watch their money grow tax-free until the money is withdrawn). Lower-paid employees are the least likely to participate because they reap fewer tax benefits, seldom receive a company match, and are often living paycheck to paycheck. But the biggest reason lower-income employees don't participate is the hassle factor. The forms are a bother to fill out. They don't know much about investing. They can't decide where to put their money. They choose not to choose.

Understanding this, some clever officials in the Clinton administration changed the rules governing 401(k)s to allow for "automatic enrollment." Henceforth, firms could choose to automatically put aside a percentage of all employees' wages in 401(k) accounts. Employees would have the ability to "opt out" of the program, thus retaining the right to choose, but would have to take the initiative themselves in order to exercise that right. In practice, few do. A study of companies that instituted automatic 401(k) enrollment, by economists Bridgette Madrian and Dennis Shea, found that participation rates for employees making under $20,000 annually rose from 13 percent to 80 percent.

Imagine if every company in America automatically enrolled its employees in 401(k)s, IRAs, or similar retirement accounts? That one simple step might do more to strengthen America's retirement system than any number of changes to Social Security (at no cost to the federal treasury).

Scholars think this "opt-out" concept could be applied to a wide range of policies that are vitally important, broadly supported politically, but plagued by low participation rates. Why not automatically enroll all owners of homes on floodplains into the federal-flood insurance program? Why not automatically enroll all eligible low-income working families into SCHIP, the health-insurance program for children of such famlies?

A related strategy for dealing with the natural human reluctance to choose is the one used by Cisneros: compel people to make a choice. The New America Foundation has proposed making health insurance mandatory, as auto insurance is, with federal subsidies for lower-income workers to be able to buy private policies.

That idea could be combined with another one popular in liberal circles: A universal health-care initiative that would allow individuals to buy into the health-insurance program for civil servants, the Federal Employees Health Benefits (FEHB). Under FEHB, workers choose from an array of private insurance plans pre-selected for quality and efficiency by the government. Also, those plans must disclose price, coverage, and other information in standard ways, so that employees can make apples to apples comparisons before choosing. It's no coincidence that federal workers report higher levels of satisfaction with their health care than most Americans working in the private sector.

Education is another area where structured choices might be beneficial. New Democrats have long supported giving parents more choice via charter schools. The jury's still out on whether charter schools produce any real educational benefits, and the schools themselves are prey to sabotage by the education bureaucracies. But studies suggest charter schools do have two advantages. First, parents who chose them for their kids do seem to like them. Second, the act of choosing tends to inspire more parental involvement and a more cohesive school culture, two attributes typical of successful schools.

One way to capture those benefits within larger school systems with large numbers of failing schools would be to make choice mandatory. Parents would have the option of putting their children into one of several schools in the district, including their neighborhood school. But not choosing would not be an option. Several districts have experimented with this idea. The most famous was District 4 in East Harlem, New York. In the 1970s, the district launched an experiment which combined mandatory choice with relaxed rules that allowed groups of administrators, teachers and parents to form small schools-within-schools focused on unique curricula—art, science, technology etc. The results were public schools with strong cultures and more parental involvement, and while not all students benefited, test scores rose substantially.

There are plenty of good reasons, then, for progressives to embrace the idea of designing more choice and individual control into government programs. But doing so means facing down some major opposition—from corporations that don't want to be regulated to liberal interest groups that often oppose choice initiatives. Liberals also have to stop accepting the right-wing proposition that choice and empowerment are somehow inherently conservative ideas.

But it's conservatives who face the bigger obstacle. They are committed to a strategy of using choice as a Trojan horse to undermine government, yet it's impossible to make choice work in the real world without strong measures from government. With choice, as with so much else, conservatives have mastered the art of winning elections with abstract language voters agree with, even as they push policies voters don't much like. They can't pull that trick off forever. At some point, conservatives themselves are going to have to make a choice.

POSTSCRIPT

Will the Creation of an Ownership Society Make the American Economy More Efficient and More Equitable?

The Bush administration seeks to expand ownership in American society. This effort involves initiatives in several different areas. One area is health care and the actions include the creation of Health Savings Accounts, Association Health Plans, and the new Medicare Part D drug prescription program. A second area is housing and the actions include the American Dream Downpayment Initiative and the Affordable Housing Tax Credit. Small business constitutes a third area and the actions are centered primarily on tax cuts. Retirement is the fourth area and President Bush has proposed personal savings accounts and is exploring other changes in the Social Security System. President Bush believes "The more ownership there is in America, the more vitality there is in America, and the more people have a vital stake in the future of this country."

Paul Glastris begins his analysis of President Bush's ownership society by noting that conservatives want to dismantle "big government" but cannot effectively reduce spending in such areas as retirement, health care, and education. The solution to this apparent dilemma is to switch the spending from public to private—to privatize. In other words, the way of getting government out of these areas is privatization. He notes that the ideas of vouchers for school choice and private accounts for Social Security go back to the writings of Milton Friedman in the 1950s and 1960s. He then reviews three of the privatization efforts and their "failure." Bush's efforts to create private retirement accounts has been rejected by the public; participation in the Medicare Part D prescription drug program is lower than expected; and the exercise of choice under the No Child Left Behind Program has been very low. Glastris explains this rejection of privatization and greater choice in two ways. First, people refuse to choose "when they lack the information or the expertise to decide confidentially." Second, people will not trade security for greater choice. But Glastris endorses the concept of choice and reviews some cases when choice programs have worked. The lesson he draws from this review, and one that conservatives should heed, is "that it is impossible to make choice work in the real world without strong measures from government."

Many of President Bush's proposals that encompass his ownership society are examined as separate issues in the this book: Issue 4 examines the Medicare Part D drug benefit, Issue 5 covers the Health Savings Accounts, and Issue 18 takes up the No Child Left Behind Act. For philosophic perspectives on conservative and liberal positions, see *Free to Choose* by Milton and Rose

Friedman (Harcourt Brace Jovanovich, 1980) and "The Social Consensus and the Conservative Onslaught," by John Kenneth Galbraith in *The Millenium Journal of International Studies* (Spring 1982). For another analysis of the ownership society as described by President Bush, see "Defining an Ownership Society" by David Boaz at http://www.cato.org/special/ownership_society/boaz.html.

Contributors to This Volume

CO-EDITORS

FRANK J. BONELLO received his B.S. from the University of Detroit in 1961, his M.A. from the University of Detroit in 1963, and his Ph.D. from Michigan State University in 1968. He is currently associate professor of economics at the University of Notre Dame, where he also served as Arts and Letters College Fellow. He writes in the areas of monetary economics and economic education. This is his sixth book. He is the author of *The Formulation of Expected Interest Rates* and coauthor of *Computer-Assisted Instruction in Economic Education*. In addition to *Taking Sides*, he has co-edited, with T.R. Swartz, *Alternative Directions in Economic Policy* (Notre Dame Press, 1978); *The Supply Side: Debating Current Economic Policies* (Dushkin, 1983); and *Urban Finance Under Siege* (M.E. Sharpe, 1993).

ISOBEL LOBO received her M.A., M.S.A., and Ph.D. (1998) from the University of Notre Dame. She is currently assistant professor of economics in the International Business and Economics Department at Benedictine University. She has also taught at the University of Notre Dame and Saint Joseph's College in Renesselaer, Indiana. This is her first book. She writes in the areas of general economics and economic education, and has presented papers at the Academy of International Business Conference, the Association for Global Business Conference, and the Hawaii Conference on International Business. She is planning to write an international economics text specifically for non-economics major.

STAFF

Larry Loeppke	Managing Editor
Jill Peter	Senior Developmental Editor
Susan Brusch	Senior Developmental Editor
Beth Kundert	Production Manager
Jane Mohr	Project Manager
Tara McDermott	Design Coordinator
Nancy Meissner	Editorial Assistant
Julie Keck	Senior Marketing Manager
Mary Klein	Marketing Communications Specialist
Alice Link	Marketing Coordinator
Tracie Kammerude	Senior Marketing Assistant
Shirley Lanners	Pemissions Coordinator

AUTHORS

ROBERT ALMEDER is a professor of philosophy at Georgia State University. He is the editor of the *American Philosophical Quarterly*, co-editor of the annual book series *Biomedical Ethic Reviews*, and former member of the editorial board of the *Journal of Business Ethics*. He earned his Ph.D. in philosophy at the University of Pennsylvania, and he is the author of *Harmless Naturalism: The Limits of Science and the Nature of Philosophy* (Open Court, 1998).

RICHARD APPELBAUM is professor of sociology and global and international studies at the University of California at Santa Barbara. He currently serves as director of the Institute for Social, Behavioral, and Economic Research (ISBER) and co-director of the ISBER's Center for Global Studies. He is the founding editor of *Competition and Change: The Journal of Global Business and Political Economy*. He earned his Ph.D. from the University of Chicago.

DEAN BAKER is the co-founder and co-director of the Center for Economic and Policy Research. His books include *Social Security: The Phony Crisis*, co-authored with Mark Weisbrot (University of Chicago Press, 1999), *Getting Prices Right: The Battle Over the Consumer Price Index* (M.E. Sharpe Press 1997), and *Globalization and Progressive Economic Policy*, edited with Jerry Epstein and Bob Pollin (Cambridge University Press, 1998). He holds a Ph.D. in economics from the University of Michigan.

LENNY BERNSTEIN has a Ph.D. in chemical engineering from Purdue University. He has authored more than 30 articles on the social, economic, and environmental consequences of climatic change. Currently he heads L.S. Bernstein & Associates, L.L.C., a corporate consulting firm that focuses on the political and scientific developments associated with climate change and other global environmental issues.

GERALD W. BRACEY is an associate professor of education at George Mason University and an associate of the High/Scope Educational Research Foundation. His most recent book is *Setting the Record Straight: Responses to Misconceptions About Public Education in the U.S.*, 2nd ed. (Heinemann, 2004). His prior books include *The War Against America's Public Schools* (Allyn & Bacon, 2002) and *Put to the Test: An Educator's and Consumer's Guide to Standardized Testing* (Phi Delta Kappa, 2002). His education includes a Ph.D. in psychology from Stanford University.

LESTER R. BROWN holds degrees form Rutgers University, the University of Maryland, and Harvard University. In 1974, he founded Worldwatch Institute, the first research institute devoted to the analysis of global environmental issues. At the Institute, he launched a number of publications, including the annual *State of the World* reports. In 2001, he founded the Earth Policy Institute to "provide a vision and a road map for achieving an environmentally sustainable economy." He has authored or co-authored 49 books including *Eco-Economy: Building an Economy for the Earth* (W.W. Norton, 2001).

PATRICK J. BUCHANAN sought the Republican nomination for the presidency in 1992, 1996, and 2000. He is frequently seen on television, and has served as a co-host on CNN's *Crossfire*. He writes a twice-weekly syndicated column and is the author of *The Great Betrayal: How American Sovereignty and Social Justice Are Being Sacrificed to the Gods of the Global Economy* (Little, Brown, 1998). He holds degrees from Georgetown and Columbia.

WILLIAM A. DARITY, JR. is a research professor of Public Studies, Africa and African American Studies, and Economics at Duke University. He is also the Cary C. Boshamer Professor of Economics at the University of North Carolina. He is co-author, with Samuel L. Myers, Jr., of *Persistent Disparity: Race and Economic Inequality in the U.S. Since 1945* (Edward Elgar, 1998). He holds a Ph.D. from the Massachusetts Institute of Technology.

DEMOCRATIC STAFF OF THE HOUSE COMMITTEE ON EDUCATION AND THE WORKFORCE. The names of the individuals who serve as members can be found at http://edworkforce.housegov/democrats/staff.html.

PETER DREIER is the Dr. E. P. Clapp Distinguished Professor of Politics and the director of the Urban & Environmental Policy Program of the Urban & Environmental Policy Institute at Occidental College in Los Angeles, California. He joined the Occidental faculty in January 1993, after serving 9 years as the director of housing at the Boston Redevelopment Authority and as senior policy advisor to the mayor of Boston. He previously taught at Tufts University. He is the author of *Place Matters: Metropolitics for the Twenty-first Century* (University Press of Kansas, 2004) and the forthcoming *The Next LA: The Struggle for a Livable City* (University of California Press).

CHRIS EDWARDS is the director of Tax Policy Studies at the Cato Institute. He has also been an economist with the Tax Foundation, a consultant and manager with PriceWaterhouseCoopers, and senior economist with the congressional Joint Economic Committee. He holds an M.A. in economics from George Mason University.

JOEL FRIEDMAN joined the staff of the Center on Budget and Policy Priorities in September 2000 as a senior fellow. He divided his time between federal tax and budget issues and the International Budget Project. Immediately prior to coming to the Center, he worked in the South African Ministry of Finance, where he spent nearly 4 years as the U.S. Treasury's resident budget advisor. Before moving to South Africa, he was the director of budget analysis for the Democratic Staff of the House Budget Committee and a financial economist in the Budget Review Division of the Office of Management and Budget. He holds an M.P.A. from the Woodrow Wilson School of Public and International Affairs and a B.A. from Pomona College.

MILTON FRIEDMAN received the 1976 Nobel Prize in Economic Science for his work in consumption analysis and monetary history and theory and for demonstrating stabilization policy complexity. In 1998, he received both the Presidential Medal of Freedom and the National Medal of Science. He and his wife, who also writes on economic topics, co-authored several publications including *Two Lucky People* (University of Chicago Press, 1998) and *Free to Choose: A Personal Statement* (Harcourt Brace, 1990). Professor Friedman served as a senior research fellow at the Stanford University Hoover Institution on War, Revolution, and Peace from 1977 until his passing in 2006.

DIANA FURCHTGOTT-ROTH is a senior fellow at the Hudson Institute and director of Hudson's Center for Employment Policy. She is a former chief economist at the U.S. Department of Labor and has also served as chief of staff of the President's Council of Economic Advisors. She is the co-author of *Women's Figures: An Illustrated Guide to the Economics of Women in America.* She has appeared on a number of radio and television shows including C-SPAN'S Washington Journal and The NewsHour with Jim Lehrer.

PAUL GLASTRIS is the editor in chief of *The Washington Monthly* and a senior fellow at the Western Policy Center in Washington, DC. He holds two degrees from Northwestern University and spent 10 years at *U.S. News & World Report*. He also served as a special assistant and senior speechwriter for President Bill Clinton from September 1998 to January 2001.

JAGADEESH GOKHALE holds the position of senior fellow at the Cato Institute where he works with Cato's Project on Social Security Choice. His previous positions include consultant to the U.S. Department of Treasury, senior economic adviser to the Federal Reserve Bank of Cleveland, and visiting scholar with the American Enterprise Institute. He is co-author of *Fiscal and Generational Imbalances: New Budget Measures for New Budget Priorities.* He holds a Ph.D. in economics from Boston University.

ALFREDO GOYBURU held the position of policy analyst in the Center for Data Analysis at The Heritage Foundation. He previously worked as a regional and energy economist for WEFA, a leader in economic information and forecasting. Before that, he worked as an economist for the New York state legislature, studying the impact of tax policy. Goyburu holds a bachelor's degree in economics from Cornell and an advanced economics degree from the University of Albany.

ROBERT GREENSTEIN is the founder and executive director of the Center on Budget and Policy Priorities. Greenstein is considered an expert on the federal budget and, in particular, the impact of tax and budget proposals on low-income people. Greenstein has written numerous reports, analyses, op-ed pieces, and magazine articles on poverty-related issues. In awarding him a MacArthur Fellowship, the MacArthur Foundation cited Greenstein for making "the Center a model for a non-partisan research and policy organization." In 1994, he was appointed by President Clinton to serve on the bipartisan Commission on Entitlement and Tax Reform. Prior to founding the Center, Greenstein was administrator of the Food and Nutrition Service at the U.S. Department of Agriculture, where he directed the agency that operates federal food assistance programs, with a staff of 2,500 and a budget of $15 billion.

JAMES J. HECKMAN is Henry Schultz Distinguished Service Professor of Economics at the University of Chicago and senior fellow of the American Bar Association. He received the 2000 Nobel Prize in Economic Science for his development of theory and methods for analyzing selective samples. He is co-editor, with Burton Singer, of *Longitudinal Analysis of Labor Market Data* (Cambridge University Press 1985). He received his Ph.D. in economics from Princeton University.

HOUSE EDUCATION AND THE WORKFORCE COMMITTEE was established on January 7, 1997, and has five subcommittees. It oversees education and workforce programs that affect and support many Americans.

IRA T. KAY is global practice director for executive compensation at Watson Wyatt Worldwide and co-author of the forthcoming book *Myths and Realities of Executive Pay*. His previous publications include *CEO Pay and Shareholder Value: Helping the U.S. Win the Global Economic War* and *Value at the Top: Solutions to the Executive Compensation Crisis*. He earned his undergraduate degree in industrial and labor relations from Cornell University and his Ph.D. in economics from Wayne State University.

NICHOLAS D. KRISTOF is a columnist with *The New York Times* and served for 14 years as one of that newspaper's Asia correspondents. He is co-author, with Sheryl WuDunn, of *Thunder from the East: Portrait of a Rising Asia*. He received, with Sheryl WuDunn, the 1990 Pulitzer Prize for coverage of the Tiananmen democracy movement in China and its suppression.

EDWARD L. LANGSTON, RPh, MD, is a family physician in private practice in Lafayette, Indiana. He is also chair-elect of the Board of Trustees of the American Medical Association. He holds an undergraduate degree from Purdue University and received his medical degree from Indiana University School of Medicine.

LOS ANGELES COUNTY ECONOMIC DEVELOPMENT CORPORATION is a private nonprofit organization established in 1981 with the mission to attract, retain, and grow business and jobs in the Los Angeles region.

D. W. MACKENZIE teaches economics at the State University of New York at Plattsburgh.

STEVEN MALANGA is a contributing editor of *City Journal* and a senior fellow at the Manhattan Institute. He previously held the position of executive editor of *Crain's New York Business*. His articles have also appeared in such publications as *The Wall Street Journal, New York Daily News*, and the *New York Post*. His education includes an M.A. in English literature and language from the University of Maryland.

ROBERT D. MANNING is a professor of finance at Rochester Institute of Technology and research associate of the Center for Comparative Immigration Studies at the University of California, San Diego. He is the author of *Credit Card Nation: The Consequences of America's Addiction to Credit* (Basic Books, 2000). He holds a Ph.D. from Johns Hopkins University.

PATRICK L. MASON is an associate professor of economics at Florida State University and director of African American Studies. He is also an associate editor for the Southern Economic Association. He is a past president of the National Economics Association and the co-editor of several books including *Readings in Black Political Economy* (Rowland and Littlefield, 2005).

MARK McCLELLAN has just left his potion as administrator for the Centers for Medicare and Medicaid Services in the U.S. Department of Health and Human Services and accepted a position of visiting senior fellow at the AEI-Brookings Joint Center. He has also served as commissioner for the Food and Drug Administration. He holds an M.D. degree from the Harvard-MIT Division of Health Sciences and Technology, a Ph.D. in economics from Massachusetts Institute of Technology, and a M.P.A. from the Harvard University Kennedy School of Government.

MICHAEL F. McENENEY is a partner in the law firm of Sidley Austin Brown & Wood L.L.P. and represents the Consumer Bankers Association. He earned his J.D. degree from Boston University School of Law. In his practice, he focuses primarily on regulatory and legislative issues impacting financial institutions with special emphasis on retail banking.

JOHN M. MELLE is deputy assistant U.S. Trade Representative for North America. At USTR since 1987, his previous positions include senior director for North American Affairs and deputy director of the Generalized System of Preferences. He holds a M.A. degree in Public Policy from the University of Michigan.

NORBERT J. MICHEL is a policy analyst with The Heritage Foundation's Center for Data Analysis. His areas of expertise include corporate finance and monetary economics. Before joining The Heritage Foundation, he worked for Entergy, a global energy company. He earned his Ph.D. from the University of New Orleans.

SANDRA POLASKI is a senior associate with the Carnegie Endowment for International Peace, serving as the director of the Trade, Equity and Development Project. Before moving to her current position, she served as the U.S. Secretary of State's special representative for international labor affairs. She holds M.S. degrees from both the University of Wisconsin and John Hopkins University.

RALPH A. RECTOR is a research fellow at The Heritage Foundation and is the project manager of its Center for Data Analysis. Before joining The Heritage Foundation, he worked inn the Tax Policy Economics Group at Coopers & Lybrand, L.L.P., where he supervised the construction of microsimulation models used to analyze the impact of tax reform on businesses and individuals. He has managed projects involving the use of large-scale relational databases and economic models. He has also served as a tax analyst and revenue estimator at the state and federal levels. He obtained his Ph.D. in economics from George Mason University.

MURRAY N. ROTHBARD (1926–1995) was a professor of economics at the University of Nevada, Las Vegas, and the vice president for academic affairs at the Ludwig von Mises Institute. Over his 45-year professional career, he wrote 25 books and thousands of articles, critical of socialism, statism, relativism, and scientism. He was instrumental in reviving an interest in the Austrian school of economics.

CHARLIE STENHOLM is a former member of the U.S. House of Representatives, serving the 17th District in Texas for 13 terms, from 1979 to 2005. He has two degrees from Texas Tech University and has operated a cotton farm in Texas. He is currently a senior policy advisor at a Washington, D.C. law firm and is a member of the board of directors of the Committee for a Responsible Federal Budget and the Concord Coalition.

U.S. DEPARTMENT OF HEALTH AND HUMAN RESOURCES is the "U.S. government's principal agency for protecting the health of all Americans and providing essential human services, especially for those who are least able to help themselves." For fiscal year 2005, it had a budget of $581 billion and over 67,000 employees.

THE WHITE HOUSE can be reached at http://wwwwhitehouse.gov/. At this location is an "Issues" link. Utilizing this link, persons can find prepared statements presenting the position of the Bush administration, on variety of issues including Social Security and the ownership society.

JEANNETTE WICKS-LIM is an economist and research fellow at the Political Economy Research Institute at the University of Massachusetts–Amherst. She holds an undergraduate from the University of Michigan and earned her Ph.D. in economics from the University of Massachusetts–Amherst.

JACKSON WILLIAMS, at the time he wrote his essay, was the legal counsel for Public Citizen's Congress Watch concentrating on civil justice issues. Previously, he was manager of public affairs for Defense Research Institute, the bar association of insurance defense counsel, where he also specialized in civil justice policy issues. He is a graduate of Loyola University of Chicago School of Law.

EDGAR S. WOOLARD, JR. is the CEO and chairman of the board of directors of Dupont. He is the current chairman of the New York Stock Exchange's compensation Committee. He is also a former director of Citgroup Inc. IBM, Apple Computer, Inc. and Bell Atlantic Delaware. He received his undergraduate degree in industrial engineering from North Carolina State University.

SHERYL WuDUNN is a correspondent with *The New York Times* and served for 14 years as one of that newspaper's Asia correspondents. She is co-author, with Nicholas Kristof, of *Thunder from the East: Portrait of a Rising Asia*. She received, with Nicholas Kristof, the 1990 Pulitzer Prize for coverage of the Tiananmen democracy movement in China and its suppression.

Index

Acknowledgments

The editor and the publisher have made every effort to trace the ownership of all copyrighted material and to secure permission from copyright holders of such material. In the event of any question arising as to the use of any material the publisher and editor, while expressing regret for inadvertent error, will be pleased to make the necessary corrections in future printings. Thanks are due to the following authors, publishers, publications and agents for permission to use the material indicated.

ABINGDON PRESS, for excerpt from *I Have A Stewardship*, Robert Spaulding Cushman, copyright renewed 1967 by Maude E. Cushman; for excerpt from *The Divine Yes* by E. Stanley Jones, copyright (c) 1975 by Abingdon Press.

ASSOCIATION PRESS, for excerpt from *The Meaning of Prayer* by Harry Emerson Fosdick.

THE CHRISTIAN CENTURY FOUNDATION, for excerpt by J. Maurice Trimmer, from the January 12, 1944, issue of *The Christian Century*, copyright 1944 by Christian Century Foundation.

DOUBLEDAY & CO. INC., for excerpt from *How to Believe* by Ralph W. Stockman, copyright 1953 by Ralph W. Stockman; for excerpt from *How Can I Find You, God?* by Marjorie Holmes, copyright (c) 1957 by Marjorie Holmes Mighell; for excerpt from *Peace With God* by Billy Graham, copyright 1953 by Billy Graham.

HARCOURT BRACE JOVANOVICH, INC., for excerpts from *Letters to Malcolm: Chiefly on Prayer* by C.S. Lewis, copyright (c) 1963, 1964 by The Estate of C.S. Lewis and/or C.S. Lewis.

O Merciful God, be Thou now unto me a strong tower of defence, I humbly entreat Thee. Give me grace to await Thy leisure, and patiently to bear what Thou doest unto me; nothing doubting or mistrusting Thy goodness towards me; for Thou knowest what is good for me better than I do. Therefore do with me in all things what Thou wilt; only arm me, I beseech Thee, with Thine armour, that I may stand fast; above all things, taking to me the shield of faith; abiding Thy pleasure, and comforting myself in those troubles which it shall please Thee to send me, seeing such troubles are profitable for me; and I am assuredly persuaded that all Thou doest cannot but be well; and unto Thee be all honour and glory. Amen.

Lady Jane Grey

REACH ME YOUR HAND

Reach down to me Your Hand! The way is steep
That I must go alone; and undefined.
Still blindly, I, who have too long been blind,
Must grope the stony trail and, prostrate, creep
Its weary length. Reach down to me! and keep
My fumbling fingers closely intertwined.
I have been told that earthly shepherds bind
The broken and the wounded of their sheep.

How much more gentle, then, Your touch to form
Anew; to bind the heart and to expand
The soul! And I, though shattered by the storm
That breaks about me now, shall rise—shall stand
Erect, enveloped lovingly and warm;
No more alone. Reach down to me Your Hand!

Ruth Crary

CRUSADER'S HYMN

Fairest Lord Jesus,
Ruler of all nature,
O Thou of God and man the Son;
Thee will I cherish,
Thee will I honor,
Thou, my soul's glory, joy, and crown.

Fair are the meadows,
Fairer still the woodlands,
Robed in the blooming garb of spring:
Jesus is fairer,
Jesus is purer,
Who makes the woeful heart to sing.

Fair is the sunshine,
Fairer still the moonlight,
And all the twinkling, starry host:
Jesus shines brighter,
Jesus shines purer,
Than all the angels heaven can boast.

Anonymous

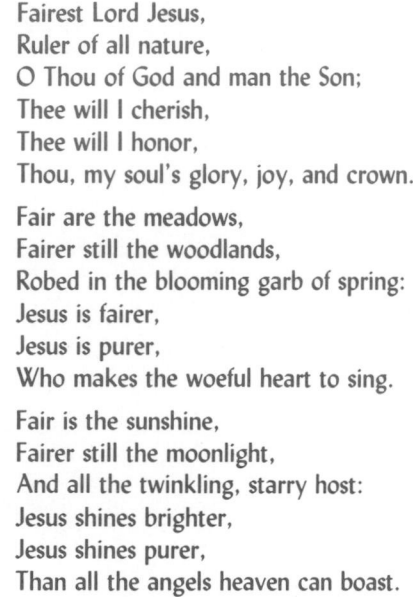

Help us, God, and give us light so that we don't stand in our own way; let us do from morning till night what should be done, and give us clear ideas of the consequences of our actions.

Johann Wolfgang von Goethe

The day returns and brings us the petty round of irritating concerns and duties. Help us to play the man, help us to perform them with laughter and kind faces; let cheerfulness abound with industry. Give us to go blithely on our business all this day, bring us to our resting beds weary and content and undishonored, and grant us in the end the gift of sleep.

Robert Louis Stevenson

Lord, I know not what to ask of Thee. Thou only knowest what I need. Thou lovest me better than I know how to love myself. Father, give to Thy child that which he himself knows not how to ask. Smite or heal, depress me or raise me up: I adore all Thy purposes without knowing them. I am silent; I offer myself up in sacrifice; I yield myself to Thee; I would have no other desire than to accomplish Thy will. Teach me to pray. Pray Thyself in me.

Francois de Fenelon

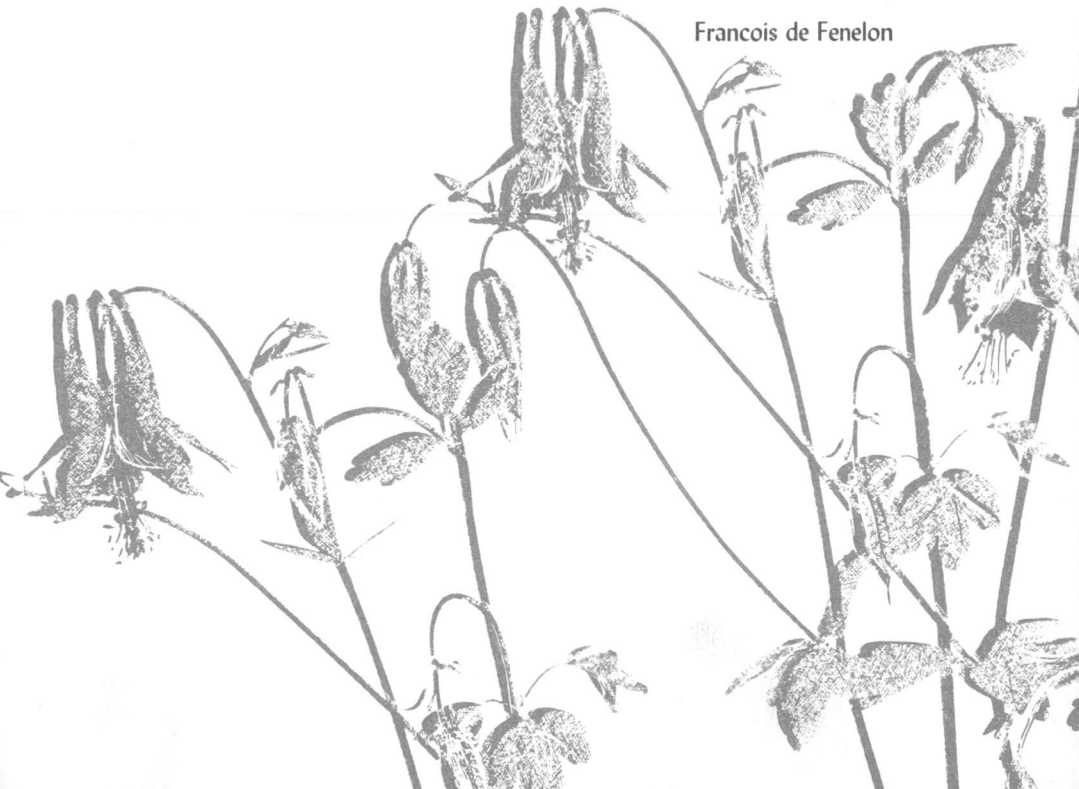

Let us unite in imploring the Supreme Ruler of Nations to spread His holy protection over these United States to turn the machinations of the wicked, to the confirming of our Constitution; to enable us at all times to root out internal sedition and put invasion to flight; to perpetuate to our country that prosperity which His goodness has already conferred; and to verify the anticipations of this government being a safeguard of human rights. *Amen.*

George Washington

AWAY IN A MANGER

Away in a manger, no crib for his bed,
The little Lord Jesus laid down his sweet
    head.
The stars in the bright sky looked down where he
    lay,
The little Lord Jesus, asleep on the hay.

The cattle are lowing, the baby awakes,
But little Lord Jesus, no crying he makes.
I love thee, Lord Jesus, look down from the
    sky,
And stay by my cradle till morning is nigh.

Be near me, Lord Jesus, I ask thee to stay
Close by me for ever, and love me, I pray.
Bless all the dear children in thy tender care,
And fit us for heaven to live with thee there.

Anonymous

A PRAYER FOR EVERY DAY

Make me too brave to lie or be unkind.
Make me too understanding, too, to mind
The little hurts companions give, and friends,
The careless hurts that no one quite intends.
Make me too thoughtful to hurt others so.
Help me to know
The inmost hearts of those for whom I care,
Their secret wishes, all the loads they bear,
That I may add my courage to their own.
May I make lonely folks feel less alone,
And happy ones a little happier yet.
May I forget
What ought to be forgotten; and recall
Unfailing, all
That ought to be recalled, each kindly thing,
Forgetting what might sting.
To all upon my way,
Day after day,
Let me be joy, be hope! Let my life sing!

Mary Carolyn Davies

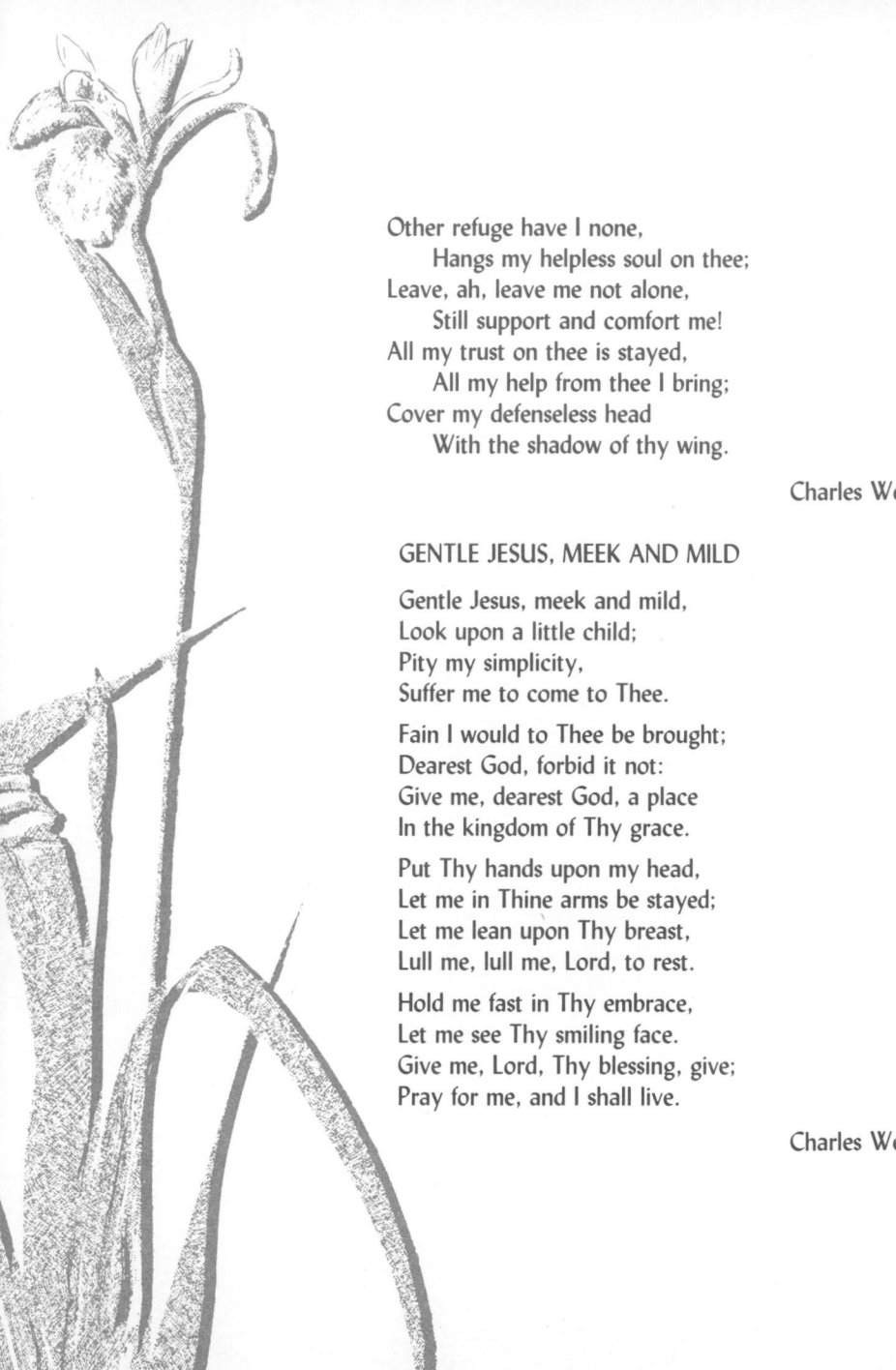

Other refuge have I none,
 Hangs my helpless soul on thee;
Leave, ah, leave me not alone,
 Still support and comfort me!
All my trust on thee is stayed,
 All my help from thee I bring;
Cover my defenseless head
 With the shadow of thy wing.

Charles Wesley

GENTLE JESUS, MEEK AND MILD

Gentle Jesus, meek and mild,
Look upon a little child;
Pity my simplicity,
Suffer me to come to Thee.

Fain I would to Thee be brought;
Dearest God, forbid it not:
Give me, dearest God, a place
In the kingdom of Thy grace.

Put Thy hands upon my head,
Let me in Thine arms be stayed;
Let me lean upon Thy breast,
Lull me, lull me, Lord, to rest.

Hold me fast in Thy embrace,
Let me see Thy smiling face.
Give me, Lord, Thy blessing, give;
Pray for me, and I shall live.

Charles Wesley

SEND ME

Use me, God, in Thy great harvest field,
Which stretcheth far and wide like a wide sea;
The gatherers are so few; I fear the precious
    yield
Will suffer loss. Oh, find a place for me!
A place where best the strength I have will
    tell:
It may be one the older toilers shun;
Be it a wide or narrow place, 'tis well
So that the work it holds be only done.

                        Christina Georgina Rossetti

Lord, help me to live from day to day
In such a self-forgetful way
That even when I kneel to pray
My prayers shall be for others.

Help me in all the work I do
Ever to be sincere and true,
And know that all I do for Thee
Must needs be done for others.

Others, Lord; yes, others.
Let this my motto be.
Let me live for others
That I may live like Thee.

                        Anonymous

THE PILLAR OF THE CLOUD

Lead, kindly Light, amid the encircling gloom;
    Lead thou me on!
The night is dark, and I am far from home;
    Lead thou me on!
Keep thou my feet: I do not ask to see
The distant scene; one step enough for me.

I was not ever thus, nor prayed that thou
    Shouldst lead me on;
I loved to choose and see my path; but now
    Lead thou me on!
I loved the garish day, and, spite of fears,
Pride ruled my will: remember not past years.

So long thy power hath blest me, sure it still
    Will lead me on
O'er moor and fen, o'er crag and torrent, till
    The night is gone;
And with the morn, those angel faces smile
Which I have loved long since, and lost awhile.

John Henry Newman

BELIEF IN PLAN OF THEE

Whatever else withheld, withhold not from us,
Belief in plan of Thee enclosed in Time and Space;
Health, peace, salvation universal.

Is it a dream?
Nay, but the lack of it the dream,
And, failing it, loves lore and wealth a dream,
And all the world a dream.

Walt Whitman

O Lord, let us not live to be useless. Amen.

John Wesley

GOD, MAKE ME BRAVE

God, make me brave for life: oh, braver than this.
Let me straighten after pain, as a tree straightens
    after the rain,
Shining and lovely again.
God, make me brave for life; much braver than this.
As the blown grass lifts, let me rise
From sorrow with quiet eyes,
Knowing Thy way is wise.
God, make me brave, life brings
Such blinding things.
Help me to keep my sight;
Help me to see aright
That out of dark comes light.

Anonymous

O Lord our God, grant us grace to desire Thee with our whole heart; that so desiring we may seek and find Thee; and so finding Thee may love Thee; and loving Thee, may hate those sins from which Thou hast redeemed us. Amen.

St. Anselm of Canterbury

PRAYER

Lord, grant us eyes to see, and ears to hear,
And souls to love, and minds to understand,
And confidence of hope, and filial fear . . . .
Lord, grant us what Thou wilt, and what Thou wilt

Deny, and fold us in Thy peaceful fold;
Not as the world gives, give to us Thine own;
Inbuild us where Jerusalem is built
With walls of jasper, and with streets of gold,
And Thou, Thyself, Lord Christ, the corner-stone.

Christina Georgina Rossetti

THE POET'S PRAYER

If there be some weaker one,
Give me strength to help him on;
If a blinder soul there be,
Let me guide him nearer Thee;
Make my mortal dreams come true
With the work I fain would do;
Clothe with life the weak intent,
Let me be the thing I meant;
Let me find in Thy employ,
Peace that dearer is than joy;
Out of self to love be led,
And to heaven acclimated,
Until all things sweet and good
Seem my natural habitude.

John Greenleaf Whittier

We thank Thee for what Thou hast given to this nation far beyond the' gifts to any other nation! Let us remain thankful for it, so that we may overcome the dangers of shallowness of life and emptiness of heart that threaten our people. Prevent us from turning Thy gifts into causes of injury and self-destruction. Let a grateful mind protect us against national and personal disintegration. Turn us to Thee, the source of our being, eternal God! Amen.

Paul Tillich

The Light of God surrounds me.
The Love of God enfolds me.
The Power of God protects me.
The Presence of God watches over me.
Wherever I am, God is.

Anonymous

O God, from whom all holy desires, all good counsels, and all just works do proceed; Give unto thy servants that peace which the world cannot give; that our hearts may be set to obey thy commandments, and also that by thee, we, being defended from the fear of our enemies, may pass our time in rest and quietness; through the merits of Jesus Christ our Saviour. Amen.

Book of Common Prayer

A BIRTHDAY THOUGHT

I ask and wish not to appear
    More beauteous, rich or gay:
Lord, make me wiser every year,
    And better every day.

Charles Lamb

DIVINE CARE

Even as a nurse, whose child's imperfect pace
Can hardly lead his foot from place to place,
Leaves her fond kissing, sets him down, to go,
Nor does uphold him for a step or two;
But when she finds that he begins to fall,
She holds him up, and kisses him withal:
So God from man sometimes withdraws His hand
Awhile, to teach his infant faith to stand;
But when He sees his feeble strength begin
To fail, He gently takes him up again:

Lord, I'm a child; so guide my paces, then,
That I may learn to walk an upright man:
So shield my faith, that I may never doubt
    Thee,
For I must fall, if e'er I walk without Thee.

Francis Quarles

Whether Thou comest in sunshine or in rain, I would take Thee into my heart joyfully. Thou art Thyself more than the sunshine; Thou art Thyself compensation for the rain. It is Thee and not Thy gifts I crave.

George Matheson

Give me Thine own self, without Whom, though Thou shouldest give me all that ever Thou hadst made, yet could not my desires be satisfied.

St. Augustine

A PRAYER FOR FAMILY LOVE

Father,
Grant unto us true family love,
That we may belong more entirely to those whom
    Thou hast given us,
Understanding each other, day by day, more instinctively,
Forbearing each other, day by day, more patiently,
Growing, day by day, more closely into oneness
    with each other.

Father,
Thou too art love:
Thou knowest the depth of pain and the height
    of glory
Which abide continually in love:
Make us perfect in love for these our dear ones,
As knowing that without them we can never be
    made perfect in Thee.

Anonymous

Make me, O Lord, the instrument of Thy love, that I may bring comfort to those who sorrow and joy to those who are regarded as persons of little account. In this country of many races, make me courteous to those who are humble and understanding to those who are resentful. Teach me what I should be to the arrogant and cruel, for I do not know.

And as for me myself, make me more joyful than I am, especially if this is needed for the sake of others. Let me remember my many experiences of joy and thankfulness, especially those that endure. And may I this coming day do some work of peace for Thee.

Alan Paton

How shall I call Thee Who art always here?
How shall I praise Thee Who art still most dear?
What may I give Thee save what Thou hast given,
And Whom but Thee have I in earth or heaven?

Eliza Scudder

Here, Lord, is my life. I place it on the altar today.
Use it as you will.

Albert Schweitzer

Lord,
    make me an instrument of Your
        peace.
    Where there is hatred let me sow
        love;
    Where there is injury, pardon;
    Where there is doubt, faith;
    Where there is despair, hope;
    Where there is darkness, light; and
    Where there is sadness, joy.

O divine Master,
    grant that I may not so much
    Seek to be consoled as to console;
    To be understood as to understand;
    To be loved as to love;
    For it is in giving that we receive;
    It is in pardoning that we are par-
        doned; and
    It is in dying that we are born to
        eternal life.

St. Francis of Assisi

Thou that hast given so much to me,
Give one thing more—a grateful heart;
Not thankful when it pleaseth me,
As if thy blessings had spare days;
But such a heart, whose pulse may be
Thy praise.

George Herbert

God grant me the serenity to accept the things I cannot change, courage to change the things I can, and the wisdom to know the difference.

Reinhold Niebuhr

Hallowed be Thy name,
not mine,
Thy kingdom come,
not mine,
Thy will be done,
not mine,
Give us peace with Thee
Peace with men
Peace with ourselves,
And free us from all fear.

Dag Hammarskjold

FOR GOD'S LITTLE WILD THINGS

God bless the little things this Christmastide
All the little wild things that live outside,
Little cold birds and animals in the snow,
Give them good faring and a warm place to go,
All the little young things for His sake Who died,
Who was a little Thing at Christmastide.

Margaret Murry

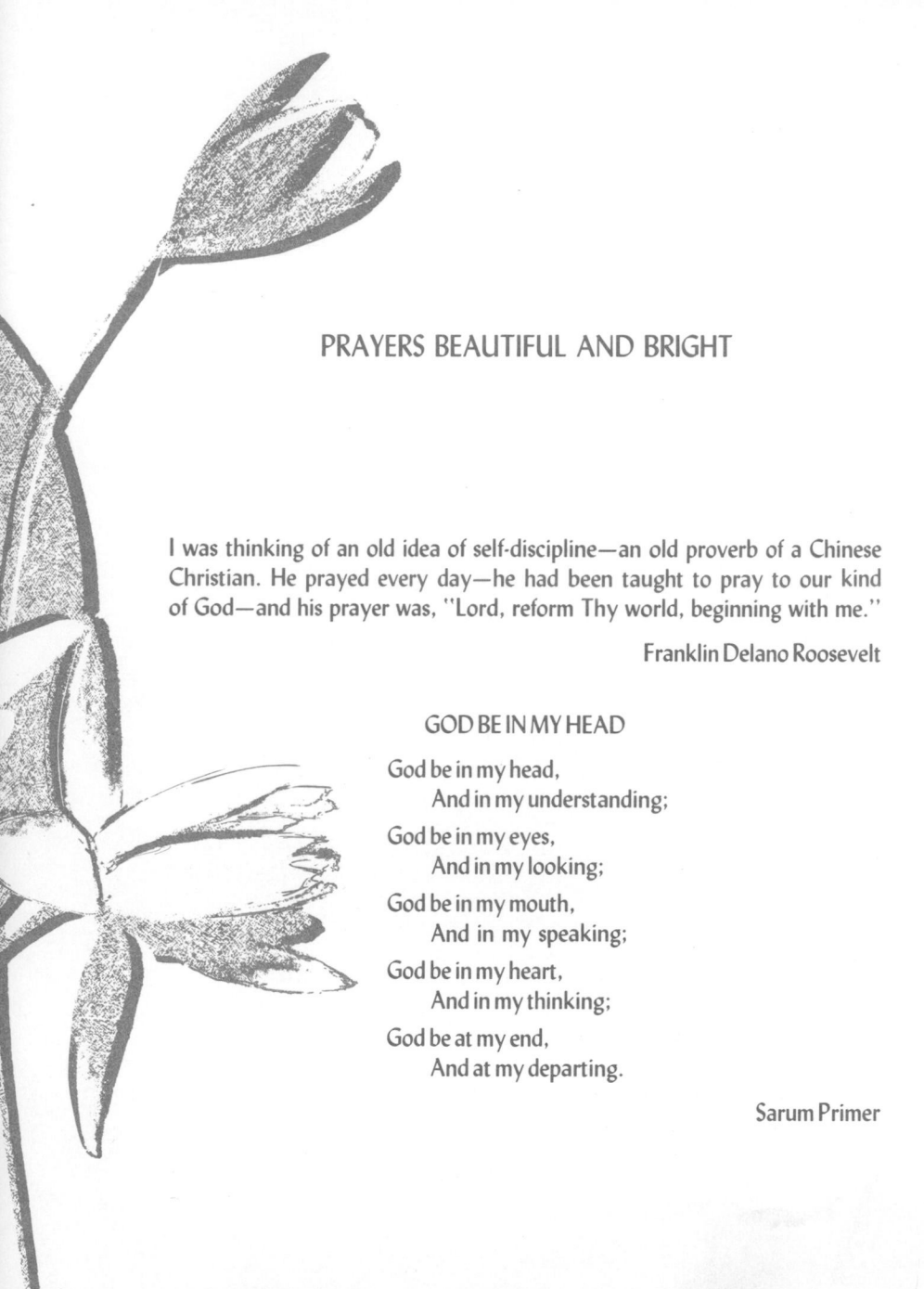

PRAYERS BEAUTIFUL AND BRIGHT

I was thinking of an old idea of self-discipline—an old proverb of a Chinese Christian. He prayed every day—he had been taught to pray to our kind of God—and his prayer was, "Lord, reform Thy world, beginning with me."

Franklin Delano Roosevelt

GOD BE IN MY HEAD

God be in my head,
  And in my understanding;

God be in my eyes,
  And in my looking;

God be in my mouth,
  And in my speaking;

God be in my heart,
  And in my thinking;

God be at my end,
  And at my departing.

Sarum Primer

We do not come to prayer to *impose* our wishes and our will upon God, to insist that He but rubber-stamp our plans, but to submit them to Him for approval, correction or rejection. Many times the things we ask for so feverishly would be not to our advantage but to our detriment. Like little children asking for a bottle labeled "Poison!", we often ask for things which would prove fatal to our spiritual life. In His infinite wisdom God favors us by withholding them.

Submissiveness to the divine will is then an essential requisite for true and fruitful prayer. Who has better illustrated this fact than Christ Himself? Kneeling in the Garden of Gethsemane, the God-man perceived the Passion and death which He was about to undergo. His human nature cried out in agony: "Father, if it is possible, let this cup pass away from me." Then He added the all-important words, "Yet not as I will, but as thou willest." These made it a perfect prayer and a model for all supplications.

John A. O'Brien

As we forgive, divine love is flowing out from us. As we pray for our enemies, we are loving divinely . . . . The greatest rewards of prayer come when we learn to set aside specific periods every day to pray for those who despitefully use us, to pray for those who persecute us, to pray for those who are our enemies—not only personal enemies because there are some people who have no personal enemies, but religious, racial, or national enemies. We learn to pray, "Father, forgive them; for they know not what they do." When we pray for our enemies, when we pray that their eyes be opened to the Truth, many times these enemies become our friends.

Joel S. Goldsmith

The prayer of the morning will determine the day. Wasted time, which we are ashamed of, temptations that beset us, weakness and listlessness in our work, disorder and indiscipline in our thinking and our relations with other people very frequently have their cause in neglect of the morning prayer. The organization and distribution of our time will be better for having been rooted in prayer.

Dietrich Bonhoeffer

Human life is a battlefield of conflicting prayers. The strongest forces in this world are these importunate desires, and when a multitude of people share a common desire, when a great prayer rises within millions like the tide called by the sky and filling all the bays and crannies of the human shore, it is irresistible. Prayer, when it is a caricature, is a futile retreat from reality. Prayer, when it is real, can turn the stream of centuries into new courses. Look to your prayers, then, your deep, real, genuine demands on life. Only when a great multitude that no man can number stands before the throne and with a voice like many waters cries, We are through with war and poverty; we demand peace and justice and brotherhood—only then will men invent the instruments on which such music can be played.

Harry Emerson Fosdick

We are to approach our praying as the trained mountaineer goes at the mountain trail, with slow, short, persistent steps. The novice who rushes at the mountain trail soon finds himself breathless and exhausted. The fruits of praying are given to us by God so imperceptibly that often we do not detect them. We are to be content to pursue our praying at God's pace for us, and never to seek to anticipate God's providence.

Charles Francis Whiston

The Devil will fight you every step of the way. He will cause the baby to cry, the telephone to ring, someone to knock at the door—there will be many interruptions, but keep at it! Don't be discouraged. Soon you will find that these periods of prayer are the greatest delight of your life. You will look forward to them with more anticipation than to anything else. Without constant, daily, systematic prayer your life will seem barren, discouraging, and fruitless. Without constant prayer you never can know that inner peace that God wants to give you.

Billy Graham

The Lord is a good worker, but He loves to be helped.

Martin Luther

When I lose such a thing as a key, I ask the Lord to direct me to it, and I look for an answer to my prayer; when a person with whom I have made an appointment does not come, according to the fixed time, and I begin to be inconvenienced by it, I ask the Lord to be pleased to hasten him to me, and I look for an answer; when I do not understand a passage of the word of God, I lift up my heart to the Lord that he would be pleased by his Holy Spirit to instruct me, and I expect to be taught, though I do not fix the time when, and the manner how it should be; when I am going to minister in the Word, I seek help from the Lord, and . . . am not cast down because I look for his assistance.

Frederic W. H. Myers

Pray as if everything depended upon God; act as if everything depended upon you.

St. Ignatius of Loyola

And perhaps, as those who do not turn to God in petty trials will have no *habit* or such resort to help them when the great trials come, so those who have not learned to ask Him for childish things will have less readiness to ask Him for great ones. We must not be too high-minded. I fancy we may sometimes be deterred from small prayers by a sense of our own dignity rather than of God's.

C. S. Lewis

Our true life lies at a great depth within us. Our restlessness and weaknesses are in reality merely strivings on the surface. That is why we must daily retire into silence, far into the quiet depths of our spirits and experience the real life within us. If we do this our words and actions will come to be real also.

Emanuel Swedenborg

All great souls have prayed receptively.
"I will hear," said the psalmist, "what God the Lord will speak." Prayer is the hospitality of the soul entertaining the Most High.

Harry Emerson Fosdick

The man who says his prayers in the evening is a captain posting his sentries. After that, he can sleep.

Charles Baudelaire

If you are still not clear as to what God would have you do, consider the method privately described by a devout and educated woman. She says that sometimes trying to find God's will is like standing beside a stream which is so placid and still that the eye at first cannot tell which way it is flowing. But if you throw a twig into the water and watch it for a few moments, you can detect the drift. So when she is in doubt as to the direction God would have her take, she makes some venture of faith, and that venture, like the floating twig, reveals the drift of the divine will.

Ralph W. Sockman

How ill-natured it is, if you believe in prayer, not to ask for everybody what they want.

Florence Nightingale

Sometimes special techniques are vital, as a keen-thinking minister knew, who told a parishioner, an invalid, to keep a chair in the room for no visitor to use. When this man had difficulty thinking of Christ, he was to imagine Jesus seated in that chair. It may be too simple a procedure for some. It may seem childish to others. But whatever makes Christ real is a helpful form of prayer. It is extremely important to find those methods which suit each of us in our present situation.

G. Ray Jordan

If we with earnest effort could succeed
To make our life one long connected prayer,
As lives of some perhaps have been and are;
If, never leaving thee, we had no need
Our wandering spirits back again to lead
Into thy presence, but continue there,
Like angels standing on the highest stair
Of all the sapphire throne—this were to pray indeed.

But if distractions manifold prevail,
And if in this we must confess we fail,
Grant us to keep at least a prompt desire,
Continual readiness for prayer and praise,
An altar heaped and waiting to take fire
With the least spark, and leap into a blaze.

Richard Trench

For a long time I had been disturbed about the problem of a wandering mind during my time of prayer. I would be trying to pray and suddenly my mind would jump to a business appointment I needed to make. For years I had forced these things out of my mind to get back to "spiritual things." But now, thanks to another Christian friend, I began to keep a list by my side; and when the thought came to me to call someone, to make an appointment, or to do something for the family, I began to jot it down and then go back to God. I was at last realizing that He is interested in my total life and that these things which came into my mind during my time of prayer might be significant things for me to do, or places for me to go. This also made it easier for me to get my mind immediately back to my other prayers.

Keith Miller

To pray as God would have us—this is what at times makes me turn cold in my soul. Believe me, to pray with all your heart and strength with the reason and the will, to believe vividly that God will listen to your voice through Christ, and verily do the thing that he pleaseth thereupon—this is the last, the greatest achievement of the Christian's warfare upon earth. Teach us to pray, O Lord!

Samuel Taylor Coleridge

Sometimes when you need rest most you are too restless to lie down and take it. Then compel yourself to lie down and to lie still. Often in ten minutes the compulsion fades into consent and you sleep, and rise a new man . . . So if you are averse to pray, pray the more.

Peter Taylor Forsyth

When you cannot pray as you would, pray as you can.

Dean Goulburn

The way to change your thought about a thing is to take that thing into your prayers. Remind yourself of the omnipresence of God. Make it clear, make it real to yourself, realize that God is present where the trouble seems to be . . . The foreign thoughts that come in, foreign to God and Truth, such as thoughts of fear, doubt, inadequacy, opposition, competition, and so forth, must be handled by supplanting them with the thought of the goodness and love of God.

Emmet Fox

The secret of what we are seeking to do is to confirm ourselves in a continual state of resting in God. We can emphasize this relationship, and help to make it inwardly real, by saying (aloud if need be and if we are alone) "I am Thine"; or we can just use the word "Thine," repeating this silently and inwardly throughout the day, remembering and resting in the wonder of this relationship with our heavenly Father.
At another time we can make our initial mental prayer a realization of deep thanksgiving. Thinking of all we owe, we murmur to God an Infinite, "Thanks." Throughout the day that is the keyword for our mental praying. Or, as we go about the world, the very name of "Jesus" may be our shield and watchword. To spend a day praying His name in this way of ceaseless, interior prayer is an experience indeed.

Cyril H. Powell

There is no need to search so wide,
Open the door and stand aside—
Let God in!

Charlotte Perkins Gilman

My prayers seem to be more of an attitude than anything else. I indulge in very little lip service, but ask the Creator silently, daily, and often many times a day, to permit me to speak to Him through the three great kingdoms of the world which He has created—the animal, mineral, and vegetable kingdoms, to understand their relations to each other, and our relations to the Great God Who made all of us. I ask Him daily and often momently to give me wisdom, understanding, and bodily strength to do His will; hence I am asking and receiving all the time.

George Washington Carver

. . . I've discovered it helps to pray aloud. When prayer is totally thought, the mind is inclined to wander. It drifts from a dialogue with God to plans and programs, an argument, a discussion, something read. Or you'll be asking God's help with a problem and the problem itself takes over: "If Jimmy wouldn't be so stubborn, we've told him that car's not *safe*—"
But if I address myself to God aloud, if I say the words aloud or in a whisper, my own ears keep order. I pay attention so God can pay attention. This means I do have to find a time and place in which to pray—at least pray comprehensively—and privacy is hard to achieve. But if I really want it, I'll find that time and place. With God nothing is impossible.

Marjorie Holmes

There will be times when the results are not what we yearn for: not all for whom we pray are restored to health. Honesty and honest sharing is necessary here. The skeptic has a point when he accuses some Christians of sweeping negative experiences under the rug. True, but I have never known a hospital to shut down because it lost some patients. Despite disappointments, the Christian is obligated to pray for the sick because we are bidden to do so (Luke 10:9) and because the crumb of our caring is but a morsel broken from the whole loaf of the Father's infinite and tender love.

Catherine Marshall

No one in his senses, if he has any power of ordering his own day, would reserve his chief prayers for bed-time—obviously the worst possible hour for any action which needs concentration. The trouble is that thousands of unfortunate people can hardly find any other. Even for us, who are the lucky ones, it is not always easy. My own plan, when hard pressed, is to seize any time, and place, however unsuitable in preference to the last waking moment.

C. S. Lewis

When is the time for prayer?
In every hour, while life is spared to thee—
In crowds or solitude—in joy or care—
Thy thoughts should heavenward flee.
At home—at morn and eve—with loved ones there,
Bend thou the knee in prayer!

Anonymous

God has come to you to save the sinner. Be glad! This message is liberation through truth. You can hide nothing from God. The mask you wear before men will do you no good before Him. He wants to see you as you are. He wants to be gracious to you. You do not have to go on lying to yourself and your brothers, as if you were without sin; you can dare to be a sinner. Thank God for that; He loves the sinner but He hates sin.

Dietrich Bonhoeffer

Our prayers must mean something to us if they are to mean anything to God.

Maltbie Babcock

The abundance of a grateful heart gives honor to God even if it does not turn to Him in words.

Paul Tillich

Often in the urgency of need or concern there come flashes of doubt or brief eclipses of faith. The problem looms so large that we forget that God is still running the universe. At such a moment we may recover our assurance by recollecting God's previous loving-kindness to us and others. The testimony of the past has a powerful ministry to perform in us if we would only stop to remember. When the children of Israel were in doubt of their future, Moses restored their faith by reviving their memories. "Ask now of the days that are past."

John Magee

We may pray most 'when we say least, and pray least when we say most.

St. Augustine

Frederick Douglass said that in the days of his slavery he used often to pray for freedom, but that his prayer was not answered until it got down into his own heels and he ran away.

Harry Emerson Fosdick

I have resolved to pray more and to pray always, to pray in all places where quietness inviteth, in the house, on the highway, and on the street; and to know no street or passage in this city that may not witness that I have not forgotten God.

Sir Thomas Browne

Ten minutes spent in Christ's society every day; aye, two minutes, if it be face to face and heart to heart, will make the whole life different.

Henry Drummond

Do not lose the habit of praying to the unseen Divinity. Prayer for worldly goods is worse than fruitless, but prayer for strength of soul is that passion of the soul which catches the gift it seeks.

George Meredith

God entrusts very definite and particular persons to each of us to intercede for, just as he entrusts us to definite persons who pray for us . . . . We do not need to use written prayers, nor a book of prayers, nor memorized prayers. Love knows how to give utterance to its concerns. We speak lovingly, simply, directly, and in our own words—stammeringly and falteringly perhaps at first. The words are not for God's sake, but to articulate our thoughts and desires for us. God reads our hearts and knows our desires and thoughts long before we express them in words. All that we need to do is to turn our hearts toward God; name the person; then offer to God our loving and unselfish concern for him.

Charles Francis Whiston

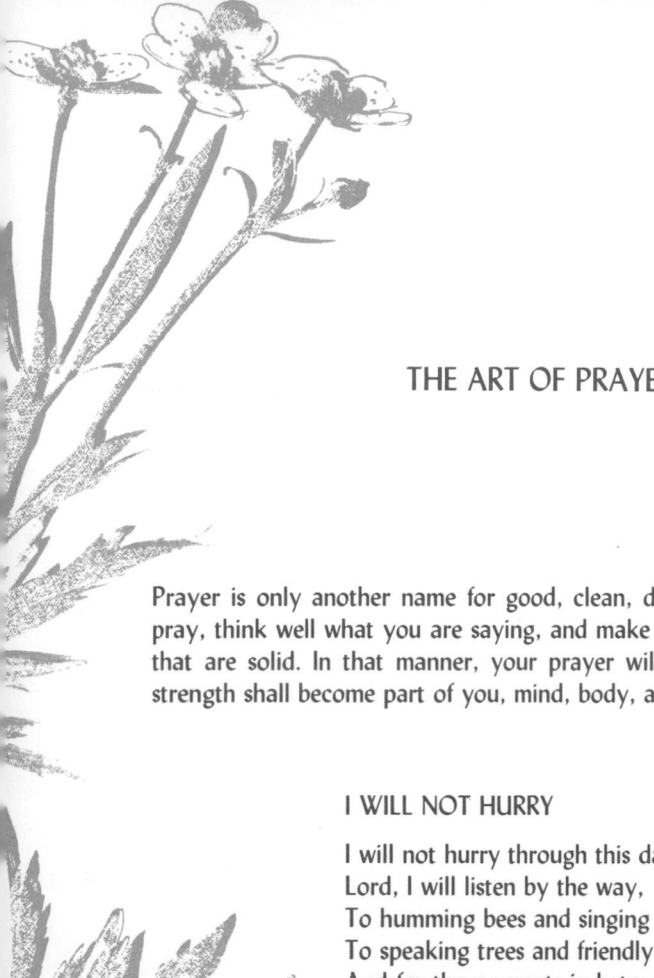

THE ART OF PRAYER

Prayer is only another name for good, clean, direct thinking. When you pray, think well what you are saying, and make your thoughts into things that are solid. In that manner, your prayer will have strength, and that strength shall become part of you, mind, body, and spirit.

Richard Llewellyn

I WILL NOT HURRY

I will not hurry through this day!
Lord, I will listen by the way,
To humming bees and singing birds,
To speaking trees and friendly words;
And for the moments in between
Seek glimpses of Thy great Unseen.

I will not hurry through this day;
I will take time to think and pray;
I will look up into the sky,
Where fleecy clouds and swallows fly;
And somewhere in the day, maybe
I will catch whispers, Lord, from Thee!

Ralph Spaulding Cushman

We pray for God's help, but we forget in how many small and quiet ways it comes to us all the time. In a helpful thought which emerges in our mind when we specially need wisdom, in a spoken or printed word which restores our confidence when we are downhearted, in an intruding duty which forces us to pause when we are about to make a misstep, in an unexpected delay which changes for the better a major decision—in and through these experiences God gives us His help. He gives it, not by working spectacular miracles in the external world, but by utilizing the mechanisms present in the minds of human beings and available for His use. His help comes, not once or twice in a lifetime, but continually. It comes, not to a few divine favorites, but to every human being who lives steadily at his best.

Anonymous

. . . *Bless.* What a beautiful word. Lively and musical and full of joy. And holding within itself one of prayer's dearest secrets. For the happiest prayers of all are when we call down blessings on people. Send a blessing winging their way for no good reason except a sudden desire to wish them well.

Marjorie Holmes

It may be your prayer is like a ship, which, when it goes on a very long voyage, does not come home laden so soon; but when it does come home, it has a richer freight. Mere "coasters" will bring you coals, or such like ordinary things; but they that go afar to Tarshish return with gold and ivory. Coasting prayers, such as we pray every day, bring us many necessaries, but there are great prayers, which, like the old Spanish galleons, cross the main ocean, and are longer out of sight, but come home deep laden with a golden freight.

Charles Haddon Spurgeon

FAITH

I will not doubt, though all my ships at sea
    Come drifting home with broken masts and sails;
    I shall believe the Hand which never fails,
From seeming evil worketh good to me;
    And, though I weep because those sails are
        battered,
Still will I cry, while my best hopes lie shattered,
                                "I trust in Thee."
I will not doubt, though all my prayers return
    Unanswered from the still, white realms above;
    I shall believe it is an all-wise Love
Which has refused those things for which I yearn;
    And though, at times, I cannot keep from grieving,
    Yet the pure ardor of my fixed believing
                            Undimmed shall burn.

Ella Wheeler Wilcox

The act of praying is the very highest energy of which the human mind is capable.

Samuel Taylor Coleridge

God is ever-active and ever-seeking those who will cooperate in his purposes of love. Answers to prayer are like the replies of a dear and trusted friend in conversation or by letter. They are assurances of love and illuminations of wisdom. They do not cause the heavens to fall or arrest the stars in their courses, though to us they may indeed open heaven and make us lords of creation and send us out with joy to act and suffer for the truth.

Gordon S. Wakefield

Within! within, oh turn
Thy spirit's eyes, and learn
Thy wandering senses gently to control;
Thy dearest Friend dwells deep within thy soul,
And asks thyself of thee,
That heart, and mind, and sense, He may make whole
In perfect harmony.

Gerhard Tersteegen

After the meeting my husband had gone alone into a spot in the woods to continue to pray by himself. Suddenly, from head to foot, he was shaken with what seemed like a magnetic thrill of heavenly delight, and floods of glory seemed to pour through him, soul and body . . . The whole world seemed transformed for him, every leaf and blade of grass quivered with exquisite color . . . Everybody looked beautiful to him, for he seemed to see the Divine Spirit within each one . . . . This ecstacy . . . was the beginning of a wonderful career of spiritual power and blessing.

Hannah W. Smith

Prayer is and remains the native and deepest impulse of the soul of man.

Thomas Carlyle

I that still pray at morning and at eve,
Thrice in my life have truly prayed;
Thrice stirred below my conscious self, have
   felt
That perfect disenthrallment which is God.

James Russell Lowell

Some of our soldiers who were trying to hold an important beachhead at Munda used up their drinking water, and then prayed frantically for a new supply. Suddenly one of the shells in the barrage which the American battleships in the distance were laying down struck the beach near these soldiers, buried itself in the sand, and exploded. In exploding it formed a deep crater, and instantly that crater began to fill with fresh water gushing up from secret springs far below. Thus God answered the prayers of those soldiers. Thus he gave them the water they needed.

The Christian Century

It is by the benefit of prayer that we reach those riches which are laid up for us with the Heavenly Father.

John Calvin

When you close your doors, and make darkness within, remember never to say that you are alone; nay, God is within . . .

Epictetus

On all my expeditions prayer made me stronger, morally and mentally, than any of my non-praying companions. It did not blind my eyes, or dull my mind, or close my ears, but, on the contrary, it gave me confidence. It did more; it gave me joy and pride in my work, and lifted me hopefully over the one thousand five hundred miles of forest tracks, eager to face the day's perils and fatigues.

Henry M. Stanley

Who rises from his prayer a better man, his prayer is answered.

George Meredith

The aim of prayer is to attain the habit of goodness, so as no longer merely to have the things that are good, but rather to be good.

Clement of Alexandria

To pray is to expose the shores of the mind to the incoming tide of the Holy Spirit.
This incoming tide of the Spirit may be so still "that moving seems asleep, too full for sound or foam." But that stillness proves a source of new suggestions. True prayer is not merely the asking for what we want; it is the hearing of what we need. And when we open our minds and hearts to God, fresh glimpses of duty flash upon us, new needs call for help . . . . Though at times we may think we are praying in a void, the overwhelming testimony of experience is that sincere prayers are heard by a "Power not ourselves that makes for righteousness."

Ralph W. Sockman

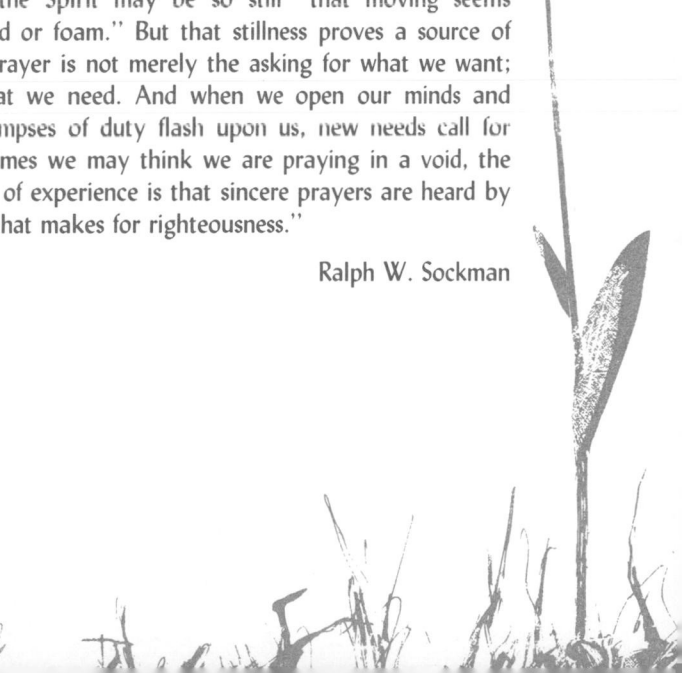

More things are wrought by prayer
Than this world dreams of. Wherefore, let thy
    voice
Rise like a fountain for me night and day.
For what are men better than sheep or goats
That nourish a blind life within the brain,
If, knowing God, they lift not hands of prayer
Both for themselves and those who call them friend?
For so the whole round earth is every way
Bound by gold chains about the feet of God.

Alfred, Lord Tennyson

We pray as much as we desire, and we desire as much as we love.

St. Anthony

The privilege of prayer to me is one of the most cherished possessions, because faith and experience alike convince me that God himself sees and answers, and his answers I never venture to criticize. It is only my part to ask. It is entirely his to give or withhold, as he knows is best. If it were otherwise, I would not dare to pray at all. In the quiet of home, in the heat of life and strife, in the face of death, the privilege of speech with God is inestimable. I value it more because it calls for nothing that the wayfaring man, though a fool, cannot give—that is, the simplest expression to the simplest desire. When I can neither see, nor hear, nor speak, still I can pray so that God can hear. When I finally pass through the valley of the shadow of death, I expect to pass through it in conversation with him.

Sir Wilfred Grenfell

Prayer is religion in act; that is, prayer is real religion.

Auguste Sabatier

Many reasons are given us why we should not pray, whilst others are given us why we should. But in all this very little is said of the reason why we do pray, which is simply that we cannot help praying. It seems probable that, in spite of all that "science" may do to the contrary, men will continue to pray to the end of time . . . Prayer is the very soul and essence of religion.

William James

GOD MAKES A PATH

God makes a path, provides a guide,
And feeds a wilderness;
His glorious name, while breath remains,
O that I may confess.

Lost many a time, I have had no guide,
No house but a hollow tree!
In stormy winter night no fire,
No food, no company;

In Him I found a house, a bed,
A table, company;
No cup so bitter but's made sweet,
Where God shall sweetening be.

Roger Williams

SERENITY

Let nothing disturb thee,
Nothing affright thee;
All things are passing;
God never changeth;
Patient endurance
Attaineth to all things.
Who God possesseth
In nothing is wanting:
Alone God sufficeth.

St. Teresa

Why should I wish to see God better than this
    day?
I see something of God each hour of the twenty-
    four, and each moment then,
In the faces of men and women I see God and in
    my own face in the glass,
I see letters from God dropped in the street, and
    every one is signed by God's name.

Walt Whitman

"WITH WHOM IS NO VARIABLENESS, NEITHER SHADOW OF TURNING"

It fortifies my soul to know
That, though I perish, truth is so:
That, howsoe'er I stray and range,
Whate'er I do, Thou dost not change.
I steadier step when I recall
That, if I slip, Thou dost not fall.

Arthur Hugh Clough

Prayer is like opening a sluice between the great ocean and our little channels, when the sea gathers itself together and flows in at full tide.

Alfred, Lord Tennyson

The using up of strength is in a certain sense still an increase of strength; for fundamentally it is only a matter of a wide circle; all the strength we give away comes back to us again, experienced and transformed. It is so in prayer. And what is there that, truly done, would not be prayer?

Rainer Maria Rilke

PRAYER

Say, what is prayer, when it is prayer indeed?
The mighty utterance of a mighty need.
The man is praying who doth press with might
Out of his darkness into God's own light.

Richard Trench

There is a tablet at the back of a church in Lucknow, India, which reads: "Near this spot Stanley Jones knelt a physically broken man and arose a physically well man." The story back of the tablet was this: After eight and a half years in India, I had had a ruptured appendix and as a result tetanus set in. This caused me to have a nervous collapse when everything would leave me in a state of confusion. I thought I would have to give up the mission field and the ministry to try to regain my shattered health.
I was in this church in Lucknow, kneeling at the back alone when God said to me, "Are you yourself ready for the work to which I have called you?" My answer was, "No, Lord, I am done for. I have reached the end of my resources and I cannot go on." His reply, "If you will turn that over to me and not worry about it, I'll take care of it." I replied, "Lord, I close the bargain right here." I arose from my knees knowing I was a well man.

E. Stanley Jones

I asked a man what made his life so radiant
and bright.
He answered: "Looking, looking toward the
Light!"

Anonymous

If radio's slim fingers can pluck a melody
From night—and toss it over a continent or sea;
If the petaled white notes of a violin
Are blown across the mountains or the city's din;
If songs, like crimson roses, are culled from thin blue air—
Why should mortals wonder if God hears prayer?

Ethel Romig Fuller

Happy the heart that keeps its twilight hour
And, in the depths of heavenly peace reclined,
Loves to commune with thoughts of tender power,
Thoughts that ascend, like angels beautiful,
A shining Jacob's-ladder of the mind.

Paul Hamilton Hayne

He who prays lives, and he who lives prays.

Alexandre Dumas

I cannot do it alone,
The waves run fast and high,
And the fogs close chill around
And the light goes out in the sky;
But I know that we two
Shall win in the end—
God and I.

Dan Crawford

I sought the Lord, and he heard me, and delivered
  me from all my fears.
They looked unto him, and were lightened: and
  their faces were not ashamed.
This poor man cried, and the Lord heard him, and
  saved him out of all his troubles.
The angel of the Lord encampeth round about them
  that fear him, and delivereth them.
O taste and see that the Lord is good: blessed
  is the man that trusteth in him.

Psalm 34: 4-8

Faith will turn any course, light any path, relieve any distress, bring joy
out of sorrow, peace out of strife, friendship out of enmity, heaven out of
hell. Faith is God at work.

F. L. Holmes

Oh! there is never sorrow of heart
That shall lack a timely end,
If but to God we turn, and ask
Of Him to be our friend!

William Wordsworth

Ask, and it shall be given you; seek, and ye shall find; knock, and it shall
be opened unto you: For every one that asketh receiveth; and he that
seeketh findeth; and to him that knocketh it shall be opened. Or what
man is there of you, whom if his son ask bread, will he give him a stone?
Or if he ask a fish, will he give him a serpent? If ye then, being evil, know
how to give good gifts unto your children, how much more shall your
Father which is in heaven give good things to them that ask him?

Matthew 7: 7-11

Prayer comes to us as a decision of God, who shares his will, his power and his love with man, whom he calls upon to pray through the instrumentality of human speech. Prayer is not a discourse. It is a form of life, the life with God.

Jacques Ellul

MY GIFT

What can I give Him
Poor as I am?
If I were a shepherd,
I would bring a lamb,
If I were a Wise Man,
I would do my part,—
Yet what can I give Him,
Give Him my heart.

Christina Georgina Rossetti

When my soul fainted within me, I remembered the Lord.

Jonah 2:7

Prayer is the very sword of the saints.

Francis Thompson

O, the starting holes that the heart hath in the time of prayer! None knows how many bye-ways the heart hath and back lanes to slip away from the presence of God.

John Bunyan

VISION AND PRAYER

I turn the corner of prayer and burn
In a blessing of the sudden
Sun. In the name of the damned
I would turn back and run
To the hidden land
But the loud sun
Christens down
The sky.
I
Am found.
O let him
Scald me and drown
Me in his world's wound.
His lightning answers my
Cry. My voice burns in his hand.
Now. I am lost in the blinding
One. The sun roars at the prayer's end.

Dylan Thomas

I have never lacked guidance—only obedience.

Rufus Moseley

As one whose whole life has been concerned with the suffering of the human mind, I believe that of all the hygienic measures to counteract depression of spirit, and all the miserable results of a distracted mind, I would undoubtedly give first place to the simple habit of prayer.

Dr. Theo B. Hyslop

"There were other hands than mine on those oars."
This is James C. Whittaker's reference to his experience with friends on a raft adrift at sea, after their plane plunged into the Pacific. Weakened by exposure, and near starvation for twenty-one days, Whittaker and his two companions apparently faced death. But when he prayed again, power came to him. Explain it how we may, the fact remains that, with arms which were little more than skin and bones, the men were able to fight their way against the current until their rubber boat reached an island, and safety.

G. Ray Jordan

Much keeping company with God will teach us who God is.

Charles Francis Whiston

Prayer! I couldn't live without it; I would have died a dozen times if it had not been for my chance to talk it over with God, and gain strength in it from him.

Dale Evans Rogers

GOD MAKES A PATH

Prayer does not change God, but changes him who prays.

Sören Kierkegaard

I have been driven many times to my knees by the overwhelming conviction that I had nowhere else to go; my own wisdom and that of all around me seemed insufficient for that day.

Abraham Lincoln

Speak to Him, thou, for He hears, and Spirit
    with Spirit can meet—
Closer is He than breathing, and nearer
    than hands and feet.

Alfred, Lord Tennyson

Prayer is a force as real as terrestrial gravity. As a physician I have seen men, after all other therapy had failed, lifted out of disease and melancholy by the serene effort of prayer.

Dr. Alexis Carrel

PRAYER IS

There is a lovely old prayer used by fishermen on the coast of France: "O God, thy sea is so great and my boat is so small!"
The prayer goes no further. Some say this is not a prayer at all. Yet we have here the groundwork and basis for all prayer: man standing consciously in the presence of God.

William Arthur Ward

Copyright (c) MCMLXXVIII by
The C. R. Gibson Company, Norwalk, Connecticut
All rights reserved
Printed in the United States of America
ISBN: 0-8378-1794-3

PRAYER . . .
Its Joys
Its Wonders
Its Power

compiled by Frederick Drimmer

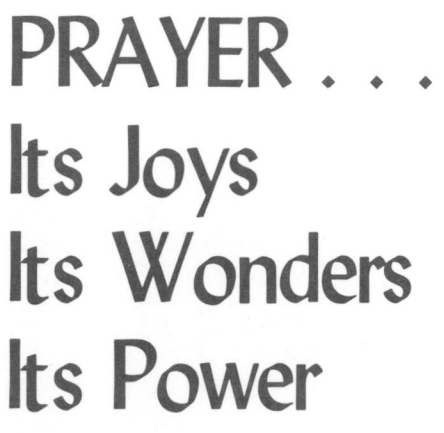

The C. R. Gibson Company
Norwalk, Connecticut